INTRODUCTION TO

SOCIAL PSYCHOLOGY

INTRODUCTION TO

SOCIAL PSYCHOLOGY

DAVID J. SCHNEIDER

The University of Texas at San Antonio

HARCOURT BRACE JOVANOVICH, PUBLISHERS

San Diego   New York   Chicago   Austin   Washington, D.C.
London   Sydney   Tokyo   Toronto

Dedicated to the memory of Joseph C. Schneider

Printed in the United States of America

ISBN: 0-15-581571-7

Library of Congress Catalog Card Number: 87-81164

Copyrights and Acknowledgments and Illustration Credits appear on pages 586–588, which constitute a continuation of the copyright page.

PREFACE

This book was written for the traditional one-semester, undergraduate social psychology course. *Introduction to Social Psychology* can be used in courses consisting almost entirely of psychology majors, or in those that include students from business, communications, and criminal justice, as well as other social science majors. All psychological concepts are explained in enough detail to allow the motivated student to comprehend the material without previous psychology courses.

The book focuses on theoretical issues and the use of empirical methods to test these theories: I have emphasized larger themes over the description of specific studies and "facts." The smaller details of social psychology, so important to research scientists, are crucial building blocks, but they nevertheless change and decay with some rapidity. I would like to see students emerge from a social psychology course with some sophistication about the major theories in the field and with a healthy respect for both the values and the pitfalls of empirical research. I would also hope that students would incorporate many of the basic themes of social psychology—the importance and subtlety of social pressures, the shaping of our knowledge about the immediate world by social and cultural factors, the interplays between biological and social–cultural forces—into a working knowledge about their worlds, and that this would enrich and broaden their lives.

I have been guided by a strong belief that social psychology, like the rest of psychology, is an integral part of the liberal arts, and that a study of social psychology is an important route to a humane perspective on the world. I have given some emphasis to philosophical foundations of our discipline and to its historical evolution. While I have tried to point out problems with the purely empirical approach

and with various experiments and experimental paradigms, I hope I have also communicated the highest respect for the basic aims of empirical social psychology. We do not dominate the truth market, but we have an important corner of it. In the final chapter, I explicitly discuss problems with traditional social psychology approaches, empirical and theoretical. I have not avoided value issues. In my version of the liberal arts, social psychology should contribute to the abilities of students to be morally committed yet epistemologically tolerant. It is not my purpose to promote any particular political, moral, or ideological view other than that generally held within our scientific community, and in both my writing and my teaching I try to avoid preaching and hectoring. However, students do need to confront value questions in the context of science, and we ought not assume that the "is" of science and the "ought" of morality and politics are as easily separated in the complexities of modern civilization as they can be within the classroom.

"Real-world" examples introduce most chapters. These examples come from a political or historical event, are drawn from ethnographic studies of other cultures, or are reproductions of conversations and descriptions of less-cosmic everyday events. They are meant to capture attention and to illustrate some (but not all) of the major issues of the chapters they introduce in a context that I hope will remind students that social psychology does have a voice in the real world.

The book is organized into four parts. In Part One, Chapter 1 introduces the field and its major guiding theories, and Chapter 2 deals with research issues. Part Two deals with social cognition, with chapters on social cognition (Chapter 3), person perception (Chapter 4), the social self (Chapter 5), language and communication (Chapter 6), attitudes and attitude change (Chapter 7), and internal versus external controls over behavior (Chapter 8). Part Three concerns social behavior, with chapters on socialization (Chapter 9), groups (Chapter 10), social influence (Chapter 11), interpersonal attraction (Chapter 12), relationships (Chapter 13), prosocial behavior (Chapter 14), aggression (Chapter 15), and prejudice and discrimination (Chapter 16). Part Four, consisting of Chapter 17, surveys issues of application and the state of our present knowledge.

The ordering of the chapters is based partially on philosophical grounds and partially on practical ones. In terms of the former, a case can be made for beginning with the cognitive bases of social behavior, a case that reflects the continuing, strong phenomenological bases of social psychology. An understanding of social behavior presupposes an understanding of how people think about their social environments. Practically, given the present status of the field and the recent emphasis on social cognition models, it is simply easier to begin with the social cognition material. I fully recognize that no reader of any text approves fully of the author's ordering of chapters. I would hope that the integration I have attempted would not interfere with those who prefer to order chapters differently in class presentation. I strongly encourage anyone who wishes to read or teach the chapters in a different order to do so.

Although *Introduction to Social Psychology* begins with a substantial emphasis on the cognitive underpinnings of social behavior, I have also emphasized traditional motivational and social variables whenever appropriate. Social cognition plays a more central role in this textbook than in many others, but I strongly believe that the study of social behavior is the ultimate raison d'être of our field. I therefore have tried to make a strong case for that perspective throughout. For example, the chapter on language and communication reinforces the

idea that social and cultural variables not only affect the meanings we give to verbal and nonverbal behaviors but also structure their manifestations. Similarly, the chapter on the self suggests that both our identities and our self-evaluations are based on reactions of other people, cultural definitions, and socialization experiences, as well as on more purely cognitive processes. In the chapters dealing with social behavior, social and group variables, of course, are given even more weight.

Most of the chapters are traditional in content, but there are in this (as in any) text some chapters less bound by consensus. One of these is Chapter 9, on socialization, traditionally a foundation of the field. Chapter 6, on language and communication, also deals explicitly with what historically have been major issues within social psychology, but which are issues often ignored in modern texts. Furthermore, this chapter allows an extended treatment of nonverbal behavior in the context of social communication—its rightful home, in my opinion. It is also unusual to have a special chapter on the self (Chapter 5), yet research on self-schemata, self-perception, and self-evaluations is now so extensive as to justify separate treatment. The fact that our selves are forged in the crucible of social interactions is a point worth making strongly. Chapter 8, on internal and external controls over behavior, deals explicitly with attitude–behavior relationships and the prediction of behavior from personality variables. This chapter provides a bridge between purely cognitive and largely behavioral approaches to social phenomena.

There are no separate chapters on applications issues; rather, I have elected to include discussions of applications in appropriate chapters. For example, issues of crime are discussed in the aggression chapter, eyewitness testimony in the social cognition chapter, juries in the groups chapter, sex roles in the socialization and prejudice chapters, and behavior in large organizations in the communications and groups chapters. I believe that applications ought to be discussed at their point of origin, so to speak, lest they get lost in the shuffle at the end of the course and lest they become divorced from basic research and theories. Thus, the decision not to have separate chapters on applications to real-life problems has been based on my respect for the importance of those issues rather than on any desire to hide them away.

A number of people have worked hard and effectively to get this book done. Alice Jimenez typed an early draft before I discovered the magic of computers. My colleagues at the University of Texas at San Antonio have been tolerant of my demands for lengthy periods of time each week free of major responsibilities. The following people provided many helpful suggestions in their reviews of the manuscript: Jennifer Crocker (State University of New York, Buffalo), John Dovidio (Colgate University), Frederick Gibbons (Iowa State University), E. Tory Higgins (New York University), James Hilton (University of Michigan), George Levinger (University of Massachusetts, Amherst), Norman Miller (University of Southern California), Richard Moreland (University of Pittsburgh), Suzanne Pallak (Georgetown University), Bernadette Park (University of Colorado), James Weyant (University of San Diego), and David Wilder (Rutgers). I especially want to thank Marcus

Boggs, College Department editor at Harcourt Brace Jovanovich, for his sage advice, warm support, and friendly conversations; Karl Yambert, manuscript editor, for his many good suggestions for improvements and for his good humor and tolerance in dealing with mine; Maggie Porter, art editor, for her work on the photos and art; and Amy Dunn and Martha Berlin, production editors, for turning the manuscript into printed pages. It has been a pleasure to work with all of them.

Finally, although writing books does have its pleasant moments, the pleasures tend to be vague, distant, tied to future accomplishments, and ethereal. The costs and pains, however, are clear, immediate, and insistent. Unfortunately one's family has to share those costs but experiences few of the larger and higher pleasures. My family has been tolerant and supportive. Doris did far more than her share to keep the home fires burning while maintaining her own career and did so with a minimum of grumbling and a maximum of good humor and support. My daughters, Kris and Caitlin, tried to stay out of my way, forgave my bad moods (I hope), and helped with various typing and bibliographical tasks. These remarkably nice and special people deserved better than they got.

David J. Schneider

TABLE OF CONTENTS

PART ONE

INTRODUCTION

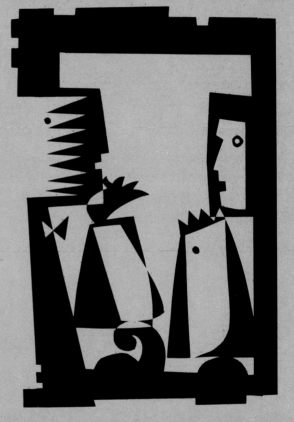

CHAPTER

1

INTRODUCTION

Most of the time I go about my business of being a social psychologist and hardly think what the field is, let alone what it could or should be. I doubt that most physicians, lawyers, or stockbrokers (or for that matter students) spend much of their time wondering about the higher meanings of their chosen roles either. But occasionally I spiral to a higher plane and am forced to think about what it is that I am.

One such occasion is at a party when talking to a stranger who asks me what I do. I usually say I am a social psychologist. At that point I get one of several reactions. Once in a while I am talking with someone who knows something about social psychology, at least enough to pose an interesting question or make a provocative observation. But, in my experience, other reactions are more common. People I call (privately to be sure) *Fraidy-Cats* stammer a bit, look frightened that I am about to "psych" them out, and then depart quickly in search of a freshened drink. Little do they realize that most psychologists are about as inept as the next person in figuring others out and behaving gracefully in social situations. *Mini-Experts* take the opportunity to instruct me in their favorite theories of why various parts of the social world do or do not function effectively; unfortunately, this is often about as illuminating as hearing a medieval monk discuss the workings of a modern automobile. *Know-It-Alls* (often lawyers or businesspersons, in my experience) insist that formal social psychology is irrelevant to the Real Social World (which seems to reach its richest manifestation in courtrooms and advertising agencies, I guess). When I draw a Know-It-All as my conversational partner, I usually suggest that *my* drink needs freshening.

But the response I like best, and the one that is also most common, usually begins somewhat along the lines of "that must be interesting, but I guess I'm not exactly sure what so-

Social psychology is the study of how people think about, evaluate, and respond to their social experiences.

cial psychology is." Rather than define the field (which seems vaguely pompous when one is balancing crackers and cheese, a drink, and the demands of polite conversation), I usually try to give a catalog of topics social psychologists study: conformity, attitude change, why people do or do not get along with one another, how groups function, leadership, aggression, helping, and how we form impressions of one another. Most people then seem to relax a bit because there's nothing so very threatening about these topics. In fact most seem to find them interesting.

THE NATURE OF SOCIAL PSYCHOLOGY

DEFINITION

This isn't a cocktail party, of course, and here I can be considerably more precise. *Social psychology* may be defined as the study of how people think about, evaluate, and respond to their social experiences.

Thinking about Social Experiences   Social psychologists are deeply interested in how people *think about* their social worlds. Often we are more interested in how people perceive things than in what those things are really like. For example, last week I handed back an exam in a statistics course and commented that the students needed to study more. Students in statistics courses tend to grumble (as I did when I took such courses), but on this day several students were muttering in a more hostile fashion than usual. When I talked to several of them later, they complained that I had a hostile attitude toward students. Because I did not feel this was accurate, I asked how they came to this conclusion. They said that I had made my comment about more study in a surly tone of voice (perhaps true—I was disappointed in the exams) and that they felt I was trying to make them the culprits when I had not spent enough time in class on the material. My past behavior also had contributed to their perceptions: after the last exam I had apparently smiled when talking about the lowest grades and this was interpreted as evidence that I relished giving low grades. The students had been discussing me after class for some weeks, and the consensus was that I was out to get them. From my perspective their perceptions were wrong, but the important point is that it was their perceptions of my attitudes toward them, and not my "true" attitudes, that affected their reactions to me.

Evaluating Social Experiences   Social psychology deals with *evaluations*. My statistics students decided that I was angry and hostile and they evaluated me negatively as a consequence. Such evaluative responses (usually called *attitudes*) are important. You probably took this social psychology course because you have at least mildly positive attitudes toward psychology courses, the professor, or the time it was offered. You like some people, dislike others, have more or less positive attitudes

about a whole range of political and social issues. Almost all your social experiences have an evaluative tinge to them, and such evaluations affect your social behavior. Although such matters are complex, as a first approximation we might say that you are likely to approach (cognitively or behaviorally) those things you like or evaluate positively and avoid those you dislike.

Evaluations are social in another way as well: almost all your attitudes have been acquired in a social context. For example, many of your political, social, and religious attitudes show clear influences of your socialization by parents. In a way, your evaluations and attitudes are a partial summary of your entire social experience.

Responding to Social Experiences   Finally, social psychologists are interested in our *behavioral responses* to our social situations. Much, if not quite all, of our everyday behavior is explicitly or implicitly social. It is explicitly social when it directly affects others. The fact that my comment to the students about studying harder affected their attitudes and their behavior toward me makes my comment social. Sometimes behavior is more implicitly social. For example, when you study instead of watching TV because you want to please your parents by making good grades, we can think of your behavior as social, even though your decision is made alone.

Thus, thoughts, evaluations, and behavior are social when they are related to people or social events. They may also be social in the added sense that our relationships, real or imagined, with others affect them. Social psychology deals both with cognitive and behavioral responses to social stimuli and with social causes and consequences of such responses.

THE CONCERNS OF SOCIAL PSYCHOLOGY

A Scientific Discipline   Social psychology is far from unique in dealing with a wide range of human social behavior. For example, great novelists and playwrights provide provocative analyses of human behavior. Philosophers speculate systematically about the psychological underpinnings of social life. The analyses of novelists and philosophers are often penetrating and often convincing. What gives social psychologists the right to think they can improve on this?

One problem with literary and philosophical analyses is that we have no compelling way of knowing whether they are incorrect, incomplete, or misleading. You may or may not be convinced by Proust or Plato, but in either case someone will disagree with you for reasons that are not demonstrably false. On the other hand, most social psychologists share the fundamental conviction that their ideas and assertions are to be tested through empirical, scientific methods. Such methods do not guarantee truth, but they do force their practitioners to be clear and explicit about most of their assumptions, and they do specify criteria for making statements about truth. We will have more to say about such methods in the next chapter.

Thus, most social psychologists are committed to the scientific study of social behavior and experiences. Science has marched on throughout this century, and as social psychologists have joined the parade with their methodological drums and bugles, they have left their literary and philosophical approaches behind. Whether this has been a wise development can be debated, because science does not solve all intellectual problems and in fact introduces constraints that create others. But most social psychologists would agree that scientific methods, with all their faults, still provide the best means of validating the general principles of human social behavior.

Relationships with Other Disciplines   So social psychology differs from literary and philosophical approaches in the use of empirical methods, but other psychological disciplines and social sciences also study social behavior empirically. How does social psychology differ from these other areas?

Social psychology overlaps other areas of psychology such as developmental, personality, and abnormal psychology. In one sense social psychology serves as a basis for these other disciplines. For example, developmental psychologists might use principles of conformity to explain how parents influence their children. The clinical psychologist might be interested in whether people with mental or behavioral problems perceive others differently than do those who are more "normal." One could put the matter that way, but in point of fact, each of these areas is just as likely to contribute to social psychology as to borrow from it. It would be an impoverished social psychology indeed that could not learn from the rich processes of social influence inherent in child rearing or that could not find sources of hypotheses in the study of deviant behaviors. However, although there is considerable overlap among these specialties, they do differ in their focus, with social psychologists attending most closely to the social context of human thought and behavior.

The relationship between personality and social psychology is special enough to require extended comment. Historically the two disciplines have dealt with the same basic phenomena—complex human behavior in a social milieu—but have approached them from different perspectives. Social psychologists have concentrated on how social situations and stimuli affect the generalized, "average" person. Personality psychology, on the other hand, has been more concerned with the study of individuals and how they differ.

Naturally the two approaches complement one another. On one hand, situations clearly have a great deal to do with how people behave. For example, most people are relatively quiet in the library, more animated in the cafeteria, and loud and excited at a close football game. People in the same situation often behave similarly (glance around when you attend your next large lecture class). Given all the ways your fellow students could be dressed and could be behaving, you might be struck by how little variability they display. On the other hand, it is also clear that even in the same situation (such as a lecture) there are some, even major, differences in the ways people act. Not everyone is smiling at the professor's jokes, a few people seem to be asleep, and some are attentive and taking notes—some even look interested.

It is surely important to recognize both that people do differ fundamentally and that people in similar situations often show remarkably similar behavior. You have surely discovered the necessity of using a logic both of situational forces and of individual differences. For example, most of your friends understand general rules about being polite so you can predict that almost all of them will help you with something minor such as loaning you a pencil. On the other hand, if you need a special favor such as borrowing a car or getting a ride to a city 50 miles away, you will probably think a bit about which friend to approach and how to tailor your request to his or her personality. So to understand social behavior we will need to know something about social forces, such as rules of politeness, as well as about how different kinds of people behave in similar situations. In Chapter 9 we will consider in detail the relationships between situational controls on behavior and individual differences.

Finally, what is the relationship of social psychology to the other social sciences, especially sociology? Many sociology departments teach courses in social psychology: social psychology actually has deep historical roots in sociology as well as in psychology.

Today sociologists and psychologists tend to have different perspectives and methodologies. It has become popular to speak of the two social psychologies—the *sociological* social psychology and the *psychological* social psychology—and to urge that there be more intellectual interchange between the two (Backman, 1983; House, 1977; Stryker, 1983). Naturally, psychologists look to other psychologies for their bearings. Therefore psychological social psychology tends to be heavily in-

fluenced by learning, perception, and cognitive psychologies, and focuses on the thoughts and behaviors of individuals. Sociologists, on the other hand, are more interested in the behavior of aggregates of people and in the mutual relationships between people and their social, economic, and political structures. So, for example, in an election the psychologist would be interested in how individual voters process election information and perceive the candidates, whereas the sociologist might lean more toward examining socioeconomic determinants of voting behavior. There are also differences in the research methods the two groups use. Psychologists tend to do experimental studies, whereas sociologists are more inclined to study social phenomena in their natural forms. This text focuses on the psychological perspective but we will also borrow heavily from the sociological tradition at various points. Both perspectives are necessary for a full understanding of social behavior.

HUMAN NATURE AND MOTIVATION

Although social psychology as a formal area of study is relatively recent, concern with social behavior is not. From ancient times, philosophers, historians, and storytellers have been interested in the causes of human behavior in social situations. As people have continued to speculate about these matters, it has usually been assumed that certain motives, desires, passions, and impulses are basic and shared by all people. There is, or so it is asserted, a basic human nature that may be modified by experience, or that may be repressed, inhibited, or redirected by society, but that remains a basic ingredient in all behavior.

Basic Motives   When we consider people and their social relations, one obvious question is whether people are naturally social or naturally egoistic (that is, oriented to the needs of others or interested principally in one's own individual welfare). This question has been debated for centuries, but the opposing positions were articulated most clearly by two opposing schools of Greek and Roman thought—the Stoics and the Epicureans. The Stoic school, which began about 300 B.C., preached that all people are a part of a natural, rational world order and as such have responsibilities toward fellow humans, namely to help others and promote the happiness of all. The Stoics recognized that people can be selfish but believed selfishness could be overcome if people would only submerge their emotions and remain detached from the world. To Stoics, human nature was fundamentally socially oriented but could easily be corrupted by emotional concerns for pleasure, fame, and material reward.

The opposite position was taken by the Epicurean school, which began about the same time. Epicureans believed that people were essentially interested only in their own pleasures and survival. Society and concern for others are not natural but arise because people need to band together for protection and to secure a satisfactory economic life. People can learn to be helpful and cooperative but it is not a part of their basic human nature to be so.

According to one view, people are naturally cooperative and have the strong potential for being concerned for others; according to the other, people seek their own pleasures, often at the expense of others. Each position has trouble accounting for the full range of human behavior. If you are inclined to believe that humans are naturally concerned with others, you must contend with the record of countless wars and thousands of years' evidence of our cruelties to one another. You will have to find convincing reasons for these corruptions of human nature. You might, like philosophers Jean-Jacques Rousseau and Karl Marx, suggest that the corrupting element is society itself and therefore look with suspicion at any social form, afraid that it will thwart whatever is genuine in people.

If, on the other hand, you believe human nature is basically egoistic and pleasure-seeking,

you will not be surprised by war and cruelty. Instead your main problem will be how to account for the emergence and maintenance of society. If individuals are basically looking out for their own welfare, why should they become civilized? How can order and cooperation arise from the competition of individuals? Why should self-interested people subject themselves to the limitations and restraints of society?

Naturally these are not the only themes in the history of social thought, but they have been amazingly persistent and they echo strongly in modern psychology. However, modern psychologists have generally been reluctant to make strong claims about basic human nature because any theory of human behavior must be flexible enough to incorporate learning and culture in addition to biological influences. Each of us is capable of behaving in a given situation in any number of ways depending on many factors—past experiences, what we have been taught, how present circumstances are perceived, inherited abilities—and it is hard to make strong statements about our basic human nature in light of this realization.

Modern Assumptions   This does not mean, of course, that psychologists can avoid making assumptions about general motives underlying human behavior. In this chapter we consider several basic approaches social psychologists have taken to questions of basic human tendencies. Those who have proposed these models have generally been seeking answers to the question, What makes people behave the ways they do in social situations? It will be convenient to refer to each of these models in terms of a metaphor: (1) person as animal, (2) person as profit seeker, (3) person as physical field, (4) person as scientist, and (5) person as actor. These metaphors are meant to suggest that people have some of the behavioral attributes characteristic of other animals, business people, objects subject to physical forces, scientists, and actors. It is not necessary to choose among these metaphors; each of them is a partial and, within limits, valid description of human motivational and behavioral tendencies.

PERSON AS ANIMAL: BIOLOGICAL ASPECTS OF MOTIVATION

INSTINCT

Darwin   For centuries people believed that human nature was something vaguely biological. With the development of Charles Darwin's (1859) theory of evolution, such ideas finally acquired a firm scientific basis. Darwin suggested that certain biological structures (for example, long legs) and behavioral dispositions (for example, the desire to compete) help animals survive long enough to reproduce themselves. Natural selection will favor certain characteristics in the sense that those individuals possessing them are the most likely to survive and to have offspring that inherit the favorable characteristics. Darwin tended to emphasize competition as a master biological imperative, because animals who could compete successfully for the best breeding privileges, feeding territories, and sites to rear young would naturally have a greater likelihood of passing on their competitive advantages. Those who followed Darwin also argued that many other behavioral tendencies would also have survival value.

Charles Darwin

Instinct Theories   During the late nineteenth and early twentieth centuries, many social scientists argued that social behavior is governed by inborn behavioral tendencies, called *instincts.* The basic idea behind such instinct theories was that animals must do certain things (such as eat) to survive as individuals and do other things (such as reproduce) for the species to survive. Because such tendencies promote survival, they may well be genetically based. Thus we are all endowed with certain compelling instincts that both energize and guide behavior.

Sigmund Freud, an influential instinct theorist, argued that there are two large categories of such instincts: aggressive and sexual. But he faced the problem of how to account for the enormous diversity of human behavior with

Natural selection at work.

The Far Side © 1986, Universal Press Syndicate. Reprinted with permission. All rights reserved.

Sigmund Freud

TABLE 1.1 McDOUGALL'S CATEGORIES OF INSTINCTS AND CORRESPONDING EMOTIONS.

Primary	
Instinct	*Emotion*
1. Flight	Fear
2. Repulsion	Disgust
3. Curiosity	Wonder
4. Pugnacity	Anger
5. Self-abasement	Subjugation
6. Self-assertion	Negative and positive feelings about self
7. Parental	Tenderness
Less Definite	
8. Reproduction	
9. Gregariousness	
10. Acquisition	
11. Construction	

only two sets of instincts. He argued that because both sexual and aggressive tendencies create social mischief, their expression is severely limited and repressed. However, because these instincts are so powerful, so urgent, they must find release somehow, typically in disguised and nonthreatening ways. Throughout our childhoods we all learned many ways of satisfying our sexual and aggressive urges, and hence our behavior is almost infinitely diverse.

William McDougall (1908) took a different approach. He argued that human behavior was complex and diverse because there were many different instincts at work. Table 1.1 gives one of his lists of instincts. So one kind of behavior (for example, earning a living) might satisfy gregariousness, parental, and acquisition instincts, whereas another (such as watching violent television) might satisfy curiosity, pugnacity, and self-assertion needs.

By about 1920 instinct theories had fallen on hard times in psychology. One major problem was that the postulated instincts were not demonstrably attached to actual biological processes: it may seem reasonable to suppose that aggressiveness has survival value, but where do we find the biological sources of aggressiveness? (See Chapter 15 for further discussion.) Indeed if an instinct is a certain ten-

dency that promotes survival, all manner of behavioral predispositions might qualify as instincts: cooking, sitting in classes, being calm in an emergency, knowing how to fly an airplane, watching educational programs on TV. Yet it is highly unlikely that such tendencies have a direct biological basis. Thus, because the biological core of early instinct theories was mushy, psychologists turned to alternative concepts.

DRIVES

By the 1930s the concept of *drive* had replaced that of instinct as the dominant motivational construct in American psychology. In many respects drives were similar to instincts, but they were based on clearly identifiable biological processes such as hunger, sex, and thirst.

The concept of drive was especially prominent in Clark Hull's theory of motivation and learning, which dominated psychology from about 1940 to about 1960. Hull believed that drives energize behavior, but that they are general and do not guide specific behaviors. There

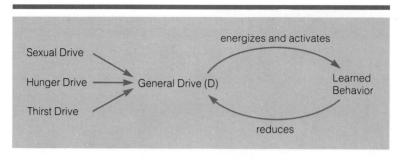

FIGURE 1.1   Hull's Drive Theory.

is a **generalized drive** (D, sometimes called "Big D"), which is a summation of all active drives. For example, a person who had not eaten for 8 hours and who was sexually deprived would have a higher D than one who was merely hungry.

Hull realized that food-starved and sexually starved people tend to do different things, but he thought this was a result of learning, not biology. To oversimplify, the organism reacts to increased D with increased activity (the pacing behavior of the hungry dog is an example), but it has to learn which behaviors pay off in the sense of reducing the dominant drive. When I am hungry, I head for the kitchen, but this behavior is learned and not wired in biologically. The fact that this behavior has, in the past, reduced my hunger drive has reinforced the behavior (see Figure 1.1). In general, D determines the vigor or strength of behavior but not its specific expression: the particular behaviors that reduce particular drives must be learned.

AROUSAL

Hull had postulated a general drive state, one which provided the impetus behind behavior without directing it to any particular goal. In recent years this idea of a general drive has been transformed into the concept of **arousal.** Everyday experience confirms that sometimes we feel highly aroused and active, while at other times we are subdued and relaxed. Consider how you feel after getting a bad grade compared with drinking your third beer with friends after your last exam. The differences in your feelings and excitement would be due, in part, to biological arousal.

Several propositions about arousal have proved useful to social psychologists. First, arousal is arousal no matter what the source. Anxiety, fear, hunger—all add to a general state of arousal. Second, performance on a variety of tasks is best at an intermediate level of arousal. If there is too little arousal, the person isn't energized and simply doesn't do anything; at high levels, the person is disorganized, frantic, and inefficient. At intermediate levels, the person is energized but not disorganized. Third, with increasing arousal, the person becomes increasingly inclined to respond with a well-practiced or natural behavior. So as arousal increases we are more likely to run from a dangerous situation or to perform a highly developed skill effectively. Fourth, with increasing arousal, we focus our attention on fewer stimuli. Finally, although arousal contributes to how emotional we feel, the specific emotion we experience depends heavily on our interpretation of events. The differences between feelings of anger and fear rest less on the internal state of one's body (which is generally aroused in either case) than on stimuli in the environment that help us label the general arousal.

Many psychologists feel that the arousal notion has limited utility at the biological level—the energy and arousal activities of the human body are far too complex to be reduced to a simple notion that sources of arousal add together. Nonetheless we will encounter the concept of arousal throughout this book because it has generated a great many research ideas.

SOCIOBIOLOGY

Modern biologists do not doubt that human physiology, anatomy, and biological processes fit nicely within a broad evolutionary framework. But behavior? One problem with fitting behavior into an evolutionary perspective is that, although the survival value of certain behaviors, say aggressiveness, is clear, it is tricky to trace the precise physiological and hormonal causes of such behaviors.

Another classic problem is that evolutionary theory can account for some types of behavior more readily than others. For example, aggression, which may be manifested through fights among males for breeding privileges, is biologically advantageous because it tends to ensure that the strongest males will mate and contribute their genes to the gene pool. Similarly one could make a case for the survival value of intelligence, caution, creativity—all characteristics that help an animal (or person) survive long enough to reproduce and pass along its genes for such traits.

However, people do more than fight, behave intelligently, and engage in sexual behavior. For example, sometimes we engage in altruism; that is, we help one another. But this altruistic behavior is hard to square with classic evolutionary theory—an animal that helps another often exposes itself to risk and lessens the likelihood of its own survival, which means it is less likely to reproduce and pass

along its altruistic genes. Suppose an animal gives a distress cry when it sees a predator: it thereby helps others find safety before they can be eaten, but only by giving away its position and running the risk of being eaten itself. There would seem to be no competitive advantage to altruism. Indeed, competition would seem to select *against* altruism: the nonaltruistic nonyellers survive, but the altruistic yellers get killed and thereby fail to pass along whatever genes they have for altruistic yelling. So how do we account for the existence of altruism?

Obviously we have a problem here from the standpoint of strict evolutionary theory. Classic Darwinian theory can easily account for aggression and competition but has difficulties with altruism, which doesn't seem to have survival value for the individual. A new field of biology, **sociobiology,** began with several ingenious attempts to integrate cooperation and helping with evolutionary principles. Sociobiology received its major impetus with the publication of E. O. Wilson's provocative *Sociobiology* (1975).

Sociobiology is a complex theory involving principles of evolution, population genetics, and ecology, among other areas. In the case of altruism, for example, sociobiologists have pointed to certain mechanisms, such as kin selection, that might favor the survival of genes for altruism. Although it is true that the individual altruist may die before she or he reproduces, the act of altruism may well promote the survival of close kin (say siblings) who share with the altruist the genetic predisposition for being helpful. Thus, if we consider the survival of the larger gene pool rather than that of individual genes, evolutionary theory can account for how individuals might have a genetic disposition to be helpful. This does not prove, of course, that altruistic behaviors are based on genetic programs.

It is hard to resist the many examples sociobiologists offer of animals that behave in socially wondrous ways because of the pushes and pulls of their genes. However, social scientists have properly been quite skeptical of the approach. There are major differences between lower animals and humans, not the least of which is the much greater role of cultural factors and learning in the control of human behavior. Furthermore, sociobiologists have generally been no more successful than their predecessors earlier in the century in spelling out precise biological mechanisms for translating genetic predispositions into concrete and observable behaviors.

Although there have been some guarded attempts to apply sociobiological perspectives to social psychology (Campbell, 1975) and to the larger field of human behavior (Barash, 1977), most social scientists are critical about the ability of the perspective to explain complex human behavior. At the moment such attempts have a high ratio of speculation to evidence and should be evaluated accordingly.

BIOLOGY AND CULTURE

No social psychologist would deny that we have a biological side to our nature and that we share some features with other animals. Clearly our bodily structures and our capacities for certain behaviors such as walking and talking are heavily dictated by our genetic heritages. However, for the most part our thoughts and behaviors, though influenced by biology, are not directly caused by biological factors. To understand how biology influences these more psychological aspects of our nature, we must examine how biology works in conjunction with social and cultural factors.

There are at least three ways biological and cultural factors might be related. First, cultural factors may inhibit or overcome biological ones. For example, most adults have learned that they cannot usually act upon their sexual urges immediately, and even hunger drives can be submerged when dieting: biology is not necessarily stronger or more compelling than psychological factors in determining behavior.

Second, our cultural heritage regulates the range of stimuli that arouse our biological urges. For example, in Western culture the smell of cooking beef stimulates most people's appetites, and for males the sight of female breasts is often sexually arousing. However, people from other cultures might find cooked beef repulsive, and female breasts far less sexually stimulating than the shape of the lips or the buttocks.

Third, social and cultural factors constrain our choices about which behaviors are appropriate manifestations of biological demands. In our culture heterosexual intercourse is considered more appropriate than homosexual relations or masturbation, and we believe that eating three defined meals is preferable to eating whenever we feel hungry. We do not urinate in public and devote fairly large sums of money to building rooms so that elimination functions can be carried out in private. So the culture encourages us to express our biological urges in particular ways.

BIOLOGICAL THEMES

We should be wary of assuming that each distinct form of human behavior has an equally distinct biological urge accompanying it. Men seduce women (and the reverse) for reasons other than pure sexual urges: sometimes the seducer is trying to demonstrate power or to prove to self and others that he is attractive and worthwhile. Similarly, many people eat more than they need to sustain their survival, so eating behavior must fulfill other needs as well. There is no neat one-to-one correspondence between biological urge and behavior:

- Biological drives and needs usually play a larger role in energizing behavior.
- Cultural, cognitive, and situational factors play a larger role in determining which behaviors are performed.

PERSON AS PROFIT SEEKER:
HEDONISM

Probably the most obvious and popular theory of human nature has been **psychological hedonism,** which asserts that people seek pleasure and avoid pain. One does not have to be especially perceptive to see that people do like their pleasures. We assume that pleasure, joy, and feeling happy are natural goals of behavior. However, most theories of hedonism go beyond that to assert that our *only* basic motives are seeking pleasure and avoiding pain, that *all* our behavior is preceded by an analysis of what is in our best interests. Hedonism has been a mainstay of both classical social philosophy and modern psychology—both Freud and most behaviorist learning theories, for example, assume that people perform behaviors because they are pleasant or rewarding (typically called *reinforcing* in learning theories). Of the many versions of such theories in social psychology, we describe briefly three: exchange theory, social learning theory, and impression management theory.

EXCHANGE THEORY

Several theories (Blau, 1964; Homans, 1961; Thibaut & Kelley, 1959) have suggested that people seek rewards and avoid punishments by engaging in social interactions that are heavily structured by the *exchange* of material and psychological commodities. (Other closely related theories, called *equity theories,* suggest that people prefer situations where rewards and costs are apportioned fairly and equitably.) We will concentrate on the exchange theory of John Thibaut and Harold Kelley because it has been the most influential and is the most elaborately developed.

Thibaut and Kelley postulate that people seek situations with the best profits, or reward–cost ratios. Thus, at least implicitly, people calculate expected rewards versus costs

Harold H. Kelley

for any potential behavior and adjust their behavior accordingly. Because interactions among people are viewed in terms of exchanges of rewards and costs, this theory is usually called an **exchange theory.** The theory suggests that I will want to interact with you and you with me only to the extent that we each receive more rewards than costs. Generally anything that increases my rewards (for example, you make good martinis) or lowers my costs (you don't care if I wear shorts and an old T-shirt) will make our interactions more profitable (enjoyable) to me. For your part, you are also evaluating my suitability as a companion by deciding whether I am stimulating or a bore.

When people have a relationship with one another, their outcomes in any interaction are affected to some extent by what the other does. Suppose that you and a friend have earned a night off from studying and are trying to decide whether to watch TV or go to the movies. If you both agree that you want to see the new movie at the campus center, Thibaut and Kelley (as well as common sense) suggest that you will go to the movie together, assuming you can get the details of what time to go and the like worked out.

However, consider a more interesting possibility: you want to watch TV but your friend (Sandy) prefers to go to the movie. You thus have a problem requiring some negotiation. You may be willing to forego your immediate preference for TV to have the pleasure of Sandy's company, so you might suggest that you go to the early movie and watch TV later. Or you may agree to watch TV tonight and go to the movie tomorrow. In any case, as you negotiate how you will spend your evening you will quite consciously be evaluating the relative rewards and costs of the various possibilities. These outcomes (the rewards and costs) will be affected not only by your own individual preferences but by your knowledge about what the other person wants.

This kind of analysis has proved to be particularly valuable in understanding social influence (Chapter 11), cooperation and competition (Chapter 14), and how we establish and maintain relationships with others (Chapter 13). In those chapters we will provide a more elaborate description of the Thibaut and Kelley exchange model.

Before moving on, however, it is worth making two additional points. First, Thibaut and Kelley are not concerned with *why* you like TV and your friend likes movies. Indeed you may even be mistaken that on a given evening you would actually have more fun watching TV rather than going to the movie. But your behavior is guided by what you *think* will be rewarding or costly, not by what is actually in your best interests. Second, although you seek the best deal for yourself in any given situation, it does not follow that you are selfish or egotistical. It is quite possible, for example, that you find that making your friend happy is rewarding to you. In that case, you can increase your own rewards by going to the movie with her. Thibaut and Kelley insist that you are calculating, but not that you are unconcerned about others.

SOCIAL LEARNING THEORY

Social learning theories emphasize the social context of our learning, particularly our learning by observing others. The most prominent

Children (and adults) learn important lessons from observing others.

of the social learning models, that of Albert Bandura (1969, 1973, 1977), also proposes that people decide how to behave on the basis of whether they think potential behaviors will yield positive or negative outcomes. Hence the motivational basis of the theory is thoroughly hedonistic.

Learning How   According to Bandura, we can learn two things from observing others: (1) how to do things and (2) what will happen to us if we do. Consider first the question of how we learn to perform behaviors and skills effectively. Traditional theories of learning did not place much emphasis on learning from watching others but instead suggested that most learning involves trial and error. For example, we might teach a person to drive a car by selectively rewarding safe and effective driving practices while ignoring or punishing poor ones. You *could* teach a person to drive this way, but this would be inefficient. To be sure, there will be some trial and error involved as our driver learns that a too-heavy foot on the brake stops the car too suddenly and causes her passengers to scream, but most of what she learns will come from observing others and listening to instructions.

Consequences   In addition, by watching others we can learn what kinds of things might happen to us if we do certain things. I have never actually fired a gun at my neighbor (or anyone else), but I think I have a good sense of what might happen if I did from watching movies and reading newspaper accounts of such things. Typically when we enter a new situation, one in which we are uncertain about which behaviors are appropriate, we carefully watch others who seem to know, hoping to get the right clues. For example, standard advice to the person attending his first formal dinner, where there will be more forks and spoons than seem necessary for the job at hand, is to watch and imitate the hostess. Similarly you will find it fairly easy to avoid making a fool of yourself in a strange church by following the lead of others.

There is an important difference between what you have learned to do and what you choose to do in a given situation. More formally this distinction is one between *learning* and *performance*. We have all learned to do certain things we may choose not to perform because the expected outcomes are so negative. I know how to fire a gun, but I have thus far preferred to keep this skill to myself. When people do not perform a certain behavior, it may be because they do not know how to, or it may also be because they do not feel it is in their best interests to do so.

Goals and Values   We have emphasized the *social* and *learning* parts of social learning theory, but it is important to remember that

the theory is basically a hedonistic one—it emphasizes the proposition that we perform those behaviors that will pay off. Strictly speaking, what we learn from watching others is what will happen to us if we behave in certain ways; the observation does not tell us whether that outcome is good or bad. You may have learned that if you miss examinations in your social psychology course you will fail the course. For most of you failure would be a negative outcome, but there may be those who would find this outcome appealing because they want to convince their parents that they are not cut out for college life.

The point is simple but easily forgotten: consequences of behavior are fairly brute facts about the way the world operates, but what meaning we make of those consequences depends heavily on our own values and goals. I know that one probable consequence of my killing an irritating neighbor is a long prison sentence. Because my personal values and goals emphasize freedom and respectability, I regard this as a highly punishing outcome. It would, however, be wrong for me to assume that everyone shares these values. For some, prison may not be a negative outcome, or at least may not be negative enough to overcome the joy of solving a long-term problem with the neighbor by getting rid of him. What is similar about people is that we all want to do things that lead to rewarding outcomes; what is different is that we do not all find the same consequences equally rewarding. Figure 1.2 shows all this somewhat more analytically.

Self-efficacy   Bandura's more recent theorizing has been concerned with feelings of *self-efficacy*, or competence. According to Bandura (1977), our behaviors are often mediated by feelings of whether we can perform the behavior. Generally we choose to do things we feel we can do and we persist in doing activities that yield rewarding feelings of competence or self-efficacy. Thus what you do in a given situation is affected not only by such

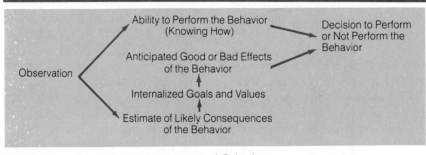

FIGURE 1.2   A Social Learning Account of Behavior

external consequences of behavior as praise from others but also by your self-evaluations.

Feelings of self-efficacy arise most readily from our own experiences. However, we can also assess how well we might do at some task by observing others ("I can do what he is doing") or by having others persuade us ("You can do it"). In addition, Bandura emphasizes that people often structure tasks to achieve success and feelings of efficacy. For example, it might be best to break complex tasks into subgoals and to try to achieve these subgoals rather than try immediately for the larger goal of success on the total task (Bandura & Schunk, 1981). Also, explicit goals and concrete feedback about performance are often helpful (Bandura & Cervone, 1983).

Self-efficacy theory is a significant advance over earlier social learning theories that saw behavior as controlled mechanically by situational forces. In self-efficacy theory a person's cognitions about the task and expectancies play a major role. The theory is still hedonistic because it stresses our desires to achieve satisfying outcomes, but the control over behavior has passed to the acting person.

IMPRESSION MANAGEMENT THEORY

Up to this point we have discussed our desires for rewards in a general sense, and we have paid little attention to specific kinds of rewards or pleasures. Indeed, most hedonistic theories do not distinguish among money, status, invitations to parties, being liked, sex-

ual satisfaction, having a good laugh, and relaxing one's normal cares, among others, as important classes of rewards. However, for the social psychologist one source of reward is especially salient and central: the approval others can provide. There may be nothing quite so important to most of us as winning and keeping the approval of others, as being liked and respected. Not only is approval rewarding for its own sake, it is also a means to other ends. Job promotions, popularity, and sexual gratifications may depend heavily on whether others approve of you and your behaviors.

Approval itself is, of course, dependent on how others perceive you. All things being equal, a person who is perceived as being nice will be liked, will be invited to more parties, and will have more friends than someone who is seen as hostile. A person who is seen as ambitious, competent, and hardworking will probably go further in most careers than the person who is seen as lazy and not very bright.

Because how others perceive us will affect their reactions to us, their approval of us, and ultimately our rewards and costs, those who care about such rewards and costs will be tempted to manufacture a favorable public image. The psychology of managing impressions is ancient, and nearly everyone who has written on social life has been aware that impression management is an ever-present possibility.

Edward E. Jones (1964) initiated a major line of social psychology research with his model of ingratiation. According to the ingra-

Edward E. Jones

tiation model, when people want to win the favor of others, they may use a number of strategies such as conforming to others, expressing approval of others, and presenting themselves to others in particular ways. Self-presentational strategies in particular have been intensively studied. If a student wants me to think she is particularly smart, she may simply tell me directly that she is smart or she may use some more subtle strategy of declaring her intelligence.

Impression management models (Baumeister, 1982; Schlenker, 1980; Tedeschi, 1981) generally focus on several variables. First, they suggest that the person's desire to create a good impression may be affected by personality variables such as need for approval or by situational demands such as a job interview. Some people seem always to be obsessed with the impression they make on others, whereas others never seem to care much; presumably such differences are related to personality. On the other hand, most of us are not inevitably or always trying to win approval, but do so only when our own goals in a particular situation encourage trying to win approval. Second, the nature of the desired impression will depend heavily on the values of the audience. You may want your professors to think you are smart and hardworking but prefer that your friends think you kind and warm. There may even be circumstances in which you want others to think you have some quality that is normally undesirable. For example, when you walk down a dark street late at night you may

want to convey an impression of hostility, even meanness. Third, there are many strategic considerations in conveying a desired impression. As many of you know from job interviews, there is often a subtle distinction between seeming to brag and seeming self-confident about your abilities. We consider some of these strategic concerns in Chapter 12.

It is important to note that not all or even most impression management is deceitful. People sometimes lie about themselves simply to create a favorable impression, but being sincere and honest can also have the same effect. You may be smart and still make sure your professor knows that fact. Moreover most impression management is not even conscious. Most of us pick our wardrobes, obey rules, behave morally, and do assigned tasks not from some specific desire to create impressions but more from a generalized concern to appear normal and well-socialized. Thus the impression management model is a general one that has wide application to a variety of situations. However, because approval concerns are so pervasive, the impression management model may be too general to make precise predictions (Tetlock & Manstead, 1985).

HEDONISM THEMES

There are three major themes which emerge from our discussion of this most ancient of theories about human motivation:

- The behavior of people is motivated by a desire to achieve rewards and avoid costs. Because different people value different things, these rewards and costs depend on the values and psychological processes of each individual.

- From observing other people we learn how to accomplish our goals and what consequences will likely occur if we perform certain behaviors.

- Because the approval of others is highly rewarding and mediates other rewards, people seek to win the approval of others and to avoid their disapproval by behaving in appropriate ways and by presenting a favorable image of self to others.

PERSON AS PHYSICAL FIELD: RESOLVING MOTIVATIONAL CONFLICT

THE PHENOMENOLOGICAL APPROACH

It is a commonplace fact of elementary physics that the "behavior" of a physical object results from several physical forces. For example, when you throw a ball, its trajectory (behavior) results from the forces of your throw, gravity, wind, and the spin on the ball, among other things. Similarly we could think about the behavior of people as the result of various forces.

Kurt Lewin (1935, 1951) argued that our overt behavior and thinking are constant struggles to resolve conflicting motivational forces. We want to do mutually incompatible things at the same time or we want to be doing something other than what we are presently doing. For his analysis, Lewin insisted that the basic unit was the individual person in her or his environment. The environment, called the **life space,** consists of both the person and the immediate psychological environment. This environment is divided into regions corresponding to important aspects of the physical and social world as perceived by the individual.

Note that the life space is a *psychological* environment. Lewin suggested that we respond not to the real environment but to our conceptions of it; this is sometimes called the **phenomenological approach.** For example, just now I am hungry, my back hurts from typing for so long, I would like to listen more carefully to a lovely Mozart sonata playing in the background, and I want to finish this section of the chapter before lunch because I have a series of boring and distracting meetings all afternoon. Like the thrown ball that is subject

Kurt Lewin

to all kinds of pushes and pulls, my own behavioral inclinations are also being jerked around by the forces of my phenomenological environment just now. My resolution: I will type faster, turn off the radio, and get up for lunch at 1 P.M., whether I am done or not.

A great deal of Lewin's work was devoted to an analysis of forces in the life space, their tensions, and the reduction of such tensions. Throughout this analysis he always had the model of physics before him. Because he tried to understand behavior in a psychological field as physicists try to understand the behavior of objects in a physical field, his theory has sometimes been called *field theory.*

INTERNAL AND EXTERNAL CAUSALITY

Much of the research of Lewin and his students was addressed to how groups make decisions and how these decisions affect the individuals within the groups (see Chapter 11 for a summary). One of the things he observed was that people respond differently to their own desires than to what others want them to do. They conform to the dictates of others but only when others are in position to reward and punish them. When left to their own devices, people tend to do what they want to do and not what others tell them. Lewin called the forces initiated by other people, such as threats of disapproval and punishment as well as promises of rewards, *induced forces,* whereas those motives from the person's own desires he called *own forces.*

Social psychologists continue to find this distinction highly useful although these days the induced forces tend to be called **external forces,** reflecting their origins exterior to the person, and own forces are now typically called **internal forces,** reflecting their origins within the person. A good deal of modern research in social psychology is based on this distinction. For example, when we consider social influence (Chapter 11), we distinguish between true *conformity,* wherein people behave in certain ways because they want to, and *compliance,* wherein the change is often a superficial response to the external forces of others' desires. You can help your roommate with his project because you really enjoy it (internal or own forces) or because you know he will loan you his car if you do so (induced or external forces). Attribution theories (Chapter 4) claim that in our perceptions we also make a sharp distinction between causes of behavior that are internal ("he was nice because he's a nice guy") and those that are external ("he was nice because his mother told him he had to be"). Research on intrinsic motivation demonstrates that people work at tasks differently when they are intrinsically (internally) motivated than when they are extrinsically (externally) motivated. Thus, the Lewinian distinction between own and induced forces has powerful echoes a half century after he introduced it.

In many ways Lewin is the father of modern social psychology. His personal qualities as a person, teacher, and researcher exerted a strong influence on the work of his students, many of whom became leading social psychologists in their own rights. Lewin's insistence that our needs and desires involve competing tendencies and that stable, "normal" behavior occurs only when equilibrium is achieved has been highly influential.

LEWINIAN THEMES

Two broad themes suggested by the seminal work of Kurt Lewin remain important today:

- Our behavior is a response to various, often conflicting, forces from the external world and our own needs and values. Behavior is a function of how these forces are represented in our consciousness; that is, our behavior is a response to our cognitions about the world rather than to the actual world we inhabit.

- Behavior is different when it results from external pressures than when it results from internal desires and personality dispositions.

PERSON AS SCIENTIST: COGNITIVE MOTIVATION

Partially because of the influence of Lewin, social psychologists have, in recent years, been receptive to models of cognitive motivation. According to such models, people have natural desires to understand, to keep their worlds consistent and predictable, and to exert some control over their environments. Because these are exactly the sorts of things that scientists care about, it has often been suggested that people are like scientists.

Scientists do many things, of course, but there are several motivational tendencies that seem to underlie their work. First, they must be curious, and must try to build a theory or explanation of what they seek to explain. Second, in so doing they will try to formulate a set of internally consistent and well-ordered propositions. Finally, they will use their theories to make predictions and ultimately to control some aspects of the environment. Those who feel that people are like scientists argue that everyday people also have those same concerns although they may not be as rigorous in their methods. The scientist simply has a more formal way of doing what we all do much of the time: explore and ask questions, formulate theories, make observations, predict, and control.

THEORY BUILDING

Before 1960 or so American psychologists did not concern themselves very much with cognitive processes. Behavior was assumed to be a learned response to some internal or environmental stimulus. Now, however, most psychologists argue that people do more than respond passively to their environments. Rather, they are active in trying to make sense of the world. And in trying to subdue the complexities of the world, everyday people do what scientists do—they construct models or theories about the ways the world operates. Many of these theories are acquired from the culture through socialization, whereas others come from personal experience.

No matter how they are acquired, theories are more than useful—they are essential. Without theories you could understand nothing. One reason our nightmares are so disturbing is that they usually violate the theories we have about the world. Every time you use language, name some object, or label a behavior you invoke an implicit theory about the world. When you try to understand some new event or person in terms of your past experiences, you must use a theory about the past. Some of these theories are explicit and easily verbalized, but at other times you use theories you probably cannot put into words. So by the end of a course you probably have a pretty good idea of how the professor assigns grades ("what he wants on exams"), but you may be quite inarticulate about the rules you use to decide why one professor is interesting and another boring.

Theories help us simplify the complexities of the world by focusing attention on essential details, but there is a significant cost in the use of theories. Sometimes they lead us to miss important information or to misremember what actually happened. When you see your professor on the first day of class, you will attend to what she says about course requirements and whether she seems to have a good lecturing style but you will probably not pay close attention to the color of her shoes. That is generally efficient because shoe color is probably not a part of your theory about what makes college professors tick. But there might be circumstances when that item of information is important. Countless murder mysteries revolve around skilled detectives who note such items of information that most of us ignore. We will have a good deal to say about the relative costs and benefits of informal theories in Chapter 3.

COGNITIVE CONSISTENCY

The Importance of Consistency   Theories are important, but they are almost always simplified models of the ways things actually work. Rather than try to capture the full complexity of some phenomenon, a scientist tries to simplify by finding the essential qualities. But in so doing the scientist must also strive to find an inner coherence among the qualities; the parts of the theory must be consistent with one another. So if you developed a theory that everyone is essentially kind but that everyone is also out to get you, we might dismiss your theory as implausible just because it is internally inconsistent.

During the 1950s many social psychologists argued that having consistent thoughts is so important that we have a fundamental drive or need for cognitive consistency. We discuss such theories in more detail in Chapter 3, but here we describe the essential features of Festinger's (1957) theory of cognitive dissonance, which has been the most influential of the consistency theories.

Cognitive Dissonance   Festinger assumes that two cognitions can be either *consonant* (consistent) or *dissonant* (inconsistent) with one another. Thus "I do not smoke" and "I know smoking is bad for my health" are consonant cognitions because they are consistent psychologically on the reasonable assumption

"I smoke" and "smoking is bad for me" are dissonant cognitions.

that I value my health. On the other hand, "I smoke" and "I know smoking is bad for me" are dissonant cognitions. The fundamental assumption of the theory is that people find dissonance uncomfortable and hence are motivated to reduce it. The magnitude of the dissonance is a function of (1) the number of dissonant cognitions relative to the number of consonant ones and (2) the importance of the cognitions. With cognitions of equal importance, the person who has four consonant cognitions (I smoke, smoking relaxes me, I don't think I could quit smoking, smoking helps me keep my weight down) and one dissonant cognition (smoking causes lung cancer and heart disease) will have less dissonance than the one who has only two consonant and one dissonant cognitions. But we also have to take into account the importance of the cognitions: in the above example, the person who values his health more than his weight will have more

dissonance than the person who values these two equally or who values keeping a slim figure more than living to a ripe old age (see Table 1.2).

As the magnitude of dissonance increases, so does the desire to reduce dissonance. There are three basic ways to reduce dissonance: (1) change a cognition, (2) add new cognitions, and (3) reduce the importance of the dissonant cognitions. So our smoker could change the cognition that smoking is harmful to his health; cognitions that "I smoke" and "Smoking is *not* harmful" are not dissonant but consonant. Or he could add several other reasons why he should continue smoking (adding cognitions), thus overwhelming the one cognition that says smoking is bad. Finally, he could change the importance of the dissonant cognition, for example, by deciding that because he will die anyway smoking is not that big a risk.

Cognitive dissonance theory has been a major theory in social psychology since 1955. Indeed, it may be the most used (and abused) theory in modern social psychology (see Box 1.1, pp. 22–23).

TABLE 1.2 DISSONANCE MAGNITUDE AND REDUCTION.

Small Dissonance	
I smoke	Smoking causes
Smoking relaxes me	lung cancer
I can't quit smoking	
Smoking helps with my weight	

Large Dissonance	
I smoke	Smoking causes
Smoking relaxes me	lung cancer

Larger Dissonance	
I smoke (important)	Smoking causes
Smoking relaxes me (trivial)	lung cancer
	(very important)

Dissonance Reduction	
I smoke	Smoking causes
Smoking relaxes me [change]	lung cancer
	I do not smoke

BOX 1.1

COGNITIVE DISSONANCE THEORY

Festinger's theory of cognitive dissonance has been the most widely used and durable theory in modern social psychology. Like all theories, this one was not totally original; the idea that people dislike inconsistent ideas can be found in major philosophical theories for centuries past. However, Festinger added the strong assumption that we are *motivated to reduce* this inconsistency.

There were many sources for the theory. Festinger's teacher and mentor, Kurt Lewin, had emphasized the importance of resolving tensions between conflicting demands and desires within the psychological life space. Lewin and his students had done research on the effects of group decisions (see Chapter 11); people tend to agree with decisions when they have been a part of a group that made them. Festinger suggested that the group decision forced a realignment of cognitions in support of the decision; it reduces dissonance to be in a group with which one agrees. Also some of Festinger's early research on conformity pressures in groups (Chapter 11) suggested that groups did not like disagreement (inconsistency) and tried to restore unanimity by either converting or expelling dissidents. Cognitive dissonance can be thought of as the individual, internal, cognitive counterpart of these group tendencies.

Perhaps the most important immediate stimulus to the theory was work Festinger did with Henry Riecken and Stanley Schachter on how people respond to disconfirmations of central beliefs. This work, reported in the classic *When Prophecy Fails* (1956), was based on field research with a group of people who had predicted that the world would end on a particular day. Before the crucial day, the group had been secretive and did not seek converts to its cause. After the prophesied destruction failed to occur, the group actively sought to convince others that its views were correct (although admitting they had miscalculated the date of destruction). Festinger and his colleagues argued that garnering social support is one way to affirm the correctness of one's beliefs: the substantial dissonance engendered by the failure of the prophecy led the group members to seek converts as a way of reducing dissonance.

Cognitive dissonance theory was embraced by social psychologists for at least two major reasons. First, the theory helped explain many otherwise quite different phenomena. Second, many of the predictions of dissonance theory were contrary to predictions made by common sense. Social psychologists generally like theories that seem to fly in the face of conventional wisdom.

To get an idea of the range of phenomena covered by the theory, consider some of the early research problems stimulated by dissonance theory. Imagine that you have just bought a new computer, say a Macintosh, after also considering an IBM. Dissonance theory suggests that after you have made the purchase you will emphasize the wonderful features of the Mac (it is small, does graphics nicely, is cheaper) and the negative features of the IBM (it is big, the dealer was arrogant, a friend has had all sorts of problems with her IBM). Knowing that the IBM has good features and that the Mac has deficiencies creates dissonance, so you minimize the IBM's virtues and the Mac's shortcomings. The theory also predicts that when you get back to your dorm, you will try to convince others that the Mac is better than the IBM; gaining converts is a further validation of your choice. Further, when you read computer magazines, you will prefer to read about Macs than IBMs because you don't want to increase your dissonance by reading good things about the IBM.

What are your feelings about that class you are taking that is giving you fits and that has stimulated several all-nighters? When it's all over, aren't you likely to tell everyone how much you hated the stupid course that kept you awake nights? Not necessarily, according to the theory. Sometimes you decide to love the things you suffer for. In this case dissonance between the beliefs that (1) you worked hard and that (2) you hated the course can be reduced by deciding that you liked the course (Aronson, 1961). Similarly, if you have to jump through hoops to get into a group you want to join, you may actually like the group more than if you were admitted routinely, without initiation. The knowledge that you suffered a severe initiation is dissonant with hating the group, but suffering to get into a group that you have decided is attractive is not dissonant (Aronson & Mills, 1959). Even being forced to eat a disliked food can make you like it more—on that score your mother knew what she was talking about (Brehm, 1960). Conversely we may come to hate the things we can't have. Children who are kept from playing with a valued toy come to dislike it as a kind of sour-grapes phenomenon. Again, liking something is dissonant with knowing that you can't have it, but disliking something you can't have does not arouse dissonance (Aronson & Carlsmith, 1963).

In one of the most striking predictions from the theory, we may under some circumstances change our attitudes to match our behaviors. The cognitions that one has said one thing and that one believes another thing are dissonant; this dissonance can be reduced by changing the attitudes to match the behavior. Cognitive dissonance theory has been used to explain classic psychoanalytic defense mechanisms such as projection. If you believe you have undesirable characteristics, this should arouse some dissonance; you might reduce the dissonance by convincing yourself that other people have the same nasty traits (Bramel, 1962).

Note that several of the theory's predictions are not ones you would generate from your own intuitions. Most of us probably feel that we decide we like the things we choose *before,* not after, we have chosen them. And it seems odd that we would like things such as courses and groups that make us suffer. Surely being forced to do something can't make us like it. Usually we imagine that attitudes affect behaviors and not the reverse.

Like most scientists, social psychologists prefer theories that predict the novel and the unexpected. In general we do not feel the need for elaborate theories to explain the common, the routine, the expected. So the ability of dissonance theory to generate predictions that violate everyday understandings of thought and behavior is an important reason for its popularity. In addition, the theory is capable of fairly precise predictions. We do not always like the things we choose nor do we modify our attitudes to be consistent with our every action, but the theory allows the careful psychologist to determine when such effects will occur.

The theory of cognitive dissonance neither explains everything nor inevitably makes correct predictions; in fact, minor modifications have been made to the theory over the years to accommodate unpredicted data from experiments. Although the theory is no longer a major generator of research hypotheses, its established validity allows us to use it as an explanation for a wide range of human behavior.

CONTROL AND PREDICTION

Prediction   Scientists and the rest of us develop theories for many reasons, but among the most important is that theories allow for prediction of events and control over the environment. Our every action is based on the sense of a predictable world. You would hardly venture from your room unless you could be reasonably certain there is something firm to place your feet on outside the door. Feelings of security and safety, so essential to our feelings of well-being, are largely based on our beliefs that we can predict what will happen.

Prediction has an added benefit. Events we can predict we often can also control. If you theorize that professors give high grades to students who praise their lectures, you will be in position to raise your grade through some well-chosen remarks—assuming, of course, that your theory is correct. In recent years psychologists have emphasized fundamental needs for control and prediction.

Reactance   Feelings of being able to predict and control situations enhance feelings of freedom. And most of us like to feel free. Jack Brehm (1966) has argued that people experience a state called *psychological reactance* when their freedoms are threatened, and this reactance motivates attempts to reassert control. For example, suppose an overbearing friend tells you that you must, simply must, agree with her about abortion. Might you be inclined to dig in your heels a bit at this point and even be contrary enough to take the opposite position just to prove that you are independent and cannot be pushed around? The experience of having one's feelings of control threatened is common enough, and reactance theory suggests that in such circumstances you will often be motivated to prove that you still have control.

SOCIAL REALITY

Scientists and everyday people are curious, have theories about the world, try to keep their ideas consistent with one another, and predict and try to control their social and physical worlds. The end result of all this activity is a sense of reality, a more or less consistent set of beliefs about the whys and wherefores of the world. *Reality* is a tough term to define exactly, but informally it refers to those things about the world we take for granted and rarely question.

Much of our reality is occupied with things we can directly test through informal tests and

In most cultures, religious leaders help structure important realities.

experiments. I feel relatively confident that pressing the "e" key on my computer terminal will produce an "e" on screen now just as it has for the past several minutes. Turning the steering wheel to the right surely will make the car turn right. Such theories about the physical world get informally tested many times throughout the day. Other beliefs might be directly tested but only with great inconvenience. You believe that the world is round, but you have probably not tested this directly for yourself; indeed you have less direct evidence for this belief than the ancients did for theirs that the world was flat. It is doubtful that you will test your belief that hammer blows dent car fenders by hammering on your own car, but the test is begging to be run if you suddenly are overwhelmed with doubt.

Moreover, many of our beliefs are not subject even to inconvenient tests. How could you test theories that God exists, abortion is wrong, capitalism is better than communism, psychology courses are better than accounting courses, or Ronald Reagan is a poor president? The validity of many of our most cherished beliefs cannot easily be demonstrated through direct tests, although that does not necessarily make them wrong.

The Nature of Social Reality   Much of what we know to be true about the world derives from other people and from our cultures. Social scientists usually refer to such socially generated beliefs as *social reality.* Most of your social realities have been drummed into your head early and often. Your culture provides a language, a set of regularly used categories, a rather constrained set of religious beliefs, and so forth. But the culture also does something else important—it designates certain people as authorities on particular aspects of reality. For example, most societies have a priest class that interprets the higher mysteries of the universe to the less enlightened. In our society many people regard scientists as having

special insights into truth. An important part of our reality systems is that they tell people whom to turn to for help in defining reality.

Even if a priest, scientist, or guru is not at hand when you are confused, you can seek clarity by speaking to or watching others. An important part of the socialization process is learning how, when, and from whom to seek information. As we emphasized in the discussion of social learning theory, you can learn a lot about how to behave and think just by watching others, and often the behavior of others is used to define a reality. Because beliefs that cannot easily be proved need confirmation from others, communities of believers are important in religion, politics, and social ideologies.

Elaboration of the Social World   When social scientists speak of social reality, they usually are referring to the beliefs about religion, politics, social relations, and economics that are central to a given culture. However, there are also less-cosmic realities created in our social interactions, and our socialization helps ensure that everyday social interactions are meaningful. We are taught how to behave properly so that our behavior will be meaningful to others and not cause them undue stress and anxiety.

In this regard, it is important to note that the physical and social worlds differ in fundamental ways. The world of physical objects is basically a predictable one: my house does not move and my car responds in predictable ways to my behavior. Indeed large parts of the physical world can be controlled because the objects in that world have an essential inertia and tend to respond to physical forces in lawful ways. Matters are different with people because they insist on having wills of their own. People do not merely react; they do what they want to do.

However, social life is not entirely unpredictable. We are socialized and taught rules of behavior that everyone in a given culture tends to follow, so we do not all march to the beat of different drummers. Through our behavior and adherence to these rules we project images of ourselves and our situations. So when I give a party I am not merely creating the circumstances for people to have a good time. I am also implicitly suggesting that I am sociable, that I know how to pay back social obligations, that I have the skills to create a good party atmosphere, and that I have interesting friends. A guest who refuses to accept this definition by behaving obnoxiously not only creates a primary unpleasantness by insulting others, but he also calls into question my images of being a good party-giver and a person who has good taste in friends. To protect against such awkwardness there are fairly strong though implicit rules that say guests at parties should not be obnoxious and that everyone should conspire to confirm my definition as a good party-giver by acting as if the most boring party is great fun. Rules of politeness keep all our social apples in their carts so we can have smooth interactions with one another.

We all learn rituals of tact and rules for various remedial and supportive interactions that tend to confirm existing definitions of situations (Dreitzel, 1970; Garfinkle, 1967; McHugh, 1968). Unless reasons for alarm are great (as when you walk through a dangerous neighborhood), it is simply easier to believe that what seems to be true is true.

COGNITIVE THEMES

Many social psychologists believe that the complexity of human social behavior cannot be grasped without theories about how people try to understand their worlds. Many have assumed that everyday people are much like scientists in that regard. Four major themes have animated the cognitive approach to social behavior:

- People develop and use theories about the behavior of others and social events. Such theories aid our processing of information but at the cost of oversimplifying reality and producing error.

- Inconsistency among cognitions is unpleasant, and our behavior and cognitive processes seek to reduce such inconsistencies.

- People desire to control their environments and to predict events and the consequences of their behavior. People attempt to avoid threats to this control.

- Social and cultural forces create realities that guide our behavior and thought, and much of our behavior supports such realities.

PERSON AS ACTOR

SOCIAL SCRIPTS, RITUALS, AND HABITS

When you stop and think about it, much of your behavior is habitual and ritualized. You say hello to friends you meet on campus, you say "you're welcome" when someone says "thanks." You sit quietly in class, act in certain specified polite ways in the company of your minister, priest, or rabbi, dress in particular ways, often without much thought, and drive familiar routes lawfully and safely but without much conscious attention to road signs.

The fact that much of our social behavior is fairly routine and ritualized has long been noted (James, 1890). If you are inclined toward mechanical explanations of human behavior, you can see such examples as evidence of conditioning; that is the way they have been viewed for much of this century. But there is a better perspective. Consider a dramatic play or some formal ritual such as a wedding. When a play is performed, there is a physical stage setting and a set of lines that tightly constrain the behavior of the actors.

The bride, her father, and the attendants play their roles in the "giving away the bride" portion of the wedding script.

Similarly, in a wedding, the bride, groom, attendants, minister, parents, and guests all have assigned roles and typically know what they are supposed to do at any given juncture. However, neither the behavior of actors nor that of brides and grooms is exactly controlled in the same way that the behavior of a rat performing a trick is controlled. People perform their assigned roles on the stage and in life because they have some conception of the overall plan and their place in it. For actors, the script constrains and organizes behavior without controlling it in detail: actors can say their lines in several ways and, within limits, can move as they wish.

Sociologist Erving Goffman's (1959, 1963a) *dramaturgical perspective* suggests that our so-cial lives are affected by such scripts. We do not usually have to think deep thoughts about how to behave in a given situation, because the script tells us. Sometimes such behavior becomes so automatic that it is performed unthinkingly; it becomes habitual. A person extends his hand and you shake it without thinking much about what this means or why you are doing it. But your behavior is free in the sense that you could, if you wished, kiss his hand, or slap it, or ignore it. Other times scripts are acted out with considerable thought and skill: you probably monitor your behavior carefully as you enact the role of interviewee in a job interview, for example.

Rom Harré (1979; Harré & Secord, 1972) suggests that we follow social rules, but he emphasizes the extensive thought we use in understanding and obeying them. When you enter a new situation, you may not be perfectly clear what rules are appropriate. Your professor invites you to his house for dinner. Is your role that of dinner guest? student? friend? As the evening progresses you will pick up cues about the role you are supposed to play and govern your behavior accordingly.

According to Harré, behavior in social situations cannot be understood as a mechanical response. How the person understands the rules and their application to behavior are crucial features of organized social behavior. If we are to understand fully why people behave as they do, we must examine behavior in natural settings and uncover the rules that govern that behavior. Harré has been quite critical of experimental studies of social behavior that typically provide artificial and unfamiliar settings in which normal rules do not apply.

The perspective of person as actor also has implications for our constructions of reality. Our understandings of the world are based in part on the stability provided by social rules and scripts (Schank & Abelson, 1977). At some level you have no trouble understanding what is happening at a wedding because the behaviors follow a well-defined script. We take on social identities through the roles we play, we understand others in the same way, and we behave in terms of expectations based on the roles we play.

THEME OF THE ACTOR PERSPECTIVE

The dramaturgical perspective suggests that in some respects "life is a stage." Like actors, we use scripts provided by our culture to guide our behavior; like actors, our behaviors are guided but not controlled by the script we have.

■   Human behavior is rule-governed. The rules we use for our social behavior are provided by the larger culture and are supported by our continuing adherence to them.

THE COMPLEXITY OF
SOCIAL BEHAVIOR

We have discussed five theories of social behavior and thought. This is a far from complete list of relevant models and theories, and you will encounter others throughout the text. However, these theories have been widely used and they capture the flavor of most theories in social psychology. You may have noted some considerable overlap among the theories as well as major differences. Sometimes social psychologists have played up the differences and have waged theoretical wars over which was more correct. Such conflict has been healthy and productive, but in the final analysis there is no reason to assume that one perspective has a monopoly on truth. Sometimes we act as if we were entrepreneurs in seeking interpersonal profits while at other times we seem more like dispassionate scientists. Biological impulses guide behavior but so do the theories we have about the world and the roles we enter.

William McGuire (1983) argues that all social psychology theories are both correct and

incorrect. Each theory provides a useful way of thinking about some but not all aspects of our behavior. When students discuss their exam performance with me, I am taken with their concerns with rewards and costs; hedonistic theories provide a reasonable way of understanding negotiations over grades. On the other hand, students also exhibit considerable curiosity on occasion, even staying up late to learn about something that interests them with no immediate rewards but with considerable costs. For that behavior the scientist model is more appropriate. Each theory could probably explain both grade negotiations and late-night learning, but each theory has an easier time with one type and explains the other only with considerable effort and strain. So it is best to think of theories not as correct or incorrect but as more or less appropriate.

Thus different theoretical perspectives are best used for different phenomena, a fact reflected throughout this book. At times one perspective will be emphasized simply because it provides a broad way of organizing the data we have. At other times a different theory will move to center stage for the same reasons. But the important point is this:

■   Human behavior is complexly organized and motivated because human physiological and cognitive systems and their environments are complex.

PLAN OF THIS BOOK

In Chapter 2 we continue with a discussion of the scientific methods social psychologists employ and some of their advantages and problems. Then we launch into discussion of various topics central to the field.

SOCIAL COGNITION

As social psychology has evolved during this century, the many problems and issues have tended to group themselves into two large categories: social cognition and social behavior. Although neither is more important than the other, there is a sense in which our behavior in social situations is based on our social cognition, on how we think about those situations. As we noted earlier, many theories make use of the phenomenological approach—our social behavior is affected by our thoughts. Furthermore, our thoughts are influenced by our social circumstances. We see the world though glasses composed of our values, attitudes, self-concepts, beliefs, and cultural understandings. Thus social cognition is concerned with how culture, experience, and language affect our thinking.

In Chapter 3 we consider some general models of social cognition. Chapter 4 shows how social cognition models apply to our perceptions of other people. This approach continues in Chapter 5 by examining our perceptions of ourselves. Chapter 6 discusses language and communication; Chapter 7 discusses attitudes and how they are formed and changed; and Chapter 8 considers how our attitudes, values, and beliefs interact with our understanding of the external situation to produce behavior.

SOCIAL BEHAVIOR

The second large grouping of topics in social psychology deals with social behavior. For all the importance of social cognition as a foundation for social behavior, it is unlikely that we would be very interested in how people think about their social worlds if their thoughts did not have immediate relevance to their behavior directed toward others. Social psychology exists as a field primarily to explain salient behavioral facts of social life: people interact with and form attachments with others, they belong to groups, they help and hurt others, and they conform to social pressures. Although we cannot fully understand these facts without reference to social cogni-

tion, these and related behavioral concerns are the classic core of social psychology.

Chapter 9 discusses the important question of how we become social beings through socialization processes. In Chapter 10 we discuss the nature of groups, what functions they fill, why people join them, and how they are organized. In Chapter 11 we consider how people influence one another: why and under what circumstances do we conform to the desires of others? Chapters 12 and 13 take up interpersonal attraction (liking and loving) and the closely related topic of interpersonal relationships. In Chapters 14 and 15 we consider two broad groupings of social behavior: behavior designed to help others (prosocial behavior) and behavior designed to advance one's own interests at the expense of others (competition and aggression). Chapter 16 extends this discussion to the topics of prejudice and discrimination.

Finally, in Chapter 17 we review topics of central concern to social psychology and discuss how much we can or should rely on the facts and concepts of social psychology. We also consider applications of social psychological knowledge.

CHAPTER SUMMARY

This chapter has focused on assumptions made by various social psychologists about the fundamental tendencies of human behavior. Typically these are expressed as assumptions about basic motives. In this discussion we isolated several themes, which by way of summary we repeat here:

■ Biological drives and needs usually play a larger role in energizing behavior, whereas cultural, cognitive, and situational factors play a larger role in determining which behaviors are performed.

■ The behavior of people is motivated by a desire to achieve rewards and avoid costs.

Because different people value different things, these rewards and costs depend on the values and psychological processes of each individual.

- From observing other people we learn how to accomplish our goals and what consequences will likely occur if we perform certain behaviors.

- Because the approval of others is highly rewarding and mediates other rewards, people seek to win the approval of others and to avoid their disapproval by behaving in appropriate ways and by presenting a favorable image of self to others.

- Our behavior is a response to various, often conflicting, forces from the external world and our own needs and values. Behavior is a function of how these forces are represented in our consciousness; that is, our behavior is a response to our cognitions about the world rather than to the actual world we inhabit.

- Behavior is different when it results from external pressures than when it results from internal desires and personality dispositions.

- People develop and use theories about the behavior of others and social events. Such theories aid our processing of information but at the cost of oversimplifying reality and producing error.

- Inconsistency among cognitions is unpleasant; our behavior and cognitive processes seek to reduce such bothersome inconsistencies.

- People desire to control their environments and to predict events and the consequences of their behavior. People attempt to avoid threats to this control.

- Social and cultural forces create realities that guide behavior and thought; much of our behavior supports such realities.

- Human behavior is rule-governed. The rules we use for our social behavior are provided by the larger culture and are supported by our continuing adherence to them.

- Human behavior is complexly organized and motivated because human physiological and cognitive systems and their environments are complex.

CHAPTER

2

RESEARCH METHODS

As a social psychologist, I am often asked such questions as why people like horror movies, how people can walk on hot coals, whether school uniforms at private schools are justified, why cars slow down at accident sites, why John McEnroe is such a brat when he plays tennis, whether pornography is harmful, and why hijacked hostages speak so favorably about their captors. But among the questions I get asked most frequently is whether televised violence has bad effects on kids. As we see in Chapter 15, this question does not have a straightforward answer. In casual conversation I usually respond that televised violence can't do much good and it might do some harm. But sometimes the questioner wants a more profound answer. In that case I say that a child will not turn into a murderer by watching violent TV but that on the average children do become more hostile after watching violent television. That is, I believe, an accurate assessment of current psychological research, but it often fails to satisfy my interrogator.

"How can you say that? I watched lots of action programs when I was a kid and I didn't become a violent person." "The research shows," I respond. But then my questioners sometimes suggest that psychological research shows everything and nothing. This is a most frustrating response. Apparently we are prepared to believe social science research only when it supports our preconceptions.

Psychologists who do competent research frequently reach conflicting conclusions, and sometimes research findings are complex indeed. But this does not mean that research on such questions is worthless or useless. How else but by research would we seek to answer important questions? Informal wisdom is sometimes incorrect. Public opinion once held that women were too stupid to attend college, and there is no reason to believe that public opinion on the TV-aggression question is more

Careful observation of behavior is an important aspect of empirical research.

accurate. Do we exchange compelling personal stories? Such experiences would probably add up to a draw of sorts: from my own experience I have sometimes been grouchy and hostile after watching a violent movie, and at other times I have been my usual sweet self after a similar movie.

At a minimum we need to be systematic and careful in trying to answer the question. The methods of empirical research are designed to help us do just that. Let us then examine why and how we do empirical research.

HOW DO SOCIAL PSYCHOLOGISTS DO RESEARCH?

PURPOSES OF EMPIRICAL RESEARCH

Why Empirical Research? Social psychologists, like most other people, try to make sense of the social world. However, unlike Mr. or Ms. Everyperson, the social psychologist is likely to set about the task of understanding by doing some sort of systematic empirical research.

Such research has as its primary objective the understanding of some phenomenon. *Understanding* can mean many things, but for the scientist it implies finding general and regular relationships among variables of interest. *General* means that the relationship exists across various entities and *regular* that the relationship occurs under a wide variety of circumstances. Not every relationship among variables will be of scientific interest. Some are too specific and particular. For example, to say that Jimmy always beats up his little brother after watching "Miami Vice" certainly states a regularity about Jimmy's behavior. However, because it is not general over targets, actors, or behaviors it has limited scientific merit (though it might be important nonetheless to Jimmy's parents or therapist).

A more general relationship might be stated thusly: young boys behave more aggressively after watching TV programs containing considerable violence. Note that "Jimmy" has been replaced by "young boys," "beats up his brother" by "behave more aggressively," and "Miami Vice" by "programs containing considerable violence." Such a relationship, if it were true, would, because of its generality, have scientific relevance. And ideally it would apply to and help explain the concrete behaviors of Jimmy; his specific behavior would be considered a special case of the more general formulation.

So we seek general relationships among variables, but as bold statements such general relationships may leave us with an incomplete feeling. There are relationships and there are relationships. Some merely express correlations among events whereas others refer to causal connections. For example, here is a general statement: people who live in high-crime areas watch more violent television than those who live in low-crime areas (Doob & Macdonald, 1979). Almost immediately the alert reader will want to know why such a relationship exists. Are we to assume that crime-filled neighborhoods are pervaded with TV-crazed hoodlums looking for people to beat up? Or perhaps people who live in dangerous neighborhoods are afraid to go outside and therefore stay in their homes with TV as their main solace. Either of these explanations (and many others) is possible, but the point for now is that we do feel the need to make some statement about what produced the relationship. In that regard note that both of the explanations we offered had strong causal implications: either watching TV causes violence, or violence causes fear, which in turn causes people to stay inside and watch TV. But the initial statement of relationships is silent on the nature of the cause, and that silence leaves us feeling somewhat unsatisfied.

Causality Generally we have in mind several related ideas when we assert that one thing causes another. Consider a simple physical example: I cause a ball to roll by pushing it. There are at least two necessary conditions for my making such a statement. First, the push must come before the rolling—the cause must *precede* the effect. Second, every time I push the ball it must roll—there must be a *regularity* to the relationship. Yet even these two conditions are not quite enough. Suppose that someone has diabolically glued the ball to the floor so that my usual push does not make it roll. Although this violates the regularity of the push–roll relationship, we surely would not suggest that on this account pushes do not cause rolls. We must add a third condition: I cause the ball to roll by pushing it only in the absence of glue—the causal relationship holds *so long as other factors do not interfere.* Obviously there are many things that make balls roll or keep them from doing so, but when we concentrate our attention on one of them (a push) we have the right to demand that the others mind their business. Usually this is expressed as an "all other things being equal" condition. Balls roll when pushed, all other things being equal (that is, all other forces being absent or controlled). In general terms then, variable *A* causes variable *B* when (1) *A* precedes *B*, (2) *A* regularly produces a change in *B*, and (3) all other things are equal.

Let us now apply this definition to a concrete example. Does Jimmy's watching violent TV cause him to beat up his younger brother? The answer would be yes provided we could show that (1) the TV watching comes before the beating, (2) watching TV always produces this aggressive behavior, and (3) there are no other variables that interfere with or cause the aggressive behavior. Of course, in everyday life the last condition may be hard to meet. Surely there will be times when Jimmy watches aggressive TV programs but is too tired to hit his poor brother or is inhibited by an observant parent. And Jimmy may be aggressive for reasons other than his TV fare. However, we are asserting that Jimmy's TV habits are *a* cause and not the *only* cause of his behavior.

This latter qualification may seem like cheating, but it is not. When we say that Jimmy's behavior is caused by his watching TV, we do not assert that this is the only cause of his behavior any more than my pushes are the only reasons balls roll. Human behavior, even more than that of balls, is complex and subject to many causes. And some of these causes may work at cross-purposes, may contradict one another. This is important to keep in mind as you read through this text. In every chapter, when we say such things as that watching TV violence causes aggression or that attitudinal similarity causes liking, we are not suggesting that these are the only, or even the most important, causes at work.

Prediction and Control   We seek causal relationships in part because they help us understand behavior. We also search for causes because they aid our efforts at prediction and control. The ability to predict is quite different from the ability to understand. I can safely predict that it will be hot on a July day in San Antonio without understanding anything about the weather, and I have discovered that students who sit near the front of my classes make better grades than those who sit near the rear, although I have no clear idea why. In fact, most of the predictions we make every day are based on observed regularities without benefit of deeper causal understanding.

Sometimes, however, we wish to change, or control, something. Observed regularities are then an ambiguous guide. Suppose a student asks me how to improve his grade. Should I urge him to move to the front of the class? Surely this will help only if something about sitting near the front (such as being able to hear lectures better) actually causes one to make better grades. On the other hand, the regularity may have a different causal explanation—perhaps people who are smarter make better grades and also like to sit near the front. In this case the student's changing his seat will have no effect on his grade.

If you wanted to stop Jimmy from hitting his brother by cutting down on his TV, you would have to know whether something about the TV caused him to be more aggressive. Generally speaking we can better control behavior to the extent that we have a clear understanding of what causes the behavior. If the violence on "Miami Vice" causes Jimmy to be aggressive, we can control his behavior to some extent by forbidding him to watch this and similar programs. However, it may not be the violence that causes the aggressive behavior after all. Suppose that Jimmy is aggressive after he watches "Miami Vice" because that is the last program he watches before he goes to bed, and that as he thinks about bed he also is reminded that he has a dreaded piano lesson the next day. In this case the cause of the behavior is not the violent content of the program but rather its position in the evening's events. Keeping him from watching "Miami Vice" will not reduce his aggression as long as the piano lesson still looms before him.

Formulating the Problem   We usually do empirical research to uncover causal relationships. However, there are several steps in doing the research properly. The first step is to formulate the problem, and perhaps also state predictions in terms of past research and theory.

A general problem that might concern a researcher is, Does watching violent TV programs encourage aggression? The researcher will have to define carefully what he or she means by *watching, violent, encourage,* and *aggression* in this general question.

What does "watching violent TV programs" mean in this context? Does *watching* mean merely that the person is in the same room with a TV on, or do we require that he attend closely to the content of the program?

What does *violent* mean? What is a "violent" TV program? Surely this category includes programs in which people get shot and stabbed, but do we also include slapstick comedy, professional sports, and Saturday morning cartoons? What about the verbal arguing and shouting in many dramas and soap operas? In deciding what to count as a violent TV program, the researcher will probably use past research practices and theories as guides. The researcher might even avoid the question to some extent by creating his or her own programs that contain precisely defined amounts of particular sorts of violence, but even here a theory will serve as a guide in selecting the kinds of violence to show.

Next, consider the term *encourage.* Does this mean that watching violent TV increases motivation to be aggressive, or do we require that the TV watching actually increase aggressive behavior? The scientist will also have to decide whether *encourage* will be taken in a causal sense or in a sense that indicates some less-direct connection.

Finally, we will have to define *aggression.* Hitting or knifing another person would surely count. But would shouting at another person? Again the scientist will have to make some decisions guided by theory and past practices. Someone influenced by Freudian theory might be inclined to look for instances of unconscious hostility, whereas the social learning

theorist would prefer more obvious behavioral measures.

Thus far we have considered decisions about translating the general terms of the problem into more clearly defined categories. Once having decided what the relevant terms mean, the researcher must think about the strategy for actually conducting the research. Most generally, the social psychologist has to worry about the status of the independent and dependent variables.

Types of Variables   Researchers try to study the effects of a small number of variables (**independent variables**) on one or a small number of other variables (**dependent variables**). The independent variables are *causal* variables and the dependent variables are the *caused* or *effect* variables. In the example we have been using, TV watching is the independent variable and aggressive behavior is the dependent variable. Throughout the preceding discussion we have emphasized that there are many other important variables at work in the world—watching TV may cause many things

"Glad you brought that up, Jim. The latest research on polls has turned up some interesting variables. It turns out, for example, that people will tell you any old thing that pops into their heads."

Drawing by Saxon © 1984, The New Yorker Magazine, Inc.

besides aggression, and aggression may be caused by variables other than TV watching. Such **extraneous variables** may be important in other contexts, but they are not directly relevant to the causal relationships under investigation. If an investigator wants to show that watching violent TV causes aggression, the child's success in school would be an extraneous variable. Of course, failure in school may be an important cause of aggression, probably far more important than what the child watches on TV, but for the purposes of the problem as formulated for study, such a variable is extraneous because the researcher defines it as such.

All research involves making choices about what is worth studying (the dependent variables), what possible causes are most interesting or important (independent variables), and what variables will be treated as irrelevant and controlled (extraneous variables).

The primary research question is whether the dependent variable (in our case, aggressive behavior) changes or varies when the independent variable (watching TV violence) varies. As the level of TV watching increases, does the level of aggression increase too? If so, should we interpret this relationship in a correlational or a causal sense? If the independent variable is allowed to vary naturally and the extraneous variables are uncontrolled, the research is *correlational;* if the independent variable is manipulated (say by assigning people to watch specified amounts of violent TV) and an attempt is made to control the extraneous variables, the research is *experimental.*

of murders. In the case before us we might correlate the number of violent TV programs watched per week by a group of elementary school children with their aggressiveness on the playground.

The problem with correlational research is that it is hard to know what causes what. Our working assumption is that causes (independent variables) must precede effects (dependent variables) and that no extraneous variable could be a cause. Suppose we find that children who watch a great deal of violent TV are more aggressive than those who don't. Can we be sure from this correlation of aggression and TV watching that the TV watching was prior to the aggressiveness? Can we be sure that no other variables entered the causal mix? The answer to both is no. Although it is reasonable that TV watching might have caused aggression, it is just as possible that the causal connection runs in the opposite direction— perhaps children who play aggressively are stimulated to watch action programs on TV. A correlation between two variables does not, by itself, tell us which variable causes which. In addition, an uncontrolled extraneous variable may have produced the relationship. For example, it is possible that aggressive parents encourage their children both to behave aggressively and to watch lots of violent television. In that case a third and extraneous variable, namely parental behavior, might produce the correlation between the other two. This problem arises because the extraneous variable has not been controlled and varies with both the independent and dependent variables.

CORRELATIONAL RESEARCH

In **correlational research** the independent and extraneous variables are not manipulated or controlled. The independent variables are simply correlated with the dependent variables. For example, we might examine the correlation between smoking and age of death, or between economic conditions and number

EXPERIMENTAL RESEARCH

Traditionally, most research in social psychology has been experimental. In **experimental research** the investigator does at least two things: (1) manipulates one or more independent variables and observes reactions to this manipulation and (2) attempts to control the extraneous variables usually by assigning sub-

Opinion data can be collected in a variety of settings.

jects to conditions randomly and by selecting stimuli randomly.

Manipulation of Independent Variables Manipulation of independent variables can be accomplished by assigning different groups of subjects to watch different amounts of violent TV. In this way the experimenter determines both the strength of the independent variable and the temporal ordering of variables. When we manipulate the independent variable and observe its effects on the dependent variable, we have, in effect, made sure that the causal direction goes from the independent to the dependent variable.

Controlling Extraneous Variables Several other variables may be correlated with, and could thereby produce the correlation between, both independent and dependent variables. In an experiment we want to be sure that such variables are no longer correlated with the independent variable and can therefore no longer be active causes. In our earlier example we suggested that parental aggressiveness might be correlated with the independent variable of TV watching and hence might ac-

tually produce the aggressiveness. We need to make sure that parental aggressiveness is not related to TV watching.

There are two ways to do this. The first is to make sure that everyone in the experiment has the same level of parental aggressiveness; we *fix* the extraneous variable at a particular level. Because the parental variable does not vary, it cannot be a causal force. One problem with that strategy is that we cannot be sure that our results generalize to families with parents who are more or less aggressive than our sample. Furthermore, other extraneous variables also demand to be controlled. For example, school failures and abusive parenting might also be correlated with TV watching. In principle we could seek to fix all such extraneous variables at a particular level, but in practice we would soon run out of time, energy, and a sample of children with identical parents and experiences.

A less precise but effective strategy for controlling extraneous variables is ***randomization.*** In this experiment we randomly assign children (and their families) to groups that watch certain amounts of violent television every day. If we successfully do this, we should have close to equal numbers of aggressive parents represented in each group. Because the low–violent TV and the high–violent TV groups have about the same number of aggressive parents, we can be relatively certain that any effects we find for TV watching on aggressiveness are not due to the behavior of the parents; all other extraneous variables are likewise controlled by randomization.

QUASI-EXPERIMENTAL DESIGNS

We have emphasized two basic kinds of research: correlational, in which independent, dependent, and extraneous variables vary naturally, and experimental research, in which the experimenter exercises control over the independent and extraneous variables. In a third kind of study, *quasi-experimental designs* (Campbell & Stanley, 1963), the researcher measures the independent variable as it varies freely in its natural state, while attempting to eliminate the effects of any extraneous variables statistically (see Kenny, 1979, for a fuller discussion).

Such strategies require both statistical and methodological sophistication, but we can explore the general logic with a simplified example. In the present case we would measure our dependent and independent variables, and as many potential extraneous variables as we could. Imagine that the researcher has measured parental aggressiveness as one such variable. Assuming that a correlation between

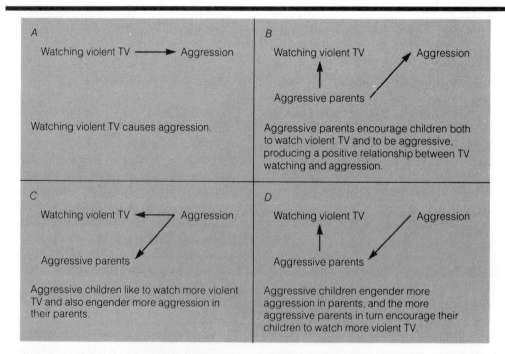

FIGURE 2.1   Some Possible Causal Relationships among the Variables: Watching Violent TV (independent), Aggression (dependent), and Parental Aggression or Hostility (extraneous). Hypothesized causal relationships are shown by arrows.

Donald T. Campbell

watching violent TV and later aggressiveness is found, there are several possible explanations. Figure 2.1 proposes several different causal relationships among the three variables: remember that the researcher in this case *knows* which variables are correlated with which other variables but must *infer* causal direction. Model A says that TV violence causes aggression, and assumes no relationships between parental aggressiveness and either of these variables. Model C assumes that aggression in children should be correlated with TV violence and with parental aggressiveness, because the child's aggressiveness causes these other variables. However, because there is no assumed causal link between TV violence and parental aggressiveness, these two variables should not be correlated. So the patterns of correlations uncovered in the research should help us decide between models A and C. If model A is correct, the correlation between TV violence and aggression should be high and there should be little or no correlation of those variables with parental aggressiveness. If, on the other hand, aggressiveness in children seems to correlate highly with parental aggressiveness as well as with TV violence, model C would be a more likely candidate.

Matters are not so simple with models B and D, unfortunately. They both assume correlations between aggression and aggressive parents and between aggressive parents and watching violent TV. Taken together, these relationships produce the correlation between TV watching and aggression. Therefore, a set of correlations would not, by itself, help us distinguish between these models.

Models B and D differ primarily in that model B assumes that aggressive parents cause their children to be aggressive, whereas model D assumes that aggressive children make their parents more aggressive. To determine which causes the other, we could make use of the simple rule that causes precede effects in time. In practical terms we would sample both the parents' and their children's aggression at several points in time to determine which variable produces changes in the other. If we found that whenever the parent is aggressive the child tends to become more aggressive but not vice versa, we would accept model B and reject model D.

Even with this simple example, you can see that the use of quasi-experimental designs requires considerable skill and foresight on the part of the investigator, who must keep in mind any number of causal possibilities in order to measure not only dependent and independent variables but also extraneous ones.

COMPARISON OF DESIGNS

There are advantages and disadvantages of both correlational and experimental designs. The main advantage of the correlational approach is that both independent and dependent variables are measured in their naturally occurring state, lending a certain amount of realism to the research, in turn increasing our feelings that the results can be generalized to many other situations. On the other hand, a major problem with correlational research is that we usually have trouble knowing exactly what has caused what.

Therefore most scientists prefer to exert control over the independent and extraneous variables. One disadvantage of the experimental approach is that often we simply cannot manipulate variables as we would like. It would not be ethical to raise some children with brutal mothers to see whether this can cause schizophrenia, and it would be practically difficult to get a large sample of people to drive more slowly to see whether such driving reduces traffic accidents. So even when a scientist wants to perform experimental tests, he or she may not be able to do so for ethical or practical reasons.

Interactions   There is an additional, more subtle problem with manipulation of variables: causal variables interact with one another to produce effects. That is, the presence of one independent variable alters the effects of a second. For example, some researchers have hypothesized that watching TV violence increases aggression when children are frustrated but not when children are not frustrated. In such a case, we might expect to find data similar to those in Figure 2.2. It is obvious from these hypothetical data that watching violence on TV produces aggression primarily for the frustrated children. Hence we

would say that frustration and TV violence *interact* in their effects on aggression.

Such interactions are common. For example, criticism may stimulate people who are confident to work harder but make those who are less confident want to quit; bullies may be more likely than nonbullies to be aggressive when around weaker people and less likely to be aggressive when around stronger people.

These interactions are often more important than are single variables. Yet up to this point we have been pretending that variables such as TV violence affect behavior without considering interactions with other variables. It is surely possible that TV violence does not affect behavior strongly by itself but only in interaction with other variables. So televised violence might affect boys one way and girls the opposite, or have different effects on younger and older children, or lead to more aggression if parents seem to approve the program but actually decrease aggression if parents disapprove.

There is nothing in principle to stop an investigator from studying two, three, or even four or five independent variables in the same experiment. But practically it is difficult to study all the variables that might interact with televised violence to affect behavior, however important these combinations might be. Hence the research paradigm that is limited for theoretical or practical reasons to relatively few variables might obscure important relationships among potential causes or independent variables.

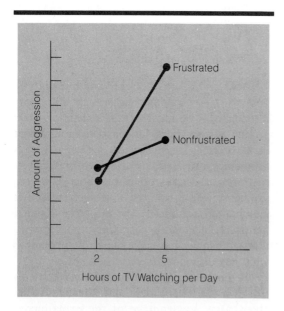

FIGURE 2.2   Hypothetical Relationships between TV Watching and Aggression for Frustrated and Nonfrustrated Children.

Realism   Careful control is an important feature of the experimental method, but may require that the independent variables as manipulated in the experiment do not represent their real-life analogs very well. For example, if we were to set up an experiment in which people were forced to watch several hours of violent TV each day, the subjects may resent having to watch so much TV or having what they watch so rigidly controlled. It might be this resentment rather than the content of the programs as such that makes them aggressive.

Ironically, then, the experimental situation itself may be an extraneous variable that must be taken into account in the causal mix. There is often a tension between realism and the need to manipulate variables precisely. There is no strict rule for how to resolve the conflict. In the first place, it is not necessarily the case that what people do in artificial experiments will differ from what they would do in real life. Subjects' behaviors might or might not be affected by having the decision about which programs to watch made for them. In the second place, the main reason we do experiments is to tame the complexities of the world. We should not be surprised that this bears costs in reduced realism. Nonetheless, the fact that experiments are often contrived is a potential problem to which we need to be alert.

The Psychology of Being in Experiments
Another problem with experiments is that the subjects usually know they are taking part in an experiment and may adjust their responses accordingly. Rosenthal (1966), among others, has pointed out that people in experiments may do what they think the experimenter wants them to do; this is especially likely if the proposed outcome of the study is obvious. In such cases, the researcher can never be sure whether the subjects changed because of the independent variables or because they are being cooperative and doing what is expected of them. The problems with such bias are discussed at length in Chapter 17.

Deception Research   In experiments with humans we often have problems making sure people respond to the "correct" stimuli in the experimental situation. A fruit fly in an air-conditioned lab is probably not distracted by the hot weather outside or by the fact that the lab assistant is an attractive blond football player, but a human subject might care.

Therefore experimenters often try to direct the cognitions of their subjects. However, because the subjects cannot be depended on to turn their cognitions and feelings on or off at the whim of the experimenter, the situation must be structured so that the subjects have the "right" thoughts in their heads at the right time. This may involve telling subjects untrue things about the experiment—often subjects are deceived about what the experiment is about.

For example, if subjects in our hypothetical experiment on watching violent TV knew that we were interested in their aggressive behavior, some might feel that they had to be on their best behavior and would not be aggressive even if they felt like it. Others might respond more aggressively than they truly felt, because they thought that is what we wanted. So we might try to disguise the true purpose of our experiment, perhaps by telling subjects that we are interested in how much they like various programs.

Or suppose we were interested in how people respond to obnoxious others. If the subjects knew what we were interested in, their behavior might be determined more by what they thought we wanted them to do than by the actual other person. Therefore we would need to make the obnoxious person—a confederate of the experimenter—seem to be a routine part of the experiment. (People whose behavior is actually programmed but who act as if they are regular subjects are called **confederates,** and they are used often in social psychology research.) Perhaps we introduce the obnoxious person to the subjects as a person waiting for another experiment to begin.

For some kinds of experiments, deception is necessary for proper control. This can be cruel (for example, telling people they have failed an important task), but usually researchers make sure that subjects are aware of the deception before they leave the experiment and arrange to talk to subjects long enough to answer their questions. A properly conducted debriefing can be an educational experience for both the subject and the experimenter. The ethical question of whether an experimenter has the right to deceive people is discussed further in Chapter 17.

Laboratory versus Field Experiments   For reasons of convenience and experimental control, most social psychology experiments are conducted in formal laboratories. There is, however, no necessary relationship between the type of research and its setting. Experiments can be performed in people's homes or in the streets. For example, some of the best studies on the effects of TV violence have been done in nursery schools or institutions with captive populations. One advantage of doing research

Social psychology research somtimes relies heavily on technology.

in such settings is that subjects need not know they are in an experiment and the manipulations of independent variables therefore can have considerable realism. If nursery school children are used to watching a few minutes of television every day during their juice break, one can easily manipulate what they watch without their being aware they are in an experiment. We can then measure their behavior without fears that they are behaving in particular ways to please an experimenter.

Field experiments, which are conducted in "the field"—outside the laboratory—have their own problems, however. Compared to laboratory studies, there is generally less control over extraneous variables, and the independent variables may also be manipulated less precisely. Measurement of the dependent variables may be limited to what one can easily observe in a public place. Still there are the obvious advantages.

Some social psychologists believe that laboratory research is so hopelessly artificial that it tells us more about the behavior of people in labs than about their behavior in natural settings. Others believe that, despite all the problems of the lab setting, its control and precision are worth the costs. The great majority of social psychologists would accept the results of either kind of research, provided the research has been carefully performed. Ideally one would have research findings from various kinds of studies—correlational as well as experimental, field as well as laboratory experiments—that converge on a single set of conclusions. One reason most psychologists now believe that televised violence is harmful is that we have such convergence. Highly controlled laboratory studies show that children imitate what they see on television (including violence), correlational studies show that people who watch lots of violence are more aggressive, and field experiments find that manipulations of amounts of televised violence affect aggressive behavior.

WHERE DO SOCIAL PSYCHOLOGISTS GET RESEARCH IDEAS?

THEORY

Obviously, one must have ideas before undertaking research of any sort. Usually these ideas are stated in the form of formal hypotheses or predictions. Where do these hypotheses come from? A common source is formal theory.

For example, the hypothesis that television violence ought to encourage aggression can be derived from social learning theory (see Chapter 1), which suggests that models (including those in the mass media) not only teach us how to perform behaviors (such as aggressive ones) but also teach us the consequences of behaving in certain ways. Violent people on TV typically reap the rewards of their activities, if only in the short run. What makes matters interesting is that other theories might make a different prediction. For example, Freudian theories suggest that aggressive energy builds up over time and requires release. On the assumption that watching televised violence is one form of release, such theories would argue that televised violence might lower rather than raise aggressive behavior.

Science seeks not only to test the validity of theories but also to discover crucial tests that help us say which of several competing theories is the most nearly correct. So one reason there has been so much research attention to the TV-violence issue is because several theories make plausible but competing predictions about its effects.

ALTERNATIVE EXPLANATIONS

A related source of research ideas is the alternative methodological explanation. Often, experiments manipulate several things simultaneously. Thus there may be plausible alternative accounts of why the study came out as

it did. Additional research may be needed to clarify which of the alternative explanations is correct.

For example, suppose that children in an experiment were made to watch either 0, 2, or 4 hours of selected, violent programs. Assume also that aggression levels at home and school rise in proportion to the amount of violence watched. This would seem to support strongly the proposition that televised violence causes aggression. However, another psychologist might suggest that the real reason the kids who watched 4 hours per day were more aggressive than those who watched 2 or 0 hours is that the former group was angry or frustrated at having to watch so many programs they did not pick. That is, their aggression was caused by the control exerted over their lives rather than by the content of the programs.

This is a perfectly reasonable alternative explanation for the results. We would have to devise a new experiment to determine whether the control or the violent content was responsible for the behavior. The most straightforward additional experiment would be to have several groups of children watch the *same* number of hours of programs per day but vary the mix of violent and nonviolent programs. Every subject would watch 4 hours per day but some would see all violent programs, some would see all nonviolent programs, and others would see a mixture. In this way we would eliminate the possibility that being told to watch television could cause the results, because all the children have been forced to watch the same amount. Because the content varies across groups, however, any difference among the groups in aggressive behavior might be attributed to the content of the programs. Of course, later someone else might have a different alternative—say that the children who watched 4 hours of violence are angry at having to watch so many trashy programs—and we might have to do yet another study to rule out this possibility. There will almost inevitably be alternative explanations for the results that can lead to additional research studies.

EVERYDAY EXPERIENCES

Thus far we have emphasized the testing of hypotheses derived from a particular theoretical position. However, one does not need theory to do good research. You need never have heard of social learning theory or Freud to be interested in whether TV violence affects behavior. Your common sense may suggest that it does or does not. In either case, you might seek to confirm your hunch through formal research.

Throughout this text you will see many examples of research findings that may violate your intuitions about social behavior. However, sometimes our intuitions turn out to be correct. The important point is that just because people think something is true based on their own experiences does not make it so. Empirical research is a surer guide to truth.

SOCIAL ISSUES

Social psychologists as a group tend to be concerned about major social and political issues in our society. Often their research ideas come from salient real-life problems. For example, research on the effects of televised violence increased markedly during the 1960s and 1970s when violence rates in our society were on the increase.

Another example of a social issue that led to formal research is the murder of Kitty Genovese outside her apartment in New York. None of her many neighbors who heard her cries for help helped her or even called the police. The so-called Kitty Genovese phenomenon—the failure of people to help in an emergency—has been replicated in the laboratory (Latané & Darley, 1970) and is a major area of research (see Chapter 14).

CONCLUSIONS

This is not a complete listing but it does show that there are many ways we get research ideas. Theories are nice but not necessary. Sometimes research is done to tie up loose ends, sometimes just to explore some phenomenon. However, one point should be clear: a textbook account of how research gets done can never convey the full flavor of the experimental enterprise. It is rarely as neat and concise as the discussion might imply. Research is done to promote careers, to get important grants, to prove wrong someone one doesn't like. But most research is stimulated by curiosity. Most scientists find doing research (especially when things are going well—and they often aren't) one of life's most exhilarating experiences.

CHAPTER SUMMARY

■ Empirical research generally seeks to find general and regular relationships among variables. Not all relationships among variables can be interpreted in causal terms, but scientists typically want to discover which variables cause which others. In such cases the cause must precede the effect temporally and the cause must always produce the effect, unless the effect is influenced by the action of other variables. Thus we say that *A* causes *B* when *A* precedes *B*, when *A* regularly produces a change in *B*, and when all other things are equal.

■ All relationships between variables allow us to predict the occurrence of values of one variable from another, but only when the relationship is a causal one will we be able to control the effect by changing the cause.

■ In *experimental* research, scientists study how independent variables cause dependent variables. This requires that the independent variable be manipulated by the experimenter and that other, extraneous variables not of interest to the research effort be controlled. Typically such control is exerted through random assignment of subjects to conditions. Experimental designs can show causality but often suffer from problems with artificiality. In addition, for practical reasons experimenters are often limited in the number of causal variables they can study. Experimental research is not restricted to laboratory settings. Research done in real-life settings, whether experimental or correlational, is called *field research*.

■ In *correlational* research, the researcher does not exert control over the independent variables. This means that often one cannot determine which variable causes which, or whether some extraneous variable may have produced the result.

Although correlational designs do not allow unambiguous causal interpretation, they do allow studies of variables in their everyday setting with considerable realism.

■ In *quasi-experimental* designs, the experimenter does not manipulate the independent variables but does try to rule out extraneous variables through controls and does try to establish causal direction through patterns of correlations.

■ Ideas for research come from various sources. Perhaps the most common and important is formal theory. Another is the attempt to show that results in previous experiments were produced by some extraneous, uncontrolled variable. Some ideas come from real-life experiences or from major social issues.

PART TWO

SOCIAL
COGNITION

CHAPTER

3

SOCIAL COGNITION

The following example is an interaction between me (DJS) and a student (HM) after a lecture in which I claimed that most stereotypes are not so much false as unverifiable. As an illustration, I had suggested that I could not prove that Mexican-Americans were *not* lazy any more than prejudiced people could prove they *were*, simply because *lazy* is a vague term. After class the student asked to speak to me, and when we were alone the following ensued:

HM: I appreciate why you had to say what you did because there were minorities in the classroom. But now that we're alone, wouldn't you admit that Mexicans [a South Texas term for Mexican-Americans] really are lazy?

DJS: I meant what I said. *Lazy* is a vague term subject to all sorts of interpretations, but if we could agree on a meaning I suspect we'd find that Mexican-Americans are no lazier than anyone else.

HM: Well, I know what I mean by it. I've done farm work with Mexicans all my life, and believe me they don't work very hard.

DJS: What do you mean?

HM: They just don't work hard. You have to tell them how to do everything, and if you don't threaten them with being fired they'll do hardly anything at all.

DJS: And you do work hard all the time?

HM: Well, of course not. Nobody does. But I sure work a damned lot harder than they do.

DJS: But maybe if someone was watching you they might catch you loafing from time to time and say you are lazy too.

HM: I always got the job done.

DJS: And did your Mexican-American co-workers?

HM: Sometimes, but only because they were being threatened.

DJS: So if I have your theory down, it's this: if people work only when they are being threatened, they are lazy. That right? [Agree-

If we think we know who are the introverts and who are the extroverts in a group, we may pay most attention to information that confirms our views.

ment.] So let's talk about this course for a moment. You're not doing so well, and my perception is that you don't do most of the reading.

HM: I get most of it done.

DJS: But only because I threaten you with exams, right?

HM: I see where you're leading, but it's different. See school work is basically irrelevant to me. I just want to get my degree so I can get a job, and as long as I get my degree I don't really care about my grades.

DJS: But you would agree that you are lazy given the evidence I have.

HM: But I've just explained that isn't fair. I could do the work if I wanted to. I want to make something of myself, but I'm just not very interested in all the stuff you make me read. I work hard in other places.

DJS: But following that logic you might reason that the Mexican-Americans you were talking about weren't generally lazy; they just didn't like their job. Did you find farm work fun?

HM: But the logic isn't the same. Sure I didn't like the job, but I knew I was going to do something different. These Mexicans aren't ever going to do anything else. It's their job.

DJS: That doesn't make the work any more enjoyable does it?

HM: Well it ought to.

The conversation went on for some time. I tried to record as much of this as possible immediately after the fact because I was impressed by HM's tenacious ability to defend his theories. You can guess that HM was not convinced by my arguments, and, as he correctly pointed out to me, I was also unwilling to change my theory that Anglos and Mexican-Americans were equally lazy (or hard-working).

INTRODUCTION

Psychologists have long been interested in how our cognitive systems transform and change what the outside world presents to us. Just as food must be digested and transformed to be useful to the body, so our perceptions of the world must undergo a cognitive digestion process before we can understand them. The spit and bile of cognitive digestion are theories, past knowledge, and preconceptions. Social psychologists have especially stressed the importance of values, culture, language, and social backgrounds in establishing and maintaining our theories.

In this chapter we begin a discussion of social cognition—the study of how people perceive, interpret, and remember social stimuli (Fiske & Taylor, 1984). This is a large topic and it will take several chapters to cover it.

Social cognition theorists dote on the kind of example we have just presented. Both HM and I allowed our own theories, our preconceptions, to shape our information. We are rarely in position to perceive and think about things exactly as they are. The social world is inherently ambiguous: not only are social events and the behavior of others complex, but much of the meaning of behavior and events depends on psychological states we cannot observe. HM and I see the same behavior as lazy or hard-working because of our different inferences about *why* the actors are performing the behavior.

It is easy to point to errors, biases, and faulty logic in our thinking about social events. On the other hand, the same cognitive processes that produce such problems also allow us to tame the complexities of the world so we can behave effectively. Our cognitive systems are specialized for efficiency, for quickly extracting important information about the world from enormously complex stimuli, and we pay the price of sometimes making errors.

PROCESSING INFORMATION: SCHEMATA AND SCRIPTS

You cannot perceive the world without preconceptions. To be sure, some people claim that they can, through mental discipline or the use of drugs, return to something like a childhood apprehension of the world, a direct contact with reality unsullied by the taint of culture and past experience. But for most of us, most of the time, there is no way to erase the effects of past experiences from the cognitive system. Nor would we want to ignore the results of our hard-fought battles to subdue the complexities of inner and outer worlds.

Past experiences leave residues in the form of cognitive structures that affect processing of information. Several terms have been used for these cognitive structures: *stereotype*, *construct*, *theme*, *prototype*, *world knowledge*, and *frame*, among others. Although there are important differences among these various terms, we will emphasize their similarities and will use the term **schema** (plural *schemata*) to refer to implicit theories or models about people and things, and the term *script* to refer to theories about behavior sequences. (We will often use *schemata* as the general term to encompass both schemata and scripts.)

Our knowledge structures, or schemata, include much more than collections of facts about something. Think about your schema for a classroom. Your visual image will differ depending on whether you focus on a large lecture hall or a small seminar room. But most of the images will have common features: four walls, chairs, a special place for the instructor, perhaps with a podium and chalkboard, and so on. Furthermore, if given the opportunity, you could discourse on why classrooms have the special features they have. You could easily explain why the room has a chalkboard and why it is near where the instructor stands or sits. In short, you have a fairly simple, but useful, theory (schema) about classrooms.

The same might be said of scripts, which are theories about action sequences and how they unfold over time (Abelson, 1976). Consider

Robert P. Abelson

the script for the first day of class. Typically the professor enters the room after most of the students have arrived, walks to her appointed place, hands out syllabi, explains the readings and where they can be purchased, discusses her examination policy, makes preliminary remarks about the nature of the course, and (if you are lucky) dismisses class early. Of course, different professors act out this script differently, just as different classrooms present variations on a basic theme. But the script provides a general framework and the elements of that framework fit together in a meaningful way. Your knowledge of the script is a theory of sorts about the action sequence.

FUNCTIONS OF SCHEMATA AND SCRIPTS

Generally, schemata and scripts allow us to understand the world we encounter and thus provide feelings of familiarity. On the first day of class your schema for the classroom helps you know where to sit, your schema for the professor allows you to know that the woman who enters the room and goes to the front is the professor, and your script for the first day of class tells you what the professor is up to as she begins to hand out materials. Without these schemata and scripts, every new experience would have little meaning, and we would be constantly confused.

When we encounter new information, there are several interrelated steps we must go through to process it. The steps are rarely so

Although the students in this class are atypical of students generally, they understand the schemata of the class.

clearly ordered as the following discussion might suggest (we often jump around in the sequence), but in any case our theories—our schemata and scripts—guide us through each step.

First, schemata (and scripts) *direct our attention and our information-seeking.* They tell us what the important features of an object or situation are. If you enter a room and want to know if it is a classroom, you would surely check for chalkboards and desks before looking to see whether the floor was carpeted or the lights were fluorescent.

Second, our schemata help us *recognize and label new experiences.* You would more readily recognize and label a lectern in a classroom than in a living room just because your schema for classroom has prepared you for seeing things like lecterns. This provides a preliminary, fairly automatic, and somewhat superficial meaning analysis.

Third, schemata *guide deeper meaning analysis* as we integrate the new material with what we already have stored in our memories. Schemata affect what we remember. They help organize our experiences so we can effectively code and retrieve them from memory. You would more easily remember that a classroom had chalkboards than how it was lit. However, our schemata also aid memory for radical departures from the expected. You would be likely to remember quite well a classroom with easy chairs and a wet-bar just because these details are so incongruous from a classroom schema.

Fourth, schemata allow us to *infer beyond what we immediately experience* and to anticipate what is likely to happen. When your professor enters class the first day with a stack of papers, you will assume they are syllabi rather than exams even though you cannot see them. Schemata and scripts tell us what *ought* to be present so we do not need to check on details all the time.

So schemata and scripts are useful in simplifying and categorizing information and thereby help make efficient the processing of information. However, there is a cost. Generally whenever we find rules, theories, or hypotheses that help make our processing of information more efficient, we also find that they are prone to produce errors through miscategorization or oversimplification. Our schemata sometimes direct attention to the wrong things. They help us recognize the familiar but sometimes lead to mislabelings, and they sometimes create errors of memory and judgment. Throughout the remainder of this chapter we will confront a constant tension: our need for efficient ways to understand the complex world also produces many mistakes.

SCHEMA AND SCRIPT ACTIVATION

Any piece of information, any fact, anything you can see or do can be construed in terms of many alternative schemata. My friend is a person, a woman, an extrovert, a professor, a psychologist, and hardworking. How I react to her at any given time is heavily affected by which schema I use to classify her and interpet her behavior. Each of us probably has favorite personal schemata (Higgins, King, & Mavin, 1982)—some people tend to think of others in terms of gender and others in terms of age, height, or ethnic group—but social psychologists have also emphasized situational factors that affect schema use (Higgins & King, 1981).

Expectations   Schemata may become activated because of our expectations. The an-

E. Tory Higgins

imal down the street could be a wolf, but it is more likely that I will perceive it and react to it as a dog. I encounter dogs every day and wolves only infrequently, so I keep the dog schema ready and activate the wolf schema only at zoos because I *expect* to see dogs and not wolves on city streets.

Situational Requirements   We do not go through life passively letting our environments wash over us. We enter most situations with a set of plans and goals we want to accomplish. These may be as simple as walking through the room without making a fool of yourself or as complex as finding your grandmother's friend, whom you have never seen, at the airport. If you are trying to find your grandmother's friend, you will activate schemata having to do with elderly women. This will allow you to ignore all the men and younger women and to concentrate attention on four or five women whom you try to match with your grandmother's description. Having captured your new friend, you then activate schemata (scripts in this case) for retrieving luggage, finding your car, and getting home from the airport. Thus we turn schemata on and off depending on where we are, whom we are with, and what we want to do.

Frequency and Recency   Schemata are more accessible when they have been used frequently or recently (Wyer & Srull, 1981). We have all had the experience of working on something in a particular way and then finding that we cannot turn that specific mind-set off. For example, I find that after a long stretch of grading student papers or correcting a manuscript, I tend to spot grammatical errors in newspapers quite readily.

ATTENTION

Attention is selective; we do not perceive everything around us. Normally you are unaware of the feeling of clothing, and during an engrossing movie you may not be aware of the touch of a friend's hand or the pressure of your bladder. On the other hand, a joke during a complex lecture may restore your wandering consciousness to matters at hand, and you will probably attend closely to details about an upcoming examination.

Directive Factors   Why do we pay attention to some things and not others? Surely strong and vivid stimuli capture attention, but often we direct attention to things we want to label or understand. In that case, available schemata tell you what to look for. For example, suppose you are asking your friend to loan you her car for the evening. You will probably process information about her behavior in terms of a helpful-person schema or a request script. Is she playing her part properly? As you monitor her behavior you will be especially concerned with how friendly she seems, and whether she is reaching for her car keys. You will pay close attention to her nonverbal behaviors and what she says (as well as how she says it), but you will largely ignore the fact she is wearing no shoes and that she has been working on a chemistry assignment.

We pay attention to information that our schemata tell us is important. In an experimental study by Berscheid, Graziano, Monson, and Dermer (1976), subjects thought they were part of a dating study in which the experimenter had assigned them a date whom they would see either once or exclusively during a five-week period. Then the subjects were asked to watch a videotape of a discussion that included the potential date, and they could choose which of the participants they would watch during the interaction. As expected they preferred watching the date to the other discussion participants, and this preference was especially strong when the dating relationship would be long-term.

Attention is hard work, and our schemata also tell us when we can relax. If your friend gives early evidence that she will loan you her car, you cease monitoring her every behavior because your schema allows you to predict the outcome. In an experiment by White and

Carlston (1983), subjects watched a videotape of two people carrying on separate conversations at opposite ends of a table. As subjects watched, they were allowed to manipulate how loud each conversation was; presumably the conversation they most wanted to hear would be made louder. All this was designed to allow for measurement of attention, but schema salience was also manipulated. Before the tape began subjects were given information about the two people; in one case the information was rather bland, but in the other the information conveyed that one of the conversationalists was likely to have a particular personality trait (for example, kindness). In the early part of the tape, subjects preferred to listen to the conversation of the person with the trait, presumably to determine whether his behavior conformed to their schema for that trait. Because the person did generally provide confirming evidence, subjects gradually shifted their attention to the other person for whom they did not have a relevant schema. In the last part of the videotape, the first person began to act inconsistently with his alleged trait, and subjects once again monitored his behavior carefully.

Selective Attention   Our goals and purposes activate schemata that in turn direct our attention to particular features of the environment. Sometimes this can lead to our being so engrossed in something that the rest of the world seems to disappear. Yet this introduces a paradox of sorts. If you are totally wrapped up in reading an exciting novel, does this mean that nothing else can enter your consciousness until you decide to put the novel down? Surely not. Someone's yelling "fire" might manage to penetrate, although a meaningless remark might not.

Cognitive psychologists are far from agreeing how this might be explained, but for our purposes we might imagine that there are particularly important schemata idling below conscious awareness, ready to be activated. So

if you are concentrating hard on something, some stimulus related to one of these important schemata might immediately capture your attention. Self-relevant schemata seem especially important so you might well register the sound of your name spoken softly across a crowded room even if you have been absorbed in conversation. Emotionally arousing stimuli such as sexually explicit words also have this capacity to steal attention away from on-going activities (Nielsen & Sarason, 1981).

So schemata regulate attention in at least two ways. First, our goals, expectations, and values activate certain schemata that in turn direct attention to information central to the schema. If everything seems clear, attention may be relaxed. Second, even when we are concentrating hard on something, information

Sometimes we must focus our attention to shut out distractions.

that is highly relevant to normally important schemata (such as self) refocuses attention on information relevant to this new schema.

PERCEPTION, RECOGNITION, AND INTERPRETATION

Recognition   Your recognition of the things in the world is usually automatic and nonreflective, although sometimes it entails considerable cognitive effort. You ordinarily recognize a dog as a dog almost immediately and without any conscious thought because schemata related to familiar objects are readily accessible. However, you may have to heat up your cognitive juices a bit (that is, explicitly activate a past-roommate schema) to decide whether the guy across the room is indeed your roommate from three years ago. In either case, when a particular schema is activated it facilitates recognition of schema-related stimuli (Neisser, 1976).

Labeling   Events, people, and things can be classified many ways. For example, a gun may be a murder weapon, an heirloom, an investment, or a source of protection. The behaviors of others are especially amibiguous because the meaning of behavior rests on what it was intended to accomplish, and intentions are not readily observed. Schemata become especially crucial in aiding our interpretations of ambiguous stimuli. In the opening example of this chapter, the student HM labeled

Mexican-Americans as lazy and, implicitly, himself as hard-working because—according to his schema—different motivations lay behind the farm work he and Mexican-Americans both did.

Interpretation   Several experiments demonstrate the role of salient schemata in behavior interpretation. Duncan (1976) asked subjects to watch a videotape of two people who heatedly discussed a problem until one shoved the other. The subjects were all white: the major independent variable was the race of the discussants. When a black man did the shoving, most of the subjects rated the behavior as violent, whereas only a small percentage of subjects rated the white shover as violent (see Table 3.1). One suspects that, because violence is a part of a white stereotype of blacks, the stereotype acted as a schema for interpreting the ambiguous behavior. This is not a case of simple racism, however, because black students in a desegregated school also classify the ambiguous behavior of blacks more negatively (Sagar & Schofield, 1980).

In these studies there is only a strong suggestion that it was the race of the stimulus people that activated the schemata of the subjects, but other experiments have manipulated the salience of schemata more directly. Higgins, Rholes, and Jones (1977) had subjects read descriptions of behavior that could be labeled in various ways. For example, "By the way he acted, one could readily guess that Donald was

TABLE 3.1 PERCENTAGES OF SUBJECTS WHO PERCEIVED THE PUSHES AS "PLAYING AROUND" OR AS "VIOLENT." *Note that subjects were more inclined to see the black than the white shover as violent and more likely to see the white than the black shover as playing around.*

	Black Pushes Black	Black Pushes White	White Pushes Black	White Pushes White
Playing around	0	3	25	19
Violent	69	75	13	13

SOURCE: Duncan, 1976.

well aware of his ability to do many things well" could be interpreted as evidence either of self-confidence or conceit. Before reading such sentences, subjects had read a list of either positive or negative words applicable to the story: for example, *self-confident* or *conceited*. After reading the story, subjects who had previously read positive words saw Donald in more positive terms than did those who had read the negative words. Presumably the reading of the words activated a schema that in turn affected interpretation of the ambiguous stimuli.

The fact that active schemata affect interpretations is important and has many ready applications. Consider just one example. Carver, Ganellen, Froming, and Chambers (1983) found that when subjects had a hostility schema activated they saw more hostility in the behavior of others and were themselves more hostile. Given these data it is probably no accident that policemen who live with a constantly activated hostility schema (Rubinstein, 1973) may misinterpret the behavior of others as hostile, sometimes with tragic consequences, such as, perhaps, shooting a young man who was reaching into his pocket for matches, because he "looked hostile" and "was going for a gun."

MEMORY

The human memory system is not like a photocopying machine that faithfully records everything passed through it. Not everything we see or hear is stored in memory, and that which is put away for cognitive safekeeping is often distorted. The classic demonstration was provided by Bartlett (1932), who asked subjects to read a short North American Indian folk tale entitled, "War of the Ghosts." It is hard for most of us to understand and remember this story because of the rich interplay between supernatural and realistic elements. When subjects were asked to recall it, they tended to organize their reproductions around certain themes, to forget material that

did not fit the themes, and to distort what they had read to be consistent with the themes.

Memory for Schema-related Material Bartlett proposed that during both comprehension of new material and subsequent recall, people use schemata (or themes) to guide their cognitive activity. When people think about information in terms of larger information structures, they often remember it better than when they are explicitly trying to memorize it (Hamilton, Katz, & Leirer, 1980; Srull, 1983). One clear implication is that details will be better remembered if they are given meaning by being anchored in a general schema pattern. In everyday life, knowledge about the goals and intentions of people helps us understand and remember their behavior (Hoffman, Mischel, & Mazze, 1981; Owens, Bower, & Black, 1979).

The kinds of judgments we make about information also affect what we remember. In general we tend to remember best the information that is relevant to a schema invoked for a decision (Carlston, 1980; Lingle et al., 1979; Wells, 1982), that supports a decision already made (Snyder & Cantor, 1979), or that is in line with the perspective adopted when the information was first incorporated (Wegner & Giuliano, 1983; Wyer, Srull, Gordon, & Hartwick, 1982). If you meet someone for the first time and think about that person as a potential date, you would be more likely to remember that person's physical features and other personal qualities that you consider relevant to date-worthiness than, perhaps, what clothes were worn or what the person said. This latter information is less relevant to your schema for deciding to date the person, and thus is less memorable in this context.

Schemata improve memories about certain kinds of details. Consider your script (which is a schema for behavioral sequences) for how you get to your first class on Monday. Such a script would include central, defining information such as the route you take, the activities you perform along the way (stopping for mail, getting breakfast), and the identities of your usual companions. These defining details we will call *relevant* or *schema-related* details. There will also be information irrelevant to the script, such as what clothes you wear (unless, of course, you are accustomed to dressing the same way every Monday) and how warm the day is.

Now suppose I ask what you did three Mondays ago. If you are like most people, you will say you can't possibly answer such a question. Who remembers Monday mornings? And three weeks ago? But if you probe a bit, you might find that you can remember a great deal about those things you usually do on your Monday walk, though perhaps not the irrelevant details such as what you were wearing or what the weather was like. People usually remember schema-related details better than schema-irrelevant ones (Cantor & Mischel, 1977; Rothbart, Evans, & Fulero, 1979).

Schema-based Errors There is a price, unfortunately, to be paid for schema-enhanced memory in the form of schema-based error. Specifically you might recall things that never happened but should have. Suppose your script for getting to class includes stopping to check your mail. When I ask what you did three Mondays ago you dutifully report that you checked your mail. However, it is possible that the Monday in question was a holiday and you did not check your mail. You "remember" something as having happened that did not. Or if you were to meet an extroverted person at a party, you might remember that he did lots of extroverted things, but not be as clear as about which of many possible extroverted behaviors he actually did perform. When we use schemata to aid memory we may make errors, particularly by remembering schema-related details that were not, in fact, present (Graesser, Woll, Kowalski, & Smith, 1980; Read & Rosson, 1982).

Memory for Schema-inconsistent Details Presumably you have a schema for your social psychology professor. You easily remember central details of this schema: appearance, speech mannerisms, whether you like her or him, what kinds of exams he or she gives and so on. But suppose one day your professor danced into class dressed in the latest punk fashions, muttering incantations about student devils. It is very likely you would remember that day for a long time. Surely we have good memories for events that depart radically from what our schemata lead us to expect.

Research confirms this. In one classic study, Hastie and Kumar (1979) had subjects read behavioral descriptions, some of which were consistent and some inconsistent with the subjects' impressions of a person. Subjects were later asked to recall the behaviors. They remembered best the behaviors that were inconsistent with their impressions. That is, if they thought the person was friendly, they tended to recall the unfriendly behaviors especially well. Generally, then, schema-inconsistent material is remembered better than schema-consistent material, which in turn is remembered better than schema-irrelevant material (see Box 3.1 for an extended discussion of this research). You would probably remember quite well that three Mondays ago was the day you met a special friend (schema-inconsistent information), less well that you went to class along your usual route that day (schema-consistent information), and hardly recall at all what you wore or what the weather was like (schema-irrelevant information). Actually the tendency to recall schema-inconsistent information has a major advantage: it allows for ready individuation of experiences. I forget students who are just like most other students (that is, who fit the student schema) more quickly than those who don't fit the mold. The other day I encountered a former student in a shopping mall. Neither of us could remember the name of the other, but she recalled that I told silly, but instructive stories about my dog in class and I recalled that she, unlike most other students, liked my jokes. We each remembered individuating information about the other.

BOX 3.1

SCHEMA-BASED MEMORY: INCONSISTENT ITEMS

Standard schema theories predict that information consistent with the schema ought to be better remembered than information irrelevant to or inconsistent with it. Why? Consider your schema for college students. At a minimum your schema would include some information about what characteristics college students generally have: they are intelligent, hard-working, self-centered, grade-conscious, sloppy dressers, loud and rambunctious on weekends, anxious, sincere, and so on.

When you are presented with information about a person, you will draw on your schema of college students and attach relevant items of information to your person image. Some of the information will fit the schema: "Joe is hard-working and grade-conscious." Other information is irrelevant to the schema: "Joe comes from Newark" or "Joe works out at the gym on weekends." In one sense the first type of information ought to be easier to remember because it is not new information: you already know it is likely to be true given that Joe is a student, and all you have to do is make sure the information gets attached to the particular student, Joe, in your memory. The irrelevant information ought to be harder to learn, however, because you have no way of knowing whether it might be true of Joe just by knowing that he is a student. You have to remember something new *and* attach it to the Joe image. But what if you learned that Joe is stupid? This information not only does not fit the schema, it violates one of its central assumptions. Such information ought to be doubly hard to learn: you have to learn information for which you have not been prepared *and* you have to unlearn one key assumption *and* you

have to apply this information only to Joe in your memory.

Yet, research by Hastie and Kumar (1979) finds that people actually remember the inconsistent information quite well. This is not predicted. How can we explain it? Let us discuss the actual research in more detail. Subjects were told they should try to form impressions and remember information about a fictional character. To make a personality schema salient, each subject was told to read aloud eight traits that characterized the fictitious person. Suppose that the relevant schema was *intelligent*. Thus the subject would read the eight traits—intelligent, clever, bright, smart, quick, wise, knowledgeable, and decisive—traits that previous subjects had rated as connoting intelligence. Then the subject read aloud 20 behavior sentences, 12 of which were congruent with the intelligence schema (for example, "won the chess tournament"), 4 of which were incongruent (such as, "was confused by the television show"), and 4 of which were irrelevant (neutral) to the schema (such as, "ordered a cheeseburger for lunch"). Subjects were then asked to recall as many of the behavioral items as they could. Under these circumstances they recalled 43% of the congruent items, 38% of the neutral ones, and 54% of the incongruent items. The results confirm the prediction of schema theories that congruent items are recalled better than irrelevant ones, but the more interesting result is that incongruent items are better recalled than congruent ones. In a second study, the proportion of congruent and incongruent items was varied. As Table B.3.1 shows, subjects recalled a higher percentage of the incongruent items when there were

TABLE B.3.1 RECALL FOR CONGRUENT, INCONGRUENT, AND IRRELEVANT ITEMS. *Note two features of the data. First, subjects recall a higher percentage of incongruent than congruent items and a higher percentage of congruent than irrelevant items. Second, subjects always got 16 items, but as you move across columns from left to right, the percentage of that number that was incongruent increases and the percentage of the incongruent items that were recalled decreases.*

	Number of Items in List			
Congruent items	12	11	9	6
Incongruent items	0	1	3	6
Irrelevant items	4	4	4	4
Percentage of incongruent items	0	6	19	38
	Percentage Recall			
Congruent items	56	55	49	50
Incongruent items	—	77	61	59
Irrelevant items	48	47	42	42

SOURCE: Hastie and Kumar, 1979.

relatively few of them. That is, when the list was composed of 11 congruent, 1 incongruent, and 4 irrelevant behaviors, the incongruent item was recalled 77% of the time. But when there were equal numbers of congruent and incongruent items this percentage dropped to 59%.

How might these results be explained? There have been various theoretical explanations offered (Hastie, Park, & Weber, 1984), but the one that has produced the most research is usually called the Srull–Hastie model (Hastie, 1980; Srull, 1981). This model proposes that congruent and incongruent items are processed differently during the encoding stage, when the subject reads or hears them. For example, when a subject encounters an item congruent with the intelligence schema, she can simply attach that item to her image of the fictitious person in the Hastie and Kumar experiment—she doesn't need to think much about why an intelligent person wins chess matches because her schema of intelligence already tells her that he does.

The congruent item need simply be attached to the person image in her memory. However, when she encounters an incongruent item such as "Joe failed to understand the TV program," she will have to try to understand how an intelligent person could perform this behavior, a process that requires time and attention. As a result, the incongruent item will be well integrated in her memory not only by its attachment to the person image but by its attachment to congruent items as well (see Figure B.3.1). Finally, irrelevant items receive very little processing and will be loosely linked to the person image but will not be linked to other items.

From this model several predictions follow. First, subjects will attend more to the incongruent than to the congruent items, which they do (Stern, Marrs, Millar, & Cole, 1984). Second, if subjects are prevented from giving this extra attention to the incongruent items, they will no longer recall them better than the congruent ones; again this has been demonstrated

BOX CONTINUED

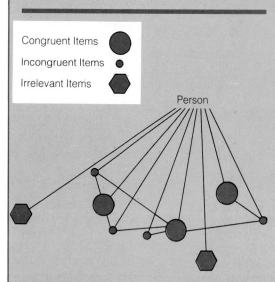

Congruent Items

Incongruent Items

Irrelevant Items

Person

FIGURE B.3.1   Network of Memory Associations among Congruent, Incongruent, and Irrelevant Items. *Note that the irrelevant items are attached only to the person, whereas there are associations among the congruent and incongruent items that aid the recall of the incongruent items.*

clearly (Bargh & Thein, 1985; Srull, 1981). Third, there will be a memory preference for the incongruent over congruent items only when the person is actively trying to form an impression. When the person is merely trying to memorize the items, she will not be especially motivated to link incongruent to congruent items. Several studies have shown that impression-formation instructions facilitate memory for the incongruent items (Srull, 1981) and that thinking about the psychological implications of information also aids subsequent recall (Crocker, Hannah, & Weber, 1983; Hastie, 1984). People who have a tendency

to think about relationships among things also show better recall of the incongruent items than those who do not have this tendency (Srull, Lichtenstein, & Rothbart, 1985). Fourth, the effect should occur only when the person is relating the items to a single entity, say a person or a group, because focusing on a single entity ought to encourage concern with explaining the incongruent items (Srull, 1981). Fifth, given that the incongruent items are attached to so many congruent items, the congruent items ought to be particularly good cues for the incongruent ones. Accordingly if the person recalls an incongruent item, that recall ought to have been preceded by recall of a congruent one (Srull, 1981; Srull et al., 1985).

The Srull–Hastie model generates several clear predictions (there are even others not discussed here), and it has generated so much research just because it is so easily and cleanly tested. But this discussion illustrates an even more important point about the relationship between theory and empirical tests. The model evolved gradually to explain a single result that traditional schema theories had trouble with—enhanced memory for incongruent items—but through this evolution we have arrived at a general model that can be used to explain a wide variety of effects in memory for people. The model also has drawn the attention of social and cognitive psychologists to important variables such as how we think about the material we are trying to encode into memory and how we store different kinds of information. In the process we have learned a good deal about how we come to think about others.

Eyewitness Testimony Schema-based memory is especially important in those situations that depend on accurate memories. One such situation is the legal context, where the guilt or innocence of a defendant may depend on what crime witnesses say. Eyewitness testimony is often the most important influence on jury verdicts; experimental data confirm that when eyewitnesses testify to the guilt of a defendant the rate of convictions increases (Weinberg & Baron, 1982). Unfortunately eyewitnesses are often wrong in what they report, and the confidence of a witness in his or her testimony is not always highly correlated with its accuracy (Deffenbacher, 1980; Leippe, 1980). Yet juries believe confidently presented testimony more (Wells, Lindsay, & Tousignant, 1980).

Why are people inaccurate in such a situation? For one thing, crimes usually happen quickly and witnesses may not be able to process information effectively at a time of emo-

Drawing by Charles Addams, © 1982, The New Yorker Magazine, Inc.

tional stress. But what people believe they see is also affected by the expectations provided by their schemata. Furthermore, people testify about crimes long after they have happened, and in the interim memory of the crime may be affected by subsequent events.

A study by Loftus, Miller, and Burns (1978) provides an instructive research example. In it, subjects saw a series of slides depicting an accident involving a car that turned right after stopping at either a yield or a stop sign. Then subjects were asked whether another car had passed the car when it was stopped at the *stop* sign or at the *yield* sign. This meant that some subjects were asked a question implying the existence of something they had seen (they had seen a stop sign and were asked about a stop sign) but others were asked a question implying something they had not seen (they had seen a stop sign but were asked about a yield sign). Then they were shown slides both of the car stopped at a yield sign and of the car stopped at a stop sign and were asked to identify which was the slide they had seen previously. Those who had been asked the "correct" question made the correct discrimination 75% of the time. However, when they had seen one sign but were asked about the other, their level of accuracy fell to 41%, thus indicating that what they remembered was influenced by the question they had been asked. Another experiment showed that estimates of speed could be affected by the wording of a question. After viewing an accident, those who were asked how fast a car was going when it *smashed* into another car gave higher estimates than those who were asked a more neutral version (Loftus & Palmer, 1974).

Such results suggest that eyewitnesses do not simply report what they see and hear but present an elaborated version that fits their schemata for what "must have happened." People continue to think about salient events such as crimes and accidents, and their subsequent testimony may be affected by unintentional desires to produce a coherent story.

Other factors may also influence testimony. Sheppard and Vidmar (1980) staged a crime and then had subjects interviewed by purported defense or prosecution lawyers. The subjects' subsequent testimony was biased toward the side that first interviewed the eyewitnesses.

Most research on eyewitness testimony has emphasized errors in the accounts given. However, as we earlier emphasized, our theories about the world are essential for understanding and recall of events. Errors are the price we pay for effectiveness and efficiency.

This was made clear in a study of the Watergate testimony of John Dean (Neisser, 1981). The major breakthrough in the Senate Watergate hearings on the involvement of the Nixon White House with the Watergate break-in came with Dean's detailed testimony on what had occurred in several conversations with the president. At the time many expressed doubt that Dean could remember such details months after the actual conversation. Fortunately for our purposes (if not for President Nixon's) transcripts of the actual conversations were later made public so that Neisser could compare what was actually said with Dean's recollections. Was Dean accurate? Yes and no. He had reasonably good memory for the gist of what was said, the tone of the meetings, and who said what. However, he was also inaccurate in many details. He tended to move comments from one conversation to another, made each of the conversations more coherent, and often remembered his own role in a way that excused his own not inconsiderable culpability. Thus Neisser concluded that Dean was broadly correct in terms of general meaning but wrong in many details. This, of course, illustrates the general message of this section. Schemata allow us to store meaning while allowing or even encouraging the forgetting and distortion of some details. Without general knowledge structures we could remember little, but at times the remembering we do is skewed or just plain wrong. When careers and prison sentences are at stake, we ought to remember that our memories are rarely as accurate as we would like to think.

STRUCTURAL SCHEMATA: BALANCE THEORY

Up to now we have focused on **content-specific schemata:** theories about particular classes of events, people, or things. We have schemata about classrooms, professors, terrorists, the first day of class, the Fourth of July, and selecting lunch at a cafeteria. But we also have theories about the ways information ought to be related: about how causal factors operate, how things are organized logically. These may be called **content-free** (or *procedural*) **schemata** (Fiske & Taylor, 1984). For example, if I tell you that Jim is taller than Bob and Bob is taller than Jennifer, you will use your theories about size relationships to infer that Jennifer is shorter than both Bob and Jim. Theories about cause and effect and orderings of size do not refer to any particular kinds of things and so are content-free; we use such schemata as kinds of logical rules or procedures for judging a range of events. In the remainder of this section we will focus on a

John Dean's testimony was a crucial breakthrough in the Watergate case.

particular kind of procedural schema: the tendency to order our cognitions consistently.

We try to keep our thoughts in order and in some consistent relationship with one another. As our minds go to war with reality, our cognitive generals like their ideas in close formation, like a well-drilled army. So you might find it most disconcerting to discover that you like a particular professor but hate her course material. Although we all tolerate some inconsistencies among our beliefs, we generally find inconsistencies somewhat disconcerting, sometimes so much so that we change beliefs or invent elaborate theories that seem to explain them.

As you will recall from Chapter 1, cognitive consistency theories have been used by social psychologists for many years. In part this reflects the Lewinian emphasis of the 1930s on reconciling tensions in the life space, but it also fits well with the emphasis of social psychology on attitude and belief change, because one of the obvious reasons we change our attitudes is to reduce perceived inconsistencies. We have previously discussed cognitive dissonance theory (Chapter 1), and now we turn to balance theory.

Balance Theory   Balance theory was first formally proposed by Fritz Heider (1958), although he readily admits that the theory has a long philosophical pedigree. Heider was influenced by Lewin's emphasis on tensions in the life space and both were influenced by Gestalt psychology. The latter emphasized that our perceptual apparatus structures our sensations so that they are ordered, meaningful, and well patterned. Thus Heider began with the strong assumption that patterns of beliefs and feelings would seem more natural, more pleasing, and easier to comprehend if they were well structured. In that sense, balance is a procedural schema we use to judge how natural certain cognitive structures are.

In balance theory, cognitive structures are composed of three entities and the relationships among them. These entities can be almost anything: people, things, even ideas. Heider assumed that each pair of entities has a positive (+) or negative (−) relationship. For example, you (Entity I) like (positive sentiment) your social psychology course (Entity II) but George (Entity III) hates (negative sentiment) the course (Entity II).

Heider notes that some sets of relationships among entities seem more natural than others. For example, if Dave likes (+) Jane, Jane likes (+) punk rock, and Dave also likes (+) the same type of music, this seems like a fairly natural state of affairs. On the other hand, suppose Martha favors (+) nuclear disarmament, Jim disapproves (−) of disarmament, and Martha likes (+) Jim. Although we may not feel that this relationship is hopeless, it may be at least mildly distressing to imagine that two friends could disagree on such a vital matter.

Any triad is *balanced* if the number of positive signs is odd and is *imbalanced* if the number of positive signs is even. Put differently, if you multiply the signs of all three pairs in the triad and the product is positive, the situation is balanced. For example, the student HM had a negative sentiment toward laziness, perceived a positive relationship between Mexican-Americans and laziness, and had a negative sentiment toward Mexican-Americans. The triad is balanced because there is a single (odd number) positive relationship (or if you prefer: the product of a positive, a negative, and another negative is a positive). Figure 3.1 shows examples of balanced and imbalanced situations more graphically.

Heider emphasized the idea that balanced states are preferred, feel right, look good, and are easy to think about and remember. They are good gestalts. Imbalanced states on the other hand feel bad, don't look right, cause one to wonder what has gone wrong, and motivate attempts to restore balance. From this framework, therefore, four testable propositions emerge: (1) balanced triads are more natural and pleasant than imbalanced ones; (2) when only partial information about the relationships in the triad is given, people are

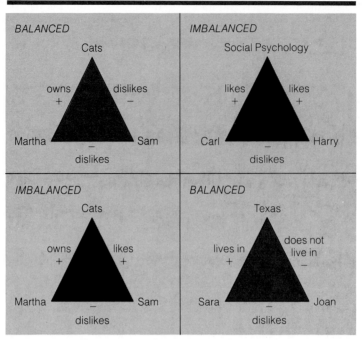

FIGURE 3.1   Examples of Balanced and Imbalanced Situations. *Note that the balanced situations all have an odd number of + signs.*

likely to infer additional information to perceive the triad as balanced rather than imbalanced; (3) balanced states are easier to learn and remember than imbalanced ones; and (4) there are strong tendencies to change one or more relationships in imbalanced states to produce balance.

Pleasantness   To test the first prediction that people should prefer balanced to unbalanced triads, subjects can be presented with hypothetical situations involving relationships among a person (*P*), and other (*O*), and some object (*X*), and then asked to rate how pleasant or unpleasant the situation is. An experiment by Rodrigues (1967) illustrates some typical results. Subjects were given all eight possible combinations of relationships among *P*, *O*, and *X* (see Table 3.2) and asked how unpleasant each would be. Subjects experienced the least tension in the balanced + + + triad in which everyone likes everything. They also rated little tension or unpleasantness in

the balanced + − − triad in which *P* likes *O* and they both dislike *X*. So far so good. But what about the two other balanced triads when *P* dislikes *O* and they disagree in their reactions to *X* (− + − and − − +)? These two situations were both rated as moderately unpleasant, whereas balance theory says they should be pleasant because they are balanced.

The ratings in Table 3.2 reflect three independent tendencies. First, the balanced situations were generally preferred to the unbalanced. Second, subjects preferred situations in which *P* liked *O* to those in which *P* disliked *O*. Third, there is also an agreement bias: subjects liked the situations more when *P* and *O* agreed than when they disagreed.

All three of these tendencies are commonly found in this type of research (Markus & Zajonc, 1985). Cacioppo and Petty (1981) have argued that agreement and attraction tendencies may be fairly immediate reactions to the situations; it doesn't take much brainpower to

TABLE 3.2 RATINGS OF UNPLEASANTNESS FOR HYPOTHETICAL SITUATIONS. *Note that for these data lower numbers indicate more pleasantness. Below the eight distinct combinations, mean unpleasantness ratings are given for balance, agreement, and positiveness tendencies.*

P likes O	P likes X	O likes X	+ + +	B	A	P	20.18*
P likes O	P likes X	O dislikes X	+ + −	U	D	P	61.43
P likes O	P dislikes X	O likes X	+ − +	U	D	P	64.37
P likes O	P dislikes X	O dislikes X	+ − −	B	A	P	34.73
P dislikes O	P likes X	O likes X	− + +	U	A	N	66.61
P dislikes O	P likes X	O dislikes X	− + −	B	D	N	54.21
P dislikes O	P dislikes X	O likes X	− − +	B	D	N	59.75
P dislikes O	P dislikes X	O dislikes X	− − −	U	A	N	64.57

B = Balanced	42.22*	
U = Unbalanced	64.25	
A = P and O agree about X	46.52	
D = P and O disagree about X	59.94	
P = P likes O	45.18	
N = P dislikes O	61.29	

*High numbers indicate unpleasantness.
SOURCE: Rodrigues, 1967.

decide whether you like situations in which people like one another or agree. On the other hand, a preference for balance may require a more thoughtful and careful analysis. Such results do not invalidate balance theory, but they do suggest that sometimes preferences for balanced situations may be overridden by more powerful and immediate preferences such as those for agreement and mutual liking.

Inferences   The second prediction is that when people are presented with partial information about a triad they will infer the missing information in a way which implies balance. For example, suppose that you know only that Jose likes the Chicago Cubs and that Gertrude likes the Cubs; what if anything would you infer about Jose's liking for Gertrude? You might claim that you don't really have enough information to say, but if you were pushed you would probably admit that Jose ought (all other things being equal) to like Gertrude, who shares his sentiments. Similarly you might infer that a staunch conservative and a socialist (who disagree about their atti-

tudes toward government) would have problems being friends. A large number of studies have explored the inference predictions and by and large they are consistent with the balance prediction (Crockett, 1982).

Learning and Memory   Generally it is easier to learn material that is well organized and clear. Because balanced structures supposedly have those properties, they should be more readily learned than imbalanced ones, a result usually but not universally found (Crockett, 1982).

Two major effects of balance on memory have been examined. First, balanced situations ought to be better remembered than imbalanced ones. The actual research on this is mixed: some studies find the predicted effect (Zajonc & Burnstein, 1965) but others find the reverse effect (Gerard & Fleischer, 1967).

However, other studies have shown that balance may affect what is remembered and may also produce some distortion; in that sense balance is like any other schema, of course. Spiro (1980) gave subjects a brief story about two people who were in love but who either agreed (balanced) about the desirability of having children or disagreed (imbalanced). Subsequently the subjects were told that the two had gotten married or had not. Spiro argued that because balanced triads are consistent and imbalanced ones inconsistent with marriage, subjects should remember as much evidence of balance as possible for married couples even to the point of distorting the information. By the same logic, those who learned no marriage had taken place should tend to distort the previous balanced states to make them seem more imbalanced. The data support these conjectures, and the study suggests that we may tend to remember a situation as more balanced than it was when it is subsequently clear that balance is now appropriate, and as more imbalanced when imbalance is appropriate.

Cognitive Change   A final prediction is that people who experience a lack of balance should be motivated to change one or more elements to achieve balance. For example, if you like President Reagan and your best friend does not, you could restore balance by changing your attitude toward Reagan or by picking a more congenial friend. These kinds of balance predictions are important in the areas of attitude change (Chapter 7) and interpersonal attraction (Chapter 12). For the moment it is sufficient to note that the bulk of the data support the change prediction.

SCHEMA CHANGE

One of the classic problems in psychology is cognitive change. How do teachers change the beliefs of students? How can a therapist get a depressed person to change her outlook on life? How can religious missionaries or political candidates change the views of people? What would it take to convince HM that his schema about Hispanics as lazy is false? Clearly we do change our beliefs and values, but such change is rarely easy. It is probably fair to say that most of us dislike changing our beliefs and theories, that is, that our schemata resist change.

Theory Perseveration   There are several demonstrations of the tendencies of schemata to resist change (Ross & Anderson, 1982). One research tradition shows that people are reluctant to change theories they have developed, even when the data on which these theories rest are shown to be invalid. For example, Anderson, Lepper, and Ross (1980) asked subjects to read case studies in which risk-taking predicted either success or failure as a fire fighter. As you might expect, subjects developed beliefs congruent with the data they had received. Subsequently, however, the subjects were told that the cases had been made up and that the data were fictitious. At this point perfectly rational people would realize that their beliefs were based on faulty data and would admit that they didn't know if risk-taking predicted fire-fighting ability or not. However, subjects continued to maintain their beliefs that risk-taking was related to fire-fighting ability.

How can we account for such theory perseveration? One possibility is that when subjects read an account suggesting that risk-takers make good (or poor) fire fighters, they construct miniature theories about why this should be. Arguments that explain the data continue to affect judgments even after the data are discredited (Anderson, New, & Speer, 1985).

A similar possibility suggested by Wegner, Coulton, and Wenzlaff (1985) is that people have a tough time storing and recalling negation and denial information. When information is stored in memory, it is not automatically erased when it is subsequently denied but rather is tagged as having been refuted. However, if this refutation tag is forgotten or lost, the original, unrefuted information is retrieved instead. Thus over time the person may remember the basic data but forget that they were later judged invalid.

A related effect has been termed the *innuendo effect* by Wegner, Wenzlaff, Kerker, and Beattie (1981). Sometimes famous (and not so famous) people are branded as guilty of something merely through suggestion or association. "Is it true that Politician X is corrupt?" may serve to identify the politician with crime if people forget the qualifiers (that is, that the association of the politician with crime was phrased as a question) before they forget the central message. It is also possible that in response to innuendo people might invoke theories to explain the association, theories that persist even after the details have been forgotten. At any rate Wegner and his colleagues did demonstrate that ratings of guilt of people could be raised by innuendo-type questions.

Does this mean that we construct theories that inevitably then blind us to reality? Obviously not. We *can* recognize the control our theories exert, and we often do realize how provisional they are. For example, theory perseveration is dramatically lessened when people are urged to pay attention to both sides of an issue (Anderson, 1982; Lord, Lepper, & Preston, 1984). Likewise, many of your professors hope to foster in you a lifelong critical attitude about facts and concepts just so your theories do not enslave you and you can continue to learn and grow cognitively.

Biased Evaluation of Information   However, unless we are vigilant our theories do tend to burrow into the recesses of the mind, becoming relatively inaccessible to examination and change. Even when people are confronted with evidence that contradicts their theories, they evaluate it in biased ways: if you can convince yourself that the information that threatens to disconfirm your theory is wrong, you will be able to maintain your theory intact. In one demonstration, Lord, Ross, and Lepper (1979) exposed proponents and opponents of capital punishment to articles that presented research data supporting one side or the other. Subjects rated the arguments that supported their prior position as more convincing, and as a consequence they became even more extreme in their views.

Gilovich (1983) examined why people persist in gambling despite losing more than they win. In his study, subjects were asked to explain their bets on professional football games, and as expected they spent more time explaining losses than successes. Explanations for failures emphasized that the game outcome might have been different, whereas explanations for successes emphasized the inevitability of the outcome. Again, the data were evaluated in biased ways so the theory that gambling could be economically successful was preserved.

Selective Exposure   Searching for information may also be biased toward confirming schemata and hypotheses. Social scientists have long emphasized the tendencies of people to expose themselves to information that supports their previous views, a tendency usually called *selective exposure.* Can you think of times when you have resisted getting an exam

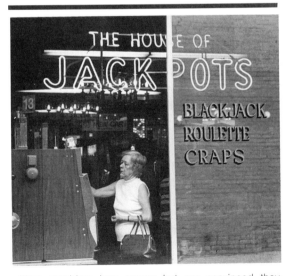

Most gamblers lose money but are convinced they can beat the odds.

back for fear that it might disconfirm your positive self-concept? And don't you generally prefer to hear politicians you agree with than those with whom you do not? The selective-exposure hypothesis has been used extensively to explain political behavior. For example, Sweeney and Gruber (1984) examined data on preferences of Nixon supporters and nonsupporters during the Watergate revelations (which were quite negative to Nixon's image) in the early 1970s. Nixon supporters reported that they paid less attention to Watergate news, discussed it less often, and knew less about it than did people less favorably inclined to Nixon.

The selective-exposure hypothesis has been extensively investigated experimentally. The major stimulus for this research was Festinger's theory of cognitive dissonance, which clearly predicts that people will avoid information dissonant with their existing beliefs. However, although many studies confirm the cognitive-dissonance prediction (Frey, 1986), a surprising number do not. It is clear that there is more to seeking information than simply avoiding dissonance.

One reason you might not avoid or might even seek dissonant information is that it is useful to you (Canon, 1964). For example, in a political year you might find it advantageous to know what the "other side" is saying so you can better refute them in argument. Or you might fear that the comments on a term paper will be painful to read but hope that they will help you do better next time. And you might be willing to seek out dissonant information if you are confident that you can refute it (Frey, 1981). Finally, there are individual differences in tolerance for bothersome information or ambiguity (McPherson, 1983): some people are more willing to confront uncomfortable information in hopes of refuting it while others prefer to deal with potential anxiety by avoidance (Olson & Zanna, 1979). People do have a desire to avoid dissonant information, but other factors will determine how important such desires are in any given situation.

Generally people prefer information that confirms rather than disconfirms their theories (Fischhoff & Beyth-Marom, 1983). We often structure social interactions so that information confirms our hypotheses about other people. In a study by Snyder and Swann (1978a) subjects were given the opportunity to test hypotheses about others by choosing questions to ask. The subjects were led to believe that a person was an introvert or an extrovert and they could pick from among questions such as "What would you do if you wanted to enliven things up at a party?" or "What things do you dislike about loud parties?" When testing the hypothesis that the other was an extrovert, subjects tended to pick questions like the first, which is almost certain to elicit an extroverted answer. Short of saying that you do not ever want to enliven a party (which is a vaguely rude answer), almost any response to the question will provide evidence that you are extroverted. Thus subjects began with a hypothesis and tended to ask questions that all but guaranteed that their hypotheses would be confirmed. Only when subjects are explicitly asked to disconfirm the hypothesis do they ask disconfirming questions (Snyder, 1981a).

Although the Snyder paradigm suggests that subjects may seek biased information, it is important to remember that the questions used in the study are actually not very diagnostic, because they virtually guarantee a particular answer. In everyday life, people are not so constrained in how they ask questions and probably don't ask such undiagnostic questions most of the time. If I wanted to determine whether someone was introverted, I might ask a question such as "Do you like loud parties?" This form of the question does not constrain the answer. When subjects are given the opportunity to ask less biased questions, they do not show such powerful biases toward confirmation (Bassok & Trope, 1983–84). This is not to suggest that we are never biased in the ways we seek information but only that people are capable of being reasonably unbiased in their attempts.

Self-fulfilling Prophecies   Social factors also affect how we get information. Suppose you interact with someone you think is hostile. You might be inclined to be defensive, vigilant for any signs of hostility on the part of the other, and primed to respond to his first remotely hostile remarks with hostility of your own. And the result? From the standpoint of the other, you must present a far from pleasant picture yourself. That, in turn, might induce him to become hostile or unpleasant. Now you will have good evidence that he is as hostile as you first thought (see Snyder & Swann, 1978b, for an experimental demonstration). Such a paradigm is often called a *self-fulfilling prophecy* because the perceiver's behavior, based on his or her preconceptions, draws out behavior from the other that validates or fulfills the prophecy (perceptions).

In another demonstration by Snyder, Tanke, and Berscheid (1977), men talked to women over the phone. Half the men were told that their female partners were attractive, whereas the other half were told she was unattractive. Those who thought they were talking to an attractive women behaved more warmly toward her, and the partners (who were not necessarily attractive and did not know that the males had been told anything about them) themselves became more social and friendly. Thus the men who thought they were interacting with an attractive female structured the interaction to produce behaviors that are part of an attractive-woman stereotype (see Figure 3.2).

Such self-fulfilling interaction patterns are probably quite common in everyday life and account in part for why the same person seems to have somewhat different personalities with different people (Darley & Fazio, 1980). Of course, such effects are not inevitable; for example, someone who knows that a perceiver

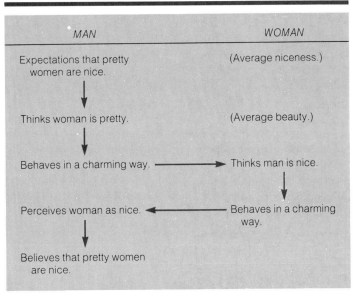

FIGURE 3.2   A Possible Scenario for Self-fulfilling Prophecies. *The man's expectations affect his behavior, which in turn affects how the woman responds. Her behavior then confirms his initial expectations.*

has a negative expectation may actively try to disconfirm it (Hilton & Darley, 1985). In Chapter 16 we will discuss such effects further as one of the ways stereotypes are maintained.

SUMMARY

We have covered a wide range of material, but it is central to the ways social psychologists deal with social cognition. It might help to refocus on the central point: our knowledge structures—schemata and scripts—help us cognitively negotiate a complex and potentially confusing world, but they do so at the cost of producing error. Schemata direct attention, help us recognize people and objects, provide meaning, affect memory, and allow us to go beyond the information given in our inferences. The general rule is that if material fits the schema, it is processed fairly effortlessly and efficiently, but not in an individuated way. Material that is basically irrelevant goes unattended, unrecognized, and unremembered. However, material that does not fit the most accessible schemata may receive additional attention and meaning analysis that, among other things, may result in its being better remembered. The cost in all of this is that our tendencies to see the world in terms of existing knowledge structures may lead us to ignore relevant information, to mislabel, and especially to misremember the world as more consistent with schemata than it was. Schemata are basically conservative—they resist change—and there is always the danger that we are so efficient and glib in our analyses of the world around us that we hold on to our theories too long even when they are clearly wrong.

EMOTIONS AND MOODS

Since the time of the ancient Greeks and the early Christian thinkers, Western thought has made a sharp distinction between *reason* and *emotion*. Those of us who are part of that tradition find it easy to assume that emotions somehow corrupt our abilities to think clearly and logically. And emotion does affect thought, although its effects are not always damaging.

We have all had the experience of wishing so hard for something to happen that we become convinced it will. The great psychologist, William Shakespeare, nailed it down, "Thy wish was father, Harry, to that thought" (*Henry IV*, Pt. 2). In a less poetic demonstration, Stephan, Berscheid, and Walster (1971) aroused sexual desire in male subjects by having them read a romantic seduction scene from a novel. Sexually aroused subjects rated a potential date as more attractive and as more sexually receptive than did nonaroused subjects, suggesting that needs skew our perception of reality. However, the aroused and nonaroused groups did not differ in their ratings of women who were *not* potential dates, suggesting that needs operate in conjunction with reality in determining judgments.

Weinstein (1980) has shown that people are generally optimistic about their life chances, expecting that positive events are more likely and negative events less likely to happen to them than to most people. Such wishful thinking is perhaps a fundamental bias, but without some wishful thinking most of us would probably not act strongly on our desires. When specific needs are aroused, the belief that they are likely to be fulfilled may aid effective behavior in pursuit of those needs.

Wishes and desires affect thoughts and behaviors, but do moods? Yes. People who are in good moods react to the world in different ways than people who are in neutral or bad moods. For example, Isen, Shalker, Clark, and Karp (1978) manipulated positive moods by giving people in a shopping mall a small gift. When asked to evaluate their cars and household appliances, the subjects who had received a gift (and who were presumably in a good mood) rated them more positively than those who had not been given a gift. Other studies show that ratings of slides of neutral scenes

(Isen & Shalker, 1982), interviews involving self (Forgas, Bower, & Krantz, 1984), and one's own performance (Wright & Mischel, 1982) are also affected by moods. Our moods affect us whether we see the world through rose- or grey-colored glasses. In addition, good moods aid efficient problem-solving (Isen & Means, 1983) and affect cognitive structures in ways that may promote creativity (Isen, Johnson, Mertz, & Robinson, 1985). As we see in subsequent chapters, moods affect our self-evaluations as well as our tendencies to be helpful or aggressive.

Emotions and moods also affect memories. People tend to remember material that is emotionally congruent with their mood at the time of recall. For example, Isen, Shalker, Clark, and Karp (1978) had subjects learn positive and negative words. When subjects were later asked to recall the words after they had succeeded or failed at a task, they recalled more of the positive words after success and more of the negative words after failure. Other studies by Bower (1981) and his colleagues have shown that even when mood is hypnotically induced, recall is congruent with the mood (see Figure 3.3).It might be noted that whereas good moods promote positively toned memories, negative moods are less likely to produce unpleasant memories. In general, negative moods produce more complex behavioral and cognitive effects than do positive moods (Isen, 1984).

In Chapter 7 we consider further the effects of moods on our self-evaluations and on depression. For the moment, however, it is important to remind ourselves that our thoughts are affected by our feelings, emotions, and moods. This is not necessarily bad. Our feelings probably facilitate as often as they inhibit or corrupt our efforts at efficient thinking.

JUDGMENT MODELS

We have been dealing with the question of how such basic cognitive processes as atten-

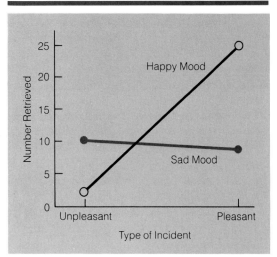

FIGURE 3.3   Number of Pleasant and Unpleasant Childhood Incidents Recalled When the Recaller Was in a Happy or Sad Mood. *Note that pleasant memories are more likely when the person is in a happy mood and that unpleasant memories are facilitated by a sad mood. However, sad moods lead to equal numbers of pleasant and unpleasant memories, whereas happy moods greatly favor pleasant memories.*
SOURCE: Bower, 1981.

tion, perception, and memory allow us to make sense of our social worlds. However, once we have made sense of the world and stored our interpretations, we still must apply our knowledge. Often we do so by making some sort of judgment: the criticism is unjust, Margaret should be admitted to law school, Seattle will not win the Super Bowl. There are, of course, many types of judgments, but in this section we emphasize two: comparisons with a standard and relationship judgments.

COMPARISONS WITH A STANDARD

Thousands of times each day you make judgments in which explicitly or implicitly you compare one thing with another: the day is cold, the man is attractive, the administration's foreign policy is horrible. There are no readily used absolute scales of temperature, attractiveness, or goodness of government policy. When you say the day is cold, you really mean something like, "the day is colder than average for this time of the year" or "the day is colder than yesterday." And we all recognize that a cold day in Tampa might seem warm in Minneapolis and that one woman's "too expensive" is another's "easily affordable."

For dimensions such as weight, heat, loudness, beauty, and values, judgments are affected by what has happened previously. **Assimilation effects** occur when current stimuli are drawn toward or seen as similar to previous stimuli. If you have been working outside on a cold day, a cool house may not seem especially cool or uncomfortable to you. On the other hand, a warm house may feel uncomfortably hot. The latter would be an example of a **contrast effect** where feelings (in this case sensations of warmth) are contrasted with or displaced away from previous feelings.

Contrast effects are more commonly reported in research literature (Eiser, 1980). Consider for example one important type of contrast effect, namely judgments of happiness. How happy you feel may depend in part on what you have recently experienced. Most of us feel particularly happy just after recovering from a bad cold or a tough week of work. And you may feel happy about your own situation when you compare yourself with others less fortunate.

However, there are also some paradoxical effects. Suppose something wonderful has happened to you. Common sense suggests that you should be quite happy, and so you might be in the short run. But what about the long run? The ordinary pleasures of life may pale beside the "big event," leading to long-term unhappiness. Brickman, Coates, and Janoff-Bulman (1978) compared the happiness ratings of ordinary people and winners of lotteries (all of whom had won at least $400,000). As the previous argument suggests, the lottery winners rated the mundane pleas-

Although people play lotteries because they believe winning a large sum of money will make them happier, lottery winners are often no more happy than other people.

ures of life as less satisfying than the controls and in general were no more happy than the controls.

Thinking about good things in the past or future may make the present less satisfying by contrast. Dermer, Cohen, Jacobsen, and Anderson (1979) exposed subjects to positive and negative materials and measured changes in satisfaction with present life. In one study this was done by emphasizing the positive or negative features of life in 1900, and in a second study subjects were asked to imagine good (winning a vacation) or bad (being in a serious accident) events. In both studies life satisfaction increased after exposure to negative events and slightly decreased after exposure to positive events. Present satisfaction is affected by contrast with past conditions or possible (future) conditions.

Contrast effects are not limited to judgments of happiness. They have been demonstrated for ratings of physical beauty (Kenrick & Gutierres, 1980), judgments of the seriousness of crime (Pepitone & DiNubile, 1976), evaluations of seriousness of psychopathology (Manis & Paskewitz, 1984), and judgments of extremity of political attitudes (Judd & Harackiewicz, 1980), among other areas. Such contrast effects can create mischief: to an opponent of abortion, the prochoice position seems quite extreme by contrast with the attitudes of self and like-minded friends; a prochoice person also finds his or her opponent extreme by contrast. By making our opponents out to be more extreme than they are, we create conditions for misunderstanding, self-fulfilling prophecy, and, ultimately, hostility. The literature on international relations is filled with examples of misunderstandings caused by one national leader who thinks an opposing leader is extreme and unyielding (Jervis, 1976).

RELATIONSHIP JUDGMENTS

Similarity   One important judgment we make continually is that two objects, people, or events are similar in some way, despite other obvious differences. For example, people and elephants are both mammals, though people are closer in size to desks and elephants to trucks. The judgment of similarity is affected by the context of comparison: we would find people and elephants more similar to each other when judged in comparison to insects but less similar in comparisons involving a wider range of sizes.

Moreover, similarity judgments can be affected by which object is taken as the focus. Consider the perceived similarity of the Soviet Union and Cuba. It might seem that the similarity is symmetrical in that Cuba is as similar to the USSR as the reverse, but that is not the case. Most people judge Cuba more similar to the Soviet Union than the reverse. According to Tversky and Gati (1978), people take the most prominent of the two items as a referent; the nonreferent is judged closer to the referent than the reverse.

Because similarity judgments are crucial to so much of our thinking, it is important to remember that similarity is never absolute but is relative to the particular dimensions that are relevant, to the context of comparison, and to the referent chosen. This is not to say that similarity is totally in the eyes of the perceiver, but only that a perceiver's judgments are affected by cognitive variables in addition to objective features.

Perceived Correlations   Perhaps one of the most primitive perceptions we have is of the world as essentially nonrandom, of it as having an order. Even when exposed to random patterns of events, people often invent elaborate explanations for relationships (Peterson, 1980).

Our theories about the world that emphasize relationships among events may lead us to see stronger relationships than we could objectively justify. For example, most people probably overestimate the correlations between such traits as good grooming and general character, church attendance and morality, and mental illness and aggressiveness. Such overgeneralizations have been called *illusory correlations* (Chapman & Chapman, 1967, 1969). One way of understanding stereotypes such as the ones HM had about Mexican-Americans is to recognize that people often assume an illusory correlation between group membership and personal characteristics.

Our theories create illusory correlations in various ways. For example, many people assume that women are worse drivers than men, despite considerable evidence to the contrary. The assertion that women are poorer drivers may be a nonreflective, culturally based prejudice. But even a person who tries to think about the data as objectively as possible may still run aground by using methods that maintain the theory in the face of disconfirming data (see Rothbart, 1981, for a discussion). For example, the person may define poor driving differently for males and females: the woman who changes lanes frequently may be defined as dangerous but the man who does the same thing may be defined as alert and defensive. Also the person might selectively remember many instances of poor driving by women and selectively forget instances by men. Further, the person may place too much emphasis on instances that confirm the hypothesis, in this case that women are poor drivers. When judging relationships, people often emphasize evidence that confirms their theories.

The evaluation of relationships is difficult under the best of circumstances, and it is easy to conclude that relationships are stronger or more pervasive than they really are. Most of us find it difficult to deal with the ambiguities of moderate relationships (sometimes *A* is related to *B* but sometimes it is not), and our cognitive systems cooperate by making them seem stronger.

Causality and Control   Our perceptions of causality are influenced by our feelings that the world cannot be random. Strickland, Lewicki, and Katz (1966) asked people to bet on throws of dice either before the dice were thrown or after they were thrown but before the outcome was known. Subjects were willing to bet more before the dice were thrown, probably because they had a primitive feeling that they might control an event before it occurred but could not afterwards. Langer (1975) found that people value the lottery tickets they choose themselves more than those someone else chooses for them. Langer argues that people have the *illusion of control* over chance events such as the roll of dice or the choice of a winning lottery ticket when they actively participate in the chance outcome. Of course, I

am not actually more likely than you to roll a winning dice combination or to pick a good lottery ticket, but if I have actively done the rolling or picking I seem to feel I have more control, that I somehow cause the outcome.

JUDGMENT HEURISTICS

Many of our everyday judgments are more complex than simply deciding similarity or causality. For example, a prediction that the Cleveland Indians will win the World Series involves many sources of data and possibly a complex set of rules for combining the data. Similarly a doctor uses complex information in complex ways in making a diagnosis, as do stockbrokers and businesspeople. Because the world is complicated and the relevant data for decisions are legion, most of us seek cognitive shortcuts. For example, some women complain that their physicians use a shortcut rule, something like "women with ill-defined complaints are neurotic," and do not dignify their problems with a fuller attempt at diagnosis. Similarly, a student recently told me that he rarely took courses with more than three books on the syllabus because that meant that the professor was a tough grader. Professors are often accused of using shortcut rules, such as "people who write long exam answers know more than those who are brief."

In recent years psychologists have devoted considerable attention to the shortcut rules, or **heuristics,** people use (Nisbett & Ross, 1980; Tversky & Kahneman, 1971, 1973, 1978). People use heuristics because the rules have stood the test of time, and they often work. But as you should realize by this point, any cognitive rule or theory that reduces the complexity of the world also leads to errors. Thus much of the research on heuristics has emphasized the biases they create. We will consider several examples.

The Representativeness Heuristic   Often when we need to make a decision or prediction we are confused by lots of seemingly relevant information. One way to sort the information is to use the **representativeness heuristic** (Kahneman & Tversky, 1972): rather than use all the available data systematically, we treat the person or event to be explained as a representative of a relevant category and then use our general knowledge about that category to make a decision. Suppose you are trying to predict whether a course will be easy or hard. Instead of trying to take into account everything about the course—by consulting people who have had the course, by checking out the reading assignments, by talking with the professor—you may take a shortcut: does this course resemble more of the hard courses or the easy courses you have taken?

This is often a useful decision rule, but it can also lead to problems. For example, suppose you were to judge which of the following exact sequences of heads (H) and tails (T) for successive coin tosses is the more likely: HHHHH or HTHTT. Most people probably feel the second is more likely, because it looks more similar to (that is, it is more representative of) a typical mixed sequence of heads and tails. Actually, of course, the two sequences are equally likely. Many parents who have been disappointed by a string of same-sexed children discover when they try again that Mother Nature does not understand that a different sex is "due." The parents may be caught up in a representativeness heuristic because families with at least one child of each sex are more common than families with all boys or all girls—and families with mixed-sex offspring are therefore more representative of the typical family pattern.

Several other problems are associated with the representativeness heuristic. **Conjunction error** (Tversky & Kahneman, 1983) can most easily be illustrated with a concrete example. In one course I asked my students what percentage of the psychology faculty they thought (1) were liberal, (2) drank wine, and (3) were both liberal and drank wine. The mean per-

centages were 83% for liberals, 65% for wine-drinkers, and 73% for the combination, that is, for liberal wine-drinkers. This seems to make sense until you realize that some of the 65% who are wine-drinkers may support conservative causes: the total percentage of liberal wine-drinkers cannot be greater than the percentage of total wine-drinkers. Stated generally, the probability of the *conjunction* (co-occurrence) of two events cannot be higher than the probability of the least likely one. In this case, the explanation in terms of representativeness is straightforward. A wine-drinking liberal seems a more representative image of a psychologist than someone who is simply a wine-drinker. Hence my students judged by whether the data fit a stereotype rather than by pure probabilities.

A second type of error, the **dilution effect** (Nisbett, Zukier, & Lemley, 1981; Zukier & Jennings, 1983–84), is the improper use of diagnostic and nondiagnostic information in making predictions. Suppose you are trying to predict a student's GPA (grade point average). If you know she made an A in advanced calculus, you would probably predict a high GPA for her because she is representative of the image most of us have of people who make good grades. Now suppose you also learn that she likes soap operas and drives an old truck. Her nonintellectual interests do not fit well our image of a student with a high GPA, and most people would probably lower, or dilute, their estimates of her GPA given this additional information. And they should *if and only if* they know that liking soap operas and driving a truck are negatively related to GPA. But if (as is likely) these are nondiagnostic attributes—that is, if they have nothing to do with GPA—lowering the predicted GPA would be an error.

Another problem with the representativeness heuristic is that individual cases that seem representative are often given more weight in decisions than are more stable and generally predictive category probabilities. We might call this the *concrete case bias.* If you are trying to decide what courses to take next semester, a statistical summary of the evaluations of past students for the courses would probably be more useful in the sense of predicting the best courses for you than would the overheard comment of a single student. Yet most of you would probably prefer a concrete testimonial from a representative student than the abstract data based on several students.

It may well be that people like to believe that individual cases are highly predictive. You may, for example, find yourself saying something like, "This guy I met is just like George, and since George turned out to be entirely untrustworthy, I'll bet this guy will also." Of course, using clear and prototypic cases may be a highly effective strategy, provided that such cases truly represent the category and that similarities between present and past cases are based on important dimensions. Unfortunately, superficial appearances are often the

American help train Contra rebels in Nicaragua. Is this similar to the early days of American involvement in Vietnam?

basis for reasoning from case to case. For example, Lewicki (1985) had subjects meet a friendly person, and they subsequently met two other people, one of which looked like the first person and one of which did not. Subjects judged the similar-appearing person to be friendlier. It would be hard to defend the notion that a person who has the same hair style and type of glasses as a friendly person is thereby also friendly, yet this is in effect what the subjects concluded.

When we feel that one situation is similar to another, we use the previous one as an object lesson. In a simulation of foreign-policy decisions, Gilovich (1981) presented subjects with a situation involving conflict between nations. Some subjects read a description that included phrases reminiscent of World War II (such as calling the briefing room the Churchill Room) whereas others read the same basic description with phrases recalling the Vietnam War (such as mentioning Dean Rusk Hall). Note that all this information is irrelevant to the decision at hand, although it is likely to draw subjects' attention to past foreign-policy situations and scripts. The parallels to World War II suggest that stopping aggression early is important, while the parallels to the Vietnam War might counsel greater caution. Accordingly, subjects were more likely to recommend an aggressive resolution to the crisis when parallels to World War II were salient.

There is nothing inherently wrong with using concrete cases to make decisions. The problem arises when people are blinded by similarities between the present and past without considering that there are alternative models. And often one situation is judged similar to another on relatively superficial characteristics.

The Availability Heuristic and Frequency Judgments   One of the important judgments we make is how frequent events or instances of categories are. Usually our frequency judgments are comparative; we say that crime is increasing or that there have been more rainy days this spring than last. It is unlikely that our memories keep counters on such events; so how do we estimate their frequency? Tversky and Kahneman (1973) suggest that we typically make frequency judgments by sampling relevant instances from memory and by using what we can easily bring to mind for the estimate. Such a strategy is called the ***availability heuristic,*** because we judge real-world frequencies on the basis of the availability of instances in memory. Such a shortcut is efficient and may be accurate. But it can also lead to error, especially when our memories have a biased sample of instances or when we draw a biased sample from memory because some instances are more salient than others. In the classic demonstration, Tversky and Kahneman (1973) asked subjects to read a list of names of famous men and women. In some lists the males were more famous than the females, and the reverse was true in the other lists. Then subjects were asked to estimate how many male and female names had been on the list they had read. They generally overestimated the gender with the more famous names, presumably because the famous names are easier to think of (that is, they are more available).

What makes certain concepts available? The most obvious variable that affects availability is the frequency or recency of use (Higgins & King, 1981; Wyer & Srull, 1981). Being exposed to a particular category of stimuli makes that category more available in subsequent processing (Gabrielcik & Fazio, 1984; Powell & Fazio, 1984). In addition, some things simply stand out in memory because we care about them or because they are inherently salient. People seem to enjoy reading about especially gory murders, for example, and it is likely that they would overestimate the occurrence of such crimes because it is far easier to think of gory murders than bland household murders, because the former get more publicity.

Similarly, most people think that murder is more common than suicide and that death by fire is more likely than death by drowning. Yet statistics show that suicides are more common than murders and that death by fire and by drowning are equally likely (Slovic, Fischhoff, & Lichtenstein, 1982). The most probable reason for such mis-estimates is that murders and fire-related deaths are more prominently reported in newspapers than are suicides or drownings: the more commonly reported events are more available in memory when people make judgments about likelihood.

What we think about affects our behavior in various ways, so it is not surprising that when certain ideas become more available behavior is affected. Wilson and Capitman (1982) manipulated the availability of a boy-meets-girl script by having male subjects either read or not read a story related to this theme. Subsequently the subjects met a young woman, and those who had read the story were more friendly in both verbal and nonverbal ways. Thus script availability apparently affected their behavior. Gregory, Cialdini, and Carpenter (1982) had certain subjects imagine using a cable-TV service. These subjects were subsequently more likely to subscribe to the service later than those who had not gone through this imagining processing. Evidently thinking about subscribing made the actual behavior seem more probable. So availability of instances in memory not only affects estimates of frequency and likelihood but affects behavior as well.

Are We Doomed to Irrationality?   It may have occurred to you that social psychologists seem to be quite enthusiastic about showing all the ways people can be irrational. Of course, this is not a new perspective. For hundreds of years philosophers and psychologists have argued that emotions corrupt our best attempts to be rational. This "new irrationality" seems to make a more serious charge, however: namely, that the same features that make people enormously efficient processors of information also lead those people to make frequent errors.

It is important to recognize the limitations on our abilities to make complex decisions, but it does not follow that people are inevitably irrational and biased. In the first place, subjects are assumed to be irrational if they do not follow fairly sophisticated rules of logic and statistics, yet neither logic nor statistics can be regarded as the only forms of rationality (Cohen, 1982; White, 1984).

In the second place, people often *do* use logical and statistical rules. Kruglanski, Friedland, and Farkash (1984) have, for example, shown that statistical information can be used appropriately when its relevance is obvious. Nisbett, Krantz, Jepson, and Kunda (1983) have suggested that people have the capacity to reason logically and statistically but that situational circumstances affect whether they will in fact use these capacities. The social world is often inherently more complex and less clear than the physical worlds of playing cards and roulette wheels, and it is often difficult to know how to apply statistical and logical rules in these more complex domains. Also there are cultural prescriptions about when to apply statistical arguments. Baseball fans can hardly avoid statistics, but most people feel it is vaguely unseemly to argue statistically about whom you will marry or whether you are likely to get a good job.

Under any circumstances it is probably less important to argue that people are or are not "rational" than to discover the forms of reasoning they actually use in concrete situations.

AWARENESS

Throughout this chapter you have seen a good many ways your mind can play you false. Our past experiences and schemata allow us to attend to, recognize, label, and remember information efficiently, but the price of this efficiency is error. This might not be such a great problem except that we are usually not aware when we have misconstrued or misremembered something. "I saw it with my own eyes" is a claim meant to stifle all doubts about what really happened, but what we think we see or what we remember seeing may not be what happened at all.

Not only are we unaware of our biased thinking, but some psychologists have argued that we may be fundamentally unaware of many of our cognitive processes. Well-practiced cognitive operations are performed without much attention precisely because we do not have to devote many of our cognitive resources to them to use them efficiently. For example, most adults can perform simple addition without much thought and find that thoughtful adding actually slows them down. Cognitive psychologists usually refer to well-practiced activities as **automatic cognitive processing,** which they contrast with **controlled cognitive processing** (Bargh, 1984). Although automatic processing is usually quite efficient, it is not without its costs. For example, people tend not to remember information processed automatically as well as that processed more thoughtfully (Smith & Lerner, 1986).

AWARENESS OF PROCESS

The claim that we are not always aware of how we think is now universally accepted (Bargh, 1984). However, a much stronger claim is made by Nisbett and Wilson (1977a), who argue that, although we are usually aware of the products of our mental machinations, we are generally not conscious of the cognitive operations or thought processes themselves. In the social realm, people may be unaware of what has affected their thinking; their knowledge about why they think the ways they do often is based less on insight into their own mental processes than on implicit, culturally given, theories about thinking.

Consider a demonstration cited by Nisbett and Wilson. Women were asked to judge which of several articles of clothing lined up in a row was the best. Empirically the women showed a strong position bias, preferring the items on the right more than those on the left (as part of the experiment, the particular items were systematically varied in position). When asked about their preferences, the women denied that position had played any role in their choices despite the obvious fact that it had. Here, then, is a case in which people are unaware of the factors that affect the decisions they make.

In another demonstration, subjects watched a film under one of three conditions: a distracting noise was present, the projector was out of focus, or under normal viewing conditions. The subjects were asked to rate the film, and the actual mean ratings for the three groups were quite similar. Even so, those who had had the noise or improper focus felt this had affected their ratings although on the average it had not. Here then are conditions in which people feel something affects their thinking when it does not.

From these and other demonstrations we cannot conclude that people *never* know what affects their thinking. But the demonstrations suggest that at least some of the time we may be ignorant, confused, or incorrect about why we think as we do. Where then do we get our ideas about how we think? Nisbett and Wilson argue that we have theories about how we think, and that we draw on these models rather than on our actual phenomenological experiences when we try to explain the mysteries of our thoughts. In the movie study most people probably feel that a badly focused projector would lower their enjoyment of the movie and so they report that it did (even though it probably did not).

In a study by Nisbett and Bellows (1977), subjects were asked to rate applicants for a counseling job. They rated how much they liked her, how sympathetic she would be to a client's problems, how intelligent she was, and how flexible she would be. Different groups of subjects read different descriptions of the applicant's characteristics: her academic credentials, her physical attractiveness, and whether she had been in a serious accident. Subjects were asked to report which factors had affected their decisions, and the experimenters could easily determine objectively which factors actually affected the ratings. Subjects accurately assessed what had affected their judgments of intelligence—correctly reporting that academic credentials played a larger role in their decisions than did attractiveness or having had an accident. However, the subjects were less accurate in reporting the factors that affected their decisions about the ratings of liking and sympathy. For example, subjects felt that academic credentials played a larger role in liking and a lesser role in sympathy ratings than they actually had.

Why were subjects accurate about some things and not others? Nisbett and Bellows suggest that they were accurate in knowing what affected their judgments about intelligence because they had culturally provided theories that academic credentials should affect intelligence judgments but that physical attractiveness should not. In other words, when asked how they judged intelligence, the subjects did not report their actual experiences (because they have no direct awareness of how they made their decisions) but reported a culturally based theory that happened to be correct. On the other hand, they were inaccurate on other judgments because they reported what most people would think ought to affect their judgments and the cultural theory happened to be incorrect. For example, subjects agreed with cultural theories in reporting that they would have more sympathy with the person who had been in a serious accident even though the previous accident had no effect on their actual ratings of sympathy. The point of this fairly complex experiment is actually simple—people do not have a clear sense of what affects their judgments. We rely on cultural models of what we should pay attention to rather than on our actual experiences when we report how we think.

Taken at face value, the Nisbett–Wilson claim makes for a depressing conclusion. People are biased, but because in principle they can never be aware of how these biases affect them, it is hard or impossible to achieve accurate and rational thinking. Can Nisbett and Wilson be correct in their strong claim that people are not aware of cognitive processes?

There have been many criticisms of the Nisbett–Wilson contention (Adair & Spinner, 1981; Rakover, 1983; Sabini & Silver, 1981; Smith & Miller, 1978; P. White, 1980), and it is now clear that Nisbett and Wilson were extreme in their initial claims. Perhaps most damaging are data that show that people can be introspectively aware of how they solve problems (Ericsson & Simon, 1980) and can accurately assess which factors affect their decisions (Kraut & Lewis, 1982; Wright & Rip, 1981).

So the argument that people cannot be aware of how they think about problems is clearly wrong. It may even be wrong to suggest that people are *usually* inaccurate in assessments of how they think. On the other hand, Nisbett and Wilson have shown that people might be unaware of how they reach the conclusions they do, so we cannot invariably trust what people say about how they think.

MINDLESSNESS

Most of us do not usually want to worry about how we think about problems. The 6-year-old who is learning to add may be best off thinking through the details of the addition process and counting mental fingers, but I would prefer to be spared such meaningless activity. Indeed, one of the goals of education is to instill in people effortless and efficient ways to think about routine problems.

Ellen Langer has proposed that some mental activities and behavioral sequences may be performed automatically or mindlessly, whereas others are more thoughtful, conscious, and mindful. Frequently performed activities are understood in terms of well-learned scripts, and we often perform them in a condition of **mindlessness.** If someone asks you a small favor, one that your cultural norms suggest you should honor quickly and gracefully, it is hardly worth thinking about what to do. Who would want to spend the time thinking about whether to answer someone's request for the time of day? Of course, if the requester is menacing and the night is dark, or if he wants to check the time by holding your watch, you would be well-advised to give the request some thought. But this thought would be instigated precisely because the request no longer fits the normal script for asking the time.

In an experiment by Langer, Blank, and Chanowitz (1978), a behavioral script related to honoring requests was used. In this case the subjects were waiting to use a photocopying machine and were approached by someone who asked if she could do her photocopying first. According to Langer and her colleagues, when the request can be accommodated within the normal request script (perhaps by being polite and having relatively few pages to copy) people should comply without much thought. If, on the other hand, the request was out of the ordinary (the person had many pages to copy), compliance would no longer be automatic and mindless and might not occur at all. In the actual study, the size of the request and also the reasons given were varied. When the request was small (and fit within the usual request script), compliance was high and the kinds of reasons given had no real effect on compliance, as if the subjects played their part in the script without thinking. However, when the request was large (and therefore less representative of the typical request in such situations) the reasons made a difference; subjects complied more when the reasons for the request made some sense ("May I use the machine because I'm in a hurry?") than when they did not ("May I use the machine because I have to make some copies?"). Subjects obviously had to think about the request and whether they would comply.

This and other experiments suggest that people will be fairly mindless and unaware when their behavior fits into normal and normatively regulated interaction sequences. However, when things do not appear normal or when there is no well-developed script, people will be more thoughtful and mindful of what they are doing.

CHAPTER SUMMARY

- Social cognition deals with how we perceive, interpret, and remember social stimuli.

- Our cognitive processes transform incoming information and are specialized for efficient processing. The cost of this efficiency is that we make frequent errors.

- Many social and cognitive psychologists emphasize the importance of schemata for the processing of information. A *schema* is a theory about some category of people, things, or events, and *scripts* are schemata that refer to behavioral sequences.

- There are several stages in our processing of information, and schemata/scripts aid that processing at each stage. Schemata direct attention, aid in recognition and labeling, affect what we remember, and allow us to make inferences that go beyond the information given.

- Schemata have to be activated to affect information processing. Our expectations about a given situation lead us to activate relevant schemata. In addition, schemata that have been recently or frequently used are likely to be readily accessible.

- When schemata are active they direct attention. In particular we look for information that assures us that the schema is appropriate to the situation; when it is, attention to schema-relevant material relaxes. Some schemata, particularly those relevant to oneself, are easily activated by incoming information so that one's attention can be quickly directed to the self-relevant information.

- When a schema is active, it facilitates recognition of schema-relevant stimuli, and we tend to label ambiguous stimuli in terms of currently active schemata.

- Schemata have three general effects on our memories. First, we tend to remember information better when we think about it in terms of schemata or theories. Second, we remember both schema-congruent and schema-incongruent information better than schema-irrelevant information. Third, we often distort our memories to become more schema-congruent and we falsely remember that schema-congruent information was present. These effects of schemata on memory have important implications for eyewitness memory of events.

- We have knowledge structures for categories of people, events, and things but also procedural schemata that suggest appropriate reasoning strategies; one example is balance theory. According to balance theory, cognitive entities have positive or negative relationships to one another. Three of those entities are in a balanced relationship when the number of positive signs is odd and are imbalanced when positive signs are even. Research suggests that people prefer balanced to imbalanced situations, that they infer otherwise missing information to create balance, that they tend to increase balance in memory, and that they will be motivated to change one or more cognitions to restore balance.

- Schemata resist change through several mechanisms. We tend to remember our theories better than the supporting (or nonsupporting) data. We tend to discredit incoming data that might disconfirm our schemata. We also prefer to seek information that confirms rather than disconfirms our theories and schemata and we may even structure social situations to encourage such confirmation.

- Sometimes our thinking is biased by our moods and wants. People in good moods as compared to those in neutral or negative moods typically evaluate information more positively, think more efficiently, and remember more positive information.

- Many judgments involve comparisons with a standard. Commonly we judge new information as farther away from the standard than it is—a *contrast effect*—although sometimes we see the new information as closer—an *assimilation effect*.

- Similarity judgments are affected by the range of stimuli compared and by which stimulus is considered to be the referent.

- How closely events or people are related—perceived correlation—is hard for us to estimate and is affected by our knowledge about how closely they should be related as well as by our biases in memory and attention.

- People have distinct preferences for seeing events as causally related and seem to dislike the idea of randomness.

- *Heuristics* are shortcut rules people use in judgments, and they are often efficient but are also error-prone. The *representativeness heuristic* is used when we judge on the basis of how close some new event is to representative examples of a larger category. The *availability heuristic* allows us to estimate frequency or probability of events on the basis of how available relevant memories are.

- Some have claimed that we are fundamentally unaware of how our cognitive processes operate. This is not true in principle although many of our cognitive processes do take place outside awareness.

CHAPTER

4

PERSON PERCEPTION

n 1979 Gary Dotson was tried for allegedly raping teenager Cathleen Crowell. Dotson claimed he was innocent and produced friends who gave him an alibi. But Crowell positively identified Dotson as her rapist and some laboratory evidence was consistent with Dotson's guilt. In addition, Crowell was clearly bruised and scratched and Judge Samuels felt her testimony was highly credible and consistent with that of a rape victim. After a short trial Dotson was convicted and sent to serve a 25–50-year sentence in an Illinois prison. This was a fairly routine case remarkable mainly for the long sentence decreed even though guilt was not absolutely certain.

However, in 1985 Cathleen Crowell Webb (now married) recanted her testimony that Dotson had raped her. She now said that her wounds were self-inflicted and that she had claimed she had been raped because she feared she was pregnant. She had identified Dotson as her attacker because he fit the fictitious description of the rapist she had given the police, but she was now a born-again Christian and her conscience would not allow her to let Dotson stay in jail for a crime he did not commit. Dotson's case was reheard before the same Judge Samuels. To the surprise of the public (but not of the legal profession), Judge Samuels let the original verdict stand and sent Dotson back to prison. (The legal system takes a dim view of recanted testimony because guilt, bribes, and pressure by others may induce such recantation.)

Ultimately the interesting question is this: which testimony do you believe? It is possible to imagine a young woman charging a man with rape to protect herself, and later feeling guilty and recanting. But many who have studied the case are convinced Webb is lying now. But what possible motive could she have for helping to free a man who had attacked her six years ago?

Cathleen Crowell Webb and Gary Dotson.

I recently spent a good part of an evening talking to a woman I met at a party. Barbara wasn't especially amusing, intellectually stimulating, or physically attractive, but I found her oddly intriguing. She was clearly intelligent, had a professional job, talked coherently about current events, and laughed at my jokes. I also concluded that she was highly achievement oriented and materialistic (she wanted to talk about her "first" Porsche and her power contacts). She was honest enough to tell me I didn't know what I was talking about when we discussed President Reagan's economic policies, though in most other respects she was anxious to please almost to the point of being ingratiating. But as the evening wore on I began to detect some underlying hostility. She made a couple of nasty remarks about our host, said the party was boring (which it was), and complained that most people at the party wouldn't talk to her as an equal and were scared of her. She made some semiderogatory remarks about racial and religious groups.

As I thought about Barbara over the next day or two, I found myself wondering what made her tick. How can someone be honest, nice, and hostile all at the same time? Clearly, honesty is one way of being hostile, but what about the niceness? I eventually decided that Barbara was really quite insecure and that her niceness to me had been a cover-up for her basic hostility. I remembered that she had said early in the conversation that she had always been a bit nervous about psychology. I began to feel that she probably disliked me as much as she seemed to dislike everyone else but that she had been afraid of what I, the psychologist, might think of her. So perhaps she had tried to impress me with her car and the people she knew. After I had drawn that conclusion, she no longer seemed as intelligent to me as she had before.

INTRODUCTION

These examples involve **person perception:** the study of how we perceive and think about other people. It is impossible for any of us to know whether Cathleen Crowell Webb was lying then or now, although we certainly might infer things about her veracity. My impression of Barbara is filled with trait ascriptions, assumptions about the causes of behavior, and attempts to paint a total impression of her.

Sometimes our inferences, like those about Barbara, are well thought out, but at other times they are not nearly so well considered. You label the salesperson as rude without much thought, and you just know that your friend is still angry with you because she seemed cool this morning. Nonetheless, whether or not our perceptions of others are based on deep thought or less reflective processes, they are important because they mediate our behavior. Your votes in the next election will depend heavily on your impressions of various politicians, and you will prob-

ably react differently to your friend depending on whether or not you decide she is still angry.

These examples provide an introduction to some of the enduring problems of person perception. In the case of Cathleen Webb we have the question of how to interpret behavior in terms of its causes. Was her behavior caused by fear several years ago? Is it caused by misguided compassion now? The "Barbara" example suggests an attempt to form a general impression. In the section on attribution immediately following, we consider the first set of questions concerned with the causes and interpretation of behavior. In the section after that, we consider how our interpretations are unified into general impressions.

ATTRIBUTION

BASIC ISSUES

One of the most important judgments we make about others is why they behaved as they did; why did Cathleen Webb lie, either during the trial or more recently, and what kind of a person is she for doing so? Why was Barbara so hostile? We infer (attribute) motives, abilities, personality traits, and values to people in an effort to explain their behavior, and we call these inferences about people **attributions.**

The Stimuli of Person Perception   Any judgment we make must be based on some sort of information, and this information can come from any number of sources: gossip, a newspaper, observation of behavior, even bumper stickers. Indeed, we often have powerful impressions of people we have never met just from seeing them in public or reading about them. However, most of our person-perception activity is stimulated by observations of familiar people doing something. I see Joe, and more than likely I will also see him behaving—he seems to be shouting at a woman. Moreover, I note that this all takes place in a particular setting, say at a concert. These then are the crucial stimuli for person perception: *person, behavior,* and *context.*

Snap Judgments   Sometimes we infer things about people by using well-worn but convenient rules, such as dark-haired women are serious, people in suits are stuffy, and men who dance at discos are extroverted. I suspect that one reason I thought Barbara was so intelligent was that she wore glasses, and we all know people who wear glasses are smart. Such judgments are based on obvious but superficial cues, and they are likely to be nonreflective, even nonconscious, and often are wrong (such as the glasses example). But such judgments are common and have been called **snap judgments** (Schneider, Hastorf, & Ellsworth, 1979) to emphasize both their quick and their nonreflective nature.

Such snap judgments probably have many sources. Our culture pushes certain beliefs ("blonds have more fun"), and each of us has idiosyncratic experiences (people with blue eyes are rude because so many blue-eyed people have been rude to me). Beliefs may be based on (perhaps unconscious) metaphors; baby-faced adults, like children, are judged to be submissive, for example (McArthur & Apatow, 1983–84). However, whatever their sources and validity, such rules can be used quickly and require little cognitive effort.

In recent years several psychologists (for example, McArthur & Baron, 1983) have argued

Leslie McArthur

that many of the stimuli of person perception—behavior and physical appearances—are informationally rich and do not necessarily require much in the way of conscious analysis. For example, although we *can* go through an elaborate analysis to decide whether a person is working hard at some task, it is simpler to observe if the person sweats, frowns, and grunts at the task: effortful behavior *looks* effortful. But most person-perception theorists assume we usually must make some cognitive effort to figure out behavior.

Causal Judgments   Snap and other nonreflective judgments usually do not involve inferences about the causes of behavior. However, we often want to interpret or explain the behavior in terms of intentions and motives. If someone compliments you, you may care whether she really means what she says or is trying to win your approval. Is she sincere or a flatterer? You may go even further. She is trying to win your approval in this instance because she needs a special favor. Or she is kind to you because she has a general disposition to behave kindly—more informally, she is kind because she is a kind person. In other words, you *attribute* intentions, traits, motives, and dispositions to people to explain why they behave as they do.

THE NAIVE ANALYSIS OF BEHAVIOR

Although people have speculated for centuries about how we infer the characteristics of others, Fritz Heider's (1958) account is the most influential modern theory. Heider called his model the *naive analysis of behavior,* because he assumed that everyday people who were naive about science still analyzed behavior. He suggested that in trying to understand any behavioral or physical phenomenon we usually ask what caused it to happen. In the case of objects, we realize that they have properties that *dispose* them to be moved in certain ways. For example, balls are disposed to roll by virtue of their roundness, and the flatness of a block disposes it to slide. The "behavior" of an object is thus a joint function of its own properties (such as roundness) and the external forces applied to it; balls are capable of rolling, but only when pushed.

Heider assumed that a similar situation exists with people. All people are subject to environmental forces, such as pressures from others, norms, and laws. In addition we each have different dispositions, such as attitudes, values, motives, and personality traits, that allow these forces to work in different ways. To understand behavior we need to know about the interaction of environmental forces and personal dispositions. Your abilities, motives, and personal dispositions surely affect behavior, but you sometimes behave in certain ways because of strong external or environmental forces. For example, you probably will attend your next exam in spite of and not because of your natural inclinations. And social and legal pressures keep us from doing naughty things we otherwise would like to do.

The interplay of these internal, *dispositional forces* and external demands constitutes the breeding ground of attribution models. One essential question for most attribution models is whether a person performs some behavior because of his or her own inclinations or because of some strong external force. When a student says she likes my course, does she really mean it (her behavior is caused by her own values and attitudes) or does she say it because of the approval (in the form of good grades) I might offer (external forces)? Is Cathleen Webb motivated by her religious (internal) ethics to claim now that Dotson never raped her, or does she have some ulterior (external) motive for saying that?

The distinction between internal and external forces is important in person perception, but it has its flaws. For example, suppose we ask a group of students why they have shown up for class on a blustery, cold winter morning. Carlos announces that he came because he likes the course and the lectures—this is an

Fritz Heider

internal cause. Ann says that she came because she thinks the professor is angry with her for missing class so much and with an exam coming up she feels compelled to attend to get back in his good graces—this is an external cause.

However, neither explanation is pure. Carlos wants to be in class, but he certainly doesn't sit in this classroom all day. The class meeting time (an external demand) controls his behavior as much as his desires do. And the fact that Ann responds to the professor's watchful eye indicates that she cares about her grade in the course. Her desire to do well (an internal cause) is as influential as the demands of the professor. So a full explanation of the behavior of Carlos and Ann requires that we take account of both internal and external forces and their interplay.

Despite these problems, Heider was on to an essential point about everyday perceptions: namely, that we distinguish between those times when our behavior seems to spring from the inner wells of personality and other times when we do something because we feel we have to. This distinction is usually easy for people to make and has been critical to subsequent work. However, Heider did not really offer a precise theory, and his work was not oriented toward empirical testing. Recently, however, several social psychologists have built on Heider's ideas and have proposed several attribution models that have been widely subjected to experimental testing.

PERSON VERSUS ENTITY ATTRIBUTION

Types of Attribution   Harold Kelley's (1967) influential attribution model extends the Heiderian emphasis on internal and external causality. Attributions made to internal or dispositional qualities such as abilities, motives, intentions, and traits are collectively called *actor attributions* in the Kelley model. Kelley calls attributions to external, situational, or environmental forces *entity attributions* to indicate that often our behavior is dictated by the nature of some thing or person in the environment. More recently it has become customary to add *circumstance attributions,* which refer to more variable features of the environment.

Let's introduce all this with a concrete example. Suppose a friend, Judith, knows that you are looking for a course to take. She has just recommended that you take a course in person perception because she really liked the course and thinks you would also. You ask yourself why Judith liked the course. You want to know whether to attribute her reaction to the entity (the course is really good), to the actor (Judith is the sort of person who likes courses generally), or to the circumstances (perhaps she was in a good mood when she gave you her evaluation). Now obviously you will follow her advice to take the course only if you make an entity attribution—that is, only if you think that she made the recommendataion because the course really is good. If Judith's reactions were produced by her course-loving nature or by personal circumstances you might not share, you will probably not see her advice as especially relevant to your decision.

Types of Information   Kelley says you need three kinds of information to make an attribution in this sort of situation. *Consistency information* refers to whether the actor (Judith) makes the same response (liking) to the same entity (the course) under a wide variety of circumstances. If she liked the course throughout the semester, we would say that her reaction was consistent. If, on the other hand, she liked the course some days but not others, consistency would be low. *Consensus information* refers to whether other people agree with Judith's reaction. If nearly everyone agreed with her that the course was good, consensus would be high; if there was considerable disagreement, consensus would be low. Finally, *distinctiveness information* refers to how the person reacts to similar entities. If Judith likes all courses, we would say her reaction to person perception is not distinctive (low distinctiveness), whereas if she likes this course but few others, her reaction to person perception is highly distinctive.

Empirical Tests   According to the Kelley model, entity attributions ought to be high when there is high consistency, high consensus, and high distinctiveness. In other words, you are likely to think the course really is good (entity attribution) if Judith always likes it (high consistency), everyone else likes it also (high consensus), and she likes few other courses (high distinctiveness). On the other hand, if consistency is high but Judith is alone in liking the course (low consensus) and she likes almost all the courses she takes (low distinctiveness) you might be correct in assuming that Judith just likes courses—she has a course-loving nature. Finally, when Judith's reactions are inconsistent—say she likes the course some days but not others—we might be inclined to feel that Judith's moods or her personal circumstances have more to do with her reactions than do her dispositions or the nature of the course. To return to the example of my encounter with Barbara, I concluded that she was hostile because she made disparaging remarks about a range of topics (low distinctiveness) though no one else was making such comments (low consensus).

Data from an extensive study by Leslie McArthur (1972) confirm that subjects generally follow these rules, and other studies (for example, Smith & Miller, 1979) also support the Kelley model in broad outline. There are, however, some consistent peculiarities regarding both information and attributions in such experiments. First, regarding information, although both distinctiveness and consensus information ought to be high with entity and low with actor attributions, McArthur's subjects tended to rely much more on distinctiveness than on consensus information in making that distinction. Subjects were biased in underutilizing consensus information to distinguish actor from entity attributions. Second, regarding attributions, subjects tended to favor actor over entity attributions. Subjects were more likely to say that Judith's personal characteristics rather than the course caused her reactions. We will return later in this chapter to these tendencies because they have important implications for certain problems in attribution processing.

DISCOUNTING

The attribution models of Heider and Kelley are general in the sense that they help us decide whether behavior was caused by external or internal forces, but they do not give us much of a handle on *which* internal or external forces could be at work.

There are usually several plausible reasons for why a person behaved in a particular way, and it may be hard to decide which of the many possibilities was crucial in producing the behavior. Naturally if we could eliminate several of the possible causes, we might have more confidence in the remaining possibilities. Kelley (1972) argues that when there are many possible causes of a behavior you will not feel confident than any one was the "real" cause—you will **discount** any one as the key cause. On the other hand, to the extent that there is only one plausible cause, you will be certain that it is the effective one.

In the example of Barbara, I was initially taken with how nice she seemed and I assumed that she was a genuinely nice person—I made an actor (internal) attribution. Then I remembered that she had asked whether I might be

able to help her with a project and also that she said psychology made her a little nervous. Now I was in the position of having three possible causes of her nice behavior. She could be genuinely nice (my initial actor attribution), she could be trying to butter me up (an attribution to me, the entity), or she could be the kind of person who becomes nice when she gets nervous (circumstance attribution). As the discounting principle suggests, I was much less certain that the first explanation was the correct one because I now had tripled the number of candidates. The opening example of Webb's testimony also illustrates the discounting principle. One reason recanted testimony is suspect is that it could be recanted due to external pressures, changed feelings about the defendant, and so on, as well as by a sincere

"You say you're sorry. You act sorry. And you look sorry. But you're not sorry."

Drawing by Geo. Price © 1977 by the New Yorker Magazine, Inc.

desire to reveal the truth. So the possibility that recanted testimony is an expression of the truth is discounted when the other possibilities are considered.

Sometimes potential causes or reasons for behavior are all internal. For example, a person could work hard in her courses because (1) she loves to work hard, (2) she wants to make good grades, (3) she enjoys the course material, (4) she is infatuated with the professor, or (5) she is trying to take her mind off personal problems, among other possibilities. Thus, similar behaviors may be expressions of different motives and personality traits (Jones & Davis, 1965). The student above could be (1) a workaholic, (2) achievement oriented, (3) genuinely enthusiastic, (4) smitten with the professor, or (5) neurotic.

The perceiver may also want to decide whether the behavior was due to personal dispositions rather than environmental pressures. Professors who require their students to attend class, alas, never can be sure how popular their lectures really are. Because the external pressures are sufficient to account for the bodies in the lecture hall, the possibility that students really want to attend the lectures must be discounted. A child I know has been known to refuse to perform requested household chores when she claims she was going to do them anyway, because her parents will think she did them because of the command and not because of her desires. It is hard to get personal credit for mandated behavior.

Role-playing   Often we find ourselves performing behaviors that go against our inner values and attitudes in order to play it safe, gain popularity, or avoid ridicule. This presents an attribution problem for the perceiver of our behavior. When you compliment your hostess on a meal or tell a professor that you enjoyed her course, there is some risk that your genuine appreciations will be discounted because external politeness norms are so salient.

Or the politician who takes a popular stand—say, giving a pro-ERA speech to a feminist group—may raise doubts about the sincerity of his or her beliefs (Mills & Jellison, 1967). A speech delivered to an audience expected to favor it might have been given either because the speaker actually believed in its content or because the speaker wanted to win the approval of the audience. The speech may accurately reflect the speaker's views, but the audience cannot be certain of this because of the other plausible motive for the speaker's statements. On the other hand, the only plausible explanation for a speech given to an audience expected to be hostile to its content is that the speaker must truly believe what he or she says.

Similarly, when people do what their jobs or social roles say they should, we should discount the possibility that they perform the behavior because of their own dispositions. But if those people do something their roles do not mandate, we would have high confidence that their behavior is caused by internal or dispositional factors.

In an experimental demonstration by Jones, Davis, and Gergen (1961), subjects listened to recordings of people applying for jobs. Half the subjects heard the applicants apply for a job that required introversion; for the other half the job required extroversion. Within each of these conditions, sometimes the applicants described themselves as introverted and sometimes as extroverted. As expected, the subjects were more confident of what the applicants were really like when they described themselves in the way that went against the role demands (for example, the person applying for the introverted job who said she was extroverted must really be extroverted). When a person describes herself to fit job demands, you cannot be sure whether it is the demands or her real personality that produced the description, but when she goes against the demands, her personality is the only likely reason for her response.

However, this effect is not found for every characteristic. Consider the woman who is incredibly brilliant in class. Even if you know there are strong pressures on her to act smart, you probably will not discount her intelligence as a cause of her behavior because of this. Why? Because intelligence is not the sort of thing that comes and goes with situational demands: if someone acts smart, she must be smart. On the other hand, the person who acts stupid might be responding to situational forces, because it does not require unusual ability to act stupid. So for dispositions that involve abilities there may be an *asymmetrical* attribution: the person who displays the ability must have it but the person who does not display it may or may not in fact lack it, depending on situational forces (Reeder & Brewer, 1979; Reeder, Messick, & Van Avermaet, 1977). Similar asymmetry exists for attributions of moral behavior: a person who behaves honestly in a particular situation may or may not be honest, but a person who behaves dishonestly is seen as dispositionally dishonest (Reeder & Coovert, 1986). Thus immoral behavior generally elicits attributions of an immoral disposition, even though we need to know more about the situation before we can judge moral behavior.

Attitude Attributions   Not only behavioral motives but expressed attitudes may vary according to situational pressures. Often we feel compelled to say things we do not fully believe. For example, you must compliment a host on the pig's liver and artichoke souffle he has served you, no matter what your private opinions are. The host will have little information about your true attitudes under such circumstances.

In an experiment by Jones and Harris (1967), subjects read an essay either defending a popular position (Cuba's Fidel Castro is bad) or an unpopular position (Castro is good). Half of the subjects were told that the essay they read was written by someone who had

We are prone to assume that people who perform immoral behaviors, such as this shoplifter, have immoral dispositions.

had no choice about which position to take, and the other half that the writer had had a choice. Theoretically, subjects should infer nothing about the true attitudes of writers who have no choice. But subjects should have no problems attributing expressed beliefs to writers' true attitudes when the writers do have a choice.

Certainly the second prediction was confirmed. As Table 4.1 shows, subjects did infer that the person with a choice had attitudes consistent with what he or she had written. However, in the no-choice condition the results were more perplexing: subjects inferred that the writer of the pro-Castro essay was more favorable to Castro than the writer of the anti-Castro essay (44.10 to 22.87), even though neither writer had had a choice about

TABLE 4.1 MEAN ATTRIBUTIONS OF ATTITUDE.
When the essay writer had a choice of which side to defend, subjects infer attitudes in line with the essay position. This tendency is reduced, but still apparent, even when the essay writer did not have a choice.

	Speech	
Condition	Pro-Castro*	Anti-Castro*
Choice	59.62	17.38
No choice	44.10	22.87

*10 = maximum anti-Castro score; 70 = maximum pro-Castro score.
SOURCE: Jones and Harris, 1967.

what to write. The tendency to infer attitudes from behavior is *less* in the no-choice than in the choice condition, but is nonetheless still present.

This tendency to infer attitudes from even strongly constrained behavior is in effect a *failure to discount* information that may plausibly be uncertain or incorrect. This tendency has been replicated with many variations of experimental details (Jones, Riggs, & Quattrone, 1979; Jones, Worchel, Goethals, & Grumet, 1971; Schneider & Miller, 1975). In one striking demonstration (Gilbert & Jones, 1986), subjects dictated to others what answers to give to political questions, yet still inferred the political attitudes of the others from their answers.

Personality Attributions   As with attributions of motives and attitudes, we tend to make attributions of the personalities of people consistent with their behaviors even when the behaviors are constrained (Napolitan & Goethals, 1979; Miller, Jones, & Hinkle, 1981). Eagly and Steffen (1984) have shown that women are perceived to be more selfless and concerned with others than are men, and less self-assertive and mastery oriented, because the traditional female role of homemaker encourages the former but not the latter qualities. We tend to attribute the behavior of women (and men) to qualities of personality at

the expense of fully recognizing the real cultural and social pressures that encourage role-consistent behaviors. We often fail to discount personal causes of behavior when entity or circumstance attributions are just as appropriate. In the example of Barbara, I assumed that her nice behavior at the party reflected her personal disposition to be nice, even though I should have realized that the party situation puts nearly everyone on his or her best behavior.

Ability Attributions   Ability attributions are also subject to this failure to discount information. In a classic study by Ross, Amabile, and Steinmetz (1977), a general information quiz was arranged in which subjects tried to ask questions to stump a contestant. Could you succeed at this task? If you are like most of us you probably know more about some area (such as baseball trivia, names of legendary rock groups, or facts of geography) than most other people do. In other words, you have a huge situationally determined advantage in choosing which questions to ask the contestant. You are not necessarily smarter than the contestant, but you have been allowed to pick an area that you know better. Yet Ross and his students showed that people who observe and participate in such contests attribute greater intelligence to the questioner than to the contestant; this occurs even when they are fully aware of the situational constraint (Johnson, Jemmott, & Pettigrew, 1984). It is an irony of sorts that some of my students think I am smarter than they because I can ask them questions about psychology they cannot answer, but that sometimes my daughters think I am incredibly stupid because I cannot answer their questions about physics or calculus.

The discounting principle is a useful one and there is clear evidence that people use it routinely. However, the research reviewed in the last three sections suggests that people do not always use the rule in an optimal way. We should discount the possibility that any one potential cause of behavior is the actual cause when there are many possibilities. Yet we often do not discount personal dispositions (actor attributions) when there are strong situational constraints on behavior. As we will see later in the chapter, this is part of a more general bias to see the internal causes for others' behaviors as more important than the external causes.

ATTRIBUTION OF RESPONSIBILITY

One of the reasons Heider made such a sharp distinction between internal and external causality is that he assumed people would be held responsible for their behavior only when it was internally caused. But the concept of responsibility is philosophically, legally, and psychologically vague (Shaver, 1985). Let us focus on just three meanings of the concept. When you say a person is responsible for an action, you may mean that he or she (1) caused some effect through his or her behavior, (2) is morally responsible for the effect, or (3) is legally culpable. These meanings are related but they are not identical. Suppose that Sam Smith killed another person. If he shot a man in battle or killed an armed intruder in his home, we would agree that Smith caused the death of the other but normally we would not hold him either morally or legally responsible for the killing. In some cases, Smith might be legally responsible without bearing full measure of moral responsibility, such as if he were to kill his wife's lover in what is defined (and partially excused) as a crime of passion. Finally, there are cases of legal or moral responsibility without direct causal responsibility. For example, if Smith drives the getaway car in a robbery in which a murder is committed, he may be legally responsible for the murder even though he did not cause it directly. Or Smith could be legally and perhaps morally responsible for the misdeeds of his minor children even though his direct causal responsibility is minimal.

Generally, responsibility attributions seem to have moral overtones that are usually absent from purely causal descriptions, and legal responsibility often involves the assignment of sanctions in addition to moral responsibility. Further, although we generated plausible examples of various combinations, the typical case is one in which moral responsibility attribution is based on causal ascriptions: we usually do not hold someone responsibile for an outcome unless he or she also caused it. Legal sanctions in turn typically begin with moral responsibility attributions—commonly we seek to punish primarily those we believe to be morally culpable.

Causal Responsibility   Sometimes, to decide whether a person caused something or to determine how much causal responsibility he or she is to bear is a tricky issue (Einhorn & Hogarth, 1986). A major problem is that there are usually many causal factors at work in any situation. For example, in 1986 President Reagan ordered American planes to bomb

During the 1960s and 1970s, the Vietnam War provoked intense public debate about moral and legal responsibility.

Libya. During the raid innocent people may have been killed by Libyan missiles shot at American planes as well as by American bombs. So the behavior of the Libyans, Reagan's decision, the behavior of American planes, the larger geopolitcal context of international terrorism, and the behavior of the Israeli government toward Palestinians all count as potential causes in the sense that the innocent people would not have been killed had any one of these factors been substantially changed. How then do we decide which factor is most important in a causal sense?

One general rule of thumb suggested by philosophers (Feinberg, 1965; Hart & Honoré, 1959; Mackie, 1974) is the **abnormal conditions test.** To use an example of Einhorn and Hogarth (1986), when we tap a watch with a hammer, sometimes the watch breaks. We normally assume the hammer tap to be the relevant cause of the broken watch, although logically the fragility of the watch is a contributing factor—we take fragile watches for granted but consider hammer taps unusual. On the other hand, if the context were switched such that the hammer tap occurred during the normal testing of watches in a factory, the cause would probably be seen as a defective watch—hammer taps are common during tests but fragile watches less so. Similarly, when an old man dies from a relatively mild case of the flu, we blame the flu, although a younger man would not have died. Age is a background, taken-for-granted, normal condition, whereas the flu bug is less normal. Thus we tend to ascribe causal responsibility to the condition that seems most abnormal in the context.

Moral Responsibility   In the case of moral responsibility, usually the person must have caused the relevant act before moral responsibility is assigned. But clearly something else must be added. I cause harm and benefit to many people each and every day without being morally responsible. Suppose that I am in a store and that I stumble, fall

against someone, and cause her to injure herself. Assuming that my stumble was purely accidental, I am not likely to be held morally responsible for her injury even though I clearly caused it. Under what circumstances would I be responsible for the injury?

There is general philosophical agreement and some research support for the notion that responsibility attributions involve (in addition to causality) elements of voluntariness and foresight (Shultz & Schleifer, 1983) as well as appreciation of the moral implications of the behavior (Shaver, 1985). In the example above, I will be off the hook morally if my stumble was purely accidental but not if I was "horsing around," because in the latter case I had some voluntary control over the behavior. I will also be more responsible if I should have foreseen what might happen. One does not, of course, oridinarily anticipate stumbles, but if I stumbled while trying out a pair of stilts in a crowded store, the woman might well hold me morally accountable—I should have been able to foresee that I might stumble. Finally, before I am held fully morally responsible I must have the capacity to realize that hurting others is wrong.

Legal Responsibility   Perhaps the central difference between legal responsibility and causal and moral responsibility is that legal responsibility is oriented toward imposing sanctions (usually punishments) on behavior (Hamilton, 1980). Legal responsibility may depend on judgments about fairness, appropriateness, and deterrence in addition to judgments about degree of causal and moral responsibility.

Although a comprehensive review of the issues in legal responsibility is beyond the scope of this text (for further discussion see Fincham & Jaspers, 1980; Lloyd-Bostock, 1983; and Shaver, 1985), it is important to understand that there are fundamental and interesting differences between moral and causal responsibility and legal responsibility. One cherished principle of our legal system is that definitions of crimes and responsibility should not depend on the status of the victim. Stealing $200 from a friend is legally as wrong as stealing the same amount from the phone company by making fraudulent calls, even though moral responsibility might be different. Murder is murder whether the victim is nice or mean. Yet a certain amount of legal lore suggests that defendants have an easier time before juries when their victims were less than morally pure. Furthermore, experimental research (Landy & Aronson, 1969) and studies of actual court cases (Myers, 1980) show defendants fare better when their victims are of low status or are morally deficient in some way. So sometimes moral responsibility would seem to corrupt legal responsibility.

This is a particularly salient issue in recent debates about rape. Part of the traditional fantasy for some males has been that women enjoy rape, or at least invite it, so that rape has been seen as at least partially the fault of the victim. One of the major problems in rape prevention has been getting law enforcement officials and the public to stop blaming the victim. Rape victims sometimes even blame themselves (Janoff-Bulman, 1979). Certainly there have been cases where women have explicitly invited rape, and a good many rape victims could have been more cautious, but legally such matters are largely irrelevant. A person who leaves his car unlocked may invite its theft, but the thief is still a thief. Similarly, no amount of stupidity or sexually provocative behavior justifies sexual contact once the woman becomes an unwilling participant.

Several factors can contribute to blaming victims. Janoff-Bulman, Timko, and Carli (1985) point out that victims may be blamed because of **hindsight bias:** when we know some event has actually happened, we tend to assume that it seemed likely beforehand. Once

Defensive attribution tendencies sometimes lead us to blame people, such as these victims of a tornado, for events they could not control.

a rape has occurred, we may blame a victim for not having taken precautions against what now seems to have been so likely. In addition, some blame may be defensive: blaming rape victims for stupidity or "loose" behavior may serve to protect one against thinking about a similar fate for oneself. Also, rape victims may be blamed because our culture encourages the idea that women beguile helpless men through their sexual charms.

However, we should keep in mind that blame is not the same as legal culpability. Perhaps the more serious question is whether reactions to rapists are affected by such legally extraneous variables. We do not have definitive evidence, but the data we do have suggest that blame for the victim does not reduce the perceived legal responsibility of the rapist (Pallak & Davies, 1982; Wyer, Bodenhausen, & Gorman, 1985).

ATTRIBUTION BIAS

Attribution models purport to show how people function more or less rationally to arrive at causal explanations for behavior. Yet we know people do not always follow the attribution rules or make unbiased attributions about the causes of behavior. Some have suggested that people are biased because of motivational or emotional factors. For example, people often blame others for their own mistakes to protect their own self-esteem. We will consider other examples in Chapter 5 on the social self. However, we concentrate here on more purely cognitive biases that limit the ways we process information.

Perception of Self and Others   Jones and Nisbett (1972) stimulated much of the current interest in attribution bias by arguing that for the behavior of others we favor internal, dispositional explanations but for our own behavior we tend to use external, situational explanations. If asked why you take psychology courses, you might say that they are in-

teresting (a typical entity or situational attribution) whereas your friend might ascribe your choices to your particular personality.

Lee Ross (1977) has termed this tendency to overattribute the behavior of others to internal forces the **fundamental attribution error.** We have already seen several examples of this tendency. Perhaps most striking is the tendency of subjects to feel that a person believed what he said or wrote even when he was under strong external compulsion to do so. This amounts to a propensity to favor internal attributions for the behavior of others.

Several studies support the general position of Jones and Nisbett about differences between perceptions of self and others. However, a careful review of research studies (Watson, 1982) indicates some important qualifications. Though both actors and observers tend to perceive behavior as dispositionally caused, people perceive stronger situational causality for self than for others. Indeed it is possible that the differences between attributions to self and to others reside more in overperception of situational causes for one's own behavior than in overassigning dispositional causes to others (Funder, 1982).

How might these differences between perceptions of self and others arise? One possibility is that we have more information about self than others (Monson & Snyder, 1977). In particular, each of us probably has a clearer sense of how we have behaved in the past than we do of how others have behaved in the past. If

Richard Nisbett

you know that you are sometimes generous and sometimes not (as would be the case with most of us), you would naturally tend to see situational reasons for your present generous or ungenerous act. On the other hand, because we often see others only in a single situation, we typically do not have information on situational variability for them. However, this is not automatically true. If you are sure that you have some personality trait such as generosity and that your behavior is fairly consistent with regard to that trait, you might be more inclined to see present behavior as a reflection of basic dispositions (Monson & Hesley, 1982). Similarly if you have background information about another person, you will also assess the consistency of present behavior with past behavior; consistent behavior will favor dispositional attributions (Kulik, 1983). Thus the attribution of the behavior of both self and others to either dispositions or situations depends on both the amount and the kind of information you have about past behavior.

Jones and Nisbett also argued that different features are salient when we process information about self and about others. I know I am basically the same person, and as I observe my behaviors change, I will also note situational changes. On the other hand, when I examine others, it is the situation that seems to be the stable element. For example, at a baseball game I notice that Jim is behaving in a boisterous way but that Sam is sitting quietly and talking to friends. Although upon reflection I realize that the baseball game represents different constellations of situational forces for Jim and Sam, I am more immediately aware that the two people are behaving quite differently in the "same" situation, and I tend to attribute this to differences in their personalities. When I observe others I am struck by differences between people in a common situation.

This argument suggests that differences in attributions are due to focus of attention. Several experiments have shown that attributions depend particularly on visual perspective. We are more inclined to ascribe internal causality to those people we look at. In a conversation I look at you and see your behavior as more dispositionally caused than mine. But if the perspective changes so do attributions. In a clever experiment by Michael Storms (1973), conversations were videotaped and subjects saw tapes in which the camera had focused on them—in other words, they now saw themselves much as the other person had seen them in the original conversation. Those subjects now saw their own behavior as less situationally caused.

A study by Pryor and Kriss (1977) manipulated salience of actors and situational forces in another way. Sentences written in a subject-oriented mode (for example, Judith liked the course) tended to elicit actor (Judith) attributions, whereas sentences written to make the object more salient (the course was liked by Judith) elicited less actor and more circumstance attribution. These and similar results suggest that attributions are biased toward that part of the stimulus field that is salient (Rholes & Pryor, 1982; Sherman & Titus, 1982; Smith & Miller, 1979).

Salience Effects   More generally this salience argument suggests that those we pay attention to should also be seen as exerting a fair amount of causal force (McArthur, 1981; Taylor & Fiske, 1978). For example, Taylor and

Shelley Taylor   Susan Fiske

Fiske (1975) found that after a conversation involving several people, subjects were more likely to ascribe traits (taken as evidence of dispositional attributions) to those who sat across from them, presumably because they tended to pay more attention to those people.

There are important implications for everyday life. Anyone who stands out (a woman in a top managerial position, a black male among white females) is likely to capture attention and be seen as causally responsible for what goes on in the group (Taylor, 1981). Likewise famous politicans and people accused of highly publicized crimes will tend to be held responsible for the effects of their behavior even if there are strong situational forces at work. It is axiomatic in politics that the president gets blamed for economic woes and high crime rates and praised for a surging economy and low crime rates. He has little direct control over the economy or crime, but he is salient, and salient people tend to get more than their share of both credit and blame.

Consensus Effects   So far we have discussed two possible reasons for differences in perceptions of self and others: (1) we may have different amounts and kinds of information about the two and (2) the focus of attention affects salience, which in turn affects perceptions of causality. There is yet a third possibility for which we have already seen considerable evidence. McArthur (1972) and others have shown that people tend not to weigh consensus information as highly as other kinds of information. Consensus information, as discussed above, tells us how many people perform a particular behavior or, more generally, how likely the behavior is. When consensus is high, the behavior is popular— that is, many people perform the behavior— and ordinarily we would look to strong norms or situational pressures to explain the behavior: the fact that most of the guests at a large wedding are dressed in their best attire would not usually be taken as evidence that

We do not assume that high-consensus behavior reflects much about individual dispositions.

people have strong internal desires or dispositions to dress this way. So information about consensus (that is, about how many people perform a behavior or have a reaction to it) ought to give us indirect information about the strength of cultural norms and other strong situational forces and should therefore affect attributions to these forces. Yet people seem to ignore or play down such information. Why? There are several possibilities (Kassin, 1979).

One possibillity is that consensus information is not ordinarily very salient, so people may not pay much attention to it. Knowing how many people did something can be abstract and may not seem very interesting. Consensus information typically has more effect when experimenters make special efforts to ensure that people pay attention to it (Feldman, Higgins, Karlovac, & Ruble, 1976).

People may also mistrust consensus information, particularly when it violates what they think most people would do. If you are told that Alice and many other subjects were willing to take strong shocks in an experiment, you might discount the information because you feel sure that you and the people you know would not be so stupid. Indeed people do think that they know what their peer group would do, so that experimenter-generated consensus information about peers is likely to be mistrusted and to receive less weight than consensus information about nonpeers (Higgins & Bryant, 1982).

False Consensus Effects   This raises an additional interesting possibility. Most people think they have a clear idea of what "most people" think, and it's sad to report that they are often in error. For example, in my part of the country, which is politically conservative, students routinely underestimate the percentage of people in the country at large who are prochoice on abortion and who favor gun control. However, people do not simply make errors; they make a particular kind of error—they tend to assume that others agree with whatever position they hold.

Misestimating consensus in this way is such a common bias that it has its own label—the *false consensus effect.* This vividly demonstrated experimentally by Ross, Greene, and House (1977), who asked subjects to walk around the Stanford campus wearing a signboard saying either "Eat at Joe's" or "Repent." They were also asked to predict what others would do. Subjects who agreed to perform the behavior also felt that a majority of their fellow students would do so, whereas those who refused also felt that a majority of their fellow students would also refuse. In other words, subjects inferred that others would do as they do and they generated a false consensus for their behavior.

There are several demonstrations of the false consensus effect (Mullen et al., 1985), and it is socially important and interesting even apart from its importance for attribution bias. Why do people think that others think as they do? One possibility is that they tend to associate with like-minded others and hence fail to appreciate that there are other types of people in the world. Another possibility is that, to make our own views seem valid and reasonable, we transform our *hopes* that others agree with us

Selective interaction with others is one reason we think our attitudes and values are more widely shared than they are.

into feelings that they *do* agree with us. In line with that possibility, people who perform mildly deviant acts such as smoking or who hold socially undesirable positions on major issues overestimate the percentage of people who agree with them (Sherman et al., 1983; van der Pligt, 1984). Failure also increases false consensus tendencies (Sherman, Presson, & Chassin, 1984), suggesting that those people who most need reassurance that they are correct are also most prone to overestimate the number of people who agree with them.

We began this discussion of false consensus by discussing the role of consensus in attributional biases. The fundamental attribution error suggests that people are too dispositional in their perceptions of others. The data we have examined suggest that consensus information is generally underutilized, a tendency exacerbated by the false consensus effect when people mistrust consensus information that violates their own ideas about what people think and do.

THE NATURE OF ATTRIBUTION PROCESSING

Attribution theory has now become a central part of social psychology and is increasingly used by personality, developmental, and clinical psychologists. After such a record of use (and abuse), the theory can claim a certain validity—not only does it fit with many of our commonsense notions of how we judge others, but even more importantly, there is massive empirical support for the approach. Like most theories that acquire a kind of establishment status, the theory has often been taken for granted and accepted uncritically. In recent years, however, attribution models have been subjected to substantial criticisms and revisions. In this section we review some of the work that addresses questions critical of attribution theory.

Motivation for Attributions   One important question is, What motivates attribution? Several conditions seem to favor attributional processing (Hastie, 1983). One main reason we try to figure people out is to predict how they will behave in the future. But when would you need to predict the behavior of others? The most obvious circumstances are when you have to interact with others or when they have the power to affect you in some way. Research generally confirms that we are more likely to seek causes of behavior under such circumstances (Berscheid, Graziano, Monson, & Dermer, 1976; Monson, Keel, Stephens, & Genung, 1982).

However, the need to predict is not the only reason we try to determine what causes behavior. Sometimes we are simply curious

about people who cannot affect us in any way. I am curious why Cathleen Webb decided to recant her rape testimony, even though I will never meet her. Is she lying now? If so, why? In general, when the behavior of others is extreme, novel, unexpected, or non-normative, it seems more interesting, and such behavior does lead to greater attributional processing (Holtzworth-Munroe & Jacobson, 1985; Pyszczynski & Greenberg, 1981; Weiner, 1985).

Deciding what caused another's behavior can also serve other motives. For example, if you and a friend have an argument, you might prefer to see his behavior as caused by his immaturity and hostility and your behavior as a reaction to his immature and hostile behavior: your attributions may be motivated by a desire to protect your self-esteem (Cunningham, Starr, & Kanouse, 1979; Knight & Vallacher, 1981).

In our everyday lives we do not always seek to discover the causes of another's behavior, but experimental data suggest that the need to predict, curiosity about strange or deviant behavior, and the desire to protect our own self-images can all engender attributions.

Attributional Processing   Attribution theory is explicitly based on a metaphor of person as scientist (see Chapter 1). Heider, Kelley, and other attribution theorists have argued that people try to explain the behavior of others much as a scientist would, employing less precise data to be sure, but using many of the same rules about causal inferences. To perform an attributional analysis of why a person did something, the perceiver must be prepared to be systematic and careful, although inevitable biases creep into the process for everyday perceivers (as they do for scientists as well).

Surely, however, we do not perform such elaborate analyses every time we decide what someone is like. Most of us rarely have conscious experiences corresponding to a full attribution analysis, although such analyses could occur automatically and below the conscious level. Indeed data suggest that some attributions are nonconscious, that trait attributions are made spontaneously when we learn about a person's behavior (Winter & Uleman, 1984; Winter, Uleman, & Cunniff, 1985). Box 4.1 discusses the hows, whys, and wherefores of this research in greater detail.

Alternative Approaches   Even if we assume that attributions are made consciously and deliberately, there is still reason to believe that people may use less elaborate models than those discussed in this chapter. Consider, for example, the Kelley model, which claims we use consensus, distinctiveness, and consistency information in forming attributions. Although Kelley proposed a quasi-statistical model for how people used this information, there are simpler methods. One version suggested by Hilton and Slugoski (1986) builds on the idea that conditions perceived to be abnormal (or unusual) are seen as effective causes. If we apply that to the Kelley model, we come up with something like the following: if consensus is low (the target is the only person who does something), the target person seems abnormal and gets the causal ascription. On the other hand, high distinctiveness (the person responds only to this stimulus) indicates that it is the stimulus that is unusual and therefore causal (entity attribution) and low consistency (the persons responds differently in different situations) indicates that the particular circumstances are unusual and therefore causal (circumstance attribution). This kind of model requires the perceiver to look for only the unusual condition or conditions to find the causes of behavior.

Another possibility is that perceivers rely on causal templates or schemata, often based on previous experience (Anderson, 1983, 1985). For example, when a student comes to my office complaining about a low test grade, I could ask how he is doing in other courses (distinctiveness) and compare his recent grade with other grades (consistency) or with other students (consensus). But I am more likely to

have a ready diagnosis (template, schemata) waiting to be activated. For introductory courses, my experience has been that students often don't spend enough time reading the texts. My causal template for poor test performance therefore is lack of effort on the part of the student. On the other hand, in more advanced courses my experience has been that ability is more pertinent, and my causal template is likely to be that the student may be taking too hard a course for his ability.

Another approach is based on script theory (Chapter 1). Recall that Schank and Abelson (1977) suggest that we have cognitive representations of common behaviors and scenarios, such as going to class or ordering a hamburger in a restaurant. Lalljee and Abelson (1983) note that these scripts may carry their own explanations as well. For example, it hardly makes sense to ask why a person sitting in class opens her notebook, because in that context opening a notebook is usually a prelude to taking notes. Similarly, I usually do not go through an elaborate analysis of why a student asks me for advice about how to study better; his behavior fits so well within my script for student-after-doing-badly-on-the-first-exam that I just assume—perhaps correctly, perhaps incorrectly—that he is asking for help because he is worried about his grade. Of course, not all behavior can be made to fit a well-designated script, and in that case more complex forms of attributional processing may go on. We have already suggested that this is likely when behavior is uncommon or deviant (meaning, among other things, that it is not well scripted).

SUMMARY

In terms of published work, attribution models have dominated social psychology in recent years. One reason is that they attempt to get at one of the fundamental features of our everyday social lives: our attempts to explain the behavior of others. This is a common

BOX 4.1

ARE TRAIT ATTRIBUTIONS AUTOMATIC?

It is an important question whether trait attributions are deliberate and conscious or spontaneous and nonconscious. Clearly, people in attribution experiments can produce judgments about internal versus external causality, personal dispositions, and the like, but that does not tell us whether they *spontaneously* make trait attributions in everyday life.

How would you determine whether attributions are more spontaneous or more deliberate? Simply asking people whether they form attributions spontaneously is out of the question because such processing is assumed to take place nonconsciously. Winter and Uleman (1984) solved this problem by sneaking up on it and addressing it indirectly. They made use of a well-known memory phenomenon, the *encoding specificity effect*. Tulving and his associates (Tulving & Thompson, 1973) have shown that when one is trying to remember material previously read or heard, stimuli that were present at the time of encoding are especially effective cues. That is why sometimes when you are trying to remember a fact while taking an exam it may be helpful to try to remember what music you were listening to when you read the information. Accordingly, if subjects form trait attributions immediately upon hearing information about a person, then the trait attribution (which was present at the time of encoding) should be a good cue for recalling the behavioral information.

Winter and Uleman performed two experiments. Subjects saw slides of behavioral sentences for 5 seconds each; there were 18 slides in the first study, 12 in the second. The sentences were of this sort: "The pro-

fessor has his new neighbors over for dinner." After reading the sentences, subjects were given a brief distractor task (to abolish short-term memory material) and then were asked to recall as many of the sentences as they could. Some subjects were merely asked to recall with no cues given; others were given cues. One kind of cue was a dispositional trait cue related to the *subject* of the sentence. For example, Winter and Uleman assumed that when subjects read the professor sentence, they would be likely to have spontaneously inferred the trait *friendly* (or something very similar) so that trait would be a good cue to stimulate recall of the sentence. Other subjects were given a semantic cue related to the *meaning* of the sentence. Such cues are usually effective in improving memory, and the investigators wanted a baseline of how well cues that were presumably not present at encoding worked. In the first experiment, the semantic cue was related to the subject of the sentence, the actor—thus, for the professor sentence, the cue was *teacher*. In the second experiment the semantic cue was related to the action of the sentence—in this case *party* was the cue.

The results were quite clear (see Figure B.4.1). Subjects recalled far more of the sentences when they had the dispositional traits cues as compared to the no cue condition. The trait cues were also more effective than the semantic action cues in the second study and somewhat more effective than the semantic actor cues in the first. There was one exception—the actor cue in the first study was more effective than the disposition cue in helping subjects remember that the professor (the actor) did something. By contrast

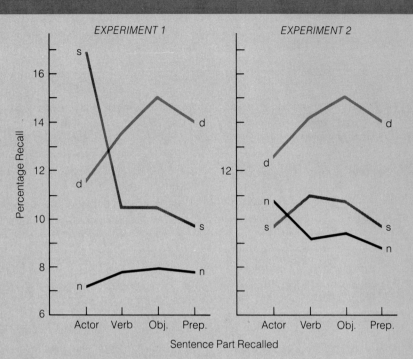

FIGURE B.4.1   Percentage Recall of Sentence Parts for Dispositional Cues (d), Semantic Cues (s), and No Cues (n). Note that in both experiments the dispositional cues generally produce more recall than the semantic cues or no cues, except for recall of the actor in Experiment 1.

Winter and Uleman, 1984.

the trait cues were more effective than the actor semantic cue in aiding recall of the verb expressing action *(having over)*, as well as the object *(neighbors)* and the prepositional phrase *(for dinner)*.

This first set of studies demonstrated that dispositional traits were good cues for memory of sentences. The most straightforward explanation is that when subjects read the sentences they had immediately, spontaneously, and nonconsciously formed a trait inference that, having been present at the time they read the sentence, was subsequently a good cue for recall. However, in this study it was possible (although not very probable) that subjects may have explicitly formed trait inferences when they read the

sentences. If that were the case, the results would not be especially interesting because no one doubts that explicitly inferred traits could be good cues for recall. Winter and Uleman, however, argue that trait inferences are formed spontaneously.

To test this idea further, an additional study was performed (Winter, Uleman, & Cunniff, 1985). The logic behind this study is that if the subjects were not focusing on the behavioral sentences they would not form inferences consciously, although they still might nonconsciously. Subjects were told that the study concerned memory for digits. They saw several digits and then they were presented with one of the target sentences, which they thought was to distract

BOX CONTINUED

them from remembering the digits, followed by recall of the digits. In reality, of course, the digits were to distract subjects from forming trait inferences. Finally, subjects were given a surprise recall test for the sentences. Again the dispositional cues were generally more effective than the semantic cues or no cues. According to the previous logic, these traits must have been inferred at time of encoding because they were such effective cues for recall. However, in this study it would have been virtually impossible for subjects to have formed the inferences deliberately when they read the sentences because they were trying hard to memorize the digits. To be absolutely sure about this the subjects were asked directly about any thoughts they had about the sentences. Only a small percentage (19%) reported any such thoughts and the extent to which subjects reported having thoughts about the sentences correlated minimally with the actual recall.

This work has not been without its critics, in part because it challenges our notions about what attribution work is. Generally, attributions are assumed to be the product of sciencelike reasoning that ought to take time and attention. Furthermore, a rich body of literature suggests that attributions are affected by motives and therefore that it is unlikely that attribution formation

is always automatic. Bassili and Smith (1986) argued that if trait attributions are purely spontaneous they should *not* be affected by instructions and motives that should require some conscious attention. These authors replicated the Winter and Uleman results under memory instructions (trait cues being better than semantic or no cues) but showed that memory is also improved when the subjects are instructed to form an impression of the person in the sentence. Therefore it cannot be the case that trait attributions are *always* formed spontaneously, because instructions and motives can play a role in trait inferences. Of course, the Bassili and Smith results really do not rule out spontaneous inferences. You may give your name or telephone number without any conscious processing much of the time, but this does not mean that you could never do the same task deliberately and with full consciousness.

The main reason we have considered this work is because it represents a clever way of getting at the ways people process information when that processing is presumed to be nonconscious and hence unavailable for report. Usually experiments are fairly direct in their logic, but in this case Winter and Uleman had to resort to a roundabout way of assessing what subjects were doing as they read the sentences.

---

activity and is important because our inferences about the reasons for the behavior of others dictates how we behave toward them. A critical comment will be received quite differently when it is perceived to be good natured teasing than when it is seen as motivated by inner hostility.

Another reason for the popularity of attribution models has been their assumption that

people reason logically and rationally—rather like scientists are supposed to reason. There are really two aspects to this "naive scientist" view. First, attribution models assume that, like scientists, people want to comprehend the underlying causes of behavior so as to predict and control phenomena. In particular, attribution models assume that when behavior is seen to be caused or produced by internal motives—wants, attitudes, values, and personality characteristics (collectively called dispositional properties)—the person's behavior will be predictable across situations. Second, attribution theories suggest that the rules people use in making such judgments have a firm basis in logic and rationality. Thus the Kelley model suggests that people should infer situational causes when consistency and distinctiveness of behavior as well as consensus are high, and this becomes almost a logical rule that must be followed. Similarly there is logical sense to the notion that when several forces could have produced behavior, the rational perceiver should discount the importance of any one of them. Not only do these rules make logical sense, they are well anchored in common sense.

It has therefore been something of a challenge to deal with data suggesting that people are not always good naive scientists. People do not always make the sorts of attributions the theories say they should. In particular, people do not discount dispositional causes enough in the face of strong situational forces—the so-called fundamental attribution error. Many reasons have been advanced for this bias within attributional processing, including not paying enough attention to consensus information and seeing the salient part of the social field (typically the person) as being a causal factor. In more recent years the whole basis of attribution models has been challenged by newer models of explanation that suggest that people use fairly simple rules when they make attributions.

IMPRESSION FORMATION

Attributional questions concerning how we perceive the causes of behavior have dominated person perception research for the past

What kinds of impressions do you have about these two people? What kinds of cues do you use and what inferences do you draw from them?

twenty years or so. Yet, this is not the only or even the most important aspect of person perception. Remember the opening example of Barbara, where, after a 2-hour conversation I decided that she had several traits, some of which seemed to contradict others. But then I organized my impression, partly by inferring new traits, such as insecurity and a desire to please, that helped me relate the traits that didn't fit together well. All this cognitive activity of inferring, organizing, and reconciling is called **impression formation.** More formally we might define impression formation as the process of organizing information about another person.

THE ASCH STUDIES

It is rare for a single person to initiate a completely new problem in psychology. This is, however, what happened when Solomon Asch published his classic paper (1946) on impression formation. He presented his subjects with a list of stimulus traits (for example, *practical, intelligent, skillful*) and told them that these traits characterized a particular person. After reading the traits, the subjects wrote their descriptions of the person. They then read a lengthy list of additional traits and were asked to check those that most likely would also characterize the stimulus person.

Think about a person who is practical, intelligent, and skillful. Would you also see this person as generous? cold? happy? This was the

kind of task Asch's subjects worked on. In the most famous of his experiments, often called the warm–cold experiments, the subjects were asked to form an impression of a person who was intelligent, skillful, industrious, determined, practical, and cautious. When just these traits were presented, 55% felt the stimulus person would be generous, 71% felt the person would be happy, and 69% thought the person would be good-natured.

Next the trait *warm* was inserted into the middle of the stimulus list. With this list, 91% felt the person would be generous, 90% that he would be happy, and 94% that he would be good-natured. Inserting *cold* in the place of *warm* reduced these inferences considerably. It is fair to say that the person defined by the list with *warm* in it was perceived quite differently than the person who was cold. Asch explained his results by using certain principles of Gestalt psychology. He believed that the subjects tried to fit all the traits together to form a unified whole (gestalt) and that in this particular context *warm* and *cold* became central traits that organized or crystallized the total impression. The subjects were responding not merely to differences between *warm* and *cold* as psychological qualities but to two quite different impressions built around these core qualities.

Asch was also interested in the question of how people combine contradictory information. You may, for example, discover that a person you have just met is intelligent, witty, cruel, ambitious, and honest. Most of us would find it difficult to fit those traits together. Asch was especially concerned to show that people changed the meanings of the traits to form the gestalt, and he studied this by presenting either the positive or the negative traits first in the list, followed by the opposite kind of information. For example, had you been a subject in his studies, you might have been asked to form an impression of someone who was kind, happy, intelligent, silly, illogical, and rigid (positive information first) or silly, illogical, rigid, kind, happy, and intelli-

Solomon Asch

gent (negative information first). Asch found that subjects generally weighted the information that came first more strongly: impressions were more positive when the positive information came first and more negative when negative information came first. This has come to be called the *primacy effect.* Asch felt that this happened because the first information provided the context or central meaning to which the later information could be fit.

INFORMATION COMBINATION

Two major programs of research have been stimulated by attempts to show that Asch's results could be explained in somewhat simpler ways. One, to be discussed in the next section, deals with how we infer one set of characteristics from another. The other, discussed in this section, concerns how information is combined into a single reaction. It derives from Asch's discussion of the primacy effect.

Asch's discussion of the primacy effect led to research questions of broader significance. When we try to resolve contradictions between positive and negative information, we try to combine information to make a single judgment. We do this sort of thing all the time. The employer who decides to hire someone after an interview, the member of a graduate admissions committee who rejects an applicant after reading the applicant's file, you who decide to invite a person you have just met to a party—in each case the perceiver makes an evaluative judgment based on some combination of behaviors, traits, test scores, appearances, grades, and other kinds of information. Often in everyday life when we are asked for our impressions of someone, we respond with a single evaluative judgement: "Sara is a jerk"; "Joe is nice."

Averaging Models   Considerable research addresses the question of how we combine information about others into evaluative judgments. Norman Anderson has performed

many research studies that show that relationships between the final evaluative judgment (typically likability) and the social desirability of the stimulus traits are precise and predictable. In particular the final evaluation is a function of the average desirability of the stimulus traits.

Anderson (1965) presented subjects with sets of four traits that varied in positiveness. Some where highly positive (H), such as *truthful*; some were moderately positive (M+), such as *painstaking*; some moderately negative (M−), such as *unpopular*; and others were highly negative (L), such as *spiteful.* Subjects read various combinations of these four kinds of traits and were then asked how much they would like a person described by these sets of traits. The liking ratings increased regularly with the average positiveness of the traits (See Table 4.2).

A simple *averaging model* (that is, a model postulating that subjects average the values of the traits) can describe the results of many experiments, but it is sometimes necessary to use a more complex model. In a **weighted averaging model,** Anderson assumes that people weigh the stimulus information differentially before averaging it. That is, when you make a decision you do more than add up a list of positive and negative traits. Certain traits—

TABLE 4.2 LIKING FOR A STIMULUS PERSON, BASED ON THE POSITIVENESS OF THE STIMULUS INFORMATION. *As the information gets more positive (going up the rows of the table), the evaluation becomes more positive.*

Traits	Liking*
H H H H	79.39
H H M+M+	71.11
M+M+M+M+	63.20
M−M−M−M−	39.50
L L M−M−	25.67
L L L L	17.64

*High numbers indicate more liking.
SOURCE: Anderson, 1965.

positive or negative—will weigh more importantly in your decision than other traits.

Various factors may influence the way you weigh the traits that affect your decision. One is the nature of the judgment. In deciding how much you like someone, you may weigh his friendliness more than his height, but if you were picking an intramural basketball team his height might contribute more to your selection. There may also be individual differences, so that some people weigh some factors more than others (Ostrom & Davis, 1979). For example, your wittiness might contribute heavily to my decision to invite you over for dinner, whereas another person might be more inclined to invite you because of your kindness. Finally, some kinds of information seem to be weighted more by nearly everyone. Negative (Ronis & Lipinski, 1985) and extreme (Fiske, 1980) information is typically weighted heavily in our judgments of others. Your unkindness (a negative trait) may be more important to me than your positive trait of honesty, and extreme honesty will probably count more than everyday versions of honesty. I think I must have weighted Barbara's few negative behaviors more than her positive ones in determining my final impression of her.

Primacy and Recency   The weighted averaging model was introduced in part to describe primacy effects in impression formation. As discussed above, Asch found that people tend to base their evaluative impressions more on the first information they encounter. According to the weighted averaging model, primacy effects could easily occur if for some reason subjects give more weight to the first than to the latter traits. Subjects might, for example, assume that the first traits are more important because they come first, or subjects might get bored and simply pay less attention to the later traits. The clear implication is that if people were forced to pay equal attention to all the traits, the primacy effect (which depends on unequal attention) should be

erased, as has in fact been demonstrated (Anderson & Hubert, 1963). Some studies (for example, Dreben, Fiske, & Hastie, 1979) even find a *recency effect* in such circumstances—that is, later rather than earlier information weighs more heavily in impression formation.

Kruglanski and his colleagues have argued that situational demands may also affect our receptiveness to new information. When people have a high need for structure (say they are under time demands or the task is complex), they tend to freeze a particular set of beliefs and reduce their attention to new information. Conversely when they are afraid of being wrong, they will resist freezing. This would suggest that primacy effects ought to be strongest when people have high needs for structure and do not have strong fears of being wrong; exactly this pattern has been found in several studies (see Freund, Kruglanski, & Shpitzajzen, 1985).

An important occasion for primacy effects is when performance changes over time. Suppose you improve during a course. How does that affect the attributions others (say your professor) make for your behavior? In a classic study by Jones et al. (1968), subjects watched another person working on 30 intelligence type problems. This person (actually a confederate of the experimenter) always got 15 of the 30 correct. However, some of subjects saw the confederate begin poorly and gradually improve (*ascending* performance), others saw performance deteriorate over the 30 trials (*descending* performance), and still others saw a constant level of performance. At the end of the experiment the subjects were asked to indicate how many correct they thought the person had got, how well she would perform in the future, and how intelligent she was. The results indicated that the subjects perceived the descending person as smarter than either the random or ascending person—presumably because the descending person had performed better earlier and thereby created a better ini-

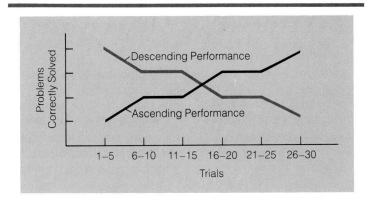

FIGURE 4.1 *Descending and Ascending Patterns of Performance. Over all 30 trials, the two groups perform equally well, but the descending group performs best at the beginning and the ascending group best at the end of the sequence.*

After Jones et al., 1968.

tial impression among the subjects. Moreover, subjects predicted that the descending person would perform better in the future.

When information that comes first is seen as due to stable factors, later information is assimilated to that earlier information (Jones & Goethals, 1971). In the Jones et al. (1968) experiment, after the first 10 trials the descending person had solved more problems correctly than the ascending person (see Figure 4.1). Subjects might reason that the descending person is smart and the ascending person not so clever. Intelligence is normally assumed to be highly stable, so when subjects make their initial attributions they might interpret subsequent behavioral information to fit: they remember the descending person as solving more problems than she had. Subjects may also be more attentive to the first few trials, which also could account for why their final assessments are affected more by the first than by the later information (Newtson & Rindner, 1979).

For whatever reasons, such primacy effects, where the first (primary) information is weighted more than the more recent informa-

tion, are quite common when we see behavior unfold over time. Once we think we know what a person is like, we interpret and even distort later behavior to conform to the early impression.

Much of the time, people do not fully analyze new information for people they already know. For example, if I decide that I like someone, my future judgments may be based more on that previously remembered summary impression than on the actual facts that went into it. Once summaries are constructed, they often become the basis of future judgments (Carlston, 1980; Lingle et al., 1979; Sherman, Zehner, Johnson, & Hirt, 1983). This is particularly likely when the new judgments are similar to the old (Schul & Burnstein, 1985). So once I have formed an impression of you as intelligent, I am likely to base new judgments about you more on my memory of my old impression than on new data.

First impressions do count, then. But can we ever change the first impressions others have of us? It all depends. Sometimes the perceiver forms such a clear first impression of you that he or she doesn't really process additional information. In that case your initial encounters and behaviors are crucial. On the other hand, if the perceiver continues to think about the kind of person you are, the impression may continue to be modified.

Asch's Theory Revisited   Although his original work stimulated a great deal of research on information combination, Asch's Gestalt hypothesis has not fared well. The work of Anderson and others has shown that both evaluative impressions and primacy–recency effects can be predicted quite well by knowing how subjects evaluate and weigh the component information they use for their judgments. These models assume that each of the component traits has a particular evaluative meaning independent of the other traits, whereas Asch had assumed that the individual traits changed their meaning depending on the context.

Intuitively Asch seems correct. For example, the quiet, reflective happiness of a mature person seems different from the silly happiness of someone who is immature. And *intelligence* seems to connote something different when paired with *warm* than with *cold*. Some studies (Hamilton & Zanna, 1974; Woll et al., 1980) find evidence for Asch's meaning change in different contexts, but others find more mixed results (Watkins & Peynircioglu, 1984). It would appear that, although traits can change meaning in different contexts, this is generally not as strong a phenomenon as Asch thought; nor can meaning change fully account for our evaluative impressions.

More generally, people seem to employ various modes of resolving contradictions among information (Asch & Zukier, 1984). For example, if you know someone is both intelligent and foolish, you might segregate domains by deciding that this person is intelligent in abstract matters but hopelessly naive and foolish in practical matters. Or you might infer a third trait that helps to explain the contradiction between the other two traits: with Barbara I inferred insecurity as a way of explain-

ing how a nice person could be hostile, and, having done so, I found that the niceness was not as nice anymore.

IMPLICIT PERSONALITY THEORY

Asch's Gestalt position has also come under attack in other ways. Recall that in his studies Asch presented subjects with a list of stimulus traits that defined a person and asked subjects to say what other traits the person would likely possess. Asch felt that the stimulus traits were first combined into a general Gestalt-like impression that was then used to generate the trait inferences. A much simpler assumption would be that subjects infer other traits directly from the given stimulus traits. One reason that the intelligent, skillful, industrious, *warm,* determined, practical, cautious person was seen as more generous and happy than the intelligent, skillful, industrious, *cold,* determined, practical, cautious person may be simply that *warm* directly implies generosity and happiness more than *cold* does (Wishner, 1960).

People seem to have a good idea of what traits go together. Does it not seem more likely that a happy person would be mature rather than immature? that a stupid person would be careless rather than careful? Subjects can generate many such inferences without much prodding, and most of us do this sort of thing all the time. Once I have labeled a student as responsible I may be inclined to feel she is also smart, even in the absence of any particular evidence for her intelligence. I readily inferred that Barbara was insecure from knowing that she was hostile.

People not only have ideas about what traits go together, they also have ideas about *how* traits and other characteristics fit together. A person's assumptions about which traits go together and how are usually referred to as his or her *implicit personality theory* (Schneider, 1973). Such theories are important because they allow us to begin with some initial information about another person and to infer other information we have not observed directly. If you think a professor is arrogant, you may infer that he is not helpful when it comes to giving assistance on term papers, though you have no direct experience to support that inference. Implicit personality theories also allow us to fill in the gaps in our information, to provide intepretative bridges between known characteristics. The Barbara example illustrates this: my inference of her insecurity helped to redefine her niceness and relate it to her hostility. Implicit personality theories perform many of the same functions as cognitive schemata (see Chapter 3).

Experiential Bases   Suppose you think that warm people are usually generous. Why might you assume this? The most obvious reason is that, in your experience, warm people (however you define this trait) have been generous (however defined). In support of that position are studies that show that people can use information about the coocurrence of traits in individuals to estimate trait relationship (Berman & Kenny, 1976). Furthermore, people's judgments of trait relationships often match quite closely actual relationships as determined by correlations among personality tests (Lay & Jackson, 1969).

However, other studies show that people's estimates of trait relationships are often different from actual relationships. Berman and Kenny (1976) exposed subjects to a number of made-up stimulus persons, each defined by a pair of traits. Subjects were then asked to estimate how often the traits had appeared together. Supporting the experiential position, traits that had actually been paired together several times were seen as more highly related than those traits that had not appeared together often. However, pairs of traits (for example, *understanding* and *tolerant*) that subjects felt *ought* to go together were reported by subjects as having appeared together more often than they actually had. Thus the Berman and Kenny study showed that people respond to their experiences but also to preexisting

theories about what kinds of traits ought to go together.

Evaluative Bases   Another reason (besides experience) that traits such as *warm* and *generous* seem to go together is that they share a common evaluative meaning. Early in the history of empirical psychology, Thorndike (1920) noted that raters tend to assume that a person who has one positive trait also has others, a phenomenon he labeled the **halo effect.** Such effects have been well documented (Cooper, 1981). In a modern demonstration, Nisbett and Wilson (1977b) found that people who watched a college professor act in a warm manner rated his physical appearance, mannerisms, and even accent more favorably than did people who had seen the same professor behaving in a cold manner. In other words, when the professor had one positive characteristic (warmth), he was also evaluated as having other positive traits, even ones that were probably logically and empirically unrelated to warmth. Halo effects are found even when subjects are warned what the effect is and are encouraged to avoid it (Wetzel, Wilson, & Kort, 1981).

The halo effect suggests that one basis for perceived trait relationships might be evaluative similarity; that is, traits that seem alike (or are evaluated as similar) are seen as belonging together. It has been clear for some time that perceived trait relationships mirror evaluative similarities quite well (D'Andrade, 1974; Shweder & D'Andrade, 1979). However, important as evaluative similarity (the halo effect) is in our judgments of others, it is probably not sufficient to account for all perceived cooccurrence (DeSoto, Hamilton, & Taylor, 1985; Gara & Rosenberg, 1981; Romer & Revelle, 1984). So generosity and warmth are both positive, and that contributes to perceived similarity, but there is more to judgment than evaluative similarity.

Schemas   Another reason you might think warm people are generous is that you have a schema or personality prototype of nice people in which both of these traits occupy a central position: warmth and generosity might be related because they are both manifestations of a nice person or helpful person prototype. More generally, when traits are embedded within the same cognitive schema they seem to go together. Schneider and Blankmeyer (1983) tested one implication of this. They reasoned that if traits are related because they are both manifestations of a prototype or schema, the traits should be seen as more highly related when the schema is salient than when it is not. Their results supported this conclusion.

There is no simple answer to the question of why traits and other characteristics seem to go together. Our experiences with people surely play some role, perhaps the most important one, but it is also clear that our schemata and our sensitivity to the meanings of trait words also contribute. In any case, our implicit personality theories are important elements in our information-processing schemata because they allow us to infer one kind of information from another and to go beyond what is immediately given in experience.

CHAPTER SUMMARY

- For the social psychologist, the study of person- perception—how we perceive and think about other people—is central.
- The stimuli for person-perception activity include people, their behaviors, and the situations in which the behaviors take place.
- Sometimes we make snap judgments about others by inferring traits and other characteristics immediately and nonreflectively from behavior, but we may also seek to understand what internal traits and motives cause behavior.
- Heider's analysis of causal judgments suggests that we infer dispositional qualities of people (such as motives, traits, desires, and

abilities) because such internal characteristics predict behavior across situations. We may also feel that behavior is caused by external factors such as social pressure, laws, rules, and the like.
- Kelley's model of attribution suggests that we infer that behavior was caused by external entities when the person's behavior is consistent over time, applies mainly to a particular entity (is distinctive), and is shared by most others (high consensus). However, the behavior will be seen as due to the person's disposition when the behavior is consistent, nondistinctive, and low in consensus.
- The discounting rule says that when several potential causes of a behavior are present, we tend to discount any one of them as being crucial.
- Research on role-playing and attitude attribution suggests that perceivers attribute beliefs to people consistent with their behavior, even when the behavior is strongly constrained.
- One of the key assumptions from early attribution models was that judgments about causality influenced judgments about responsibility for actions. However, responsibility is now known to be multidimensional and includes moral and legal variables as well as those related to psychological causes.
- People do not always use attribution models as the theories say they should. In general, people see more situational causality for self than for others and tend to overplay dispositional attributions in their perceptions of others; this latter tendency is called the *fundamental attribution error*. Differences between perceptions of self and others may be due to our having more information about self than others or due to the greater salience of the situation when perceiving our own behavior. In addition, people tend to ascribe causal significance to salient stimuli, and other people are

more salient than the situational forces that affect them.

- Another reason for differential perceptions of self and others may be that we downplay consensus information that ought to help discriminate behaviors that are popular and hence likely due to situational pressures from behaviors that only a few people do, presumably because of their own desires. One reason is that consensus information is typically not very salient. Also, people may mistrust consensus information that does not fit their own notions about what most people like and do. There is a *false consensus effect* such that people tend to assume that their own behavior and attitudes are more common than they are.

- There have been recent debates about how conscious and deliberate attributional processing is. Some research suggests that attributions are done fairly automatically and may not require elaborate analyses of the sorts demanded by the theories. It is possible that people use simpler rules based on scripts or schemata.

- Impression formation deals with inferring new information and organizing the infor-

mation available about another person. Asch's initial studies were based on a model that traits and other information unite to produce an impression not easily predicted from the component parts. Subsequent work by others has tried to refute this position.

- One line of research suggests that the evaluative impression of another can be predicted clearly by knowing the evaluations of the component information. This component information may also be weighted differentially. In particular, it is often the case that perceivers pay more attention to information early in a sequence. This is the *primacy effect*, whereby first impressions count most.

- People also use known information about others to infer new information. The matrix of assumed relationships among various kinds of information is known as *implicit personality theory*. These theories are based partially on our experiences about which characteristics *do* go together and partially on cultural models that suggest that certain personality characteristics *ought* to go together.

CHAPTER
5
THE SOCIAL SELF

When I speak to or about a friend, I usually use his or her first name or a nickname. For people I know less well, I often use last names, perhaps in combination with a social or occupational title, such as "Mrs. Smith," "Professor Jones," or "Dr. Johnson." For relatives I use either first names or a relationship name, or both, such as "Grandma" or "Uncle Bob." There are several ways, then, that we can refer to or address people: first names, last names, occupational titles, and relationship names.

People in Bali also can refer to a given individual in a variety of ways, but their system of names is quite different from our own (Geertz, 1973). Each child is given a *personal name* at birth, but the name has no special meaning and is rarely used by self or others. Socially, a more important designation is the *birth-order name,* also given at birth. There are only four such names, designating the first- through fourth-born, and for those families lucky enough to have more than four children the naming cycle begins again. Thus within the same family the first, fifth, and ninth children would have the same birth-order name, and the firstborn in one family would have the same name as the firstborn of another.

There are also *kinship terms* (such as "father," "uncle," and "sister") but these are rarely used in everyday conversation except to clarify possible misunderstandings. The most important designation for the Balinese are *teknonyms,* assigned to an adult at the birth of his or her first child. A teknonym has the form "mother- (or father) of-Jim." The parent is then known by this teknonym until he or she has a first grandchild, when the name switches to the form "grandmother-of-Mabel." The Balinese also have a complex set of *status titles* that designates prestige and that are tied to the complex Hindu caste system. Finally, for those

people who acquire certain public distinctions, there may be *public titles,* much as if we called the chief of police "chief" or the mayor "mayor" even in private.

Imagine yourself in this society. Shortly after birth you would be named, say, "Masjof," but most people would refer to you as "Firstborn." When you married you would keep your name until you had your first child, when you would become known as "mother-of-Roshed." This would be your name until Roshed or one of his siblings produced a child, when your name would change again to "grandmother-of-Nowkan."

As you might be able to infer from this example, the Balinese have quite different conceptions of selfhood, individuality, and identity than we Westerners do. It is a society governed by a rich and complex set of social conventions dealing with politeness. Within this system people are reacted to less in terms of personal characteristics than in terms of their social status, which in turn is based on age, parenthood, caste type, and acquired designation. The Balinese recognize that people are different, but most of the differences that we would count are not given much attention. In such a society the sense of self as an independent agent acting for or against the common good is likely to be blunted. There is considerably less sense of self as alienated from the society, that is, as a person who cannot fit in.

INTRODUCTION

THE NATURE OF THE SELF

How we view ourselves constrains our behavior and influences how others respond to us. In addition, most of us find our own selves the most intriguing objects of study in our lives. Certainly the self is the object of intense evaluative feelings; terms such as *pride, shame,* and *self-esteem* point to such feelings. In that regard, the self is an important bridge between the individual and society, because most of our feelings about ourselves reflect what others think of us and are based on culturally defined standards. Indeed, as the Balinese example suggests, our identities are intimately bound up with the forms of social recognition from others. Thus, although the self is in some ways the most private element of experience, it is evaluated by public, shared criteria.

However, despite the fact that for thousands of years billions of people have tried to understand themselves, the exact nature of the self has been the subject of intense controversy for most of this time. The ancient Greeks contrasted the self with the purely physical aspects of existence, whereas the early Christians added the notion that the self is not only separate from the body but transcends it and participates in the divine. Later the self was more closely identified with the purely thinking functions of human existence. To most of us today it seems natural to identify the self with our cognitive activities; the self is the agent of thought.

The notion of the self has had a halting career within modern psychology. Many early psychologists were convinced that the self was the central element in our experiences and helped to guide both thought and behavior. Yet for many decades most psychologists considered the self too elusive, too private, too subjective to be a fit topic for scientific analysis. In recent year, however, the self has regained some of its previous eminence, particularly in social and personality psychology. Before considering some of this recent research on the self, let us review some classic theories about the self by early psychologists.

THEORIES

William James   The philosopher–psychologist William James presented a detailed and articulate analysis of the self in his 1890 textbook, *The Principles of Psychology.* James was struck by the phenomenological fact that thoughts are personal, that when you are thinking you are often conscious of an "I" who selects certain thoughts or who pays attention to certain stimuli. This "I" is an element in experience that one infers or feels, something that is necessary to complete an analysis of one's thought processes, rather than something one sees with the mind's eye. The "I" is the self as subject or as experiencer. However, in addition, there are elements of experience that can be direct objects of thought, and these James called the "me."

At the core of your experience of yourself are your body, your clothes, your possessions. Your own body is a primary object of

William James

experience—you identify with the body you are stuck with, the bodily "me." As the child grows into maturity, family and worldly possessions become extensions of this bodily "me." Furthermore, James argues that your feelings of self-worth are partially dependent on what others think of your body, its extensions, and your accomplishments, but only to the extent you care about the "me" under consideration:

> I, who for the time have staked my all on being a psychologist, am mortified if others know much more psychology than I. But I am contented to wallow in the grossest ignorance of Greek. My deficiencies there give me no sense of personal humiliation at all. Had I "pretensions" to be a linguist, it would have been just the reverse. (James, 1890 [1950], Vol. I, p. 310)

Thus our feelings of self-worth are at least partially dependent on what others think of us, and we are particularly affected by their evaluations of things we care deeply about. On the other hand, this is also likely to vary depending on the person doing the evaluation. I care what my students think of my teaching, but not what my next-door neighbor thinks of it. I do care (just a little) whether he thinks my yard is attractive, but this almost never comes up with my students.

> Properly speaking a man has as many social selves as there are individuals who recognize him and carry an image of him in their mind. To wound any one of these, his images, is to wound him. But as the individuals who carry the images fall naturally into classes, we may practically say that he has as many different social selves as there are distinct groups of persons about whose opinion he cares. He generally shows a different side of himself to each of these different groups. Many a youth who is demure enough before his parents and teachers, swears and swaggers like a pirate among his "tough" young friends. We do not show ourselves to our children as to our club-companions, to our customers as to the laborers we employ, to our own masters and employers as to our intimate friends. From this there

results what practically is a division of the man into several selves. (James, 1890 [1950], Vol. I, p. 294)

This Jamesian insight that we organize our self-evaluations around the several others who evaluate us has important implications for social psychology. In some sense, you change as a person, at least to the extent you are concerned about different things, when you are with different people.

George Herbert Mead   George Herbert Mead was strongly influenced by James. It is therefore no accident that he made a theory of the self central to an understanding of social psychology. The fundamental question for Mead is, "How can a person get outside himself (experientially) in such a way as to become an object to himself?" (Mead, 1934, p. 138). Mead's answer to that question goes to the heart of the Jamesian insight: the individual experiences the self, not directly, but from the viewpoint of other people.

The easiest way to approach Mead's answer is through a developmental perspective. Young children are aware of the evaluations that others, particularly parents, make of them, and they apply these parental evaluations to themselves directly. As they grow older, children also learn that most social situations involve interactions with several people who may have conflicting expectations for the children's behavior. Individual behavior must fit into a complex normative matrix. For example, as a shortstop in a baseball game, a youngster must coordinate his or her behavior with what the other team members and coaches expect. A still later stage is reached when children learn the efficiency of adopting the perspective of the generalized other: in many situations the precise expectations of every other are not known, so a person must react to the expectancy that is most general or common.

For Mead the self grows primarily through the incorporation of evaluations from others. Because one continues to have to coordinate

One of the most important tasks children learn in school is to adapt to the expectations of others.

behavior with others, and because one has to care what others think in order to be successful, the self continues to grow throughout adulthood. However, the self is much more than the residue of other, past evaluations; it is a process of continual evaluation in terms of constantly changing perspectives.

James and Mead not only provided powerful insights about the self, but they also set the agenda for much research on the self of primary interest to social psychologists. In particular, they alerted us to three basic questions: (1) What is the role of the self in processing information? (2) What is the basis of identity? and (3) How do people evaluate themselves as a function of their identities? In the next sections we take up these questions.

THE SELF AND INFORMATION PROCESSING

Throughout this chapter we will concentrate on the self as an object of evaluation, but clearly the self also plays some role in our general cognitive processes. Historically it has proved difficult to know how to talk about the self as knower. When we try to make something of the "I" in sentences such as "I thought the lecture was interesting," there seems to be nothing very concrete about the "I-ness" of the experience. To be sure, it is I who had the experience and not you, but is the "I" in this case anything more than a linguistic marker to discriminate one person from another?

Surely the answer is "yes." For one thing our own experiences have an intensity that can rarely be duplicated at second hand. It is also possible that the "I" in experience plays an important role in organizing that experience. Not only do I see what I see and hear what I hear, but most of what I see and hear is encoded with special relevance to myself. The self helps organize the world of experience.

It has long been a staple of commonsense psychology that we tend to view the world in terms of our own concerns. Aren't you just a bit inclined to think that what you like must have something approaching universal appeal? Don't you secretly wish that others were as sensible as you? Don't you remember things that happened to you better than things that happen to others? Although you do not invariably view the world solely from the standpoint of self, it would be strange if you did not use the person who is most familiar to you, namely your own self, as a structure for your cognitions of the world.

Greenwald (1980) has argued that we are *egocentric* in the sense that we view ourselves as central actors on life's stage. For example, people are typically better at remembering what they have said in a group discussion than at remembering what others have said

(Wagner, 1984). People also tend to see themselves as more influential in groups than others rate them (Ross & Sicoly, 1979). We also tend to see ourselves as the focus of the behavior of others. Fenigstein (1984) had professors comment favorably or unfavorably on a particular but unidentified exam before exams were handed back. Students were asked whether it was more likely that the exam that had been singled out belonged to them or to the person sitting next to them. The students were much more likely to believe the exam was theirs rather than the other person's.

On a grander stage, Jervis (1976) has argued that political leaders often feel that their own actions make more of a difference to the course of world events than they do. For example, during the Vietnam War, President Johnson and his advisors interpreted almost all actions of the North Vietnamese in terms of the heavy bombing the United States used against that country. Whether the North Vietnamese seemed to change strategy or not, their actions were interpreted as responses to the bombing. The American leaders therefore saw themselves as controlling their enemy's behavior, no matter what the enemy did.

SELF-SCHEMATA

Recently psychologists have studied the use of the self as a device for understanding experience. Many people have argued that the self has schema properties (see Chapter 4): the knowledge we have and the theories we hold about the self may act as more general knowledge structures for understanding others as well as self (Kuiper & Derry, 1981; Markus & Smith, 1981; Rogers, 1981). There are several testable implications of this view.

Accessibility of Self-dimensions   One implication that has been empirically supported is that characteristics or dimensions that are a salient or accessible (see Chapter 3) part of one's own self-image might be used to judge others (Higgins, King, & Mavin, 1982;

Hirschberg & Jennings, 1980; Shrauger & Patterson, 1974). People who feel they have particular characteristics are more likely to seek out information about others relevant to those characteristics and are more confident in judging others on those self-relevant dimensions (Fong & Markus, 1982). For example, if you have some particular investment in your intelligence, you are likely to be especially alert to information about how smart the people you meet are, in part because this self-relevant dimension is highly accessible.

Efficiency   Another implication of the idea that self is a master schema for perceiving people is that it should be easier to judge information relevant to that schema, because schemata facilitate quickness and sometimes accuracy of decisions about schema-relevant material (see Chapter 3). In a classic demonstration, Markus (1977) divided subjects into groups based on their self-ratings of their independence and dependence. Those who described themselves as either dependent or independent, and who therefore presumably had schemas for those traits, made judgments about traits related to independence–dependence more quickly than did those subjects who did not have strong feelings about their own independence or dependence (see Figure 5.1). People are also able to make finer and more expert distinctions about the behavior of others that are relevant to a self schema (Markus, Smith, & Moreland, 1985).

Bargh (1982) has argued that processing information relevant to the self is efficient and should require little attention. He studied this in a clever way, reasoning that if a task is fairly simple (say counting), it should not interfere with other on-going tasks as much as more complex tasks (such as solving equations) might. Bargh showed that dealing with information about the self interfered less with another on-going task than did processing information not related to the self. So information about the self readily captures attention

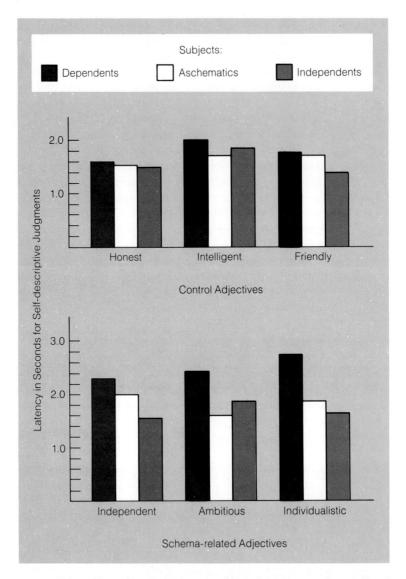

FIGURE 5.1   Mean Response Latency for Independence-schema-related Adjectives and Control Adjectives. Note that the dependent- and independent-schematic subjects do not differ much in how fast they respond to the control adjectives (unrelated to independence or dependence) but that the independent-schematics are faster than the dependent-schematics in responding to independence-related adjectives.

Markus, 1977.

but requires less cognitive effort to process, probably because we are so practiced at making judgments about the self.

Memory   As we saw in Chapter 4, theories help us comprehend and remember new material. Similar effects have been shown for self-schemata. Several studies have shown that when people are asked to judge whether traits describe them, they remember the traits better than when they are asked to make some other judgment about the traits, such as whether the traits describe another person or have particular semantic properties (Kuiper & Rogers, 1979; Lord, 1980; Rogers, Kuiper, & Kirker, 1977). This implies that self-schemata act as particularly available knowledge structures that help us retain memories.

Cognitive Reference Points   When people are asked to judge the similarity between two objects, they tend to see less-salient objects as more similar to more-salient objects than the reverse (see Chapter 3). Research confirms that others are judged more similar to the self than the self is to others, supporting the view that the self is a cognitive reference point (Holyoak & Gordon, 1983; Srull & Gaelick, 1983). We seem to have a particularly well-differentiated view of the self that acts as a kind of anchor for our judgments of others.

Is the Self a Schema?   Although these results suggest that the self has schema properties, it is fair to point out that there are non-schematic interpretations. The self is familiar, so many of the effects may simply reflect the use of a familiar set of stimuli—rather than the self itself—as a referent. For example, judging whether a trait describes a familiar other enhances memory (Keenan & Baillet, 1980), so the fact that self-referent judgments increase memory for traits may simply be a special-case manifestation of the general "familiar other" result: the self is the most familiar person you know. Or perhaps making self-judgments encourages organization of the material, which in turn aids memory (Klein & Kihlstrom, 1986); the same organization would aid memory whether or not self-encoding had occurred. It has also been argued that self-judgments are easy to make and enhance memory because we can easily think of relevant experiences associated with the self,

and these experiential cues may act as cues for judgments and memory (Bellezza, 1984). For example, when you judge whether *kind* describes you, you may readily think of a time when you were kind or unkind. When you are later asked to recall traits, the experience you generated may help you remember that *kind* was one of the traits presented. However, such experiences may be less easy to generate for others or be less effective cues for recall. These criticisms are important in our attempts to understand whether the self can be thought of as having schemalike properties. Whatever the resolution of that issue, even the critics of self-as-schema readily admit that the self has central organizational properties and has some privileged status in our thinking about others (see Greenwald & Pratkanis, 1984; Higgins & Bargh, 1987; and Kihlstrom & Cantor, 1984).

SELF-AWARENESS

The idea of self-schemata suggests that the self may help us focus material about others as well as about self. Of course, sometimes we think about the self directly; Duval and Wicklund (1972) suggest two basic ways we experience the world, two states of consciousness that are close to what James and Mead called the "I" and the "me." In *subjective self-awareness,* the self is the thinking subject (the "I") and consciousness is directed toward the outside world as object. In *objective self-awareness,* attention is directed to the self as object (the "me"). It is this latter state of self-awareness that has been the subject of most research and that most concerns us here.

What leads to objective self-awareness? In everyday life, a problem may lead people to focus on self. Or when people are uncertain about why they are experiencing a particular inner state, they may also focus on the self in an effort to explain the inner state (Wegner & Giuliano, 1980). There are also strong individual differences in the extent to which people focus attention on self (Fenigstein, Scheier, &

Objective self-awareness focuses our attention on how well we measure up to our ideals.

Buss, 1975). In research settings, objective self-awareness is typically manipulated by having subjects perform some task before a mirror or in the presence of a television camera. Subjects sitting before a mirror or camera tend to use more self-references, suggesting that they are thinking about themselves more (Carver & Scheier, 1978). It is as if subjects are watching themselves as others watch them.

According to Duvall and Wicklund, when you are in a state of objective self-awareness, you will implicitly or explicitly be thinking about how good or bad you are relative to some socially acceptable standard. Ordinarily you will attempt to reduce any discrepancies between your present self-image and this standard by changing behavior to more closely match the standard. For example, most male subjects feel it is wrong to hurt a female; when asked to shock females, male subjects are less likely to do so when they are in front of a mirror than when they are not (Scheier, Fenigstein, & Buss, 1974). But when it is clear that shock is appropriate and approved, subjects

give *more* shocks when they are objectively self-aware (Carver, 1974).

Early versions of self-awareness theory (Wicklund, 1975) suggested that we should be motivated to avoid a state of objective self-awareness because it induces us to think about how we are failing to match a standard. However, Carver (1979) has argued that focus on self is not inherently aversive: as long as we have the opportunity to improve our self-image relative to the standard, we will not feel uncomfortable, though objective self-awareness should be uncomfortable for those who feel they cannot improve. Studies have shown that persistence is increased by self-awareness so long as people feel confident they can meet the standard, but that persistence falls off as confidence declines (Carver, Blaney, & Scheier, 1979a, b). Thus it appears that being in a state of objective self-awareness can motivate people either to work harder to meet standards or to avoid the state of awareness, depending on the perceived efficacy of their behaviors.

Interestingly enough, there may be circumstances in which attention focused on the self interferes with effective performance, perhaps because people become so concerned with the impressions they are creating that they fail to monitor their behavior properly (Baumeister, 1984). For example, in professional basketball championships, the home team wins 70% of the first four games but only 39% of the championships decided in the seventh game. According to Baumeister and Steinhilber (1984), the self-presentational concerns of winning the championship before the home crowd engender too much self-awareness for effective performance.

Thus, self-awareness theory suggests that when we view our behavior and bodies as others might, we tend to be highly evaluative, just as others might be. On the other hand, evaluative concerns are less salient when we focus on the task at hand rather than on how we are doing. In other words, the self as "I" is not especially concerned with self-evaluation, but the self as "me" engenders such concerns.

SUMMARY

There is abundant evidence that we use self-relevant information to judge others and that thinking about self and others encourages particularly efficient ways of dealing with that information. On the other hand, this may simply imply that the self is familiar and salient rather than that there is something unique about the self as such. Work on self-awareness suggests that when we feel we are the object of attention (by others or self) we tend to think of ourselves in evaluative ways and generally try harder to meet social standards.

IDENTITY

Our second major question about the self concerns identity. When you think about yourself, you recognize that you are you, that certain objects are yours, that your family is tied to you in important ways, and that the behavior you just performed and the thought you just had are yours and yours alone. In short, you have a sense of identity. Baumeister (1986) suggests that identities are built on continuities and unities of behavior over time. Your identity may evolve and change over time, but you have the sense that throughout these changes there is a common element of identity that differentiates you from others. Even if you and I have the same basic job, live in the same house, and do most things together, we will each have the sense that we are distinct people because we each have a sense of continuity in our lives, a unique personal history, and because we know we have different personal characteristics.

It is important to note that the significance that people from modern, Western, economically developed societies assign to identity is

Drawing by H. Martin © 1982 by The New Yorker Magazine, Inc.

served how children behaved while the children watched themselves in the mirror. Small babies take little notice of mirror images, but by the middle of the first year the child recognizes the personness of the mirror image without realizing that the image is of herself. How do we know whether a small child recognizes herself? Lewis and Brooks-Gunn placed rouge on the children's noses and observed their behavior to their mirror images. If a child looks in the mirror and attempts to touch her real (not the mirror image) nose, this is compelling evidence that there is recognition of identity between the mirror image and the self. By 15 months some children show such recognition and by 21 months most children recognize mirror images of the self.

As the child acquires cognitive skills, the sense of self expands dramatically. In broad outline, self-understanding parallels the ability to understand others (see Chapter 3) but there are also important differences. According to the summary provided by Damon and Hart (1982; Hart & Damon, 1986), young children conceive of the self in physical terms, confusing mind, self, and body. Self is distinguished from others in terms of external appearance and physical abilities and activities. After children enter school, the recognition of internal qualities—that different people have different thoughts and feelings—becomes the basis of identity. Children then also learn that their own characteristics are consistent and stable over time (Rotenberg, 1982). Adolescents develop abilities to predict and monitor what they think, and they learn that real feelings can be masked by conscious ones.

As a result of these gradual changes in self-understanding, self-descriptions become more abstract. In addition, Damon and Hart (1982) argue that different domains are especially important at various ages. For example, physical and material properties are crucial for preschoolers, relative capacities for the elementary school child, social and personality characteristics for the early adolescent, and beliefs and values for the older adolescent. In

not universally shared. The ideas common to our culture that adolescence is a time when one forges an identity and that at various stages in life one will have "identity crises" would be quite foreign to the Balinese, for example. For the Balinese you are basically what your social status says you are. There is little room for the notion that one's inner self, one's personality, and one's ideals and goals set one apart from others. Indeed, the modern notion of identity is just that—modern—and only within the last century or two has personal identity come to be central to our sense of being.

DEVELOPMENT OF IDENTITY

Developmental Trends   A sense of identity appears gradually in the life of the young child. Lewis and Brooks-Gunn (1979) ob-

general, our identities grow by moving from external to more private and internal bases of identity.

Social Bases   At each age, there are potentially many sources of identity. Why does a child say she is red-haired, or an adult that he is a doctor? Clearly one important reason is that certain categories are dictated by the culture. In Western culture, gender and occupation cast long definitional shadows. In Bali, identity is more heavily governed by one's birth order and status as a parent. In other cultures, religion might be more crucial. To a large extent we are who our culture says we are.

But even within a given culture certain characteristics might become sources of identity because of their relative rarity in the social environment. When McGuire and Padawer-Singer (1976) asked elementary school children to describe themselves, those who were much older or younger than classmates more often gave their age, those who had been born in a different place from where the school was located tended to mention place of birth, and those with unusual physical characteristics were likely to mention these. Members of ethnic minorities or children whose gender is in a minority in a given classroom are more likely to give their minority status as a defining characteristic (McGuire, McGuire, Child, & Fujioka, 1978). This research suggests that to some extent our identities are based on the ways we think we are different from other people. It follows that how we think about ourselves will vary from situation to situation, depending on what sets us apart and makes us feel unique in each situation.

It would also seem reasonable that people's identities are affected by what they think they are good at doing. Thus my teaching (at which I am reasonably competent) is more central to my self-identity than my ability to repair cars, and my local mechanic undoubtedly feels the opposite. Experimental data confirm that people reduce the importance of tasks on which

Gymnastics is an important part of the self-concept of this young woman.

they perform poorly and enhance the importance of those on which they do relatively well (Tesser & Campbell, 1980; Tesser & Paulhus, 1983). Moreover, the positiveness of self-ratings on traits also predicts how relevant those traits are for our judgments of others (Lewicki, 1983, 1984). I, who rate myself as reasonably intelligent, tend to think about how smart others are, whereas my brawnier but less intellectual friend views the social world in terms of athletic abilities and manual dexterity.

When we think that the things we are good at doing are important, we are certainly biased, but it is also a highly functional way to think. Those who insist on wearing identities that fit them poorly often seem pathetic just because they try so hard to do things they cannot. Self-images channel our behavior along productive lines, so that when we think that our important features are those things we are good at doing, this tends to ensure that we will be at least minimally successful.

Behavioral Sources of Identity   If you base your self-image on your intelligence, you need to know that you are, in fact, smart. But how do you know that you are intelligent (or hard-working, extroverted, happy, shy, silly, pretty, or nice)? Sometimes the evidence is objective: it is a fact that you are male or female, that you are taller or shorter than average, that your IQ score is higher or lower than average. In addition, you may have been told that you are attractive, fat, or rich; any self-description would likely include such objective or consensually validated information.

Your identity also includes your values, attitudes, goals, and personality traits, matters less subject to verification. But how do you know that you are a liberal, value kindness, admire certain political figures, are introverted, or feel hostile? "Well," you say, "there's no great mystery about this. I know what I feel, think, and want because . . . well, because, I just know." And in your defense (should you indeed say something like the above) there is a sense in which we all feel we have direct and immediate access to such internal matters. But where does this sense of your self come from?

Suppose I ask you if you are kind. You say yes, you are kind. I ask you how you know you are kind. You say you just know you are kind. If I press you further and ask you where and how you first knew you were kind, you might reply along the following lines: "I've just always known that I was a kind person. I value kindness in others, and I seem to behave more kindly to others than most of the people I know do. As long as I can remember I've enjoyed helping people." Now we're getting somewhere. You have, in effect, suggested that you infer your traits from your behavior. In fact, it is hard to know how else you might discover your kindness—other than to be told you are kind by other people.

Historically, the idea that self-identities mirror behaviors developed from research on attitude change. Normally we think that behaviors change to reflect changes in attitudes and values, but can behavior change lead to attitude and value change? If it can, does this also suggest that identity is based on behavior to some extent?

COUNTER-ATTITUDINAL BEHAVIOR

The Cognitive Dissonance Approach Festinger's theory of cognitive dissonance suggests that a change in behavior can indeed lead to a change of attitude and therefore of identity. The basic question for dissonance theory is what happens when a person says something he or she does not believe. The answer is that there should be some dissonance between the cognitions (1) "I believe X" and (2) "I said I believe non-X," a dissonance that is distressing and can be most easily reduced by coming to believe non-X.

The dissonance between beliefs and knowledge that one has acted contrary to them should be lessened if the person has good reasons for having performed the behavior. So if you pay me $2 million to endorse the proposition that social psychology is a fraud, the dissonance I would normally experience is alleviated considerably by thoughts of sports cars and nice vacations. Similarly if you threaten to shoot me unless I make the statement, I would have minimal dissonance between my speech and my private beliefs because I have a good reason for my behavior.

In a classic study (Festinger & Carlsmith, 1959), subjects took part in a long and boring experiment. There was every reason to believe their attitudes toward the experiment would be neutral or slightly negative, as was indeed reported by control subjects. But other subjects were asked to tell someone else the experiment was interesting, a behavior dissonant with their beliefs. Some subjects were paid a fairly large amount of money ($20) for saying this; according to the theory they should have had limited dissonance because they had good reason to say something they didn't believe. Indeed, when asked whether they had liked the experiment, they reported attitudes not markedly different from the control subjects. Another group of subjects was paid a minimal amount of money ($1) for the same counter-attitudinal behavior (that is, for saying the experiment was fun). Now these subjects did not have a good excuse for their behavior; they should have had considerable dissonance between their attitude that the experiment was boring and their statement to the contrary According to the theory, they should have changed their attitudes to match their behavior, and in fact, as Table 5.1 shows, they did report that the experiment was more interesting than the other subjects did.

The dissonance explanation is both simple and powerful. You will change your attitudes to match your behavior if (1) your behavior is dissonant with your beliefs and (2) minimum pressure (either reward or threat) is used to get you to perform the behavior. Theoretically, the least amount of pressure that will get you to perform the behavior should result in the most attitude change. Substantial pressure to perform the behavior gives you a good excuse for your behavior, causes little dissonance, and therefore effects little attitude change.

Refinements of the Dissonance Interpretation   The Festinger–Carlsmith experiment stimulated many other research studies (see Box 5.1). It is now fairly well established that

before people change attitudes to match behaviors they must feel some free choice in the commitment to perform the behavior (Linder, Cooper, & Jones, 1967), they must think some of the consequences of their behavior are likely to be negative (Cooper, Zanna, & Goethals, 1974), and they must believe that these negative consequences were foreseeable (Goethals, Cooper, & Naficy, 1979).

These findings refine the basic cognitive dissonance interpretation of behavior and attitude change. If you do not feel that you have freely chosen to perform a behavior, it is as if strong rewards or threats have been used, conditions that lower dissonance and induce little or no attitude change. Also, positive consequences of a behavior tend to justify having performed it, and in that sense act as a reward or an excuse after the fact, again lowering dissonance. Finally, one would probably not feel responsible for the behavior if one could not foresee the consequences, and this might act to reduce the dissonance between the behavior and attitudes.

SELF-PERCEPTION MODELS

Initially, cognitive dissonance research tested the prediction that people *change* their attitudes to match their behavior. That is, people are presumed to hold an initial attitude, to behave in an inconsistent manner, and then to change the attitude to fit the behavior. In more recent years, however, the focus has shifted to explaining how people *infer* their own attitudes and other internal states from their behavior. Of course, this is exactly what we do when we perceive others; we don't know what the other person's attitude is, and so we must infer it from behavior. So these self-perception models have basic affinities with general attribution models (see Chapter 4).

Bem's Theory   Daryl Bem's (1965, 1967, 1972) self-perception theory asserts that we do not have privileged insights into the causes of

TABLE 5.1 RATINGS OF HOW INTERESTING THE TASK WAS (WITH −5 = BORING AND +5 = INTERESTING). *The control subjects and those who had considerable pressure to say the task was interesting ($20 subjects) both report that the task was neutral to slightly boring, whereas those with minimal pressure to say the task was interesting ($1 subjects) report more interest in the task.*

Subjects	Rating
Control	− .45
$1	1.35
$20	− 0.05

SOURCE: Festinger and Carlsmith, 1959.

BOX 5.1

COMPETING THEORIES:
COGNITIVE DISSONANCE VERSUS IMPRESSION MANAGEMENT

The Festinger–Carlsmith study is one of the most influential papers in modern social psychology. It may interest you to know that this study was Merrill Carlsmith's undergraduate honors thesis at Stanford. The study was a clever test of clearly derived predictions from cognitive dissonance theory. Partially because the results of the study seem to fly in the face of common sense and many theories, they have also given rise to many attempts to show that the dissonance explanation is incorrect. We have already discussed self-perception theory in that context. Here we will discuss another such attempt based on impression management models.

As you will recall from Chapter 1, such theories suggest that people have a fundamental desire to win the approval of others by managing the impressions others have of them. Many of our behaviors change to fit situational requirements and the demands of others. How might this model explain the Festinger–Carlsmith results? Consider the high-dissonance condition from the standpoint of the subject. She has just taken part in a boring experiment and has now told an innocent bystander that the experiment was fun. In effect, she has lied about her experience. Most of us presumably do not want others to think we are liars, nor do we want to think of ourselves as liars. But how can this be avoided? In the experimental setting the easiest way to reconcile the attitude to the behavior is to report that the experiment was fun—a subject who tells the experimenter that the experiment was fun suggests that she was not lying when she told a bystander the same thing. Be-

cause the subject has no reason to believe that the experimenter knows her true attitude, she is free to report an attitude consistent with her behavior. According to this impression management perspective, the subject is chiefly motivated by the desire to avoid looking like a hypocrite in front of the experimenter and so publicly claims to have attitudes consistent with her behavior.

The task before us, then, is to find a way of showing that impression management theory provides a better explanation of apparent attitude change than the dissonance account does. We need conditions in which one theory makes one prediction and the other theory a different prediction. In the present case, impression management theory specifies that people do not so much *change* their attitudes to match behavior as they *report* attitudes consistent with the behavior to try to win the approval of others. It follows that a person should be particularly prone to report behavior-consistent attitudes when others suspect his behavior has been fradulant and when he is motivated to win approval by convincing them otherwise. One important factor then ought to be whether the experimenter knows about the subject's behavior. If I lie in telling a friend that I am in favor of a major tuition increase, but you do not know that I said this, I will not be especially concerned that you think I am a liar. So one variable we might want to manipulate is whether the experimenter knows about the counter-attitudinal behavior.

In addition, if subjects fudge their real attitudes in an effort to convince the experimenter that their behavior was honest, we might reduce this tendency by making it costly for subjects to lie to the experimenter. If one could discourage subjects from reporting false attitudes to the experimenter, there should be less consistency between reported attitudes and behavior. Fortunately there is a technique, called the *bogus pipeline,* designed to encourage truthful reporting of attitudes. With this bogus pipeline, subjects are hooked up to elaborate physiological devices that, they are told, can detect their true attitudes (Jones & Sigall, 1971). The idea behind this is that when subjects believe their true attitudes will be detected by the machine, they will be motivated to report their true attitudes lest they appear to be lying.

Let's look at one concrete version of this kind of study, an experiment by Gaes, Kalle, and Tedeschi (1978). Subjects entered the experiment and were asked to give their attitudes on several issues. These reports were ostensibly private, but a confederate secretly recorded them. All this preliminary attitude measurement was necessary for the bogus pipeline conditions that will be described shortly. In the main part of the experiment, subjects were asked to write essays on why brushing teeth is harmful, a position counter to their own beliefs; control subjects did not write these essays. Elaborate procedures were employed to manipulate whether the experimenter could know what subjects had written in the essay. In the *private* condition, subjects used fake names and emphasis was placed on the fact that their answers could not be traced to them. In the *public* condition, real names were used and emphasis was placed on identifying subjects. After this exercise was completed, some experimental and control subjects were asked to report their attitudes toward toothbrushing on normal attitude questionnaires, but others, in the bogus pipeline conditions, were told that they were to have their attitudes measured by a machine that could detect true attitudes. In a "calibration" phase (designed to enhance the credibility of the machine), the machine did indeed accurately predict the subjects' responses to the earlier attitude measures. This was not hard, of course, because the confederate had secretly copied down what these attitudes were and had given them to the experimenter who manipulated the machine appropriately. Finally, subjects were asked to indicate their own attitudes toward toothbrushing.

In the experimental situation we are considering, the prediction is that when subjects are motivated to report their true attitudes rather than attitudes designed to make them look good, they will show less correspondence between their antibrushing essays and the attitudes they express to the experimenter. Consider, first, the bogus pipeline manipulation. If impression management theory is correct in assuming that subjects lie about their real attitudes, and this machine inhibits lying, then in this condition subjects should be less willing to lie by saying that their attitudes match their behavior. Second, consider the public–private manipulation. When subjects' essays were private, subjects should have few fears that their hypocrisy would be exposed; only when the experimenter knew they had written an antibrushing essay would subjects be especially concerned to convince the experimenter that they were not lying, that they really were opposed to brushing.

The data show that only when the essay had been public and the final attitudes were measured with a traditional paper-and-pencil questionnaire did subjects report attitudes close to their behaviors. This condi-

BOX CONTINUED

tion corresponds closely to the one used in most research of this sort, and it is important that the experimenters were able to show that they could replicate the original effect under similar conditions. However, subjects did not report substantial attitude–behavior consistency when their original behavior had been unknown to the experimenter, when their attitudes were measured in a way that discouraged lying, or both. At first this seems like a victory for impression management theory. When subjects have no reason to manipulate or when they fear to try to manipulate the experimenter's impressions of them, they do not change their attitudes. This suggests that subjects are more concerned with impression management than they are with reducing dissonance.

However, the dissonance theorists have a counterexplanation that is fairly involved. According to the dissonance perspective, dissonance is an unpleasant form of arousal. To the extent it cannot be attributed to other sources, it will motivate attitude change. Indeed, experiments show that conditions that produce dissonance also increase arousal and that this arousal often leads to attitude change, although perhaps not directly (Elkin & Leippe, 1986). However, when this arousal can be attributed to other sources, the chief driving power

behind attitude change is taken away and attitude change should be lessened (Zanna & Cooper, 1974).

How does that apply to the present situation? One argument might be that the bogus-pipeline measurement device is an alternative attribution for arousal. So the subject hooked up to this device might have arousal based on dissonance between attitudes and behavior, but when she misattributes this arousal to the machine ("the machine made me nervous") her motives for reducing dissonance are lowered. Thus, the reason people show less attitude change in the bogus-pipeline condition is not that they are being more truthful but that they have less arousal to drive the change.

Can these two possibilities be distinguished? Stults, Messé, and Kerr (1984) reasoned that if subjects had more experience with the bogus-pipeline apparatus, they would not be as nervous (aroused) around it and therefore would not misattribute their dissonance arousal to it. In their experiment, subjects were asked to write an essay in favor of smoking, a position the subjects did not endorse. Subsequently, their attitudes were assessed in one of three ways. Some subjects merely gave verbal reports of their attitudes. A second group reported attitudes while hooked up to the bogus-pipeline apparatus—these subjects

our own behavior. Rather, he suggests, people follow the same rules in explaining their own behavior as in explaining the behavior of others. If you wish to know what caused my behavior, you will first ask whether the environment caused the behavior; if it did not, you will conclude that the behavior probably oc-

curred because of my internal needs, wants, or abilities. On the other hand, if external forces are strong, you will discount internal forces. Bem suggests that you will account for your own behavior in exactly the same way.

Bem initially developed the theory to explain the results of the Festinger–Carlsmith ex-

were in a condition like those in the study just described. And, to distinguish whether the bogus-pipeline subjects show less attitude change because they are more honest or because they have less arousal to motivate attitude change, an additional condition was run with the bogus pipeline: subjects were habituated to the machine to make sure that arousal would not be attributed to the machine. Presumably this group would be motivated to be honest (in that way being like the subjects in the usual bogus-pipeline condition) but would also have higher arousal due to dissonance between their essay-writing behavior and their antismoking attitude (in that way being like the verbal reports subjects). If the fear of being caught lying is crucial, their attitudes ought to resemble those in the usual bogus-pipeline condition, but if arousal is more critical, their attitudes ought to change to match behaviors as they do for the equally highly aroused verbal reports subjects. The attitudes reported by these subjects looked more like those in the verbal reports condition. That is, unlike the usual bogus-pipeline subjects, they showed some change toward the essay they had written even though they were presumably just as motivated to be honest. This suggests that bogus-pipeline subjects maintain their attitudes not because they are more honest

but because they lack important arousal —they misattribute their arousal due to dissonance to arousal due to nervousness, and therefore they have less reason to change attitudes to reduce dissonance.

It seems as if we have a standoff. Indeed, each theory is richly endowed with ways to explain predictions made by the other theory, and it may not be possible to find a definitive study that "proves" one theory right and the other wrong (Tetlock & Manstead, 1985). Does this then mean that the research is worthless? Not at all. In the first place, we learn something about the phenomenon in question by examining it from the various angles suggested by competing models. Second, each theory has become richer (and perhaps more complex and flabby) by trying to incorporate the results from the "other side." Both models have an element of truth, and each best explains results under different sets of conditions (Baumeister & Tice, 1984; Paulhus, 1982).

For our purposes, the research on this question (of which the studies discussed here are but a small sample) illustrates one important stimulus for empirical research—attempts to show that a new theory offers a better explanation for a set of results. This leads to friendly (and sometimes not so friendly) competition as the two sides attack and counterattack.

periment. Self-perception theory assumes that the subjects had no initial attitudes before they were called upon to repeat them to the experimenter. The subjects then *inferred* their initial attitudes from their own behavior rather than having been aware from the beginning of attitudes that changed after the behavior. Thus,

according to Bem, Festinger and Carlsmith's subjects inferred their own attitudes after the fact, very much like an observer of the experiment might.

How might this work? If you saw Bob tell Elsie, for $20, that an experiment was interesting, you would probably conclude that Bob

Daryl Bem

had acted under strong external pressure and you would discount the possibility that he believed what he had said. Hence you would probably feel that Bob hadn't liked the experiment as much as he said he did. But suppose you knew that Bob had performed the same behavior for $1? Because in this case there is no strong external force, you might well decide that Bob had acted from internal forces—his own attitudes; hence you would say that he had really enjoyed the experiment. Bem's argument is that Bob discovers or infers his own attitudes in exactly the same way you infer Bob's attitudes, that is, without any special knowledge about his prior attitudes.

Bem (1967) has shown that observers infer that the highly paid subjects disliked the experiment more than the lowly paid ones, which is, of course, exactly what Festinger and Carlsmith had shown with their subjects. However, Bem could not directly prove that the Festinger–Carlsmith subjects had actually inferred their attitudes as his observers had, but only that observers and subjects had arrived at similar conclusions, *as if* they had made the same inferences.

Salience of Attitudes   We do not know for sure whether subjects formed attitudes after the boring task (the initial attitudes) or whether they waited to infer them only when the experimenter asked for them. Surely subjects might have formed the attitudes initially; most of us have at least a few salient attitudes

that we simply know we hold without external prompting or the need to infer them from behavior. Bem (1968, 1972) conceded that point and has argued that the real question is salience of initial attitudes. Thus, to the extent initial attitudes already had been formed and were salient, subjects had no need to infer attitudes from behavior; however, if these attitudes were not salient, subjects would have to infer them on the spot, presumably from behavior.

There is good evidence that we will infer attitudes from behavior to the extent the behavior is more salient or powerful than our initial attitudes (Chaiken & Baldwin, 1981; Fazio, Herr, & Olney, 1984). In everyday life, some of our attitudes are likely to be perennially salient whereas others are less so; the latter should be more affected by our behaviors.

Self-knowledge   Surely you sometimes know whether or not you like a person or a course by being keenly aware of feelings of excitement and interest. Susan Andersen suggests that we not only have such self-knowledge directly, but that we feel such information about internal states to be generally more informative than behavioral information. In one study (Andersen & Ross, 1984), subjects made statements either about their own emotions and thoughts or about their behaviors. Both subjects and observers felt that the affective/cognitive statements were more diagnostic of real self than were the behavioral statements. In a second study (Andersen, 1984), observers were more accurate in matching the subject's own self-assessments when they heard the statements about inner states rather than statements about behavior, thus suggesting that the former were more informative. Such data do not prove that we have direct access to our inner states, but they do suggest that we often feel statements about such states are more informative than inferences drawn from behavior. There is probably no direct way to prove that we have direct access to such states, but common experience suggests that we do.

The Arousal Argument   There has been another important area of conflict between cognitive dissonance and self-perception models. Bem's theory makes no assumptions about motivation. Cognitive dissonance theory, on the other hand, points to the motivating power of inconsistent cognitions. Normally we think that motivation involves activation of some arousal system. If dissonance is motivating, then like other motivation states it should have arousal properties; research confirms that it does (Croyle & Cooper, 1983).

Furthermore, dissonance theory proposes that the arousal produced by dissonance is unpleasant and that people change their cognitions to lower the arousal. Now suppose we could convince a subject that her arousal was due to something other than her dissonance. In this case the person would have no reason to change her cognitions, because she would not feel that the change would lower the arousal. Several studies have supported this line of reasoning (Fazio, Zanna, & Cooper, 1977; Zanna & Cooper, 1974; Zanna, Higgins, & Taves, 1976). These studies indirectly but powerfully support the dissonance perspective. When the importance of arousal, a factor critical to dissonance theory, is reduced, so too are the effects of behavior on attitudes.

with the desired behaviors will not be internalized if these external factors are perceived as strong.

Threat   In the classic Aronson and Carlsmith (1963) study, children who were threatened with mild punishment for playing with a desired toy actually came to dislike the toy more than those who had received stronger threats. According to dissonance theory, the mild-threat children had substantial dissonance between their liking for the toy and their realization that they had not played with it. They reduced this dissonance by saying they really didn't like the toy after all, a kind of sour-grapes reaction. Those with the strong threat had plenty of justification for their not playing with the toy, had little or no dissonance, and therefore had no reason to derogate the toy.

These results can also be interpreted within self-perception theory. The high-threat children should discount their own interest in the toy because they have a salient external explanation for their behavior. The low-threat children have no such salient alternative explanation and therefore infer an internal explanation—their dislike of the toy—from their behavior. Lepper (1973) has argued that the low-threat children might also infer that they are generally compliant children and found that they were inclined to resist temptation in an entirely new situation several weeks later.

JUSTIFICATION AND MOTIVATION

I can make my students study by giving frequent examinations, but how does that affect their interest in the course? The parent who threatens the child with a spanking if she plays with matches may get her to leave them alone while the parents are present, but what about when they are gone? Both dissonance theory and self-perception theory suggest that values, motives, attitudes, and interests consistent

Mark Lepper

Overjustification and Intrinsic Motivation
What is the effect of rewards rather than threats? Teachers, parents, and other control agents often promise rewards for good behavior. However, for years educators and psychologists have worried about the effects of rewards (such as grades) on curiosity and desire to learn. The argument has been that students will work for good grades but that they will lose interest in what they are doing in the process. That is, the provision of strong extrinsic rewards for activities otherwise enjoyable (usually called *overjustification*) may lower intrinsic interest.

The effect has now been demonstrated literally hundreds of times. In a classic study, Lepper, Greene, and Nisbett (1973) showed that nursery school children liked to play with magic markers. Then the experimenters told some of the children that they would get an award for making good drawings with the markers, while other children were not told anything about awards. Several weeks later, the award children had decreased their play with the markers much more notably than the nonaward children. From the self-perception perspective, this is easy to explain. Those children who were promised an award had a strong external reason for their play and therefore discounted their own internal interest: "I played with the markers to get an award. I must not like playing with them very much." The nonaward children, on the other hand, could still infer real enjoyment because there was no salient external factor to explain their playing with markers.

These effects are quite general. For example, not only is overt behavioral interest sometimes lowered by rewards, but so are subjective feelings of enjoyment (Deci, 1971), quality of performance (McGraw, 1978), and creativity (Amabile, 1983). People who help others for a reward report lower feelings of moral obligation than people who help without the promise of a reward (Kunda & Schwartz, 1983). Many aspects of intrinsic motivation seem to be lowered when otherwise desirable behavior is rewarded.

Factors other than explicit reward also lower intrinsic interest. For example, people who work against a deadline (Amabile, De-Jong, & Lepper, 1976) or under close supervision (Lepper & Greene, 1975) show decreased interest in the task at hand. So it would seem that strong external pressures rather than rewards as such are the key factor. This makes good sense within self-perception theory, of course.

Does this mean that rewards should never be used to help people master and perform tasks? No. In the first place, in the studies we have been discussing, people were rewarded for doing something they already enjoyed, and a considerable body of research (McGraw, 1978) suggests that salient external factors affect intrinsic interest only when that interest is initially high. However, rewards often must be used to get people to do things they otherwise might not do, that is, in situations where intrinsic motivation is low. The child who hates math might never learn to add if not bribed to do his math homework, and all of us can generate examples of acquiring an interest in something only after we were rewarded for doing it.

There is another problem with these results. We have all had the experience of doing something we enjoy and having a teacher, parent, or friend praise us for our accomplishments. And we can all think of situations where that praise has increased rather than decreased our enjoyment. It is highly doubtful that Larry Bird, for example, enjoys playing basketball less because he makes the All-Star team. Sometimes rewards can raise rather than lower intrinsic motivation.

It is clear therefore that we need something more general than the self-perception account. We can begin with the fact that reward has at least two general and often conflicting effects on behavior. According to Edward Deci's cognitive evaluation theory, rewards provide information about both *competence* and *control* (Deci, 1975; Deci & Ryan, 1980, 1983). When someone tells you that you have done a good job or pays you for a job, she communicates two things. First, she implicitly or explicitly says that you have done a good job, and this information should enhance feelings of competence that presumably increase intrinsic interest. But, second, she has also provided information about her control over your behavior (she has the right to praise you, to evaluate your performance), and generally knowing that someone else can control you ought to decrease feelings of competence and lower intrinsic motivation. Whether it is the competence or the control information that is more powerful in this situation depends on many factors, such as what the other person says, what you were promised ahead of time, and the like. But generally Deci suggests that money, grades, and other highly visible rewards communicate control information, whereas verbal praise communicates competence information.

Several experiments have provided strong support for the idea that rewards generally decrease intrinsic motivation when they undercut feelings of competence but may increase motivation when they enhance feelings of competence (Boggiano, Harackiewicz, Bessette, & Main, 1985; Boggiano, Ruble, & Pittman, 1982; Harackiewicz, Manderlink, & Sansone, 1984; Ryan, Mims, & Koestner, 1983). If you are performing an enjoyable task, others can make you less interested by making you aware that you are performing only for some reward, but they can help you maintain or increase enjoyment by providing information that you are performing competently.

DEFINITION OF EMOTION

Among the most internal, private, personal, and self-owned aspects of our experiences are our emotions. You and I may reveal our attitudes and thoughts, and if we communicate well we will feel that we have understood one another. But when it comes to emotion, we all feel that there is something both unanalyzable and fundamentally subjective about these feelings, something that cannot be fully shared with others. In fact, the emotions we experience are likely to be an important part of our identities in a given situation.

Much of the empirical work on labeling of emotions was stimulated by William James' important theory of emotion. He claimed (1884) that our feelings were based on perceptions of our bodily states and behaviors. Thus one reason you feel afraid is because your gut, your breathing, your pulse—in short, your insides—have a particular fear pattern that you can recognize. However, James was probably wrong, because a half-century of research has failed to uncover specific and clear physiological patterns that correspond neatly to discrete, experienced emotions (Mandler, 1984). This is not to say that such arousal is unimportant for our feelings, but only that differences among emotions cannot be based primarily on differential visceral feedback.

How then do we know we are afraid or sad or happy? Schachter (1964) has argued that there must be some arousal for emotions to be experienced. However, such arousal is diffuse, not specific to any given emotion. How then can you know which particular emotion you are experiencing? Schachter argues that such differential diagnosis depends heavily on our interpretation of cues from the larger environment. Thus the difference between fear and anger lies less with how the stomach feels than with the situation in the outside world.

Mandler (1962) has referred to this theory as a "jukebox theory of emotion." One must first insert a coin to start the machine (corresponding to a general activation or arousal) and then select a record (the particular emotion). Without general arousal there will be no emotion at all, but without specific cues the person will not know which particular emotion he or she is experiencing.

The classic experimental test was that of Schachter and Singer (1962). The levels of general arousal and specific cues were manipulated separately. Arousal was manipulated through injections; high-arousal subjects received epinephrine (commonly called adrenaline), whereas no-arousal subjects were given an injection of an inert saline solution (placebo condition). In addition, information was provided about the effects of the arousal. Some subjects were told nothing about the effects of the injections, others were correctly told that the injection would make them feel jumpy and aroused, and still others were misinformed about the effects, being told that their feet would feel numb, they would itch, and they might get a headache.

Now let's explore the purpose of these manipulations a bit more. Subjects in the placebo condition should experience little or no arousal except from the fear of being given a shot, so they are a useful baseline of low arousal. The epinephrine-informed subjects should be quite aroused, but because they know why they are feeling jittery they do not depend on external cues for definition of their emotions. Both the epinephrine-misinformed and the epinephrine-ignorant people, on the other hand, will be aroused, but probably will not know why—these subjects should be especially alert to situational (external) definitions of their emotional states.

The situational definitions were manipulated in a later part of the study. The experimenter left the room and a confederate entered. With some subjects he acted in an extremely manic (happy) way, whereas with others he behaved in a hostile and angry fashion. Subjects' own behaviors were observed and they were also asked about their feelings.

The basic prediction is that the subjects who had been injected with epinephrine and who were ignorant or misinformed about the effects of the injection should look to the behavior of the confederate for a definition of their emotional states. The basic data were consistent with the predictions.

However, the data from some conditions in the original study did not strongly support the model, and other studies have failed to support the predictions at all (Marshall & Zimbardo, 1979; Maslach, 1979). It does seem clear that the Schachter–Singer model is not a complete explanation of emotion and works only with specific combinations of arousal and cues (Reisenzein, 1983). However, the Schachter model focused attention onto the idea that cognitive interpretations of physiological arousal are often important and more generally on the notion that how we feel is often less a matter of our internal bodily states than of the state of our minds and the environments we are in.

MISATTRIBUTION

Both Schachter's and Bem's theories place considerable emphasis on the possibility that we use our own behavior and/or external cues to infer our internal states. It may also follow that our internal states can be not only inferred but *changed* through such cues. Can changing an emotion or attitude be all that different than defining one?

One way to change an emotion or attitude is to redefine for oneself what caused it—that is, to attribute it to some other cause. The standard experimental paradigm in the study of what has come to be called **misattribution** is to present subjects with a highly salient alternative explanation for their arousal. So a person who is aroused because of some fearful stimulus (say a tough final exam) presumably labels his emotion as fear or anxiety because the external stimulus is so clear. But if the person now took a pill (actually a placebo) and was told that the pill would cause certain symptoms (such as trembling hands, perspiration, and butterflies in the stomach), which are similar to those caused by fear, he might misattribute his arousal to the pill and feel less afraid: "It's the pill and not the exam that is making me so nervous—so I must not really be afraid."

Several experiments confirm this reasoning. People avoid painful stimuli less when they misattribute pain-arousal (the symptoms of pain) to a pill (Nisbett & Schachter, 1966). In addition, people are less likely to avoid a feared stimulus (that is, they will be less fearful) when they misattribute their fear-arousal to another source (Ross, Rodin, & Zimbardo, 1969). Shy people often feel nervous around others, but when led to believe that their shyness symptoms are due to something else, they behave less shyly (Brodt & Zimbardo, 1981). Guilt is also a kind of arousal. Diestenbier and Munter (1971) gave people an opportunity to cheat, which presumably produced some guilt-arousal. Those subjects who were given a pill and told that the side effects were similar to guilt symptoms were more likely to cheat than were subjects who had been told the pill would lower their arousal: presumably, when guilt-arousal is attributed to a pill, people feel less guilty, and when they feel less guilty they are more likely to cheat.

The effects of misattribution techniques are not always strong, but they are real and potentially important. The concept of misattribution has been one of social psychology's most prominent contributions to the discipline of modern psychology.

SUMMARY

There are many sources of identity. Some things we know about ourselves because they are objective facts or because we have been told them so often that they have factual status in our consciousness. Even so, the Balinese example from the beginning of the chapter should alert us to the fact that cultural and social factors affect which of our many characteristics we emphasize. In our culture, gender, socioeconomic status, and occupation are emphasized, whereas birth order, names of offspring, eye color, and knitting prowess are not. In addition, situations affect salience of identities; you are likely to emphasize those characteristics that make you different from others, even if this might mean emphasizing different characteristics in different situations.

In recent years, social psychologists have focused on sources of identity in our own behaviors. Cognitive dissonance theory suggests that we change behaviors to match our attitudes because we are motivated to reduce inconsistencies between attitudes and behaviors. Self-perception theories, on the other hand, emphasize that we often do not have salient initial attitudes and that we must infer them from our behavior in much the same way that other people might infer our attitudes. This kind of model has been extended to the perception and identification of emotions: our emotions are particular labels applied to general arousal on the basis of salient external cues. There is evidence that our emotional definitions can be changed if our perception of the causes of the emotions is changed.

SELF-EVALUATION

The third major question about the self is how we evaluate ourselves. As a working hypothesis, it seems reasonable that failures lead to low self-evaluations and successes to higher evaluations. On the other hand, each of us can easily think of counterexamples: some people are clearly not as smart as they think, and many a psychotherapist is kept in business by people who tend to emphasize their shortcomings and to find fault with their successes. Moreover, for self-evaluations, objective performance is often less important than our subjective interpretations of events.

CORRELATES OF GENERAL SELF-EVALUATION

There has been a vast amount of research on correlates of general self-evaluations and self-esteem. Much of this research has been designed to study developmental antecedents of self-esteem, and although the data present a mixed picture (Harter, 1983), a few generalizations emerge.

Generally parents of high-self-esteem children are warmer and more approving than those of low-self-esteem children, although it is hard to know what causes what in this case. Parental approval may raise the child's self-esteem, but the causal direction may also be reversed—the child with high self-esteem may also make good grades and do other things that elicit parental approval. Junior and senior high school students who are successful in academic (Gray-Little & Appelbaum, 1979; O'Malley & Bachman, 1979), athletic (Ryckman, Robbins, Thornton, & Cantrell, 1982), and social (Rosenberg, 1979) pursuits have more self-esteem than their less successful counterparts. Among college males, muscular strength is positively related to self-esteem (Tucker, 1983), and people with less-than-ideal body types have lowered self-esteem (Gunderson, 1965).

While social, academic, athletic, and other competencies are related to general self-esteem, the relationships are often not strong

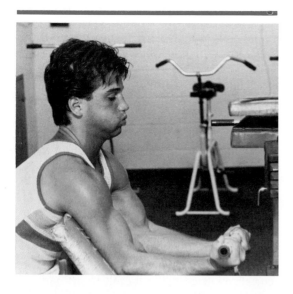

One's body type is an important part of self-esteem for many men and women.

and are mediated by many other factors, particularly the reactions of friends. For example, a good student might have relatively high self-esteem if his friends value academic performance, but his self-esteem might be unaffected or even lowered if his peer group denigrates doing well in school (Faunce, 1984). Also, although our self-evaluations usually match the evaluations we *think* others make of us, they may not always match the evaluations others *actually* make of us (Shrauger & Schoeneman, 1979). At any rate, it is clear that the reactions of others do play a role in how we evaluate ourselves, but it is often extremely difficult to disentangle the mutual causal relationships of real accomplishment, perceived accomplishment, peer-group values, perceived evaluations, and self-esteem.

Clearly then there are mediating influences between our life experiences and our self-evaluations. Social psychologists tend to examine two kinds of mechanisms that mediate the effects of success and failure on self-evaluation. First we will consider how people explain their successes and failures; attribution models have been used extensively in this area. Second we will discuss how our self-evaluations are affected by comparisons with the accomplishments of others.

EXPLANATIONS FOR SUCCESS AND FAILURE

It seems intuitively likely that the effect of success and failure on our self-evaluations must depend in part on how we attribute the causes of those outcomes. Weiner and his colleagues (1972) argued that the classic internal–external attributional distinction was too broad and that the stability–instability of forces was also an important dimension of causality. So causes can be either internal or external and either stable or unstable (see Table 5.2). Presumably, success or failure will affect self-evaluation only when it is attributed to a stable, internal force—in other words, to ability. Indeed, failure attributed to lack of

TABLE 5.2 TYPES OF ATTRIBUTIONS RESULTING FROM TWO DIMENSIONS OF CAUSALITY.

	Stable	Unstable
Internal	ability	effort
External	task difficulty	luck

ability has been shown to lower self-evaluations particularly strongly (McFarland & Ross, 1982). Generally, our emotional responses to success and failure are affected most when we attribute outcomes of our behavior to the internal factors of ability or effort (Smith & Kluegel, 1982).

Bias   One of the obvious problems with attributions for our own behavior is that we may be biased. Aren't you just a bit more inclined to see your successes as due to your own abilities and efforts and your failures as due to hard tasks or bad luck? There are many demonstrations that we are more likely than are others to give ourselves credit for our successes and to absolve ourselves of responsibility for failures (Bradley, 1978). This tendency to make attributions that favor the self is not universal, but it is common. The most obvious explanation is that people are motivated to preserve their self-esteem by seeing successes as representative of the self at its best and seeing failures as less characteristic of one's own dispositions by attributing them to external forces.

But there are at least two other types of explanation. A cognitive explanation would be that you may have information available to explain your own behavior that other people do not have. For example, if you are a typical college student you have had a fairly successful life up to this point. Therefore an experimentally increased success is likely to be more consistent with your known history than a failure would be. Because we know that high consistency favors internal attributions, it would make sense for you to say that the consistent

success was more internally caused than the inconsistent failure.

It is also possible that attributions are used as self-presentational devices. Just as we infer other people's qualities from their behavior—and from their explanations of their behavior—so too can we present ourselves to others in a good light by the way we explain our successes and failures. Certainly, attributions for one's own behavior tend to be different when given in public than in private, which supports the self-presentation reasoning (Arkin, Appelman, & Burger, 1980; Tetlock, 1981; Weary et al., 1982).

Learned Helplessness   Imagine that you have just failed an important exam, one for which you studied reasonably hard. In a couple of weeks you will have another exam. How might you react? One possibility would be for you to redouble your efforts, to study even harder. Of course, this does not guarantee that you will perform better, but at least you will have given it your best shot. On the other hand, you might conclude that you failed the first time because you are hopelessly stupid so there is no point in studying for the next exam. This would, of course, all but ensure a second failure, which would confirm your low self-evaluation.

A great deal of research with both humans and animals has been directed to variations on this theme. Martin Seligman (1975) has referred to conditions where people cease trying even when their efforts might pay off as **learned helplessness.** In experiments, people who fail at intellectual tasks where trying does not reliably lead to success subsequently show decreased performance on tasks that can be solved (Pittman & Pittman, 1979). When people fail despite working hard, they act unhappy, often cease trying, and show reduced capacities to learn how to behave effectively.

The most prominent models to explain learned helplessness employ various attribution principles. Abramson, Garber, and Seligman (1980) have suggested that responses to failure are affected by three attribution dimensions, similar to the Weiner dimensions discussed previously. If your attribution is to *internal* factors (such as ability), you will experience lowered self-esteem and self-evaluations. The *stability* dimension affects how chronic your performance deficits will be. If, after failure, you assign the causes to fairly stable factors, say lack of ability, you will be inclined to expect to fail in the future on similar tasks. If your attribution is more unstable (for example, you didn't try hard enough), you may feel you can do better in the future. Finally, you can make more or less *general* attributions. If you do poorly on a social psychology examination, you might generalize from that experience to feel you are poor at a particular kind of examination (fairly specific), incapable of learning social psychology (more general), incapable of learning psychology material (more general), or generally stupid (highly general). Thus, internality of attributions affects how you feel about your failure, whereas stability and generality affect your expectation of failure across task (generality) and across time (stability).

This kind of analysis may help us to understand when helplessness effects will and will not appear. Most of us do not decide that we are perfectly stupid and worthless based on a single experience of failure. Indeed, people sometimes react to failure by trying harder rather than by giving up (Wortman, Panciera, Shusterman, & Hibscher, 1976). However, the attribution account suggests that people will cease trying to the degree that they make internal–stable–general attributions for their failures. Thus if you fail an exam and decide that the exam was unfair, that you were under the weather, that you didn't study the right way, or that you didn't study enough, you may feel that you will do better on the next exam and be motivated to work harder. On the other hand, if you decide that your failure is a reflection of your total stupidity and that all the hard work in the world will not help you much, you may well give up.

Depression   The decreased effort and the lowered feelings of personal efficacy and self-esteem that characterize the victims of helplessness experiments appear similar to the feelings and behavior of those who are chronically depressed. In general, studies show that depressed people (depressives) are more likely than the nondepressed (nondepressives) to attribute failures to internal factors, especially low ability (Anderson & Arnoult, 1985; Anderson, Horowitz, & French, 1983). There is also evidence that depressives are more inclined to use general and stable attributions for failures (Peterson & Seligman, 1984).

In the early days of research on depression, some psychologists felt that depressed people probably focused more on their negative than on their positive qualities. However, it turns out that depressed people tend to recall both positive and negative experiences about equally, and it is nondepressed people who are biased in that they tend to remember relatively more positive information (Kuiper & Macdonald, 1982; Kuiper, Olinger, Macdonald, & Shaw, 1985; Natale & Hantes, 1982). There is also evidence that depressed people tend to respond to the affective quality of experiences. For example, Pietromonaco (1985) showed that depressed people are particularly likely to

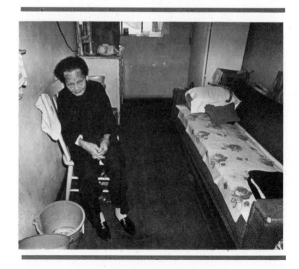

label categories of self-relevant traits in terms of positive or negative affect (for example, "my good traits"), whereas nondepressives are more likely to use neutral labels (such as "how I act with others").

Generally, depressed people have a cognitive style much like those who experience learned helplessness. They code their experiences affectively, readily remember negative events, are quick to see that they have little control over events, and tend to ascribe failures to internal, dispositional characteristics. It should be pointed out, however, that not all depressed people exhibit such styles and that people who exhibit such styles are not always depressed (Hammen, Marks, deMayo, & Mayol, 1985). Depression is a complex psychological state, but current research suggests that part of the problem stems from the ways depressed people attribute their successes and failures.

Excuses and Attributional Ambiguity

The attributional analysis of learned helplessness emphasizes cognitive responses to failure. However, other psychologists have placed more stress on motivational factors, particularly the need to protect self-esteem. If you have failed or done poorly on some task, you might be tempted to make an excuse for your failings (Snyder, 1985). One way to make such an excuse is to claim that "it wasn't my fault" or "I didn't do it" or "someone else made me do it." Another possibility would be to suggest that things aren't as bad as they seem: "I could have done better, but all things considered it wasn't so bad." A third possibility uses attributional ideas. Because internal causality is generally high when consistency of performance is high but distinctiveness and consensus are low, one way to make an excuse is to manipulate these sources of information. In one study (Mehlman & Snyder, 1985), subjects who failed a test were especially prone to make excuses by saying they would do better if they took the test again (suggesting low consistency) or that they would do better on a different sort of test (suggesting high distinctive-

ness). Interestingly, in this study subjects did not use the consensus dimension—they did not claim that everyone else probably did as poorly as they did—and this parallels subjects' underutilization of consensus information in other kinds of attribution tasks.

Sometimes we may even set up our excuses ahead of time. If you expect to fail on some task, you might be tempted to give yourself a ready excuse for the expected failure. "I'm smart enough to do it but I'm not really going to try" is one salient possibility. Or you might work on the task under adverse conditions (such as while watching a distracting TV program, or while tired, or while drunk). In effect you are making the causes of your behavior ambiguous. It could be because you don't have the ability, or it could be because you were distracted, or poorly motivated, or for some other reason.

This deliberate creation of attributional ambiguity has been termed **self-handicapping** (Jones & Berglas, 1978). Note that the basic self-handicapping strategy uses the discounting principle of attribution models. By providing a salient other cause (the handicap, such as alcohol or lack of trying) the person hopes that an observer will discount the other salient attribution (lack of ability). As Jones and Berglas point out, alcoholism and drug addiction may provide convenient excuses for people who are afraid their abilities are not up to the tasks they face. Symptoms of physical illness may serve a similar function (Smith, Snyder, & Perkins, 1983) as can confessions of shyness (Snyder, Smith, Augelli, & Ingram, 1985).

Research on self-handicapping strategies complements that on learned helplessness. People who are certain they lack important abilities may cease trying (learned helplessness), but those who are uncertain of their abilities may respond with increased trying to give their abilities a fair test. To the extent that a person concerned with the evaluations of others follows such a strategy, however, he or she runs the risk of being publicly embarrassed by failure. In that case, where self-presentational concerns are strong, self-handicapping may be a prevalent strategy (Kolditz & Arkin, 1982).

SOCIAL COMPARISON

We have discussed how people interpret the causes of their successes and failures and how such attributions affect feelings, self-evaluations, and subsequent performance. Another important component in self-evaluations is that our definitions of successes and failures often depend on our aspirations. I would be delighted to be able to run the 100-meter dash in 12 seconds, but a young woman who aspires to win the Olympics might be crushed by such a performance. Our aspirations, in turn, commonly depend on comparisons with others.

Relative Deprivation   One empirical source of the idea that our standards for judging self develop, in part, from comparisons with others comes from work on **relative deprivation,** which is the idea that our feelings of being deprived usually depend less on our objective state than on how deprived we are relative to salient others. For example, Stouffer et al. (1949) found that black soldiers stationed in the South during World War II were happier than black soldiers in the North. This was a period of overt segregation in the South, so this result may seem a bit strange. However, it makes sense once one realizes that the black soldier in the South was relatively better off than civilian blacks, whereas the soldier in the North was not so relatively advantaged and felt relatively deprived by comparison to the civilians. The same kind of idea can be used to explain urban riots. Revolutions and riots tend to occur, not when people are most deprived in *absolute* terms, but when they are making some progress and begin to feel *relatively* deprived (Davies, 1962). Perhaps people are angrier when they raise their aspirations and begin to compare themselves with people who are well off than when their major com-

parisons are with those who are as badly off as they.

Experimental studies confirm that people feel unhappiest about not having something in those situations in which they compare themselves with someone who is better off (Austin, McGinn, & Susmilch, 1980; Bernstein & Crosby, 1980). My old Mazda seems like a real jewel when I compare it with 20-year-old Chevys, but I confess to being somewhat more unhappy when I see two Mercedes in the driveway next door. Thus our feelings depend on whom we compare ourselves with. The question naturally arises as to why we compare ourselves with one person rather than another.

Social Comparison Theory   Festinger's (1954) *social comparison theory* deals with just this issue. There are four important hypotheses in the theory. Hypothesis I states, "There exists in the human organism a drive to evaluate his opinions and abilities" (p. 117). Hypothesis II says, "To the extent that objective non-social means are not available, people evaluate their opinions and abilities by comparison respectively with the opinions and abilities of others" (p. 118). These first two hypotheses are really assumptions that we want to know that we are correct—we want to have a handle on reality. If this reality can be determined through direct test, this will be preferred. However, for many abilities and opinions there is no unambiguous physical reality to use as a comparison. One cannot simply collect data to determine whether God exists, whether Ronald Reagan is a better president than Walter Mondale might have been, or whether one could climb Mt. Everest. For validation of many of our abilities and opinions, we must seek a social reality through comparisons with other people.

Festinger's third hypothesis is that "the tendency to compare oneself with some other specific person decreases as the difference between his opinion or ability and one's own increases" (p. 120). If the only people I played tennis with were Jimmy Conners and my daughter, I would know only that I was neither terrible nor great; I would gain more precise information by playing someone near my own ability. Likewise, I would not gain much information about the validity of my opinions on Russia by talking only with an extreme conservative or a member of the Communist Party.

It follows that if you want to evaluate your abilities and opinions, you should seek out someone who is roughly comparable to you. However, Festinger suggests that ability and opinion comparison differ in one important way. Hypothesis IV states, "There is a unidirectional drive upward in the case of abilities which is largely absent in opinions" (p. 124). We prefer to compare ourselves with someone who is better than we are in abilities, but because opinions (unlike abilities) are not clearly better or worse than each other, we do not have such tendencies with opinions.

Research   Most of the available research has tried to validate Hypotheses III and IV, especially for abilities. Typically, subjects are given a score on some test that they believe ranks them somewhere near the middle of the distribution. Then they are asked to pick one person whose score they would like to see. In most research, subjects want to see the score of a person who is close to them but slightly better.

However, there are important exceptions to the similarity rule. When you score near the class mean on an exam, you might want to know how well the best person did so you can gauge how much better you would have to do to receive an A. Studies have found that people often seek comparisons with the highest scorer on a test (Gruder, 1977), especially when subjects have no idea where they stand or what the range of scores was (Wheeler et al., 1969). So in addition to comparing ourselves with those who are similar we sometimes compare ourselves with the best to get an idea of standards of excellence. There are even times when

we wish to compare ourselves with those less fortunate in an effort to make ourselves feel good (Pyszczynski, Greenberg, & LaPrelle, 1985). Festinger made an important point that we can enhance our feelings of competence by comparing ourselves with people who perform slightly better, but there are also other motives that may lead us to compare ourselves with those who perform more poorly or with those who perform much better.

Festinger suggested that we compare ourselves with others who are similar on a given relevant characteristic, but there are surely other sources of similarity that are also important in choices of comparison people. Suppose, for example, that you just received an average score on an exam. It seems likely that you would want to know how others did, and you probably would prefer to see the score of a friend, a resident of your dorm, or someone of the same sex as opposed to a random person who merely scored a bit better than you did. Evidence suggests that people prefer to see the scores of those similar to them on other attributes when those other attributes are potentially related to performance (Miller, 1982; Zanna, Goethals, & Hill, 1975).

Thus, there is support for Festinger's original proposition that we seek to compare ourselves with others who have similar abilities. But it is also clear that similarity is not limited to actual scores, that sometimes highly dissimilar others (particularly those who are quite good) provide other useful information, and that we sometimes compare ourselves with others who are worse off, less for getting information than for making ourselves feel good.

BIAS AND STABILITY IN SELF-EVALUATIONS

Although we are subjected to a range of success and failure experiences each day, most of us find that we are able to maintain fairly stable self-evaluations. My estimate of my teaching ability is not dramatically affected by my blunders in class or for that matter by the occasional student who informs me that she enjoyed the course. Similarly, you are unlikely to decide that you are incredibly stupid or bright after getting a single exam score that is quite low or high. How do we maintain stable self-concepts in the face of varying and unstable information about competence?

Cognitive and Motivational Factors Earlier we discussed the commonsense idea that how we process self-relevant information is affected by a variety of motivational and cognitive factors. Social psychologists have shown a lively interest in trying to determine whether we are biased because of the ways our cognitive systems operate or because of our motivation to see ourselves in certain ways, but in reality these two kinds of factors are hopelessly intermingled much of the time. However, because motivational factors are comparatively obvious, it is probably wise for us to emphasize purely cognitive factors in this discussion.

We noted in Chapter 3 that we tend to hold fast to our theories about the world (and self) until there is strong evidence that requires their change. One relevant demonstration for self comes from an early study of theory perseveration by Ross, Lepper, and Hubbard (1975). Subjects were told either that they had succeeded or that they had failed on a task. Subsequently, the experimenter told them that the success or failure information had been bogus. One would expect that this debriefing would cancel the effects of the previous information, but the success subjects continued to feel that they would do better on related tasks than the failure subjects did.

We also sometimes rewrite our past histories to conform to present realities. For example, as a professor of psychology, it is easy for me to remember that I was especially interested in psychology when I was, say, 16, although I doubt that anyone at that time would have seen my interests as lying especially in that direction. In one experimental demonstration,

Ross, McFarland, and Fletcher (1981) changed people's attitudes about health care practices and then asked them to recall their own past behaviors relevant to those practices. As expected, people recalled behaviors more in line with the new than with the old attitudes. Conway and Ross (1984) had subjects participate in a program to improve study skills, a program that had no demonstrable effects on actual grades. Those who took part in the program retrospectively remembered their initial study skills evaluations as more negative than they had been, felt that their study skills had improved, and six months later remembered their grades as better than they had actually been. The net result was that subjects who participated in a program that they thought should change them saw themselves as changing even though they had not.

Sometimes, of course, we get evidence that directly contradicts cherished theories about the self. In Chapter 4 we explored many of the ways we have of dealing with inconsistent information. We attend to only some new information, label our experiences in biased ways, and selectively recall what has happened. Thus you may pay less attention to information inconsistent with your self-image, may label it as uncharacteristic, and may, in time, forget it. Our memories may be particularly prone to bias. For example, we tend to remember more positive than negative information (Bower & Gilligan, 1979; Holmes, 1970), and negative information may be remembered as less negative than it was (Steiner, 1968). We may also be prone to exaggerate our own contributions to group efforts (Ross & Sicoly, 1979). Thus, we tend to process information about the self in ways that lead us to have positive rather than negative self-concepts.

However, it would be wrong to overemphasize these biases. Surely even the most biased student cannot easily maintain a view of himself as a gifted student after he fails his tenth course. Much as I would like to think of myself as a good teacher, I could not keep this belief if students refused to take my classes or if my teaching evaluations were each year the lowest in the university.

It is probable that we are more biased when we are uncertain about our self-evaluations. For example, Felson (1981) found that athletes tended to rate themselves higher than their coaches did on attributes, such as mental toughness, that are relatively ambiguous. However, for more objective attributes, such as strength, the athletes and coaches were in closer agreement. In an experimental demonstration, Jones and Schneider (1968) created either certain or uncertain low self-evaluations in subjects who were then given positive or negative evaluations from others. Subjects liked the negative evaluator less when they were uncertain than when they were certain that they had poor abilities. These and other studies suggest that we display self-esteem biases primarily when there is some uncertainty about self-evaluations.

Social Factors   Cognitive and motivational factors have lots of support from social interactions in maintaining stable self-evaluations. Many of our self-evaluations are based on evaluations we receive from others. If those evaluations are fairly constant or biased, our self-evaluations might be similarly constant or biased. One such social factor is *selective social interaction.* It is not uncommon for students to avoid taking courses with professors who have given them bad grades in the past, and while most of us have some appreciation of honest criticism, we hardly select our friends because they are usually critical of us. We tend to like and associate more with—we selectively interact with—those who agree with us about our self-evaluations (Backman & Secord, 1962).

Mark Snyder (1981b) has argued that people tend to select situations that allow ready confirmation of their own personal dispositions. So an extroverted person is likely to prefer noisy bars to quiet libraries whereas the introvert may prefer the library. Such choices of situation confirm both our own self-

Nancy Cantor   William Swann

conceptions (it is easier to behave in an extroverted manner at a bar than at a library) and the evaluations of others (the extrovert's loud jokes will win more approval at a bar than in the library).

Nancy Cantor and her colleagues have suggested that people have cognitive prototypes of who is likely to be successful in given situations. People want to interact with people who are prototypic for a given situation (Cantor, Mackie, & Lord, 1983–84). Furthermore, our choices of situations are influenced by the extent to which we are prototypic for that situation. Niedenthal, Cantor, and Kihlstrom (1985) had subjects rate the typical person who lived in various kinds of campus housing. Subjects preferred to live in situations where their own self-ratings were close to the prototype. We could safely predict that such choices would lead to interactions with people who were similar to them and who would reinforce their own self-images as good and proper. For example, if a student felt that sorority people were rich and socially conscious, and that these traits also described her, we might expect that if she joined a sorority she would find her own self-assessment validated by people who shared her traits.

Within a given situation, we may also selectively interact with other people. Swann and Read (1981b) showed that people preferentially seek information that confirms rather than disconfirms their self-evaluations. We may also behave in ways that elicit confirmatory feedback from others (Swann & Read, 1981a). So if you consider yourself to be kind, you would probably be inclined to behave in ways that lead others not only to see you as kind but to report their perceptions to you.

What happens when others seem to hold erroneous views of what you are like? Ordinarily you will try to change their views either through direct challenge or by behaving in ways consistent with your self-concept and inconsistent with their concepts of you, at least if you care what they think of you. The important question is how such activity might affect your own self-concept. Swann and Hill (1982) have shown that if you had reason to believe that you had successfully supported your self-image publicly, there would be no reason to change that image. If, however, you have no opportunities to change the others' views of you, you would probably be more likely to change your self-concept to meet the others' conception. So, if someone erroneously thinks you are lazy, you might try to convince him otherwise; however, if you cannot change his view, you might come to think of yourself as lazier. Thus, the ability to engage in remedial activity may be an important device for maintaining a stable self-concept.

Sometimes our friends insulate us from discrepant information, which is another means to maintain our self-evaluations. Swann and Predmore (1985) gave subjects feedback that disagreed with their self-concepts (either more positive or more negative) and then had them talk to a stranger, a friend who also disagreed with the subject's self-concept, or a friend who agreed. Then subjects reported their own self-concepts. Generally, subjects moved toward the discrepant, experimenter-provided evaluations. The one exception occurred when the subject talked to a friend who supported the subject's previous self-concept.

We also stress certain associations more than others. In one study, students were more likely to wear school-identifying colors on a

People are proud of their identification with a winner.

Monday after their college team had won rather than lost a weekend football game. Students were also more likely to say *we* won rather than *we* lost, suggesting closer identification with the winning team (Cialdini et al., 1976). This tendency to bask in reflected glory presumably maintains a positive self-evaluation by emphasizing positive associations (Cialdini & Richardson, 1980).

Approval-seeking   People would rather say nice than negative things about others (Tesser, 1978), and it is usually not hard to get approval from others. When people want to get approval, they will try to define themselves as worthy in the eyes of others (Jones & Wortman, 1973). We need not always define ourselves as successful to get this approval. Sometimes people will fail if failure seems expected of them or will be approved (Aronson & Carlsmith, 1962; Baumeister, Cooper, & Skib, 1979).

In Chapter 12 we discuss the nature of self-presentation in some detail. However, for the moment we will concentrate on the effects of self-presentations on self-evaluations. There is a paradox of sorts here. Suppose that I want your approval; to get it I behave in ways that I know you will approve and I may even brag about myself a bit. And suppose you play your part and provide the approval. But isn't your approval tainted somewhat by the fact that neither of us may have been quite truthful? I have worked to get your approval, perhaps by behaving in uncharacteristic ways, and you have followed the strong norm in our society that we should generally agree with others about themselves.

However, several experiments suggest that even when people solicit approval deliberately through their self-presentations, they seem to accept and believe the approval (Gergen, 1965; Jones, Gergen, & Davis, 1962). According to self-perception theory, the approval might not even be necessary—people may infer their self-evaluations from their own behavior. In several experiments by Jones, Rhodewalt, Berglas, and Skelton (1981), subjects who were induced to describe themselves positively subsequently had higher self-evaluations than those who used negative self-presentations, even when there was no approval given.

For whatever reasons, it seems that we believe our own self-presentations, at least some of the time. Because there are fairly strict norms about how we should present ourselves (don't brag too much, don't be overly modest, don't say things about yourself that are untrue, and so on), the probable result is that most people say moderately positive things about themselves. These presentations may then come to define the self, either because of approval or through self-perception processes.

SUMMARY

Perhaps the most salient feature of the self is that it is the object of our most intense evaluative feelings. The most obvious source of such evaluations is our successes and failures with our physical and social environments. Data from several sources suggest that successful people have somewhat higher self-evaluations than unsuccessful people, but that the correlation between success and self-evaluations is remarkably low. One reason for this is that people tend to explain away failures as due to external causes beyond their control and to see the causes of successes as internal and dispositional. There are, however, individual differences in these tendencies. Depressed people in particular are likely to take more credit for failures and less for successes than nondepressed people. In addition, people may use any of several cognitive excuse strategies so that attributions for failure focus on unstable features such as not trying, illness, alcoholism, and the like. While attributions helps us to interpret the causes of successes and failures, comparison with the performances of others helps us evaluate performance and self. We have several ways to maintain stable self-evaluations. We tend to want to interpret our own performances in the best possible light and we tend to remember information as more consistent with our self-perception than it was. In addition, we sometimes structure our social interactions both through our selection of people with whom we interact and through our self-presentations, so that we get feedback consistent with our self-concepts.

CHAPTER SUMMARY

- While philosophers have argued for centuries about the nature of self, the early psychologists William James and George Herbert Mead argued that the self is both the agent of experience and the object of evaluative feelings. We learn to evaluate the self by thinking about ourselves as others do.

- In modern social psychology there have been three basic questions about the self: (1) What is the role of the self in processing information? (2) What is the basis of identity? and (3) How do people evaluate themselves?

- Clearly the self occupies a central role in our experiences because it is the "I" with its individual history and unique concerns that thinks and processes new information. Beyond that, it has been argued that the self also has schemalike properties that aid the efficient processing of information. In support of that argument, it has been shown that characteristics of the self are accessible in judging others, that judgments about characteristics of self are made rapidly, and that judging whether something applies to self improves memory for that material. Others have argued that many of these results could be explained equally well by assuming simply that the self is familiar and that the self has no unique processing advantages.

- When people focus on themselves as others do (objective self-awareness), they typically find this state aversive and are inclined to behave in more normative ways.

- There are many sources of identity. Our cultures emphasize certain characteristics and those of our characteristics that are unusual in a given situation are often salient parts of identity. In addition, we tend to emphasize the things we are good at doing.

- Research stimulated by cognitive dissonance theory has shown that when people behave in ways discrepant from their attitudes, they will often change their attitudes to match their behaviors. This effect works best when people have freely committed themselves to perform the behaviors and the behaviors have the potential of negative consequences for others.

- Bem developed his self-perception theory to explain the results of research stimulated by cognitive dissonance theory. According to this model, people do not have initial attitudes but infer them after the fact from their behavior. More recent versions suggest that some attitudes are salient parts of memory and do not need to be inferred, but when attitudes are easily accessed they will be inferred from behavior.

- Research suggests that emotions require a state of general arousal, which is then labeled by environmental or internal cues. This has led to the idea that people's emotional states can be changed through misattribution, whereby a salient cue suggests an alternative label for the arousal.

- Self-evaluation is an important component of self. Generally, people's self-evaluations are responsive to their successes and failures; however, the fit is far from exact, because successes and failures have to be explained through attributions, and sometimes these attributions are biased. Depressed people are especially prone to assume that their successes are due to internal, stable, and general characteristics. We also make excuses for our failures and sometimes arrange conditions so our failures will be attributed to unstable or environmental causes rather than to our abilities.

- Our successes and failures also acquire meaning when we compare our outcomes with others through social comparison. Social comparison theory suggests that we compare our abilities with people who perform at a similar but slightly better level. Although research offers some support for this hypothesis, there are also times when we compare ourselves with those who perform much better or much worse.

- One of the remarkable features of the self is that our self-evaluations remain stable despite variability in outcomes. Several mechanisms help to promote stable self-concepts. We are inclined to interpret and remember information consistent with past self-concepts. We also selectively interact with those people who will support our self-concepts and sometimes we structure social situations to gain consistent feedback about ourselves.

CHAPTER

6

LANGUAGE
AND COMMUNICATION

A high school English teacher once asked me for advice about problems she was having with a particular student, a young black man. She felt he was hostile and asked him why he was so angry. He replied that she, the teacher, hated him but he would not give specific evidence. The teacher suspected that race was an issue and so she told the student that she tried to treat the Negro boys and girls and the white boys and girls just alike. The student looked up suddenly and muttered, "I'm no Negro—I'm black; and I'm no boy—I'm a man." The teacher continued to talk to the student but reported that the tone of the conversation did not improve.

The teacher asked me what she should have done. We focused on why the student was so upset that she had called him a Negro boy. She claimed that he was a Negro and he was a boy (a freshman in high school). I pointed out that most blacks now preferred to be called *black* rather than *Negro* and adult black males had been called *boy* for so many decades as a means to mark their inferior social status that it was surely understandable that the student would resent the term. But the teacher would not give up. She got out her dictionary and showed me that *Negro* is a perfectly acceptable racial designation, and she asked me to confirm that a person of age 14 could reasonably be called a boy. I suggested that although *Negro* and *boy* are acceptable words in certain contexts, it is at best rude to call people by terms they do not like and at worst morally and politically wrong. But she refused to go along, pointing out that it wasn't all that many years before that the student in question would have been called *nigger,* and she was proud of the fact that she had never used such a term. She claimed she was not prejudiced (and I think she is not), but she did demand the right to use clear and accurate words; wasn't that what her entire life as an English teacher was for? After all, *black* is inaccurate because the average black person is brown and not black. So why should she substitute a grossly inaccurate term for one that is perfectly accurate and useful?

INTRODUCTION

Communication is complex. Communication involves the use of symbols and their meanings, and any given symbol may have several levels of meaning. For example, the terms *Negro* and *boy,* while perfectly accurate designations in their narrow senses, also communicate meanings that are unacceptable in a wider sense. In this examples the symbols are words, but symbols may also be deeds, gestures, or even the failure to act. But whether the symbols are verbal or nonverbal, they communicate meanings.

Communication is one of the central aspects of our social lives. It is social because at least two people are involved—one who provides a symbol and one who interprets it. But, more important, communication is social because our interpretations of symbols are affected by our cultures. Our verbal language is a product of culture; we have to learn to use words reasonably precisely and to interpret them more or less correctly. We also have to learn how to make and interpret the gestures appropriate to our cultures. We learn the language of words, gestures, and actions during childhood and continually throughout life.

WORDS AND BEHAVIORS

Any behavior—saying *thank you,* falling asleep in a lecture, crossing your legs, staring at another person—can convey meaning and is, therefore, potentially a part of the communication enterprise. Although we often think of language purely in verbal terms, communication is not limited to words. Verbal language is, of course, extremely important. It aids our private thought processes and allows us to say what is on our minds efficiently. Asking a friend to pass the salt is usually more efficient than grunting, pointing, or gesturing to get the salt to your end of the table. On the other hand, using words is sometimes inefficient or ineffective; there are times when a hug, a smile, or a tear can convey a richer meaning more quickly than words can.

Verbal and nonverbal behaviors interact to produce and enrich meanings. Sometimes we use our gestures to reinforce our words; typically you smile when you compliment someone and frown when you criticize. But at other times the two domains produce different meanings. This can produce confusion or a perception of insincerity, as when your friend does not quite smile the right way when she tells you she likes your new hairstyle and you decide she really doesn't mean what she says. Sometimes we deliberately create conflicting messages. Sarcasm, irony, humor, and kidding all depend heavily on the ability of behavioral and vocal cues to tell others that the words are not to be taken at face value.

THE GOALS OF COMMUNICATION

There are many specific goals of communication (Higgins, 1981a). For example, you may try to get someone to help solve a problem ("Please shut the door."), or you may seek information ("What did he say?"). Communication may also be used for persuasion or to establish a common social reality; "We all agree that this proposal is silly, don't we?" Sometimes we talk to, touch, or hug someone to initiate or maintain a social bond such as friendship. We can also use words and expressions as forms of self-advertisement; we brag or otherwise promote ourselves to others. Sometimes we communicate just for the joy of it, as when we tell jokes or stories. This list is not exhaustive and these goals are not mutually exclusive. Surely when you ask a question

in class you may be seeking information, but you are probably not oblivious to a desire to impress the professor or your classmates with your wisdom. Agreeing with a friend may secure her friendship *and* cement a social reality.

A major theme of this chapter is that normative and social contexts affect not only what we ourselves do and say but also how our words and gestures will be interpreted by others. You simply do and say different things when you are participating in a class discussion, helping a friend with a research project, or attending a party. In the first situation, you may want to communicate information; in the second, warm support; and in the third, something about your own sterling qualities. Therefore, saying that "Wundt used the method of introspection" would be entirely proper in the class context but would be thought odd at the party. Moreover, the tone of your voice and your expressions will likely be different in each situation. The exuberance common at parties is out of place in most classes, and the pompous tones of the classroom would likely be resented by your friend if you were helping him with a project.

LANGUAGE AND MEANING

MEANING AND CONCEPTS

As long as people have been using words and gestures, there have been problems of miscommunication and concerns with **semantics,** what words mean. Our cave-dwelling ancestors probably argued around the campfire about whether Og grunted an insult or a request for more meat. Certainly concerns with meaning and miscommunication are manifest in the works of Homer, the Greek philosophers, and the Bible, which are among the oldest writings still in use.

The Concept Model   One of the oldest theories of meaning is based on the obvious fact that many words denote certain objects or classes of objects. The word *dog* refers to four-legged, generally furry animals of a particular range of sizes and appearances. If you wanted to teach a small child what the word *dog* means, you could point to relevant beasts while saying the word. Before long the small person would show that she understood what the word means by correctly labeling new dogs. (Of course, she may make a few errors; children are prone to charming linguistic mistakes such as calling a large cat *doggie* or a strange man *daddy*.)

This model suggests that we use words to refer to abstract concepts. When we develop the concept of *dog*, we look at several relevant instances and determine the essential qualities they have in common: four legs, a restricted range of size, fur, and the like. The term *dog* then is simply a label for this category of instances sharing an essential quality. Knowing what is common about dogs helps to distinguish them from cats, birds, houses, and other categories.

However, there are so many problems with this model that it is no longer taken seriously as a complete model of meaning. One basic problem is that many words are difficult to define this way. We can learn what *dog* means by seeing instances, but suppose you were trying to teach someone what the word *beauty* means. You might point to works of art, roses, particular men and women, and certain spring days. But beauty is more subjective and ambiguous than dogness, and you would have trouble getting the meaning across by reference to particular instances. Other words such as *truth, love,* and *happy* are also hard to define by denoting instances.

The philosopher Ludwig Wittgenstein (1958) has pointed out that some terms, such as *game*, do not even refer to things or events with common properties. There is probably no single quality common to the games of bridge, chess, football, charades, solitaire, and poker. Wittgenstein proposed that a word's meaning depends on its social uses, on implicit agree-

ments within a community of language users. Often the group sharing a meaning is quite large, so that in the United States hardly anyone would fail to understand what I mean by *car* in the statement "I'll be in the green car." However, there are smaller language communities. For example, Back, Bunker, and Dunnagan (1972) analyzed disagreement in a meeting of theologians and scientists. Such words as *authority, manipulate,* and *knowledge* had quite different points of reference for the two groups, and such differences contributed to misunderstandings and interpersonal tensions.

Prototypes   An additional problem with traditional categories is that some instances are seen to be better examples of categories than others. Somehow a shirt is a better example of *clothes* than a glove, and a robin seems more birdlike than a penquin. Rosch (1978) has argued that our concepts (and the words denoting them) are based on prototypic representations. According to Rosch, **prototypes** are instances of categories that are typical in the sense of resembling the other objects in the category more than nonprototypic instances do. Your basic easy chair is probably physically closer to most other chairs than is a modern Danish chair, so the former is more and the latter less prototypic; when you think of chairs, it would be more likely that the prototypic example would spring to mind. Research shows that people can make judgments faster (Rosch, Simpson, & Miller, 1976) and can remember more (Reed, 1972) about prototypic than nonprototypic examples of categories.

Basic Categories   Why do you call that beast *dog* rather than *mammal* or *collie*? Rosch (1978) and her colleagues have argued that when we arrange categories into hierarchies of generality, we rely on certain **basic categories** that are neither too specific nor too general for our given purposes (see Figure 6.1).

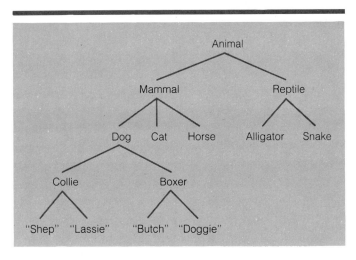

FIGURE 6.1   Hierarchy of Categories Including Basic Categories. Note that basic categories are usually found at intermediate levels of generality—in this case *dog, cat,* and *snake* would probably be basic categories.

Usually the *collie* designation is too specific: if I want to warn my children to stay away from animals that might bite, it matters little whether the animal is a collie, a boxer, or a wirehaired pointing griffon. By the same token, calling the animal a mammal is too broad, because I don't wish to include stray cats in my warnings. In this case the basic category *dog* is specific enough to make a difference in behavior but not so specific as to provide irrelevant information. However, as our purposes change, so too might our basic categories: at the local dog show, *dog* is too broad and the basic category may shift to, say, *collie.*

Connotative Meaning   Even prototype theories of concepts and meaning tend to miss one essential aspect of meaning: words not only label specific things, they also arouse affective and emotional reactions—what is termed **connotative meaning.** The teacher in the example at the beginning of the chapter did not realize that what for her was a neutral

designation *(Negro)* was a word filled with negative connotations for the student. Thus, a given description may evoke greatly different reactions from different people or in different situations. Furthermore, a given instance can be described in various ways—a person can be black or a Negro or an Afro-American—and these different descriptions can convey quite different emotional connotations.

One of the most widely used techniques to measure connotative meaning is the **semantic differential** developed by Osgood and his colleagues (Osgood, Suci, & Tannenbaum, 1957). Subjects are simply asked to rate concepts on several adjective scales. For example, one might rate *college professor* on such scales as strong–weak, responsible–irresponsible, good–bad, happy–sad, and light–dark.

Three major dimensions commonly underlie the adjective ratings—good–bad, active–passive, and strong–weak. Figure 6.2 shows the semantic space positions of several concepts. Note that certain concepts such as *God* and *America* are similarly good, active, and strong,

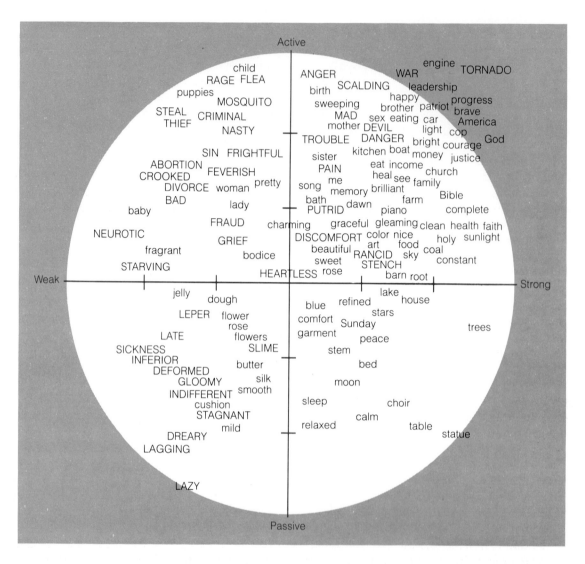

FIGURE 6.2   Locations of Selected Concepts in the Semantic Differential Space. Concepts rated "good" are in lower-case letters; those rated "bad" are in capitals.

Carrol, 1964.

giving them a connotative similarity despite their otherwise quite different meanings. On the other hand, although the closely related concepts *lady* and *mother* are both good and active, *lady* is much weaker. This relative weakness of the term *lady* may account for why it is not favored by many modern women. Such subtleties are often quite important in our social lives, and techniques like the seman-tic differential help us understand the vague, somewhat emotional ways in which words differ.

CONTEXTUAL VIEWS OF MEANING

Words as symbols take on part of their meaning by their reference to objects or concepts. But words also take on at least part of their meaning from the context in which they appear (Clark & Clark, 1977). In this sense it is not so much the words as the word combinations that carry meaning.

Most words have a range of meanings and, of course, there are often several words which have nearly identical meanings. Therefore, the choice of words is often predicated on quite subtle cultural understandings of the context. For example, though the class I teach from 7 to 8 P.M. is a night class, the meal I eat afterwards is my evening meal, not my night meal. At 9 P.M. in winter I can say that night has fallen, but my wife wears an evening gown and not a night gown when we leave for a fancy party. The words *night* and *evening* mean nearly the same thing and could perhaps be used as synonyms in some contexts, but in other contexts, such as in the examples above, one word is culturally appropriate and the other is not.

Types of Context   Words take on a part of their meanings from the context in which they are used. This context is partially *grammatical*—thus "Carlton Fiske was knocked down defending home" will be understood by baseball fans (who know Fiske is a catcher) as meaning something entirely different from "Carlton Fiske was knocked down defending *his* home." The simple addition of *his* makes all the difference. The context may also be situational. The word *foul* has quite different meanings in conversations about food, baseball, and basketball. Contexts may also be social and normative. If I ask a colleague in the hall, "How are you?" she would not be likely to give me a rundown on her mental and physical health. I was greeting her rather than asking for information, and as members of this culture, we both understand this convention. On the other hand, the same question at the beginning of a visit to the same person in the hospital would be seen as a request for health information because the situation emphasizes different norms.

Thus, meaning is affected by grammatical, situational, and normative contexts, among others. One classic demonstration of the effects of such contexts was provided by Barclay et al. (1974). Words such as *piano* were embedded in different contexts, such as "the man tuned the piano" versus "the man lifted the piano," making either the musical or the weight aspect of the instrument salient. Recall of the sentence was best when it was prompted by a cue (something musical or something heavy) related to the original context. Thus, subjects had encoded the word *piano* in terms of the meaning made salient by its original context.

Contexts can also make otherwise quite dissimilar words similar in meaning. If you are driving down the road and your friend screams, "Look out for the _____!" a great many words such as *tree, woman, car,* or *elephant* could meaningfully be placed in the blank. In that context they all have roughly equivalent meanings, even though no one asserts that *cars* and *trees* have much in common otherwise.

Direct and Indirect Speech Acts   According to the theory of speech acts (Austin, 1962; Searle, 1969), people write or say sentences to accomplish some goal such as asserting something ("It was a dog."), gathering information ("Was that a dog?"), or commanding ("Stop that dog!"). People who understand English have a clear understanding of these (and other) forms. If we say these sentences aloud, we will find that our voice tone and inflection vary, which indicates that we use ways of speaking to enforce the particular meanings.

More formally, several kinds of speech acts have been distinguished (Clark, 1985): (1) assertions (statements of belief, predictions, confessions, and so on), (2) directives (including requests and questions), (3) commissives (commitments to act in certain ways, such as, "I will meet you at 3"), (4) expressives (statements about feelings), (5) effectives (statements that change situations, such as "You're fired"), and (6) verdictives (statements that declare truths, such as "Strike two!" shouted by a baseball umpire.) One major problem for speakers and hearers is that these kinds of speech acts do not map directly onto the four major types of sentences: declarative, interrogative, imperative, and exclamatory. A directive request may be phrased as an interrogative ("Would you pass the salt?"), as an imperative ("Pass the salt."), or as a declarative sentence ("I think the steak needs more salt.").

A distinction may be made between direct and indirect speech acts. **Direct speech acts** are those with a fairly clear and unambiguous interpretation in terms of their form. **Indirect speech acts** are those whose appearances belie their functions. As I return a set of exams, a student asks, "Did you have fun last night?" I understand this not as a serious question but as a tease and respond with a question of my own, "Do you look happy?" He treats my question as an assertion of sorts and groans. The conversation that appears to be about my

"To all employees: It has been recently observed that when Mr. McCutcheon says 'How are you?' certain employees have taken this simple greeting as an invitation to 'let it all hang out.'"

Drawing by Stevenson © 1977 by The New Yorker Magazine, Inc.

happiness is actually, if indirectly, about how well the students did on their exams.

Commands are often expressed indirectly because of politeness norms. My wife sometimes has trouble getting four people to the dinner table on time. She usually begins her indirect command sequence by saying something like "Dinner is almost ready." If this is not followed with compliance, she will follow with "Dinner is on the table" and still later by "The dinner is getting cold." Technically, each of these statements is an assertion, but woe betide any of us who fails to understand them as commands. We often hesitate to command directly, but we are socialized to understand quite well that questions and assertions can function as indirect commands.

The fact that sentences don't always mean what they seem to say was once conveyed to me when I called a friend and asked, "Is Irene [his wife] there?" He answered "Yes," but said nothing more. "Could I speak to her?" was similarly answered. Not knowing what to expect next, I commanded directly: "I would like to speak to Irene. Please call her to the phone." Being a mathematician, he respected my precision and promptly did as he was told. Irene thought it was funny, but then she's a physicist.

Normative Principles Modern linguists have argued that communication and meaning depend heavily on normative principles. Grice (1975, 1978) has noted that several rules govern conversational exchanges. Perhaps the most important is that we should make our contributions *informative* enough to satisfy the demands of the situation but not so loaded down with information as to overwhelm the other person. If I ask a colleague how a class went, she knows (usually) that I want a summary statement and not a blow-by-blow description. One should also be *truthful* and as *clear* as possible. Finally, one should be *relevant,* the relevancy established culturally or situationally: for example, "you are crazy" is normally understood as a tease rather than as a precise diagnosis.

Sometimes these rules come into conflict, as when you discover that you must simplify to be informative, which causes you to distort the truth. And on occasion we are allowed to relax the rules a bit. When I tell a story among friends, I am allowed a certain amount of embellishment of facts by nearly everyone but my wife, who believes strongly in the truth principle. We are often encouraged to violate norms of truth and informativeness by other norms of politeness, which strongly suggest that indifferent meals be complimented and ugly Christmas gifts praised (and worn or used).

These principles guide not only what we say but also how we are understood. Consider the relevancy principle as one example. People will assume that my comments are coherent and responsive to what went before. You ask, "How was the concert?" and I reply, "I was home by 9." Although these statements could refer to very different things, you will take my answer as a response to your question and assume that I mean to say the concert was boring.

We understand relationships among sentences because we assume they are related, and therefore we form cognitive bridges between them (Clark & Haviland, 1974). Suppose I say the following: "I went to the concert last night," "the music was too loud," and "I didn't stay long." Although I never directly said that the loud music was at the concert or that I left because of the loud music, nearly everyone will assume that is what I meant to say. In other words, my listeners form inferences that help them bridge the gaps in what I have said.

Such bridging allows for economy of communication. If a speaker or writer had to fill in every missing link, books would be far too long and conversations would never end. Sometimes, of course, we leave gaps that are too big and the listener does not understand what we are trying to say. The communication

partner who leaves big gaps will often be seen as unresponsive. Research confirms that we have more trouble understanding and remembering unresponsive (that is, irrelevant) comments and that we evaluate people who are unresponsive somewhat negatively (Davis & Holtgraves, 1984).

Thus, there is more to communication than producing words. Words have a range of meanings, and their exact meaning is very much a product of their grammatical context, how they are said, social norms, and informational context. Shortly we will show that nonverbal and expressive behaviors provide yet another context that affects what words mean.

LANGUAGE AND COGNITION

It has long been asserted that language determines or at least affects thought. This hypothesis was most strikingly articulated by Benjamin Whorf (1956). Whorf's general hypothesis was that language categories and grammar make possible certain forms of thinking. But this is too general to be especially helpful: does language merely facilitate thinking or does it determine it? This is a difficult question to answer, but most psycholinguists feel that evidence for the strong deterministic hypothesis is hard to come by.

On the other hand, many would be prepared to argue that language facilitates our thinking to the degree that it makes certain categories and discriminations more salient. Consider a famous Eskimo example (Brown, 1965). Eskimos have names for several kinds of snow, whereas for most Americans *snow* is simply *snow*. It is reasonable to expect that their varied snow vocabulary somehow corresponds to the Eskimo's ability to discriminate more kinds of snow than the average American can (skiers may be one American exception). But do the names make the perceptual discriminations easier or are the names merely passive labels for discriminations already present?

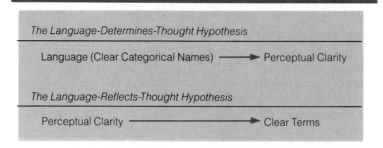

FIGURE 6.3   Two Possible Relationships Between Language and Thought.

One famous test of this question came in studies dealing with memories for colors. Brown and Lenneberg (1954) assumed that the color spectrum was continuous and that to label particular parts of the spectrum with color names was essentially an arbitrary process, although culturally and linguistically convenient. They further argued that having clear, easy-to-remember color names facilitates our abilities to perceive and remember certain colors—in other words, language facilitates thought. For example, imagine that you are at a store and want to buy a sweater to go with a particular shirt you have at home, so you try to find a shirt in the store that is the same color as the one you have at home. Brown and Lennenberg would assume that if the color has a clear name (short and with general agreement on the name), such as *rust* or *lemon yellow,* you would be more nearly able to find the color in the store than if the color you are looking for is harder to describe (such as, *kind of a misty green with a bit of yellow in it*). In their study, subjects were shown colors and then asked to pick them from an array from memory; this was easier to do for the colors with clear names. Brown and Lennenberg interpreted these findings as supporting the Whorfian idea that clear, culturally defined labels facilitate the discrimination and recognition of colors, or of objects generally.

However, there is another obvious interpretation. Perhaps we have clear names for certain colors because they are easier to discriminate in the first place. When you examine blue colors at a paint store or look at several blue shirts, you may feel that certain of the blues stand out as especially good blues. This is not a judgment about beauty but about closeness to some ideal ("Now that's a real blue"). If such good examples exist, it would not be surprising that we have names for them and that these names are fairly clear and agreed upon. Thus, it may be that salient perceptual experience produces clear names rather than that clear names produce perceptual clarity (see Figure 6.3).

This is hard to test empirically, but there are some useful data from different cultures. Although not every culture draws the boundaries between colors in quite the place we do, there is general agreement across cultures in the primacy of certain colors such as black, white, blue, green, red, orange, pink, and purple (Berlin & Kay, 1969). And although a given language may not have distinct names for all these colors (green and blue are often given the same name), its speakers are likely to have names for at least some of them. Furthermore, people from vastly differing language groups tend to agree on the best and most representative colors for each word. That is, if two cultures both have a name for red, people from those cultures will agree on which shade is the best red. Moreover, the names of these so-called focal or prototypic colors are generally the more commonly used color names within a given culture (Heider, 1972).

In an even more crucial demonstration, Rosch (formerly Heider) showed that even when people do not have a distinct name for a color, they can still learn names for focal colors better than for nonfocal colors (Rosch, 1973). So people who have no name for red could still learn a name for what you and I would consider a good red better than for what we would consider an off-red. These results suggest that physical stimulation and our perceptual apparatus make certain experiences salient, for which we then develop clear names. To return to the original Brown–Lenneberg research, it now appears possible—even likely—that people can pick out certain colors readily not so much because the colors have clear names but because the colors are somehow perceptually salient. That does not, of course, rule out the possibility that in domains other than color the names may exert more control over the thought than the reverse. Surely thought and language are so intimately bound together that they cannot ultimately be separated.

SUMMARY

A given word can have many shades of meaning (and sometimes quite distinct meanings). One reason that words may have many meanings is that for some, such as *beauty*, the referents are unclear. In addition, we often use words to refer to loose collections of things, and Rosch has argued that we think about categories in terms of prototypic instances rather than in terms of defining features. Words also have connotative meanings—a general emotional tone in addition to their strict definition—that affects our responses to them. Words also take on at least part of their meaning from cultural, normative, and grammatical contexts. The ways we think about things affect our use of words, and our use of words affects our thought.

NONVERBAL COMMUNICATION

It is easy to assume that communication is verbal, that words carry the primary messages from one person to the next. Our whole educational system is geared to the study of words, and much of the important information we get comes from reading and speaking. However, in everyday social interactions, words are not the only ways we have of communicating. Gestures, facial expressions, tone of voice, and even how we stand or sit have their own messages. Sometimes these nonverbal messages enrich verbal ones—a joke told aloud with appropriate gestures and expressions is usually funnier than one read from a book, and a spoken avowal of love, again with appropriate gestures and expressions, is likely to be more successful than the same words sent as a valentine. Furthermore, nonverbal cues "say" some things better than words ever can. There are times when a hug is more comforting than a verbal expression of sympathy. The language of gestures, expressions, and behaviors is especially important in conveying emotion, affect, and information about social relationships. In addition, nonverbal behaviors play an important role in regulating verbal communication such as conversations.

What do nonverbal behaviors mean? There is no easy answer to this. Some nonverbal behaviors, called **emblems** by Johnson, Ekman, and Friesen (1975), are gestures with fairly concrete and stable meaning within a given culture. Gestures signalling "sit down," "stop," and various obscene messages are examples. However, except for such emblems, there are generally no one-to-one dictionary correspondences between nonverbal behaviors and their meanings. That should be no surprise; meanings of words change depending on contextual factors, and matters are no different with nonverbal behaviors. In a sense, we all have a dictionary of the range of meanings a nonverbal cue may have, but the precise meaning is determined by the situational and

Some gestures have a clear meaning.

verbal context. Consider the smile. Our nonverbal dictionary tells us that smiles generally reflect pleasure, but the specific pleasure may derive from a humorous incident, sexual feelings, a good mood, an overture of friendship, a reaction to approval, encouragement, a social greeting, or even sadistic delight in hurting someone. The verbal, situational, and other behavioral contexts will determine which kind of pleasure is signalled by the smile.

Interpretations of nonverbal cues are sometimes affected by duration and intensity of display. A small amount of eye contact indicates shyness or embarrassment, larger amounts show liking, and larger amounts still (as with staring) convey hositility. Absence of smiling shows unhappiness, moderate amounts of smiling convey pleasure, and prolonged smiling suggests lunacy.

The study of nonverbal behaviors is far younger than the study of verbal behaviors, and there is still much to be learned. However, the general outlines are fairly clear, and we can turn to a consideration of various classes of nonverbal behaviors. In this chapter we will be concerned with three kinds of nonverbal behavior: (1) *paralanguage,* the *way* something is said rather than *what* is said, (2) *proxemics,* which is the use of space and touch to convey messages, and (3) *body language,* including gestures, posture, eye contact, and facial expressions.

PARALANGUAGE

Paralanguage refers to such vocal behaviors as rate of speech, pitch of voice, hesitations, and silences—speech without the words. Many of these paralinguistic features are affected by stress or strong emotion. For example, speech disturbances such as hesitations are more common under anxiety conditions (Cook, 1969; Mahl & Schulze, 1964). When people lie, their pitch rises (Streeter et al., 1977). Emotional states such as anger or fear lead to a higher voice pitch and greater variability in pitch. Thus, observers often infer lying, nervousness, and aroused emotional states from higher voice pitch and increased speed of talking (Apple & Hecht, 1982; Apple, Streeter, & Krauss, 1979). On the other hand, sorrow leads to lower and less variable pitch.

PROXEMICS

Distance is an important aspect of social relationships. Metaphorically, I might say that a person is "close to me" even though he literally is 5,000 miles away. I may also tell someone who bothers me to "stay out of my hair" or the person who tries to be too intimate to "keep your distance." The anthropologist Edward Hall (1959, 1966) has suggested that distance is not mere metaphor, however. He was particularly struck by cultural differences in how close people stand while in conversation. For example, Americans tend to feel that people ought to stand about two or three feet apart when talking, but Arabs feel more comfortable conversing at a distance of inches, practically nose to nose. The study of messages conveyed by distance cues is called proxemics.

Personal Space   Although Hall's hypotheses about cultural differences in preferred interaction distance have been only partially confirmed (Hayduk, 1983), another of his ideas has received substantial support. He proposed that distance is a cue for intimacy, and therefore we should regulate our distances from others according to how close we feel to them. Research supports this basic idea. We do stand or sit closer to people we like (Heshka & Nelson, 1972) and farther away from strangers (Becker, 1973). Nonhandicapped people also tend to keep their physical distance from handicapped people (Comer & Piliavin, 1972; Kleck et al., 1968), presumably because interactions with the handicapped are somewhat uncomfortable for the nonhandicapped.

We all have an envelope of two to three feet around us, called a **personal space,** which we prefer relative strangers not to enter. When others violate this space, we show discomfort, stress, and physiological arousal (Evans, 1978). The person who violates the personal space is also uncomfortable (Efran & Cheyne, 1974). This you can demonstrate for yourself. Just sit next to someone on a nearly empty bus or stand very close to a person to whom you are talking. You will discover that not only do you feel anxiety doing this, but the other person also shows visible signs of discomfort and often hostility.

Territoriality   Members of many animal species keep other animals away by trying to maintain territorial boundaries. There have been some suggestions that humans are also territorial animals. Certainly we tend to manufacture spatial boundaries between what is ours and what is not. Even in public places we mark off space for our temporary but exclusive use, and we expect others to respect these boundaries. We might, for example,

The man on the left is leaning back slightly, in part as a reaction to a violation of his personal space.

claim an unoccupied table at a crowded cafeteria by piling coats and books on it while we stand in the food line. We would probably be annoyed or upset if someone chose to ignore our territorial claim and sit at "our" table in our absence. Personal items left as territory markers are generally effective in keeping others away. Interestingly enough, when a person leaves such personal markers, the person sitting in the next chair will act to defend the marked space against an invader even if he does not know the person who was sitting next to him (Sommer & Becker, 1969).

People also stand close to or touch items they want to mark for their personal use (Werner, Brown, & Damron, 1981). It is one of the social world's minor comedies to watch someone waiting to use an occupied phone in a public place. She must stand close enough to ward off others who also want to use it, but not so close as to seem to invade the privacy of the person already talking on the phone. Typically all this will be communicated by impatient behaviors (amplifying the message that "the phone is mine next") accompanied by looks of studied indifference, as if to say, "I couldn't be less interested in your conversation." The use of touch to communicate ownership reaches perhaps its fullest manifestation at department store sales, where people try to claim temporary ownership of as many sales items as possible through touch and grasp.

Touch   Touch is probably the most basic of all nonverbal intimacy cues. Parent's initial communication with their children is largely through touch, and the classic research by Harlow (1962) suggests that baby monkeys (and probably human infants as well) seek warm, cuddly mothers or mother surrogates. As we grow older, touch remains the primary way we have of communicating warmth, reassurance, and love. People touch one another more when they are in an intimate relationship (Heslin & Boss, 1980).

Henley (1977) has argued that touch also carries status and dominance overtones, so that it is more likely that adults touch children, bosses touch their workers, and men touch women. However, research does not strongly support this interesting hypothesis (Stier & Hall, 1984). Nevertheless, while there are powerful social norms about who can touch whom on what parts of the body (Jourard, 1968), touch is a subtle cue. It is still possible that status (particularly gender) differences in touching occur, but only for particular kinds of touching.

BODY LANGUAGE

Eye Contact   The idea of body language has been popular in recent years, and many have claimed that the body reveals secret messages. There is a particularly rich lore about eyes and their role in communication. We supposedly gaze fondly at those we love, look downcast when ashamed, and look the other in the eye when confident or honest. More metaphorically, eyes can be bashful, roving, even evil. Social psychologists have not yet found support for the evil eye, but they have isolated several more prosaic functions of gaze and eye contact.

In the first place, eye contact serves an affiliative or intimacy function. For example, eye contact is greater among those who like to be with others (Exline, 1963); it occurs at particularly high levels with those we like (Exline & Winters, 1965) and love (Rubin, 1970). However, as with other nonverbal behaviors, the interpretation of eye contact depends heavily on its context, intensity, and amount. For example, too much looking, what we usually call staring, is most often perceived as hostile (Ellsworth, Carlsmith, & Henson, 1972).

Eye contact also has dominance and respect properties. It is considered polite to look at people when they are talking (although in many cultures young people are taught not to make eye contact with older adults), and people tend to look at others more when listening than when they are talking themselves. However, high-status people seem to convey their power by looking at others more when they talk and less when they listen than do low-status people (Ellyson, Dovidio, & Fehr, 1981).

Eye contact is important in initiating and regulating interactions among people. Gazing at another is often a signal that communication is possible; for example, we try to get the attention of waiters and salespeople by locking in on their eyes. Hitchhikers seem also to feel that making eye contact with passing motorists improves their chances of being picked up. Eye contact even plays a role in traffic jams. If you are determined to cut another person off and wish to signal that fact, you will studiously stare straight ahead and refuse to make eye contact with him or her.

Smiles Smiles can be ambiguous nonverbal behaviors. There are smiles of derision, comfort, joy, sarcasm, sexual fulfillment, and even embarrassment. However, there are probably two major classes of smiles: we smile when we are happy and we smile when we want to communicate a positive social message such as "I like you." Research by Kraut and Johnston (1979) suggests that smiles may be more often social than emotional displays. For example, bowlers are only slightly more likely to smile after a strike than a nonstrike, but they smile more when other people are present. And smiles are effective social cues of warmth, understanding, and encouragement (Brunner, 1979). This does not suggest that people do not smile when happy, but it does suggest that smiling can be more a social behavior than a manifestation of inner joy.

Gestures Most people gesture a great deal when they talk. Indeed some of us would feel very uncomfortable if we were forced to carry on a conversation with our hands tied behind us. McNeill (1985) has argued that gestures, like words, have an inherent order, a complex system of meanings—what we might call a grammar. In fact, he argues that gestures and words mutually support one another in the communication enterprise, each class helping to structure meaning for the other.

McNeill notes several kinds of frequently used gestures. Some gestures give pictorial support to the verbal message. For example, a person may raise her hands if she is talking about something going up or may subtly shape with her hands an object she is discussing. Other gestures include manual representation of more abstract meanings, such as placing the hands as if to support something when one is talking about emotional support. In addition, there are gestures used to comment on the verbal messages. For example, the speaker might make a circular motion of the hands as if to say this part of her commentary repeats what was stated before—the gestural equivalent of

We use a language of gestures to help explain some things.

et cetera. Gestures also have important roles to play in the regulation of conversations, which we will discuss shortly.

CUES IN COMBINATION

Up to now, we have discussed the various nonverbal cues one at a time. We have seen that each of us can communicate a variety of messages, depending on the context and intensity of our display, so there are many ways to convey our liking or disliking, our interest or disinterest in another person. Therefore, another way to approach nonverbal behavior is to examine the message itself and try to determine how people manage to communicate specific feelings through *combinations* of cues.

For example, messages of dominance and status are central to everyday life and are often communicated almost entirely nonverbally. Of course, you do not need nonverbal cues to know that the average student has lower status than the average professor, and you will likely know who is boss when you enter your doctor's office. However, many situations are not so culturally structured, and the people who seem to dominate others in those situations will do so largely through nonverbal cues.

Higher-status and dominant people behave differently than their lower-status and less dominating fellows. The highly dominant people tend to touch more than they are touched (Leffler, Gillespie, & Conaty, 1982); to sit higher, stand rather than sit, and stand in front rather than behind the other (Schwartz, Tesser, & Powell, 1982); to talk more and interrupt the other more (Leffler et al., 1982); to claim a larger physical space (Leffler et al., 1982); to act more presumptuously by restating the comments of the other and by issuing commands (Cansler & Stiles, 1981); and to maintain more eye contact while talking and less while listening (Dovidio & Ellyson, 1982). This is merely a sample of nonverbal cues for dominance (see Edinger & Patterson, 1983, for a fuller discussion), but even this sample suggests not only that dominance is communicated in various ways, but also that many of these cues may substitute for one another.

Suppose you want to play down your status or dominant position. You might have a tough time doing that, because there are so many ways others might infer what you are trying so hard to hide. When I am trying to encourage informal talk with a student, I might sit with him in front of my desk and be very careful not to interrupt him or touch him. But despite my deliberate attempts to eliminate nonverbal cues of dominance, it is likely that I will still convey some of my culturally defined higher status, such as through my gaze or by restating and clarifying what he is saying. It is difficult to control all of our nonverbal behaviors consciously toward a particular end.

EMOTIONAL EXPRESSION

Nonverbal behaviors communicate approval, liking, intimacy, dominance, and other social messages. Emotions are another large category of messages we need to explore. We may or may not talk about our feelings, but our expressive behaviors are surely the most important ways we have of telling others what we are feeling.

Accuracy of Judging Emotion   Charles Darwin (1872) postulated that human emotional expressions evolved from more primitive behaviors shown by animals. For example, our facial expressions of anger look something like the anger shown by dogs and other carnivores. We cannot directly prove Darwin's theory, but there are implications that can be tested empirically. If human emotional expressions have an evolutionary basis, they ought to be universal across human cultures. Furthermore, because it would seem strange that millions of years of development of behavioral tendencies would occur without corresponding abilities to recognize these basic and universal behaviors, we ought to be able to recognize what emotion someone (even from another culture) is experiencing just by looking at that person, especially his or her face.

The ability to recognize emotional expression was an early research problem for psychology. Surprisingly, much of the early research suggested that people could not recognize emotions accurately. But if this were literally true, you would have trouble knowing what your friends are feeling and we would be eternally puzzled by plays and movies, because actors could use only words to tell us what they were feeling.

It is now clear that we can accurately perceive basic emotional expressions (Ekman, Friesen, & Ellsworth, 1972; Schneider, Hastorf, & Ellsworth, 1979), even cross-culturally (Ekman & Friesen, 1971). Sophisticated measurement techniques have shown that there are standard muscular movements associated with major emotional categories. Sometimes these are so subtle and fleeting that ordinary observers cannot catch them, but they can be captured by sensitive measurement devices (Cacioppo, Petty, Losch, & Kim, 1986; McHugo et al., 1985). Thus, Darwin's original

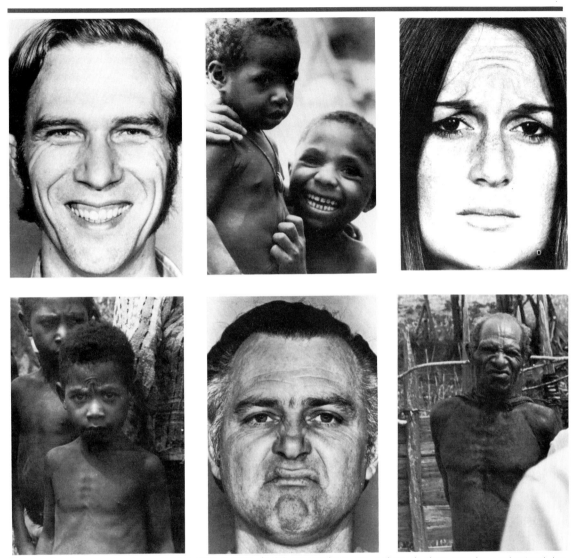

Cross-cultural research demonstrates that certain facial expressions are universal: they can be understood by anyone, regardless of cultural background.

claim seems to be vindicated: there are standard facial expressions associated with basic emotions, and people can recognize them.

Individual Differences   Although we can all express and infer emotions, some people can express and/or infer emotions better than other people can. Some people seem to wear their hearts on their sleeves, while others are inscrutable, poker-faced, or simply look confused. Some of us seem to have uncanny abilities to know what others are feeling, while others of us seem more limited in this regard.

Research confirms individual differences in abilities both to express emotions and to decode or interpret them accurately (Buck, 1984). Perhaps the most stable correlate of these abilities is gender. Females communicate their emotions more accurately than men (Hall, 1979; Rosenthal & DePaulo, 1979) and, within a given gender, those who are more feminine are also better able to portray what they are feeling (Zuckerman, DeFrank, Spiegel, & Larrance, 1982). Women also are generally more accurate at inferring emotions than are men (Hall, 1978).

INCONSISTENCIES AMONG VERBAL AND NONVERBAL BEHAVIORS

Often—perhaps usually—verbal and non-verbal channels support one another. Your disgust at an accident, anger at the umpire's decision, or joy at getting a good grade will most often be communicated both by what you say and how you behave. Nonetheless, there are circumstances in which the two types of behaviors "say" different things. For example, following Freud, many psychotherapists have made much of the possibility that the unconscious speaks through errors and mannerisms that belie a person's verbal statement. And our folk wisdom generally supports the notion that nonverbal cues that are inconsistent with the verbal message convey lying. For example, many people believe that a liar cannot look you in the eye, that liars will sweat and stammer and generally appear nervous when the verbal statement would imply no reason for nervousness. Is this correct? Do people give away their lies through nonverbal behaviors?

In most of the relevant research, people are asked to answer questions or describe their feelings either truthfully or deceitfully as they are videotaped. The psychologist then can determine what sorts of behaviors differentiate the honest and dishonest communicators. However, even if objective differences emerge, we cannot be certain that ordinary people attend to these cues or make optimal use of them. Therefore, to determine which cues are used, the tapes are usually shown to subjects

who are asked to discriminate the honest and dishonest communicators. Often it is helpful in such research to show the subjects only a part of the behavior of the communicators. For example, a subject might see only the body or only the face of the communicator. Indeed it is possible to present subjects with just about every combination of verbal, paralinguistic, facial, and bodily cues.

First, consider what kinds of nonverbal behaviors actually predict lying. Liars tend to use a higher voice pitch (Ekman, Friesen, & Scherer, 1976; Krauss, Geller, & Olson, 1976); to have nervous hands (Ekman et al., 1976); to give shorter answers with more hesitations and "ums" (Kraut, 1978); to have more negative-looking faces (Zuckerman et al., 1979); and to provide verbal messages perceived to be more ambiguous and tense (DePaulo, Rosenthal, Green, & Rosenkrantz, 1982). Contrary to popular belief, liars do not seem to have trouble making eye contact (Bond, Kahlar, & Paolicelli, 1985; Riggio & Friedman, 1983).

Second, now consider what use everyday people make of these and other cues. People can discriminate truthful from deceitful communications (Zuckerman, DePaulo, & Rosenthal, 1981), although they are far from perfectly accurate. Generally, we use many of the cues that are objectively related to lying, but we do not make optimal use of them, and we often use cues that are poor indicators of lying, such as lack of eye contact. This may produce errors of judgment. For example, facial animation is used by most people to infer truthfulness, even though it does not empirically predict either lying or truth telling. Thus, extroverted people, who tend to be animated, might be judged to be honest simply because of this irrelevant behavioral style (Riggio & Friedman, 1983).

Ekman and Friesen (1969) have argued that most people can control their facial expressions even when lying but are less able to control their bodily behavior, presumably because they have their cognitive hands full controlling the verbal lie and their faces quite apart from their bodies. Ekman and Friesen propose that lies might more readily leak forth in body behavior, and therefore we might be more accurate in judging lying if we concentrate on the communicator's body. This **leakage hypothesis** has been widely supported (Ekman & Friesen, 1974; Zuckerman, Kernis, Driver, & Koestner, 1984). However, even though the face and vocal cues may be less rich in deceit information, deception can also be judged from these areas (Zuckerman et al., 1984).

SUMMARY

Like words, nonverbal cues typically do not have narrowly restricted and well-defined meanings. The interpretation of such cues is affected by social, situational, and verbal contexts. The intensity and duration of many important cues, such as smiling and eye contact, also affect their meaning. In some cases, nonverbal cues support one another and can substitute for one another. So liking or dominance, for example, can be displayed by smiles, posture, eye contact, and other cues, either singly or in combination. At other times, these cues conflict, either with each other or with verbal messages, which may lead us to mistrust the verbal messages. At some level we are aware of this and we usually try to control our nonverbal behaviors when we try to deceive others with verbal statements. However, people are often very good at interpreting nonverbal displays and at detecting deception from nonverbal cues, especially from the body rather than the face.

INFORMAL COMMUNICATION

The many forms of communication range from the casual conversation to a formal speech, from the phone conversation to the class presentation, from the note to a friend to an international treaty. When we consider groups and social influence (Chapters 10 and 11), we will discuss formal modes of communication, which are typically marked by explicit rules about who says what to whom in what ways. However, for the moment let us concentrate on more informal communication settings, where most of us spend most of our time. The face-to-face or telephone conversation is the prototypic example of informal communication. As with formal communication, there are a great many norms and rules about the processes of informal communication, but these are typically implicit and not formally articulated; they tend to be matters of politeness rather than formal policy.

Informal communication typically involves both verbal and nonverbal messages. In this section we will emphasize how nonverbal behaviors help to regulate the course of informal verbal interchanges. Your facial expressions and paralinguistic cues convey their own messages about your feelings, whether you are lying, and the like, but they also help the verbal conversation to move along smoothly.

LANGUAGE STYLES

There are many ways, or styles, to communicate the same message. "Come here," "Get in here," "Could you please come over here?" and a wave of the hand all communicate roughly the same command, although at the purely linguistic level they differ in many ways. Moreover, each of the phrases could be said in different ways to convey a more or less imperious tone. Even waves of the hand have different styles. So let us consider some of the determinants of our styles of speaking.

Target and Situation Effects   Surely you do not speak the same way to your professors as to your close friends. With your professor you probably use less slang, talk in more complete sentences, use bigger words, and employ a more respectful vocal tone. And if you want to press the case, most professors talk differently to one another than to their students. People also say different things in different ways to children and adults, and even children alter the speech patterns for different classes of adults and children (Giles & Powesland, 1975). Indeed this may persist seemingly forever. Most adults at least occasionally resent the fact that their parents still talk to them as if they were children.

You can generally tell fairly quickly whether two people have a formal or informal, intimate or nonintimate, pleasant or unpleasant relationship by what they say and how they say it. There are powerful, although largely implicit, norms that govern all this. Not only do you talk differently to your minister and your best friend, but you are aware that you are *supposed* to do so.

The most obvious way this is displayed is in terms of address (Brown & Ford, 1961; Kroger, 1982). People who are on intimate terms with one another generally use first names or sometimes nicknames. One is supposed to address people of higher status by formal title and last name, whereas those of lower status are almost always called by their first names or no name at all. So in a university, professors are usually addressed as "Dr. Davis" or "Professor Peters," whereas students and secretaries are called "Jim" or "Hazel." My physician calls me "David," and try as I might I cannot quite get up the courage to call him "Carl." Some languages, such as German, make these status relationships even more explicit by having differing pronouns for differing degrees of intimacy (just as in English *thou* once indicated a more intimate relationship and *you* a more formal relationship).

Situations also have a role to play in all this. The president of my university prefers to be addressed as "Dr." in faculty and committee meetings, but he seems more relaxed about this in more informal circumstances. An adult student who gladly calls me "Dr. Schneider" in class may wonder how she should address me at a PTA meeting, where first names are almost universal.

Communicator Variables   Our language styles are powerfully affected by our region of the country, race, ethnic group, social class, and gender. Some of these differences are slight. For example, in New England I order a *hamburg* and *frappe* (or *tonic*), but in Texas I order a *hamburger* and *milkshake* or *soda*. But sometimes the differences are more profound. Black English differs grammatically from Standard American English, which also differs from British English. Tex-Mex Spanish spoken in South Texas is different from Spanish spoken in Southern California, and both of these differ dramatically from the Spanish spoken south of the border and even more from Castilian Spanish spoken in Spain.

There are also social class differences in communication patterns. For example, lower-class people tend to use a more restricted code (Bernstein, 1967) with fewer different adjectives and adverbs, fewer passive verbs, and more personal pronouns than middle-class people, who use a more elaborate code. However, these differences are not large (Higgins, 1976).

Functions of Language Styles   Although linguists are inclined to stress the proposition that one way of speaking is not inherently superior to another (Hudson, 1980), most lay people do not share that assumption. There is ample evidence that some ways of speaking are valued more than others (Giles & Powesland, 1975). For example, in Great Britain the English spoken by the upper classes is considered superior to Welsh-, Scottish-, or Irish-accented speech, as well as to the various lower-class accents. French-accented speech in Montreal (Lambert, 1967) and Spanish-accented speech in the southwestern United States (Ryan & Carranza, 1975) have been considered inferior. White people generally evaluate speakers of black English negatively (McKirnan, Smith, & Hamayan, 1983).

Of course, a great deal depends on who is doing the evaluating. New Englanders look down on Texas accents, while Texans reciprocate this sentiment. In the case of ethnic group accents and ways of speaking, it is hardly surprising—given other evidence of discrimination—that people in the dominant culture reject those whose language indentifies them as a part of a minority. Yet some studies find members of the minority also evaluate their own language negatively (Ryan & Carranza, 1977). This is surely no accident, because members of minority groups receive massive amounts of socialization from schools and the media to promote the dominant language at the expense of the minority language. For example, in San Antonio, which has a majority Hispanic population, there are many Hispanic television reporters, but few of them speak English with a highly noticeable Spanish accent. Given this kind of example, even parents who value their own culture may encourage their children to use standard forms of English to get ahead (Edwards, 1979).

Our speech styles clearly are powerful cues for status, power, competence, and education, whether these inferences are fair or not. Then why don't we all try to talk like New York bankers? One obvious and important reason is that many people do not care enough about status to imitate the speech mannerisms of the rich and influential. But a more interesting reason is that our ways of using language are components in our ethnic, racial, and regional cultures. Texans talk like Texans rather than Bostonians in part because they are proud to be Texans. Jews use Yiddish expressions and Hispanics use Spanish words partly to provide salient contacts with rich cultural heritages and partly to distinguish themselves from a dominant culture that seeks homogenization. Culture surely involves language, and it is no surprise that distinctive language patterns persist when people seek to preserve cultural identities (Fishman, 1977).

An extreme form of the use of language to preserve ethnic identity is reported by Grumperz and Wilson (1971), who studied a small (population 3,000) village in India and found three mutually incomprehensible languages in use, each by a different caste. Some people spoke more than one of the languages, of course, yet it is still interesting that people living closely together have maintained caste-based languages over several centuries as a way of reaffirming identities. In an experimental demonstration, Bourhis and Giles (1977) had subjects in a Welsh-language class hear a speech that suggested that the Welsh language is dying. The subjects had stronger Welsh accents after hearing the speech, probably because the speech strengthened the stubjects' Welsh ethnic identity.

Slang is also important in reinforcing group identities. College students, drug users, musicians, gamblers, bureaucrats, and college professors, among many others, all have their specialized languages. These languages include various jargon and slang terms that undoubtedly aid communication, but also build a sense of solidarity and fence off outsiders. For example, slang terms used by college students tend to persist about two to four years, and I would guess that as their use filters out into the general population (especially into high school groups), new terms have to be invented to preserve the relatively more-sophisicated college identity. Slang and jargon can also be used to impress outsiders. McNeill (1966) has shown, for example, that the use of long, imposing space terms by NASA officials is more common in lay-oriented publications than in internal NASA documents.

Language styles are thus important parts of our group identities and also affect how we react to others and they to us. It is understandable that debates about bilingual education and making English the official language of our society are intense. More, much more, than language is involved. How we speak tells us and others who we are.

COMMUNICATION ACCURACY

Verbal language and nonverbal behavior have many functions, but the central function is the accurate transmitting of information. But being able to describe something accurately to another is not merely a matter of using the proper words and gestures. In the give and take of informal communication, it is often as important to know what *not to* say as to know what *to* say. For example, if you were trying to tell someone who is unfamiliar with your campus how to get from your classroom to the library, you could provide too much information. Suppose you said, "Walk out the door and take four large steps, then turn right. Walk twelve steps then turn left. Then . . ." —clearly the stranger would never get to the library.

Therefore you would probably try to give a more abstract set of directions. To do so you would have to have a pretty good cognitive map of the campus that you could translate into the language of turns, distances, and landmarks. You would have to make some assumptions about what the visitor already knew. If she were familiar with the campus slang, you might say "Turn left at MemChu," but otherwise you might be better off saying something like "You will come to a church called Memorial Church. Turn left there." You would also try to avoid idiosyncratic references. "Turn left at the ugly building where I took biology" might help you, but it wouldn't help someone who did not share your experiences.

Public versus Private Languages   The latter point is important. We often code things and events in terms of a private language. However, while saying that someone looks like Sam Smith in your hometown is a highly efficient way of coding the person for yourself,

it will hardly help someone who does not know who Sam Smith is. To communicate well you must use words with public rather than purely private meanings.

In one study (Krauss, Vivekananthan, & Weinheimer, 1968), subjects were given several colors. Some subjects were asked to describe the colors so they could recognize them later (nonsocial coding), others so that another person could recognize them (social coding). These descriptions were then shown to self and others who tried to pick out the correct colors. Subjects were most accurate when they used their own descriptions, regardless of whether they were social or nonsocial (see Table 6.1). The second highest level of accuracy was with the social codings provided by others; subjects were least accurate with nonsocial codings others had provided for themselves. Of course, in our actual conversations, the feedback we get from our listeners helps us speak a mutually understandable language by coordinating what we say with what our listeners need to know (Kraut, Lewis, & Swezey, 1982.

Development of Communication Skills It has long been recognized that young children use idiosyncratic languages and only

TABLE 6.1 MEAN PROPORTION OF CORRECT IDENTIFICATIONS IN THE SIX DECODING CONDITIONS. *Note that subjects are most accurate at identifying colors when using their own descriptions, regardless of social or nonsocial coding, and that they are better with socially coded than nonsocially coded descriptions provided by others.*

Original Encoding Condition	Decoding of Messages Encoded by		
	Self	Other: Social	Other: Nonsocial
Social	.74	.62	.58
Nonsocial	.74	.62	.54

SOURCE: Krauss, Vivekananthan, and Weinheimer, 1968.

gradually learn to use the more public forms during communication (Piaget, 1958; Vygotsky, 1962). Children also have some problems in taking the perspectives of others (see Chapter 9), which further reduces their abilities to use public language. They often do not realize they are not communicating well.

Consider an experiment by Glucksburg, Krauss, and Weisberg (1966). Children were asked to describe designs to someone who could not see them. Children who were 4–5 years of age were almost totally unsuccessful at this task. Other children could not use their descriptions to pick the correct design. One gets some feeling for the idiosyncracy of description when we realize that a single figure was described by five children as "man's legs," "airplane," "drapeholder," "zebra," and "flying saucer."

Children will have trouble with this kind of communication task because of their inability to evaluate the adequacy of their own messages and to utilize feedback from their errors (Asher, 1979). However, the major problem children (and many adults) have in this type of task is a failure to use words that have a clear, culturally defined meaning. A child who uses a private language to explain things to others will have trouble communicating, as will a professor who lectures to undergraduates in the esoteric jargon of his or her profession.

CONVERSATION

Although we communicate with others in many ways, the prototypic form of informal communication is the conversation. It may seem at first that there is nothing special or interesting about conversations. One person speaks, the other answers, and so it goes. However, if things were that simple, why is it that some people are so much better at the art of conversation than others? Good conversationalists are often amusing and witty, but they also seem to possess special skills such as

the ability to keep from monopolizing the conversation and to use nonverbal cues to enliven the conversation without being distracting. This art is not easily learned. Adults engage children in conversation from an early age, giving them implicit and sometimes explicit lessons in such conversational graces as relevancy, turn-taking, and verbal facility (Clark & Clark, 1977).

Implicit Meanings Consider the following conversation between me (DJS) and a student (RT):

RT: I got it.
DJS: Good. Did you have any problems?
RT: You mean besides having to wait forever?
DJS: That doesn't even count anymore.
RT: Not to you, it doesn't.
DJS: I don't get paid to wait.
RT: What do you get paid for?
DJS: Dealing with obnoxious students, I guess.

As you read this brief part of a longer conversation, you may be struck by several things. In the first place, you probably don't have any idea what the converstion is about. What did the student get? "It" is hardly informative to you, but it was to us. Second, the conversation has many loose ends. RT never answers the question about whether he had any problems, but redirected the conversation to a seemingly unrelated topic. Yet neither he nor I had any problems with the transition. Third, from merely reading the conversation you get little sense of its tone. On the face of it, there seems to be a fair amount of hostility toward the end, but the words are not entirely clear. For example, did I mean the reference about obnoxious students to apply to RT? How do you know whether I did or not?

Most conversations take place in incomplete sentences with pronouns (such as "it") and other terms of dubious reference. In this case the "it" was a tape recorder the student had tried to get. When I asked RT whether he had problems, he clearly understood that I meant to ask about getting the recorder and not about, say, his financial situation. But he did not answer the question as if it were really a question (and it really wasn't—I asked it more from politeness than genuine interest in his problems). He therefore felt free to ignore the literal request for information and used the opportunity to tell me that he had to wait, although he phrased this as a question ("You mean besides having to wait forever?"). By not answering my question, he made it clear that there had been no major problems; by asking a question of his own, he made clear his irritation at having had to wait. When I replied that "that [waiting] doesn't count anymore," I conveyed that I understood his implied meaning.

The real change in the conversation took place when RT commented (with a broad smile) that waiting doesn't count to me. His voice and smile conveyed that he did not want to be taken as hostile—which would otherwise be a possible interpretation of his comment. The import of the remark is clearer if you know that the last time we needed a tape recorder I had waited with him, but this time I had asked him to get the recorder for me because I had some phone calls to make. In effect, then, his remark is a tease about my being too important to wait. He does not say this directly, but my reply indicated that I knew exactly what he was implying and that I accepted the tease by being willing to carry it forth. I affirmed his implicit accusation that I considered myself too important to wait, and his question (not really a request for information, of course) suggested that he felt comfortable enough to extend the tease. My reply about obnoxious students was clearly meant to apply to him as a way to assert my superior status and suggest that the game is over. He had no ready answer for the comment, and indeed his next comment was a quick return to business. However, all this had been accomplished with no hurt feelings, without even any explicit recognition that power games were being played.

The important point about all this is that there are multiple levels of meanings here (see Table 6.2 for a summary of the above analysis, which is only one of many possible analyses). At one level we were exchanging information, although the information was not always explicit. But much more was involved. There were implicit meanings about how RT and I were to take one another and what our relationship might be. As sociologist Erving Goffman has suggested, "what talkers undertake to do is not to provide information to a recipient, but to present dramas to an audience. Indeed, it seems that we spend most of our time not engaged in giving information but in giving shows" (Goffman, 1974, p. 508). Conversations are cooperative enterprises, but we also use them to tell ourselves and others what kinds of people we are. We converse to show our wit, our abilities, our knowledge. Moreover, conversations inevitably say something about interpersonal involvements (Goffman, 1963b). Every time we make appropriate responses to the other, whether it be an answer or a nod, we reaffirm both our involvement in the conversation and the implied worth of the other person. RT and I maintained our status relationships through the tone of the conversation, but we also reaffirmed the warmth we felt for one another and our comfort with one another. In addition, much of the conversation was involved with our making clear that we had understood one another, that we shared a common set of meanings.

Thus, conversations are implicitly "about" the mutual involvement and shared meanings of the conversationalists as well as about the explicit content of the conversations. Nonverbal cues are especially important in conversations. You are not supposed to yawn or glance at your watch in a conversation, because to do so would imply that you are not fully involved with matters at hand. Laughs, nods, tone of voice, and facial expressions are also used to communicate involvement as well as being

TABLE 6.2   IMPLIED MEANINGS OF CONVERSATIONAL INTERCHANGE.

Actual Comment	Implied Meaning
RT: I got it.	I got the tape recorder you asked me to get.
DJS: Good. Did you have any problems?	Did you have any specific problems getting the tape recorder?
RT: You mean besides having to wait forever?	I didn't have any problems, but the wait was a nuisance.
DJS: That doesn't even count anymore.	I understand your irritation, but it's not my problem.
RT: Not to you, it doesn't.	You told me to get the tape recorder because you had something you thought was more important to do. You are clearly too important to have to do mundane tasks, but I will tease you about that. (I am smiling, so don't take my remark as hostile.)
DJS: I don't get paid to wait.	You're quite right that I am more important than you are and far too important to wait. And I know you are not being hostile; I accept the tease.
RT: What do you get paid for?	You're being awfully nice about all this—letting me tease you and all. Let's see how far I can take this.
DJS: Dealing with obnoxious students, I guess.	You are in danger of stepping out of line. Let's be friends, but remember that I have the status and power here.

cues for what words mean. The nonverbal cues not only enhance (or contradict) the verbal message but also provide a kind of running commentary on the verbal conversation.

The Formal Structure   You do not ordinarily enter into verbal interchanges randomly. You have a purpose. But how do you start a conversation and negotiate its subject matter? During the course of the conversation, how do you determine what to say and make sure that you have the opportunity to say it without turning it into a monolog? How do you and your partner arrange to take turns in talking? When the conversation has run its course, how do you arrange to end it gracefully? You may never have posed these questions to yourself, because they deal with matters that seem simple, routine, and obvious, but matters are more complex than they seem.

Conversations may be initiated in many ways: the phone rings and you pick it up; the person across the room waves or tosses you

an inviting smile; someone bumps into you. If you follow our cultural rules, each of these situations could well lead to verbal interchanges, although some people are more adept at using nonverbal cues to initiate conversation than are others (Purvis, Dabbs, & Hopper, 1984). Conversations usually begin in a relatively low key with a fair amount of ritualized chatter ("How you gettin' along?" "Nice weather." "How's the family?"), and people who fail to heed the normal opening moves are often thought rude. Why do we seem to require greeting and opening ceremonies? One reason might be that conversations are time-consuming and require total involvement, at least ideally. Thus, we may take on this commitment gradually so that both people have the opportunity to break off before things get too heavy. This becomes especially clear when you have to speak to someone about an embarrassing or delicate topic; in that case you will probably ease into it gently.

Once the conversation begins, people take turns talking. It is considered rude to dominate a conversation, precisely because the dominator fails to provide evidence that he or she is involved with the other. It is also rule to interrupt or to talk while someone else is talking. If you listen carefully to conversations, you will find that although there are occasional interruptions, people are usually good about taking turns.

This turn-taking is regulated almost entirely by subtle cues. Some cues are purely linguistic: when a question is asked or a thought is completed, turn-taking is likely (Sacks, Schegloff, & Jefferson, 1974). But there are also nonverbal cues. Starkey Duncan and his colleagues have uncovered many of these cues through intensive analysis of videotaped conversations (Duncan, 1972; Duncan & Fiske, 1977). Typically, the speaker is assumed to have the floor until she gives some signal that she is about to relinquish her turn, and there are several ways this is done: (1) she may end a sentence with either rising or falling intonation; (2) she may drawl on the final syllable (or final stressed syllable) of the last word; (3) she may cease a

We often use nonverbal cues to regulate our verbal conversations.

hand gesture or relax a tensed hand; (4) she may use any of a number of meaningless expressions such as "you know" or "or something"; (5) there may be a drop in her pitch or loudness; and (6) she may finish a sentence.

When one or more of these cues are displayed, there is a tentative permission for others to speak. However, the permission is not automatic. The speaker may decide she wishes to continue. Or she may not fully understand the meaning of her own behavior, so although her behavior gives others permission to talk, she does not realize this and continues on. Increased hand gestures are often an important "cancelation cue" that overrides signals to the listener to begin talking. In general, however, the probability of the listener's talking is proportional to the number of turn-taking cues that the speaker presents (Duncan, Brunner, & Fiske, 1979).

It is important to note that although these cues give the listener permission to speak, they do not force him to. Even when as many as three cues are present, turn-taking takes place only about one-third of the time (Duncan et al., 1979). What happens the other two-thirds of the time? There may be a major pause, but usually the speaker continues to talk. However, the listener will often provide prompts to continue, such as nods, smiles, or an "un huh." Through the use of such prompts, the listener explicitly registers the offer of a turn and declines it. He also provides information that he is fully involved in the conversation and that he understands what the speaker is saying.

Of course, actual conversations are never quite so orderly, and the rules of conversation, like other social rules, work only part of the time. Sometimes there are interruptions or painfully long pauses in the conversation. Suppose that you were interrupted; how would you make sure that you got to finish what you were saying? Meltzer, Morris, and Hayes (1971) found that he who talks loudest generally wins the battle for the floor. In addition, the person who was already talking has an important advantage and can usually "win" if he talks at least as loudly as the interrupter.

As we indicated above, we typically ease into conversations, especially those with strangers, because they are so costly in terms of time and involvement. But given that a conversation is so involving, how can you break one off? If you listen to a conversation ending, you may discover that it is not so easy to end one. Long after everyone has said what needs to be said, there are a whole series of "I'll be seeing you." "OK," "See you then," "Take care," "Nice talking to you," and the like. Schegloff and Sacks (1973) argue that participants first have to agree that the conversation is over, something that may be easier said than done if one person wishes to continue. One way out is to claim the convenient press of circumstances. Mothers may say, "Gotta run, the kids are crying," and a business-woman may claim that the long-awaited call from Oshkosh is on hold on the other line. In face-to-face dialog, exaggerated scrutiny of one's watch with appropriate comments about pressing engagements will have to do. This does not always work, of course. Entertaining others in one's home is especially difficult in this regard; one can hardly plead pressing business to get rid of the guests who have overstayed their welcome when one has ostensibly set aside the evening for being with those guests.

However, assuming that both parties want to end the conversation, there are still matters to be negotiated. The problem comes from the dual nature of conversations: conversations are about some topic, but they are also about involvement and concern for others. Were you to break off a conversation abruptly at the conclusion of information exchange, you would be implying that the only reason for the conversation was your selfish need for information or amusement. Businesspeople are allowed to terminate conversations quite abruptly precisely because there is no pretense of

deeper involvements, and you can end a brief conversation with a salesperson quickly for the same reason. But were you to be so abrupt with a friend, his or her feelings would likely be hurt. So we slide out of our conversations with ritualized statements that communicate no real information about the content of the conversation, but speak volumes about mutual concern. Research confirms that leave-taking rituals are more complex among friends than strangers (Hornstein, 1985).

In a way, leave-taking rituals reaffirm that you like one another and wish the converstion could go on longer. This is why it is one of life's minor embarrassments to have to come back to a party you have left, say to retrieve a forgotten coat. Having spent five minutes at the door saying good-bye to the host and really saying nothing except that you like one another, it is now awkward to have to renegotiate all that again. And if you have ever had the experience of running into someone who is moving far away the day after you have said what you thought were your final farewells, you realize that there is literally nothing new to say and both of you will be embarrassed accordingly.

There are at least three central points to this extended (but far from complete) analysis of conversations. First, conversations, like other forms of social behavior, operate on several levels of meaning. In this discussion we have stressed the fact that conversations both communicate information and affirm involvement with and concern for the other person. Second, even communication as seemingly unstructured as a telephone conversation among friends has a structure, and the enforcer of this structure is generally a complex set of nonverbal cues. Third, although these conversational cues are subtle, complex, and largely implicit, they are well learned and are followed nearly automatically. One of the enduring mysteries of human psychology is how people can so readily learn and use the exquisitely complex linguistic rules that govern our understanding and production of words. Nowhere is this more apparent than when we consider speech production in informal conversation where the words flow without much conscious monitoring and where the give and take of participants follows cognitive and social rules most of us know well but cannot articulate.

SUMMARY

How we speak and the words we use are often affected by who our conversational partner is and what the situation is. Speech styles are powerful cues for relative status, education, and other situational variables. On the other hand, speech styles are also important components of regional, cultural, and other group identities, so many people may resist changing their speech styles even though their ways of speaking are disparaged by other groups. Communicating effectively with others involves mastering a number of normative and cognitive rules. One such rule is that we must use words to refer to public rather than private meanings to communicate accurately. Also, there are complex rules for beginning and ending conversations as well as for determining who talks when; these rules are largely governed nonverbally. One of the important normative features of informal communication is that, in addition to a specific topic of conversation, there is usually a range of implicit messages about dominance and concern for the other. Much of what is communicated, verbally or nonverbally, functions to maintain social relations.

CHAPTER SUMMARY

- Any behavior can convey meaning to others. Although we usually think of words as the primary vehicle for communicating meaning, our nonverbal behaviors, especially expressive gestures and facial expressions, also convey meaning.

- There are many goals of communication, including solving problems, persuading others, establishing social realities, maintaining social bonds, and presenting oneself in a favorable light.

- Early models of meaning focused on the idea that words refer to categories of objects and events. However, some words do not have clear referents in that sense, and other words refer only to loose collections of objects without a common set of defining characteristics. Recent approaches suggest that most categories are defined in terms of prototypic representations.

- Connotative meanings are affective and emotional reactions to words. Two words that refer to the same class of people or things may differ in their connotations.

- Modern psycholinguists typically emphasize the idea that words acquire part of their meaning from their context. This context can be situational, grammatical, or normative. The same word may have quite different meanings in different contexts, and may not even mean what it says literally. The grammatical forms of sentences often belie their true meanings.

- Whorf suggested that language determines thought. Early research suggested that salient words may make corresponding stimuli perceptually salient and more easily remembered, that is, that language shapes perception. However, more recent interpretations suggest that easily coded stimuli evoke commonly used words rather than the reverse, that is, that perceptions affect our selection of words.

- Nonverbal communication deals with several areas, but traditionally paralinguistics (how something is said), proxemics (use of space), and body language, including facial expressions, have received the most attention.

- Like words, most nonverbal behaviors do not have precise meanings but take on meaning from their situational and verbal contexts.

■ Paralinguistic cues such as speech hesitations and voice pitch are highly responsive to emotional states.

■ Most people prefer that others do not approach them too closely, although the preferred distance is larger for strangers and handicapped people. Violations of this personal space are uncomfortable.

■ Animals and, to a certain extent, people will defend marked territories. With humans, personal items are often used to mark territory in public places.

■ Touch is an intimacy cue and may also function as a dominance or status cue.

■ Frequent eye contact demonstrates positive affect, but also dominance and respect. It is also important in the regulation of conversation. Intense eye contact (staring) may signal hostility. Smiles may be more a social display than a sign of personal happiness. They are also important cues for positive regard for others.

■ Hand and body gestures have a grammar of sorts and often are used to support verbal messages. For many messages, such as love and dominance, several nonverbal cues alone or in combination may convey a given message.

■ People can recognize emotional expressions accurately, provided the expressions are clear and the judgment task requires identification of basic emotions.

■ Verbal and nonverbal cues usually support one another, although there may be times when one channel is used deliberately to change the meaning of the other. During deception, the nonverbal channels leak cues to deception. Such cues are especially prominent in the body as compared to the face or voice.

■ How people talk depends to some extent on whom they are talking to and in what situation. Language styles are important cues for status, but people who speak the less-valued styles may continue to do so in part because language styles are important parts of larger regional, cultural, and ethnic identities.

■ Communicating accurately depends on suppressing a private language in favor of one that is more public. Children in particular have trouble understanding that other people do not share their private references.

■ Conversations have multiple levels of meaning. One level is the explicit topic of the conversation, but other levels convey information about the relative statuses and mutual regard of the conversationalists.

■ Conversation requires many cognitive and social skills. One has to know how to start and end conversations as well as how to negotiate who talks and when turn-taking is appropriate. Much of this regulation is controlled by nonverbal cues.

CHAPTER

7

ATTITUDES

n my university, and perhaps in yours, students are given the opportunity to evaluate courses and instructors at the end of each semester. The forms that are used contain a number of questions about the beliefs of students (such as, "My professor seemed adequately prepared for class.") as well as more general attitudes (such as, "Compared to other professors, I would rate this one as much better than average, better than average, etc."). Student reactions to my courses are usually mixed. In some cases students differ in their beliefs. For example, in one recent class some students used the fact that I often lectured without notes as evidence for a belief that I was inadequately prepared for class, whereas others used the same evidence to conclude that I was well prepared. The same beliefs often lead to different attitudes. For example, several students commented on my illustrating central points with stories and real-world examples. Some felt that these stories were pointless, leading them to evaluate the course and me negatively. Others had positive attitudes, in part because they thought the stories added interest to the course. In everyday life as well as in university courses, people use the same evidence as support for differing beliefs and use similar beliefs to support differing attitudes.

Among the most successful commercials in recent years have been those for Miller Lite beer. These commercials are usually shown during weekend sporting events and largely involve sports heroes from the past arguing over whether the beer in question is to be preferred because it tastes better or because it is less filling. One remarkable feature of the ads is that no attempt is made to extol the virtues of the product in comparison to competing brands. Yet the ads have been effective in changing attitudes toward the beer and in affecting consumer buying habits. How and why?

Our attitudes affect our behavior in so many ways that they are frequently measured.

THE NATURE OF ATTITUDES

THE ORIGINS OF THE CONCEPT

Attitudes are evaluative reactions to persons, objects, and events. You not only have beliefs about courses and beers, for example, but you have positive or negative feelings about them. *Attitude* is probably the most widely used conceptual term in social psychology. It has a history of well over 50 years at center stage in the social psychology enterprise. Psychologists have long recognized that behavior is affected not so much by objective stimuli in the environment as by people's orientations to those stimuli. A college course can be a learning experience, a way to accumulate credits for graduation, a boring way to spend an hour, a long walk from your dorm, a place to meet other students, a place to hear good jokes, a requirement, or something that interferes with sleep—depending on how you approach it. So the term *attitude*, which originally meant (and still does) physical orientation or posture, was taken over by psychologists early in this century to suggest a mental orientation, a readiness to interpret the world in certain ways. In addition, during the early part of the century sociologists and anthropologists also needed a term that would reflect the internalization of culture and its effects on behavior. For these social scientists, *attitude* was used to refer to general, internalized dispositions to behave in certain ways. So attitudes have been seen as central because they both guide interpretations of our experiences and mediate the effects of experience on behavior.

THE THREE COMPONENTS

Most definitions of attitude have emphasized its cognitive, affective, and behavioral components. The *cognitive* component of attitude refers to what a person believes about something or a class of things. For example, some of my students believed that my not using lecture notes meant that I was unprepared for class. The *affective* component of attitude refers to emotional reactions, to how much you like or dislike the attitude object; in the opening example, some students liked the course while others did not. The *behavioral* component of attitude refers to how you are inclined to act toward the attitude object: you usually attend your class meetings or you are likely to recommend the course to a friend.

Research clearly shows that the cognitive (belief), affective, and behavioral components of attitude are distinct yet show moderate relationships with one another (Breckler, 1984), although there is presently lively debate about how distinct these components are (Chaiken & Stangor, 1987). You can easily imagine major inconsistencies. It is possible for you to like football even though you hate violence and believe football to be violent—the affective component of your attitude toward football does

not coincide with the cognitive component. Or you may fanatically follow a certain team's fortunes, but choose not to attend the games—in which case your behavior does not match the affective aspects of your attitude.

The relationships of the cognitive and affective components to the behavioral component are sufficiently complex that they will be treated separately in Chapter 8. How then are the cognitive and affective components related to each other? There are many possibilities (McGuire, 1985), but an influential position (Fishbein, 1967a) argues that beliefs (the cognitive component) in combination with evaluations (the affective component) lead to attitudes. In the opening example we informally discussed how different beliefs could give rise to different evaluations and hence different attitudes, but at this point, let us explore in some detail how beliefs and evaluations might combine to produce attitudes toward courses, in particular the social psychology course you are now taking. We could probably identify several beliefs about the course. For example, you may believe that (1) the course material is interesting, (2) the book is hard to read, (3)

Differing beliefs and values lead people to have quite different attitudes.

the professor is interested in her students, (4) the professor is a good lecturer, (5) the course will help you with other courses you want to take, and (6) you are likely to make a C in the course. Each of these beliefs contributes to your positive or negative evaluation of the course, depending on whether you believe the course helps or hinders your achievement of basic goals. If you value interesting courses, for example, your belief that this course is interesting, and that it therefore helps you achieve your goal of having interesting experiences, will lead you to evaluate the course positively. On the other hand, your belief that you will get a C means that the course will not help you achieve your goal of making good grades (if you consider only A's and B's to be good grades), and you will accordingly evaluate the course negatively on the basis of that belief. Also, each belief is more or less important to you; the belief that the book is hard to read may be less important to your general evaluation of the course than the belief that you will make a relatively poor grade. We could determine your general attitude toward the course by multiplying the strength or importance of each belief times its associated evaluation, and adding up all the results for all the beliefs. Table 7.1 shows one possible outcome.

There is empirical evidence that attitudes can be predicted from beliefs and evaluations in just this way (Fishbein & Ajzen, 1975). Thus, it is reasonable that people who believe abortion involves killing a human life and whose values indicate that killing is wrong will have negative attitudes toward abortion. Those who believe that the fetus is not yet human and who believe that abortions give women freedom to control their own destinies, something they value positively, will generally have more positive attitudes toward abortion.

It should be emphasized that this approach to attitude formation assumes that attitudes are products of a deliberate, rational series of cognitive processes. There is no room in such a model for pure "gut feelings." Other models, however, might place more emphasis on the affective component, independent from the cognitive (Zajonc, 1980). For example, the pride and enthusiasm that most people feel for their home town or college sports teams often seems not to be strongly based on a belief component.

ATTITUDE FORMATION

Many attitudes "feel" important. Each of us has several cherished attitudes toward friends, groups of people, family, spiritual orientation, government, and certain politicians that we could not easily imagine giving up or exchanging for others. Most of us are not afraid to speak our minds about these attitudes and we

TABLE 7.1   ORIGINS OF ATTITUDES TOWARD A COURSE.

Belief	Strength or Importance	Evaluation	Belief × Evaluation
Course material interesting	3	+2	+6
Books hard to read	1	−2	−2
Professor interested in students	2	+1	+2
Professor good lecturer	2	+2	+4
Course will be helpful	1	+3	+3
Likely to make a C grade	3	−3	−9
TOTAL ATTITUDE (sum of belief × evaluation)			+4

are often eager to find out what attitudes others hold. Several major industries conduct attitude surveys and thereby affect the TV programs we watch, what our cereal box looks like, and how our congressperson votes on important issues. What factors influence these important beliefs, evaluations, and attitudes?

Socialization   Perhaps the most obvious reason we hold the attitudes we do is because that's what we were taught. As we grow up, we are exposed to a limited range of attitudes and most parents try to make sure that their children have the "right" attitudes. It is no accident that the attitudes of parents and their children are fairly similar on a variety of political and religious issues even after the children have become adults (Jennings & Niemi, 1981), though as children get older their peers also help to steer them attitudinally.

Experience   Given that attitudes reflect combinations of beliefs and evaluations, we might ask how *experiences* affect the beliefs and evaluations we have. Consider beliefs. At one level, the development of beliefs is trivially easy to explain. The man who has just received his fifth dog bite of the week undoubtedly will believe that dogs bite. If your professor knows every student's name in a class of 250 and manages to see each for a conference during the semester, you will probably entertain the belief that she cares about students. We do, of course, have to keep in mind the lessons of Chapter 3—that beliefs are not always a faithful portrait of reality—but most of us find that reality unavoidably colors our beliefs considerably.

It is also fairly easy to explain the development of the affective component of attitudes. As we argued earlier, generally we like those things that promote the achievement of our goals and dislike those that inhibit our getting or doing things we want. Thus, my belief that dogs bark at night carries a negative evaluation because noise interferes with my goal of sleeping through the night. Your belief that getting an A in a course will help you get a

good job encourages a positive feeling about A's. It is important to realize that because people have different goals, they may also have different evaluations of objects even though they share the same beliefs. A defense contractor and a world-peace advocate may have the same belief that arms negotiation will reduce military expenditures, but have different evaluations of that outcome; we might expect the contractor to have a more negative attitude toward arms negotiations than the peace advocate does.

On the other hand, some—perhaps most—of our affective reactions are not based on such calculated reasoning. For example, Zajonc (1968) has shown that familiarity with objects leads to positive affect. You may come to like your room, car, dog, and professor just by being around them often. (Chapter 12 has an extended discussion of this phenomenon). Classical conditioning models also suggest that objects or events that are paired repeatedly with positive experiences are evaluated more positively than those associated with negative ones (Zanna, Kiesler, & Pilkonis, 1970). It would be hard to argue that the positive feelings most of us have for the moon spring from experiences in which the moon has helped us achieve goals. More than likely our positive feelings for the moon and moonlight result from, for example, associations with positively evaluated romance in song and fable.

Inferences from Behavior   In Chapter 6, we discussed the influential self-perception theory of Daryl Bem. Bem's perspective emphasizes that people infer their own internal states (such as attitudes) from their behavior when their prior attitudes are weak, nonsalient, or poorly organized—an emphasis confirmed by data from several experiments (Chaiken & Baldwin, 1981; Fazio, Chen, McDonel, & Sherman, 1982; Fazio, Herr, & Olney, 1984; Wood, 1982).

It is unlikely that you carry around with you well-formed and easily accessible attitudes toward every person you know or every object or situation you have encountered. Surely you cannot automatically remember whether you liked or disliked every course you have taken. If you were asked to give your attitude about your high school algebra class, nothing may come to mind at first. Then, as you think about specific experiences (you got a good grade, the teacher was as fun as math teachers ever are, you met the love of your high school life in the course), you may "calculate" that you must have liked the course; that is, you infer your attitude from your past behavior.

This is not to suggest that all or even most of your attitudes are formed on the spot. You probably don't need to think about past church attendance to come up with an attitude toward religion, and your attitude toward President Reagan is not formed anew each time you think about him. Some of our attitudes are well formed and salient and are not substantially affected by our behaviors.

Attitudes and Personality   It has long been an article of faith among psychologists that attitudes reflect personality dynamics. In one study (Adorno, Frenkle-Brunswick, Levinson, & Sanford, 1950), researchers developed measures of anti-Semitism and then conducted interviews with people identified through these measures as anti-Semitic. The general conclusion of the researchers was that people who hated Jews frequently also hated blacks and other minority groups. Furthermore, prejudiced attitudes were related to political conservatism, to preferences for structured social hierarchies where everyone knows his or her place, to beliefs that destiny is controlled by fate, and to strongly moral attitudes about sex—among other kinds of attitudes. This general cluster of attitudes made up what was called the **authoritarian personality**, which is conventionally measured by the **F-scale** (for potential *fascist*, to emphasize the personality similarities of authoritarians and followers of Hitler). The television character Archie Bunker was a perfect example of such an authoritarian personality.

Despite many problems with the research and criticisms of the F-scale, this kind of research has been historically important in drawing the attention of social psychologists to the intimate relations between attitudes and other aspects of personality. In particular, it is now apparent that attitudes fulfill many functions for people besides merely summarizing their experiences (Katz & Stotland, 1959; Smith, Bruner, & White, 1956). For example, some people hold negative attitudes toward others not because of particular bad experiences with those others, but as a way of making themselves feel good by comparison. Some people may be against abortion not because they or someone they know had a bad experience with abortion, but because their expression of disapproval is a way of reaffirming their religious commitments.

Generality and Stability   The attitude construct was originally introduced to provide an internal, stable, and general mediator between outside stimuli and behavioral responses. However, our attitudes differ in how general and stable they are. You may reasonably like college courses in general, dislike psychology courses, like the social psychology course you are taking, but dislike the social psychology course when the professor gives an exam. Thus, your attitudes toward college courses vary with how general the attitude object is.

In that light, it should not be surprising to find that a person who says he hates Jews may also get along famously with his Jewish neighbor. Our anti-Semite may like his neighbor because his beliefs about his neighbor (a specific attitude object) are positively evaluated, though at the same time he may have had fairly negative experiences with many other Jews (a general attitude object).

There are several reasons why it is important to consider the generality of attitudes. For one thing, if we want to predict specific behaviors, the more specific attitudes will work best. If we want to know how a person will react to his neighbor, then knowing his attitude toward his neighbor will predict his behavior better than knowing his attitude toward Jews in general.

It may also be easier to change specific attitudes than general ones. General beliefs are fairly far removed from concrete experience and may be difficult to change through single encounters with an attitude object. One unpleasant encounter with a student I do not know well may be enough to shift my attitude about that particular student from positive to negative, but it would not have much of an effect on my general attitude toward students, which is based on many, diverse encounters. Also, general beliefs may be hard to change because they are closely integrated with other important attitudes. The anti-Semitic man may have beliefs that he has never got ahead in life because Jews control the wealth in this country. We could present him with evidence that this is not true, but he may still be reluctant to change this belief because he would be forced to change other central beliefs about his self-worth and the nature of society. Sometimes, as in conversion experiences, we get a radical reorientation of several interrelated beliefs, but this is rare.

Most of our important attitudes are quite stable (Judd & Milburn, 1980). One reason for this stability is that we usually do not continually go through a systematic reanalysis of our fundamental beliefs. Rather, once we have established a particular attitude we store it in our memories separately from the particular beliefs, evaluations, and behaviors that gave rise to it initially (Lingle & Ostrom, 1981). We may originally have decided our attitude on abortion by thinking through all the pros and cons of the issue, but once the attitude is decided and stored, we may simply retrieve it without further thought or updating. Furthermore, we tend to interact with people who support our beliefs and attitudes, so that for many of our central attitudes there is strong social support and little reason to call the attitudes into question.

In addition, there are cognitive reasons for the stability of certain attitudes. In Chapter 3 we reviewed evidence that we process information in biased ways. You would not be surprised to discover that the militant atheist does not usually watch the local TV channel devoted to religious programming. You would also not be surprised to discover that he would reject the messages if he did happen to watch an evangelist some afternoon or that he might selectively remember what he had heard. Ironically, examples of attitude *change* help us see why attitudes are usually *stable*. Research shows that when people alter their attitudes, they also tend to alter their memories of past behaviors to be consistent with their new attitudes (Ross, McFarland, & Fletcher, 1981); such biased recall increases commitment to the new attitudes (Ross, McFarland, Conway, & Zanna, 1983). So the stability of attitudes, whether old or new, may be increased by selective or altered memory for those past behaviors consistent with the attitudes.

Complex attitudes toward general objects are similar to cognitive schemata in that they are constellations of beliefs and evaluations related in different ways. It would be rare that all the beliefs in a given complex attitude would point in the same evaluative direction. For example, cars can be alternatively a convenience or a nuisance, an object of pride or embarrassment, a handy mode of transportation or an instrument of mayhem and slaughter. Positive and negative elements can occur simultaneously: cars that appeal to me because they are inexpensive typically have fewer gadgets and less power than those that cost more. Furthermore, my attitude toward cars may change from day to day, not because of any fundamental change in my beliefs or evaluations, but because my experiences on any day might make salient—from among my cluster of beliefs and evaluations about cars— certain beliefs and evaluations but not others. My attitude toward cars is likely to be more negative on days when my car is in the repair shop than on days when it is running well.

Liberals as well as conservatives have constellations of related attitudes that serve many and diverse functions for the individual.

Attitudes, then, vary in how general as well as how stable they are. Some attitudes are based on quick assessments of our own behavior and may be easily changed as beliefs change with new experiences. Others are more general and are likely to be more stable because they are based on more experiences or because they have been formulated in ways that invite cognitive and social supports.

SUMMARY

Attitudes have cognitive (belief), affective (emotional), and behavioral components: most social psychologists emphasize the cognitive and affective components. One traditional approach suggests that an attitude is the total sum of the products of the importance of each belief about the attitude object (the cognitive component) times the evaluations of the outcomes of those beliefs (the affective com-

ponent). Generally, beliefs are based on our socialization, our experiences, and our inferences from our own behaviors, although some attitudes are clearly expressions of personality processes. The affective component of attitudes generally reflects the extent to which the attitude object facilitates or inhibits our achievement of our goals, although there may be other, less rationally calculable reasons why we like and dislike certain things. Because they stem from so many sources, attitudes vary in how stable and general they are; some attitudes seem all-encompassing and rigid whereas others are more specific and labile.

ATTITUDE CHANGE

In our age of democracy, political campaigns, universal education, advertising, and ubiquitous mass media, we rather take for granted persuasion as a central fact of social life. But as McGuire (1985) reminds us, our age is of the rare ones in history in which rational persuasion has been the dominant way of getting social business done. In most societies even today, and in the vast majority in the past, cultural tradition, religion, and political coercion have been sufficient for the routine demands of social, economic, and political life. We have the luxury and often the inconvenience of having to persuade people to behave in certain ways.

During and immediately after World War II, relevant concerns about propaganda and attitude change prompted a vast outpouring of research on attitude change. Indeed, the study of attitude change was perhaps the premier topic in social psychology during the 1950s and early 1960s. The complexity of the results obtained from all this research, plus the growing recognition that attitudes do not predict behavior in any simple way (see Chapter 8), led to a dramatic decrease in attitude research during the 1970s. However, at the present there is evidence of renewed interest in the topic, in part stimulated by research on the cognitive underpinnings of attitudes and attitude change (Cialdini, Petty, & Cacioppo, 1981; McGuire, 1985; Petty, Ostrom, & Brock, 1981; Wyer & Carlston, 1979).

THE NATURE OF ATTITUDE CHANGE

The Depth of Change   At a party you participate in expressing a popular political opinion even though you do not privately agree with it. Your friend attacks one of your attitudes, and you give in to get him off your back and because you can't think what to say in reply. When you go shopping, you suddenly buy a new brand of expensive soap because a favorite movie star has recently been plugging it on TV. After hearing a debate you change your attitude, but upon reflection later, you decide that your original attitude was correct after all. You hear a speech favoring nuclear

disarmament and find it so convincing that you not only change your attitude, but spend considerable time working for a local disarmament committee. After talking to a community leader about poverty, you change your position on how to deal with poverty and also find that your whole ideology has shifted—many of your attitudes about society begin to change. Or you attend a religious crusade and commit your life to wearing robes and singing religious hymns on street corners.

Obviously, some of these examples represent quite fundamental attitude change whereas others are skin deep at best. Attitude change is like that. Sometimes it is clear that you have made a major and committed change, while at other times the changes are subtle and fleeting.

Impression Management   Some psychologists (for example, Jellison, 1981) have argued that almost all of what passes for real attitude change is merely behavioral compliance and, as such, is superficial and unlikely to persist. Although most social psychologists would not go that far, they would recognize that public expressions of attitudes can be used to win friends and influence people as well as to define self for others. This position is based on the simple observation, supported by abundant empirical evidence (Schlenker, 1980), that we like others who agree with us more than we like those with whom we disagree. It is not surprising that some people some of the time seem to change their attitudes to get others to like them. Indeed, the attitudes people report are often tailored to the positions they think observers hold (Tetlock, 1983).

The impression management perspective suggests that if I want to impress you I should report that I have the same attitudes as you. Or if I am really clever, I may make a show of changing my attitudes because of your superior arguments and wisdom. On the other hand, most of us would prefer to have others think we are thoughtful and consistent, and changing our attitudes is not the best way to project that sort of an image.

The question is, When do we get approval for seeming to change and when for holding fast? Cialdini, Braver, and Lewis (1974) have shown that persuaders are more impressed with the person who changes, but bystanders are more taken with the person who is steadfast. People seem to realize this because they report more change in their attitudes when only a persuader can see their attitudes (Braver, Linder, Corwin, & Cialdini, 1977). Thus, you might impress your professor by confessing privately that she has changed your attitude about the course material, but you would impress your friends by openly holding fast to your opinions in a classroom debate.

A full discussion of impression management strategies is reserved for Chapter 12, but we have mentioned the topic here because the impression management perspective raises some important questions about the reality of attitude change (or lack of change).

THEORIES OF ATTITUDE CHANGE

Motivational Models   Most theories of attitude change have borrowed heavily from other prominent perspectives in psychology. For example, Hullian learning theory (see Chapter 1) was used extensively by Carl Hovland and his colleagues at Yale. Basically, this model argues that people change attitudes only when they are reinforced for doing so. So, for example, a person might develop a more favorable attitude toward brushing her teeth if you made her afraid of what might happen if she continues her indifferent attention to her teeth and gums. Your message arouses fear, which might induce her to brush, which in turn helps alleviate her fear. The reduction of fear would reinforce a new, more positive attitude toward brushing her teeth.

Festinger's cognitive dissonance theory has also been used extensively in attitude change research. According to this theory, the mere knowledge that someone disagrees with you is sufficient to generate dissonance. You might reduce the dissonance by derogating the person ("he's a fool" or "she doesn't know what she is talking about"), because the knowledge that an idiot disagrees with you does not arouse much dissonance. Or you might reduce dissonance by changing your attitudes to resemble more closely those attitudes held by the other person.

These motivational models have tried to explain why attitude change takes place. More recently, cognitive theories of attitude change have become prominent. Such theories place more emphasis on the *how* than on the *why* of attitude change. Cognitive models do not deny that people are motivated to change attitudes, but they tend to recognize only a single motivational tendency, namely the desire to hold correct attitudes. We will make use of various theoretical ideas throughout the remainder of this chapter, but we will focus on cognitive models of attitude change.

Attributional Approaches   The attributional approach (see Eagly & Chaiken, 1984) assumes that people want to have the most valid attitudes possible and that they change their attitudes when someone can offer a more valid opinion. Suppose you hear a speaker on your campus who advocates a substantial raise in tuition for next year, and let us make the reasonable assumption that you are strongly

Alice Eagly

Shelly Chaiken

against this policy. The attributional perspective suggests that you would want to determine the causes of this speech. The speaker could have said what he said because of something about himself (he might be the university financial officer, who is concerned about making ends meet, or a student who feels that the presence of too many lower-class students at the university demeans his own social standing)—you make a person or actor attribution. Alternatively, you might make an entity attribution—he made the speech because raising tuition really is a good idea.

You are more likely to change your attitude if you make an entity attribution rather than a person (speaker) attribution. That is one reason political and religious converts are so valuable to their sides. If, for example, a conservative politician can get liberals to support his proposed tax legislation, he thereby encourages people to make an entity attribution—the legislation is so good that even opponents support it.

According to the attributional perspective, you would be interested in how many other people advocate the same opinion (consensus information), as well as in whether the speaker's statements seem to vary across occasions (consistency) and issues (distinctiveness). You might also approach this from a discounting perspective: does the speaker have reasons other than the worthiness of his position to make the comments he has made? The attributional perspective would be especially concerned with such variables as the credibility of the communicator and expectancies about the communicator that help determine whether the communicator's views derive from personal biases or some objective truth.

Psychologic Models   The attributional perspective assumes that attitude change is based on assessments of the communicator, but psychologic models focus on relationships among beliefs. According to psychologic models, we have several attitudes that are re-

lated to one another in logical or quasi-logical ways. For example, if you believe that human life is sacred, you might oppose capital punishment because it destroys lives. Alternatively, if you believe in retribution for crimes, you might feel that some crimes should be punished with death. Of course, issues such as capital punishment are complex and many people have several strong values that lead them to hold complex and often conflicting views on these questions. But the point is that our attitudes do have some logical relationships with one another. Table 7.2 gives some examples.

Psychologic models assume that attitudes will change when logically related beliefs change (McGuire, 1960; Wyer, 1970). For example, suppose a person believes that capital punishment deters crime, that there is far too much crime, and that therefore capital punishment should be supported. If she were now convinced that capital punishment does not deter crime, then logically she should no longer favor capital punishment. Certainly this sort of persuasion does occur and it is therefore not surprising that a good many of our at-

---

TABLE 7.2   PSYCHOLOGIC APPROACH TO ATTITUDES TOWARD CAPITAL PUNISHMENT.

A
I believe human life is sacred.
Therefore deliberately taking a life is wrong.
Capital punishment is deliberately taking a life.
Therefore capital punishment is wrong.
B
People should pay for their crimes.
Some crimes are so horrible that the proper punishment is death.
Therefore capital punishment is a good penalty.
C
It is important to deter major crimes.
Capital punishment deters major crimes.
Therefore capital punishment is a good penalty.
D
It is important to deter major crimes.
Capital punishment does not deter major crimes.
Therefore capital punishment is an ineffective penalty.

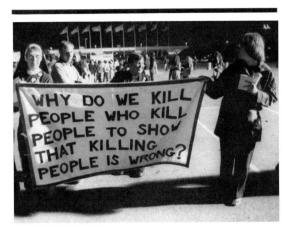

Many of our attitudes are derived logically from our basic values.

tempts to change attitudes are appeals to the logical relationships among beliefs.

However, some of our values and basic beliefs may lead to one kind of attitude while others of our values and beliefs lead to a conflicting attitude. For example, suppose that you believe both that human life is sacred and that people should pay for their crimes. These two premises might lead you to different conclusions about capital punishment. If your present attitude is based on one set of beliefs and we make the other set salient, then your attitudes might change accordingly. Thus, if your beliefs about the sanctity of life were especially salient, you would be more likely to oppose capital punishment than if your beliefs about retribution for crimes were salient. McGuire (1960) has called this effect the **Socratic effect** after the great Greek philosopher Socrates, who led his students to conclusions by making certain of their beliefs salient.

The Heuristic Model   Chaiken (1980, 1987), Petty and Cacioppo (1981), and others have distinguished between two broad ways people respond to persuasive messages. The first, called central (Petty & Cacioppo) or *systematic processing* (Chaiken), involves detailed consideration of the message and communicator; this kind of response is reviewed in the next section. The second, called peripheral (Petty & Cacioppo) or *heuristic processing* (Chaiken), involves a less thoughtful, perhaps less conscious or more automatic, response to the communication. We will use the terms *systematic processing* and *heuristic processing* because they describe more clearly the processes involved.

Suppose you listen to your professor make a speech on some political issue. Should you accept her conclusions? You might, of course, go through a full reasoning process, thinking about the logic of her statements and considering whether she knows what she is talking about on this issue—this would be an example of systematic processing. On the other hand, you might use a shortcut rule to decide whether you agree with her. You could say to yourself that because, in your experience, professors usually read a lot, keep up with current events, and reason logically, they are usually correct in what they say. Hence you should agree with this professor now. Conversely, you might have a shortcut rule that because professors live in an ivory tower, they know little about the outside world and are usually biased when they do; hence professors usually don't know what they are talking about and you should disagree with this one now.

Richard Petty   John Cacioppo

In Chapter 3 we noted that people often use shortcut rules, or *heuristics*, to think about and judge complex events. Here we are suggesting that people may use heuristics to help decide whether they agree or disagree with a persuasive communication. To the extent that you buy without much reflection a product advertised by a favorite movie star, you may be using the heuristic that people you like and respect usually steer you in the right direction. Persuasion via the heuristic route is often not very consciously determined—you just go along with what you are told without much thought. I usually prefer not to waste valuable cognitive resources on debates about which laundry soap to use, and I am happy to respond almost reflexively to advertisements on the basis of simple heuristics. On the other hand, sometimes heuristic processing can be consciously chosen. If I believe a politician has been wrong on nearly everything up to now, I may decide quite consciously not to think much about what he is saying because surely he's probably wrong on this as well. Remember that heuristics are useful because they save time and cognitive energy, but the heuristic model does not assume that we are captives of our mindlessness. I usually don't think much about politician A and what he says, but I can if I so choose.

Heuristics are likely to involve fairly superficial cues such as physical appearance (well-dressed or stylish people are more credible), likability (I usually disagree with people I dislike), similarity (I usually agree with people who share my educational background and religious preferences, among other traits), status and prestige (I like to agree with high-status people), and so on. Furthermore, it is likely that attitude change based on heuristics will be superficial and unstable compared to changes based on systematic processing (Chaiken, 1980; Chaiken & Eagly, 1983).

Cognitive Responses   The cognitive responses perspective assumes that people want to hold correct opinions. To understand attitude change, we must understand the full range of people's cognitive responses to what they read and hear. This approach emphasizes that people think about the communication, try to understand it, and accept or reject it (Petty & Cacioppo, 1986, Petty, Ostrom, & Brock, 1981).

What leads to this thoughtful mode of processing persuasive communications? Involvement in the issue is crucial. One reason I use heuristics to process television advertisements, say for laundry soaps, is that I have little interest in whether I have ring around the collar or whether my clothes have static cling or a fresh smell. On the other hand, I usually am more active and systematic in processing political information during campaigns because I care about the issues and want to make informed decisions. There are, of course, many things that create involvement. Obviously, we are generally more involved in issues that affect us directly. In addition, we may have beliefs and ideologies that predispose us to be more involved in some issues. So I am concerned with capital punishment because of a central interest in justice, even though no one I know has ever been involved in a murder. People who are involved in issues will be motivated to process relevant persuasive appeals in a more systematic, although not necessarily unbiased, way.

How do people respond cognitively to messages? McGuire (1985) and others have postulated at least a dozen stages of processing information, but we will make do here with a more generalized set. Imagine a person watching a political speech on television. How might she respond? First, she must *attend* to the message; our prototypic person may not hear what is said on the TV because she is talking to someone else or reading a magazine. Second, she must *understand* what she has seen and heard and know what position she is supposed to adopt. When issues are fairly complex, as they often are in politics, people surprisingly often do not know exactly what position has been advocated. Third, she must *remember* the message long enough for it to affect her old attitudes and produce the possibility for change. Fourth, she must actually change her attitudes, or *yield* to the communicator. Fifth, she must *maintain that change* and translate it into relevant action of some sort; presumably, the politician wants her to vote for him or to support his campaign by writing letters or by performing some other activity.

Generally, psychologists have concentrated on the yielding factor—What do we have to do to get people to change?—and have devoted relatively little attention to the other factors, though these may also be important. For example, advertisers have long kown that people may tune out TV advertisements (we go to the bathroom, refresh our drinks, or pick up the threads of a conversation), and many people remember having seen an advertisement but cannot remember what product the advertisement was pushing. Therefore, advertisers often concentrate less on convincing people to buy their product than on capturing and holding attention and getting people to remember the product. For example, the Miller Lite commercials are probably effective in part because they are amusing and grab attention; the average Sunday afternoon sports watcher probably watches the ads and remembers the name of the beer associated with them.

Factors that promote change at one level may not at another. For example, a slick ad may capture attention (thus promoting change) but be so silly that it is not convincing (inhibiting change). Smart people may be able to understand messages more easily (promoting change) but also may be more resistant to yielding (inhibiting change). It is also important to note that, to the degree that each stage of cognitive processing is necessary (and remember the heuristic models suggest that change may be achieved in other ways), it limits the amount of change possible at the next stage. For example, suppose the probability that a person will respond positively to each stage of persuasion is .75 (which is probably a

high estimate) and assume that an audience of 100 people watches a speech. Accordingly, only 75 (75%) will actively attend to the message; of those 75, only 56 (75% of 75) will understand; of those 56, only 42 (75% of 56) will remember; of those 42, only 31 will yield; and of those 31, only 23 will actually make some relevant behavioral response. Thus, it may not be surprising that so few people are changed in political campaigns.

The cognitive responses position suggests that we must understand the effects of the persuasive appeal at each of these various stages, although in practice most attention is directed to the yielding stage. The basic assumptions of the cognitive responses approach are that people respond actively to what they see and hear and that attitude change must be understood less in terms of people changing others than of people changing themselves. Imagine that you have just heard a speech with which you agree, which means that you find that your cognitive responses are basically positive. In this case you may adopt the advocated position not because the speaker has convinced you but because you have convinced yourself. The speech has stimulated you to generate your own convincing arguments. But when you hear a talk advocating a position you dislike, you may find that your cognitive responses are basically negative and you present compelling counterarguments to yourself. It is unlikely that your attitudes would dramatically change under these circumstances.

What factors encourage positive or negative cognitive responses? Motivational factors are crucial. For example, if you like the speaker or find her credible, you may be so charmed that you are disinclined to counterargue. On the other hand, if she begins her speech by insulting you or by telling you that she is going to change your attitudes, you may feel challenged to generate arguments opposed to hers, counterarguments that inhibit your changing.

Ability factors are also important. Sometimes recipients of persuasive communications have, by virtue of knowledge or involvement, a great number of pro and con arguments to draw on. So if someone tries to convince you that tuition should be raised at your university, you might immediately think of several reasons why this is a bad idea and construct counterarguments of your own. For other issues, however, you may have fewer arguments at your disposal. A speaker advocating a new policy on wasteland management may find that her audience has few con arguments to offer in rebuttal. Such issues may lower the abilities of people to resist change by counterarguing, but they may also lower attention, comprehension, memory, and pro arguments, so the end result is that people still may not change.

The rule of thumb concerning all this is fairly simple: if the persuasive communication helps the recipient generate favorable arguments, it is likely that the recipient will change in the direction advocated by the communication, assuming that she understands and remembers the relevant parts of the message. On the other hand, if the communication or communicator encourages counterarguing, persuasion is likely to be inhibited. So the speaker wants, first, to inhibit counterarguing and, second, to get the recipient to generate positive, supporting arguments of her own (see Figure 7.1).

THE SOURCE OF THE COMMUNICATION

We focus attention here on three classes of variables pertaining to attitude change and persuasion: the *source* of the communication, the *communication* itself, and the *recipient* of the communication. One of the most obvious influences on attitude change is the source. We all have stereotypes of the unscrupulous used-car salesman, may feel that all politicians are biased and cynical, or buy advertised products because they are endorsed by favorite movie stars. Everyday experiences suggest that source credibility, prestige, and personal attractiveness affect attitude change.

If so, there is a paradox of sorts. It may seem reasonable that credible, trustworthy, knowledgeable, nice-acting people should elicit more change. After all, we associate such people with truth and wisdom. But these factors are not directly relevant to the validity of the message. The Miller Lite commercials use a number of ex-athletes to make claims about their beer, but it is doubtful that the average ex-athlete knows any more about beer than the average beer-drinker. Although it may be true that a respected political commentator may more often be right than your local bartender, on any given issue the truth of what each says must stand on its own merits. So these source variables may be *cues* for the validity of the message (and thus whether we ought to change in the direction of the message), but the message itself is the ultimate test.

Recall that heuristic processing relies more heavily on cues for validity, whereas systematic processing is a more thoughtful approach. When people are less involved in the issues and are therefore more likely to process information in terms of heuristics, these source cues are more important (Chaiken, 1980; Petty, Cacioppo, & Goldman, 1981). For example, Petty et al. showed that, with high involvement in issues (and, presumably, systematic processing), it was the quality of the arguments that determined attitude change, whereas with lower involvement (and, presumably, heuristic processing), speaker credibility was more influential.

Credibility   A classic study by Hovland and Weiss (1951) shows the effects of credibility, which is some combination of expertise and objectivity. Subjects were given articles to read, half coming from high-credibility sources, such as a medical journal, where both expertise and objectivity were judged to be high, and half coming from low-credibility sources, such as *Pravda*, where both expertise and objectivity were judged to be low. Gen-

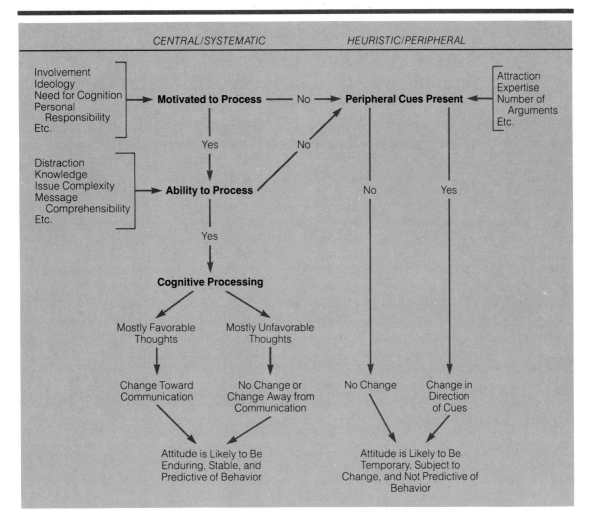

FIGURE 7.1   A Model of Attitude Change.

Adapted from Petty and Cacioppo, 1986.

erally subjects changed their attitudes more after reading the high-credibility sources.

When Hovland and Weiss measured the subjects' attitudes several weeks later, they were greeted with a surprise. As Figure 7.2 shows, the credibility effect had disappeared. It is perhaps not so surprising that those subjects who had read the highly credible message showed less change after two weeks than immediately—they may, for example, have forgotten what they read. The real surprise is that the people who had read the low-credibility sources changed slightly more after two weeks than immediately. One explanation is that there was a **_sleeper effect_**, which results when people remember the message but not necessarily who said it. If this were true, it would have important implications. For example, an irresponsible politician could make extravagant but groundless claims, confident that people would remember his message and forget that it was proposed by an idiot. Fortunately, the typical result in experimental studies is that, although the high-credibility source loses effectiveness over time, the low-credibility source either gains effectiveness only slightly or not at all (Gillig & Greenwald, 1974). The slight gain in effectiveness sometimes shown by the low-credibility source is in fact apparently due to a disassociation between the message and the credibility information over time (Gruder et al., 1978).

It is at least theoretically possible that over time people remember the content of messages better than their validity or credibility. They may even disregard credibility information. How would you feel if a notoriously unreliable scandal sheet reported that you were a criminal and people remembered the charge against

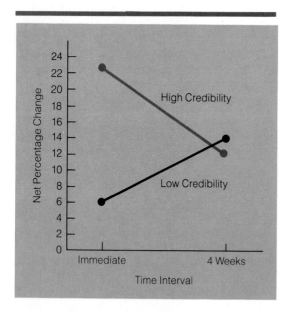

FIGURE 7.2   Changes in Extent of Agreement with Position Advocated by High-credibility and Low-credibility Sources. The sleeper effect is the tendency for the low-credibility source to get more attitude change over time.

Hovland and Weiss, 1951.

you but forgot where they had read it? Even worse, suppose that someone read in the newspaper that you were *not* guilty of a crime, but only remembered that you somehow had been associated with the crime. In research by Wegner, Wenzlaff, Kerker, and Beattie (1981), subjects read newspaper headlines about public figures. Headlines that asserted that the person had done something wrong naturally led to low evaluations of that person. But, surprisingly, headlines that merely raised a question about guilt or that explicitly denied guilt also led to lowered evaluations. This research on the innuendo effect suggests that people may not process credibility information as well as they process the actual assertions.

What happens when we consider the expertise and objectivity components of credibility separately? Generally, expert sources produce more attitude change than do nonexpert sources (Cook, 1969; Maddux & Rogers, 1980). There may be several reasons for this. If messages are being processed heuristically, expertise may be a cue for change. In times of systematic processing, people may also pay more attention to experts: there is evidence that people counterargue less with expert sources (Cook, 1969). Because counterarguing typically retards change, the net result would be that people change their attitudes more to agree with the expert with whom they argue less.

There is also evidence that objective, trustworthy communicators produce more change than less trustworthy sources (McGinnies & Ward, 1980). The attributional perspective suggests that one way we gain the trust of an audience is to overcome obvious bias (Eagly, Wood, & Chaiken, 1978). For example, you would normally expect people with business interests to oppose environmental restraints on economic growth. So when a businessperson makes a proenvironment speech to a probusiness group, his proenvironment speech will be seen as more trustworthy because he has presumably overcome his "natural" biases.

Attractiveness   Advertisers seem to feel that pretty and likable people are more persuasive than their less attractive peers. Political lore has it that handsome and seemingly personable political candidates also seem to win more than their share of elections. Experimental research confirms that likable (Hass, 1981) and physically attractive (Chaiken, 1986) sources do generate more attitude change, especially for those recipients who are processing information heuristically rather than systematically. Box 7.1 discusses this research in more detail.

THE COMMUNICATION

If I wish to convince my class of something, I can hardly do much (in the short run) to change how biased, expert, or pretty they think I, the communicator, am; they have probably long before reached conclusions about such matters. Nor can I do much to change the nature of the recipients; I have to take the audience much the way I find it. What I can do, however, is try to make my message itself as persuasive as possible. I will try to find the convincing argument, work on the emotions of the audience, and package what I say in the most palatable way. This happens informally as well. If you are getting ready to approach someone for a loan, you will undoubtedly think about what you might say, how you should structure your arguments, and how impassioned your plea should be.

Broadly speaking, there are two basic categories of approach to packaging the message. Some persuasion attempts are fairly blatant attempts to manipulate *affective* or emotional reactions to attitude objects. Other approaches are more *cognitive* in orientation, seeking to change beliefs about the object. Suppose you were trying to convince someone to support a policy of reduced welfare spending. At the affective level, you might try to associate welfare with sloth and sin in your

listener's mind by providing lurid examples of welfare recipients who commit crimes. Alternatively, you could work directly on your listener's beliefs through cognitive appeals. For example, you might try to convince your friend, with appropriate statistics, that the general citizenry is adversely affected by the high taxes levied to cover rising welfare costs.

Affective Reactions: Positive Associations   One of the most common strategies of advertising is to associate products with positive experiences. Beautiful women jump into snazzy cars and whiz away through beautiful scenery, carefree and happy. Or a gorgeous man runs his hands through the freshly laundered hair of a woman with a faultless complexion, high cheekbones, and an elegant but understated wardrobe. A sweaty, muscular kind of guy earns his Blah Beer after a hard day's work being macho. Firesides, ski slopes, pounding waves, San Francisco hills, and clean mountain scenery figure prominently in many advertisements. Humor, as in the Miller Lite advertisements, is another effective device to associate products with positive experiences.

In each of these cases there is an effort to mate the product with happy experiences and associations. When words or ideas are associated with pleasant or unpleasant experiences, they take on a similar emotional coloration through conditioning. Even mood can affect attitude change. For example, Janis, Kaye, and Kirschner (1965) exposed subjects to several persuasive communications. Some subjects were offered food during this process while others were not. Those who had the food and were therefore presumably happier changed their attitudes more.

Affective Reactions: Fear Arousal   One strategy for attitude change that is probably used more than any other is fear arousal. Advertisements for cosmetics and personal care products play on our fears of rejection should we look unlovely or smell bad; some preachers incorporate themes of hellfire and damnation

BOX 7.1

ATTRACTIVENESS AND ATTITUDE CHANGE

Source characteristics are usually irrelevant to the basic truth of the communication. For example, despite the emphasis placed on physical beauty in our culture, most of us would hesitate to defend the proposition that how attractive someone is affects the validity of his or her message (except perhaps advertisements for beauty products). However, the data from several studies suggest that a pretty face helps even those appeals not relevant to beauty.

Perhaps beautiful people are more persuasive because they seem more confident or can argue better. As we will see in Chapter 12, attractive people tend to be more outgoing and socially skilled. It is therefore reasonable to hypothesize that attractive communicators may also be more skilled in the persuasive arts.

Shelly Chaiken (1979) directly tested the idea that attractive people may be more persuasive because they are more skilled. She recruited college students to try to persuade other students that the dining halls should stop serving meat during breakfast and lunch. Each of the communicators was rated for attractiveness. The results showed that the attractive communicators were more successful in getting agreement with their position. In addition, Chaiken obtained several other measures on each communicator and found that the attractive and unattractive people differed in several ways. For example, the attractive communicators were more verbally fluent and reported higher SAT scores. However, Chaiken found that the relationship between attractiveness and persuasion was not due entirely to the greater persuasive skills of the attractive communicators.

So we must look to other possibilities. A second explanation is built on the following logic. Attractive people are liked more than unattractive ones; we like to please and be liked by people we like; one way to please other people is to do what they ask, such as by changing our attitudes toward theirs. Therefore, attractive people get more attitude change because we want to convince them to like us. Although this kind of hypothesis can explain the greater effectiveness of pretty friends, it stretches matters to think that movie stars sell products because people in the TV audience want the stars to like them. Moreover, this idea is fairly easy to test. If true, the attractiveness effect should be strongest when the subject knows the communicator and expects that the communicator will find out whether he changes. Yet research suggests that attractiveness produces attitude change even when the communicator cannot find out whether the subject has changed (Chaiken, 1986). So the idea that changing attitudes for attractive people is an effort to win their approval cannot explain all the results.

A third possibility is based on the notion of heuristic processing. We may have learned that we generally agree with people we like or with whom we are similar. Balance theory, for example, suggests that a triad made up of you, another person, and an attitude object would be balanced if you like the other person or are similar to her and have the same attitudes toward the attitude object (see Chapter 3). Thus, you may assume that by having the same attitudes as the communicator you will be similar to her in other ways—including, perhaps, attractiveness. This is not the height of rational reasoning, but it does fit the kinds of identifications one typically sees with adolescents who imitate the clothing patterns and behavior styles of rock stars and with grown people who also imitate the lives of the rich and famous as much as possible. This idea of a balance heuristic is difficult to test directly, but it does have one testable implication. Because the change is supposedly mediated by using a simple rule almost without thought, it follows that the rule will be used more when people are encouraged to process heuristically rather than systematically. Thus, attractiveness ought to be more important when people are processing information heuristically.

As partial support for this proposition, Chaiken (1980) has shown that likable communicators get more change than unlikable ones primarily when recipients are not deeply involved in the issue. In addition, Pallak and her students (Pallak, Murroni, & Koch, 1983–84) showed that when the message encourages systematic processing, attractiveness does not have a major effect on attitude change. However, when the message is more emotional and encourages heuristic processing, attractiveness has more of an effect.

Usually, attitude-change researchers think about attractiveness as a cue used only when subjects process information heuristically. However, Pallak (1983–84) has argued that the relationship could also be reversed. Perhaps physical attractiveness itself could be a cue for how people should respond to the message—in other words, when attractiveness is salient, it is a cue to process information heuristically. In Pallak's study, subjects read a statement from an art critic that advocated more funding for the arts. Some subjects read a fairly strong set of arguments, while others read weaker arguments. If subjects think about what they are reading, they should be more persuaded by the strong arguments. If, on the other hand, they process the information heuristically, the quality of the arguments might not make much difference. Pallak did not manipulate the attractiveness of the art-critic communicator (he was handsome in all conditions), but rather how *salient* his appearance was. This was cleverly done by giving some subjects a high-quality color photograph (high salience) and some subjects a low-quality photocopy (low salience) of the communicator. The predictions were that when handsomeness was not salient, subjects would process the information systematically and would be more influenced by the strong than by the weak arguments. On the other hand, when handsomeness was highly salient, the qual-

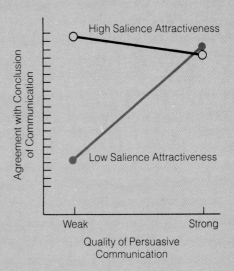

FIGURE B.7.1   Agreement as a Function of Salience of Attractiveness and Strength of Argument. Note that when attractiveness of the communicator is not salient, strong arguments are more persuasive than weak ones, but that when attractiveness is salient, the nature of the arguments makes little difference.

Pallack, 1983–84.

BOX CONTINUED

ity of arguments might not make much difference. As Figure B.7.1 shows, this is exactly what happened. In addition, Pallak had subjects write down what they had thought about while they read the message. When attractiveness was salient, subjects listed more thoughts about the communicator. When the attractiveness was not salient, the subjects listed more thoughts about the communication. Thus, salient attractiveness was a cue to pay (heuristic) attention to the communicator rather than (systematic) attention to the message.

So it would seem that attractiveness is an important cue for attitude change primarily when the recipient is not thinking deeply about the communication. In addition, appeals to attractiveness may also lead us to process the communication in less systematic ways. You might keep this in mind as you watch many television ads. Is there anything to the ad other than an appeal to beauty? Is the focus on attractiveness a clever way to divert you from thinking carefully about the actual merits of the product?

for those who refuse to mend their ways; politicians assure us that if their opponents are elected, the world as we know it will end, soon.

In an early discussion of how fear arousal works, Hovland et al. (1953) proposed a learning model. They suggested that fear is aroused during the communication (you might have ring around the collar). This fear is an aversive state. Later a type of action (using Brand X Soap) is advocated, which if followed should solve the problem and alleviate the fear. Reduction of fear, in turn, should be rewarding and should therefore strengthen or reinforce adoption of the new attitude or behavior.

This seems sensible enough as a working theory, but the research evidence has not been altogether cooperative. Some studies have found that high fear-arousal retards rather than enhances attitude change (Janis & Feshbach, 1953), but most recent research has supported the opposite conclusion, namely that high fear-arousal leads to more attitude change (Higbee, 1969). Nonetheless, it is also clear that fear arousal works only under some

circumstances and probably does not work by drive reduction or simple reinforcement. If fear-arousal were always effective, health professionals would have a far easier time convincing people to lose weight, to stop smoking, and to get frequent checkups. Yet it is common to find women with large and visible breast cancers who have resisted getting an examination or men who later die of cancer who insist that the pains in their stomach will go away in due course. Sometimes fear makes people so afraid that they avoid the whole topic rather than take effective action.

This might suggest that the problem with some studies is that they have aroused too much fear. One possibility is that fear-arousal is most effective at some moderate level (Janis, 1967). Too little fear is not motivating and too much leads to avoidance. At least one study did find that an intermediate level of fear was most effective (Krisher, Darley, & Darley, 1973).

However, most recent attempts to explain the effects of fear-arousal have concentrated on perceptions of both the fearful situation and abilities to cope with it rather than on the fear itself (Leventhal, 1970; Rogers, 1983). We can perhaps make this clearest with a concrete example used by Maddux and Rogers (1983). Suppose you were trying to convince your father to stop smoking. Rather than trying to make him tremble with fear, you might appeal to his reason in four stages. First, you might stress how potentially dangerous smoking is; it leads to cancer as well as to heart and lung disorders. Second, you might try to convince him that he is extremely likely to encounter these problems if he continues to smoke. Third, you could suggest that if he stops smoking, he may arrest or even avoid these problems. Fourth, you could try to convince him that he will be able to do what you have requested, namely to stop smoking. This latter stage is close to what Bandura (1977) has referred to as self-efficacy, meaning that the person feels he or she has the ability to affect the fearful situation. In general, there is experimental support (but with several conflicting findings) for the idea that each of these stages affects attitude change, but in one study that examined all four stages (Maddux & Rogers, 1983), the last three, especially self-efficacy, were all shown to have effects on intentions to stop smoking.

We began this section by asserting that fear arousal is a strategy widely used to effect attitude change, but recent research suggests that arousing fear may not be the crucial element. It is probably more important to pay attention to people's cognitions about the dangerous situation and their abilities to change it. Thus, what appears to be an affective or emotional approach to attitude change now appears to be more heavily cognitive.

Changing Beliefs: Discrepancy   A persuader who faces an audience must decide how extreme to make his or her presentation. Sherif and Hovland (1961) divide the attitude continuum of the audience into three parts: (1) those positions that recipients find acceptable (the latitude of acceptance), (2) those positions the

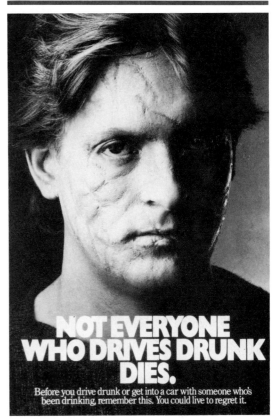

Fear arousal is a standard attitude-change strategy. Courtesy Reader's Digest Foundation.

recipients definitely reject (the latitude of rejection), and (3) those positions of relative indifference (latitude of indifference). Sherif and Hovland maintain that when the communication is too far away from the recipient's position (in the latitude of rejection), it will call into question the communicator's expertise and wisdom. On the other hand, if the communication is too close, the recipient may not recognize that the position is different and will have little reason to change. Maximum attitude change should occur when the communication is discrepant enough to motivate change, but neither so discrepant as to engender rejection nor so acceptable that it stimulates no change of attitude. In other words, according to this model, we would expect the least amount of attitude change to occur in the latitudes of rejection and acceptance and the most to occur somewhere in the latitudes of indifference (see Figure 7.3).

For example, imagine that you are one of a number of liberal senators proposing bills to establish national health insurance. You are perhaps not surprised to find your message immediately rejected as extreme by doctors and conservative Republicans. But you may be surprised to find little support for your plan among liberal Democrats—your plan may be so close to some of theirs that they see no reason to abandon their plans to support yours. It may be that your chief source of potential support would be among moderate senators, who are close enough to you politically that they do not automatically reject your arguments, but who are far enough from you that there is room for them to change toward your views.

Results tend to support the Sherif–Hovland model. The more discrepant the communication, the larger the attitude change (Hovland & Pritzker, 1957), until the discrepancies become extreme, at which time there is less attitude change (Hovland, Harvey, & Sherif, 1957). As the communication becomes more extreme, recipients either reject the speech automatically or generate counterarguments that retard attitude change (Cacioppo & Petty, 1979).

The Quality of Arguments   The cognitive responses position also places great emphasis on the quality of arguments offered in the communication. Generally, as one might expect intuitively, arguments that are readily understood produce more change than those that are relatively incomprehensible (Eagly, 1974), and good arguments usually produce more change than do bad ones. However, the effectiveness of arguments often depends on other

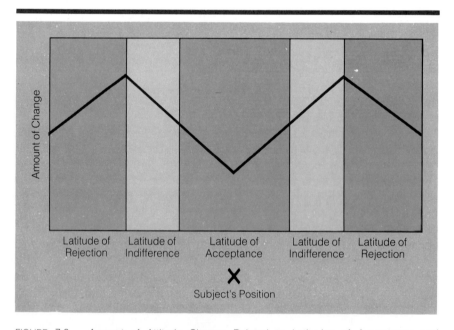

FIGURE 7.3   Amount of Attitude Change Related to Latitudes of Acceptance and Rejection. Note that because the person's attitude is moderate, there are latitudes of indifference and rejection on either side. If the person were initially extreme, there might be only one latitude of indifference and one latitude of rejection.

factors. When people care about the topic at hand, there is generally more attitude change as the arguments get better, but those people who don't care are usually not responsive to the quality of arguments (Petty & Cacioppo, 1979b, 1984). People who have substantial previous knowledge and can therefore better evaluate the communication are also more affected by message quality than are those who have little knowledge (Wood, Kallgren, & Preisler, 1985).

A related issue is whether the number of arguments makes a difference. In general, it might seem that the more arguments the better, especially if they are good ones. And some studies find that more arguments lead to more change of attitude (Calder, Insko, & Yandell, 1974), but other research has shown that there may be limitations on this result. For one, both the number of arguments and the length of the communication seem to affect attitude change, primarily in situations of low involvement when people process information heuristically (Petty & Cacioppo, 1984; Wood et al., 1985). In such cases, people may reason (fairly superficially) that truth is associated with many arguments, thereby disregarding the quality of the arguments. On the other hand, when people process more thoughtfully and systematically, a large number of arguments may overwhelm their efforts to understand the communication and lead to less change (Petty & Cacioppo, 1981).

Types of Presentation   Say you are organizing an ad campaign for a political candidate. Do you spend your limited funds primarily on newspaper and magazine ads or do you invest in television and radio ads? Research generally supports the proposition that visual and audio media are more effective than the written media, though for complex reasons (Chaiken & Eagly, 1976). In the first place, most material is better understood when written than when spoken, so, for complex material, the written media ought to have an advantage. You can't be changed by something you fail to understand. On the other hand, audio and visual media have other advantages. Various visual and vocal nonverbal cues may enhance the credibility and display the attractiveness of the candidate, which can increase persuasion. Such cues may also distract the recipients from counterarguing to some extent, also increasing persuasion. Chaiken and Eagly found that with complex issues there was more attitude change with written materials, but with the simpler issues audio and visual presentations were more effective. There is additional evidence that recipients think more about the communicator with audio or visual presentations, and under those circumstances communicator characteristics, such as likability, play a larger role than in written persuasion attempts (Chaiken & Eagly, 1983). These results suggest that politicians would be well advised to use television if they are attractive and likable but to rely on the written media otherwise. One cannot help but believe that President Reagan (who projects attractiveness and likable qualities) gets his messages across better on television, whereas President Carter (who projected a much cooler image) might have done better to stick to the written word.

THE RECIPIENT OF THE COMMUNICATION

Some people are stubborn and refuse to listen to reason, at least on some issues. At the other extreme are people who never seem to hold their own in an argument, who cave in to others without a whimper or a fight. Do these two kinds of people have different overall personality characteristics? In general, the influenceability of a person is not strongly related to his or her other personality variables nor does it preclude a large amount of situational control over attitude change (Eagly, 1981).

One much-studied individual difference variable is gender. Many people have long felt that women are more easily persuaded than men. To some extent that may reflect the fact that women more than men are more often placed in subordinate roles where conformity to the opinions of superiors is culturally expected (Eagly, 1983). However, in experimental settings—which probably reduce such expectations—women are only slightly more likely to change attitudes than men. For example, Eagly (1978) reports that in 62 experimental studies that reported attitude change by gender, 82% found no gender differences and 16% found that women were more influenced. When all the studies are combined, about 60% of the women are more likely to change attitudes than the average man (Eagly & Carli, 1981). Furthermore, those gender differences that do exist are more apparent in studies done before 1970, suggesting that changing women's roles and consciousness may have reduced the small differences almost to nothing. Another partial explanation for whatever sex differences exist is that many attitude-change experiments (particularly those of some years ago) used male-oriented topics. Because men may know more about these topics, they may also be better able to resist changing. Both Sistrunk and McDavid (1971) and Karabenick (1983) have shown that males conform more on female-oriented topics and females more on male-oriented topics. So, although there are theoretical explanations for observed sex differences in attitude change, the differences are actually quite small when subjected to experimental scrutiny.

More generally, the nature of the situation and the issue typically plays a much larger role in who changes their attitudes than do personality characteristics. There has been relatively little contemporary research on the role of the recipient in attitude change. In part, that reflects a general conclusion that social behavior is typically not closely related to personality variables (see Chaper 8). But it also reflects a practical consideration. If you want to persuade people, you may have considerable control over your communication and some control over your presentation of self as a communicator. What you cannot control is your audience. In many attitude-change situa-

tions (say a political campaign), your audience will be quite heterogeneous, made up of men and women, young and old people, smart and dull people, and so on. Therefore it would be hard to tailor a persuasive communication that could appeal to all those people.

THE RECIPIENT AS ACTIVE PARTICIPANT

Throughout this chapter we have emphasized the cognitive responses approach, that sees attitude change as dependent on the quality of arguments that subjects generate in an attitude-change situation. In general, if people are motivated and have the ability to generate favorable arguments, they will change toward the communication, whereas if they generate counterarguments, they will resist change.

Inoculation   The research that perhaps most directly led to the current emphasis on cognitive responses was done by McGuire and his colleagues on what they called *inoculation* against change. Metaphorically, inoculation can be compared to the medical situation in which exposure to a weakened form of a virus (an inoculation) stimulates the body to develop defenses against a more virulent form. McGuire used cultural truisms (such as, you ought to brush your teeth) for which the person has never been exposed to effective counterarguments—did your mother, health teacher, or dentist ever give you reasons why you *shouldn't* brush your teeth? As a result, if you were to be exposed to strong arguments for not brushing your teeth, your own beliefs might collapse because you had never developed refutations of these arguments, just like the person who is vulnerable to smallpox because of never having been exposed to it. On the other hand, if you were exposed to some of the arguments you might expect to hear (like an inoculation), you might be able to develop your own defenses.

McGuire's research involves having subjects read a strong communication arguing against a cultural truism; subjects might, for example, read why they should not brush their teeth.

Those subjects who simply read the communication reported afterwards that they agreed they should not brush their teeth; their attitudes were changed because they had never had to develop counterarguments. Other subjects received supportive immunization; that is, before reading the communication they read an additional communication supporting their previous views that brushing teeth was good. They were also persuaded by the antibrushing communication; this is not surprising because nothing in the probrushing communication gave them arguments to refute the antibrushing communication. However, other groups of subjects were inoculated against change. Before reading the antibrushing communication, they read probrushing counterarguments to the antibrushing reasons for not brushing their teeth. These subjects were largely not influenced by the antibrushing communication. When they read it they presumably refuted it with the counterarguments they had just read. They were motivated to counterargue and had lots of ammunition (McGuire & Papageorgis, 1961, 1962).

It would seem that attempts to shield people from alternative ideas by exposing them only to supportive propaganda may leave them more vulnerable than to inoculate them by exposure to even-handed presentations that give them opportunities to develop counterarguments to the other side. Such research certainly offers a lesson for those who feel that the best educational strategy in teaching their children is to *protect* their children from all views contrary to the "right" ones. However, our main interest in this research is that it was perhaps the first attempt to show that acceptance or rejection of persuasive communications depends on whether the recipient has the ability to counterargue.

Forewarning   Another line of research also showed the importance of counterarguing. Imagine that you have just been told you will hear a speech taking a position directly opposed to your own. The fact that you are warned about what the speaker will say might give you an opportunity to think through your own position, to review the possible arguments the speaker might use, and to prepare your counterarguments. This forewarning might then give you both the motivation and the ability to counterargue and, hence, to be able to resist the persuasive speech. In an experiment by Allyn and Festinger (1961), one group of high school subjects was told that a speaker would argue for raising the driving age and was told to concentrate on the speech, while another group was not told about the topic of the speech and was told to concentrate on the personality of the speaker. Results showed that the forewarned group changed toward the speech less than those who were not told what the speech was to be about.

Subsequent research has generally confirmed that forewarning inhibits attitude change, although occasionally some change takes place toward the communication even before it is seen or heard. Such **anticipatory belief change** may represent attempts to preserve self-esteem (McGuire & Millman, 1965), as if the recipients try to convince themselves that they had changed on their own before the communication had a chance to affect them.

However, it is probably more common to find that forewarning does induce resistance to change, the original Allyn and Festinger result. This seems especially likely when recipients know that someone is deliberately trying to persuade them (Hass & Grady, 1975; Watts & Holt, 1979), perhaps because most of us like to think we cannot be cognitively coerced. Forewarning also gives subjects the time and motivation to develop counterarguments (Petty & Cacioppo, 1977). Thus, the research is fairly consistent. When subjects are motivated to counterargue (because the topic is involving, the communicator is trying to persuade, and the communication is likely to be quite discrepant from the recipient's views) and when subjects have the time and ability to generate counterarguments, subjects will show less attitude change.

Distraction   Consider the Allyn and Festinger study again from a different angle. Recall that subjects who were forewarned about what the speaker would argue changed their attitudes less than those who had been told to concentrate on his personality. Heretofore, we have interpreted this as evidence that forewarning retards attitude change. But there is another possibility. Suppose that both groups were motivated to counterargue, but that the subjects who monitored the speaker's personality were thereby distracted from the arguments of—and therefore the counterarguments to—the speech. So perhaps the Allyn–Festinger study does not show that forewarning retards attitude change; perhaps it shows that distraction inhibits counterarguing and thereby promotes attitude change.

This possibility was tested in a clever study by Festinger and Maccoby (1964). Fraternity members were exposed to an antifraternity speech. Half the subjects saw a movie of the speech, while the other half heard the speech as the soundtrack of a silent comedy. Festinger and Maccoby reasoned that the latter group might be distracted from counterarguing as they watched the movie, and, consistent with that reasoning, the distraction subjects did change their attitudes more than the subjects who watched the speech normally.

The distraction effect is usually but not always found. If you think about it for a moment, distraction is a tricky effect. If the person is not distracted at all, she may counterargue and resist attitude change. But if she is distracted a lot, she cannot counterargue but she also can't change her attitudes toward those of the communicator because she can't comprehend what is being said. Thus, it follows that attitude change is facilitated when the distraction is sufficient to retard counterarguing but not sufficient to obstruct understanding (Osterhouse & Brock, 1970). It also follows that a given amount of distraction might facilitate attitude change for a simple message but retard change for a more complex message (Regan & Cheng, 1973): because the simple message can be easily understood, the distractor interferes with counterarguing but not with understanding; however, for a more complex message, the distraction interferes with comprehension as well as counterarguing. Generally, people do not change toward arguments they fail to understand.

Generating Positive Arguments   We have been arguing that people will often be convinced by the arguments of others unless they can actively resist by generating counterarguments. But now we need to examine the other aspect of active processing of information, namely, generating arguments in favor of a particular position.

It seems intuitively likely that if you were encouraged to generate arguments in favor of a position (say by explicitly having to prepare a speech), you might inadvertently convince yourself by the arguments you prepare for others; at any rate, preparing speeches does promote attitude change in the direction of the speech (Janis & King, 1954). In preparing a speech you would ordinarily think about and explicitly prepare more arguments in favor than against the proposition, and just as you would be convinced by a speaker who offered more arguments for one side than the other, you may convince yourself in a similar manner (O'Neill & Levings, 1979).

But beyond these kinds of effects that basically assume you convince yourself just as any other communicator might, it is also clear that we sometimes strengthen or even change our attitudes about objects just by thinking about them. Tesser and Conlee (1975) had subjects think about issues, and the longer they thought the more extreme their attitudes became—if initially negative they became more so and if initially positive they were more positive at the end of the thought period.

Tesser (1978) has argued that such effects result from schema processing. Most of us have complex attitudes toward important issues and objects, typically with a mixture of positive and negative feelings about different aspects. For example, there are things I like and things I dislike about my job, and we can think about my schema for my job as incorporating both positive and negative features. When I think about my job, I may become more positive as I emphasize the positive features or more negative as I emphasize the negative ones. If my general attitude is positive, it is likely that I will think about, and thus make more salient, the positive features, resulting in change in the positive direction.

One implication of this view is that there should be more attitude extremity or polarization when the person has such a well-developed cognitive scheme. Tesser and Leone (1977) had male and female subjects think about their attitudes toward women's fashions and football. As expected, the men showed more polarization for football and women for fashions. Chaiken and Yates (1985) have further shown that people with well-developed knowledge structures show more polarization.

Generally, then, merely thinking about an object can lead to attitude change toward that object. This may be common and important in its own right, but it also provides a foundation for the idea that when we are changed by an external communication, some of the effect may be produced by the way the communication stimulates us to think about the issue for ourselves.

ATTITUDE CHANGE IN EVERYDAY LIFE

Experimental studies show that many source, communication, and recipient variables can and do affect attitude change. But do these variables also have an effect in everyday life? One way to answer that question is to examine the role of the mass media in changing attitudes, especially on political issues.

The Mass Media and Politics   Television and, to a lesser extent, newspapers, radio, and magazines are important sources of information about a range of issues, people, and events (Roberts & Maccoby, 1985). Therefore, it would seem reasonable to examine how successful the mass media are in changing attitudes. This is a topic of particular concern because many people have been fearful that the media, especially television, can be used to control the attitudes of people. You may recall the emphasis George Orwell placed on television manipulation of behavior in his novel *1984*.

However, when we examine political campaigns, where the use of the media to try to change attitudes is most obvious, we quickly discover that the effects of the media are subtle at best and are hardly strong enough to support the idea that the American electorate is hostage to the media. At any rate, there are few changes in preferences during a given election campaign. Probably fewer than 10% of voters actually switch preferences from one candidate to another, and those who do switch do not do so because of what they have seen in the media (Comstock et al., 1978). The strongest predictor of voting preference, especially in presidential elections, is party preference (Kinder & Sears, 1985). Independents, who provide most of the swing votes in elections, are less likely to vote (and to expose themselves to political propaganda) than are those committed to one of the two major parties.

This does not, however, mean that the media have no effect on voting. Political campaigns do lead to fuller and more informed impressions of candidates and to greater consistency of political attitudes with party identification (Kinder & Sears, 1985). Perhaps even more important, campaigns strengthen political attitudes and affect decisions to vote. Thus, although people may not change their attitudes toward candidates much, they may become more or less willing to vote. Consider the results of the presidential debates in the 1960, 1976, and 1980 elections. The debates actually changed few preferences. After the

1976 debates, for example, only 6% of Carter supporters switched to Ford and only 5% of Ford supporters switched to Carter. After the 1980 debates, Carter lost 10% of his supporters to Reagan and Reagan lost 5% to Carter (Kinder & Sears, 1985). There was more switching after the 1960 debates between Kennedy and Nixon, but the strengthening effect was probably still more important. In those debates Kennedy made a much better impression than Nixon. Because doubtful Kennedy supporters became stronger in their beliefs than did doubtful Nixon supporters (Deutschmann, 1962), the debates may have been a major factor in what turned out to be a close election by getting more Kennedy than Nixon supporters to the polls. In general, data on more recent debates also points to strengthening rather than to changing effects (Kinder & Sears, 1985).

A frequent theme of recent years is that the media, especially television, affect the images we have of candidates. There is little doubt that perceptions of traits such as competence and integrity affect preferences for candidates (Kinder & Sears, 1985). Additional research has shown that many people have complex emotional reactions towards candidates that affect preferences (Abelson, Kinder, Peters, & Fiske, 1982). However, there are still few data that show that the media have a major effect on images (Kinder & Sears, 1985), even though most people get the bulk of their political information from television and newspapers, and it would be strange if they did not form images based on that information.

Some social scientists have also argued that television performs an indirect but important function by affecting public interest in issues. This so-called *agenda setting* is most vividly illustrated by the media coverage of the Watergate story. Watergate clearly was not a major concern of most Americans early in the series of revelations, but came to be a focal concern with increasing and unremitting media coverage. In one experimental study, Iyengar, Kin-

Kennedy's better speaking style and appearance in the 1960 presidential debates may have helped him defeat Nixon in the election.

der, Peters, and Krosnick (1984) had subjects watch news stories. The researchers manipulated how many stories referred to a particular problem. When the stories emphasized a particular area (such as energy policy), performance of President Carter in the energy area better predicted subjects' general evaluation of Carter than did his performance in other, unemphasized areas—in other words, subjects' ratings of Carter depended more on the media-emphasized areas than on other areas. It would seem that media attention to a particular area indirectly affects the performance ratings of politicians.

The Laboratory versus the Real World
Contrary to popular belief, it is fairly difficult to change people's attitudes through the media. For example, research on the effectiveness of advertising shows highly limited effects of most advertisements (Comstock et al., 1978). Most advertisements affect the product preferences of fewer than 5% of the people who come into contact with them, although that 5% may represent a lot of money. On the other hand, it seems trivially easy to change attitudes in a controlled, laboratory situation. Why is there this discrepancy?

Carl Hovland (1959), the father of modern attitude-change research, addressed this question and isolated several factors that differentiate the two situations. First, whereas the real world contains all sorts of people, most laboratory research uses reasonably bright college undergraduates who are in an environment that stresses open-mindedness and willingness to change. Second, subjects in laboratory experiments are cut off from their usual social ties, and they are therefore unable to perceive the subtle social cues that guide them to accept or reject communications. Even if you were trying to be unbiased in watching a political campaign speech, you would probably interpret, remember, and judge it quite differently watching with a supportive, a hostile, or a neutral audience, or alone (Kelley & Woodruff, 1956).

Also, the nonlaboratory researcher usually wants to study factors that influence change on important issues—it is the issues that are the focus. For the laboratory researcher, on the other hand, it is the change that is the focus, and the issues typically are trivial ones, for which change can occur easily and often.

Finally, laboratory research is usually more precise and refined than the typical real-life study. This means that change can be more easily detected and that there is more control over confounding variables in the laboratory. Just as it is easier to see a faint star in the countryside, away from bright city lights, so it is easier to detect change in the well-controlled (that is, simplified) laboratory environment.

These differences do not invalidate laboratory study. Most of what we have learned about the major variables that affect attitude formation and change come from such studies. However, by the same token we should not be surprised when we discover that what appears to be simple in the laboratory turns out to be complex in everyday life.

SUMMARY

Throughout the 50 or so years of active empirical research in social psychology, attitude change has been perhaps the most enduring single issue. Because there is such a vast amount of research, the area is filled with complex and conflicting results. However, there are some ways of bringing order to the area. One important distinction is between systematic or central processing, whereby the person makes an effort to understand the message and to think about it logically, and heuristic processing, whereby the person uses simplified rules such as "I usually agree with people I like" to decide whether to change. Generally, systematic processing is more common when the person is involved with the issue and heuristic when the person is less involved. When the person is processing heuristically, such variables as the appearance of the communicator are likely to be important, but when the processing is systematic, the quality of the arguments is more critical.

One popular approach to systematic processing has been the cognitive responses perspective, which assumes that people try to understand a message and that their own responses affect subsequent attitude change. In a sense, people change themselves through the responses they generate to the message. If people have the ability and motivation to understand, then to the extent they generate positive thoughts about the message, they will change toward it. If, on the other hand, their attempts at comprehension lead to negative thoughts, attitude change will be inhibited. When people have negative reactions, they may try to counterargue with the communication and this counterarguing retards attitude change. Generally, forewarning people that they will hear a discrepant communication retards attitude change because the forewarning increases counterarguing, whereas distraction may interfere with counterarguing and lead to more change.

Attitude change is generally more easily obtained in controlled, laboratory situations than in everyday life. In particular, the concern that the mass media, especially television, control and change attitudes receives little support from research on advertising and political campaigns. Change is often easier to get in experiments than in the everyday world because experiments use subjects who are willing to change, they remove social supports for previous attitudes in experiments, they use more trivial attitudes, and they have a greater ability to detect small changes.

CHAPTER SUMMARY

- There is general agreement that attitudes have cognitive (belief), affective (emotional), and behavioral components, although most social psychologists em-

phasize the cognitive and affective components in their research.

- Generally, beliefs are based on our socialization, experiences, and past behaviors, and the affective component also reflects the extent to which the attitude object facilitates or inhibits our achievement of certain goals. But attitudes also reflect personality factors.

- Most social psychological research on attitudes deals with attitude change. Some attitude change is superficial in that it rarely persists, whereas other change is more stable and may eventually effect changes in other attitudes.

- Older theories of attitude change were oriented more toward the various motivations people have for changing; most modern models are oriented more toward how people think about their attitudes and the communications that seek to change them.

- In systematic processing, the person makes an effort to understand the message and to think about it logically; in heuristic processing, the person uses simplified rules, such as "I usually agree with people I like," to decide whether to change. Generally, systematic processing is more common when the person is involved with the issue and heuristic processing when the person is less involved.

- The cognitive responses perspective assumes that, when people are processing systematically, they try to understand a message and that their own responses affect subsequent attitude change. If the person understands the message and generates basically positive responses to it, he or she will change toward the message. If he or she generates negative messages, attitude change will be inhibited.

- Credible (trustworthy and unbiased) communicators produce the most attitude change. Attractive communicators also produce more change than unattractive ones, but typically only when the recipient is processing heuristically.

■ Some communications primarily work on affective components. Research suggests that when the attitude object elicits positive associations, people will also have positive attitudes toward it.

■ Fear arousal is an effective means of changing attitudes, but only if the person feels that by changing attitudes he or she can reduce the fear.

■ Communications that are somewhat discrepant from the recipient's views are effective in changing attitudes. Beyond the optimal discrepancy, increasing discrepancy leads to increasing rejection. Less-than-optimal discrepancy produces agreement, but of a kind insufficient to motivate a change of attitude. People also generally change more when the arguments are better and more numerous, and primarily when they are processing the arguments systematically.

■ People seem to differ in how easily they change their attitudes, but this characteristic does not seem to be related to other personality characteristics.

■ A considerable body of research suggests that people may resist changing their attitudes by posing counterarguments to the communication. Generally, forewarning people that they will hear a discrepant communication retards change because it increases counterarguing. In contrast, distraction may interfere with counterarguing and lead to more change. People may scan their reactions in biased ways, which may also lead to change.

■ Attitude change is typically harder in the everyday world than in experimental laboratories. For example, most research on political campaigns suggests that they are largely ineffective in changing attitudes, though they may motivate people to vote. Attitude change in the real world must deal with stable attitudes and must counteract social tendencies against changing.

CHAPTER

8

INTERNAL AND EXTERNAL CONTROL OF BEHAVIOR

once was involved with a prison reform group that sponsored meetings where some of the prisoners could talk to people from the community about their lives. I chaired one such meeting at a local Unitarian Church. The men had been chosen by the warden for their abilities to make a good impression and to be articulate. The large audience on this particular evening consisted mostly of well-educated, middle-class liberals.

Each of the prisoners talked about his background (almost all were working-class men from the Boston area) and about his crime (which spanned a range of offenses). They all admitted that they had done the crime for which they had been convicted and said that they were sorry and hoped to go straight when they got out. Most of them were vague about their plans, but they all hoped to get jobs or finish their education. Overall, they made a good impression.

After an hour or so, I opened the floor for questions, and several predictable questions were asked: What was prison like? Were the educational programs in prison any good? What advice would they give to youngsters? The men replied in different ways, but collectively they conveyed an impression of articulate men who cared about their lives and the lives of others. They were sometimes quite passionate in their statements, and the audience loved it.

I knew the evening had reached a high point of sorts when one woman announced that these men were really just like her own sons, although perhaps not as well educated, and she hoped there was something she and others could do for them. For example, she asked the warden if the men could come to live in the community in homes like hers. The warden suppressed a smile and said that this wasn't officially possible. But she persisted. These men could benefit from living in the commun-

ity, and she was sure they would straighten up if only they were in better living conditions. The prisoners began to exchange knowing looks and to tap one another under the table. Finally one of them said, "Lady, I don't think you understand. We're not nice people, or we wouldn't be in prison."

It was a revealing incident at several levels. The woman had the interesting theory that the nice young men sitting at the table in front of her could not possibly be bad men. Perhaps if we had pushed her, she might have held forth a theory of how their bad behavior was really a matter of circumstance. There are no bad men, only bad situations. (If that were her theory, she managed to ignore some relevant data. The men had been carefully selected by the prison authorities and had been briefed by me on how to make a good impression. In other words, she was surely seeing them at their programmed best. In a way, the woman was expressing surprise that prison convicts could act civilized and normal.) On the other hand, the prisoner who replied had seen his fellow convicts at their worst, and he had no illusions that what they were presenting was "real." But he might also have considered the possibility that the criminal behavior he and his comrades had performed was as much a response to situations as was their present "good" behavior and was not necessarily due to a "not nice" disposition.

INTRODUCTION

Most psychologists have traditionally assumed that our attitudes, motives, values, personality traits—in short our personal or internal dispositions—control or at least strongly affect behavior. Social psychologists have long studied attitude formation and change on the assumption that attitudes predict behavior. Clinical psychologists have generally assumed that therapy ought to be directed to a rearrangement of motivational and cognitive forces because only by changing such variables will meaningful behavioral change ensue. Personality psychologists have measured personality traits in hopes of better predicting behavior.

Of course, not all psychologists have made such assumptions. For example, behaviorists traditionally emphasized situational rather than conscious control over behavior. And, for all their interest in attitudes and values, social psychologists have long suggested that social and normative forces had major effects on behavior. So there has been a debate over the years about whether personal dispositions or external forces exert more control over behavior. In this chapter we discuss the relative effects of internal and external forces on behavior as that behavior is predicted from (1) attitudes and (2) personality traits.

ATTITUDES AND BEHAVIOR

Attitudes do not always predict behavior well. Before discussing ways that current models attempt to explain this, we first consider some of the classic research on attitudes and behavior and then discuss some problems with this research.

RESEARCH EVIDENCE

LaPiere's (1934) classic study remains provocative. At a time when anti-Chinese prejudice was high in America, LaPiere set out on a cross-country trip with a Chinese couples. They stayed at hotels and ate at restaurants, and LaPiere recorded how they were treated. He judged the treatment to be average or above average most of the time, and the group was refused service only once. When he returned, LaPiere wrote to each of the more than 200 places they had visited and asked whether Chinese guests would be acceptable. Of the half that responded, 90% said that they would *not* welcome Chinese guests. Here is a case in which behavior did not match attitudes.

Later research has used more precise measures of both attitude and behavior but has generated similar results. DeFleur and Westie (1958) asked Southern white students during a period of considerable overt racial prejudice whether they would be photographed with a black person of the opposite sex. Although the prejudice of the white students did predict willingness to be photographed and how openly they would allow the photo to be displayed, about 30% of the students displayed major inconsistencies between the amount of their prejudice and their behavior.

In well-controlled laboratory studies, there is usually a statistically significant relationship between attitudes and behavior, but generally these relationships are modest and far from perfect. Interpretation of such evidence depends on one's frame of reference. We could either emphasize that the predictions are significant or that they are weak and inconsistent. Given their natural tendency to assume that attitudes and behaviors *ought* to go together, social psychologists can perhaps be forgiven for focusing on the fact that they often *do not* go together.

EXPLANATIONS

Several factors may account for attitude–behavior discrepancies (Liska, 1974). One is the spirit-is-willing-but-the-flesh-is-weak syndrome. For example, I may approve of participation in community affairs but, when asked to do something, I find that I am lazy or do not have the time. There is nothing in attitude theory that suggests that all attitudes must always be expressed in overt behaviors.

We also all have competing internal controls over behavior. The hotel managers contacted by LaPiere may have disliked Chinese people but also may have disliked provoking a scene; and, of course, even prejudiced business people like to make money. So before we can understand the behavior of these managers, we have to know *all* their relevant attitudes, not just how prejudiced they are.

Another problem is that the object of the attitude is often not well defined and may not be the same in the attitude and behavioral responses. For example, it is entirely reasonable that in 1934 many hotel managers may have had negative stereotypes of Chinese people as uncouth, strange, even bizarre. Of course, a manager probably does not want such people in his hotel, but a nicely dressed, well-behaved Chinese couple was not the object of the attitude. LaPiere might have found more consistency between attitudes and behaviors if his Chinese friends had more closely conformed to what we may assume was the object of the hotel managers' attitudes.

Lord, Lepper, and Mackie (1984) have confirmed the importance of this reasoning. They measured subjects' stereotypes of certain groups (fraternities and homosexuals) and their attitudes toward working with members of these groups. The subjects were then asked whether they would like to work with actual individuals, who either matched closely or departed significantly from stereotypes. As expected, the subjects' previous attitudes predicted their behavior (the decision to work with the person) well when the person fit the stereotype but poorly when the person did not fit the stereotype. Attitude–behavior consistency is greater when the object of the attitude and the object of the behavior are closely re-

lated than when they are different. As we noted in the previous chapter, a man may be quite anti-Semitic but still like his Jewish neighbor who is not similar to what he considers to be the typical Jew.

THE FISHBEIN–AJZEN MODEL

Reasoned Action Theory Predicting behavior from relevant attitudes is not simple or straightforward. One model developed for more precise prediction, and which has generated both considerable research and considerable controversy, was proposed initially by Fishbein (1967b) and is now generally termed the *reasoned action theory* to emphasize the idea that behavior often results from explicit reasoning about the implications of the behavior. Further details of the model have been spelled out by Fishbein and Ajzen (1975) and by Ajzen and Fishbein (1980).

A major assumption of this model is that attitudes predict behavior to the extent they agree in target (object of the attitude), behavioral act, and time. The claim is that violations of this rule have led to less than optimal attitude–behavior similarity. For example, sometimes attitudes are measured long before the relevant behavior, leaving room for many additional and unforseen factors to affect behavior. Similarly, as we have already suggested, there may be attitude–behavior discrepancies when the attitude is measured toward general classes of people but the behavioral object is a single person.

Perhaps the most mischievous problem is that we typically measure attitudes as general dispositions whereas behaviors are quite specific. Suppose we measure you as having a generally positive attitude toward religion, and from that we hope to predict whether you go to church next Sunday. We surely would expect to find some correspondence, but we would also be forced to recognize that other factors affect your church attendance. For example, you may have been out late on Saturday night, or you may have an even more

Martin Fishbein

favorable attitude toward playing golf than toward going to church. If, on the other hand, we measured a more specific attitude (corresponding to the specific behavior), we would probably find greater attitude–behavior correspondence (Ajzen & Fishbein, 1977). Asking you on Sunday morning whether you plan to go to church in an hour would predict your behavior better than would asking you if you like going to church or if you think religion is good.

Does that mean that measurement of general attitudes is worthless? No. Attitudes predict behavior to the extent that they are similarly specific or general. Our problem is that we have been using a general attitude to predict a specific behavior. But specific attitudes (say, toward going to church in an hour) predict specific behaviors (actually getting there) quite well. If we want to enhance the predictive power of general attitudes, we ought to find that they predict general behaviors. But behaviors are, by their nature, specific, so how is this possible? It's not so hard when you think about it. General attitudes are really summaries of how we feel toward some general class of objects, and so general behaviors might be thought of as summaries of behaviors toward a class of objects. In the case of religious behavior, we might measure how many times you went to church last year, how much money you give to the church, whether you pray before meals, and whether you participate in church educational

activities and missionary work. So a general index (perhaps merely the sum of all these behaviors) would provide the required measure of general behavior. General religious attitudes should predict such a general index of religious behaviors quite well (Fishbein & Ajzen, 1974). The general attitude may not predict any one behavior very well, but it does predict a more general measure of behavior.

Thus, the general rule is that, for good prediction, attitudes and behaviors should correspond in their specificity or generality. General attitudes predict a general behavior index better than they do a specific behavior. Similarly, if we want to predict a specific behavior, we should measure attitudes toward that specific behavior.

Fishbein and Ajzen argue, however, that attitudes do not predict behavior directly. Rather, attitudes control behavior by affecting *intentions* to act in a certain way. This intermediate step of behavioral intentions is added because there is another factor (besides attitudes) that affects intentions, namely *normative feelings* about whether one *should* perform a particular behavior. For example, you may attend church because your parents pressure you or tell you that you should; in other words, you are doing something because of norms. Both your attitudes toward attending church and your feelings of obligation to your parents (normative feelings) will affect your intentions to attend, which are in turn will affect your actual behavior. The clear emphasis of the theory of reasoned action is to predict intentions, which are in turn a function of attitudes and norms. These two forces—one representing internal forces (the attitude) and the other an internal representation of external forces (normative beliefs)—are added together to predict intentions (see Figure 8.1).

The theory of reasoned action further specifies the determinants of both attitudes and normative beliefs. As we saw in the last chapter, Fishbein assumes that attitudes have several belief components, each accompanied by an

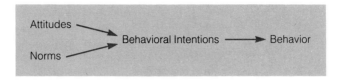

FIGURE 8.1   Fishbein–Ajzen Model of Attitude–Behavior Relation.

evaluation. Consider your attitudes toward going to church on a particular Sunday. You may well have the salient belief that you will feel better about yourself and the world if you go to church; because that probable outcome is positively evaluated it will contribute a positive attitude toward attending church that morning. Then you think about the refreshments and comradeship after services, which are again positively evaluated. You also like to sing at the service—another positive element. On the negative side, you have a splitting headache and feel sure the organ music and singing will make it worse. Because this outcome is negative, it will subtract from your positive attitude toward attending services. And as you think about it, you decide there is a middling probability of a boring sermon (highly negative). As you add together all these positive and negative elements you will finally arrive at an attitude toward attending the morning services.

Just as the effect of attitudes is influenced by the strength of their positive or negative evaluations, so too are normative forces influenced by the motivation to comply with the norms. For example, your mother has recently made it clear that you should attend church more often. Conversely, your new friend down the hall will surely make fun of you if you go. Now you are surely aware of these pressures, positive in the case of your mother and negative in the case of your friend, but before they can influence your intentions you must be motivated to comply with them. You must *want* to please (or not please) your mother or your friend for her pressure to affect your in-

tention to go to church. Thus, each of your normative beliefs must be multiplied by your motivation to comply with it to determine the total effect of normative forces on your behavioral intentions.

If we want to predict whether you will go to church this Sunday morning, the best predictor will be your intention to go. This intention in turn results from your total attitude toward attending church that morning as well as your total normative forces: the attitudes and normative forces together produce intentions. In the example in Table 8.1, your attitudes are positive, because all the positive aspects (feeling uplifted, comradeship, and singing) are more important than the negative (your headache and the possible boring sermon). The normative forces are also positive in this case, because we have assumed that your desire to comply with your mother is stronger than your desire to comply with the friend. However, because the attitudinal and normative components of intentions are additively related, either component could overcome the other in a given context. For example, you might have a positive attitude about going to church but be so strongly motivated to do the opposite of what your insistent mother wants that you refuse to go just to spite her. Alternatively, you might hate going to church (negative attitude) but go every Sunday to please your mother. Such normative pressures are one of the major reasons attitudes do not always predict behaviors. We have all done something we did not want to do or *not* done something we *did* want to do, because of social pressures.

TABLE 8.1   THE FISHBEIN–AJZEN MODEL APPLIED TO CHURCH ATTENDANCE.

| Belief | Attitudes toward Attending Church | | |
	Strength (probability of outcome)	Evaluation of Outcome	Product
Feeling uplifted	.7	10	+7
Comradeship	.5	6	+3
Singing	.8	5	+4
Headaches	.8	−5	−4
Boring sermon	.4	−5	−2
Total attitude			+8

| | Normative Beliefs | | |
	Outcome	Motivation to Comply	Product
Mother pressures	+5	2	+10
Friend ridicules	−3	1	− 3
Total normative belief			+ 7

$$\text{Intention to Go to Church} = \text{Attitude} + \text{Normative Belief}$$
$$= \quad 8 \quad + \quad 7$$
$$= \quad 15$$

In the example given in Table 8.1, your intention is positive and we would predict that you will shortly be getting ready for church. However, note that we have measured your attitudes as closely as possible in time to the actual event. The theory of reasoned action clearly asserts that attitudes most closely predict behavior when the attitudes and behaviors are close together in time. Suppose we had measured your attitude last night. The attitude might have been quite different. On the one hand, you wouldn't have had a headache, and on the other hand, you might not have had such a strong desire for being uplifted. In any event, attitudes can change in a short time because our beliefs and evaluations change. It is sometimes easier to have a positive attitude toward church on Thursday than on Sunday morning.

Research Evidence   Research has generally supported the theory of reasoned action. Intentions predict behavior well, especially when they are measured just before the relevant behavior (Ajzen & Fishbein, 1970, 1973,

1980). However, there has been some question about whether attitudes and normative beliefs have their effects on behavior only through the mediation of intentions or whether there may also be more direct routes to behavior. For example, you may have a positive attitude toward some act and therefore perform it without forming any intention at all. A person who has a warm feeling and positive attitude toward babies may smile at a baby or even pick it up without forming any explicit intention—it is almost an involuntary and direct expression of the attitude. In this way attitudes could affect behavior without going through an intention.

In some cases, behavior that seems intended and purposive may be caused neither by intentions nor by attitudes. You may find that you go to church on Sunday not because you have a positive attitude or because of pressure, but simply because it has become a habit.

There is empirical support both for the possibility that attitudes affect behavior directly (without mediation by intentions) and for the possibility of habitual control over behavior (that is, behavior caused by neither intentions nor attitudes). Bentler and Speckart (1979, 1981) have shown that attitudes exert some direct control over behavior, apart from whatever indirect effects they exert through intentions. These authors, as well as Bagozzi (1981) and Fredricks and Dossett (1983), have also found that past behavior can affect subsequent behavior independently of intentions. If you had a positive attitude toward attending church or you were in the habit of going (past behavior), these components could act directly on the behavior without first affecting a relevant intention.

Matters are thus somewhat complicated, but it seems that most purposive behaviors are strongly affected by intentions and that intentions result from attitudes and normative factors. However, it may also be important to include other kinds of variables in the prediction model. Perceived *ability* or *control of the situation* is one strong possibility. I intend to grade a pile of term papers that are sitting on my desk before tomorrow morning, but somehow I doubt that there are enough hours for me to be able to get the job done. Asking people whether they expect to perform a behavior (which takes account of perceived capabilities) predicts behavior better than asking them about their intentions (Warshaw & Davis, 1985). More generally, our confidence in our ability to perform behaviors and accomplish goals strongly influences our behavior (Bandura, Adams, & Beyer, 1977). For example, for people who are dieting, weight loss is better predicted by perceived control over weight than by dieting intentions (Schifter & Ajzen, 1985). Again, such data do not invalidate the basic reasoned action theory, but they suggest that attitudes may affect intentions and behavior most strongly when the behavior is fully under the control of the person.

EXPERIENCE AND ATTITUDE ACCESSIBILITY

The theory of reasoned action requires highly specific measures of attitudes to predict specific behaviors well, which might imply that there is little utility in measuring general attitudes. However, some social psychologists have not been so eager to give up on the predictive power of general attitudes: perhaps general attitudes predict some behavior, some of the time, for some people. One possibility that we explore later in the chapter is that some people are more situationally controlled while others behave more in line with their internal attitudes, values, and other, general dispositions.

Another possibility is that experience with the attitude object determines attitude–behavior consistency. Imagine that we have measured the attitudes of incoming freshmen toward psychology courses. Assuming that most of these students have had limited exposure to psychology, their attitudes would be uninformed, vague, and nonsalient; it seems intuitively likely that such attitudes would not predict behavior (such as whether they will take a psychology course) very well. On the other hand, suppose we came back a year later and measured the attitudes of students who had just finished taking one psychology course. Again, intuitively, it seems that these students would have more knowledge about the course and that their informed attitudes would predict their decisions about whether to take another course. Or perhaps they have a greater psychological investment in attitudes formed on the basis of experience—there is evidence that attitudes predict behavior better when there is more investment in the attitudes (Sivacek & Crano, 1982). At any rate, attitudes predict behavior better when the attitudes are based on some experience with the attitude object (Fazio & Zanna, 1981).

In Chapter 7 we reviewed evidence that suggests that, when subjects have experience with attitude objects, their attitudes are more accessible and such accessible attitudes are better predictors of behavior (Fazio, Chen, McDonel, & Sherman, 1982). Also, when people have a chance to think about their attitudes or past behavior, their attitude–behavior consistency

Russell Fazio   Mark Zanna

increases (Sherman, 1980; Zanna, Olson, & Fazio, 1981). Making salient the relevance of attitudes to behavior has the same effect (Snyder & Kendzierski, 1982).

Although experience and thought generally make attitudes more salient and stable, which in turn promotes their control over behavior, this effect is not inevitable. At least one set of experiments suggests that too much introspection can *reduce* attitude–behavior consistency. Wilson et al. (1984) found that asking subjects to analyze the reasons for their attitudes lowered how well their attitudes predicted their behavior. The authors speculate that in searching for reasons (for example, in why they like their boy- or girlfriends) subjects may end up actually changing their attitudes, thus reducing the ability of the previous attitudes to affect behavior. For example, at Time 1 you report that you like your friend, but after thinking about it for a while you are now, at Time 2, not so sure. If we now (Time 2) measured some behavior that reflected liking, we would probably find that your attitude at Time 1 predicts your behavior less well than the newly formed (Time 2) attitude. Unfortunately, we are trying to predict with the old (Time 1) attitude. If attitudes become more stable or are more accessible as a function of thought, we would expect attitude–behavior consistency to be increased, but if such thought actually forces a change of attitudes, attitude–behavior consistency might be reduced.

SUMMARY

It seems reasonable to assume that attitudes would predict behavior, but social psychologists have long known that attitudes predict behavior relatively poorly. One reason for such attitude–behavior discrepancy is that people are not always motivated to act consistently with their attitudes; another reason is that a person may hold different attitudes, which may conflict when predicting the same behavior. Fishbein and Ajzen's theory of reasoned action suggests that attitudes will predict behavior to the extent that the attitudes and behavior are similarly specific or general and to the extent that the relevant attitudes are measured as close in time to the behavior as possible. Their theory suggests that the best predictor of behavior is an intention to perform the behavior and that attitudes and norms together predict intentions. Some psychologists have argued that the model is overly restrictive and that other variables also predict behavior. There is good evidence that attitudes sometimes affect behavior directly without being mediated by intentions and that past behavior may predict future behavior as a kind of habitual response. In addition, perceived ability to perform the behavior may also be important. Fazio and his colleagues have argued that attitudes will predict behaviors better when the person has experience with the attitude object and when the attitude is relatively accessible.

PERSONALITY AND BEHAVIOR

The attitude–behavior relationship is only one part of an enduring problem in psychology. More generally, we often ask to what degree and under what circumstances behavior is controlled more by situational forces (external forces) or more by personal qualities (internal forces). Of the internal variables, attitudes are important, but motives, values, and personality traits are also presumably crucial.

Although there are many kinds of personality theories, American personality psychologists have emphasized the measurement of personality traits. Such traits as self-esteem, need for approval, authoritarianism, dogmatism, need for achievement, power orientation, cognitive differentiation, and need for affiliation have extensive research literatures. Once these and other traits are measured, researchers often try to see whether they correlate with or predict other traits and behaviors. For example, one would expect to find that people who have a high need for approval also have low self-esteem and readily conform to the expectations of others.

THE MISCHEL CRITIQUE

Despite the search for correlations between personality traits, such traits often fail to correlate with one another or to predict accurately concrete behaviors. This has led some to question the validity of measuring personality traits. Although criticisms based on such data go back a half century (Epstein & O'Brien, 1985), the most substantial attack in recent years was made by Walter Mischel:

> Several main findings have emerged from the data on traits and states . . . and it is now instructive to summarize them briefly. First, behavior depends on stimulus situations and is specific to the situation: response patterns even in highly similar situations often fail to be strongly related. Individuals show far less cross-situational consistency in their behavior than has been assumed by trait–state theorists. The more dissimilar the evoking situations, the less likely they are to lead to similar or consistent responses from the same individual. Even seemingly trivial situational differences may reduce correlations to zero. Response consistency tends to be greatest within the same response mode, within self-reports to paper-and-pencil tests, for example, or within directly observed nonverbal behavior. Intraindividual consistency is reduced drastically when dissimilar response modes are employed. Activities that are substantially associated with aspects

of intelligence and with problem-solving behavior—like achievement behaviors, cognitive styles, response speed—tend to be most consistent. (Mischel, 1968, p. 77)

Mischel's position has been controversial, and it is fair to say that defenses and criticisms of his work have dominated the study of individual differences during the past 20 years.

Situations versus Traits   We argued earlier that general attitudes often do a poor job of predicting specific behaviors. Mischel has similarly argued that relatively general needs, values, motives, traits, and psychic entities (such as conscience) also fail to predict concrete behavior. This is not necessarily to deny that people differ in need for approval or in aggressive tendencies, but Mischel has forcefully argued that by themselves such entities do not predict much.

Mischel feels that a major reason personality traits cannot predict behavior is that most behavior is situationally specific and under the control of cognitive factors such as how the person understands the situation. Thus, the dominant person does not always try to lord it

Aggressive behavior is more often a function of the situation than of individual personality.

over other people and may in fact be quite submissive in some situations. To understand why he is dominant sometimes and submissive others, we need to know such things as how he construes the situations, what payoffs he anticipates in each situation, and what he values in the way of rewards (Mischel, 1973).

Criticisms of Mischel's Position   There have been several critical responses to the Mischel position. First, we may ask whether Mischel has been entirely fair to traditional personality research. He has argued that personality variables cannot predict behaviors well because behaviors are caused by many factors that vary from situation to situation. In some situations you desire approval and act accordingly, whereas in others your behavior may be dictated by other needs. People are aggressive in some situations but not others, because the situational forces are different and hence promise different consequences for aggressive behaviors.

However, the seeming inconsistency of behavior from situation to situation may be more illusory than real. Consider John, who is your basic aggressive and hostile person. We follow John around and discover that he is demanding and rude to a salesclerk, insults his professor, and tells his roommate to go to hell—we find that John is aggressive in several situations. But then we notice that when his best friend tells John that he is sometimes obnoxious, John says nothing. Surely he is not being aggressive now. However, it we look

Walter Mischel

beneath the surface, we may find that John has decided that his friend will be more hurt if he fails to acknowledge the criticism than if he yells back. So while his behavior doesn't seem, on the surface, to be aggressive, in reality it is an expression of his general aggressiveness. Similarly, a person who generally tries to gain the approval of others may, on occasion, refuse to engage in an obvious approval ploy because it seems so fawning and obvious—he figures he will gain more approval by acting as though he doesn't care about the approval. The point is this: behaviors may seem inconsistent from situation to situation, but when we pay closer attention to what the behaviors *mean* they may exhibit a greater coherence (Bem & Allen, 1974; Bowers, 1973; Rausch, 1977).

It is also possible that seeming inconsistencies among personality dispositions and relevant behaviors are caused by failures to measure behaviors properly. Recall that Fishbein and Ajzen argued that we should not expect general attitudes to predict specific behaviors, because behaviors are subject to many forces other than attitudes. The same is true when we try to predict behaviors on the basis of personality dispositions. Just as the religious person may not behave religiously in every situation because of competing pressures and attitudes, so the hostile person has reasons other than his hostility for behaving the ways he does. Personality variables often do a better job of predicting general indexes of behaviors than they do of predicting single behaviors (Buss & Craik, 1983a, 1983b).

Furthermore, aggregated behavioral indexes show greater stability over time than do single behavioral indexes (Epstein, 1979, 1980). John may not yell at his roommate next month as he did today, but if he performed many hostile behaviors today he will probably still be hostile (although perhaps in different ways) next month.

So temporal consistency is increased if we use many behavioral measures of the personality disposition. What about consistency across situations? If John is hostile to his roommate, will he also be hostile to salesclerks and to his professors? Some have reported that specific behaviors (such as yelling) show little cross-situational consistency, but if behaviors related to a common trait are combined (say yelling, hitting, swearing, and using obscene gestures, which are all related to hostility), they will be consistent from one situation to the next (Conley, 1984; Epstein, 1979, 1983; Moskowitz, 1982). In other words, yelling in one situation might not predict yelling in another, but if the person is somehow hostile in one situation he will tend to be hostile in another, although perhaps in a different way. However, Mischel and Peake (1982, 1983) have reported no real improvements in consistency using such aggregated indexes of behavior. Box 8.1 provides an extended discussion of this controversery.

What has and has not been shown here? First, Mischel is largely correct that personality dispositions usually do a relatively poor job of predicting single behaviors, just as general attitudes do. He is also largely correct that individual behaviors are often inconsistent across situations. However, personality dispositions are better predictors of *general* indexes

of behavior, and there is greater temporal and situational consistency of general behavior compared to specific behaviors. This is, of course, exactly what we would expect from the research reviewed in the last section on the attitude–behavior relationship.

THE INTERACTIONIST POSITION

If Mischel's position is correct, it should follow that, for any given behavior, situational forces should predict behavior better than do personality variables. This idea has received research support. For example, Endler, Hunt, and Rosenstein (1962) gave subjects a list of anxiety-provoking situations (such as you are crawling along a ledge high on a mountain side, or you are entering a final examination) and a list of symptoms (such as heart beats faster and nausea), and asked subjects to indicate to what extent they would experience each symptom in each situation. The analysis showed that situations accounted for the responses better than did differences among subjects. In other words, it is more likely that two people will both be anxious in an exam than it is that the same person will be anxious both in the exam and on the mountain ledge.

BOX 8.1

THE CROSS-SITUATION CONSISTENCY DEBATE

In the debate over whether personality traits predict behaviors, a central issue has been whether behavior is consistent across situations. Mischel argued that personality traits do not predict behaviors well because behavior is inconsistent across situations. Obviously, if our behavior changes dramatically from situation to situation, our relatively constant traits cannot be the major predictors of the behavior. So the assump-

tion of at least some cross-situational consistency in behavior is essential for trait theorists. Epstein and others have argued that behavior is consistent across situations *if* it is measured carefully and *if* the behavior is measured and observed in the aggregate—that is, as a general index of behavior.

In a controversial paper, Mischel and Peake (1982) reported preliminary data

BOX CONTINUED

from what would seem to be a definitive study of cross-situational consistency. Sixty-three Carlton College students were assessed on conscientiousness over a 10-week period. Conscientiousness behavior included such things as class attendance, assignment neatness, time spent studying, class participation, bed neatness, lecture punctuality, and desk neatness. All these behaviors were observed on at least three occasions so there was aggregation over time. For most behaviors there was a fair degree of temporal stability; that is, a student who attended class on one day was also likely to attend on another. A neat desk early in the period accurately predicted a neat desk later.

Then the authors correlated different single behaviors across subjects and found that the average correlation was quite low ($r = .08$). This means that a person who was conscientious in one way on a given day (say getting to class on time) was not necessarily conscientious in another way. On the average, the individual behaviors were not related to each other. To address the Epstein argument, Mischel and Peake then aggregated behaviors over occasions so that the total number of classes attended might be correlated with the total neatness of the desk. Some of the individual correlations were quite high (the correlation between aggregated class attendance and aggregated assignment punctuality was .53—students who got to most of their classes were also likely to get their assignments done on time), but the general average of all correlations was only .13. Thus, aggregating the measures over time increased the correlation from .08 to .13, a difference hardly worth the increased computer time. Because different measures of

the same trait, conscientiousness, failed to show even promising correlations, Mischel and Peake concluded that there was little cross-situational consistency.

However, the "other side" has counterattacked (Epstein & O'Brien, 1985; Jackson & Paunonen, 1985). First, consider the partial list of behaviors that Mischel and Peake called *conscientiousness*. It is easy to understand that these behaviors were grouped together because they all seem to have something in common. But if you think about it, the behaviors can be quite different. Imagine a person who participated in a class discussion. Is he likely to have made his bed? It's possible that he's so conscientious that he did both, but it may be that if he's in the habit of talking a lot in class he has more important things to worry about than making his bed. So we might expect a *negative* correlation between some of the behaviors (meaning that a person who was likely to do one would be unlikely to do the other), and, in fact, some of the behaviors were negatively correlated.

Now what do we make of that? Mischel and Peake say the specific behaviors are all examples of conscientiousness, but because conscientious behavior is controlled by situational forces, and because situations differ, it is not surprising that some examples are unrelated or even negatively related. But their critics argue that these behaviors are not all good examples of conscientiousness and that it is not surprising that the behaviors fail to correlate with each other.

So who is right? One way to solve such matters is to have a theory of sorts that specifies what conscientiousness is and what counts as behavioral examples of it. If we had such a theory and if we concluded that all the behaviors were good conscientious behaviors, the low correlations would be powerful support for the Mischel position—the same person can be conscientious in one situation but not in another. Unfortunately, Mischel and Peake did not provide any theory or definitional criterion for their selection. The behaviors were chosen informally and without regard to any theory of conscientiousness. So perhaps some of the behaviors are not examples of conscientiousness at all, and in that case it is not surprising that there are low correlations among them—apples and oranges are being compared. The point is that, in the absence of a formal theory and definitional criteria, one can call behaviors anything one wants, but then anyone has as much right to claim that class participation is *not* conscientious behavior as Mischel and Peake have to claim that it *is*.

Fortunately there is a way to make an end run around the definitional issue. When one constructs a personality test—say of self-esteem—one usually does not know ahead of time what good self-esteem behaviors are. The standard way to deal with this is to assemble behaviors that look likely to measure the construct and then to see which are empirically related to the others. We assume that the behaviors that correlate well together do so because they are all measuring the same general trait. Those that don't correlate may be perfectly good measures of something but not of the trait under consideration. One could view the present situation analogously. Because we may not agree on what conscientious behaviors are, we will correlate behaviors and use the ones that work well together to measure conscientiousness. If Mischel and Peake had followed this process, they would

have had to throw out several behaviors. So, according to their critics, they have tried to correlate good examples of conscientiousness with poor examples. No wonder the correlation is low.

A second problem with the study is that it fails to speak directly to the aggregration issue. Mischel and Peake seemed to have assumed that each of the conscientiousness behaviors took place in a different situation, but this is arguable. Unfortunately, we do not have a clear idea in this study what is to be defined as a "situation." Is one's dorm room a situation? If so, Epstein would want to aggregate all the conscientious behaviors in the dorm and compare them to a similar aggregate in another situation, say the classroom. The Epstein argument has been that we must aggregate behaviors *within* situations in order to compare the (aggregated) behaviors *across* situations and *across* time. The important issue for Epstein is whether conscientiousness properly measured will transfer from the dorm to the classroom. Epstein and O'Brien (1985) have argued that when the data are aggregated within situations and are analyzed across situations and time, there is substantial evidence of cross-situational consistency, a conclusion supported by Jackson and Paunonen (1985).

The point is this. Mischel and Peake are probably correct that behaviors we think of as examples of the same trait often do not correlate well with one another. However, if one selects the behaviors with care, using standard test-construction procedures, and aggregates the behaviors carefully within situations, there is evidence for cross-situational consistency, and in some cases the evidence is strong.

Situation–Trait Interactions However, this kind of result should not be taken to mean that situational forces are invariably stronger than personality variables: through appropriate manipulation, either one can be made to look more important than the other. For example, if I observed a wide range of people on a battlefield and then the same people all reading books, I should likely be impressed by how important situations are in controlling anxiety. After all, almost everyone is more anxious in the first situation than in the second. On the other hand, if I observed the behavior of the same people in a physics exam and in a calculus exam, I would note relatively few situational differences and might be overwhelmed with the degree to which Mary seems more anxious in both exams than Joe. Or if I observed quite different types of people (say a seasoned Marine and a small child) in the same situation (say a mock battle), I would surely note tremendous differences between their behaviors. In short, whether personality or situation seems more important depends in large part on the range of situations and individuals considered. There is some evidence that personality predicts behavior best when situational forces are relatively weak (Monson, Hesley, & Chernick, 1982).

Some reflection might also indicate that there are bound to be enormous interactions between people and situations. That means that different situations affect different people differently. Even a moderately anxious person is not always anxious but is anxious only in some situations. For example, I tend to be moderately anxious in the dark but not in giving public lectures. Many people would have the reverse reaction, fearing audience reaction more than ghosts and bogeymen. And to complicate matters even more, different people display anxiety (and other classes of behaviors) differently. My stomach gets the brunt of my anxiety although I can easily maintain outer calm; other people may twitch more but rarely get a nervous tummy.

Many people would be anxious on a deserted bridge at night, but others would not be—or would not show it so clearly in their facial expressions.

At this point it is hard to talk sensibly about whether one person is more anxious than another. John is more anxious than Ruth in some situations but not in others, and he shows his anxiety in one way while she shows hers in another. So in recent years there has been increased concern with studying these kinds of interactions between personality and situation. For example, Mischel (1973, 1977, 1981a) now emphasizes how different kinds of people perceive different kinds of situations, and he sees personal continuity as more a matter of consistent ways of perceiving than of behaving. In particular, social learning theorists such as Mischel (see Chapter 1) suggest that people behave in ways they think will yield good rather than bad consequences. To understand whether you think a situation will provide rewards or punishments, we would need to know how you construe the situation.

Is it threatening or relaxing? Do you think the others present like or dislike you? So, even if you are usually anxious you may not be anxious in a situation where you feel others like you. And, in the same situation, the person who is usually less anxious than you might act more tense if he construes the others present as hostile.

Situational Forces Revisited   Because the situation plays such an important role in behavior, psychologists recognize that situations, like people, have "personalities" in the sense that they encourage or discourage certain types of behavior (Moos, 1976). To begin with, there is usually a broad consensus as to appropriate behaviors (Price & Bouffard, 1974). Most everyone would agree that praying is more appropriate in church than at a disco and that wild dancing goes over better at a disco than at a church service.

Furthermore, situations can be characterized by **templates** of personality tendencies, which are patterns of characteristics that represent different ways of being successful (Bem & Funder, 1978). For example, one university might be represented by a template of high grades and an intellectual orientation, whereas at another university beer drinking and fraternity life might be the dominant means to success. Thus, we can characterize situations—universities in this case—by patterns of behavior (or templates) that are encouraged in those situations.

Other psychologists have examined more directly how people construe situations. In Chapter 6, we noted that people have implicit personality theories, notions about which traits go together. Similarly, people tend to see situations as related to one another, at least in certain contexts. For example, a classroom may be seen as similar to a dorm room because both are chilly, or as similar to a snack-bar because you see your best friend in both places. Reading a novel at home is similar to jogging in the park in that both may be relax-ing, though they are dissimilar in their physical characteristics. Lord (1982) found that behavior is more consistent in situations perceived to be similar. The person who sees playing golf and attending a concert as similar in that they both involve opportunities to make business contacts will behave relatively similarly in these two quite different physical and social settings. The person who sees the two settings as quite different will show almost no similarities in behavior.

So, people may perceive situations differently and hence see different consequences for their own potential behaviors. In addition, our personal dispositions may lead us to prefer and seek out some situations over others, thereby reinforcing our dispositions (Alker, 1977; Olweus, 1977; Snyder, 1981b). For example, the introverted person who prefers to spend time alone, and does, will have few opportunities to develop his interpersonal skills. Conversely, the extrovert may prefer loud parties where the social situation will further encourage him to be socially oriented. There is now considerable evidence that personality traits predict what situations people prefer (Diener, Larsen, & Emmons, 1984; Gormly, 1983). There is also some correspondence between the personalities of married people (and probably close friends as well), suggesting that people not only select compatible mates, but may change one another to become more similar (Buss, 1984). So people tend to select environments and companions that are consistent with their personalities, and that kind of selection reinforces their personality traits.

INDIVIDUAL DIFFERENCES

Internal variables such as attitudes and personality traits do not always do a good job of predicting concrete behaviors unless they are measured with care and unless we respect their interactions with situational variables. Our attitudes, traits, motives, needs, and the like affect what we do, but generally they are not so powerful in themselves as to lead to certain kinds of behavior under any and all circumstances. Rather, they guide our intentions, goals, and perceptions, which may nonetheless vary considerably across situations.

Having said all that, however, simple observation also leads us to believe that some people are more consistent than others. We all know people who really do seem to be hostile in a wide range of situations and others whose hostility seems far more situationally specific. Some people are almost invariably kind; others are kind only to some people some of the time.

Consistency   Bem and Allen (1974) asked subjects to assess their consistency of behavior. Some people reported that their behavior was fairly consistent from situation to situation, whereas others reported their behavior as more inconsistent. Bem and Allen also found that people who said they were consistent for a particular trait actually were more consistent. Such consistency effects have also been demonstrated by Underwood and Moore (1981), although Mischel and Peake (1982), Chaplin and Goldberg (1985), and others have found no support for the idea that people differ in their consistency across situations. It is probably safe to conclude for the moment that self-described consistency has not yet been securely linked to actual individual differences in consistency across situations.

Self-monitoring   Although people's descriptions of their own consistency may or may not predict their actual consistency, it is still possible that there are individual differences in cross-situational consistency. Mark Snyder (1979) has argued that consistency of behavior may itself result from a stable personality disposition, which he calls *self-monitoring.* People who are high in self-monitoring are especially concerned about the appropriateness of their behavior and hence adjust their behavior according to situational cues about such matters. Low self-monitors, on the other hand, pay less attention to information about normative cues and hence vary their behavior less from situation to situation. In support of these claims, it has been found that, compared to low self-monitors, high self-monitors (those who are concerned about norms of behavior) pay more attention to social information (Berscheid, Graziano, Monson, & Dermer, 1976), are more likely to seek out information about others (Elliott, 1979), have better knowledge about how others behave in prototypic social situations (Snyder & Cantor, 1979), show more varied emotional responses (Lippa, 1976; Snyder, 1974), are more affected by situational demands in their choice of work partners (Snyder, Gangestad, & Simpson, 1983), and offer more situational explanations for their behavior (Snyder, 1976).

This research offers impressive support for the proposition that high self-monitors are both more aware of situational determinants of behavior and more motivated to comply with them. Given that such situational forces usually vary across situations, it is not surprising that their behavior also varies across situations (Bem & Allen, 1974; Snyder & Monson, 1975). Thus, compared to low self-monitors, high self-monitors are relatively inconsistent across situations. Low self-monitors show more consistency across situations, and their behavior is also better predicted by their individual dispositions. As one would expect, general attitudes predict behaviors better for low self-monitors (Snyder & Swann, 1976; Zanna, Olson, & Fazio, 1980).

Obesity   Strangely enough, another promising area in the study of the relative influences of internal and external forces is obesity. Stanley Schachter has speculated that the eating behavior of obese people tends to be regulated by external cues, such as when it is the appropriate time to eat, whereas normal-weight people eat according to perceptions of internal hunger cues.

In a famous experiment by Schachter and Gross (1968), subjects arrived at an experiment at 5 P.M. They sat facing a prominent clock that for half the subjects was rigged to run slow (so that when the real time was 5:50 the clock showed 5:35) and that for the other half was fast (so at 5:50 the clock showed 6:20). During various procedures, the subjects were told they were free to eat crackers that were available on a table. The dependent measure was the amount of crackers eaten. Physiologically, most of the subjects probably were beginning to get hungry about the time the cracker-eating phase began. If eating behavior is regulated by external cues, the subjects who watched the fast clock should have more reason to eat than those watching the slow clock. As predicted, the obese subjects ate more crackers when the external clock told them it was time to eat (the fast clock).

Another prominent external cue is the quality of food. As the Schachter hypothesis sug-

Judith Rodin

gests, the eating of obese people is affected more by the taste of food than is the eating of normal-weight people (Nisbett, 1968). Obese people are also affected more by the external variable of how hard it is to get at food. For example, whereas normal-weight people eat nuts whether they are shelled or not, fat people eat less when they have to work by shelling the nuts (McArthur & Burstein, 1975).

Obese people eat more because external time and food cues tell them to do so. Are they generally more affected by external cues? Several studies suggest they are. Obese subjects score higher on a standard measure of dependence on external visual cues (McArthur & Burstein, 1974), are more distracted by extraneous environmental cues in a learning situation, and are more likely to decide whether to comply with a request based on how nice the requester is (Rodin & Slochower, 1974). It is fair to conclude that a general responsiveness to external cues plays some role in the eating behavior of obese people, but there are other, probably more important psychological and physiological factors that also cause obesity (Rodin, 1981).

SUMMARY

Just as general attitudes often do not predict specific behaviors well, so too do general personality traits predict specific behaviors weakly. Mischel has argued that this is because behavior is controlled more by perceptions of situational forces than by internal dispositions such as personality traits, and that there-fore—*in principle*—traits cannot predict be-havior. There have been several responses to Mischel's arguments. First, behaviors may not mean what they seem to mean, so that seem-ingly nonaggressive behaviors, for example, might actually be stimulated by hostility. Sec-ond, Epstein and others have argued that, just as general attitudes predict general behaviors best, so predictions from general traits ought to be strongest for generalized behavior indexes. Thus, Epstein has suggested that we predict indexes based on aggregated behaviors. Other personality psychologists have em-phasized the idea that different kinds of people react differently to different kinds of situa-tions. In recent years this interactionist posi-tion has been extended to include the idea that our personality dispositions may encourage us to favor certain kinds of situations, which then reinforce our dispositions. Finally, it has been argued that some people are more consistent than others. People who are high in self-monitoring respond more to situational forces (and hence are less consistent) than those who are low in self-monitoring and who therefore are governed more by their internal qualities. Obese people are also more responsive to external forces than are normal-weight people.

CONTROL OF BEHAVIOR

In our considerations of both the attitude–behavior relationship and the prediction of behavior from personal dispositions and traits, we have mentioned briefly that behavior is in-herently ambiguous. In the first instance, the same behavior can mean different things, depending on the intentions of the actor. When your friend teases you about something, he could merely be trying to restore your good mood by showing you that you take yourself too seriously or he could be hostile and trying to get your goat. Second, what behaviors mean to actors and observers depends heavily on sit-

uational contexts. Joking loudly about the sex-ual affairs of a friend would be interpreted dif-ferently depending on whether they were said at his funeral, to his wife at a party, or to the friend over a drink. How we identify or label our own behavior also affects how we behave. When I exhort my students to try harder, I see my behavior as "trying to motivate them," un-til someone makes me realize that my behavior may also be seen as "taking out your own frustrations on your poor students."

ACTION IDENTIFICATION THEORY

In their *action identification theory,* Robin Vallacher and Daniel Wegner (1985) suggest that the labels or identifications that people at-tach to their behaviors vary in their generality or abstractness. One can think of eating a steak as chewing (low level, or fairly concrete) or as having a pleasant experience (higher level, or more abstract). Generally, low-level identifications correspond to the ways we do things; so eating (high level) is accomplished by chewing (low level). High levels are the rea-sons for which we behave ("I chew because I want to eat"). Vallacher and Wegner's theory suggests that people will try to identify their behavior at as high a level as possible because the higher-level identifications give more meaning to behavior and because ordinarily we prefer not to think about the grubby,

Robin Vallacher   Daniel Wegner

mechanical details of our actions. So you would rather think of your munching as providing essential nutrients or as allowing you to enjoy a pleasant meal rather than as simple chewing of food matter.

Emergent Identification   However, when an action sequence identified at a relatively high level becomes problematic, a lower-level identification will be sought. Suppose you are performing a series of actions you call studying (high level) and you find you are being distracted and are having trouble concentrating. You may then begin to think about the details of how to study, and if someone asked you what you were doing, you might say something like "I am trying to understand this page" or "I am trying to memorize these terms." Problems with the behavioral sequence have forced you to use a lower-level identification. However, remember that people prefer to use high levels of identification. When low levels are adopted, the behavior becomes subject to other high-level identifications through a process Vallacher and Wegner call *emergence.* When your studying becomes difficult and you move to a lower-level identification by saying you are memorizing or understanding or underlining, you may subsequently move back to a higher level once the behavior is under control again. However, the high-level identification may not be the one you formerly had. You now may think of your behavior as being bored or as missing a favorite TV program. According to action identification theory, you then have moved from "studying" (high level) to "memorizing" (lower level) to "being bored" (a different higher level) while performing exactly the same behaviors throughout.

Wegner et al. (1984) assessed whether lower-level identifications give rise to emergent redefinitions of behavior. In one study, students were given coffee to drink. Normally we would think of this activity at a high level; there is nothing problematic about drinking

This person might describe herself as preparing for a career, trying to do well in a course, studying, or reading a book.

coffee. However, the experimenters caused some of the subjects to have to think about the details of their behavior by making them drink from unwieldy cups; this resulted in lower levels of identification ("raising the cup to my lips"). Then the experimenters suggested a new, or emergent, high-level identification of coffee drinking, either as seeking stimulation (for some subjects) or as avoiding stimulation (for other subjects). Action identification theory predicts that those who had previously concentrated on the low-level identifications should be affected by these emergent high-level identifications, whereas the subjects who stayed with high-level identifications ("drinking coffee") would not be subject to new identifications. One measure of whether the subjects had taken on the new emergent identification as stimulated or unstimulated was how loud they set the volume on some music they were asked to rate—the presumption being that stimulated people would prefer louder music than would unstimulated people. As expected, those who had been forced to think about the details of drinking coffee were affected by the new identification; in particular those who were told that coffee was stimulating played the music more loudly than those who were told that coffee was not stimulating. But those who had maintained the previously high-level identification (drinking coffee) were not affected by the suggested emergent interpretation of being stimulated or not stimulated. Other experiments (Wegner, Vallacher, Kiersted, & Dizadji, 1986) have shown that people who generally identify behavior at a low level are more subject to new identifications that affect behavior than are people who generally use higher levels.

Attention and Impulse   Vallacher and Wegner have also suggested implications for control of behavior. Action sequences with high-level identifications tend to be performed with little attention to the details of the behavior. Often this is good: we often want routine behaviors to remain routine and not require us to think much about them. However, there are times when a little more attention to detail might come in handy. For example, one problem that obese people have is that they eat without thinking; similarly, people with drinking problems often drink almost reflexively. Wegner and Vallacher (1986) have confirmed that heavy drinkers and alcoholics tend to identify their drinking behavior in more general terms than do occasional drinkers. Their general identification of their behavior keeps them from thinking about the details of how to do it, and thus they sacrifice some conscious control over it. On the other hand, people who tend to identify behavior at lower levels are also more impulsive. According to action identification theory, this is because those people with low-level identifications are open to new, emergent identifications that redirect their behaviors.

Although there are obviously many forms of control over behavior other than whether or not the behavior is identified at a high or low level, the theory of action identification is important for reminding us that how we think about what we do affects what we do.

FORMS OF CONTROL

Throughout this chapter we have been considering the complexities of behavioral control. It is easy to find cases in everyday life and from your own experiences where external control has been very salient and others where feelings of freedom have been more prevalent. Yet, in most cases, neither form is absolute. Let us consider three kinds of cases.

Involuntary Control   Some behaviors are involuntary and are controlled almost entirely by internal and external stimuli. People with certain diseases may twitch and lurch uncontrollably, for example; their behavior is surely controlled by internal neural events, but there is little that the afflicted person can do about it. More commonly, you may find your behavior under the control of external stimuli, such as when you jump involuntarily when startled by a loud noise.

Voluntary Control   Some behaviors are clearly affected by thought and are seemingly under the control of our wills; most social behavior falls readily into this class. As we have seen, there are a great many ways in which external stimuli and thoughts may be related. At one extreme we have what might be called impulsive behavior, in which a person responds to a situation almost totally in terms of his or her immediate needs and wants. We have suggested that such impulsive behavior is most likely for those people who are thinking about their behavior in fairly concrete ways. At the other extreme is behavior that seems controlled by the situation.

If questioned, most of you would probably say that you were not free to go to a large party the night before an exam or to go skiing at the time the exam is given. You don't *feel* free. You feel controlled and put upon. And yet this manner of speaking (which we all use) is not fully accurate. You are not forced to attend the exam. Your behavior is not involuntary like the actions of your digestive system or of someone who has been conditioned to blink when his name is said. You will surely think, and think hard, about what you will do. That is not to deny the reality of the strong external force of the examination, but we need to remember that if you do study for and attend the exam, it remains your choice to do so.

The research we have covered in this chapter on attitude and personality influences on behavior makes this point forcefully. It is rare for most of us to do exactly what we want to do in the sense that the only effective controls over our behavior are our attitudes and personality dispositions. As we have seen, situational forces also affect what we want from our behavior and what the potential consequences of the behavior will be. You may have a more positive attitude toward skiing than toward taking an exam, but in the larger sense you have a more positive attitude toward graduating from college in a timely fashion than in momentary pleasures—or at least you do if you elect the exam over the ski slopes. Thus, you show up for exams not because you have to but because you want to in terms of some larger attitude or value.

Habitual Behavior   There is another form of behavior somewhere between calculated, purposive behaviors and fully controlled, automatic behaviors. What we usually call *habitual* or *routine behavior* seems automatic and mechanical in the sense that it tends to be performed about the same way without benefit of conscious control. I walk to my first class of the day in about the same way, following the same route, and usually without a moment's thought. On the other hand, such behavior can be brought under conscious control, could be different than it is.

Much of what most of us do throughout each day is in this way mindless and habitual. I smile at those who smile at me, drive to work without any conscious control of my driving behavior, answer the telephone "hello," walk to my classes, and pet friendly dogs without the slightest relevant thought. Or at least I do until something goes wrong, such as encountering a detour sign or hearing a growl from the "friendly" dog. Many learning theorists have assumed that habitual behavior is controlled by external stimuli rather than by thought. However, one can usually seize control over such behavior. You can answer the phone "goodbye," say "bah, humbug" at those who smile at you, and kick friendly dogs. Habitual behavior is fairly automatic and fairly determined at one level, but at another it awaits redirection of attention and a seizing of conscious control.

Action identification theory, of course, makes this point explicitly. So long as we have learned action sequences well and continue to identify them at a high level, there is no reason for conscious control. On the other hand, when there are problems, a lower-level identification results, there is more concentration on

Driving is often habitual and does not require full concentration.

details, and the behavior is subject to a new, higher-level identification where it goes into automatic pilot again.

How we control our behavior has been an enduring question for thousands of years. Yet even the highly selective discussion here should be sufficient to alert you to the fact that most of our behavior is controlled by our personal attitudes, wants, desires, and values, while situational forces affect which of these are salient and most powerful.

CHAPTER SUMMARY

■ It seems reasonable to assume that attitudes would predict behavior, but in fact attitudes predict behavior relatively poorly. Several reasons exist for this attitude–behavior discrepancy. One is that people are not always motivated to act consistently with their attitudes. Second, the same behavior may be encouraged by one attitude and inhibited by another—that is, different attitudes held by the same person may conflict with each other. Third, attitude objects are not always the same as behavior objects—that is, attitude objects may be more general or more specific than behavior objects.

■ Fishbein and Ajzen's theory of reasoned action suggests that attitudes will predict behavior to the extent that both are similarly specific or general and to the extent that the relevant attitudes are measured as close in time to the behavior as possible. Their theory suggests that the only predictor of behavior is an intention to perform the behavior and that attitudes and norms together predict intentions. They assume that the normative component consists of concerns about proper behavior and motives to comply with these norms.

■ Some psychologists have argued that the theory of reasoned action is overly restric-

tive and that other variables also predict behavior. There is good evidence that attitudes may affect behavior directly, without being mediated by intentions, and that past behavior may predict future behavior as a kind of habitual response. In addition, perceived ability to perform the behavior may also be important.

■ Another model of the attitude–behavior relationship suggests that attitudes best predict behavior when the attitudes are based on direct experience with the attitude object and when the attitudes are more accessible. On the other hand, sometimes it is the case that thinking about attitudes can *lower* the predictive power because the attitudes are changed by thinking about them.

■ Just as general attitudes often do not predict specific behaviors well, general personality traits also predict specific behaviors only weakly. Mischel argued that this was because behavior is controlled more by perceptions of situational forces than by internal dispositions such as traits, and that therefore traits in principle cannot predict behavior.

■ There have been several responses to Mischel's arguments. It has been argued that behaviors may not mean what they seem to mean, so that superficially inconsistent behaviors may in fact stem from a consistent disposition; for example, seemingly nonaggressive behaviors might actually be stimulated by hostility.

■ Just as general attitudes predict general behaviors best, so predictions from general traits ought to be strongest for generalized behavior indexes.

■ Other personality psychologists have emphasized the idea that different kinds of people react differently to different kinds of situations. In recent years, this interactionist position has been extended to include the idea that our personality dispositions may encourage us to favor certain situations, which has the effect of confirming and reinforcing the dispositions.

- It has also been argued that some people are more consistent than others. People who are high in self-monitoring respond more to situational forces (and hence are less consistent) than those who are low in self-monitoring (and who are governed more by their internal qualities). Obese people are also more responsive to external forces than are normal-weight people.

- The action identification theory suggests that people may identify their actions at fairly global or at fairly specific levels. The latter usually suggest *how* actions are done and the former suggest reasons *why* they are done. People try to identify behavior at the highest level, but when the behavior becomes problematic they typically reidentify it at a lower level. This opens the possibility that a new, higher-level identity can emerge. Generally, habitual behaviors are identified at higher levels and lower-level identifications lead to impulsive behaviors.

- A few human behaviors are purely involuntary in the sense that we have no control over them. However, most behaviors are controlled by our needs and purposes, although we often feel that such behavior is controlled externally. Habitual behavior is fairly automatic but is nonetheless purposive in that it can easily be brought under conscious control.

PART THREE

SOCIAL BEHAVIOR

C H A P T E R

9

SOCIALIZATION

n 1797, peasants near Aveyron in Southern France observed a wild and naked boy running through the woods. He was captured, caged, and exhibited in the public square. After several escapes he was permanently captured in 1800 at which point he was estimated to be about 12 years old. Nothing was known of his background, but evidently he had lived alone for many years because he was devoid of both speech and social graces. He preferred raw food, seemed oblivious to pain, did not respond to sounds, disliked wearing clothes, and readily defecated and urinated on the floor or even in his bed.

This boy, quickly dubbed the *enfant sauvage de L'Aveyron* was not the first nor the last child who had spent most of his childhood in the wild (Zingg, 1940, discusses several cases). But the Wild Boy of Aveyron case has been especially well documented (Lane, 1979) and is historically important. For he was seen by the French philosophers and scientists of the time as an almost perfect test case for competing theories of human nature—one that people were naturally good and perfect, although usually corrupted by society, and a second theory that people are born as mental blank slates upon which experiences then write.

Unfortunately for the first of these notions, the boy displayed so little orientation toward anything except his own immediate biological needs that it would be hard to classify him as either social or nonsocial, as either bad or good; indeed, he was initially seen as severely retarded. He probably would have lived the rest of his life in an institution if not for the concern of a young physician, Jean-Marc-Gespard Itard, who had a long-standing interest in working with the deaf. Through painstaking training methods, Itard was able to accomplish what had seemed impossible: the young man (by now named Victor) learned to dress himself and to restrain his impulses somewhat. Victor could smile and express his

Truffaut's film *The Wild Child* shows Victor before any attempt to civilize him.

appreciation; he learned to defecate in appropriate areas. In time he could even follow simple commands written out for him. However, he never learned to talk, and although he lived into his 40s, he never became a self-sufficient human being. So perhaps the theory that experience could inscribe civilization onto Victor's blank slate also did not fare very well.

While we can applaud the good work of Dr. Itard, we are still struck by how uncivilized Victor was. He was not economically self-sufficient, could not express complex feelings or thoughts, had limited control over his impulses, had little conception of morality, and could not participate meaningfully in any complex social situation. We cannot rule out severe retardation as the cause, but we also cannot eliminate the possibility that Victor had missed out on the important social experiences of infancy and early childhood that we now believe to be crucial for learning how to adapt to adult society.

INTRODUCTION

Although our interests in Victor are not those of the scientists who studied him at the time, his case still raises instructive questions about the process of socialization. *Socialization* is the process of learning how to behave effectively in groups and adjust to particular cultures. It is the process of learning how to become effectively social. Ordinarily we think of socialization as a process that occurs in childhood as the child learns the rules of his or her society and acquires the skills necessary for reasonable success as an adult. It is in that sense that we may think of Victor as incompletely socialized. On the other hand, socialization is not restricted to children. We may speak of socialization to a particular career, to physical disability, to being a college student, or to marriage or parenthood, because these various statuses all carry well-defined rules for behavior and self-definition. In this chapter we concentrate on socialization of the child, although much of the remainder of the book will speak broadly, if indirectly, to socialization of adults in various contexts.

THE TASK OF SOCIALIZATION

Children are not born with many social skills. The newborn can signal distress by crying. Soon after she will smile at others, and within the first year she will be able to laugh, hold out her arms to be picked up, and crawl toward another person. But during the first year she will not be able to communicate much more than her diffuse emotional states. She cannot engage effectively in complex forms of social behavior such as sharing, cooperation, or aggression. She cannot control her impulses or biological processes. She has no sense of morality and little or no consciousness of herself as distinct from the environment or as part of a complex social matrix. The 1-year-old has a great deal to learn about becoming a part of her family and the larger society, and her parents will devote much of their time for the next several years to teaching her what she needs to know to be an effective member of her society.

Knowledge, Skills, and Motivation   Consider briefly some of the general characteristics we expect to find in a well-socialized adult in our society. First, she must have a fairly extensive knowledge about her language and culture. Most obviously she should have a clear conception of the values, norms, morals, and rules of her society, although we might not expect her to share all of them. She will also need a large amount of practical information such as where to find groceries, whom she should consult for medical problems, and how the everyday economic system functions.

We would also expect her to have various cognitive and physical skills. She should know how to read, write, and do enough math to

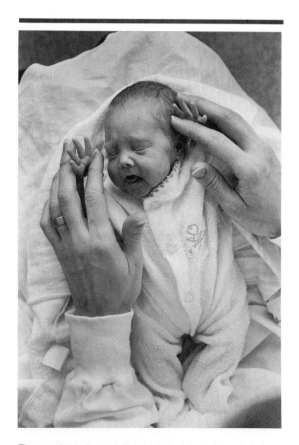

The newborn human is nearly helpless.

hold down a job. It would be nice if she had social skills such as the ability to help others, to communicate effectively, to be sympathetic and empathetic, and to listen and understand what others say to her. If she marries and has children, we would hope she would know how to be an effective spouse and parent.

Internalization   In addition, we expect that well-socialized people want to do the things society says they should do. To be sure, we do not all jump out of bed every morning eager to get to work, but most of us manage to get to work, more or less on time, and to do more or less what is required of us. Of course, a person may have many reasons for performing what we think of as well-socialized behaviors. Consider that there are selfish economic advantages in robbing an elderly widow of her life savings, but most of us do not rob widows and orphans (or anyone else for that matter). Why?

One obvious reason is that people who rob and cheat run a sometimes small but always present risk of getting caught and punished; the police and judges take a dim view of people who cheat elderly women. Even if you managed to escape detection by the legal system, you might still suffer the negative consequences of loss of status and reputation among friends and family.

But that is not sufficient. We hope that you do not cheat the elderly woman because you have some sense that it is wrong. Your own values and moral sense—your conscience—keep you from performing such behaviors. In the language of the last chapter, you have internal as well as external controls over your behavior. This process of acquiring internal controls is ***internalization.***

THE HISTORY OF CHILDHOOD

In an influential book, Aries (1962) argues that for much of recorded history childhood was not seen as a unique period of being hu-

man and that parents did not have the same emotional investment in their children as most modern parents do. Until the last century, about half the children died before reaching maturity; in some societies infanticide was sanctioned and common. Children who survived were rarely given much education and were put to work as soon as they were able. As a rule, children ate, slept, and participated in adult recreations with the adults around them. Furthermore, Aries argues there were no special strategies for raising children. They were socialized through participation in adult activities.

The Aries argument is probably too simplistic. It is certainly possible to find evidence that medieval and later peoples recognized children as a special category of people, and there have been explicit theories of what children are like and how they should be trained for at least 1,000 years (Borstelmann, 1983). On the other hand, many of these theories had more to do with religious ideals than with close observation of children and realization of their unique needs.

Major changes took place in the eighteenth century. Two psychological models evolved around this time, both of which argued against the religious notion that children are inherently evil. John Locke (1693) believed that there are no innate ideas and that learning is all-important. For Locke, children are essentially vessels to be filled with experiences, and he emphasized the importance of the training in and practice of proper social behavior. Jean-Jacques Rousseau (1763), on the other hand, felt that children did have inborn, but largely good, tendencies, and that if children could be protected from the corrupting influences of society, they would acquire virtue on their own. Adults should not preach and command but rather guide the natural unfolding of capacities. Given the conflicting theories of Locke and Rousseau, you can perhaps appreciate why the study of Victor was of such interest at the time.

In the nineteenth century, concerns with the effects of child labor focused additional attention on the status of children, but the major theoretical impetus came from the evolutionary theory of Charles Darwin. While Darwin (1877) pioneered the careful observation of children, the main impact of the theory came through the popularly accepted but erroneous view that the development of the individual child recapitulates the development of the species in general. Thus scientists became interested in the study of children largely for the light that their development supposedly shed on the evolution of the human species.

In our century three broad conceptions have dominated: Freudian, behaviorist, and Piagetian. *Sigmund Freud* (1856–1939) felt that the child is born as a creature of pure impulse, and the task of socialization is to control, repress, and channel these primitive impulses. In the well-socialized adult, behavior is controlled not only by environmental contingencies (through the ego) by also by strongly internalized prohibitions and standards fueled by guilt (the superego).

The *behaviorists,* led by John Watson (1878–1958), continued the Lockean tradition of seeing learning as crucial. For example, from a behaviorist perspective, prohibitions must be learned through punishment and standards must be acquired through rewards. Social learning models (see Chapter 1) stress the ability of the child to learn through observation of others and emphasize cognitive controls over behavior. However, what remains even in this highly cognitive version of learning theory is an emphasis on the learning of relatively discrete behaviors and their consequences. In other words, there is no general, integrated product of socialization such as conscience, but only a set of situationally specific rules; you may recall Mischel's arguments from Chapter 8.

Jean Piaget (1896–1980) stressed Rousseau's notion of unfolding. There are innate developmental programs, but these are stimulated by and acquire much of their content through experience. Moreover, children pass through various developmental stages, and at each stage thoughts and behaviors are integrated together in a particular way. So young children differ from adults not only in being more impulsive or in having fewer experience-based rules, but also because they think about the world differently from adults.

PARENT–CHILD INTERACTIONS

It seems natural to assume that socialization is something forced on the child initially by parents and later by schools and other agents. Indeed our culture asserts that parents have a substantial duty to turn the creature, dominated by biological impulses, that they bring home from the hospital into a well-behaved person by shaping his or her behaviors and inculcating their values. Not surprisingly, therefore, most of the early research on socialization processes concentrated on particular techniques, such as punishment, toilet training, and explicit instructions.

However, useful as this approach is, it ignores the mutual *interactions* between parents and their children. Bell (1968) pointed out what many parents had always known, namely, that children are full if often unwitting participants in their own socialization. For example, the parents of an active youngster will find themselves closely supervising his activities and responding to his propensity to "get into things." The child may for his part resist the supervision through struggling, crying, or even hitting, which will in turn initiate a series of controlling behaviors by the parents. The parents of a calmer child may interact with their child with less control and perhaps with different results.

It is usually impossible to assign causal influence in such interactions. Consider the example in Figure 9.1. The parent punishes the child because of what the child does, but the

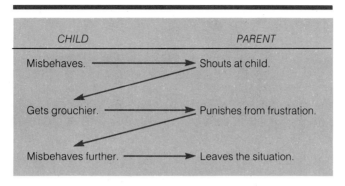

CHILD	PARENT
Misbehaves. ⟶	Shouts at child.
Gets grouchier. ⟶	Punishes from frustration.
Misbehaves further. ⟶	Leaves the situation.

FIGURE 9.1   Mutual Parent–Child Interaction.

child's behavior is also affected by what the parent does. If we discover that an aggressive child has parents who tend to use more physical punishment, we cannot be sure whether the punishment causes the aggression or the reverse. Indeed it is likely that each causes the other. So as we consider various parental behaviors we must always remember that parents react to their children and children react to their parents.

EARLY INTERACTIONS

Parents and children react to one another almost immediately after birth. A newborn who nurses quietly will elicit quite different responses from her mother than the child who is fussy and hard to feed. Of course, infants do not have elaborate behavioral repertoires, but behavioral coordination between infants and their mothers has been observed in the days immediately after birth. For example, mothers and children coordinate their movements when the child is being held, and when either mother or child gazes at the other the gaze is often returned. Later, when the child begins to make sounds, vocalizations are also likely to be exchanged (Maccoby & Martin, 1983).

During the first year or so of life, parents do not generally engage in explicit socialization strategies. However, after the first year, the in-

creased mobility and strength of the child make control a more central concern. Physical skills such as eating and elimination begin to be shaped. As the child acquires language and can understand simple requests and commands, mothers and fathers usually begin the process of teaching the child behavioral controls, physical skills, and the rudiments of correct behavior.

TYPES OF PARENTAL BEHAVIOR

Socialization research has investigated a wide range of parental behaviors, such as the use of physical punishment, reasoning, restrictions on freedom, severity of toilet training, and the like (see Hoffman, 1970; Maccoby & Martin, 1983). For the most part, studies that examined specific parental behaviors have found low and often negligible correlations of such parental variables with the later behavior of children.

Dimensions of Parental Behavior   In recognition of the difficulties in using single parental variables, socialization researchers have tended to examine larger dimensions of parental behavior. Maccoby and Martin (1983) have suggested that the crucial dimensions of parental behavior are (1) demanding and controlling versus undemanding and uncontrolling and (2) warm accepting, child-centered versus rejecting, parent-centered behaviors. Note that the emphasis is less on particular parental techniques than on general parental style.

In general, there is agreement that child-centered, warm, accepting parents produce more socially and morally competent youngsters (Maccoby, 1980). The restrictiveness or control dimension has provided more conflicting results, perhaps because both too much and too little control can produce problems. Another reason is that control combined with warmth intuitively seems different than control combined with hostility. For example, parents can set a child's bedtime (controlling) because they recognize the child needs rest (accepting, child-centered), or they can do so because they want to get their children out of their hair relatively early in the evening (rejecting, parent-centered). Conversely, parents may give a child freedom about bedtime (uncontrolling) either because they want to foster feelings of autonomy in the child (child-centered) or because they don't want to fight with their children about going to bed (parent-centered). So neither control nor freedom is good in itself but the effect of each is, in part, dependent on the spirit in which it is administered.

Although not specifically designed to test predictions about the dimensions above, a series of studies by Baumrind (1967, 1971) was instructive. She divided parents into three categories: *permissive* (child-centered, but not demanding), *authoritarian* (demanding, but parent- rather than child-centered), and *authoritative* (both demanding and child-centered). Generally, she found that the authoritative parents had more mature children than either the authoritarian or permissive parents.

Communication   Another important aspect of parent–child interactions is how parents communicate their wishes, demands, warmth, and the like. Hoffman (1970) pro-

posed that such communication can be broken down into two large categories. ***Induction strategies*** involve reasoning and explanation. The parent may be fairly demanding but attempt to support his or her demands with verbal explanations and clarifications: "I know you are angry, but I don't want you to hit your sister because it is wrong to hit other people." Alternatively, ***power-assertion strategies*** involve less reasoning and less concern for the needs of the child: "Stop hitting your sister; that makes me so tense. I'm going to hit you if you don't stop."

There is good evidence that the use of induction strategies is associated with children who are mature and helpful and who have good impulse control. Hoffman (1983) argues that induction is effective because it draws attention to the social consequences of behavior and promotes empathy. Thus, Hoffman suggests that the child's affective responses are as important as his or her cognitive understandings. Of course, the content of parental communications to children cannot easily be separated from the control and accepting dimensions discussed earlier, but such research reinforces our earlier conclusion that *what* a parent does has less effect on the child than *how* the parent does it.

The Role of Fathers   In our society, mothers have had the primary responsibility for childcare, even when both parents work. Therefore, it is not accidental that until recently most parent research concentrated on maternal behaviors, but with increasing concerns about gender roles, fathers have also come under the research gun.

There are some differences between the ways moms and dads interact with their children. For example, mothers are more nurturing and play more quietly (less physically) with their children than do fathers (Clarke-Stewart, 1978; Parke, 1979). Fathers are more likely to hold even 1-year-old daughters than sons and to issue behavioral prohibitions to sons (Snow, Jacklin, & Maccoby, 1983). On the other

hand, fathers and mothers are often remarkably alike in their treatment of their children and there is no particular reason to believe that males are less equipped for the parental role than are females. Of course, this does not suggest that in every family mothers and fathers are alike in their behaviors, but only that mothers are not inevitably more involved and competent than fathers.

MODELS

Parents spank, command, caress, scold, explain, and smile warmly when they socialize their children, but they do something else that may be just as important: they provide *models* for appropriate behaviors. When mom spanks Jimmy out of frustration and anger, the most important lesson may be that hitting is an acceptable way of dealing with negative emotions. So we need to consider the role of modeling in socialization.

Parental Models   You may recall from Chapter 1 that learning through imitation encompasses two distinct processes. The first is learning how to do something. When a parent works at woodworking, her example will teach the child certain physical skills. Second,

models provide information about the consequences of behavior. If dad swears every time he has to clean the toilets, it is likely that junior will learn to see this as disgusting work. Of course, parents have long known this, and most parents strive to set good examples for their children regardless of what else they do in the way of more direct tutoring and socialization strategies.

Children will readily imitate almost any model: priests, neighbors, classmates, older siblings, doctors, and grandparents may be copied from time to time. Nonetheless, there are special reasons for emphasizing the importance of parental models, especially in the preschool years. One obvious reason is that young children simply spend more time with their parents than with most other people. Second, children are especially likely to imitate models who are nurturant and who control valuable resources, a role most parents fit (Bandura, Ross, & Ross, 1963b). Third, parents may work especially hard to set consistent examples of appropriate behaviors. Finally, parents may be particularly likely to accompany their "model" behaviors with explanations that further support the salience of the behavior. However, as children get older, other models become important, and in recent years the importance of television models has been stressed.

Television   Chidlren watch a lot of television, and they do so from an early age. Even toddlers may watch as much as 1 hour per day and school-age children typically watch as much as 4 to 5 hours per day (Pearl, Bouthilet, & Lazar, 1982). It is extremely difficult to be sure what exact effects television may have because television watching is associated with many other variables, such as type of family, socioeconomic status, and general societal trends. Moreover, at the level of the individual child, such variables as comprehension and attention, parental explanation and support for media messages, and family environment must be taken into account (Collins, 1983).

"To start with, gentlemen, I just want to say that if at times I strike you as being strange or weird or something, or whatever, it's because I'm probably the first member of this board to grow up with television."

Drawing by W. Miller © 1982 by The New Yorker Magazine, Inc.

There have been several large-scale studies of the role of television (Pearl et al., 1982; Singer & Singer, 1981; Surgeon General's Scientific Advisory Committee on Television and Social Behavior, 1972). The research is not especially comforting. As we will see in Chapter 15, television can contribute to aggressive behavior, and large amounts of daily television watching can depress cognitive skills, affect beliefs and attitudes, lead to desires to buy advertised products, and result in more fidgety behavior (Rubinstein, 1983; Singer & Singer, 1981). On the other hand, exposure to television models of helpful behavior can lead to increased cooperation and altruism as well (Wright & Huston, 1983).

SOCIAL RELATIONSHIPS
AND BEHAVIOR

Much of what we learn about how to get along with others or how to behave has been learned in the give and take of establishing and maintaining social relationships. The family, which is a rich matrix of relationships, takes the initial lead in socialization. Later, when we enter school, our teachers and peers play an increasingly important role. So it is important to try to understand how such relationships develop and prosper. In the following sections we consider how children become attached to their parents and how they develop relationships with other children. Then we consider social competence as a set of broadly defined skills for getting along with other people.

ATTACHMENT

One of the first and most important social achievements of the baby is the development of relationships with one or more adults. The typical 9-month-old child is obviously attached to her father. Although she cannot yet speak, she smiles when she sees him and gives clear evidence of wanting to be near him. He, of course, reciprocates this obvious affection, and if we observe closely we may note that the father and daughter have learned to coordinate their behaviors: she whines and he picks her up; she seems comforted and he relaxes his hold on her; she squirms and he puts her down; she smiles, and he smiles in return.

Early Social Behavior   Children are obviously not born attached to their parents, although some would argue they are born with a biological program that facilitates attachment. The newborn is not much of a social creature, although she has many behaviors such as crying, sucking, and smile-like grimacing that serve as cues for other people. However, the new baby gradually learns rudimentary social behaviors. Perhaps the earliest unambiguous social behavior shown in infancy is the social smile. Although babies smile from an early age, they initially do not smile at the sight or sound of others. But by six months or so they have begun to smile at human faces. Most parents find this especially rewarding, and they tend to smile back or talk, events that in turn strengthen the baby's tendencies to smile (Brackbill, 1958). Although these smiles are clearly social, they are not usually discriminating: baby will smile at a stranger as readily as at mother. But by 8 or 9 months he will smile more frequently at mother and may even cry when he sees a stranger. By this time he can also show his preferences for familiar people, such as parents, by crawling toward them and may hold out his arms to be picked up. At this point we can say the child is attached to his parents.

Attachment Behaviors   *Attachment* may be defined as "a relatively enduring emotional tie to a specific other person" (Maccoby, 1980). Usually, children are attached to only a few familiar adults, who are typically but not inevitably the children's parents. One problem in studying attachment is that it is itself an unobservable emotional tie, so we must look for its observable behavioral manifestations. Typically, the following are used to define attachment operationally: (1) seeking proximity with the adult, (2) crying or showing distress at separation, (3) showing joy when reunited, and (4) being especially attentive to the adult (Maccoby, 1980).

Patterns of Attachment   Ainsworth and her colleagues (Ainsworth, Blehar, Waters, & Wall, 1978) have made the most concerted effort to study the development of attachment during the second half of the first year and beyond. They use what has come to be called the "Strange Situation," in which the child and its mother are brought into an observation room containing several toys. Most children initially stick close to mother but gradually begin to explore the room. When a stranger enters, the child usually moves closer to the mother and reduces exploration of the room. Most children eventually play with the stranger, but when the mother leaves the room they whimper or cry. When mother returns, most children want to be held and try to stay close to her.

Those children who like to be near their mothers, who show some but not a great amount of fear of the stranger, who are moderately distressed when mother leaves, and who seem happy to see her return are said to show *secure attachment*. However, a minority of the children show somewhat different patterns. *Avoidant attachment* is indicated when the child seems to be little affected by the mother's presence or absence and when the child avoids mother when she returns. *Resistent attachment* is displayed by children who have trouble exploring even when mother is present, who resist the stranger, and who greet mother's return with a mixture of relief and hostility. These latter forms of attachment are usually called *insecure* or *anxious attachment,* because the child seems unsure about its ties with mother and is ambivalent about separation from her.

There have been substantial criticisms of Ainsworth's attachment classification system (Campos et al., 1983). Not all research finds such a neat pattern of types of attachment, and some studies find that attachment classifications are quite unreliable over even short time periods. Others have argued that what appear to be reactions to the mother in a Strange Situation are really only more basic temperamental differences among children (Kagen, 1982). For example, children who have trouble adjusting to stress will appear to be more frightened and will be classified as insecurely attached, whereas children who handle stress better will appear to be securely attached. However, although the exact nature of attachment awaits further research, the concept of different types of attachment has stimulated a great deal of research on the causes and consequences of parent–child bonds.

Causes of Attachments   The fact that children begin to show quite strong preferences for their parents during the second half of the first year has long been noted. The classic explanation was in terms of reinforcement.

Because mothers (and, to a lesser extent, fathers) are associated with the food that relieves hunger drives (as well as with other reductions of other biological drives), the parents become positively evaluated. However, we now know this position is incorrect.

The most striking evidence against it comes from classic research by Harry Harlow (1958) on monkeys. Baby monkeys were raised apart from their biological mothers but in the presence of artificial mothers who either were made of wire and associated with food or were warm and cuddly but did not provide food. The young monkeys strongly preferred the cuddly mother even though "she" could not provide the reinforcement of hunger reduction.

Another possible explanation for attachment is based on the idea that children learn to predict the behavior of primary caretakers (Cairns, 1979). As babies and their parents interact, both learn to adjust their behaviors to one another. In the infant's confusing world, the ability to predict and control the behavior of a parent may be reassuring. When parents play with their children, they may further enhance feelings of security and control by providing their children with experiences that are novel but nonthreatening.

Harlow's monkeys preferred the soft, cuddly "mother" to the wire "mother" that provided food.

John Bowlby (1969, 1973) has provided a highly influential model based on psychoanalytic and evolutionary perspectives. According to Bowlby, attachment behaviors have evolved for the purposes of protecting the infant from harm. For example, when the child stays close to mother or cries, the competent mother will recognize that the infant is experiencing some distress. Parents are biologically predisposed to respond to such signals with the necessary reassurance and care. Thus, attachment may be thought of as a general organization of protection-seeking behaviors and their emotional accompaniments of feeling reassured.

One implication of Bowlby's position is that attachment ought to be universal across human cultures, and this seems to be the case (Ainsworth, 1967). Another is that attachment also ought to be found among higher animal species. There is some support for this. For example, sheep (Cairns, 1979) as well as primate babies (Mineka & Suomi, 1978) show distress at being separated from their mothers. Although such results do not directly support Bowlby's theory, they do suggest that attachment has a strong biological basis.

Ainsworth has been heavily influenced by Bowlby, and her work has generally shown that secure attachment is promoted by responsive parenting. In one study (Ainsworth et al., 1978), behavior in the Strange Situation was correlated with the behavior of mothers and their children during home visits. Generally, the mothers of the securely attached children were more affectionate and responsive to the needs of their children than were the mothers of insecurely attached children. For example, mothers of securely attached infants were quicker to respond to the cries of their youngsters than were mothers of insecurely attached children. Other studies have also confirmed that mothers of securely attached children are more competent and responsive to their children's needs (Egeland & Farber, 1984). And lest we assume that fathers are left out of the attachment picture, competent and involved fathers produce children who are more securely attached to both the fathers and the mothers (Easterbrooks & Goldberg, 1984).

With recent emphases on day-care arrangements for children, there has been concern about the effects of alternative care on attachment. Might children who spend most of their days in day-care centers show diminished or insecure attachment to their mothers and fathers? Most studies find few differences in attachment as a function of where children spend their days (Brookhart & Hock, 1976; Owen, Easterbrooks, Chase-Lansdale, & Goldberg, 1984). Children do become attached to their caretakers in day-care centers, but such attachments do not replace those with parents (Anderson, Nagle, Roberts, & Smith, 1981). Also, children who are raised collectively and apart from their parents in kibbutzim in Israel do not differ in most important ways from children raised in more traditional home environments (Talmon, 1972).

Thus, attachment is not a simple function of how much time children spend with their parents, although the responsiveness and competence of parental behavior do play major roles in shaping attachment. We cannot say with assurance that early attachment has lasting effects on children's social behaviors with others, but the available evidence suggests that it does (Ainsworth, 1985).

THE DEVELOPMENT OF PEER RELATIONS

Relationships with parents, whether positive or negative, remain central to us for as long as we and they live. Nonetheless, successful socialization in our society requires that this primary bond be gradually loosened over time. Children must develop the ability to form significant relationships with others besides their parents. Actually, the years of parental domination are relatively short, as children expand their circle of friends, begin kindergarten

and school, and come under the influence of teachers and other adults. These changes may be so radical that it is appropriate to speak of socialization as a movement from one subculture to another (Higgins & Parsons, 1983).

When Janey begins school, she will meet many new children whose values and behaviors may be different from her own and she will have to learn to coordinate her behavior with theirs. Teachers will impose demands such as sitting still and quietly that may seem quite foreign. When she enters middle or junior high school, she will have to adjust to being "youngest" again, and she will face far more people whose activities are organized more extensively and formally. Clubs and extracurricular activities will become important, and she will define herself in terms of her friends and activities. In high school, the demands on social skills will increase more dramatically.

Higgins and Parsons quite correctly point out that increasing demands of ever-more-complex social situations produce not only new social experiences but new socialization pressures. Parents typically remain the single most important socialization agents even during adolescence, but they will increasingly share this task with others.

Early Social Relationships   Socialization is a gradual process, and one would not expect to find infants engaged in meaningful relationships with other infants. Indeed, it might seem implausible that such relationships exist at all before the third or fourth year. Nonetheless, even very young children show signs of special interest in one another. For example, babies as young as 2 or 3 months display obvious interest in other infants, and by the end of the first year infants direct behaviors such as smiles and touches to one another, behaviors that may be reciprocated. Infants in the last half of the first year also respond to cries and signs of distress of other infants. By 9 or 10 months, children react differently to children they know and strange children (Hay, Pedersen, & Nash, 1982).

Socially directed behavior increases dramatically during the second year. Toddlers are increasingly able to respond to one another in complex ways and to engage in rudimentary play (Eckerman & Stein, 1982). By age 2, children communicate invitations to play, demands, and protests; these communications often elicit relatively coordinated responses from peers (Ross, Lollis, & Elliott, 1982). Even social rules about possessions and social conflict can be observed in such young children (Bakeman & Brownlee, 1982).

Naturally these early social skills are quite primitive, and small children are not paragons of social virtues. They are often selfish, are interested only in their own activities, and play with others reluctantly. However, the basis of effective social behavior has roots deep into infancy. Social skills do not emerge suddenly when the child attends preschool or begins to play with neighborhood children.

Play   Play constitutes a common and important aspect of the child's (and, to a lesser extent, the adult's) life, although there are many different theories about why children play and about its effects on later social and cognitive abilities. Parents play with their child almost from its birth, and as the child acquires the ability to respond with smiles, laughs, and coordinated behaviors, the complexity of this play increases dramatically (Garvey, 1974; Stern, 1977).

At about 1 year, children rather suddenly acquire the ability for pretend play. At first this may involve simple motor sequences, as when the child pretends to feed himself or feeds a doll. Such pretend play becomes more common during the second year and seems to increase regularly at least until the early school years (Rubin, Fein, & Vandenberg, 1983). Such play also becomes more socially oriented from about 18 months onward. By age 2 or so, children often play pretend games with

others and the complexity of roles increases as well. Moreover, mutual play with toys and other objects shows a corresponding increase. What might be considered a final, but important, stage of play development occurs by age 3 or 4, when children begin to play games with defined rules. Such games may involve sports or board equipment, may simply be interaction games such as hide-and-seek, or may involve defined roles ("I'll be the mommy and you be the daddy") (Garvey, 1974).

Children play for a number of reasons, although it is reasonable to believe that play, especially that involving others, is a crucial way children learn about social rules and roles, try out important new cognitive skills, and develop conceptions of others as distinct entities with their own thoughts and desires. We might think of play as one way children have of practicing social skills.

Relations with Others   Young children show some rudimentary social recognition, but there is not much evidence of any conception of social relationships before the middle or end of the second year. However, children gradually learn to respond to others as distinct people. Certainly by age 2½ one can observe

Children learn important social skills through play.

preferences among children in play groups, and as the children move into nursery school, and subsequently primary and secondary school, they will fit themselves into an increasingly complex social fabric with roles and norms. By the time of high school there may be elaborate groups and cliques, each with its own peculiar norms and even languages (Hartup, 1983). This increased complexity demands more sophisticated behavioral skills, capacities to control impulses, and abilities to think about the social world.

There is ample experimental evidence that children reward one another for approved behavior and punish one another for naughty behavior and that these sanctions control behavior (Hartup, 1983). In addition, children may explicitly take on responsibilities of tutoring others, especially younger children, and the role of peers as models for approved behavior is also well documented (Abramovitch & Grusec, 1978). Thus, as children enter the wider and more complex social world of the school, they are exposed to a wider range of socialization agents.

SOCIAL COMPETENCE

Children enter a social world only gradually. By the time a child goes to nursery school, kindergarten, and primary school, she will have to adapt to a social world that includes other children. Psychologists refer to this ability to adapt to the social world as *social competence.* Often, such competence is indexed through popularity, acceptance by others, or status within a group. This is not to say that popularity and the ability to fit in are ultimately desirable in and of themselves (although for children as well as adults they are generally useful), but popularity or status often is a convenient way of summarizing many social skills that are desirable.

Correlates of Popularity   There are several ways in which popular and unpopular children differ. Popular children are generally friendlier, more cooperative, and more willing to share and help others (Hartup, 1970). They are also less aggressive, although, especially for boys, a complete lack of aggressiveness is not always conducive to popularity. Good grades (Green, Forehand, Beck, & Vosk, 1980) and physical attractiveness (Langlois & Stephan, 1981) also lead to relatively high status within children's groups.

One problem with many of these results is that we cannot be sure whether popularity causes or is caused by these other variables. For example, it makes good sense to suppose that children would like a helpful, nonaggressive peer more than a nonhelpful, hostile peer. But it makes just as much sense to assume that a child who is rejected by others (say because he is ugly or lacks athletic skills) will react by being less helpful and more aggressive and will be denied opportunities to practice social skills.

In recent years, to allow more definitive causal conclusions, many investigators have examined the interpersonal styles of socially competent and less competent children. Dodge (1983) assembled groups of previously unacquainted 7- and 8-year-old boys; because the boys did not know one another, differences in popularity that emerged would have to reflect behavior in the group and not vice versa. After a few hours of interaction, it was clear whether the boys would be accepted, rejected, or neglected by their peers. Those boys who were generally rejected often approached others, but their style included inappropriate behaviors and aggression so that they were often rebuffed by those they approached. Boys who were neglected by others tended to have low rates of approach and exhibited what might be called a shy style of behavior. Some boys were rejected by some in the group and accepted by others; they were active in the group and displayed high levels of both prosocial and antisocial behaviors—they may have been perceived as somewhat overbearing and bossy. Finally, the popular boys behaved appropriately, were not aggressive, and were received positively when they approached others. Generally, socially competent children are responsive to others and have a good knowledge both of appropriate social goals and strategies for achieving them (Asher, 1984; Renshaw & Asher, 1982).

The Origins of Social Competence   Because social competence includes so many features and may be affected by cultural and subcultural values, we would not expect to find that there is any single thing that parents do or do not do that encourages such competence. Nonetheless, some broad generalizations seem clear. First, those children who are securely attached to their mothers as infants seem to have a better chance at social competence than their insecurely attached peers (Waters, Wippman, & Sroufe, 1979). Second, socially competent youngsters generally have parents who show warmth and accept their children but who also place high demands on the children for maturity (Baumrind, 1971). Third, results from research on parental encouragement of prosocial behavior (positively related to social competence) suggest that such behavior is promoted when parents are warm, demand a prosocial orientation (Radke-Yarrow, Zahn-Waxler, & Chapman, 1983), and stress affective consequences to others of the child's misbehavior ("you have hurt your friend") (Zahn-Waxler, Radke-Yarrow, and King, 1979). When we examine the development of aggressive behaviors that are negatively related to social competence, we find that mothers of aggressive boys are both negative toward their sons and permissive when it comes to aggressive behaviors (Parke & Slaby, 1983). So parents of competent children encourage skills that lead to competence while they discourage those skills that lead to unpopularity.

We also know that imitation of models is important for many behaviors that apparently lead to social competence. Both prosocial (Radke-Yarrow et al., 1983) and aggressive behaviors (Parke & Slaby, 1983) are clearly affected by modeling. So we might expect that children who grow up in cooperative, sharing households would have models for prosocial behavior, whereas those who live in more hostile environments would also have models for aggressive behaviors. Models shown in the mass media can also influence prosocial and antisocial behaviors (see Chapters 14 and 15).

Finally, experiences with peers themselves may be important (Zahn-Waxler, Iannotti, & Chapman, 1982). Children not only imitate one another but they teach one another directly. It seems clear that the child who grows up with a bully for an older brother may acquire different skills and a different perception of the world than the child who grows up as an only child or with a protective older sister.

SUMMARY

Like cognitive skills, social abilities show a clear development. The earliest social relations of most children are with their parents. By the end of the first year, most children show evidence of attachment to various caretakers. Parents who are responsive to their children's needs promote secure attachment; less-responsive parenting produces insecure attachment, in which the child seems unsure of parental love and may also exhibit hostility to parents. Early evidence of peer relationships appears within the first 2 years, and from about 3 onward most children are increasingly involved with peers. Peers provide models and help the child learn social rules and roles. Play, whether solitary or with others, also seems to promote learning social skills. By the time they enter school, some children seem more socially competent and popular than others. Socially competent children tend to be helpful, nonaggressive, and appropriately responsive to others. Social competence seems to be promoted by secure attachment, by parental warmth combined with control, by explicit reinforcement for helpful behaviors and discouragement of nonhelpful behavior, and by modeling.

SOCIAL COGNITION

Most parents and other socialization agents hope that children will learn internal controls over their behavior. Children and adults do, of course, behave in certain ways because they fear social disapproval or other, external punishments for not doing so, but ideally the well-socialized person is also guided by internal feelings of right and wrong. Such internal controls have often been attributed to guilt; we behave properly because to do otherwise would invite a prickly conscience.

A recent approach has been to consider social cognition—the ways we think about social situations and other people—as an equally important aspect of internal controls over behavior. The well-socialized person not only behaves in certain ways and feels guilt at real or imagined transgressions, but also has a considered, thoughtful stance toward her social world. She not only knows the relevant dos and don'ts, but she can appreciate what these rules mean and how to apply them to different situations. For example, being polite may mean saying something in one situation and keeping quiet in another. Hurting another person is generally wrong but might be excused or even positively evaluated if the hurt achieves some larger social good. Furthermore, rules may conflict. It is sometimes hard to be both polite and honest, for example, and fairness may involve sharing equally in some situations but considering individual needs in others. So internalization must imply more than learning what to do or not to do.

PIAGET AND THE CONCEPT OF STAGES

Traditional theories of learning might see such internalization as having been gradually acquired through experience. However, many modern developmentalists have emphasized stage models, which postulate fairly dramatic changes in behavior and thought at particular points in time followed by longer periods of consolidation. Within a given stage, the components of thought and behavior are organized in a certain way, and when the person progresses to a higher stage these will be structured differently.

There have been many such stage models (psychoanalytic theory is one such example); the most important for our purposes is that of Jean Piaget. For Piaget, there are four broad stages. The first, lasting for the first 2 years or so, is the *sensory-motor stage* and is marked by the child's learning how to coordinate thoughts and movements and learning to understand the rudiments of causality and object permanence. The second stage, *preoperational thought* (2–6 years), is more crucial for our purposes. The child can begin to think with symbols, as illustrated and aided by the use of language, but her abilities are severely limited. She tends to concentrate on surface details; what is seen is assumed to be reality. Thus, according to Piaget, the preschool child cannot generally infer intentions from behavior and focuses on the consequences of behavior, such as the reactions of authority figures. Moreover, she cannot generally attend to more than one dimension of reality at a time. The preoperational child would have trouble understanding that a person can be both a father and a husband or that people can be both sad and happy at the same time. The net result is that, during the preschool

Jean Piaget

years, the child is fairly egocentric in that she assumes others see things as she does, and she fails to appreciate that there may be several valid perspectives for a given issue or event.

In the next stage, that of *concrete operations* (6–12 years), the child learns to perform real cognitive operations. She can manipulate ideas, can see things from several perspectives, can fathom some of the hidden realities behind events. However, the child still is limited to the concrete realities of the here and now. She cannot reason hypothetically. At about age 12, she enters the *formal operations* stage, where hypothetical and abstract thinking become possible. Thinking becomes more flexible.

Unfortunately for our purposes, most of Piaget's seminal work on social thinking was done in the 1930s, long before his larger theory had developed fully. Therefore, his stage model of social cognitive development does not fully reflect his mature cognitive theory (Turiel, 1983). However, the earlier work has stimulated considerable debate about whether children's reasoning about social stimuli can best be construed in a stage framework.

EGOCENTRICISM AND PERSPECTIVE-TAKING

According to Piaget the preschool (preoperational) child is highly egocentric in the sense of being able to see a given situation only from her own perspective. Therefore, the preoperational child will be severely limited in her abilities to reason about people and social events. However, there should be dramatic improvements in this regard at age 6 or so as she enters the concrete operations stage. Before discussing the research evidence, we must briefly discuss how *perspective-taking* ability is measured.

Types of Tasks   Several tasks have been used to measure perspective-taking. For example, in the classic task used by Piaget and Inhelder (1956), a child faces a three-dimen-

sional display on a table and is asked to select a picture that represents the display as seen by a person across the table. Another task involves the ability to suppress privileged information (Flavell et al., 1968). In one version, the child is shown a story in cartoon form. Subsequently, several of the frames are removed and the child is asked to tell this new (and different story) to a person who has never seen the first version. In this case, perspective-taking involves being able to suppress what the child knows from the first version in telling the new story (Higgins, 1981b).

The Development of Perspective-taking Although both of these (and several other) tasks clearly involve the ability to imagine things as others see them, each also involves other abilities and motives (Shantz, 1983). As a consequence, most research studies find that different perspective-taking tasks are not closely related to one another, at least for preschool children (Ford, 1979). Thus, a young child can be egocentric in some ways but not in others. Furthermore, even very young children can show some perspective-taking if the task is presented to them properly. For example, Flavell (1978) asked infants to position a cup so others could see what was in the bottom of it. By 18 months, the child can position the cup so that both she and another person can see the bottom. At age 2, the child will be able to turn the cup so the other can see the bottom. As early as age 3, children realize that other people prefer different drawings than they do and can give reasons for others' choices that are different from reasons for their own preferences (Hart & Goldin-Meadow, 1984). Such results admittedly do not indicate a full capacity to put oneself in the position of another, but they do illustrate that even young children have acquired some understanding of the fact that others do not always see what they themselves see.

However, what a child *can do* under favorable circumstances is not necessarily what she *ordinarily does.* Abilities develop before the capacities to use them effectively and generally. With this in mind, it would be fair to say that there is a gradual development in the sophistication in taking the perspective of others from early childhood through adolescence (Shantz, 1983). Before age 6, the child can take the perspective of others under favorable conditions but may not always do so. By age 6 or 7 the child has begun to take the perspective of others generally, and a year or so later the child not only knows that others have different perspectives but can also evaluate her own behavior from the standpoint of another. The ability becomes more complex toward the beginning of adolescence. Now a third-person perspective can be taken where social interaction can be viewed from the standpoint of a disinterested third party (Selman & Byrne, 1974). Thus, perspective-taking develops more gradually than first assumed and involves several abilities.

The end product, the ability to take the perspective of others, is a central ability for mature social interaction (Mead, 1934). For example, communication with others depends heavily on our abilities to understand what others know and need to know (Chapter 6). Moreover, your self-concept, how you define and evaluate yourself, depends in part on your ability to step outside your own concerns to see yourself as others might (see Chapter 5). And your ability to function in a group, to form meaningful relationships, or to help or hurt someone depends on understanding the feelings, values, and likely behavior of others.

PERCEIVING OTHERS

The preoperational (preschool) child is a realist according to Piaget; she concentrates on external realities and is not able to get beneath the surface to infer complex meanings. Therefore, preoperational children who observe a behavior should not be able to infer the intentions, emotions, and motives underlying the behavior and might have trouble, for example, seeing the difference between a person who breaks something accidentally and someone who does the same act intentionally. However, Piaget has overstated the case. Young children do have difficulty inferring intentions, but they *can* do so as early as age 4 or 5 (DiVitto & McArthur, 1978; Rotenberg, 1980; Ruble & Rholes, 1982).

Nevertheless, younger children are less likely than older ones to spontaneously infer intentions and motives and they are unlikely to describe others in terms of psychological characteristics. Preschool children tend to describe others in terms of overt behaviors or physical characteristics, whereas older children use fewer objective descriptions and more trait and other psychological descriptions (Barenboim, 1981; Livesley & Bromley, 1973; Peevers & Secord, 1973).

There is also a developmental progression in conceptions of internal characteristics. Children as young as 5 or 6 infer traits and personal dispositions from behavior, but not until a few years later do they indicate knowledge that these characteristics are stable (Rholes & Ruble, 1984; Rotenberg, 1982). Subsequently, at about age 12 or so an even more sophisticated notion develops, namely, that people do not always behave consistently across situations because of situational pressures.

Recall the attributional principle of discounting (Chapter 4) that suggests that to the extent that strong external forces are present we should discount the possibility that people have performed a behavior because of their own inclinations. Because children have trouble focusing on two or more perspectives at a time, they might be expected to have trouble with discounting. Some studies find that preoperational children do have difficulty discounting (DiVitto & McArthur, 1978; Karniol & Ross, 1976) but other studies find that children can discount at age 6 and before (Dix & Grusec, 1983; Peterson & Gelfand, 1984). Again, it is probable that discounting is not usually performed under normal circumstances but may be under optimal conditions. As Higgins and Wells (1986) have emphasized, alternative perspectives (such as situational pressures) may be less accessible for younger than for older children but may still be used when the situation motivates them to think about the alternative.

CONCEPTIONS OF SOCIAL RELATIONS

Children learn to reason not only about other people but also about their relationships with them. Social relationships are, of course, very complex, involving as they do the coordination of behavior among people with differing perspectives, motives, and needs. It is one thing to note that another person thinks differently than you do and quite another to be able to conceptualize a relationship that involves these differences.

Friendship   Consider first how children think about friendships. Several studies of how children describe friends differ in some details

In adolescence, friendships often become deeper, more intimate, and more exclusive.

but agree that there is a general movement away from an egocentric toward a more abstract and psychologically oriented conception (Damon, 1977; Furman & Bierman, 1983; Selmann, 1980). For the preschooler, a friend is someone who has fun toys or who lives nearby, but during the early school years the child increasingly defines friends in terms of their personal characteristics. At first these may be fairly superficial ("my friend is nice"), but later "deeper" qualities such as kindness and having a sense of humor are mentioned. Gradually, friendship is defined more in terms of reciprocal activities, and, by the onset of adolescence, the sharing of information and intimacy becomes important as friendships also become more exclusive.

Authority   Children do not live only in a social world of friendships and peers, of course. They learn that some people, particularly adults and parents, have authority over them and that they have authority over those who are younger. Damon (1977) has proposed several stages of authority conceptions. The young child wants to do what an adult wants him to do. Subsequently he realizes that he conforms because of threats and rewards and so he sees authority in terms of these external variables. By about age 6 or 7, children come to see adults as having special moral rights to command by virtue of their overall talents and expertise. By age 9, they see that authorities are people who have special talents to meet particular situational demands; therefore different people may be authorities in different situations. Leadership conceptions show similar development changes (Selman, 1980).

SUMMARY

To the extent that our behavior is controlled by the ways we think about social stimuli, it is crucial to know how children come to understand their social worlds. Research on the development of social cognition has been dominated by Piaget's theory, which stressed that children below the age of 6 or so did not have the capacity to take the perspectives of others, to infer reasons and intentions that are not immediately apparent, or to coordinate several perspectives on the behavior of others. Research confirms that preschoolers do tend to think about social situations in terms of surface characteristics. They have some difficulty taking the perspective of others, do not always infer intentions and therefore do not judge behavior according to intentions, cannot weigh internal and external pressures on behavior, tend to conceptualize others in terms of external characteristics, define friends in terms of surface features, and think about authority in terms of power to reward and punish. However, many studies have shown that younger children have some capacity to infer internal features and take the perspectives of others, but that these perspectives may not be very accessible for them and may require special circumstances to appear.

MORAL DEVELOPMENT

MORALITY AND CONVENTION

As children grow into the social world, they must learn rules and strategies for getting along with others. There are many sorts of rules that children must learn (and that parents typically teach). Let us consider various types. Some are purely *pragmatic rules* in that they tell us how to gain worldly successes and avoid problems (Tisak & Turiel, 1984); "don't put your finger in the electrical outlet" and "look both ways before you cross the street" are examples. As children get older, the rules may take on an increasingly social flavor ("grandmothers like to be shown good report cards"; "teachers get mad when you don't do your homework"). However, whether such rules deal with the physical or the social world, they are almost entirely devoid of moral content. They tell you what you should do if you want to achieve some end, not what you should do in some moral sense.

Conventions are another important kind of rule (Turiel, 1983). Conventions are basically matters of cultural prescription and sometimes of behavioral regularity. Some conventions may be quite general and important, such as our convention of driving on the right side of the road or the tendency in our society for women to be the primary caretakers of small children. Others are perfectly trivial and specific to situations. For example, many families have fairly rigid rules about when dinner is served and how family members should behave during the meal. In your classes, you may have observed that some people sit in the same unassigned seats throughout a semester and may even become somewhat upset if "their" seats are taken by interlopers.

Sometimes we feel very strongly about the importance of conventions even though they are invariably artificial creations of a culture or social group and therefore have no pretence to universality or objectivity. This does not mean they are unimportant; we have to have *some* rule about what side of the road we drive on and someone must take care of children. However, the content of conventions is usually quite arbitrary. It is not of cosmic importance whether your family eats at 5:30 or 7:00, whether you eat in the dining room or off of TV trays; we could drive on the left or right; women could wear pants and men nothing at all. But for the sake of efficiency we must have rules of some sort even if they are arbitrary and do not resonate with special moral overtones.

However, the content of *moral rules* is crucial. Moral obligations cannot be traded around to suit convenience; Mary and Tom can switch nights to wash dishes (a convention) but should not take turns being honest (a moral obligation). Shweder, Turiel, and Much (1981) list six fundamental criteria of moral rules. First, they are *obligatory* in the sense that one's moral duties do not depend on one's desires. Second, moral rules are *general* in that they apply equally to everyone similarly situated. Third, they are *important* and generally take precedence over conventions and other norms. Fourth, moral rules are *external* and *impersonal;* their validity does not depend on whether you or I agree with them. Fifth, they are *unalterable* and cannot be changed for the sake of convenience. Sixth, they are *ahistorical;* the rule does not arise directly from any particular historical context.

MORAL JUDGMENT

Clearly the ability to judge actions for their moral relevancy is a central—perhaps *the* central—aspect of morality. A child may refrain from hitting his irritating sister solely because he knows he will be punished. Although such a child is hardly immoral, he also does not merit our full moral praise, simply because he has not shown the ability to know why hitting is naughty nor to refrain from hitting his sister accordingly.

Piaget   Piaget (1932) thought that both the content and form of moral judgments change with age. In the preschool years, rules are seen as absolute, as coming from authority, and as shared by everyone. Moral judgments are made on the basis of whether rules are followed, and if rules are broken, blame is assigned on the basis of consequences rather than intentions. Thus, a child who breaks five cups while trying to help her mother is seen by the preschooler as committing a more serious offense than a child who breaks one cup while trying to get at some forbidden cookies. Also, deviations that elicit harsh punishment are perceived to be more serious than those that receive less punishment.

This early stage of moral judgment corresponds to how the preschool child supposedly reasons generally about social events. He attends to the surface features (consequences, punishment) rather than to the unseen, internal features, such as intentions. Also, according to Piaget, the young child confuses morality and convention. Rules are rules whatever their content, and their validity rests on absolute authority and likelihood of punishment. Thus, rules about playing games, household chores, and stealing would all have the same obligatory force for the young child.

As the child matures cognitively and learns how to adjust his behavior to that of peers, he will be able to take the perspective of others for his behavior. He will also learn that behavior should be evaluated according to intentions. The moral and conventional domains will become separated and the child will learn that some rules can be changed through mutual agreement whereas moral rules cannot.

Piaget's account was very influential, but it is not fully correct. Although younger children do not generally weigh intentions enough, they can and often do make use of intention information in their judgments (Karniol, 1978), particularly when the information is salient and clear (Feldman et al., 1976; Grueneich, 1982; Nelson, 1980).

Kohlberg   The most influential and controversial theory of moral judgment in recent times has been that of Lawrence Kohlberg (1969). The theory is clearly in the line pioneered by Piaget but many details are different. Most noticeably, there are three rather than two stages, each of which is divided into two substages.

At the first—preconventional—level, moral judgments are controlled by rewards and punishments and the content of rules comes from outside, usually from parents. At stage 1 of this level, the child is attuned to punishment and sees behavior as moral to the extent it avoids punishment. At stage 2, there is greater consciousness of reward, and what satisfies egocentric needs is seen as good. Morality is a "good deal."

At the second general level—conventional morality—the person has a much greater appreciation of culturally defined rules and understands that good behavior resides in conformity to these rules. At the first substage (stage 3), the person conforms out of a willingness to meet others' expectations; although the rules are still external, compliance is motivated by internal desires. Stage 4 morality consists of duty; emphasis is less on meeting the demands of particular others than on generalized respect for authority, laws, and the social order.

The third general level is attuned to principled morality. At stage 5, morality is seen to be based on societal consensus, and breaking rules is seen as an affront to a kind of contract one has with others. At stage 6, morality is based on rationally derived higher principles, such as respect for the dignity of human life, that transcend a particular society.

Kohlberg's theory has been highly controversial but has also stimulated a vast amount of research that has enriched our understanding of moral development. A number of empirical and theoretical questions have been raised about the theory. One concerns the measurement of stages. Kohlberg measures levels of moral reasoning by asking people to respond to several moral dilemmas. Consider the hypothetical case of Heinz, who needs an exorbitantly priced drug to treat his sick wife. Heinz is poor, and in desperation he breaks into a druggist's shop to steal the drug. Subjects are asked whether Heinz was right or wrong and why. The answers are scored not so much in terms of the specific answers subjects give as in terms of the reasoning behind the answers. A number of questions were raised about the scoring of earlier versions of the test (Kurtines & Greif, 1974), but many of the problems have been corrected with later and more complete versions of the scoring manual (Rest, 1983). However, scoring of the moral dilemmas test remains difficult.

There have also been concerns about the stages postulated by Kohlberg. Some of these concerns have been largely theoretical and deal with disagreements about the nature of morality itself. For example, the assumption that

stage 6 (rationally derived morality) is higher than stage 4 (respect for authority and the social order) embodies a value judgment in Western society that individuality is superior to group-derived values (Trainer, 1977). It is also debatable whether stage 6 ought to be considered higher than stage 5. Hogan (1973) has argued that stage 5 represents an ethics of responsibility whereas stage 6 represents the ethnics of conscience; a preference for one over the other may relate more to one's personality and culture than to any intrinsic ordering. In addition, consistent stage 6 reasoning is rare, and so the more recent tendency is to drop stage 6 in scoring.

Although issues concerning morals are not entirely resolvable through empirical methods, the Kohlberg argument suggests that the higher stages are higher by virtue of being associated with higher levels of maturity. More specifically, as people mature they should also show higher levels of moral reasoning. This can be tested empirically by testing the same subjects at several points in time. Such longitudinal studies support the postulated sequence (Rest, 1983), and there is also considerable cross-cultural evidence of predicted progressions through the stages (Snarey, 1985). If people change, they almost always move to a higher stage. However, many people do not change at all, particularly after the completion of formal schooling. Another problem is that even trivial manipulations of how the information is presented can affect the level of moral reasoning expressed (LaRue & Olejnik, 1980), so the importance of changes from stage to stage may be questioned. However, within broad limits the available research suggests that at least the first four stages and probably the first five stages form a developmental sequence.

Another kind of criticism of the theory comes from Eliot Turiel (1978a, 1978b, 1983) who points out that the Piaget–Kohlberg scheme confuses moral and conventional issues. Just as Piaget argues that the young child has trouble distinguishing conventions ("be home by 5:30 for dinner") from moral evaluations ("don't hit others"), Kohlberg assumes that people who reason at stages 3 and 4 in his theory adopt a view of morality based on conventions rather than on thoroughly reasoned moral principles.

However, there is now abundant evidence that children and adults can and do distinguish between conventions and moral principles (Nucci & Nucci, 1982a, 1982b; Pool, Shweder, & Much, 1983; Smetana, 1984). Such results have led Turiel (1983) to argue that reasoning about moral issues and conventions develops somewhat independently. Conventions are accepted by young children because they describe empirical uniformities (for example, a boy should not become a nurse because most nurses are women), but later there is a more sophisticated understanding that conventions are arbitrary. Still later, conventions are understood as part of a general social system with shared values. Furthermore, whereas conventions vary from group to group and situation to situation, moral rules are seen to have a more universal application. This does not mean the two domains are totally independent but only that the rules are learned in somewhat different ways and respond to different social circumstances.

Certainly the Kohlberg model has considerable empirical support, though debate will continue over important details of the theory, such as whether moral judgments form distinct, integrated stages and whether such stages form developmental sequences.

Moral Judgment and Cognitive Development   Both Piaget and Kohlberg have assumed that moral judgments reflect general cognitive development. Kohlberg has not claimed that moral reasoning is totally dependent on cognitive maturity, but he does suggest that particular levels of cognitive development set limits for moral judgments. For example, the very young child who tends to respond to external features of situations would not be able to comprehend stage 3 and stage 4 reasoning, which demand the ability to understand that moral rules are based on more than possibilities of reward or punishment. However, being able to think beyond concrete rewards and punishments does not guarantee achievement of sophisticated moral reasoning, which must depend to some extent on experiences and learning.

Data from several studies (Damon, 1975, 1977; Krebs & Gillmore, 1982; Walker, 1980) suggest empirical relationships among various measures of cognitive development and level of moral reasoning. Although these relationships are often small, they are probably about as high as one might reasonably expect, given that moral judgments are affected by factors other than cognitive sophistication.

MORAL BEHAVIOR

Societies have more immediate concerns with behavior than with thoughts. Although it is highly *desirable* that we have moral standards to guide our behavior, it is *essential* that we behave in moral and conventional ways. You *must* drive on the correct side of the road, refrain from stealing, and control your aggressive and sexual impulses. Of course, not all rules are equally insistent, and people should not conform blindly or stupidly; on the other hand, those moral rules and conventions most central to social order must have considerable adherence for social stability. Although some conventions and moral rules prescribe ways we should behave, the "thou shalt not" rules are usually more salient; most research has been directed to the learning of prohibitions.

The Learning of Control   Children want to do a great many things they should not do, and they have trouble learning relevant prohibitions because they are so impulsive. A 3-year-old can verbalize many prohibitions, but desires often battle with knowledge about prohibitions as fingers begin to go places they shouldn't go. Punishment can be effective in teaching resistance to temptation, provided the punishment is quick, sure, consistent, and strong (Parke, 1969). On the other hand, many studies of parental behavior suggest that children who are punished often (particularly physically) by their parents have less rather than greater resistance to temptation (Hoffman, 1977).

Thus, punishment can be effective in the laboratory but often is not in everyday life. Why? One reason is that parents may use poor punishment strategies. For example, they may be inconsistent, punishing the child for some infractions but not for others, or they may administer punishment long after the naughty deed, although we know that punishment must be quick to be effective. Furthermore, punishment provides information that the child has done something wrong without telling him or her what a better behavior might have been. Therefore it is helpful to have reasons accompanying punishment, and an angry parent may not be in a position to provide such reasons. We have already discussed Hoffman's (1983) argument that induction (use of reasoning) is superior to assertion of power (usually involving punishment) just because the former helps the child acquire a cognitive basis for control over behavior. The best conclusion might be that punishment can be an effective aid in teaching prohibitions but that it is often used relatively ineffectively, without cognitive supports, and by parents who lack parenting skills. Punishment is therefore not bad as such but is used inappropriately much of the time.

Given that so much of socialization seems to consist in the teaching of prohibitions, the emphasis on sanctions, especially punishment, is understandable. However, parents do not merely punish (or reward) their children; they also serve as models for their behavior. Children learn probable consequences of their behavior from observing models and hence learn to control through such observation (Bandura, 1965).

Cognitive Transformations   During socialization and cognitive maturation, children also learn cognitive strategies to cope with impulses. One perfectly useful strategy is a version of "sour grapes"—we convince ourselves that we don't want the things we can't or shouldn't have. In a classic study by Aronson and Carlsmith (1963), discussed in Chapter 5, children who were prohibited from playing with a desired toy reduced their dissonance between desires to play with the toy and knowledge that they should not play with it by deciding that they did not like the toy as much as they thought.

Walter Mischel (1981b) has investigated a related cognitive strategy in delay of gratification. The child is asked to make a choice between an immediate but small reward and a larger reward that she may have later. Most children want to wait for the larger reward but find this hard to do. One way the child might make the wait palatable is to avoid thinking about the larger reward—thinking about the big candy bar you can have later may make the smaller candy bar too appealing to resist now. Indeed, Mischel, Ebbesen, and Zeiss (1972) showed that when the larger reward was made salient or children were encouraged to think about it, ability to delay gratification was impaired. On the other hand, when they were distracted from thinking about it, ability to delay gratification was increased.

Mischel and his colleagues have also shown that how the children think about the potential rewards affects their ability to delay gratification. Children who are asked to think about the consummatory qualities of the immediate reward (such as thinking about the sweet taste of a marshmallow) have trouble waiting. On the other hand, those who are told to think about the desired object as something else ("think of a marshmallow as a cloud") have more ability to delay gratification (Mischel & Baker, 1975).

Thus, the work on dissonance-motivated "sour grapes" and the Mischel research on how thoughts affect abilities to control impulses both suggest that how we think about desired objects and activities can exert substantial control over our natural impulses to perform fun and interesting but proscribed behaviors.

Moral Consistency   The classic view of morality handed down to us from our Puritan forebears and reinforced by Freud and other Victorian moralists is that morality is a generalized disposition to behave properly. The fully moral person not only understands the differences between the moral and the immoral but feels guilty thinking about the latter and thus guides his or her behavior accordingly.

At the very least, this classic view suggests that there should be strong relationships among various indices of morality. For example, one should expect that people who have guilt should behave morally, would have high levels of moral reasoning, and could resist temptation. However, the research data have not been particularly obliging to this point of view. For example, in one classic study by Hartshorne and May (1928–1930), children were given opportunities to exhibit behavior, such as cheating on tests and stealing, that would be considered violations of moral rules. They were also given questionnaires to measure moral knowledge. The relationships among the various measures were surprisingly low, although far from negligible (Burton, 1963). Subsequently, many other large-scale studies have confirmed that relationships among various measures of morality are usually small (Sears, Rau, & Alpert, 1965).

However, such results ought not be surprising unless one assumes that morality is a general, mechanically governed activity, which it is not. In Chapter 8 we discussed at length the idea that there are many causes of a given behavior, so we would not expect a general internal variable such as conscience or guilt to predict strongly single moral behaviors any more than we would expect a general attitude toward religion to predict a single religious behavior such as going to church. Nor would we expect high consistency among single moral behaviors any more than we would among religious or conscientious behaviors.

Research addressed to the question of whether moral reasoning affects moral behavior suggests that people at higher levels of moral reasoning are somewhat more likely to perform morally (Blasi, 1980) and to behave prosocially with their peers (Eisenberg, Pasternack, Cameron, & Tryon, 1984; Eisenberg-Berg & Hand, 1979). There are also studies of political participation suggesting that people who reason at Kohlberg's stages 5 and 6 are more likely to participate in activity devoted to societal change than those who reason at the lower, conventional levels (Fishkin, Keniston, & MacKinnon, 1973; Haan, Smith, & Block, 1968; Nassi, Abramowitz, & Youmans, 1983). On the other hand, it is fair to point out that the empirical relationships, while often statistically significant, are generally low. Clearly one cannot do a very good job of predicting whether someone will cheat or steal in a particular case by knowing how he or she reasons about moral issues.

SUMMARY

One of the fundamental attributes of socialization is learning the rules for effective behavior in social situations. Some rules are purely pragmatic, others reflect conventions, and some have strong moral overtones. Piaget's influential account stressed the proposition that young children cannot make fully moral judgments because they cannot infer the intentions and motives that are crucial to such judgments. He also suggested that young children cannot discriminate between conventions and moral rules, because both are seen as emanating from authority. However, further research suggests that young children can make such a discrimination and that they can use intention information in moral judgments, although not as effectively as older children. Kohlberg's theory postulates several stages of moral development, which he sees as forming a natural sequence. Despite many questions about the measurement of such stages and whether some ways of thinking about moral issues are higher than others, research tends to support the idea that children move from making moral judgments based on rewards and punishments to judgments based on conformity to societal demands to those based on a more principled view of morality. Moral reasoning is one, but not the only, determinant of moral behavior. Children learn to control impulses through punishment and by responding to parental reasoning. In addition, a variety of cognitive mechanisms aid effective control over behavior.

SEX DIFFERENCES

There has been considerable recent interest in sex differences, fueled in part by the movement for sexual equality, but socialization theorists have a long-standing interest in this area because sex roles and differences are centrally important in this and all other societies.

BEHAVIOR AND PERSONALITY DIFFERENCES

There are salient behavioral and personality differences between the sexes, although many of the differences are not as strong or apparent as our stereotypes would have us believe. Furthermore, there is considerable overlap between the sexes on almost any psychological variable one cares to measure. For example, although men are more aggressive on the average than women, we might discover that there is so much overlap that, say, 40% of the women are more aggressive than the average male (see Figure 9.2). Before discussing the origins of sex differences, let us briefly review some of the major differences of relevance for social behavior. These and other differences

are well documented in reviews by Maccoby and Jacklin (1974), Block (1983), and Huston (1983).

Aggression　　Perhaps the best and most consistently found difference is that boys are generally more aggressive than girls, a difference that persists into adulthood. Males are more aggressive than females, especially on physical measures; the difference is less pronounced for aggression that causes psychological harm (Eagly & Steffen, 1986). This difference is also found in nearly all cultures of the world. This is not to say, of course, that men are *always* more aggressive than women. For example, Richardson, Bernstein, and Taylor (1979) have shown that women can be as aggressive as men when aggression is approved. So at least part of the difference may be due to greater social disapproval of female aggression, or at least to the perceptions of females that their aggression will be severely punished or disapproved (Eagly & Steffen, 1986).

Activity Level　　Most parents readily assert that their sons are more active and get into more trouble than their daughters. The actual activity levels of boys and girls do not differ much (Maccoby & Jacklin, 1974), but

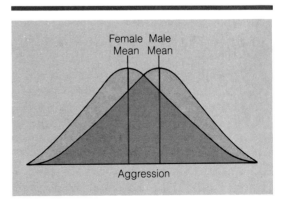

FIGURE 9.2 Possible Difference between Males and Females in Aggression, with 40% of Females Being More Aggressive than the Average Male.

boys are more adventuresome and curious in new situations (Ginsburg & Miller, 1982). Moreover, boys and girls differ in the kinds of activities they enjoy; for example, boys play more outside. Boys are also more impulsive than girls, tend to get into mischief more, and suffer more accidents requiring medical care. Boys also tend to resist their parents' attempts at control more (Maccoby, 1980). So, although boys are not always more active than girls, they do seem to engage in different and more physically vigorous activities than girls.

Dominance   In most groups, men tend to gravitate more readily to positions of leadership and power. This may result from any number of more basic tendencies. For example, males may simply have learned a more aggressive style. So it is possible that men and women both seek to exercise control over others but have quite different styles of doing so, men controlling through being bossy and women through a warmer, interpersonal style. Or it may be that men and women differ in the values they place on assertive behaviors; men rate dominant behaviors as more desirable than women do (Buss, 1981). Informal observation suggests that these values may be rapidly changing, and if they are it will be instructive to see whether women also come to occupy more informal and formal positions of leadership.

Nurturance and Prosocial Orientation   A popular stereotype is that women and girls are kinder, more helpful, more socially oriented, and more nurturant to small children than are males. There is an element of truth in this: females do tend to be more socially oriented than males, and girls tend to have smaller but more intimate circles of friends than boys. When one examines more-specific social behaviors, however, the data are mixed. Girls do not generally exhibit more prosocial behaviors, such as helping and cooperation (Radke-Yarrow, Zahn-Waxler, & Chapman, 1983), and males are more likely to help relative

strangers (Eagly & Crowley, 1986). In terms of social skills, women are somewhat better at reading nonverbal cues (Hall, 1978) but are not necessarily more empathic in their behavior (Eisenberg & Lennon, 1983).

Because in our society (and most others) women have a larger role in childcare activities, it has long been supposed that women are naturally more nurturant toward children. Although preadolescent girls are more interested in babies than are boys, this difference disappears after puberty. Adult men and women differ not in general responsiveness to babies but in how they interact with them.

Conformity   If women are more socially oriented, do they also respond more to social forces, say by conforming to the demands of others? Actually, there are few differences between males and females in conformity, although when differences appear women usually conform more. About 60% of women conform more than the average man (Cooper, 1979), hardly a massive difference. Similar results are found for tendencies to change attitudes (Eagly & Carli, 1981).

SEX TYPING

Clearly, males and females as groups differ in some important ways, especially in aggression and dominance, with the differences being less reliable for nurturance, prosocial orientation, and responses to social influence. However, such sex differences are only group averages, and there are many people whose interests, values, and behaviors are closer to the average of the opposite sex than to the average of their own sex. Furthermore, we know that some people place a great deal of emphasis on living up to a cultural ideal for their sex, whereas others are seemingly freer of such constraints.

Measurement   For many years, masculinity and femininity have been measured as a part of many personality tests. Generally, the approach has been purely empirical; an item is considered masculine or feminine if most men answer it one way and most females another. So, for example, we might expect an item such as "I would prefer watching football to a drama on television" to be a reasonable masculinity item by this definition because most men would probably answer *true* and most women *false* to that statement.

One of the major problems with such scales is that they assume that one can be either masculine or feminine in expressed values, but not both. However, these are independent dimensions (Constantinople, 1973). Empirically, people like both football and drama. You can enjoy both working on a car and cooking. A given individual can be both assertive and nurturant to small children; for that matter he or she could be neither. It is also important to recognize that when masculinity and femininity are measured in this way there is no necessary implication of homosexuality for individuals who have interests and values that characterize the opposite gender. Many males —particularly, but not exclusively, better educated ones— have a feminine interest pattern without having homosexual inclinations, and many gay men have highly masculine interest patterns. Box 9.1 dissusses further the implications of sex-typing for self-schemata.

Androgyny   Because masculinity and femininity are independent, a given person may be high on both scales. Bem (1974) argued strongly that people who are high on both scales may have special advantages because they can integrate two sets of culturally valued characteristics and can draw on several sets of skills in any given social situation. Thus, a woman who can be assertive or kind as the situation demands will presumably be more flexible and perhaps more confident and mature than the woman who has not managed to integrate the two sets.

Individuals who are relatively high on both masculinity and femininity scales are usually termed **androgynous.** A considerable body of research has accumulated, testing the notion that androgynous males and females have psychological and social advantages. Generally they do. For example, Bem and Lenny (1976) found that androgynous people were more flexible in their behaviors and preferences than people who were high in only one dimension or in neither. The androgynous people were less constrained by sex roles in their choices of tasks and were less distressed when they had to perform tasks generally thought appropriate for the opposite sex. Other studies have shown that androgynous people are particularly creative (Harrington & Andersen, 1981), have high self-concepts (Flaherty & Dusek, 1980; Heilbrun, 1981, Lamke, 1982), score high on a number of scales of psychological adjustment (Lubinski, Tellegen, & Butcher, 1981), and are evaluated especially positively by others (Major, Carnevale, & Deaux, 1981).

However, before we conclude that androgyny is an especially blessed state achieved through fusion of different values, let us examine the research a bit more closely. Bem claimed that such a fusion was necessary, but others have asserted that the real advantage of androgynous people comes from their simply having more good characteristics. That is, one does not have to *integrate* masculinity and femininity to be able to reap the advantages of being able to be one or the other when the situation calls for it.

Sandra Bem

BOX 9.1

GENDER SCHEMATA AND THE SELF

Some people work at living up to society's expectations for their gender, whereas others work just as hard to manage a life free from gender expectations. Some people think about the people of the world in terms of how masculine or feminine they are, and other people are more inclined to think of others in terms of occupation, physical appearance, or race. In short, for some people gender is an important part of the self-concept while for others it is not. In Chapter 5 we discussed the idea of a self-schema; for at least some people, gender is a part of that schema.

What would we expect if gender does function as a kind of schema? According to Hazel Markus and her students (Markus, Crane, Bernstein, & Siladi, 1982; Markus, Smith, & Moreland, 1985), the person who has a strong sense of self as feminine or masculine (that is, who is gender-schematic) has a rich and well-articulated sense of self with certain gender-linked characteristics. This in turn allows the person to process information about those gender-linked characteristics efficiently and quickly. There are several testable predictions of this perspective. One is that gender-schematic people will remember information consistent with that schema better than will people who do not hold the schema. Second, gender-schematic people will process schema-relevant information more efficiently than they will schema-irrelevant information.

Carol Mills (1983) investigated both of those predictions. Male and female subjects were given a list of adjectives and asked to check off those that applied to them. All the adjectives had previously been rated for their masculinity or femininity, and subjects were identified as masculine, feminine, or balanced depending on whether they checked mostly masculine, mostly feminine, or a relatively even number of both kinds of traits. The assumption is that subjects who check relatively more of one kind of trait have a self-schema for the related gender. In such studies there are usually a few people whose scores are inconsistent with their biological gender, but there were too few of these subjects in Mills' sample for their data to be used.

In the main part of the study, different traits, also either masculine or feminine, were presented one at a time via a slide projector and the subjects were asked to indicate whether the trait applied to them. Not surprisingly, the results supported the original classification of subjects: the masculine males responded that more masculine than feminine traits applied to them and the reverse was true for the feminine females. However, additional data were also collected on the latency of response, or how long it took subjects to decide that the trait did or did not apply to them. Schema theories clearly predict that a person with a strong schema ought to be able to make quicker decisions about schema-relevant than schema-irrelevant information. As predicted, the masculine subjects responded more rapidly to the masculine than to the feminine traits and the feminine subjects responded more quickly to the feminine than to the masculine traits. The balanced subjects, who apparently do not have a strong sense of being predominantly masculine or feminine, responded equally quickly

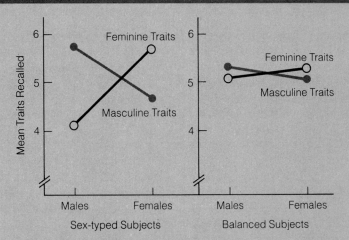

FIGURE B.9.1   Mean Number of Masculine and Feminine Traits Recalled by Masculine Males, Feminine Females, and Non-sex-typed (balanced) Subjects. Note that for the sex-typed subjects, males recall more masculine than feminine traits, whereas the reverse is true for female subjects. Males and females who are not strongly sex-typed recall equal numbers of masculine and feminine traits.

Mills, 1983.

to the two kinds of items. So the latency data clearly support the idea that gender has schematic properties for some people.

Following this task, subjects were given a brief distraction task and then were asked to recall as many of the traits as they could. Masculine subjects remembered more masculine than feminine traits, feminine subjects recalled more of the feminine traits, and the balanced subjects recalled approximately equal numbers of both kinds of traits (see Figure B.9.1).

Markus, Smith, and Moreland (1985) have assessed some additional implications. One is that people who think of themselves in terms of gender characteristics should also be more likely to label the behavior of others in terms of these same features. Male subjects for whom masculinity was highly

relevant watched films of a male performing routine activities, some of which were stereotypically masculine (such as weight-lifting), and subsequently were more likely to rate him high on masculine traits than were male subjects who were less likely to think of themselves as masculine. In addition, the subjects were asked to "chunk" the actor's behavior—that is, to divide it into meaningful units—by pressing a button as they watched the actor perform. Compared to the nonmasculine subjects, the masculine subjects used larger chunks for behavior sequences in which the actor did masculine activities but not for more routine activities. Why should this be? Imagine that you were watching someone assemble an object unfamiliar to you. You would probably concentrate heavily on the details

BOX CONTINUED

("she's soldering something," "she seems to be attaching that little thing to the bigger piece") precisely because you would not have a clear sense of what details went together. Someone who was more expert, on the other hand, would be able to think about the entire activity in terms of larger subparts and goals ("now she is making sure the X is working," "now she is putting the Y together"). So experts are able to use larger units (or chunks) in perceiving behavior. Markus and her colleagues interpreted these findings as suggesting that the masculine subjects were expert on masculine behaviors, which further supports the idea that people who see themselves as masculine or feminine have a rich knowledge about those characteristics.

There are other important theories about the ways in which gender roles affect our thinking about self and others (for example, Bem, 1981), but these theories agree that people who have a strong sense of themselves as masculine or feminine should find corresponding characteristics readily accessible in thinking about self and others. The feminine female will not only process information about femininity efficiently but will be inclined to think about others in terms of their femininity.

Much of the advantage found for androgynous people can be attributed to their high masculinity and to a lesser extent to their high femininity, without necessarily *combining* masculinity and femininity (Lubinski et al., 1983; Taylor & Hall, 1982; Whitley, 1983). To illustrate, we will make use of self-esteem data from Spence and Helmreich (1978). As you can see in Table 9.1, the highly feminine subjects are, on the average, between 2 and 3 points higher in self-esteem than the low-feminine subjects; the highly masculine subjects are between 6 and 7 self-esteem points higher than the low-masculine subjects. If we now look specifically at those subjects high in both (the androgynous people), we find that they are 2 points higher than the masculine subjects (the 2 points coming from their being higher in femininity), 6 points higher than the feminine subjects (because they are more masculine), and 9 points higher than the undifferentiated subjects. In other words, androgynous people have exactly the self-esteem one might expect for people who have two good characteristics—masculinity and femininity.

This kind of pattern is common (Taylor & Hall, 1982) and it suggests that ascribing special characteristics to androgynous people is somewhat misleading. Without trivializing the importance of having both masculine and feminine behaviors in one's repertoire, we do not need a special psychology of androgyny to account for the data. People who have more good traits (masculine and feminine) will have higher self-concepts.

HOW DO SEX DIFFERENCES ARISE?

Biology   Gender itself is biologically determined. But is there a biological basis for the psychological and behavioral differences between the sexes?

Newborns show few reliable sex differences and are hardly aggressive or dominating in orientation—the kinds of differences we observe among adult men and women—under any circumstances. Of course, sex differences could still be preprogrammed; we know, for instance, that many genetically based behav-

TABLE 9.1   SELF-ESTEEM AS A FUNCTION OF MASCULINITY AND FEMININITY.   *Note that those who score high in masculinity have higher self-esteem than those who score low in masculinity and that high-feminine subjects also score higher than low-feminine subjects. Consequently, those subjects who are high in both (androgynous) have the highest self-esteem.*   SOURCE: Spence & Helmreich, 1978

		Femininity	
		High	*Low*
Masculinity	*High*	43 (Androgynous)	41 (Masculine)
	Low	37 (Feminine)	34 (Undifferentiated)

iors such as walking and talking are not present at birth and take time to mature. Comparisons with other animals are also not especially instructive, because there is far less uniformity among animals with regard to sex differences than is commonly supposed and because it is always dangerous to extrapolate from animals to humans, given the enormously greater role of culture in human behavior.

In some ways, the most direct data on the *biology* of sex *differences* are *cultural universals* in gender-related behaviors. The logic of this comparison is that different cultures must vary considerably in the learning experiences they provide during socialization and that therefore any universals in human behavior must be based on that which is universal, namely a biological heritage. And it turns out that there are a fairly impressive number of universal or nearly universal sex differences. For example, in almost all cultures women are less aggressive, less likely to perform their economic functions away from home, and more involved in child-rearing (Ember, 1981).

However, the conclusions we can draw from this are not perfectly clear. It is true that cross-cultural comparisons tend to subtract out culturally unique learning experiences and that what is common across cultures says something about the universal human condition. The problem is that there is more to universality than biology. Different human societies may face similar demands on their ability to survive as groups and as individuals and

may respond to those demands in similar, cultural ways.

For example, in almost all societies, women are exclusively or mainly responsible for food preparation. Does this mean that women have a cooking gene? This seems silly on the face of it and, given the diversity of ways of preparing food, it is hard to imagine how one could encode such a genetic predisposition. How then can we account for this universal of human behavior? One of many possibilities is that in most societies where women must nurse or feed children several times a day and where men are inclined to be away from home because of their greater strength and consequent abilities to hunt, one obvious solution is for women to tend the home fires while the men are gone. Thus, there would be no gene for cooking. The fact that women do most of the cooking in most societies would be a culturally imposed solution to a universal problem, a solution based in part on biology but not directly caused by it.

There is no single source of data that directly proves that sex differences (other than anatomical ones, of course) are biologically based. This does not mean that biology has no role to play, but its role comes in complex interactions with cultural and learning experiences. It is also worth pointing out again and again to those who insist on biological determinism that, even if we were to discover straightforward biological dispositions, culture can and does have its own controls. So even if men and women are born as fundamentally different, culture may override much of that biological heritage.

Learning Approaches   It seems obvious that children learn how to behave like boys and girls and that parents and other socialization agents teach them to adopt behavioral styles appropriate for their gender. Certainly, each of us knows of or has experienced one of the classic scenarios: a mother counsels a daughter not to worry so much about her grades because she'll never get a husband if she is so smart; a father discourages his daughter from going to college because she's just going to get married anyway; both parents tell a son he can't take ballet lessons because ballet is for girls.

Perhaps parents have different perceptions of their male and female newborns. In one study, parents of newborns (less than 1 day old) reported that the boys are heartier, stronger, and more coordinated than girls, who were seen as softer and less attentive despite the fact that trained hospital staff could not detect these differences (Rubin, Provenzano, & Luria, 1974). Other studies, using the "Baby X" paradigm, where some people are told that the same baby is a boy and others that it is a girl, find that reactions do vary with the gender label (Huston, 1983).

At later ages, parents continue to react differently to boys and girls, but by this time we cannot be sure if it is real diffferences in the children that cause the different parental reactions or vice versa. For example, Snow, Jacklin, and Maccoby (1983) have observed that fathers tend to be more controlling with 1-year-old sons than with daughters, but that even at age 1 the boys need more control in the sense of being more likely to get into things they shouldn't. Nonetheless, there are fairly systematic differences in the ways parents (especially fathers) interact with their children as a function of sex. Fathers give their sons more freedom to explore, are more active with sons and gentle with daughters (Block

Eleanor Maccoby

1983; Huston, 1983), and are more concerned about the sex-appropriateness of toys for sons than daughters (Snow, Jacklin, & Maccoby, 1983).

Thus, there is good evidence that parents and other socialization agents treat boys and girls differently, although these differences tend to be subtle. This is not, of course, the only way children might learn sex roles. Some have suggested that children learn how to be male or female by observing their same-sex parent. However, the tendency for children to observe and imitate the same-sex parent more than the other parent is not strong, at least for young children (Huston, 1983). Furthermore, there are only weak, sometimes nonexistent, relationships between the sex-role behavior of children and that of their parents (Maccoby & Jacklin, 1974; Spence & Helmreich, 1978). So the obvious possibility that boys imitate their daddies and girls their mommies cannot be the answer.

However, sex roles could still be modeled in other ways. Perry and Bussey (1979) have argued that children learn sex-role behavior not from single (that is, parental) models but from their observation of multiple models. Girls might learn a preference for playing with dolls not so much from watching their mothers take care of children as from the more general observation that nearly all the people who take care of the young are female.

Moreover, the mass media often stereotype males and females. For example, there are far more male than female characters on television, especially in positions of authority and in hero roles. Women work outside the home less on television than in real life (Huston, 1983). Although the mass media have only weak direct effects on sex roles (Morgan, 1982), other effects of the media may be subtle. For example, stereotypic television programs may not directly create expectations that boys should be businessmen and girls secretaries, but may also not give children a clear idea of how much freedom they might have with regard to career choices. The girl who observes only aggressive and wealthy business*men* may not develop the idea that she too could perform this role. A boy who wants to help others would find few models for male nurses in television programs. Furthermore, the media convey messages about power. For example, many advertisements portray women in sub-

Children begin quite early to play with toys associated with gender roles.

servient roles, and women who watch such commercials tend to conform more subsequently (Jennings, Geis, & Brown, 1980).

Many theories of sex-typing see the formation of stereotypes as a crucial link in learning how to behave in a role (Kohlberg, 1966). A frequently suggested scenario is that the child first learns his or her own sex, subsequently realizes that this categorization is shared with half the human race, including one parent, then determines what same-sex adults do, and finally tries to copy this stereotype by engaging in stereotypic behavior. Parts of this progression are well supported by data. Generally, by age 2, children know their own gender, mostly because they have been told over and over again what they are. By age 3, children can also label adults correctly and they realize that men and women do somewhat different things and wear different clothes (Weintraub et al., 1984).

By the end of the third year, children have begun to develop a clear picture of stereotypic boy and girl behavior. We also know that children of age 2 or even younger have already begun to prefer stereotypic toys (such as dolls for girls and trucks for boys). Again, this supports the stereotype scenario. The problem with this perspective is that the preference for stereotypic activities sometimes shows up before clear conceptions of gender have developed and long before the child can report what toys boys and girls should play with (Perry, White, & Perry, 1984; Weintraub et al., 1984). In addition, children may show preferences for imitating a same-sex symbol before they have clear knowledge of gender categories (Bussey & Bandura, 1984). Clearly then, knowledge of gender categories, appropriate adult behaviors, and appropriate child behaviors do not quite match the sequence suggested by cognitive theories. This does not mean that gender stereotypes play no role in learning sex roles, but it does suggest that this learning is gradual and that sex-typing can take place without clear conceptions of appropriateness.

In this regard, it is also useful to remember a point made earlier. According to Higgins and Parsons (1983), children at different ages participate in cohort cultures that reinforce norms about appropriate behaviors. Children criticize their peers who violate the norms of appropriate sex-role behavior and reward those who conform to the norms (Carter & McCloskey, 1983–84; Lamb & Roopnarine, 1979; Langlois & Downs, 1980).

The Role of the Larger Culture   Although there are some parents and teachers who are so dedicated to existing sex roles that they try to force children into them, the learning and teaching of sex roles is as a whole subtle and multifaceted. To be sure, parents may encourage their children to do one thing over another through subtle and not-so-subtle praise and criticism, and this may be continued by teachers, but most socialization agents are not so direct. Nor do they have to be. Those who would have their children grow up to be sex-typed men and women have the whole culture on their side. The mass media, neighbors, schools, and nearly everyone else who counts will aid and abet this socialization process.

Even those parents who wish to produce children who are not sex-typed will have problems with the larger cultural expectations. What does the parent of an adolescent do when she claims with considerable justification that her popularity depends to some extent on having a closet full of designer jeans and shirts with animals on them? How do you encourage a son's desire to be a nursery-school teacher when his friends and teachers make fun of him? In a school where the boys play football and the girls lead cheers to spur them on, how do you fight the obvious message that the role of women is to look pretty and to serve while the men are the real actors on life's stage?

Every parent must, of course, make peace with the larger culture, and many parents manage to produce children who are not

trapped by their gender expectations despite the larger culture. But there are those who grow up without ever learning that there are alternatives until it is too late. The young woman who wants a medical career will "naturally" think that she should be a nurse, because most of the doctors she sees on TV are male and all the nurses are female. Given what children see around them every day, their feelings about careers may be decided long before they are in any position to think the matter through reasonably.

CHAPTER SUMMARY

- Socialization is the process of learning how to behave effectively in groups and adjust to particular cultures.

- Socialization requires the acquisition of basic cognitive skills and the motivation to achieve what a given culture considers to be appropriate goals. In addition, it is usually desirable from the culture's point of view for people to have internalized basic values so that they *want* to do what they *should* do.

- Throughout the centuries there have been various conceptions of the socialization process, but the present century has been dominated by (1) the Freudian view that society must impose controls on basic biological urges, (2) the behaviorist view that the child must learn all skills and motives through reinforcement, and (3) Piaget's theory, which stresses the interactions between experience and a biological readiness to benefit from certain experiences.

- It has been usual to think of parents as molding the child through example, explanations, and reinforcing powers, but children also affect the behavior of parents. Parental behavior varies along dimensions of control and warmth, and the data generally suggest that child-centered (warm) and controlling parental styles are most effective for producing mature children. Effective parental communication to children is also helpful in the socialization process.

- Children also learn from models. Initially, parents provide models for appropriate behaviors, but as the child gets older peers and the mass media increasingly perform this function.

- Most children are attached to one or more parental figures. Generally, secure attachment is increased by parental responsiveness to the child's needs.

- Infants show some responsiveness to other children within the first year, and by the end of the second year mutual play is possible. Play is an important way that children learn social skills.

- Socially competent children are generally nonaggressive, helpful, and responsive to other children. Social competence is produced by secure early attachment, parental warmth combined with high demands for prosocial behavior, and good experiences with peers.

- The development of social cognition has been dominated by Piagetian theory, which stressed that preschool children cannot take the perspectives of others or think about the nonobserved, psychological causes of behavior. Research has generally confirmed a developmental progression in these abilities, but has not supported the view that younger children are incapable of these skills. Thus, preschool children tend to think of friends and authorities in terms of relatively superficial characteristics, whereas older children are more inclined to stress psychological causes of behavior and have a more differentiated understanding of both friendships and authority.

- Children must learn several types of rules, but the most important are moral rules. Research has not confirmed the Piagetian idea that children are incapable of judging morality on the basis of intentions and motives, although they do have some difficulty with this. Kohlberg's theory of moral development suggests that children go through various stages of moral judgment; initially, morality is seen as based on external rewards and punishments, but gradually this concept is replaced by moralities based on the power of society and, for some people, a morality of individual conscience.

- Moral behavior requires that children not only know moral rules and know how to apply them, but also be able to control impulses. Research suggests that parental warmth and control are important factors in learning impulse control.

- Sex differences are salient in all societies, but males and females do not differ as much as most people think. Although people receive pressure to behave like typical males or females, masculinity and femininity are somewhat independent of biological gender. Androgynous people have the best features of both masculine and feminine people.

- Several theories of why males and females differ have been proposed. Biological explanations must be supplemented by examination of cultural forces. However, better explanations based on simple learning or reinforcement of sex-role behaviors are needed.

CHAPTER

10

GROUPS

On May 17, 1954, reporters and other spectators waited in the courtroom of the United States Supreme Court Building for the usual Monday announcement of decisions. Chief Justice Earl Warren read several routine decisions and then announced that the Court had reached a decision on the case of *Oliver Brown et al.* v. *The Board of Education of Topeka.* In 1952 the Court had heard arguments on behalf of black children in Topeka who were compelled to attend segregated schools. In 1896 the Court had ruled (in *Plessy* v. *Ferguson*) that separate but equal (segregated) school facilities were constitutional. Now the Court had the difficult task of deciding whether to reaffirm precedent or to chart a new course.

It had been no secret that the Court was having trouble making up its collective mind. Everyone expected a close vote with many shades of opinion represented. This was the most important case before the Court; its decision would engender considerable public hostility no matter what the Court decided.

Chief Justice Warren read the central question of whether segregated schools deprived black children of equal opportunity, and he gave the Court's answer: "We believe that it does." Warren went on to give reasons, then stated the conclusion: "We conclude, unanimously, that in the field of public education the doctrine of 'separate but equal' has no place. Separate educational facilities are inherently unequal." In a particularly fascinating example of how groups reach decisions, the Warren Court had achieved a unanimous decision on an issue that had begun to fracture the American body politic.

When the *Brown* case had been first argued in 1952, Chief Justice Frederick Vinson presided. In the conferences on the case it soon became clear that the Court would probably split 5–4 in favor of desegregation but with strong dissent and many concurring opinions

The Supreme Court's historic *Brown* decision was a compromise achieved through the leadership skills of Chief Justice Earl Warren.

(those written by members of the majority who disagree with the logic of the justice who writes the majority opinion). The result would be a decision of no moral force and considerable legal ambiguity.

At that time the Court was deeply divided over the issue of judicial restraint. On the one side stood Felix Frankfurter, who argued that all decisions must be framed in terms of legal reasoning and precedents of past decisions; in this case the *Plessy* decision had been a clear precedent saying that segregation was legal. On the other side was Hugo Black, backed by William C. Douglas, who argued that the Court had responsibilities to interpret the law in terms of larger political and societal concerns, in this case simple morality and changing public conceptions about race. Although on this case Frankfurter would ultimately abandon judicial restraint, narrowly conceived, others in his camp would not be so willing, especially when their legal logic was buttressed by Southern and conservative backgrounds. In the hopes of gaining further support, Frankfurter persuaded the Court to rehear arguments on various questions, mainly to postpone the decision.

Before the case could be reheard, Vinson died and was replaced as Chief Justice by Earl Warren, a popular governor of California, but a man of no special legal distinction. As the case was reheard in late 1953, Warren showed that although he might not have a great legal mind, he was a great leader. Initially, he proposed that in their conferences the justices not take notes or vote but simply discuss the issues. Through this he prevented positions from hardening and kept conflict to a minimum. Perhaps his most brilliant move was to present the issue in moral terms from the very outset. He made it clear that the separate but equal doctrine rested on the assumption of inherent racial inequality that had been part of the social reality of 1896 but that no longer was, at least not to morally intelligent people. He never accused his opponents on the Court of racism, but he forced them to find legal reasons for their position. Their strongest legal arguments were that a new decision would overturn the precedent of *Plessy* and that the framers of the Fourteenth Amendment to the Constitution (basically guaranteeing equality to all Americans) never meant to exclude segregation. So, according to this argument, opponents of segregation could hardly claim Fourteenth Amendment support, because the amendment had never been meant to apply to segregation. Warren met these issues head-on. He stated clearly that, although overturning precedent should not be undertaken lightly, in this case the earlier *Plessy* decision had been founded on a view of racial inequality that was clearly misguided. He virtually forced the minority to identify themselves with racism if they argued the importance of precedent. The issue of the intentions of those who wrote the Fourteenth Amendment was disposed of by a lengthy paper written by Alexander Bikel, one of Frankfurter's clerks (and subsequently a distinguished legal scholar). Bikel showed conclusively that one could conclude nothing about whether the amendment had been intended to apply to segregation; thus, the intentions of those who wrote it were irrelevant in 1954.

Throughout the winter there were group conferences, but Warren's major work was with the individual justices. He listened to their concerns and modified accordingly the reasoning he would use in writing the decision. Gradually, he won over the minority, but one remaining issue was tricky. Many members of the Court were concerned about how the decision should be implemented. How much time should school districts have to desegregate?

Warren and the Court managed a compromise that saved the day. They agreed that the initial decision would be on the relatively narrow legal and moral issues, and they would hear additional arguments on implementation after the decision was announced. This may have been a major error, because the timidity led many segregationists to believe that the Court countenanced delay. But, at the time, it allowed the contentious issues to be postponed and provided unanimity for the central decision.

The *Brown* decision was not achieved through any superhuman leadership powers; most group decisions are not. On the other hand, Warren showed what a valuable commodity leadership skills can be. Nine men who argued constantly from quite different perspectives, who had large egos and contrasting personal agendas, nevertheless agreed. Without doubt, had they been left to their own devices, the ultimate decision would have been quite different both in its wording and in its effects.

INTRODUCTION

Humans are social animals. We like other people and obtain many of our most important rewards and pleasures from interacting with them. A primitive fact for social psychology is that we spend much of our time interacting with and thinking about other people. Many of our contracts with others are fairly meaningless, as when we try to negotiate a busy sidewalk. Other times behavior seems more fully social but only in a vague sort of way. For example, as you wait in a crowded airport you will be quite aware of the presence of others and how they behave, but you probably do not respond to them in any individualized way. Our behavior is often most self-consciously social when we interact with others as a part of a group. Humans are social in many different ways, but our most highly developed forms of social behavior occur in groups of people.

THE NATURE OF GROUPS

What is a group? Most social psychologists would agree that a group is not a mere collection of people; rather, a true **group** involves people whose behavior is to some extent interdependent and who recognize a degree of mutual relationship. By *interdependence* we simply mean that each person influences the others. Also, members of a group must be con-

scious of special relationships to others within the group; ordinarily this criterion will be met if the people are willing to define themselves as members of the group—such definition presupposes feelings of relationship.

It might be useful to contrast groups with other collections of people. The least social kinds of collections are aggregates of people defined by geographical, gender, racial, or demographic characteristics. I am a Texan, a male, and a wearer of glasses, but except in certain circumstances I do not have any fellow feeling for others who share these characteristics nor am I dependent on them or they on me. We might call these groups *nominal groups,* but they are not groups in the sense of our definition. *Collectives* are people gathered together in a single place but who share neither special relationships with one another nor consciousness of kind. People waiting for an airplane or for a stoplight to change are relevant examples. People in collectives may behave similarly because of their common situation, and they may have minimal interdependencies such as when people at stoplights eye one another to see who can make the fastest

When people are gathered in the same place with no special relationship, they form a collective.

getaway when the light changes. But such interdependencies are fleeting and generally do not define a feeling of groupness.

The Group Mind   All groups develop traditions, norms, roles, and their own ways of doing things that exist apart from particular individuals in the sense that they will persist even after individual members depart. For example, the Supreme Court has elaborate traditions about how cases are heard and decided; these are largely unchanged since the early part of this century even though there have been several changes in membership of the Court during that time.

This has led some to claim that groups have a reality beyond that of the individual group members. It has even been argued that groups have a sort of mind of their own. This position was given its classic articulation by Gustave LeBon writing in 1895:

> Whoever be the individuals that compose it, however like or unlike be their mode of life, their occupations, their character, or their intelligence, the fact that they have been transformed into a crowd puts them in possession of a sort of collective mind which makes them feel, think, and act in a manner quite different from that in which each individual of them would feel, think, and act were he in a state of isolation. . . . It is precisely these general qualities of character, governed by forces of which we are unconscious, and possessed by the majority of normal individuals of a race in much the same degree—it is precisely these qualities, I say, that in crowds become common property. In the collective mind the intellectual aptitudes of the individuals, and in consequence their individuality, are weakened. (pp. 22–24)

According to LeBon, not only do crowds (and other groups such as legislative bodies) behave in a collective fashion, but this "collective mind" is unreflective, nonrational, and much the lowest common denominator of all humans. This model of the group mind exercised considerable influence on early thinking about groups.

Psychologists have tended to be very distrustful of such claims for collective realities. Floyd Allport (1924), a founding father of modern social psychology, argued that it is individuals who think and behave and not groups. Think about the Boston Celtics basketball team. Allport would claim that although the team is given credit for wins and losses, it is the shooting, dribbling, and rebounding of Larry Bird, Robert Parish, and Kevin McHale that wins or loses the games. Similarly, although we can say that the Supreme Court ruled that desegregation is unconstitutional, the decision still came down to nine individual votes.

Others would argue somewhat differently. Groups do seem to have a kind of reality that is not totally reducible to individual members. One reason Boston wins so many basketball games is the skilled integration of the individual players' moves. One of the reasons Earl Warren was a successful chief justice was that he managed to create a group atmosphere of high purpose and congeniality that submerged individual ideological and personal disagreements.

There are then really two levels of analysis. It is always important to remember that it is people and not groups who behave and think; in that sense Allport was correct and LeBon incorrect. Yet to suggest that group life is no more than the behavior of individuals is analogous to saying that a person does not perform behaviors but only her arms and legs do (Steiner, 1986). Just as we need to see movement as a property of the total person as well as of arms and legs, so too can human behavior be profitably examined from the perspective of group atmosphere, traditions, and values, as well as of individual behavior.

WHY DO PEOPLE JOIN GROUPS?

At one level it seems as strange to ask why you like and seek the company of others as to ask why you like music or prefer good health to bad. Some things just seem to be irreducible conditions for being human. Nonetheless, at another level we can still recognize that groups are valuable to us in several ways and that they fulfill various needs. Let us examine some theories about why we join groups.

Biological Models As we noted in Chapter 1, instinct theories were quite popular around the turn of the century. One theory postulated an instinct of *affiliation*, or, as it was sometimes called, the herd instinct. In more recent years, some sociobiologists have stressed the evolutionary significance of groups (Crook, 1981). There is no doubt that group membership aids survival. For example, animal groups are able to provide better defense against predators than single animals can, and food collection is often more efficient with larger groups. When animals (including humans) live together in groups, there are increased opportunities for mating, and offspring may be raised more safely and efficiently by parents in group settings. There are, of course, costs to groups as well. For some activities, group members may get in one another's way, leading to inefficient use of

available food. Diseases spread more easily in groups, and fighting may be more common in group settings as well. Still, on the whole, groups are an evolutionary bargain. However, this does not prove that humans have been born with a biological predisposition to join groups. Even if some sort of affiliative predispostion is part of our biological equipment, we still cannot specify the precise ways in which the predisposition might manifest itself in our behavior.

Freudian Theory Freud (1921) was intensely interested in the questions of why people form groups and how such groups serve to modify our strong biological natures. He essentially argued that groups are, in some ways, replacements for families. People tend to identify with strong and powerful others and to pattern their own behavior and values after these ego-ideals. Initially, the same-sex parent is the object of identification, but later strong leaders and even symbols can perform this function. Groups form when several people identify with the same ego-ideal.

Freud's theory is probably wrong in important respects. It seems unlikely that every member of a university identifies with the college president or even with the same educational ideals. On the other hand, the theory is valuable for pointing out that people join groups to fulfill certain basic needs, and that groups and their dynamics reflect the personalities of those who join. Freud was also correct in emphasizing that at least some people under some circumstances identify powerfully with some groups, and that groups can have power over individuals all out of proportion to what seems to be reasonable.

Hedonism People usually perform those behaviors they find rewarding and avoid those they find costly. Groups fit this perspective in at least two ways. First, belonging to groups often increases reward–cost ratios. Belonging to a car pool can get me to work at lower cost than driving myself, and studying for an exam with a friend might provide both people with insights they did not have before.

Second, we join some groups because the group itself offers rewards that cannot be attained elsewhere. You can enjoy exercising as a solitary activity, but it is hard to play baseball without teammates and an opposing team. You may learn more if you study in a study group, but it will also probably be more fun as well. Belonging to the Supreme Court or a social club offers prestige.

Thibaut and Kelley (1959) have argued that liking for the group will be measured against two salient standards. First, we compare the total outcomes we achieve from group membership against the average of our general rewards and costs. This **comparison level** (CL) determines whether we like the group. Thus, you will say you like a new club you have joined if you get more total pleasure from belonging and going to meetings than you typically get elsewhere.

We also evaluate groups against the next best alternative, the **comparison level of alternatives** (CL_{alt}). This CL_{alt} affects whether you will be happy remaining a member of the group. Say you have joined the local Sierra Club but now your close friend suggests you join the local French cinema society, which meets at the same time. The Sierra Club may be a perfectly nice organization (and be well above your CL) but you may still drop out because the value of going to its meetings has fallen below your CL_{alt}, namely seeing intriguing French films. Alternatively, we sometimes remain in groups we dislike because the CL_{alt} is even lower. You may dislike college (it offers outcomes below your CL) but still stay enrolled because the alternatives of going to work and experiencing parental disapproval are even worse. Needless to say, such situations (where present outcomes are below the CL but above the CL_{alt}) are not conducive to a happy group atmosphere.

Stress and Affiliation   Schachter (1959) noted that there appears to be a rather intimate relationship between anxiety and affiliation. People who are isolated for long periods seem to have anxiety attacks; Schachter wanted to know if affiliation helps alleviate anxiety.

When Schachter's female subjects entered an experiment, they were told that they would be shocked. High-anxiety subjects were told that the shocks would be painful, whereas for the low-anxiety subjects the painful nature of the shocks was played down. Following the anxiety manipulations, subjects were asked to wait in another room while the apparatus was set up, and they were given the choice of waiting alone or with others.

The results showed that the high-anxiety subjects preferred to wait with others whereas the low-anxiety subjects didn't have a strong preference (Table 10.1). A second study indicated that affiliation desires were not indiscriminate. Subjects preferred to wait with others who were also going to take part in the same experiment rather than with those who were to take part in another experiment. So the desire was to affiliate with a person in a similar plight (Table 10.2).

Schachter suggested two hypotheses to account for the results. One is that subjects felt that waiting with others would reduce their anxiety; perhaps they hoped that the others would be calm and this would help to reduce anxiety. Aversive feelings such as fear and anxiety are sometimes reduced through affiliation in both animals (Epley, 1974) and people (Friedman, 1981). However, this is not always the case. When subjects are about to experience something embarrassing, such as

TABLE 10.1   NUMBER OF SUBJECTS CHOOSING TO WAIT TOGETHER OR ALONE.

	Together	Don't Care	Alone
High anxiety	20	9	3
Low anxiety	10	18	2

SOURCE: Schachter, 1959

TABLE 10.2 NUMBER OF HIGH-ANXIETY SUBJECTS WANTING TO WAIT TOGETHER WITH SOMEONE IN SAME OR DIFFERENT STATE.

	Together	Don't Care	Alone
Same state	6	4	0
Different state	0	10	0

SOURCE: Schachter, 1959

having to suck on pacifiers and lollipops, they prefer to be alone (Sarnoff & Zimbardo, 1961). Rofé (1984) has suggested that stress leads to a desire for affiliation only when the others can reduce the stressful state.

A second possibility is that the subjects were somewhat confused about their feelings and whether the feelings were appropriate. Waiting with others might help to clarify these feelings. People presumably become aroused when threatened with shock, but several things may be unclear to them. They might wonder whether it is fear or some other emotion they are experiencing, or whether they feel more or less fear than is appropriate. Thus, the Schachter subjects may have wanted to wait with others to help clarify their emotional states. Research by Gerard and Rabbie (1961) and Gerard (1963) confirms that when people are unclear about their emotional states, they will attempt to clarify their feelings through affiliation or other means.

GROUP STRUCTURE

Groups differ in many ways. Some are quite large (say a large lecture class or the House of Representatives). Others are smaller, some as small as two people, which we technically call a *dyad.* Groups can be quite formal with elaborate rules and roles; others may be so informal that at first you don't even think of them as a group. Groups also differ in their explicit purposes, their goals: some have well-defined goals and others may have no well-articulated

goals at all other than just getting together and having a good time. Generally, larger groups have more explicit goals and a more formal structure and smaller groups typically have more diffuse goals and are more relaxed about how to achieve them.

In this section we will focus on some features all groups have in common: roles and norms, an authority structure, and ways of communicating. In formal groups such as the Supreme Court, these are quite evident. The chief justice of the United States has the role of running the meetings and overseeing the administrative details of the Court. Communication is generally in the form of written memos, except for the conference meetings to discuss particular cases. There are fairly explicit norms about how the Court conducts business. During the conferences the chief justice sits at one end of the table and speaks first on a given case, summarizing the issues and giving his own view. The most senior member of the Court sits at the other end and speaks second. The other members who sit at the sides of the table then speak in order of seniority. Formal votes are taken in the reverse order.

But there is more to the Court than this readily observable structure. For example, although the chief justice is the nominal leader, other leaders may have considerable authority. In the Warren Court, Justice Frankfurter was very influential because of the respect others had for his keen legal mind. Furthermore, although the justices hold the power of the vote, their clerks constitute a second tier of power within the Court. The clerks often discuss cases among themselves and their deliberations can affect rulings, given that individual clerks often have considerable influence on the thinking and decisions of their justices.

So, even formal groups have an informal structure. Furthermore, informal groups that may seem to have no structure at all actually do have many of the same features of formal groups. Take a husband and wife. Probably they do not have centuries of personal tradition or a written constitution that guide their actions. They might be puzzled if we were to ask who the boss is or what rules guide their activities. However, as we observe their daily routines we may discover that she usually makes dinner while he cleans the house, even though these roles may never have been deliberately decided. We may also observe that he tends to be a bit bossy on what movies they will see but she is the dominant authority on how money should be spent. They have their own family norms and rules. On Thursday nights the family watches "The Cosby Show" together but on Saturday nights Mom and Dad almost always go out. He typically initiates conversations about the children but she structures the conversations about money. Even the family unit, an informal group, has roles and norms, authority, and communication patterns.

NORMS

The Nature of Norms   All groups, except those recently formed, have **norms**, which are informal rules governing group-related activity. The Supreme Court has norms about who sits where in conferences and who can speak first. Families have norms about dinner time, bed time, and who selects the TV programs. Classes typically have norms too. You may notice that even if class seating is not assigned, people tend to sit in the same seats or at least in the same part of the room, and occasionally someone will become annoyed if another student has taken "his" seat.

Norms are the social and cultural equivalents of habits and cognitive heuristics. They simplify the social world and allow us not to think about our every action. Just as having the habit of brushing your teeth just before you go to bed makes getting to bed a little less complex, so the norm of having dinner at 6 o'clock sharp eliminates having to make decisions and lends predictability to family life. Norms provide a certain consistency and regu-

larity to behavior that allow us to focus our attention on matters more deserving of our attention. They also tend to reduce conflict, misunderstanding, and confusion: think of the chaos that would result if people could arbitrarily pick which side of the street they wanted to drive on. This does not mean, of course, that norms should never be challenged or disobeyed, but only that they provide a certain amount of social grease to keep groups moving without the friction of constantly having to make decisions. Norms also help to individuate groups. One fraternity, social group, or family may differ from another primarily in the norms of the group, and sometimes groups become very proud of these traditions and "our way of doing things."

Norms vary in many ways. Some are compelling ("do not come to class naked"), while others have a more optional quality ("I sit in the front of the class"). They also vary in how generally applicable they are. There is a norm that you shouldn't make rude faces or signs at other people, which generally applies to most situations you are in. On the other hand, a norm that you should not ask questions in class may apply only to certain classes and perhaps then only on certain days.

Sometimes norms are agreed to quite explicitly. A group of roommates may vote on when to have dinner, and any newly formed organization must initially agree on some rules of procedure. More often, norms arise from habit. Because you sat in one seat during the last class it becomes easier to sit there now. And if everyone will simply sit where he or she sat before, all will go well. A good many norms are handed down from generation to generation as a kind of tradition.

The Persistence of Norms   The persistence of traditions, norms, values, behavioral regularities, and institutions has naturally been of considerable interest to cultural anthropologists, but there have also been several experimental demonstrations of what might loosely be called cultural persistence. In one classic experiment by Jacobs and Campbell (1961), subjects were asked to judge how far a spot of light in a dark room moved. Actually, the light did not move; any stationary light in a totally dark room appears to move a small distance—typical estimates are that it moves about 3 inches. When people were in groups, their judgments about how far the light moved tended to converge on a common estimate (see Chapter 11). Jacobs and Campbell instructed confederates in some groups to give very high estimates, which had the expected effect of raising the estimates of other people in the group. Jacobs and Campbell were interested in whether the original high estimates would persist and for how long. The confederates were removed; new, naive subjects took their places; the groups again made judgments; and more subjects were replaced by new "generations" after each set of judgments. Jacobs and Campbell found that the effects of the confederates' original judgments could be observed into a fifth generation beyond their replacement. Group traditions may last even longer when they are less arbitrary and do not compete as strongly with natural perceptual tendencies (Insko et al., 1980; Weick & Gilfillan, 1971). Such demonstrations suggest that even simple groups develop traditions that outlast individual members.

ROLES

The Nature of Roles   Roles are close cousins to norms. Whereas norms are rules of behavior, *roles* are specific positions in groups that carry expectations of certain behaviors. Like norms, roles can be quite explicit and well defined; some roles you might find in a university would be professor, student, president, secretary, groundskeeper, and nurse. On the other hand, roles often may be less explicit. In a class, for example, one student may be the person who asks the professor questions other students are reluctant to ask; or in a class discussion, one student might always be

critical whereas another might be the know-it-all. In these cases, we can still speak of roles even though they have not been explicitly assigned because there is a sense of behavioral regularity. Also, as with norms, some roles are fairly general while others are highly circumscribed. A secretary may be "in role" throughout the working day, but the student critic may be "in role" only for a single class and then only when there is a class discussion.

Like norms, roles develop because they are useful to the group. Knowing that Joe will surely ask the professor what will be on the exam relieves others from having to muster up the courage to ask. In a family, knowing that dad will wash dishes keeps others from arguing about who will do them. In a business, someone must type reports, run the computer, and empty wastebaskets, and it is easier to make sure given people do each task all the time than to decide anew every day who will do what. Moreover, when a number of responsibilities are divided in this way, people may be able to do the things they enjoy and are good at and to avoid the things they hate. Roles make for efficiency.

Role Conflict   One of the inevitable problems with roles is *role conflict. Interrole conflict* occurs when a person finds that two roles he or she plays have conflicting demands. Many people experience such role conflicts in trying to be a good spouse and parent on one hand and a good company employee on the other. One cannot simultaneously be home with the kids and away on business. *Intrarole conflict*, on the other hand, arises from conflicts within the same role. Professors are expected to do considerable research to satisfy tenure committees but also to devote substantial time to students, both in and out of the classroom. In your student role you may be expected by professors to work long hours and by your friends to spend your time being entertaining.

There are several ways people insulate themselves from role conflicts. Commonly we try to perform different aspects of the same role at different times and places. I find it convenient to teach all my classes on two days and spend most of the rest of my time at home working at other professional tasks. Organizations may have explicit rules that define responsibilities to ensure that all parts of a given role are performed. For example, at many universities faculty members are required to have a certain number of office hours per week. Almost everyone in our complex society experiences some degree of role conflict every day.

POWER

A fundamental feature of any group, even the informal dyad, is that people exert power over one another. Sometimes this power is quite direct and explicit, whereas at other times it is informal and implicit. In formal groups, power relationships may coincide with established role structures, but power relations exist in groups whether or not they are a formal part of the group structure.

Sources and Types of Power   Where do people get power? An influential theory by French and Raven (1959) postulates several

OPEC, the cartel of oil-producing countries, has had considerable reward and coercive power over billions of people in recent years.

bases of social power. The first two, **reward** and **coercive power**, are perhaps closest to what we normally think of as power, namely the use of rewards and punishments to influence others. Such control can be quite blatant, as when I tell my child that I will pay her $3 to perform some chore, but often it is more subtle, as when a boss hints at a pay raise for some additional work.

Legitimate power is based on internalized feelings of one person that the other should and does have power over him or her. Such power is often quite limited in scope; for example, you may feel that your professor has the legitimate power to determine when exams will be given but not to tell you whether you should smoke or not. Legitimate power is often complex and vague, because it depends heavily on whether or not people *feel* that it is appropriate.

Referent power also depends on subtle psychological characteristics. In this case, we grant some people power because we want to be similar to them or have them like us. Women may buy a particular cosmetic because Ms. Bigteeth says it makes her look good, and men may buy a certain brand of shaving cream because Mr. Biceps uses it on TV. Presumably, by using the products advertised by the rich and famous, we gain some feelings of identification with them. However, referent power is not limited to such cases. Most families are built on considerable referent power; children do what their parents tell them because they want their parents to think highly of them.

Finally, French and Raven suggest that some people have power because they hold relevant information; this is called **expert power**. Obviously, the information must be relevant to the group's goals. My ability to read a computer program would not get me far at the local plumbers' union meeting, I suspect, and my plumber's expertise about pipes and fittings would carry little weight at a faculty meeting.

The several bases of power distinguished by French and Raven are not mutually exclusive.

In many situations a person may have several types of power. For example, a mother has the power to reward and coerce her children, her children and her husband feel that she has the right to make decisions (she has legitimate power), and her children and husband may go along with her wishes because they want her to love them and because they feel she is an expert on various matters.

Furthermore, it is important to remember that power, is not a commodity that some people have and others do not. In a business corporation, the chief executive officer may have great power to fire and hire, and certainly he had more power than his secretary. Yet she has power of her own. She may decide who gets to see the boss, she has the ability to make her boss look good or bad, and she knows how to find important information he does not. He has his sources of power, and she has others. In any group, including dyadic relationships, there are complex power relationships among the various members.

Power as a Social Commodity   Although we have stressed power as something possessed by people, in most cases power is vested in groups. In most organizations, no single person has the power to do exactly what he or she wants, and people must work together to accumulate power. The formal name for this working together to wield power is *coalition formation*. Coalitions may be quite formal, as when several relatively powerless oil-producing countries unite to form a petroleum cartel to control international oil prices. Or they may be quite informal, as when the children in a family unite to pressure Mom and Dad to get a new big-screen television.

Many models of coalition formation have been experimentally studied by social psychologists (Murnighan, 1978). Typically, three or more subjects are given votes or power points. Payoffs depend on getting a certain minimum number of votes higher than that possessed by any individual. For example, Person A might have 9 votes, Person B, 7 votes, and Person C, 3 votes in a situation where 10 votes are necessary to split a $10 prize. Obviously, in this case any two of the people could unite and gain the prize, and the major question of interest is how the winning coalition is formed. One consideration is how the payoff should be divided. An obvious possibility is that each partner should get paid in proportion to his contribution in terms of votes. Thus, if Persons B and C unite, they would get $7 and $3, respectively. Table 10.3 lists the other possibilities if the partners decide to split the winnings according to the number of votes they brought to the coalition. In this case, Person C holds more power than his 3 votes would suggest and he might be able to work out a deal to get more than his share of the loot. For example, by uniting with Person B, he would normally expect to get only $3 and Person B $7, but

TABLE 10.3 POSSIBLE COALITIONS AND OUTCOMES FOR A $10 PRIZE. *The outcomes assume that the two members of the coalition split the $10 in proportion to their relative contributions of points.*

	A's Share	B's Share	C's Share
A + B against C (9 + 7)	$5.62	$4.38	$0.00
A + C against B (9 + 3)	$7.50	$0.00	$2.50
B + C against A (7 + 3)	$0.00	$7.00	$3.00

Person B gets even less ($4.38) if he unites with Person A. So Person C might suggest to Person B that Person C get $4 instead of his expected $3, and Person B still gets more than he gets by teaming up with Person A. Typically, then, the process of coalition formation is accompanied by fairly explicit bargaining (Komorita & Chertkoff, 1973).

LEADERSHIP

One obvious feature of most groups is that they have leaders. In many cases the leader occupies a formal position. Universities have department chairpersons, business organizations have presidents, the Supreme Court has a chief justice. In fact, every formal group has one or more leaders—some with an official title or standing, others with no formal status but who are leaders nonetheless. Informal groups also have leaders. Even something as spontaneous as two or three people deciding to take a study break often involves one person making the suggestion and the other people following the suggestion.

Leadership is the power of a person to influence others in the group. Leadership is a formal and institutionalized form of power. This definition has the advantage of focusing attention on leadership as a way people relate to one another and it allows us to build on our previous discussion of power. It encourages us to recognize that sometimes the nominal leader of a group—the person elected or appointed to run things—is less a leader than is a nominal follower. The person who is "the power behind the throne" is sometimes a more effective leader than is the person on the throne.

Who Becomes a Leader?   Often we think that leaders must have some special magic. We picture the dynamic, charismatic person as our prototype leader, forgetting that the quiet accountant who runs a major corporation is also a leader by virtue of both his position and his influence over the lives of others. At any rate,

the assumption that leaders must have some special trait is clearly false (Gibb, 1969; Stogdill, 1974); with the exception of intelligence, there are few traits that discriminate leaders from followers.

If you stop and think about it, it is not surprising that leaders have no one, special trait that distinguishes them from their followers. When we consider leadership in terms of interpersonal influence, it quickly becomes clear that the nature of the influence is likely to be task specific; leadership may change from task to task. The person who dominates by power of personality may not be the optimal leader in a situation that calls for soothing the feelings of followers. Even such a seemingly obvious leadership trait as dominance will promote a person into a leadership role only under certain circumstances.

Although in most organizations leaders are chosen after many years of working their way to the top, social psychologists have been especially interested in predicting who emerges as a leader in newly formed groups. Probably the most consistent predictor of such emergent leadership is the amount of time spent talking;

Some people are leaders by virtue of election and formal position.

not even quality of comments is as important as pure quantity (Sorrentino & Boutillier, 1975).

In one classic demonstration by Bavelas, Hastorf, Gross, and Kite (1965), leaders were actually created by manipulating how much people talked. In an initial discussion, the amount of time each person talked was recorded. As expected, the person chosen as leader was almost always the person who had talked most. In a second discussion, the experimenters encouraged the person who previously had talked least to talk more. These previously quiet people who spoke up more often were now rated much higher in leadership by the other group members. In effect, Bavelas and his colleagues had created leaders by manipulating the amount of time talked.

At one level, the consistent finding that leaders are those who talk a lot makes good sense; unless you say something, others will not have the opportunity to discover your good ideas. In natural groups, leaders may talk more because they do indeed have more to say (Stein & Heller, 1979). At another level, however, the finding is a bit odd; most of us would like to think that leadership involves more than being a blabbermouth. Stein, Hoffman, Cooley, and Pearse (1979) have suggested that newly formed groups have to solve many problems, including choosing a leader. In this context, big talkers help solve the problem by implicitly making themselves candidates for the leadership role. In the absence of any obviously better-qualified candidates, a talker may become the leader by default. This does not mean that the potential leader is highly respected or liked, but only that he or she fills a need for the moment. In time, the leader might say or do something to offend others, and a new leader might emerge. But until that time, it is easier for the group members to go along with the implied claims of leadership of the person who dominates by means of his or her talking.

Status differentiation most often arises in group settings where there is a task to be performed (Berger, Conner, & Fisek, 1974). In such circumstances, it is natural that, for special help, the group will look to those members who possess special skills. Those members who seem to have the most to offer for solving group problems will be identified as having higher status and will be likely candidates for formal or informal leadership positions. Justice Frankfurter had especially high status within the Warren Court because of universal respect for the quality of his legal reasoning, even by people who did not share his values.

Another predictor of emergent leadership in groups is gender (Wood & Karten, 1986). In mixed-gender dyads, the man more often emerges as the leader, even when the female has the more dominant personality (Nyquist & Spence, 1986), although some data suggest that dominant females are just as likely as nondominant males to become leaders (Fleischer & Chertkoff, 1986). There are, of course, many reasons for male leadership, not the least of which is a cultural prescription for male leadership. But the causality may be somewhat indirect; men typically talk more and engage in active task-relevant behaviors —behaviors often associated with leadership —whereas women are more likely to engage in social behaviors (Wood & Karten, 1986). Men become leaders because they *act* more like leaders. Or, saying it another way, our expectations about how leaders should behave coincide more closely with typical male behaviors than with typical female behaviors.

Naturally, as groups get on with their business, many other qualities will become important to leadership. Leaders are endorsed more by their followers when they are competent at the group task and when the group succeeds rather than fails (Hollander & Julian, 1970; Michener & Lawler, 1975). There are, of course, a good many concrete tasks the leader must help the group perform, and these will vary a good deal from group to group and task to task.

Robert Freed Bales (1958) noted that at least two kinds of roles developed early in the life of a group. One is the **task specialist,** who keeps the group oriented to its goals. The task specialist may be so task oriented as to risk bruising the feelings of others. A second role, the **socioemotional specialist,** is filled by someone who is more oriented toward maintaining morale, giving support to people, and making sure that everyone is happy. It is important to recognize that these roles are not appointed, but when a group of strangers meets to begin working on a task these two kinds of roles emerge consistently. Many other studies of leadership also suggest basic categories of leader responsibilities that correspond closely to those of the task and socioemotional specialists (Stogdill, 1974). Obviously, leaders must keep their groups oriented to the task at hand, but it is also necessary for someone to make sure that morale stays high and that group members enjoy the interpersonal aspects of their job.

Leadership Effectiveness   How can we tell when a leader has been effective? In large formal organizations (such as corporations), where the group has well-defined goals, the most relevant criterion is group productivity. Another relevant criterion is whether subordinates like and respect the leader and get along well with one another. Because no leader in a complex organization can dictate exactly what subordinates can do in every circumstance, it is important that subordinates feel enough identification with the leader to behave effectively even if goals or procedures are not always well defined. Furthermore, where goals are diverse or ill defined, effective leadership may consist almost entirely of the ability to keep up morale. For example, in a university academic department, the success of the chairperson is almost always seen as heavily dependent on the morale of the faculty. Note that the two primary measures of leadership effectiveness—movement toward group goals and morale—correspond directly to the task-oriented and socioemotional leadership styles discussed above.

Fiedler's Model   Fiedler's (1978) **contingency model of leadership** explicitly emphasizes the proposition that leadership effectiveness is contingent on a match between leader characteristics and the situation. There are two basic styles of leadership behavior that Fiedler measures with a simple questionnaire. People are asked to describe the single person they have had the most trouble working with (the least preferred co-worker, or LPC). People with high-LPC scores describe the LPC relatively favorably, tend to be oriented toward interpersonal relationships, and seem to feel that the LPC has some redeeming qualities despite his or her bad ones. People with low-LPC scores reject those with whom they cannot get along and seem to be more task oriented and less concerned with interpersonal relations.

According to Fiedler, all leaders face situations where they have more or less control and influence. His model suggests that low-LPC leaders (those who strongly reject disliked co-workers) would function best on tasks where the leader has a great deal of control, either in situations of well-defined tasks or in situations of maximum unclarity where provision of task structure is crucial. High-LPC leaders, on the other hand, function best with moderate task and group structure. Data from both field and laboratory research broadly support the model, although its more specific details are not always strongly confirmed (Peters, Hartke, & Pohlmann, 1985; Strube & Garcia, 1981). In one study, Chemers and Skrzypek (1972) worked with groups of cadets at West Point. They measured LPC scores of group leaders and had the groups work on structured and unstructured tasks where the leaders had low or high power and were liked or disliked by the members. As expected, the low-LPC leaders were most effective with either highly structured or highly unstructured tasks, whereas the high-LPC leaders worked best with moderate structure, low power, and high acceptance. In one study of university administrators, those whose LPC scores fit with the structure of their jobs were also likely to experience less stress than those who were out of phase with the task (Chemers, Hays, Rhodewalt, & Wysocki, 1985).

Why are the two kinds of leaders differentially effective in different types of situations? One reason is that low-LPC leaders are more concerned with the task than with getting along with others (Rice et al., 1982). Thus, when the situation is unclear, they can be effective in providing structure. Alternatively, when the task is quite clear, they can devote themselves wholly to accomplishing their goals. The high-LPC leaders, on the other had, are more interested in group morale, which is likely to be most important when the tasks facing the group are only moderately clear.

Fiedler's theory has been controversial in part because the LPC measure does not have a clear meaning (Rice, 1978), and certainly his is not the only model that emphasizes the fit between leader characteristics and the group (see Hollander, 1978). However, it may be taken as representative of the kinds of complexities involved in the assessment of leadership effectiveness. No single type of leadership style works well in all situations. Winston Churchill was a great wartime leader but failed in peacetime. The basketball coach who works well with a bunch of prima donnas may not do as well with players of less talent and temperament, and the coach who consistently makes mediocre players play "over their heads" may have trouble getting good players to perform up to their abilities.

COMMUNICATION

In Chapter 6 we noted that communication is patterned in terms of intended meanings and also according to certain, largely implicit, rules and norms. For example, within a family there may be a pattern of who tends to say what to whom. In larger groups these patterns are more explicit. When 50 people try to make a decision there will almost certainly be rules about how the discussion will be run and how the decision will be made. In formal organiza-

tions communication becomes highly structured indeed, with the formal memo replacing face-to-face conversation.

Organizational Communication   As Barnard (1938) and many later theorists have made clear, the structure of complex organizations is largely one of communication opportunities and restrictions. Managers in organizations typically spend between one-third and two-thirds of their time communicating (Jablin, 1979). One kind of ideal organization is that in which information flows to the top and decisions flow to the bottom, and in most organizations people do spend much of their time in such vertical communication (Porter & Roberts, 1976).

Proper   Channels   Most   organizations have well-developed, more or less official communication networks, together with norms about how such channels should be used. If information flows in regular, predictable ways, the chances are lessened that relevant people will be ignorant of important information. If a worker were to communicate his or her grievances directly to the president of the company, the supervisor and middle executives might fail to learn about important problems that they could solve more easily than the president. Also, short-circuiting established channels interferes with delicate authority and power relations. A subordinate who bypasses a supervisor in communicating information upward not only causes the supervisor to lose face but also makes it harder for the supervisor to maintain control over both the definition and the solution of a problem.

Communication upward in a social hierarchy tends to become more abstract and less detailed, whereas downward communication tends to become concrete and detailed. For example, a floor manager might gather examples of work problems from her group, and this information together with information from other floor managers might be assembled into a summary report on work problems, which in turn becomes a small part of a more general report. Conversely, most high-ranking executives set general policy guidelines and let various levels of subordinates flesh out the guidelines with specific instructions. For example, the president of a university may decide that he wishes to increase the percentage of minority students on his campus and would communicate this to the director of admissions who would decide the means (such as making contacts with certain counselors or getting more transfers from a local junior college) to carry out the policy. Various subordinates might then use these general directives to structure a specific program of recruiting on a day-to-day basis.

Problems   This hierarchical model of upward information flow and downward decision flow rarely works ideally in practice. In the first place, people do not feel neutral about the information they receive and transmit and may decide to suppress it, speed it along its way, or pass along versions colored by their own biases. Halberstram (1972) gives several examples of how the State Department, Defense Department, and White House bureaucracies biased the kinds of information transmitted about the Vietnam War to the point where high-level decision-makers often had less-reliable information than the average reader of a major newspaper. Because they usually have a clear idea of what their superiors want to hear, subordinates are especially prone to doctor information before passing it along.

The recent *Challenger* spacecraft explosion provides another unfortunate example. When engineers at Morton Thiokol, the manufacturer of the solid rocket boosters, were informed that the *Challenger* was to be launched after a night of subfreezing temperatures, they asked for a conference with launch officials. They were concerned that the coldest temperature for previous launches had been 53° and that they had little information about the behavior of components at these much colder

temperatures. More important, a successful launch required that two rubber O-rings seal a gap between sections of the rocket caused by the stresses of the launch. It would be less likely that cold rubber rings could maintain the seal, and in fact there had been problems before with the O-rings during cold-weather flights.

The engineers were given full opportunity to express their views in a phone conference the night before the launch, but it became clear that NASA officials did not want to delay the flight. There had been previous delays, the space-shuttle program was far behind schedule, and there was a great deal of publicity for this flight because Christa McAuliffe, the first Teacher in Space, was to be aboard. The interaction between the engineers and the launch officials had a curious quality. Whereas in previous launches NASA officials had insisted that the engineers and technical staff prove that it was all right to launch, in this case Morton Thiokol officials felt they were being asked to prove that the launch should not take place. This was impossible because the components had never been tested at such

Seven people lost their lives in the *Challenger* explosion, in part because of a failure in organizational communication.

a low temperature. So the high administrators of Morton Thiokol decided to remove their objections. Unfortunately for all concerned, the O-rings did fail and the *Challenger* blew up just over a minute into its flight (Report of the Presidential Commission on the Space Shuttle *Challenger* Accident, 1986).

Thus, people may say what they think they are supposed to in order to keep their careers intact. But there are other reasons for biased communication. People are generally unwilling to communicate bad news (Tesser & Rosen, 1975). Conveying negative information makes people feel guilty. Also, bearers of bad news are often negatively evaluated, even when not responsible for the negative events they report (Manis, Cornell, & Moore, 1974).

Bad news is not the only kind of information withheld in organizations. Information is a valuable commodity and thereby creates power for those who have it. So people in organizations keep secrets, pass along important information only to trusted friends and allies, and generally guard access to their hoard of knowledge. Thus, communication structures help to structure secrecy (Zander, 1977).

One major shortcoming of the proper-channels approach to information flow is that it ignores a number of motives people have for distorting what they say and to whom they say it. A second problem stems from the sheer amount of information in most organizations and its uneven distribution throughout the organization. Information tends to pool at the top of organizations where most of the important decisions are made, but this creates two problems. First, there is often so much information available that decision-makers suffer from information overload. Second, the quality of the information is often not very high. Usually, people at the top have only abstract summaries of issues, and important details often get lost in organizations because they never get to the right person who knows how to interpret them. In the *Challenger* disaster, the top NASA officials who approved the flight were not even aware that the Morton Thiokol engineers had objected. This kind of detail was not deemed worthy of being included in the report up the line.

Matters are not quite as bleak as the *Challenger* example was, however, because in practice most organizations do not rely fully on the proper-channels model. Good executives will often ask questions that require detailed information. Sometimes clever subordinates will make use of informal communication channels to make sure that their superiors get information they must have. One reason almost every American president has been obsessed with the leaking of important information to the press is that most bureaucrats have learned all too well how to make sure that Congress and the American public learn information the administration would prefer to suppress. So informal channels not only supplement but may often supplant the more formal ones.

SUMMARY

Whether groups are formal or informal, they have a distinct structure. They have roles and norms, an authority structure and power relations, leadership, and communication patterns. Norms are informal rules governing group-related activity; by specifying appropriate behavior, they reduce the need to make decisions and they make group activity run more smoothly. Norms often persist for long periods in groups even after group membership changes radically. Roles are specific positions in groups with accompanying behavioral expectations. By making the behavior of people more predictable, they also aid behavior in groups.

There are several sources of power in groups. High-power people may have the ability to reward and punish, or power may be based on feelings that such people have legitimate authority. Referent power exists when others want to be like the person, and expert power is based on abilities to solve problems. People in groups often form coalitions to share power.

Leadership is based on the power to influence others. Leaders usually do not have any special characteristics, and the leader in one situation may not be the leader in another. In newly formed groups, people with special skills or people who talk a great deal may be seen as leaders. Fiedler's contingency model of leadership assumes that there are two basic leadership styles. Some leaders are task-directed and work best in situations of either high clarity or very low clarity. Those leaders who are more oriented toward social and emotional features of group members work best on tasks of intermediate clarity.

Communication in groups is structured. In many formal organizations, only certain channels of communication are open. Ideally, information flows upward and decisions downward, but this does not work well in practice, because group members are biased about the information they pass along and because there is too much information for high-level decision-makers to make use of easily.

GROUP PRODUCTIVITY AND DECISION-MAKING

One obvious question about groups is whether they achieve their goals and complete their tasks efficiently. In other words, are groups productive? A closely related question is whether groups are as efficient as individuals. If you had a problem, would you rather entrust a decision to a group or to an individual? These were among the first questions asked about groups when empirical social psychology developed in the 1920s and 1930s.

There are many factors that affect how productive groups are (Hackman & Morris, 1975). One is whether the group has the necessary human and material resources for the task

at hand. And surely the quality of leadership makes a difference. In addition, factors that favor high group morale and a good group atmosphere also usually aid productivity. The size of the group sometimes makes a difference; efficient groups cannot be too large or too small for the task at hand. Group productivity also cannot easily be divorced from questions about how groups make decisions. All groups must make decisions about how to define their tasks and try to accomplish them, and many groups exist almost solely to make decisions: juries, faculty committees, the U.S. Senate, and the Supreme Court are relevant examples. Much of the work on group productivity focuses on how groups make decisions, and so we will also concentrate on that issue.

GROUP DECISIONS

Consider a group trying to solve a particular problem. One could imagine that the group would stimulate individuals to find the correct or a creative solution. Conversely, we have all participated in groups that were enormously inefficient. The group could not even agree on how to go about making a decision, much less manage to focus on the decision itself. I have been in groups, and probably you have too, where one or two stupid people so dominated the discussion that the final decision was worse than no decision at all. So the question arises as to the effectiveness of groups in making decisions.

Types of Tasks   Steiner (1972) has argued that one cannot understand how groups make decisions without also understanding the nature of the task. He proposed several kinds of group tasks, but for our purposes we can focus on three. In some tasks, group performance depends on how well the least-able person performs. For example, in a classroom situation, the class's progress effectively hinges on how well the least-capable student grasps the material if the teacher does not proceed with new material until she is convinced that all the students understand. If a weakling joined an all-pro football offensive line, the quarterback would still be sacked most of the time because there is only so much that other linemen could do to compensate for the weakling's ineptness.

By contrast, in many tasks the group wants to select the best option among several possibilities proposed by group members so that performance depends on the most-able group member. In a business, the board of directors must select from several proposals a concrete course of action initially proposed by one individual. Whether the corporation makes a good decision will depend, in part, on whether they have one member who can come up with a good proposal. Only one basketball player can take a shot at any given time, and whether the

team wins or loses will depend on whether they are able to get the ball to the player in the best position to shoot.

In a third type of task, the group effort reflects the sum of individual efforts. When a group tries to raise money for scholarships, productivity will likely be measured as the sum of what all the individuals have raised. On a relay team, the team's time is the sum of the times of the four runners.

Group Performance   It seems obvious that if group performance is limited by the least-capable person, then whatever will improve his or her performance will automatically improve the effectiveness of the group. A group may try to help its least-capable member through instruction or encouragement, of course, and the improvements that

In some group tasks, the total effort is simply the sum of individual efforts.

result may be considerable. In some groups, it may be possible to assign the least-capable person to a task that makes the best use of his or her abilities or that at least keeps the person from interfering with others.

However, the most intensively studied kind of decision involves tasks in which the group has to work on a problem and accept one person's solution as the correct one. Commonly, the group is given a problem to solve, and the criterion of success is simply whether they solve it. The classic issue here has been whether groups or individuals are more successful. Shaw (1932) gave groups of four people and individuals problems for which there was an answer that was obviously correct once it was discovered. An example would be an anagram (for example, from these letters— OMNCYIUMT—what word can you make? Answer: COMMUNITY). The doctors and lawyers problem (Table 10.4), similar to the husbands and wives problem (used by Shaw), is another example. Shaw found that 60% of the groups but only 14% of the individuals solved the husbands and wives problem. Surely this is convincing evidence that groups are better.

But do not jump to conclusions. The natural assumption is that group discussion somehow stimulated group members to creative heights. Another possibility, however, is that nothing special happens during discussion but that groups have a major advantage merely because they have more people working on the problem. Is the group discussion itself important or is it simply the number of people that makes the most difference? One way to find out is to take four people who do not discuss the problem, and see whether at least one person in the group can solve it. Remember that Shaw used problems for which there was an obviously correct solution, so presumably the group would agree if at least one member got it right. It turns out that if the probability of one person being able to solve the problem is 14% and people are assigned randomly to groups, approximately 46% of the groups will have at least one person who can solve the problem (compared with the 60% of the groups that actually solved the problem). So the real groups used by Shaw got much of their advantage not from interaction but rather just by being bigger and thus having a greater chance of having a problem-solver among them. For

---

TABLE 10.4   TWO PROBLEMS USED TO STUDY GROUP DECISIONS.

The Doctors and Lawyers

On the A-side of the river are three doctors and their three lawyers. All of the doctors but none of the lawyers can row. No doctor will allow her lawyer to be in the presence of another doctor unless she is also present. Get all the lawyers and doctors across to the B-side of the river by means of a boat carrying only three at a time.

Solution: On the first trip, Doctor 1 (D1) and Lawyer 1 (L1) row across and L1 is left on the B-side while D1 rows back to the A-side. Then D1, D2, and L2 row to the B-side, leaving D1 there. D2 and L2 return to the A-side. D2, L2, and D3 then go to the B-side. D2 and L2 are left there and D3 rows back to the A-side to pick up L3.

The Horse-trading Problem

John bought a horse for $60 and sold it to James for $70. Subsequently, he bought it back from James for $80 then sold it to Donald for $90. How much money did John make in the horse-trading game?

Solution: He made $20. He expended $140 and got back $160. The fact that he bought the horse the second time for more than he previously received for it is irrelevant.

problems to which there are clearly correct answers, it makes sense to have lots of people working on solving them, though not necessarily in groups.

There is a further complication, however. Shaw's problem was the sort for which everyone would agree that the answer was obviously correct once it was hit upon. But what happens when groups work on problems with solutions that are not so self-evident? For example, the answer to one of those messy algebra word problems you loved in high school may not immediately seem correct. Another example is the famous horse-trading problem given in Table 10.4. With such problems, the group does not always accept the correct answer even if one person gets it (Laughlin et al., 1975). Indeed, the correct solution tends to be accepted only if it is supported by at least two people (Laughlin & Adamopoulos, 1980). In this case, the group is sometimes *worse* than an equal number of individuals, unless the group is large enough to have a high probability that two or more members will hit on the solution.

In summary, for tasks that have a correct solution, group performance depends, in part, on whether most people can recognize the solution as correct. If they can, then individuals in groups often are not markedly better than a similar number of individuals not in groups. When the solution is not immediately obvious, groups can actually lead to worse performance.

This is not meant to suggest that groups are never superior to individuals. Groups actually often seem to be worse than individuals when the task has a correct solution. However, most groups work on tasks for which both the problem and the solution are ill-defined. There is, for example, no "correct" way to cut expenses in a university. Each possibility has costs and benefits, and which possibility would ultimately be best may depend on factors that are unforeseen at the time the decision was made, even assuming that "best" could be defined to

everyone's satisfaction. With such decisions, no single committee member may have all the necessary information, relevant expertise, or broad perspective to make a wise decision.

Social Loafing   We have been considering tasks in which a single answer must be accepted by the group. But different sorts of issues arise for additive tasks, those for which the group product is the sum of the individual accomplishments. You might want to think about your own participation in such tasks. You are decorating for a dance or trying to get the house cleaned, and in each case the more effectively everyone works the faster the job will get done. The obvious problem here is that some people will not pull their own weight. For additive tasks, motivational issues loom large.

In one experiment by Ingham, Levinger, Graves, and Peckham (1974), subjects worked on a tug-of-war where individual effort could be easily measured. In this situation two people worked at 91% of their average individual efficiencies; that is, if each person working alone could pull 130 pounds, then two people would pull about 236 pounds, or 24 pounds less than their combined best efforts. Three people worked at about 82% efficiency (see Figure 10.1). Of course, one problem is that two or more people will have coordination problems. Perhaps one pulls hard before another is ready, or the pullers get in each others' way. Ingham et al. recognized this possibility and investigated it in a clever way. They had some subjects work alone but while blindfolded and thinking they were working as a part of a group. Such subjects still pulled less than while working alone, suggesting that behavioral coordination was not the only reason for the inefficiency—subjects were somehow less motivated when working as a part of a group.

Bibb Latané and his colleagues have referred to this tendency as ***social loafing.*** For several kinds of behavior they have shown that people

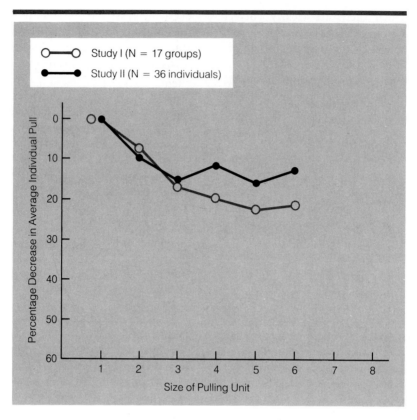

FIGURE 10.1   Mean Individual Pull Scores According to Group Size. Note that individual effort decreases as the group gets larger, at least for groups smaller than 4 people.

Ingham, Levinger, Graves, & Pekham, 1974.

generally work less hard while together than while alone. For example, Petty, Harkins, Williams, and Latané (1977) asked individuals and groups to evaluate a poem and a newpaper editorial. Individuals reported working harder than did members of groups. Latané, Williams, and Harkins (1979) asked people to clap or shout as loudly as possible while alone and while in groups. Average loudness was less when people made noise together. One possible explanation is that when people are lost in a crowd their own contributions are submerged and unidentifiable, so incentives to work hard are lost (Williams, Harkins, & Latané, 1981). When tasks are divided in such a way that individual contributions clearly count (Harkins & Petty, 1982) or when individual contributions can be clearly evaluated comparatively (Harkins & Jackson, 1985), the social loafing effect is reduced. Another possible explanation is that group members *expect* that others will loaf and hence reduce their own contributions so they will not be taken advantage of (Jackson & Harkins, 1985; Kerr, 1983).

JURY DECISIONS

Jury Competence and Accuracy   In everyday life, groups (and individuals) often are in situations where neither they nor anyone else can be absolutely sure what the correct or best solutions to problems are. One example is the jury, where a group of people have to weigh opposing arguments and evidence as to the guilt or innocence of a person.

There is a stereotype that juries are capricious, overinfluenced by silver-tongued lawyers, biased by their own prior values, and swayed by emotional factors rather than by the weight of evidence. This stereotype has relatively little basis in fact (Nemeth, 1981). We must at the outset confess that it is very difficult to decide whether a jury has or has not done a good job. At one level the criteria for performance are clear—juries should find guilty people guilty and innocent people innocent. Unfortunately, we usually have no independent way of deciding who is guilty and who is innocent. In addition, our legal system places different weights on the two kinds of errors, seeing a decision to wrongly convict an innocent person as far more serious than the error of letting a guilty person go free.

In actual trial situations, jury decisions can be evaluated against decisions reached by people with more legal training or criminal experience, although these backgrounds do not, of course, necessarily give the experts a window on truth. Kalven and Zeisel (1966) asked judges about their opinions on the outcomes of jury trials. In 78% of the cases, the judges felt that the jury had made the correct decision. Even among the 22% disagreements, the judges usually did not feel that the jury had been incompetent but had merely seen things differently than they had. When there was a disagreement between the jury's verdict and the judge's opinion, it was usually the case that the jury had voted for acquittal. Thus, even if we count these 22% as errors, the jury tends to err in the "right" direction by giving the defendant the benefit of the doubt.

Jury Processes   Because ethical and legal concerns usually forbid their observing actual juries, social scientists tend to do research on mock juries. In such cases, juries (typically college students) are assembled, hear or read an abbreviated version of a trial, and make their decisions under the watchful eye of the social scientist. The use of such mock juries has been justifiably criticized because the cases are often *too* abbreviated, because the written case cannot duplicate the pressures of judging a real person, and because college students are unlike the typical juror in age, income, and education among other factors. However, some psychologists have studied juries with people drawn from real jury lists and with fairly lengthy videotaped trials (Hastie, Penrod, & Pennington, 1983; Saks, 1977). Furthermore, much of what we have learned from mock-jury research fits with interview evidence obtained from jurors after real trials.

Perhaps the most consistent finding of such research is that jury verdicts are quite predictable from knowledge of how the jurors feel before the jury deliberations. In fact, several mathematical models have been developed to describe these relationships. Although the precise details of the various models are beyond the scope of this text (but see Penrod & Hastie, 1979; Strasser & Davis, 1981), the outlines are clear. Most research of this sort gives juries a choice only between guilty and not guilty, but the models are both more complex and less predictive when the juries have a wider range of choices (such as between first-degree murder, second-degree murder, manslaughter, and not guilty) (Hastie et al., 1983). However, for the simpler choices, when a majority goes into the jury deliberations with a particular preference, the jury generally will agree on that decision. Almost all hung juries result from situations where initial preferences were closely split. Moreover, changes in the distribution of votes from ballot to ballot are quite predictable. For example, it is far more likely for a jury split 9–3 to move to a 10–2 vote on the next ballot than to an 8–4 vote. This suggests that jury deliberations involve slow but sure social influences, with one after another of the jurors converting to a steadily growing majority—it is empirically quite rare for a single juror to convert the other 11, as happened in the movie *Twelve Angry Men*.

This does not mean that the majority necessarily bullies the minority. Juries are responsive to the evidence offered during the trial (Saks & Hastie, 1978), and many of the arguments within juries are about how to interpret and weigh the evidence. Although juries argue and pressures to conform are sometimes very strong on minority jurors (remember that all the jurors have to stay until a unanimous decision is reached), it is also possible that the majority jurors are in the majority because they have best assessed the trial evidence and therefore have the best arguments for convincing the other side.

Jury Size and Decision Rules   Much of the current research on juries was stimulated by a series of Supreme Court decisions on the

"Your honor, on the first ballot the jury voted ten to two for conviction. For three emotionally charged hours, we discussed our points of difference. On the next ballot, it was seven to five for acquittal. Over the next several ballots, the vote seesawed back and forth. One juror became ill and was replaced by an alternate. By now, we had been in session for ten hours straight. Tempers were rising and some jurors were near the breaking point."

Drawing by D. Fradon © 1986 by The New Yorker Magazine, Inc.

permissible size of juries and on whether unanimous decisions were necessary for verdicts. Although there is a long tradition in British common law (on which the American system is also based) of 12-person juries reaching unanimous verdicts before conviction, there is no rationale other than tradition for this. In 1970, in *Williams* v. *Florida,* the Court ruled that juries as small as 6 were permissible, and in 1972 the Court ruled (in *Johnson* v. *Louisiana* and *Apodaca et al.* v. *Oregon*) that in state trials even three-quarter majorities were sufficient to convict.

It is instructive to examine the concerns of the Supreme Court and how the Court tried to resolve them. Of overriding importance was whether smaller juries would affect the quality of decisions. For example, if smaller juries were more conviction prone, they would probably convict more innocent people; this would be a cause for alarm. The Court cited available social science evidence to suggest that group size would not affect the quality of decisions, but unfortunately the evidence they cited was based mostly on opinion or uncontrolled observation (Saks, 1977). Social scientists were quick to note the problem and quickly moved to study the effects of jury size on decisions.

Fortunately, the Supreme Court was basically correct in its judgment, if not for the right reasons. Several studies have found no bias toward one side or the other as a function of group size (Hastie et al., 1983). However, smaller juries are more likely to reach a decision; that is, they are less likely to be hung (Kerr & MacCoun, 1985). This makes a certain amount of sense, because smaller juries are less likely to contain one or more stubborn people who refuse to go along with the majority. Whether this is good or bad is likely to vary from case to case. However, the hung jury probably favors the defendant by encouraging the prosecution to drop the case or to plea-bargain, so in that indirect sense, larger juries may be slightly biased toward the side of the defense.

The Court was also concerned about representation of minority points of view on large and small juries. Juries are not selected randomly, but the selection processes ought not to favor some groups on irrelevant grounds such as race. The court simply asserted that 6-person juries would be as representative as 12-person ones, but any introductory text on probability would have shown the justices that they were wrong. As an example, if a particular group constitutes 10% of the general population (which is approximately true for American blacks) and if juries were selected perfectly randomly, 47% of 6-person juries would contain at least one black whereas 72% of 12-person juries would. This is not a trivial difference if one is concerned that this minority group be represented on juries. On the other hand, although there are political and moral arguments for trying to make sure that juries are racially representative, there is no direct evidence that this representativeness actually improves the quality of the decisions.

What about the Supreme Court's ruling that juries need not reach unanimous decisions? The most obvious prediction is that nonunanimous juries would less often be hung, and this has often been found (Davis et al., 1975; Foss, 1981; Kerr et al., 1976). We do not need an elaborate model of group decisions to appreciate that while a single obstinate juror can block a verdict with a unanimity rule, it will take at least four such jurors if only 9 (out of 12) votes are needed for a verdict.

Whether or not this is important is open to conjecture. One fear is that quality of discussion might be impaired with nonunanimous rules. Once the jury had the necessary 9 votes, they might close up shop and cease discussion, thus reducing the possibility of hearing valid arguments on the other side. Assuming that the minority has some important points to make, this could make for poorer decisions. The most comprehensive study of this issue by Reid Hastie and his colleagues suggests some

cause for alarm (Hastie et al., 1983). Majority juries do spend less time deliberating, especially after a majority is in hand, and jury members report that the discussions are less satisfactory in majority rather than unanimous juries. On the other hand, there is no strong evidence that the two types of juries differ in their actual verdicts.

So jury decisions that often seem mysterious turn out (if one is willing to pay attention to mock-jury research) to follow quite simple rules of group decision, especially when the decision choices are quite limited. This does not mean that strange things never happen in a jury room, but only that verdicts tend to follow predictable patterns once we know how the individual jurors responded to the trial evidence and arguments.

CHOICE SHIFTS

Fantasy time: Suppose you have just been left several million dollars by your late, lamented aunt, and for tax reasons you have to invest it immediately. Would you prefer to invest your money in a new computer software company that is likely to go bankrupt but will make a huge profit if it succeeds, or in a safe company that will guarantee you a modest but sure rate of return.

In the early 1960s, James Stoner (cited in Myers & Lamm, 1976) studied how groups make decisions of just that sort. Stoner asked groups to reach consensus on how much risk they would tolerate to get an attractive alternative. As you might expect, the individual members of the groups varied from being quite willing to take risks to being quite conservative. Two outcomes seem reasonable. First, because committees are often thought to be conservative and afraid of risk, the group might become more conservative. Second, the group might compromise individual preferences to reach some intermediate group alternative.

Stoner found neither of these results. On most of the decisions, the groups were actually riskier than the average individual. In other words, in the typical group there was a *risky shift,* as the group became more risk prone than the average group member. For example, if the group had five members who advocated risk-taking of 6, 6, 7, 7, and 8 (on a 10-point scale where 10 is a high risk), respectively, the group consensus might be 7 or 8, either of which is higher than the 6.8 average of the group members.

During the 1960s and 1970s, many studies were done on this phenomenon and they generally confirmed Stoner's results (Myers & Lamm, 1976; Pruitt, 1971). It soon became clear, however, that studies on risk-taking were only a part of a larger phenomenon. Just as Stoner's groups became more extreme in risk-taking, others have found that groups become more extreme in their attitudes (Myers & Bishop, 1970, 1971) and in prosocial behaviors (Schroeder, 1973) and aggressive behaviors (Mathes & Kahn, 1975), among other things. Because the tendency of group discussion seems to be to foster extreme attitudes, values, and behaviors, the effect is now generally termed *choice shift* (Levinger & Schneider, 1969) or *group polarization* (Lamm & Myers, 1978).

Social Comparison   Several explanations have been offered for group polarization effects. We will discuss the two most salient: social comparison and rational persuasion. The social comparison model was first suggested by Roger Brown (1965). He propsed that because American culture places a premium on risk and adventure, people would like to see themselves as riskier than average. Each person enters the group discussion feeling that he or she is indeed more risky than average, but most people will quickly discover that they are average or below-average risk-takers. In such a situation, a self-definition of risk-taking can be maintained only by trying to become more risky than the average group member. Thus, the group decision is fueled by people who are

trying to convince others that they excel as risk-takers.

Jellison and Arkin (1977) extended the Brown argument by tying the phenomenon directly to social comparison theory (Chapter 5). They argue that people want to be thought of as generally higher in ability than others and that they will be especially likely to try to present themselves as more extreme on any dimension (such as risk) that has ability overtones. So people become riskier not so much because risk itself is valued but because risk-taking is seen to reflect high abilities (Jellison & Riskind, 1970).

One clear implication of this kind of model is that group discussion is important only because it provides group members with information that they are not as able (that is, as extreme) as they thought they were. It follows, and has been demonstrated, that shifts toward the valued end of the scale might be produced without group discussion if people learned through other means that they were farther from the valued end of the scale than others (Lamm & Myers, 1978). Nevertheless, actual group discussion produces more polarization than mere exposure to information, so some other process must be in effect too.

Rational Persuasion   The other popular explanation for group polarization is based on an attitude-change model. In particular, it might be argued that the function of group discussion is to expose members to new and persuasive arguments supporting one extreme or the other (Bishop & Myers, 1974; Vinokur & Burnstein, 1974). The average group member may favor one position but during the discussion hear new arguments that convince her to change. This does not, of course, explain why the changes should be in one direction rather than the other—presumably each member would hear new arguments for both extremes.

Vinokur and Burnstein (1974) argue that in group discussions there are, in fact, more cogent arguments supporting one side rather than the other; shifts will tend to occur toward the side with the most cogent arguments. This is typically, but not inevitably, the risky side. Furthermore, the side toward which the group shifts tends to make more arguments during the group discussion (Berndt et al., 1983–84; Ebbesen & Bowers, 1974). Because both number and persuasiveness of arguments influence choice shifts (Hinsz & Davis, 1984), the favored side not only has better arguments but tends to be more assertive in making them. According to this model, group shifts take place because group members are persuaded by rational arguments.

Both social comparison and rational persuasion models are anchored in long traditions in social psychology. The social comparison model is based not only on social comparison theory (Chapter 5) but also on self-presentation models (Chapters 1 and 12), which claim that we have fundamental desires to look good in public. The rational persuasion model has basic similarities to the cognitive responses model of attitude change (Chapter 7), which suggests that people respond to how convincing arguments are. So group discussion and decision probably reflect a mixture of motives and information-processing strategies.

GROUPTHINK

We have just discussed two kinds of processes that affect group decisions. Groups may simply converge on the majority opinion, as they typically do in jury decisions, or the opinions of group members can sometimes become polarized. In this section we will concentrate on some additional factors that influence group decisions on complex matters.

Janis (1972) has discovered several pathologies of group decisions (which he calls **groupthink**) through a careful examination of American foreign policy. "Groupthink refers to a deterioration of mental efficiency, reality

Irving Janis

testing, and moral judgment that results from in-group pressures" (Janis, 1982, p. 9). Note that while Janis uses foreign policy decisions, there is nothing unique about foreign policy or even government decisions generally. For example, Henry Ford's decision to build the Edsel or recent decisions by American airlines to buy huge airplanes for which they had no ready market might also be used to illustrate groupthink. Groupthink even occurs in informal groups and committees. However, we will concentrate on American foreign policy for the simple reason that we know more about failures in this area than in the business or everyday worlds. A large corporation can conceal what the American government cannot.

Bay of Pigs   As one example of groupthink, consider the decision made by the Kennedy administration to sponsor an invasion of Cuba at the Bay of Pigs. When Kennedy's administration took over in early 1961, it was faced immediately with a CIA plan to have a small group of Cuban exiles attack Cuba. The CIA assumed that the Cuban military was so weak and the Cuban citizens so disillusioned with Castro that even this small band could precipitate a popular revolution against the government of Castro. If by any chance something should go wrong, it was assumed that the invaders could simply melt into the countryside and join up with other opponents of the Castro regime in the Escambray Mountains. Finally, Kennedy and all his advisors convinced themselves the attack could be carried out without anyone's becoming aware of the role of the American government.

On April 7, 1961, 1,400 Cuban exiles who had been training in Guatemala launched their invasion at the Bay of Pigs. The invasion was a military disaster. The Cuban military forces, which had been presumed to be so weak, easily turned back the invasion and captured all the invaders who were not killed. The mountain retreat turned out to be over 50 marshy miles away. There was no hint of any popular uprising, and it is probable that even had the invaders been more successful the Cuban people were of no mind to join them. And to make matters worse, within hours of the invasion many governments around the world denounced the United States for its role in the invasion.

The actual decision was made by President Kennedy and perhaps the most talented group of senior policy advisors ever assembled by a president, and yet they blundered horribly. Almost all the operative Bay of Pigs assumptions were flawed. Janis argues that any of the men who participated in the decision might have

This committee helped President Kennedy in the Cuban Missile Crisis, but also participated in the Bay of Pigs decision.

seen the problems had he made the decision alone. But once the discussions were underway, the group atmosphere inhibited questioning of assumptions. The fact that everyone seemed to accept the policy made everyone feel that it must be correct, and individual doubts were stifled and rarely articulated aloud.

Factors Encouraging Groupthink "The more amiability and *esprit de corps* among the members of a policy-making in-group, the greater is the danger that independent critical thinking will be replaced by groupthink which is likely to result in irrational and dehumanizing actions directed against out-groups" (Janis, 1982, p. 13). For the Bay of Pigs (as well as Watergate, the decision to get involved in Vietnam, and so on), crucial decisions were made by members of small groups who had great respect and liking for one another, factors that may inhibit criticism and close examination of suggestions. Such cohesiveness is a critical factor, though, of course, many highly cohesive groups do not make such huge blunders.

Another predisposing factor to the biases of groupthink is the illusion of invulnerability. The Kennedy advisors felt they were a privileged group; they were smart and they thought of themselves as charmed. In this kind of atmosphere, they became less critical because they assumed their skills and blessedness would carry them through. Groups subject to groupthink are likely to have strong feelings that their mission is moral and that the other side is not only immoral but stupid. The Kennedy advisors felt so strongly that their moral and intellectual position was superior to Castro and the Cubans that they failed to think about the moral implications of their own actions and they also underestimated the support for Castro among Cubans. Tetlock (1979) analyzed public records of decision-makers and confirmed that bad decisions involved more of this kind of simplistic thinking than did good decisions.

In short, groupthink involves a failure to think carefully about actions because failure seems inconceivable. In such an atmosphere, criticism is likely to be muted because it disrupts the existing social reality, and the social reality then is likely to be strengthened by the very lack of criticism it engenders. As the social reality feeds on itself and suppresses critical responses, there is a strong sense of unanimity. Members who continue to have doubts or criticisms may not express them for fear of appearing stupid or not part of the team. For example, many members of the Kennedy group involved in the Bay of Pigs decision had private doubts about the invasion but did not express them because they felt they were alone.

In addition, there may be explicit social pressures not to disrupt the general social reality. In the Bay of Pigs decision, Robert Kennedy told some who seemed to be wavering that the president needed their support. President Kennedy himself did not encourage opposition. He did not seek criticisms or alternative views. Research confirms that such a close-minded leadership style fosters groupthink (Flowers, 1977) and that leaders high in power motivation also produce more symptoms of groupthink (Fodor & Smith, 1982).

Although the immediate outcome of the Bay of Pigs was negative to all concerned, the story does have a happy ending of sorts. A year later, when Kennedy faced the problem of what to do about Cuban missiles in Cuba, his whole approach showed that he had learned from his earlier mistakes. There was no longer the sense of invincibility and certainly no consensus as to how the threat should be met. Kennedy and his advisors were more open to advice from the outside, were much less sure of themselves, and behaved in an altogether more rational fashion. This is not to say that Kennedy's decision to confront the Soviet Union was the correct one or was without flaws. Indeed, Allison (1971) argues that Kennedy and his advisors came close to making fatal decisions because of various cognitive and bureaucratic biases. However, at least the attempt was made to consider a range of options and to evaluate each critically. The absence of groupthink does not guarantee rationality or correctness, but when groupthink is present, existing biases are likely to be increased rather than decreased.

SUMMARY

Many factors contribute to group productivity, including morale, leadership, resources, and size. Another crucial factor is how the group makes decisions. The most intensively studied decision task is one in which the group must select from among individual proposals. For such tasks, the group is usually no better than an equal number of individuals, and in cases where the correct answer may not be obvious, the group may actually be worse than individuals because it fails to agree on the correct solution. For tasks in which individual effort contributes to task productivity, one relevant concern is that individuals will not work as hard in groups as they otherwise would individually.

Jury decisions are usually predictable from a knowledge of individual juror choices; the side with the most votes at the beginning of deliberation usually wins. Jury size has little effect on jury decisions except that persons from minority groups are less likely to be represented on smaller juries. Similarly, there are no major differences between juries that have to reach unanimous decisions and those that have a majority rule, other than that hung juries are more likely under the former condition. Some data suggest that majority-rule juries may be less likely to consider the evidence as carefully.

In another kind of decision, people must decide among valued alternatives. In that case, there is a tendency for the group to be more extreme than the individuals are collectively; on dimensions of value, people want to be extreme and the average person finds that he or she must move in a more extreme direction. Alternatively, the more extreme side may have more and/or better arguments.

Janis has argued that when groups are highly cohesive and have feelings of invulnerability, the members within the groups may fail to question one another and will thereby allow the group to reach faulty decisions. This tendency is called groupthink.

CHAPTER SUMMARY

- Groups involve people whose behaviors are interdependent and who recognize a mutual relationship. Sometimes group traditions and atmospheres transcend particular individuals and give rise to feelings that there is a group mind.

- People join groups for various reasons. Some biologists and instinct theories have argued that groups are evolutionarily useful, but this does not prove that we have an affiliation or gregariousness instinct. Freud argued that group affiliation stems from identification with leaders and symbols. Hedonistic theories argue that groups sometimes improve reward–cost ratios and also that groups may provide pleasure in and of themselves. Schachter's research suggests that people affiliate with others to reduce stress or to help evaluate ambiguous feelings.

- There are several structural features to groups. Every group has norms, or informal rules governing group-related behavior. Norms are useful in that they allow efficient behavior. Particular norms often characterize groups, and norms may persist even though group membership changes. Roles are positions associated with particular behaviors. Like norms, roles facilitate group behavior but they may cause problems through role conflict—conflicting demands within the same role or between different roles.

- Within groups there are multiple power relationships among individuals. There are several sources of power. Powerful people may have the ability to reward and punish others. They may also be seen as having legitimate authority, as having prestige that others want to imitate, or as being expert on something related to the group's goals. Because power is a kind of commodity, it can be shared and aggregated, as when people form coalitions.

- Leadership is basically the ability to influence others. Although many seem to feel that particular people make good leaders, in reality characteristics that make for effective leadership in one situation may not in another. In newly formed groups, people who talk a great deal or who have abilities relevant to the group may become leaders. Generally, some leaders seem to take care of task issues while others are more concerned with the emotional life of the group. Fiedler's theory explicitly suggests that those who specialize in task issues should perform better when the situation is highly structured or highly unstructured, whereas the more emotional leaders perform best in situations with intermediate structure.

- All groups have a communication structure. In large organizations this structure may be quite official and dictate who communicates with whom on which issues. In such situations, information usually flows upward and becomes more abstract, whereas decisions flow downward and become more concrete. There are many problems with this model. One problem is that people do not pass along unbiased versions of information, and another problem is that there is often simply too much information to digest.

- Groups are more or less productive, and there are many reasons for this. Among the most important is the ways the group makes decisions. On tasks where the group must select an individual's solution to a problem, groups often perform no better and sometimes worse than individuals. In groups that require more collective effort, a major problem is that some people may loaf.

■ The decisions that juries reach are usually favored by a majority of jury members before their deliberations. In this regard, smaller juries do not differ markedly from larger ones, and unanimous juries are similar to majority-rule juries.

■ Some groups must decide among several valued alternatives, and often such groups become more extreme than the individual members on some value dimension. This may occur because of a social comparison process as each person strives to be higher on the value dimension than others or because one side or the other has the better arguments.

■ For some kinds of major decisions, having groups whose members are cohesive and who get along well with each other may be a disadvantage because the members are not critical enough of decisions and they reinforce one another in believing that the group can do no wrong.

CHAPTER

11

SOCIAL INFLUENCE

The plot of *The Sorrows of the Young Werther* by Johann Wolfgang von Goethe is simple. Werther loves a young woman who chooses to marry another from a sense of duty. Because Werther cannot live without her, he shoots himself. The book is a masterpiece of early Romanticism, but one of the reasons it is remembered today is the effects it had on its readers. When the book was published in 1774, the plight of the hero captured the imagination of young men throughout Europe and for several years there was a rash of suicides clearly stimulated by people having read the book. Could suicides be affected by books (or television) today? If so, why?

In 1977, over 900 members of the People's Temple, located in Jonestown, Guyana, South America, killed themselves at the request of their leader, Reverend James Jones. Jones was a charismatic leader, and his followers, largely poor and black, were used to following his every request without question. The precipitating event for the mass suicide was the visit of California Congressman Leo J. Ryan, who had come to investigate disturbing stories about the Jonestown cult. When they arrived in Guyana, Ryan and some of his staff were murdered. Jones properly feared that his group would be held responsible and he ordered his followers (including babies and small children) to drink poisoned Kool-Aid. As far as we can tell, most went to their deaths willingly. Granted that Jones himself was somewhat demented, the question remains as to why so many other relatively sane people could be convinced to commit the ultimate act of suicide. Brainwashing?

One evening a few years ago my wife and I were talking about the fact that the older of our two cars was showing some signs of wear. Gradually the conversation shifted to the fa-

The mass suicide at Jonestown illustrates the power that one person can have over others.

miliar "Wouldn't it be nice if we could afford a new car?" scenario. Because neither of us had any idea what new cars cost, we went to the Ford–Mazda agency nearby and quickly discovered that new cars were much more expensive than we had thought. However, as we prepared to leave, we found ourselves in a separate part of the showroom looking at Mazdas. Up to that point I had only the vaguest ideas about Japanese cars other than the fact that they got good gas mileage and were cheaper than American cars. My wife and I took a Mazda for a test drive and, after inhaling new car smell for a half hour, decided that we really did want a new car. On our way back to the dealership we discussed who would look up car information in consumer magazines. When we got back, I asked the salesman about price and ordering a model more to our specifications. He told me that he could not negotiate on price and that I pretty well had to take what he had on hand. To make an embarrassingly short story even shorter, we bought the Mazda the next day despite the fact that before that evening we had never really considered buying a new car, had no pressing need for one, and had never remotely thought about buying a Mazda. Was I the victim of a clever sales technique?

INTRODUCTION

All the above examples have one thing in common. People did something they would not normally do because of the behavior of other people. In some cases, as with the Jonestown tragedy, people killed themselves because someone demanded that they do so. The Werther phenomenon illustrates the power of example. My buying a Mazda illustrates the power of a clever salesman to make me want something I didn't know I wanted.

Social psychologists use the broad term *social influence* to describe the obvious but important fact that much of our behavior is affected by what others say and do. When we considered attitude formation and change in Chapter 7, we noted the many ways attitudes are affected by how other people structure their arguments. Attitude change often results from impersonal and intellectual appeals whereas conformity usually results from direct, social forces and often appeals more to affect and feelings. In this chapter we take up two other forms of social influence: (1) conformity and (2) the conflict between impulses and inhibitions.

Conformity involves situations in which people do something they do not want to do or would not do without group pressure. In one sense, conformity pressures create a conflict between a person's own desires and external pressures. However, there is another source of social influence where the social pressure helps to resolve internal conflicts. All of us want to do things we know we should not. For example, I have always had a strong desire to throw a rock through a large plate glass window, but I have never done so for obvious legal and potential guilt reasons.

When people have such conflicts, others may alter the balance between restraints and desires by raising and lowering either or both. So it is quite possible that other people might raise my desire to throw rocks through bank windows by daring me to do so or by reminding me how much fun it would be to hear the bank alarm go off. Or they might reduce my strong restraints by convincing me we can get away before the police come or by arguing I have a silly sense of morality. Though I would never (I trust) break a bank window on my own, in a group situation the balance between my desires and my restraints might be altered in favor of performing the naughty behavior. Of course, release of previously inhibited behavior need not result in property damage or antisocial behavior. For example, most of us have a conflict between wanting to help (say, by giving blood in a blood drive) and being restrained because of inconvenience. In such a case others may encourage you to give blood by making altruistic motives salient or by reducing the restraints.

CONFORMITY

Conformity is a person's changing his or her behavior because of the explicit or implicit demands of others. It is behavior change caused by group pressures. For now, we leave open the question of whether such changes are mere behavioral changes or whether they also reflect deeper cognitive and attitude changes. But conformity must involve some behavior change.

You do not have to be convinced that people conform. We drive on the correct side of the road, face the front of elevators, wear the latest fashions, buy records, and show up for work and exams on time primarily because of the influence of others. Countless criticisms of modern society have been founded on the premise that people too readily conform to the opinions of others. Lest we become too complacent about conformity, we might remind ourselves of Nazi Germany, Jonestown, and the Watergate cover-up. By the same token, political theorists have long held that conformity to laws, customs, and norms is essential for a well-functioning society. Without some conformity, anarchy reigns and societies disintegrate; with too much conformity, societies stagnate. Given the obvious importance of conformity, it is no accident that the topic has a long history in empirical social psychology.

THREE EARLY STUDIES

Bennington College   In the 1930s, Bennington College (in Vermont) was an expensive women's college with a liberal faculty and with students whose parents were conservative. Theodore Newcomb (1943) found that freshmen were conservative like their parents but that the students became more liberal the longer they stayed in school.

Why did the students change their attitudes? Newcomb could find little evidence that this resulted directly from faculty indoctrination. Rather, he suggested that pressures from other students produced the changes. The students tended to become more liberal with time, and those who became the most liberal by the time they were juniors and seniors were also the most popular and respected. Furthermore, the liberals were more generally admired, they tended to have friendships mostly among people who shared their views, and they set the tone for the entire college. They were, in short, an in-group. Newcomb argued that many of the entering students became more liberal in

an effort to win the approval of the in-group and so become more popular themselves. This famous study suggested that people may conform to the opinions and expectations of others to win the acceptance and approval of those others.

Sherif   Muzifer Sherif argued that people conform to groups not so much to get approval as to gain a sense of reality. Sherif was a Turkish student who came to the United States for his graduate study. One of the things that impressed him about living in two cultures was the extent to which the culture imposes frames of references for interpreting essentially ambiguous information. Food that tastes good to people in one culture is repugnant to people in another. Behavior that seems right and proper in one part of the world is rude elsewhere.

Sherif felt that social groups (and cultures) do more than encourage conformity to group values; they also provide important information and interpretative frameworks. People need to know what is true, and, in the absence of structure from the physical environment, they may accept realities provided by others. To demonstrate this hypothesis, Sherif (1936) needed a situation in which the physical environment provided few cues to reality, so that social standards could operate in a relatively pure state.

Sherif took advantage of the fact that when a person in darkness looks at a stationary spot

Theodore Newcomb

of light, the light appears to move. This apparent motion is called *the autokinetic effect.* Without telling subjects that the light's movement was illusory, he simply asked each subject to make judgments about how far the light moved. (A similar study by Jacobs and Campbell, 1961, using the same strategy was discussed in Chapter 10.) Sherif found that individuals varied quite a bit in their estimates from nearly 0 inches to 10 inches or more.

In his most famous experiment, Sherif brought three subjects who had previously made private, individual judgments into the room and let them announce their individual judgments in succession and aloud. He found that the individuals converged on a single value or estimate, a kind of group norm. So the individual variability was reduced in the group. The subjects seem to have influenced

one another because of their need to define standards, a reality. One group's results are shown in Figure 11.1A.

If the group helps to define a reality for the amount of movement, once subjects have adopted that reality they should continue to adhere to it even though they are no longer in the group. When subjects made their judgments in a group before making individual judgments alone, they continued to give judgments in line with the group norm (Figure 11.1B). A later experiment by Alexander, Zucker, and Brody (1970) further supports that interpretation. When subjects know that the movement is not "real," their tendency to impose group standards is reduced.

Asch   Solomon Asch (1948) argued that people did not conform slavishly and uncriti-

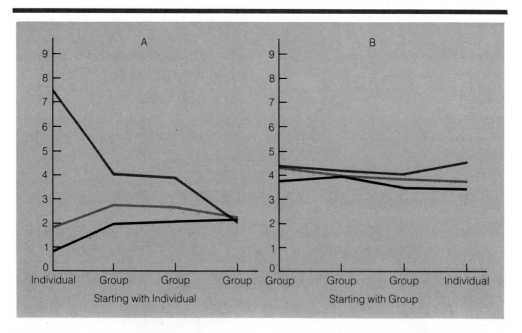

FIGURE 11.1   Median Estimates of Groups of Three Subjects Reporting an (Apparent) Movement of Light. A, Subjects first make individual judgment followed by three judgments as part of a group. B, subjects first make three judgments as part of a group followed by an individual judgment.

From Sherif, 1936.

cally. There was considerable conformity in the Sherif study because there was no clear reality, but Asch was sure that people would not go along with the majority so readily when others were *clearly* wrong. In his famous conformity study (Asch, 1952), Asch tested this idea directly and elegantly. Subjects were told they were in an experiment on perception and they sat facing a pair of white cardboards on which lines were drawn. One card had a single line—the standard; the second card had three lines of differing lengths, one of which was obviously the same length as the standard. The subjects were asked to judge which of the three lines matched the standard; the correct answers were so obvious that individual subjects rarely made errors.

The several people in the experiment made their judgments in order. Actually, there was only one real subject, who made his judgment near the end; the others were all confederates of the experimenter. For the first two trials, the confederates (and the subjects) gave the obviously correct answers, but on the third trial all the confederates gave the same incorrect answer. This occurred again on trials 4, 6, 7, 9, 10, and 12. Asch found, much to his surprise, that on these trials the average subject conformed one-third of the time. More than 80% conformed to the incorrect majority on at least one trial, and 7% conformed on all seven critical trials. Asch had demonstrated that even with a clear reality to the contrary people would still go along with the crowd. This is not what he set out to show, but science marches on.

Presumably, subjects conformed in the Asch situation because they wanted the other people to like them or because they were afraid that the others would ridicule them for not going along with the group. When Asch interviewed the subjects, they generally mentioned concerns such as these as their reasons for conforming. In addition, when he allowed the subjects to make their responses privately in writing rather than having to announce them

Asch's experiments showed that people often adjust their judgments to conform to a group, even to the point of ignoring clear evidence to the contrary.

publicly before the entire group, the amount of conformity was markedly decreased. Because people are typically less concerned about the approval of others when the others cannot monitor their behavior, these results suggest that the conformity was due to a desire to win approval.

TWO KINDS OF CONFORMITY

In Sherif's research, subjects conformed because others provided information, whereas in the Asch and Newcomb studies, need for approval seemed to be a more important motive.

Deutsch and Gerard (1955) discussed this difference by formally distinguishing **norma-tive from informational social influence.** We conform to gain either approval (normative) or information about reality (informational).

Suppose you have announced that you want to take a course in music appreciation, but your friend tries to convince you to take a psychology course she plans to take. You might conform to her pressure because you want to keep her approval. Perhaps she makes fun of the music course, so you go along with her to prove that you are a worthy person. In other words, you might conform for norma-tive reasons. On the other hand, she might try to convince you to take the psychology course by pointing out that the professor is good, the course meets at a better time, and you could study together. In this case you would con-form because she provides information you did not have before. Of course, these two sources of conformity are not mutually ex-clusive. You could follow your friend's sugges-tion both because you value her information and because you fear her disapproval.

Normative Influence   The Bennington study was one demonstration of conformity to gain approval. We all know from our own ex-periences that people conform to avoid ridi-cule, disapproval, or punishment or to gain approval, money, or a job promotion. The fashion industry (among others) depends heavily on our desires to wear whatever others will approve. You conform to laws because you fear jail, you bathe to reduce social rejec-tion, you turn in papers more or less on time to avoid failing your courses. And the list goes on. As you might expect, conformity is espe-cially high when groups control material or psychological rewards the person wants (Crutchfield, 1955; Deutsch & Gerard, 1955) and when the person is especially hungry for approval (Crowne & Marlowe, 1964). Also, as Asch found, conformity is higher when responding is public rather than private (Insko et al., 1983).

Informational Influence   As Sherif's stud-ies showed, you should be particularly subject to informational social influence when the sit-uation is ambiguous or others have important information you lack. Thus, when the Asch situation is made less clear by making the lines closer in length and harder to judge, confor-mity is increased (Asch, 1952). Also, when subjects have to make their judgments from memory rather than from direct perception of the lines, conformity is also increased; we do not trust our memories as much as our direct perceptions (Deutsch & Gerard, 1955). In ad-dition, there is more conformity when the ma-jority includes one or more experts who presumably can better assess reality (Jones, Wells, & Torrey, 1958).

MAJORITY AND MINORITY INFLUENCE

In most of Asch's studies, the lone subject was confronted by a sizeable and unanimous majority. However, both the size and unanim-ity of the majority have important effects on conformity. The number of people with whom the naive subject disagrees is important. Asch found that there is small conformity (usually less than 10%) if the subject faces a single con-federate with whom he disagrees, but the rate of conformity increases dramatically with two or three confederates. Although some studies have found that conformity continues to in-crease as the size of the majority increases, there is typically some leveling off of the amount of influence as the number reaches three or four (Latané, 1981; Tanford & Pen-rod, 1984).

Asch also showed that conformity is re-duced if the group opposing the naive subject is not unanimous. If at least one other person sides with the subject, conformity is markedly reduced. Conformity is reduced even if the minority confederate disagrees with both the rest of the group and the subject (Allen & Levine, 1969). The important factor is not so much agreement with the subject as a recogni-tion that nonconformity is acceptable.

Minority Influence   In most real-life situations, there are usually two competing points of view, and an individual is not confronted with a unanimous group against him or her. Imagine, for example, you are in a group of people deciding where to go for dinner; six people argue for one restaurant and three for another. You and two or three other people are undecided. Which group will most affect your vote?

Moscovici (1976, 1980) has argued that majorities tend to produce fairly superficial conformity because they typically rely on normative (approval-based) pressures. However, when there is a strong minority point of view, the undecided person may pay close attention to their arguments because he or she is interested in what the basis of their nonconformity might be. This ought to be particularly likely if the minority is both consistent and insistent. Thus, minorities may get more information-based conformity, which is usually deeper and more long-lasting than normative conformity even though it may take more time to develop because people may not pay as close attention to the minority initially. This suggests that while majorities may secure more change of attitudes and behavior in public, minority influence may show up in more private attitudes and dispositions. Some studies find no support for the greater effect of minorities on private change (Wolf, 1985), but several studies do support the prediction (Maass & Clark, 1984; Nemeth, 1986).

Social Impact Theory   Moscovici's model clearly proposes that people react differently to minorities and majorities and, therefore, the two factions will have different kinds and degrees of influence on undecided people. Other social psychologists have suggested that minorities and majorities operate according to the same basic social influence principles. Latané's *social impact theory* (1981; Latané & Wolf, 1981) argues that people are affected by the strength, immediacy, and number of sources of social forces acting upon them. In

Minorities often try to influence majority opinion.

general, the strength factor increases as the influence sources have higher prestige or power, and immediacy increases with proximity in time or space to the target person. The number of sources refers to the number of people who are trying to influence the target (Figure 11.2).

To account for whether majorities or minorities will have more effect, we have to examine the forces each has. Obviously, minorities will be disadvantaged with regard to number although minority influence increases with the size of the minority (Wolf & Latané, 1983). However, minorities may gain influence through the strength or immediacy variables. Minorities may be more immediate psychologically, because they seem to stand out against the background of the majority (Nemeth,

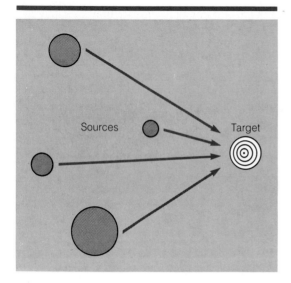

FIGURE 11.2   Social Impact Theory Proposes that a Person (target) Is Affected by the Strength (shown here as size of arrows), Immediacy (indicated by how close the source is to the target), and Number of Sources of Social Influence.

From Latané, 1981.

Wachtler, & Endicott, 1977) or because they adopt behavioral styles that make them seem strong or immediate. For example, confident nonverbal behavioral styles usually induce more conformity (Lee & Ofshe, 1981), and minorities who seem certain of their position achieve more conformity than those that are less confident (Nemeth & Wachtler, 1973). We might expect that minorities may behave more confidently than majorities because of ideological commitment and the need to defend their minority position, and these results suggest that minorities often adopt a style that leads to considerable influence over others.

The major issue still being debated is whether minorities and majorities get their influence in different ways and for different reasons. Moscovici claims that people respond to minorities differently than to majorities and that minority influence does not necessarily obey the same general rules as majority

influence. Social impact theory, by contrast, claims that the two kinds of influence can be understood within a common framework.

Under any circumstances, however, it is important to recognize that majorities are not inevitably more influential than minorities, although majorities clearly have a strong head start because of their greater numbers and control over resources. There are many historical examples of minority positions that have became majority positions over time (as in the growth of various religious sects, including every Protestant sect, and the adoption of major scientific theories). Although minority positions usually wither and die over time, we also have to account for those situations in which they do not.

GROUP DYNAMICS

Much of the research on conformity has been conducted with ad hoc collections rather than true groups of subjects. Yet, in everyday life most of the conformity pressures we face come from members of groups to which we belong. As we saw in Chapter 10, we can hardly understand group decisions and leadership without knowing something about social influence processes. The recognition of this interrelationship between conformity and group process and structure led to an approach called *group dynamics.* Although this term has come to have a broad meaning, originally it was synonymous with the research of Kurt Lewin and his students.

Group Decision   As we discussed in Chapter 1, Lewin distinguished between *induced forces* and *own forces.* People might do something because of induced social forces (someone pressures them) or because they want to (task demands correspond to their own needs). Of course, own forces may arise during group interaction, but they remain own forces only insofar as the person feels he or she is not being pressured by others.

Lewin was deeply concerned with the psychological dynamics of democratic processes. If people in a group do something because a leader tells them to do so, the forces are induced and might not persist once the leader is gone. However, if group decisions are made democratically, the forces on behavior might more readily be accepted as own forces and would continue to influence behavior even when the group is absent. Characteristic of the Lewin approach, his research on this topic was conducted in the context of a practical situation. During the early 1940s, when usual cuts of meat were hard to get because of war rationing, Lewin studied ways of encouraging housewives to buy practical but unappealing meats such as kidneys, livers, and hearts. Some groups of women were given lectures that stressed the food value of the meats and told how to serve them in appetizing ways. Other groups were asked to discuss meats with a group leader, but the emphasis was on group discussion rather than on the leader's information. After the discussion, the women were asked to indicate whether they would be willing to serve the meats. Follow-up studies showed that only 3% of the women who had the lecture format (induced forces) subsequently served any of the meats, whereas almost one-third who participated in the group discussion (own forces) did so.

Resistance to Change   It became obvious to Lewin that often the attitudes and behaviors one wants to change are deeply anchored in group identifications. If one can change the group collectively, the group members may also change as individuals; otherwise, the group may retard change. For example, one of the reasons it is so hard to change various forms of deviant and addictive behaviors such as crime, alcoholism, and drug abuse is that the deviant or addicted person continually interacts with people who put pressure on him or her to steal, drink, or use drugs: "It is easier to change the ideology and social practice of a small group handled together than of single individuals" (Lewin, 1947).

This was shown dramatically in a study at the Harwood Manufacturing Company by two Lewinians (Coch & French, 1948). At this company (which manufactured pajamas), women workers were paid for the number of items they completed. Despite the obvious fact that it was to their material benefit to produce more items, the women were not working as hard as they might because the groups clearly enforced norms about production. When one woman began to exceed the group norm, the group pressured her to slow down to almost half of what she did when she was isolated from them. The company was also distressed by the workers' resistance to necessary job changes, such as using new and better sewing machines. It took the women a long time to adjust to the changes and to get production back to an acceptable level, in part because of group pressures.

Coch and French experimented with various types of procedures for getting the workers to work harder (which was in their self-interest, remember) and to adjust to job changes. The most effective was one in which the workers were allowed to discuss the proposed changes and had a voice in approving them. Attempts to change individual workers largely failed because the group pressures to resist change were so strong, but when the group as a whole was involved in the changes, potentially induced forces took on an own-force quality.

When Lewin moved to MIT in 1945, he persuaded several of his former students to join him there. This research group, the Center for Group Dynamics, stayed at MIT for a few years after Lewin's early death in 1947. Many of the members of the center then went to the University of Michigan, where the Center remains an important center of social psychology. However, in the late 1940s the focus of attention shifted somewhat from group atmosphere and structure to group processes such as communication and social influence.

Informal Social Communication   The focus on communication and social influence is apparent in an influential paper published by Leon Festinger, one of the central members of the Lewin group. In his paper "Informal Social Communication," Festinger (1950) noted that one of the major functions of communication within groups is to maintain uniform opinions and attitudes. Just as nature abhors a vacuum and will rush to fill one, groups dislike diversity and will try to impose conformity. Why? Festinger gives two reasons. The least important reason theoretically, though not necessarily practically, is that before groups can reach some goal, the members must cooperate and submerge their differences. The second reason is that a group member whose opinions cannot be supported by physical reality must depend instead on social reality. "Thus where the dependence upon physical reality is low, the dependence upon social reality is correspondingly high. An opinion, a belief, an attitude is 'correct,' 'valid,' and 'proper' to the extent that it is anchored in a group of people with similar beliefs, opinions, and attitudes" (Festinger, 1950, pp. 272–73). Thus, Festinger, like Sherif and Asch, argued that diversity of opinion makes group members uncomfortable because it challenges their beliefs about what is real and correct.

Festinger further suggested two variables that should increase dependence on social reality. The first is the *relevance* of the behavior or attitude in question. Group members hold any number of attitudes, only some of which are relevant to the group. Generally, groups should exert more conformity pressure on issues central or relevant to the group. For example, most church and religious organizations would feel that there are certain basic beliefs all members must hold to, and they may even expect that certain behaviors (such as attending religious services, giving money, and working in church activities) should be performed by members. The church is less likely to be concerned with what brands of television sets the members own or whether they prefer reading to watching television.

The second variable that affects conformity pressure is group **cohesiveness.** Normally, cohesiveness refers to how well people in a group get along, but Festinger defined cohesiveness as pressure to stay in the group. He suggested that people would feel more pressure to stay in the group when they liked other members of the group, liked the activities of the group, and liked the group's ideology. If a group is cohesive, members care more about the group. Therefore its social reality is more important to its members, and this gives the group more power over its members. You probably care more about the opinions of your group of friends than those of members of a book club to which you might belong; hence your friends can exert more influence on you than the book club members can.

Thus, Festinger has hypothesized that groups should care more about social reality and should therefore exert more conformity pressure when (1) the attitudes and behaviors are central or relevant to the group and (2) when the group is cohesive. But what happens when there are deviants in the group, people who do not tow the party line? Festinger argues that the majority will first try to convert the deviant to the majority opinion. If these attempts at persuasion do not work, the majority may threaten the deviant with rejection and in extreme cases may actually kick him or her out of the group. The rejection of the deviant

Leon Festinger

not only removes a sore point in the group, but may actually reinforce group solidarity by confirming the shared social reality of the remaining members. In presidential politics, the people closest to the president usually insist on absolute adherence to the party line. Those who show less than complete enthusiasm soon find themselves out of the in-group; often this is accomplished physically by moving the deviant's office farther from the sources of power. In extreme cases the offender is fired or sent to another branch of government. Janis' *groupthink* (see Chapter 10) suggests additional examples of how cohesive groups try to bring deviants into line.

Empirical Evidence   One of the first studies to support Festinger's model was done by Festinger, Schachter, and Back (1950). Two housing projects had been built for MIT's married students. Festinger and his colleagues collected data from the tenants about which other tenants they liked and about their attitudes toward a prospective tenants' organization. In units where the attitudes toward the tenants' organization were relevant to the students, the more cohesive groups had more homogeneity of opinion on the issue. Also, conformers were better liked within their units than deviants were. However, in units where the attitudes were not relevant, there was no relationship between cohesiveness and opinion uniformity.

Perhaps the most direct experimental test of Festinger's theory came in a Ph.D. thesis done by Stanley Schachter (1951) under the direction of Festinger. Schachter manipulated both the group-cohesiveness and attitude-relevance variables that were important in the housing study. Cohesiveness was manipulated by assigning subjects to groups whose tasks either did or did not interest them. Presumably, subjects assigned to the groups working on the more interesting tasks would want to stay in the group more. Relevance was manipulated by having subjects work on activities relevant

or irrelevant to the stated purposes of the group.

Shortly after the groups began work, the experimenter shifted them to a discussion of the case of a juvenile delinquent. Three members of the group were confederates. One (the *modal confederate*) always supported the group consensus. The other two confederates both began by arguing that the delinquent should be punished strongly; almost all the real subjects disagreed strongly with this position. Over the course of a 45-minute discussion, one of the confederates (the *deviant*) remained firm in his position while the other (the *slider*) gradually came around to the consensus position of the subjects. Schachter measured the number of comments addressed to each group member. Theoretically, the most comments should be addressed to the deviants, especially when relevance and cohesiveness were high. Because people who do not go along with the group threaten social reality, the group should try to bring them into line by talking to them a lot. However, the data did not confirm the predictions: although many comments were addressed to the deviants, this tendency was not affected by cohesiveness or relevance. In contrast, another prediction of the theory was confirmed. The deviant was not as well liked as the slider or the modal confederate. Thus, once it was clear that the deviants could not be converted, they were rejected by the subjects, and this tendency was stronger for the high-cohesive and high-relevance groups.

Further research by Back (1951), Festinger and Thibaut (1951), and Festinger et al. (1952), among others, provides additional support for the model. Groups dependent on social reality tend to bring conformity pressure on their members, and this tendency is somewhat stronger when cohesiveness is high. In addition, rejection of deviants is also stronger when the groups are cohesive.

Social psychologists have continued their interest in group reactions to opinion deviants.

Generally, of course, opinion deviants are rejected. However, this tends to be less true for higher-status people in the group. Hollander (1958) argued that high-status people have *idiosyncrasy credits.* By virtue of their high status, which is generally earned by helping the group, higher-status people have earned the right to deviate on certain issues, provided, of course, they do not deviate so often that they use up their idiosyncrasy credits.

There has also been considerable interest in how the group reacts to the initial deviant who ultimately conforms. The subjects in Schachter's groups liked the slider reasonably well. That makes some sense. From the perspective of Festinger's model, the slider may be seen as an independent person who is won over to the group's version of reality, thus lending even greater credibility to that reality. Or perhaps we just like people we can manipulate. On the other hand, one might argue that sometimes people who change are perceived as weak and lacking in the courage of their convictions. Additional research (Levine, 1980) suggests that sliders are generally well liked as long as they end up agreeing with the group. People who change away from the group or who disagree consistently are particularly disliked (Levine, Saxe, & Harris, 1976).

PUBLIC COMPLIANCE

There is an obvious and important distinction between the person who changes her public behavior while privately maintaining old beliefs at odds with the behavior and the person who undergoes deeper change in which both behavior and attitudes are altered. For example, on essay exams, many students feel they have to write what they believe the professor wants to see, and they do so without much conviction. On the other hand, many students do change their values and beliefs during a course; the fact that their exam answers are consistent with those that the professor favors is not always the result of mere public conformity.

This distinction has been implicit in the research we have already discussed. We can be fairly certain that Sherif's subjects had changed privately as well as publicly, but one doubts that the Asch subjects who gave incorrect answers in the face of group pressure came to believe the group was right. Generally, informational influence results in belief change, whereas normative influence is less likely to do so and often represents behavioral change only. At any rate, we must be careful to note that overt, public conformity need not always reflect private change.

When social psychologists want to emphasize public conformity without private acceptance, they generally use the term *compliance.* When there is private change as well, we speak of internalization or sometimes of *conversion.* When the distinction is irrelevant or when it is impossible to tell whether behavioral change does or does not reflect internal change, we will continue to use the term *conformity.* Anytime you decide to go along with the crowd even though you don't agree, you are exhibiting compliance, but when you go along because your attitudes, values, or motives have changed, your change represents internalization. Although in many situations it is not clear whether change reflects internalization, for the moment let us concentrate on situations where it is likely that only compliance is involved.

Obedience   One line of experimentation on compliance has been so controversial and potentially important that it deserves special discussion—research on obedience to authority. We look with horror at the Nazi experience. How could such civilized people allow themselves to be involved in such outrageous acts? The answer is still not clear, but it is apparent that the German experience is not unique. The mass suicide at Jonestown reminds us that people sometimes will commit extreme acts just to comply with a leader.

In the early 1960s, Stanley Milgram conducted a series of experiments to explore the limits of obedience to authority (see Milgram, 1975, for a summary). In the Milgram paradigm, subjects arrived for an experiment and were told it concerned learning. Specifically, the experimenter was said to be interested in the effects of punishment, in this case a shock, on memory. In each pair of subjects, one person served as a teacher and one as a learner. One "subject" was actually a confederate and always drew the learner role. As learner, the confederate was taken to an adjoining room and was attached to some electrodes. Following all this rather convincing stage setting, the subject–teacher went to a different room and was told to give a shock to the learner for every incorrect response. The confederate made many errors; not only was he given a shock by the subject for every incorrect answer, but each shock was more severe than the previous one. The first shock was 15 volts, and successive shocks went up by 15-volt increments to 450 volts, which was indicated to be extremely dangerous. Of course, the confederate was not actually hooked up to the shock machine, but instead activated a tape machine which gave a standard sequence of correct and error responses. The tape also contained standard "extraneous" responses: at 75 volts, the learner groaned when shocked; at 150 volts, he asked to leave the experiment (in some variations he also complained of a heart condition); at 180 volts, he said he could no longer stand the pain; by 270 volts, his reply was an agonized scream; and at 330 volts, he stopped answering. Whenever the subject–teacher hesitated, the experimenter urged him to continue giving shocks; when the learner–confederate stopped responding, the subject was told to treat the lack of response as an incorrect answer and to continue giving shocks.

The major dependent measure was how far up the shock scale the subject was willing to go. Milgram (1975) asked several psychiatrists and lay people to predict how many subjects would give 450-volt shocks, and none of these people predicted that the subjects would go

beyond 300 volts. You probably feel that you would not give seemingly lethal doses of shock to another. Certainly I feel that I would not. Yet more than 60% of the subjects gave shocks at the maximum level (450 volts), marked "Danger: Severe Shock," because an authority figure had said to (Milgram, 1963). When subjects are free to choose their own levels of shock, only 3% give the maximum shock. But in the experiment, 65% of the subjects complied with an authority's request even when the learner had ceased to respond and might be dead (certainly this possibility occurred to some subjects). It is also clear that no matter why the subjects complied, they were extremely tense, agitated, and disturbed.

There are factors, however, that do lower the level of compliance. For example, if the learner was placed in the same room with the subject, so that the subject could see the learner's agony, only 40% of the subjects were fully compliant (see also Tilker, 1970). If, in addition, the subjects had to actually place the learner's hand on the shock plate, only 30% complied. Subjects who were merely asked to order someone else to give the shocks were

Milgram's disturbing experiments showed that even ordinary people may have the potential for extreme obedience to authority.

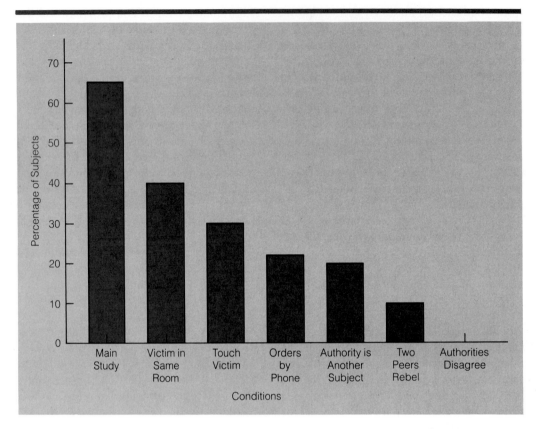

FIGURE 11.3   Percentage of Subjects Who Gave Maximum Shocks under Various Conditions.
After Milgram, 1975.

more likely to give maximum shocks than were subjects who actually had to pull the switch (Kilham & Mann, 1974).

The fact that the experimenter is a scientist seems to be critical. When the experimenter is not a scientist but another "subject" (actually a confederate) who is given the experimenter role, only 20% of the subjects complied fully with the requests to give maximum shocks. Another variable that affects compliance is the relationship of the experimenter to the subject. When the experimenter in the Milgram study was absent from the room during the shock trials and so could not monitor the subject's behavior, far fewer (21%) subjects complied. Some solved the dilemma by telling the experi-

menter that they were giving increasingly high shocks, although in fact using the lowest level of shock all the while. In addition, compliance is lowered (to about 10%) if other "subjects" (actually confederates) refuse to comply (Milgram, 1975; Powers & Geen, 1972). As in the Asch studies, the presence of a "partner" seems to lower a subject's compliance. Also, if there are two experimenters who openly disagree about whether the subject should increase the shocks, none of the subjects goes all the way (see Figure 11.3).

It is also worth noting one peculiarity of the Milgram procedure. As Gilbert (1981) has pointed out, the subject who goes all the way gets there in gradual stages. Gilbert argues that very few subjects would give 450-volt shocks if they were asked to do so from the beginning. One reason the gradual procedure is so powerful is that there is never a clear point at which the subject can say "enough is enough"; having given a 150-volt shock, what is the big deal about giving 165?

The Milgram experiment has been quite famous and controversial. It has been famous because it seems to demonstrate quite vividly that ordinary, salt-of-the-earth people can be made to perform quite harmful acts if they are pressured enough. It has been controversial, in part, because it was such a stressful experience for the subjects. Indeed, many psychologists would probably consider this experiment so stressful that it is unethical to run it. In Chapter 17 we will discuss some of the ethical issues in this research.

Foot-in-the-door   One way of understanding compliance is that once a subject decides to comply, he or she remains relatively consistent in that behavior (Kiesler, 1971). This has an interesting implication; if you can get someone to comply with a small request, it might be easier to get that person to comply with a larger one, what might be called the *foot-in-the-door technique.* Freedman and Fraser (1966) used an ingenious procedure to investigate this technique experimentally. The main compliance request was for housewives to allow a survey team of five or six people to spend two hours in their kitchens classifying household objects, a fairly major request. When subjects were simply called to see if they would allow the survey team in, about 22% complied with the request. To manipulate foot-in-the-door, other subjects were asked to comply with a much smaller request before they were asked to allow people into their kitchens. One group was approached three days before and asked if they would answer some questions about household soaps used; 33% complied with the later request. Another group not only was asked to answer questions

about soaps used, but was actually asked the questions, and 52% of these women complied with the larger request later.

There are now several replications of this basic finding that people will be more likely to comply with a large request after first doing so to a smaller one (Beaman et al., 1983; DeJong, 1979). Why does this happen? One possibility is that self-perception factors are at work. Once you have complied, you have identified yourself as the kind of person who submits to requests, and you then may feel compelled to act out this image (Lepper, 1973). This image may be reinforced when the requester responds favorably to the initial compliance (Crano & Sivacek, 1982).

For years my wife was plagued by phone calls from Kevin, who represented a disabled veterans group that sold lightbulbs. She initially bought a few (overpriced) bulbs because Kevin seemed nice and the cause worthy. Within six months, Kevin called again, and this time we bought even more bulbs after he promised never to call again. But the calls continued at ever-decreasing intervals. Kevin had learned (or had been taught) an important sales technique. People who are suckers at one point in time are likely to remain so. Having once bought lightbulbs, how do we now claim we don't need more? We always needed lightbulbs, buying them from Kevin did help a charity, and there really was no polite way to change gracefully our image as charitable lightbulb buyers.

Similarly, suppose you have just agreed to buy a new car for $12,500. Now the clever salesman suddenly announces that he has miscalculated and the car really will cost $13,000. How do you respond? Well, much as you know you should tell the salesman to jump in the lake and take his car with him, most of us would probably swallow hard and accept the higher price. Another version of the same strategy is for a salesperson to get a commitment for the basic car but then to tack on several extras such as an expensive stereo. Once having committed yourself to spending $12,500 for a car, an extra $500 for a really good stereo doesn't seem like that much more. Alternatively, you may have been asked to work "just a couple of hours" for a charity but then find that you have trouble resisting requests to work just a little more. The initial commitment almost forces you to work the extra hours.

Door-in-the-face Interestingly, another powerful strategy for getting compliance is basically the opposite of the foot-in-the-door. In what has come to be called ***door-in-the-face technique*** (Cialdini et al., 1975), people are first asked to perform a costly behavior, and when they refuse they are then asked to perform a much less costly one. Typically, compliance with the second, modest request is much larger if preceded by a large request than by no request at all. For example, Harari, Mohr, and Hosey (1980) had students phone faculty members with a request for help on a project. In some cases the professor had previously been approached with a much more costly request involving many hours of time whereas in other cases there had been no previous request. With no previous request there was 57% compliance, but with the larger previous request compliance was 78%.

This may have even played a role in the Watergate caper. During the 1972 elections, several men were caught burglarizing Democratic headquarters. Eventually the break-in was traced to the Nixon election campaign. One of the fascinating aspects of the whole business was that the break-in could not have produced information that would help the Nixon reelection campaign. Why then was it authorized? One explanation is that the first requests of G. Gordon Liddy, the leader of the burglars, for subversive activity had a price-tag of $1 million, and so when the Watergate break-in was suggested (at a much lower cost) the officials of Nixon's campaign felt they had to comply with Liddy's request because he had been so accommodating; they had to let him do something (Cialdini, 1985).

We have all been victimized by this strategy. Charities often ask me to buy five ($10) tickets so that orphans can see the circus. When I say I cannot afford the requested $50, I am then asked whether I might be willing to sponsor just one poor orphan at $10. The salesperson who shows you the super-deluxe model, which you admit you cannot afford, may then follow with the much cheaper model "with all the features you really need."

It is likely that self-perception and image factors are involved here as well. It is easy for most of us to refuse a request for $50 or 10 hours of our time on the grounds that we are poor or busy. But there may always be the vague feeling of being a cheapskate or curmudgeon for having refused. The second, more reasonable request gives you the opportunity to restore your public image of being a kind and worthy soul (Pendleton & Batson, 1979). Thus, compliance is often a self-presentational device used to restore or maintain our public (and private) images of being nice and well socialized.

The Reciprocity Norm The norm of reciprocity is also a powerful technique for securing compliance (see Chapters 13 and 14 for further discussion). One manifestation of this norm is that we should help those who help us. Regan (1971) showed the power of reciprocity for compliance in an experiment in

Robert Cialdini

which subjects worked with a confederate rating works of art. During the rest break, the confederate left the room and returned with two bottles of Coke, one for himself and one for the subject. This unsolicited favor bore fruit when the confederate later asked the subject to help him by buying some raffle tickets. Even subjects who had not been given the Coke typically bought some tickets, but those who had been given the Coke bought many more tickets, apparently because through doing so they could reciprocate the favor that had been done them. Cialdini (1985) points out one effective use of this technique. The Hare Krishna, a religious sect, were able to dramatically increase the effectiveness of their solicitations in airports simply by giving people a "free" flower before asking for the donation. For those of us who have been well socialized, it is hard to turn down a request for money after being given a free, if worthless, gift. This reciprocity norm may also account for the door-in-the-face phenomenon. When the requester lowers his or her demands, this can be read as a concession that we should then reciprocate by complying to the requested (smaller) donation (Cialdini, 1985).

By handing out small gifts, members of religious groups hope the reciprocity norm will greatly enhance donations.

Scarcity   Another factor in sales compliance is perceived scarcity. Most of us seem to want to have things we cannot have, perhaps because of psychological reactance (see Chapter 1). I have already given one example at the beginning of the chapter. Why did I buy a Mazda? It may well be that I would have bought one anyway after careful consideration, but the reason for my impulsive purchase is that the salesman convinced me that if I did not move fast I would be locked out forever. And just to prove that social psychologists do not learn from their mistakes, last week (and after writing the first part of the chapter and reliving my embarrassment over the Mazda) I did it again. This time I went to check out prices on cassette decks because my old one was showing signs of wear. I found the deck of my (limited) dreams at a price I could almost afford, and after the salesman lowered his "already fantastic sales price" a bit and agreed to throw in some tapes free, I was tempted. I told him I wanted to think it over, but he informed me that our negotiated price would not be good if I left. I now own a new cassette deck, bought that very moment.

One striking example of the scarcity principle in recent years has been the phenomenal success of Cabbage Patch dolls. Admittedly they are cute, but they were also overpriced and very scarce. People would line up outside stores hours before opening just to buy a doll. One member of my family actually bought one of the dolls just because she happened to see one on the shelves. You sure never know when you might need a Cabbage Patch doll (or cassette deck) and not be able to get one.

Those who favor censorship would profit from awareness of the perceived-scarcity principle. Telling people they cannot see or read something only whets their appetites. Commonly, antipornography crusades increase the sales of books or movie tickets. Even those who do not like pornography may want to see what all the fuss is about and want something they are told they should not have.

BRAINWASHING

Brainwashing entered American consciousness after the Korean War when a handful of American prisoners of war elected to stay behind with their Chinese captors. It soon became clear that the Chinese had used a variety of fairly subtle social influence techniques on American prisoners, ones they had developed during their attempts to convert Chinese citizens and foreigners after the Communist takeover of China in 1949. About this same time, historians and other social scientists became fascinated by the behavior of certain defendants in the famous purge trials in the Soviet Union during the 1930s. Joseph Stalin had decided to rid the Russian Communist Party and his government of those who opposed his policies. He did so by accusing them of various treasonous crimes, and many of the highest ranking of these men were publicly tried. Almost all confessed to their crimes, and the confessions resulted in their execution or their exile to Siberian prison camps where most died. At the time, it seemed possible that there might be some basis for the accusations, but by the early 1950s it was clear that most had confessed to crimes they could not possibly have committed. These purge trials were, by the way, a major source for the ideas of George Orwell in *1984*.

It seemed that Chinese and Russian Communists had developed highly effective ways of manipulating people's thoughts and behaviors. A few years later, many Americans assumed that the radicals of the 1960s had been brainwashed by political propaganda, and when religious cults began to recruit college students successfully, many parents became concerned about the ability of cultists to brainwash their children, just as James Jones surely had brainwashed his Jonestown followers. And what about Patty Hearst, a heretofore normal young woman, who was kidnapped by a radical organization and within weeks had begun to espouse the radical ideology of her captors. In due course she helped them commit at least two bank robberies. After her capture she went on trail for one of the robberies, and her major defense was that she had been brainwashed.

The Reality of Brainwashing   Can people be brainwashed? If so, how can this happen? Let us first recognize that the effects of brainwashing are usually highly exaggerated. The Chinese Communists tried to gain converts among several thousand American prisoners of war, and they succeeded with fewer than 10, although many other prisoners came home with momentarily favorable attitudes about the Chinese (Schein, 1956). In the case of the Russian purges, many of the victims confessed in the hopes of saving the lives of loved ones and to help the Party (Conquest, 1968); they were lying and they knew it. There was little evidence of internalization among these defendants, and we would hardly want to speak of brainwashing when only behavioral compliance was involved. Religious cults? To be sure, many cults have been quite successful in convincing American young people to give up their former materialistic lives for new religious values, but this kind of conversion is common in the long history of religions. If members of Hare Krishna were brainwashed, then so were many early Methodists, Mormons, and Catholics who made similar choices in centuries gone by. It is possible to think of religious conversion as brainwashing, but it seems a bit strained. Patty Hearst? Clearly she was successfully convinced that a previously alien political philosophy was righteous, but it is instructive that within days after her capture she had returned to most of her previous values.

I do not like the term ***brainwashing*** because it is used almost exclusively judgmentally to denote cases where people change from a set of values we like to ones we do not and because it connotes some sinister, mysterious source of influence. Actually, what happens in so-called brainwashing is fairly clear. Let us consider both informational and normative reasons.

Informational Factors   Many of our most cherished and deeply felt beliefs rest on unexamined foundations of cultural and social realities (see Chapters 1 and 9). If you have never had the opportunity to examine the basis of your political views, you may be vulnerable to the first person who has a reasonable alternative. Patty Hearst, who grew up in a rich and socially insulated family, was ill-prepared to defend against attacks on her family and its influence. Americans who knew nothing of the history of China hardly knew what to say when the Chinese Communists told them how America had helped to support a corrupt and cruel government before the revolution.

This is not to suggest that in these examples the brainwashers were necessarily on the side of truth or righteousness, only that they did have an effective case to make. But that is not enough, of course. If it were, we would all switch religions and political parties every time we heard a reasonable argument from the other side. As we saw in Chapter 7, most of us are able through counterarguing to resist appeals to change our attitudes, so "brainwashing" may be most effective with those basic and central beliefs that we have never examined closely enough to develop possible counterarguments against the other side in an argument.

In addition, most of us are usually enmeshed in a social framework that discourages change. A good conservative may find herself momentarily convinced by the seemingly strong arguments of a silver-tongued liberal, but she is unlikely to change dramatically, simply because she will leave this conversation and rejoin her conservative family and friends. Victims of brainwashing are almost always isolated from their usual sources of social reality. Patty Hearst listened to radical ideology hour after hour, day after day, without social support for

Immediately after her capture by authorities, Patty Hearst still espoused the radical ideology of her abductors.

her former realities; the normal stabilizing influences of her friends, family, and other people she respected were denied her. The Chinese Communists worked with some of their prisoners literally for years, keeping them isolated from former companions for the duration. One's faith in previous beliefs would have to be very strong and very well thought out to withstand such an assault.

Brainwashers also inevitably use variants of various commitment procedures we have already considered in this chapter. Recall the foot-in-the-door phenomenon in which people tend to agree to large requests after previously agreeing to smaller ones. Both Russian and Chinese interrogators used this technique masterfully. For example, the Chinese often got their prisoners to agree that there were problems with America. Surely the prisoners would agree that *sometimes* people are not treated justly in America. Often these statements were publicized, thus further increasing commitment. And after the prisoners would agree to make such a statement, it is only a short step to saying that Americans are *often* treated unjustly and another short step to saying they are *usually* given poor treatment. Similarly, the Russian interrogators usually first got their victims to admit that they had done some trivial things that were inconsistent with state ideology. Cultists often get their potential converts to admit that they are not ideally happy in their present life, thus preparing the way for stronger statements in the future. Thus, what we call brainwashing usually takes place in a series of short steps, with each new statement being only a bit stronger than the last. As self-perception and cognitive dissonance theories (see Chapter 5) have alerted us, people who make attitudinal statements varying with their beliefs may then change their beliefs.

In some cases, the door-in-the-face strategy is also used: "Well, you won't say that America is awful, but you would agree that it has some problems" or "You aren't willing to say that your parents are unloving and hypocritical, but you will agree that sometimes they are too materialistic." Backing away from extreme requests or statements makes the more moderate ones seem all the more reasonable.

Normative Factors   Still, there is something missing, and for this we must examine normative factors. You will recall that we sometimes conform because we want others to like us or to approve of what we do. For several weeks, Patty Hearst was cut off from all human contact except with her captors, and she was totally dependent on them for approval, food, conversation, and even opportunities to go to the bathroom. Furthermore, in such situations there is often an elemental fear of death, and captives may feel that their lives are in constant danger. This means that an interrogator who is nice and seemingly on the side of the victim may be liked, even loved, and the victim may be quite receptive to his arguments. You will remember that in *1984* Orwell played up this theme as Winston Smith came to love O'Brien, who had tortured him but who also seemed to care about him. As hostages come to like their captors, there would be natural tendencies to want to conform. Also, in a situation of total dependency, simple rewards such as a good meal, friendly conversation, or a pat on the back can be used as direct reinforcements for conformity.

Naturally, the particular constellation of these various factors will differ considerably from situation to situation, but what happens to victims of so-called brainwashing is hardly mysterious. With a little thought you should be able to think of a personal situation in which you heard only one side of a value position, where you were largely cut off from contact with outsiders, and where you were totally dependent on others for social and material rewards. This is called being a child, and if you are interested in the psychology of brainwashing, consider the family as by far the most successful agency of thought control in this or any other society.

TABLE 11.1 DIFFERENT CATEGORIES OF SOCIAL INFLUENCE.

	Private Change toward Source	
Public Change toward Source	*Present*	*Absent*
Present	Internalization	Compliance
Absent	Anticompliance	Independence

SOURCE: After Nail, 1986.

CONFORMITY AND INDEPENDENCE

Nail (1986) suggests that there are four types of response that a person can make when she initially disagrees with the social influence attempts of others. If she comes to agree both privately and publicly, this is of course internalization, or conversion (Table 11.1). And you will recognize the case of public agreement with no private change as compliance. The two remaining possibilities both involve the absence of public change, coupled with either private resistance (independence) or private change (anticompliance). Another form of anticompliance occurs when the target and source of conformity pressures initially agree privately but the target moves away from that position publicly as if to make a point of being independent.

The two classes of anticompliance (where the target agrees with the source privately but not publicly) have been of special interest to social psychologists. In Chapter 1, we discussed Brehm's (1966) theory of psychological reactance, which suggests that when people feel their freedom is threatened they will try to restore that freedom. When someone tells you that you have to change your behavior or beliefs, that is ordinarily a threat to your freedom to believe or do what you want. One way to restore that freedom would be to insist on disagreeing publicly. Perhaps the paradigm case is the teenager who knows his parents are correct but who insists on putting up a good battle to assert his independence.

The point to emphasize here is that what often passes for independence is in reality anticompliance. Both involve public disagreement between the source and the target, but unless we know whether the public disagreement is based on private disagreement we cannot tell whether the person is really independent or is merely trying to assert independence. She who refuses to admit publicly that she agrees with the person trying to influence her is, in some ways, just as much a captive of social forces as the person who inevitably conforms. Refusing to wear conventional clothes makes one as much a prisoner of convention, albeit in a backwards way, as always wanting to wear the latest fashions. So independence is not always the opposite of conformity, and freedom is not a necessary outcome of not conforming. To be *free from* social and physical constraints is not the same thing as to be *free to* do what is best according to self-interest (Fromm, 1941). Freedom is, in part, a state of mind and, as such, is not totally incompatible with external constraint. For example, in his study of the Bruderhof religious community, Zablocki (1973) shows that although the community imposes severe restraints on many aspects of behavior, the members feel free and act according to this felt freedom.

I hasten to return to a point made at the beginning of this chapter. Conformity is not only sometimes necessary; it is also desirable. Most people do not have the time to make an independent judgment about every possible action. Conformity in some areas frees people to be thoughtful and creative in others. Furthermore, no society or group can exist long without some compliance and a good deal of internalization of common values and goals. In

"All right, Bostock! Shape up or ship out!"

Drawing by Lorenz © 1978 by The New Yorker Magazine, Inc.

fact, those utopian societies and intentional communities that have been most successful have generally placed high demands on their members for conformity (Kanter, 1972). Full participation in any society or community requires some conformity to the desires of others and to the group norms.

SUMMARY

Most of us are asked or commanded to meet the demands of others many times a day. When we agree to do what others demand, we are conforming. We do so sometimes because we feel that others know more or can better assess reality; at other times, conformity reflects our desires to have others like us and our fears that they will reject us otherwise. Often we are subjected to conformity demands from minorities as well as majorities in groups, and the minority influence is sometimes all out of proportion to its numbers. Lewin and his student Festinger emphasized that intact groups, especially cohesive ones, would be likely to exert strong conformity pressure.

Just because people go along with social demands in public does not mean that they also agree privately. Public change without private acceptance is usually called compliance. Milgram's obedience studies are a good example of compliance, because even though subjects were quite anxious about hurting another person, they did so. The Milgram study used authority pressure, but in everyday life a number of variables affect compliance. In the foot-in-the-door strategy, people who first comply with a small request are more likely to comply with a larger request later; in the door-in-the-face strategy, those who resist a large initial request are more likely to comply with a smaller one later. We also comply because of reciprocity norms.

In recent years there has been considerable emphasis on brainwashing. However, brainwashing is not a unique or powerful form of thought control. In many cases, so-called brainwashing is merely compliance, but even when conversion is involved, informational and normative factors can explain the changes.

CONFLICT BETWEEN IMPULSE AND INHIBITION

SOCIAL DETERMINANTS OF IMPULSE AND INHIBITION

Thus far we have focused on the kinds of social influence that take place in organized groups—situations in which at least two people interact and have some interdependencies, even if only briefly. However, social scientists have long been interested in situations where the behavior of people is affected by crowds and other collectives that are not really groups. Sometimes this area of study is called *mass* or *collective behavior* to distinguish it from behavior in more defined groups. However, the more modern tradition (Turner & Killian, 1972) has been to stress similarities of social influence in groups and collections of people such as crowds. Still, the study of people in large collectives and groups highlights some features of social influence that are worthy of special attention.

Much of what happens in crowds and other large collectives can be explained in terms of enhancement of impulses or reduction of restraints against expression of these impulses. We want to do something, and this wanting can, for the sake of our discussion, be termed an *impulse*. There are also inhibitions against performing many, perhaps most, behaviors. Even trivial impulses such as getting up to get a snack may be inhibited by thoughts of diets or the inconvenience of going to the nearest refrigerator or snack machine. Of course, inhibitions against performing other behaviors, such as hitting a bore or breaking a window, may be more profound and culturally conditioned. If impulses are stronger than inhibitions, the behavior will be performed; if inhibitions are stronger, it will not be. A simple equation makes this clearer:

$$\text{Behavior} = (\text{Strength of Impulse}) \\ - (\text{Strength of Inhibitions})$$

In a situation where inhibitions are stronger than impulses, the group may release the inhibited behavior of its members either by increasing the impulse or by diminishing the inhibitions. For example, suppose that your desire to clobber a particularly disagreeable classmate has a value of 5 (on some arbitrary scale) but that inhibitions stemming from guilt and fear of disapproval or reprisal have a value of 8. In this case, because your inhibitions are stronger than your impulses, you won't hit your classmate. On the other hand, if he makes a particularly obnoxious remark and others in the class point out that this comment was directed at you and is quite insulting, you may find your impulse to hit him shooting up to 9 or 10, resulting in hostile behavior on your part. On the other hand, you might have your inhibitions reduced if others urge you to take him on and assure you that they will not allow him to hit you back.

There are many different types of inhibitions. For example, often a person simply lacks the ability to perform certain activities; this form of restraint is not likely to be lowered by social interaction. There are also external restraints that result from concern with approval–disapproval, legal sanctions, promotions, pay raises, and the like. Finally, there are more internalized inhibitions that result from guilt and other self-evaluations. Social psychologists generally have concentrated on how others affect external constraints, but others may also affect internal restraints. In the remainder of this section, we will consider various models of impulse facilitation and restraint reduction.

Social Facilitation Modern *experimental* social psychology can be said to have begun with the observation that two or more people performing the same behavior often facilitate each other's behavior. The work of Floyd Allport (1924) made this phenomenon a central part of early experimental social psychology. In a series of experiments, Allport showed that people perform a number of rather simple tasks, such as addition, better in groups, but that the effect did not seem to exist for more complicated intellectual tasks, such as arguing against the thesis of articles. Nonetheless, Allport felt that he had found a generalizable phenomenon, which he called *social facilitation.* Moreover, facilitation effects are not due simply to group interaction, because the same sorts of results occur when people perform tasks in the presence of people who merely observe them.

If the mere presence of other people facilitates certain types of performance, the question becomes, what kinds of performance? Zajonc (1965) has proposed a simple but elegant hypothesis: the presence of others acts to increase a person's general arousal, and such arousal facilitates dominant responses and inhibits nondominant responses. Although it is not always easy to specify the dominant and nondominant responses in any given situation, in general, according to Zajonc, one would expect well-learned responses to be dominant and therefore subject to social facilitation. For example, for the simple task of adding 10 and 18, the dominant response for most of us is 28. On the other hand, suppose that a teacher is trying to get a student to say "It was I" rather than his more customary "It was me." During the learning phase, the incorrect expression will be dominant over the correct, and the presence of other people will facilitate the incorrect rather than the correct (but nondominant) response. In learning situations, because the correct or desired response is not yet dominant, one would expect the arousal created by the presence of others to interfere with learning. However, having others present should aid the performance of well-learned responses. Athletes who are well practiced in, say, free-throw shooting might be expected to perform best before a crowd, whereas those whose dominant behaviors promote missing rather than hitting free throws might perform better in a secluded practice than in a crowded game.

Zajonc and others have provided some direct tests of this social facilitation model. Zajonc and Nieuwenhuyse (1964) presented subjects with verbal stimuli, supposedly Turkish words but in reality nonsense words. Some of the words were presented several times, thus becoming dominant over words presented less often. Then the experimenters showed these words to the subjects by means of a tachistoscope, a device for presenting stimuli at brief durations, so brief that they cannot be recognized confidently. The subjects were asked to report which word they had seen. The catch was that on certain trials, no word was presented, but the subjects did not know this.

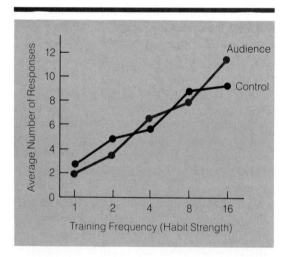

FIGURE 11.4   Number of Responses of Different Frequency Classes Emitted During Pseudorecognition Trials for Control Subjects and Those in the Presence of an Audience. Note that as training frequency (dominance) becomes greater, there are more responses for those subjects performing in an audience relative to those in the control condition.

Zajonc and Sales, 1966.

On these trials, subjects tended to report the words they had seen most often before (the dominant response, and they were much more likely to do this if they were highly aroused. Thus, dominant responses seem to be facilitated by arousal. The arousal in this experiment was not social in nature, so the study provides confirmation for only one link in the hypothesis. The other link was provided by Zajonc and Sales (1966). They used essentially the same task, but this time subjects made their responses to the blank screen with an audience either present or absent. As the model predicts, subjects gave the well-learned dominant responses more often in the presence of others—presumably an arousal condition—than when alone (see Figure 11.4).

Zajonc's hypothesis seems to suggest that there is something like a strong innate predisposition to respond to the presence of others by being aroused. However, other psychologists have been less eager to accept explanations that are based on innate tendencies. For example, Cottrell (1968) suggested that people are aroused by the presence of others if and only if they feel they are being evaluated.

To check this possibility, Cottrell, Wack, Sekerak, and Rittle (1968) repeated the "Turkish" word study and replicated the basic finding that subjects with an audience report more of the dominant and fewer of the nondominant words than subjects doing the task alone. They also ran a condition that was designed to provide an audience but that minimized evaluative concerns; in this condition, the audience was present but blindfolded. Because the audience could not see what was going on, they presumably would not be evaluating the subjects. Subjects in this condition provided responses similar to those of the alone subjects (see Figure 11.5). Thus, the social facilitation effect seems to disappear with the lowering of evaluation concerns.

Although an evaluative audience is not absolutely necessary to get the social facilitation effect (Bond & Titus, 1983), there are now several demonstrations showing that social fa-

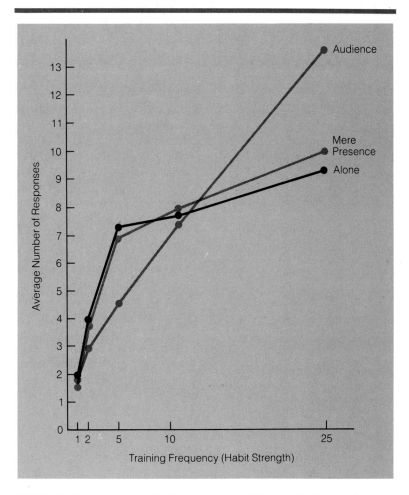

FIGURE   11.5   Number of Responses of Different Training Frequency Classes Emitted on the Pseudorecognition Trials. Note that as the responses become more dominant, they are more likely to be given by subjects who are in the presence of an evaluative audience relative to those with the blindfolded audience or no audience.

Cottrell, 1968.

cilitation is stronger with an evaluative than with a nonevaluative audience (Paulus & Murdock, 1971; Struke, Miles, & Finch, 1981). Bond (1982) argues that audiences, especially evaluative ones, increase desires to present oneself favorably. On simple tasks a favorable impression can be made by working rapidly, but for more complex tasks errors are likely and the resulting embarrassment may inhibit

performance. Another possibility is that an audience increases self-awareness (see Chapter 5), which ought to result in increased attempts to perform well, again benefiting performance on simple tasks but interfering with behavior on more complex tasks.

There has been considerable debate about the correct explanation for social facilitation effects, but the basic phenomenon is not in

Performance can be enhanced when there is an evaluative audience.

dispute (Geen, 1981; Markus, 1981; Sanders, 1981). The presence of others tends to increase dominant and inhibit nondominant responses. In terms of our concerns in this chapter, the presence of others may facilitate strong (dominant) impulses. So crowds may increase the desires of people to do certain things. As we will see, others also can change our dominant responses.

Behavior Contagion   It has long been recognized that behaviors, like diseases, are contagious in that they can spread through a group. You can observe this in almost any crowd. For example, the main performers at a rock concert seem duty-bound to show up late. If one or two people begin a rhythmic clapping, they will soon be joined by the entire audience. At classical concerts, if one or two people stand up and cheer at the end of an outstanding performance, others will stand and clap as well. And, as all musicians have learned, audience coughing is also contagious. Pennebaker (1980) studied coughing contagion in a classroom setting. As you might expect, people cough more during boring parts of lectures, but Pennebaker also found that if one person coughs the coughing is likely to catch on among others in the room.

Larger and denser crowds facilitate contagion. Freedman, Birsky, and Cavoukian (1960) had a confederate applaud at the conclusion of a movie in a science museum. Not only was the confederate imitated more with larger crowds, but the crowd density also increased clapping contagion. In another demonstration Freedman and Perlick (1979) found that people in dense crowds were more likely to imitate the laughter of a confederate during an amusing tape. Newton and Mann (1980) examined religious commitment during crusades. Larger crowds not only had more people who were willing to make a decision for Christ, but the percentage of the crowd who made such a decision also increased with crowd size. Incidentally, religious crusaders have been known to plant "deciders" in the crowd to promote decisions by others (Cialdini, 1985).

Other kinds of contagion effects on a larger scale have also been reported. Race riots, sit-ins, and student protests seemed to spread from city to city during the 1960s, culminating during the spring of 1970 when, within a period of a few days, campuses all over the country called off classes during protests of the invasion of Cambodia. Airplane hijackings also seem to show contagion effects (Bandura, 1973). Phillips (1974; Bollen & Phillips, 1982) has also demonstrated that highly publicized suicides increase suicide rates, a modern demonstration of the Werther phenomenon noted at the beginning of the chapter. Box 11.1 contains a full discussion of this effect.

It is not clear how the contagion effect works. Does hearing another person cough raise one's desire to cough, lower one's restraints on coughing, or both? If laughter is contagious, do people laugh more because hearing another laugh makes them feel more amused, or makes them lower their potential embarrassment at laughing, or both? Does a potential hijacker suddenly feel more like taking over a plane when he reads about another hijacking? Or does he come to feel it is less wrong or that he is less likely to get caught?

BOX 11.1

THE WERTHER EFFECT

At the beginning of the chapter, we noted that the publication of Goethe's *The Sorrows of the Young Werther,* in which young Werther killed himself in an outburst of romantic zeal, stimulated the suicides of young men throughout Europe. In recent years, sociologist David Phillips (1986) has investigated whether there are modern counterparts of the **Werther effect.** The main purpose in presenting that research here is to show how social scientists can use archival data to investigate phenomena that cannot be easily studied in the laboratory or even through experimental methods in the field.

Phillips (1974) studied the problem in the following way. First, he found the date of every suicide mentioned on the front page of the *New York Times* from 1947 to 1968. He did not, incidentally, assume that everyone reads the *Times,* but it is reasonable to suppose that suicides on the front page of that major newspaper would be well publicized in other papers as well. Phillips then examined the number of reported suicides nationally in the month after the story appeared. This number was compared with the number of suicides in the same period the year before and the year after the suicide. For example, Marilyn Monroe killed herself August 6, 1962, and there were 1,838 suicides in the month of August that year. This can be compared with an average of 1,641 suicides during August 1961 and August 1963, so it would seem that there were almost 200 more suicides than expected the month after Monroe's death. In general, suicides did go up the month after the suicides of famous people. Suicides are also higher the month after a suicide than

the month before the suicide (see Figure B.11.1). In addition, the magnitude of the Werther effect was greater when the suicides got more publicity and in areas where the publicity was greatest. Subsequent research by Bollen and Phillips (1982) has shown that suicides reported on national television newscasts can also have similar effects.

Phillips argues that the Werther effect exists because the publicized suicide causes people to commit suicide, contrary to other ways the data can be interpreted. For example, many deaths have ambiguous causes, and medical authorities usually like to classify deaths as accidental rather than as suicides whenever possible to spare the feelings of family members. So maybe a front-page suicide does not change the manner of death itself but merely changes the reporting patterns of coroners, leading them to report deaths as suicides rather than as accidents. If this were true, and if the number of deaths remains about the same, the increase in suicides should be accompanied by a decrease in deaths classified as accidental. But this does not occur. Or maybe the publicized suicide pushes certain people over the edge who were about to commit suicide anyway. If that were the case, one might expect to find that the suicide rate would peak immediately after the publicity but then would decline sharply because the pool of available suicide victims has been momentarily depleted. Again, no such effect occurs. A third alternative is that some environmental condition such as a drop in the stock market causes the suicide of both the public figure and the other suicides as well. However, this cannot account for the fact that

BOX CONTINUED

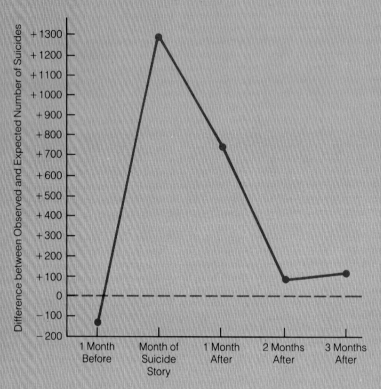

FIGURE B.11.1   Fluctuation in the Number of Suicides Before, During, and After the Month of the Suicide Story.

From Phillips, 1974.

the publicized suicide always comes before the wave of other suicides.

In his later research, Phillips (1977, 1979) has examined the number of fatal car accidents after suicides. This may seem strange, but most experts feel that many car accidents are really thinly disguised suicide attempts. Using a California sample, Phillips showed that fatal car accidents peaked about 3 days after a publicized suicide, with

Careful and controlled studies of imitation suggest that watching others may well both stimulate impulses and reduce inhibitions. For example, observation of helping tends to increase helping, presumably by making the norm of helping more salient (Bryan & Test, 1967; Rosenhan & White, 1967). There is also evidence that observation can reduce restraints. A number of studies have shown that watching others commit mildly inhibited behavior, such as jaywalking (Lefkowitz, Blake, & Mouton, 1955), or more strongly inhibited behavior, such as aggression (Bandura, Ross, & Ross, 1963a; Wheeler & Caggiula, 1966),

31% more fatal accidents than at carefully selected comparable periods. These comparable periods were matched with the period of the suicide in month, day of the week, and whether there was a holiday during the period, because these variables all affect accident rates. In addition, the dramatic increases were found more for single-car crashes than for multiple-car accidents. Presumably people who want to kill themselves in car accidents have no special desire to kill others as well, and might even try to avoid doing so. Another provocative finding was that the victims of accidents just after suicides died more quickly than those who died of accidents in comparison periods. One might suggest that, if the accident victims wanted to die, they might create more serious accidents, although, of course, there is no way to prove this.

While Phillips has focused his attention on suicides, one might expect murders also to be affected by publicity. Most studies that have examined the effects of well-publicized murders on murder rates have found little effect (Berkowitz & Macauley, 1971), but this may be because murder is front-page news almost everyday. It is hard to separate out the effects of any one murder. However, Phillips examined a violent event that would stand out more: heavyweight championship prize fights. Murder rates increased after such events (Phillips, 1983). In addition, after fights in which black fighters lose, murders of blacks but not whites increase, and when white fighters lose, white but not black murders increase. Prize fights show violence as exciting and as being rewarded, but what about cases where violence is shown as being punished? Phillips and Hensley (1984) showed that murder rates tend to decrease somewhat after well-publicized executions of murders. However, this does not make the death penalty a unique deterrent to murder: Phillips and Hensley found that well-publicized life sentences for murder decreased murder rates almost as much as did executions.

It is not easy to do this kind of research well. One is limited greatly by available data. For example, it is hard to study the effects of television on behavior because television stations do not keep careful logs of what news items are broadcast. Even collecting data on motor-vehicle deaths and on suicides requires a fair amount of diligence. One has to pick comparison periods with care to make sure they are as comparable as possible to the periods with the well-publicized events. Finally, the social scientist must have a clear sense of several alternative explanations so that the data can be analyzed or new data collected to rule them out if possible.

without punishment, increases the likelihood of a person's performing that behavior.

Why should models increase impulses and reduce inhibitions? The answers are not hard to find if we review what we already know about modeling from Chapters 1 and 9. In the first place, when we see someone else doing something, we are likely to get some information about the consequences of behavior. A jaywalker who crosses the street without being stopped by a police officer or without incurring disapproval from other pedestrians demonstrates that there are no negative consequences of jaywalking. Conversely, if one learns that the consequences of behavior are negative, then inhibitions are likely to be at least momentarily increased. Impulses may also be affected by the behavior of a model. For example, if I observe someone jaywalking, I may suddenly realize how much of a hurry I am in and how important it is to get to the other side of the street quickly. So, the behavior of others affects how we calculate the costs and rewards of a particular behavior; whether impulses and inhibitions are increased or decreased depends, of course, on what the model does and what consequences the model incurs.

There is another important effect of watching others. We often look to others for a definition of the situation, for a social reality. Normally I may think that jaywalking is vaguely naughty, but when I observe another person—or several other persons—committing this act with impunity, I may come to feel that it is not such a bad thing to do after all. The operation of these social reality factors in indirect social influence is very important and helps to explain some seemingly irrational acts.

Modern students of mass behavior have emphasized that crowds tend to form their own norms and definitions of what is right and proper; in other words, these norms tend to emerge during crowd behavior (Turner & Killian, 1972). *Emergent norm theory* suggests that crowds can actually affect the balance of impulses and restraints by making some actions seem proper and others improper. Thus, groups may determine, in part, what our dominant responses in a situation are as well as facilitating the dominant responses.

For example, consider the mass suicide at Jonestown. How could so many people kill themselves just because some highly charismatic (and perhaps mentally ill) leader says they should? One explanation is in terms of a social reality. The people at Jonestown constituted a religious community and, as such, believed that Jones was divinely inspired. Furthermore, Jones emphasized obedience and the possibility of suicide as part of his teachings. Apparently, there were dry runs of the mass suicide with unpoisoned drinks. Thus, the social reality both reduced normal inhibitions against killing oneself and also made this act seem more sacred and desirable, making it a more dominant response.

Jonestown should be no great surprise to any student of religion and cultural beliefs. The history of the human species provides many similar examples. Religious wars and political conflicts have never seemed to lack for recruits who are willing to give up their lives for God, country, and cherished beliefs. Perhaps even more vividly, the history of human sacrifice suggests additional examples (Davies, 1981). Human sacrifice has been quite common in most areas of the world until comparatively recently. The Hebrews, ancient Greeks, Romans, Indian Hindus, Chinese, and Japanese, as well as many other cultures, all used sacrifice as a religious ritual. The most impressive examples come from Aztec culture where there were frequent mass murders (by cutting out the heart) for ritual reasons. At the dedication of the Great Temple in 1487, it has been suggested that 200,000 people were killed in a period of 4 days of nonstop slaughter. While this is probably an overestimate, it is still quite clear that many thousands were killed.

Perhaps the most striking aspect of many ritual sacrifices is the apparent willingness of many of the victims to die. Of course, the victims often were promised a wonderful afterlife and were provided with every possible favor for days or even years before their final participation. In some cases of wife sacrifice at the burial of the husband, death was perhaps preferable to the conditions of remaining alive as a widow. Still, one has to be impressed with the abilities of sacrificial victims to make the best of their situations and to play out their parts for the greater glory of their gods and cultures. In this context, the events at Jonestown simply provide one more example of how social reality can affect both impulses and inhibitions.

Deindividuation   Perhaps the most popular explanation for reduction of restraints might go something like this: when a person is in a crowd, particularly among others he does not know well, he will feel a certain sense of anonymity, the sense that he is only part of the crowd. In effect, no one cares what he does. Thus, under these circumstances people may well feel a release from prior restraints, especially those based on fear of social disapproval. Something like this notion was advanced by most of the classic crowd-theorists, who felt that being in a crowd provided the proper anonymity for release from restraints. Similarly, early theorists of urban life often commented that crimes and other forms of deviance may be more common in large cities because people feel anonymous and, therefore, no one will criticize or punish them for their behavior (Simmel, 1950). This remains part of the appeal of cities such as New York and San Francisco; you can give free rein to your individuality and not worry what people think.

The importance of anonymity has sparked an extensive research literature. In an initial experiment by Festinger, Pepitone, and Newcomb (1952), the researchers were interested in whether feelings of anonymity (or what they called *deindividuation*) would affect behavior. They showed that lack of identifiability was correlated with a willingness to criticize parents, which was a more negative behavior in 1952 than it is now. In a better study, Zimbardo (1970) found that deindividuated subjects, who were dressed in lab coats, wore hoods, and were not identified by name, shocked another person more than did individuated subjects, who were dressed normally and identified by name.

In addition to anonymity, other factors can increase feelings of deindividuation: lack of concern for the group's behavior or reputation, diffusion of responsibility ("I'm not re-sponsible—they are"), high arousal, and altered states of consciousness through drugs or rituals can also contribute to deindividuation. A person in a deindividuated state loses self-awareness and consequently fails to regulate his or her behavior by considering norms, long-term plans, or self-standards. The result is behavior that is impulsive, unregulated, non-normative, and often regressive or childlike.

In an attempt to get at the underlying psychology of deindividuation more carefully, Diener (1980) has argued that the effects of deindividuation are mediated by focus of attention. In particular, Diener relies on the theory of self-awareness (see Chapter 5), which suggests that people can attend either to the outside world, where the self is a subject (subjective self-awareness), or to the self (objective self-awareness, because the self is an object). In a state of objective self-awareness, the person will be more conscious of his or her standards and will be motivated to try to meet them. When that person focuses on the outside world, however, there will be more concern with the demands of that reality.

When a person is deindividuated by being anonymous or dressed like other people, his or her attention may be directed away from self to the group. The result is that the person has less concern with meeting self-standards and more with doing what the group thinks is good. One experiment showed that deindividuation manipulations did increase a constellation of behaviors and feelings that included a

Phillip Zimbardo

lack of self-consciousness, lack of conscious planning, lessened concern with what others would say, and feelings of group unity (Diener, 1979). Deindividuated subjects were also more likely to choose to work on "juvenile" tasks such as playing in mud and painting with one's nose than were subjects who were in a state of objective self-awareness.

Other research has shown that increasing group size lowered self-consciousness, while increasing the number of observers raised self-consciousness (Diener, Lusk, DeFour, & Flax, 1980). A similar finding has been reported by Jackson and Latané (1981). They asked performers at a college talent show how nervous they were and found that people felt more nervous before a large than a small audience, but that they were less nervous as the number of performers in their group increased. This suggests that concern with audience approval decreases as the person is less identifiable by virtue of being in a larger group.

We have discussed various reasons why impulses might be increased and restraints against certain behaviors might be lowered in social situations. Certain high-arousal situations facilitate dominant responses and inhibit nondominant responses. Furthermore, observation of other people can change our conceptions of what is right and wrong and alter what consequences we expect for our behaviors. In addition, being a part of a larger crowd may promote feelings of deindividuation, in which the person has lessened internal controls over behavior. For the remainder of this chapter we will explore how these various reasons can be used to explain collective or mass behavior.

MASS BEHAVIOR

Many of the earliest speculations about social psychological matters were about the psychology of crowds and mobs. It seemed self-evident to many observers that there were striking transformations in the behavior of people when they become a part of a crowd. Otherwise law-abiding and moral people may loot, pillage, and generally behave in irrational and immoral ways. Furthermore, crowd members were seen as subject to extreme social influence in that they lost their critical faculties and followed the leader like so many sheep. The behavior of people in crowds was thought to be highly homogeneous.

Most modern students of crowd behavior disagree with that description and explanation of crowd behavior. They stress that crowd behavior is not as homogeneous as it may seem at first glance. For example, in a riot some people may loot, others may throw rocks at the police, some may cheer the others on, while the majority simply stand and watch. Furthermore, crowd behavior is irrational only by some criteria. During a riot, what is irrational about breaking into a store and stealing a color TV? It may be illegal and immoral, but that hardly makes it irrational. In fact, such behavior may be highly rational in the sense that the person decides to steal the TV only after weighing the possible costs of being caught against the rewards of having the TV. Lynch mobs may be performing repugnant acts, but they are also acting rationally, given their goals. Even in panics, say, during a fire, it is not necessarily irrational to run for an exit if holding back increases the possibility that you will be caught by the fire.

Generally, then, most modern psychologists and sociologists have emphasized that members of crowds often act in nonidentical ways and that their behaviors are rational after their own fashion (Berk, 1974; Smelser, 1963; Turner & Killian, 1972). So there is no need to postulate a general crowd psychology; the mechanisms of social influence we have been considering can be used to account for what happens in crowds as well as more organized groups.

Panics   Panics occur when people are afraid and attempt to flee from a threatening situation. When there are many people in that situation and limited means of escape, people may die from being trampled or suffocated in the crush at the exits.

One explanation for panics stresses an inner core of irrationality to human behavior that is unleashed by the terror in the situation. However, psychologists have been more inclined to emphasize panic behavior as a series of rational choices. If you are in a theater and see a fire on stage, the most immediately self-beneficial action would be to flee. In some sense that rationality is not changed by the fact that thousands of other people in the theater may have the same idea as you. If you can be the first out the door, then you have saved your life. Unfortunately, if everyone reasons this way, there will be a panic and some will die (Brown, 1965). Furthermore, in the deindividuated conditions of a panic, there will probably be lessened concerns for the outcomes of others.

Panic situations can be analyzed in terms of costs and rewards of various behaviors, but such an analysis ignores the intense emotions people feel in such situations and does not take confusion and unclarity into account. It is likely that such factors interfere with rational calculation of potential outcomes.

Other models of panic behavior have emphasized the importance of unclarity (Schultz, 1964). In panics, people are usually confused about how dangerous the situation is and what they should do. This confusion can be alleviated through the discovery that the danger is unreal or unimportant. But most of the time there is no clear source of such information and the definition of the situation must be gained from other sources, the most obvious being the behavior of other people. If everyone sat calmly, then even the most nervous person would conclude that the situation must not be all that threatening. However, the more likely alternative is that one or more people will give in to their impulses to run. Such behavior is likely to have a dramatic effect on the others. If that person way down in front is running, then the situation really must be dangerous.

The fleeing person also contributes to the panic by providing information about what seems to be the appropriate response to the danger. So the behavior of others will both magnify the danger and define running as the response of choice.

There is a closely related way of looking at panics. As we have seen, arousal facilitates a dominant response and interferes with non-dominant ones. Fear is certainly a form of arousal and fleeing is ordinarily the dominant response. So people typically run when they are afraid. Indeed, such running responses can become so dominant that they overwhelm normal inhibitions against such impulsive behavior.

Lynchings   Whereas panics show competition at its most extreme, lynchings show that cooperation is often involved in mass behavior. Like panics, lynchings display people at their seemingly most uncivilized and inhumane. For example, in 1930 James Irwin, a black man, was lynched for allegedly raping and killing a white girl.

> Irwin was tied to a tree with chains. . . . Approximately a thousand people were present, including some women and children on the edge of the crowd. Members of the mob cut off his fingers and toes joint by joint; mob leaders carried them off as souvenirs. Next his teeth were pulled out with wire pliers. . . . Irwin's mangled, but living body, was hung on a tree by the arms. Logs and underbrush [were] piled beneath. Gasoline was poured on. A match was struck. As the flames engulfed the body, it was pierced by bullets. (Raper, 1933, pp. 143–44).

No one was indicted by a grand jury for this murder.

Between 1890 and 1930 there were almost 4,000 lynchings in the United States, and about 80% were directed towards blacks (Raper, 1933). Typically, there was an "incident"; a black was thought to have harmed, assaulted, or insulted a white. In such a situation, we might suppose that the increased anger plus the arousal generated by others might facilitate the dominant aggressive response to such conditions. Just as in a panic situation, in which the group helps to define the situation as threatening and in which flight is an appropriate response, in the lynch mob the group also has a definitional role. The "incident" becomes something larger than one person's transgression; it comes to symbolize what might be expected more generally if punishment in this case is not swift and sure.

So in lynch mobs the group defines a situation as threatening and also defines the appropriate responses. However, the group must do more than define the situation and the appropriate response to it; it must also overcome members' inhibitions against the prescribed behavior. The overcoming of internal inhibitions is accomplished by defining the situation as extraordinary enough to warrant killing. Most civilizations and cultures recognize a class of such situations; otherwise, we would not have war and capital punishment. Lynching is, of course, a form of capital punishment.

It is also characteristic for mobs to define the lynching victim as somehow less than human. It is hard to kill another human. In war, the enemy is often perceived as so different as to be subhuman; similarly, the victims of capital punishment are often regarded as not particularly well socialized to middle-class values. Middle-class juries and judges may find it relatively easier to sentence such "subhumans" to death. Similarly, defining the lynch victim as subhuman is an important, perhaps an essential, part of the lynching process. Not atypically, the black victims of lynchings were described as brutes or animals.

Thus, it can be argued that social definition can overcome internal inhibitions toward killing, but what of the external constraints? It is one thing to assume that a person has a right, even an obligation, to kill another person; it is quite another to be willing to face the law for one's acts. In the popular mind, the sheriff always helps the lynchers, and in many cases he did, either by taking improper precautions or by not trying to stop the mob. Sometimes the sheriff or mayor favored the lynchings actively, and in one case a mayor was actually indicted for lynching (see Raper, 1933). After one lynching, a judge "expressed satisfaction that there had been no mutilations, and suggested that this indicated the 'orderly' way in which the lynching was effected and the 'high class' of people who did it" (Raper, 1933, p. 305). Often, newspapers were only blandly critical or actually supported the lynchings, ministers of churches refused to criticize, and juries did not indict or convict. In many cases, crowds watched and encouraged the mob members during the lynchings. Under these circumstances, the lynchers may feel, with considerable justification, that their actions are approved. Furthermore, the lynch-mob members may make some effort to conceal their identities, thus fostering deindividuation processes.

Race Riots   Most race riots in this country have involved mobs of whites attacking blacks. The riots of the mid-1960s differed from earlier riots in that the majority of the rioters were black, the primary target of the riots was property and not lives, and the behavior of the rioters was not strongly coordinated (Janowitz, 1969).

There are a number of conditions that seem to be necessary for a race riot to occur. First, there has to be a long-standing suppressed impulse of hostility. Second, there must be a precipitating incident. Third, there must be a translation of the impulse into behavior. Fourth, there must be a relaxation of usual inhibitions against violent behavior. If only the first condition was needed, there would undoubtedly be more riots. Indeed, overt racial animosity, particularly that of whites against blacks, has been a frequent theme in nineteenth- and twentieth-century American history. For their part, blacks have had long-standing grievances against the white community, grievances that have for the most part been ignored. Under such circumstances, it is likely that many blacks felt strong animosity toward whites.

The second condition is a precipitating incident. This incident need not be major. For example, the East St. Louis riots of 1917 began with the report that a black thief had killed a white store owner. The Chicago riot of 1919 began with the drowning of a black teenager and the refusal of the police to arrest the white man the blacks thought had committed the act. In Newark in 1965, a riot started when a crowd protested the injury of a black cab driver while being arrested. The Watts riots began with the arrest of a black teenager and the Detroit riots in 1967 with the arrest of several blacks at an after-hours bar.

The translation of the hatred and threat into overt behavior, the third necessary condition, involves an increase in antinormative feelings—the motives to kill and to destroy property. It is reasonable to believe that the precipitating incident serves a definitional function. It helps to focus resentments on an obvious example of unfair treatment (at least as perceived by the participants). Abstract, day-to-day, diffuse unfairness may be easier to tolerate than a vivid, concrete case (see Chapter 3). In short, the precipitating incident seems to energize people and push their anger beyond customary limits. Also, the anger and presence of others may facilitate these momentarily dominant responses.

This leads to the fourth condition, the relaxation of inhibitions against violent behavior. Normally, moral inhibitions restrain people from killing others or destroying things, and these inhibitions must be overcome before a riot can begin. In a riot situation, there may be considerable confusion, and the definition that does exist is clouded over with high emotional arousal. In this condition of ambiguity, the individual may well look to the actions and behaviors of others for clarity, because the behavior of models often helps define one's own emotional states. At this point in a poten-

Riots, such as this one in Watts, often mainly involve looting.

tial riot situation, there is often a general milling around as people wander about and discuss the situation. Sometimes a few people begin to act in a certain way, thereby helping to define the emotional state of the other people in the crowd. At the cognitive level, their behavior makes certain poles of attitudes highly salient and "more real." At other times, the process may be more extended, involving rumors circulating throughout a large community. An arrest may turn into rumors that someone has been beaten or killed by the police. In this case the collective reality that emerges is likely to be emotionally charged; the "incident" becomes a kind of collective symbol around which hatred can crystallize. People feel more angry, and whatever impulses they may have toward aggressive behavior are increased.

At the same time, the group helps to reduce inhibitions against nonnormative behavior. In this case, if enough people riot, for example, and if this activity seems to have the sanction of the group—observers as well as looters— looting will become an approved thing to do. Rioting will be normative. Finally, another powerful factor reducing inhibitions is anonymity or deindividuation; in a large crowd of strangers, people do not much fear arrest or formal sanction.

SUMMARY

Behavior in any situation can be considered a result of both desires to perform certain behaviors and inhibitions against such performance. Thus, certain behaviors may occur because the desires are high or because inhibitions are low. Other people may affect behavior either by increasing desires, by reducing inhibitions, or both.

There are many scenerios for how various inhibition and facilitation factors might combine, but for the sake of summary we may consider the following possibility. In panics, lynchings, and race riots, a situation is created in which people have a strong desire to commit behaviors that are normally controlled by effective inhibitions. The behavior of other people may act to define otherwise inhibited behaviors as appropriate, or may suggest that usual sanctions against such behaviors will not be applied. Furthermore, when people are made to feel somewhat anonymous in a group, a condition called deindividuation, they will have lessened concern for the effects of their behavior on others and will be more concerned with their own immediate outcomes. Deindividuation may also reduce concern with external punishment, because anonymity reduces the chances that one will get caught. So other people may effectively raise desires to run, kill, or loot while also lowering inhibitions against such behaviors. When the formerly nondominant behavior becomes dominant, the presence of other people may act to facilitate it, that is, to make the behavior more likely, more vigorous, or quicker.

CHAPTER SUMMARY

- Conformity refers to changing behavior to meet the expectations of others. There are two major reasons for conformity: we con-

form either because we think others have better information or because we are trying to gain approval and avoid ridicule.

- In most groups there are majority and minority points of view. Usually the majority view is more influential, but Moscovici argues that majorities typically get superficial change whereas minorities get deeper change and may even have greater effects on the behavior and thoughts of group members. Social impact theory, on the other hand, suggests that majority and minority influences operate according to the same principles. We are affected by others in proportion to their strength, immediacy, and number.

- Lewin argued that one reason it is so hard to change people is that their attitudes and values are anchored in groups. He showed that people could be changed if their groups changed and if induced social forces became own forces. Festinger further suggested that cohesive groups would use social pressures to encourage conformity and that these social pressures would be expressed as increased levels of communication to deviants and ultimately as rejection if deviants continued to deviate.

- Meeting the expectations of others publicly without corresponding private change is called compliance. The Milgram studies on obedience show that under certain circumstances people will comply with even extreme requests by authorities. Another variable that affects compliance is previous compliance pressure. If the person has previously complied with a small request, compliance with a subsequent larger request will be more likely. On the other hand, if the person has previously refused to comply with a large request, he or she may be more likely to comply with a smaller request later.

- Another form of social influence occurs when other people alter the balance between the desires to perform certain behaviors and the inhibitions against performance. The others may make the behavior more probable by lowering inhibitions or by raising the impulse to perform it.

■ The mere presence of other people may facilitate dominant behaviors and inhibit nondominant ones. This may occur because of arousal mechanisms or because people are concerned about the evaluations of others.

■ Behaviors can be contagious. When we observe others performing some behavior, the tendency to perform the same behavior may be increased, especially if the others experience favorable consequences. Observing others may lower inhibitions by showing that consequences of performing the behavior are not bad or by giving evidence that the behavior is seen as good. Deindividuation may also reduce concern with external punishment because anonymity reduces the chances that one will get caught.

■ Panics occur when people try to escape from dangerous situations. In such cases, the presence of others may increase desires to run by defining the situation as dangerous, may facilitate the dominant behavior of running through arousal, or may suggest major costs for not fleeing.

■ In lynchings, the behavior of others may define the lynch victim as especially dangerous and help to define aggression as appropriate to the situation. The lynch mob also creates a situation of deindividuation and may suggest that there will be few negative consequences for the lynching.

■ In riots, there may be considerable deindividuation, which lowers inhibitions. In addition, others may make desires to perform destructive behaviors more dominant or normative, and arousal from the presence of others may help facilitate these dominant behaviors.

CHAPTER

12

INTERPERSONAL ATTRACTION

We all know about the great lovers of history: Romeo and Juliet, Tristan and Isolde, Dante and Beatrice, Robert and Elizabeth Barrett Browning. But we probably gain more insight into what love is by asking ordinary people. The following are answers given to me during informal interviews in which I asked people to tell me what they thought love was, based on their own experiences:

JG [a 20-year-old female]: It's a nice feeling I get when I'm with X. It's not just sexual—it's just all over my body.

KP [a middle-aged, retired man]: Basically, I look at it as having everything be comfortable. I know my family loves me when no one is mad at me and everyone is happy with the way things are going. Food on the table, kids staying out of trouble. For me love is just knowing that we like and respect one another.

DA [a woman in her early 30s]: It's got to be built on respect and on caring. With a man, at least for me, there's also got be some sexual chemistry, but I wouldn't say I loved him just because I got the hots for him.

RM [a 25-year-old male homosexual]: It's having someone to care for and to care about you.

AR [a woman who preferred not to give her age]: Well, I've been through lots of kinds of love. Been married three times and I have children and grandchildren [laughs a little]. And I always said I loved my parents—my mother is still living, and she isn't easy to love, let me tell you. What is love? [pause] Damned if I know [laughs]. Well, seriously, I guess I'd have to say that it comes from being involved with people. You can walk away from a friend if she does something you don't like, but you can't abandon your kids or parents or husband (although I got rid of two of them). I'm not very romantic, and I never get itchy feelings or anything when I think about loved ones. I guess I'd have to say that

Love relationships involve differing degrees of intimacy, passion, and commitment.

it's sort of like being involved enough with someone to want to do things for them.

MJ [a woman working on her MBA degree]: It's having someone do the dishes for you when you're tired [laughs]. Actually, there's some truth to that. Well, I've had my flings but to tell you the truth what I'm looking for right now is someone to talk to. I'd just like to have someone to share a glass of white wine with in the evening and talk over the day.

INTRODUCTION

Loving and liking are forms of interpersonal attraction. Such attraction is a common and universal affective response to others. Imagine, if you will, what it would be like to go through the entire day with no affective responses to others. You would be denied warm feelings of affection; you would not care to be around someone who gives you compliments or makes you happy. Of course, matters would not be entirely bleak; you would also not hate an enemy, be bored by an idiot, or feel jealous of a friend. Nevertheless most of us would find that a world without affective reactions—either positive or negative—would be cold, lifeless, and sterile.

Obviously, liking and being liked are extremely important to most people, and most of us have a strong bias to like other people (Sears, 1983). So the study of attraction needs no special justification. But social psychologists do have additional reasons for carefully studying this area. Chief among these is that liking and disliking mediate such other important reactions and behaviors as conformity, attitude change, aggression, and altruism. Is it not more likely that you would comply with the demands of a friend rather than an enemy? Would you not be more willing to help a favorite aunt than a crotchety neighbor?

Another reason for the study of interpersonal attraction is that affective reactions are important elements in the relationships we build with other people, in how groups are structured, and ultimately in how societies function. Ordinarily, we are more likely to form enduring relationships with those we like than with those we hate, and our feelings about the leaders of society and our fellow citizens affect how well society and its institutions function.

WHAT IS INTERPERSONAL ATTRACTION?

Attraction is easier to recognize than to define. Nevertheless, there is general agreement that it refers to a kind of attitude we have toward other people. As such, attraction has affective, cognitive, and behavioral components (see Chapter 7), with the affective part emphasized. *Attraction* has been formally defined as "an individual's tendency or predisposition to evaluate another person or symbol of the person in a positive (or negative) way" (Berscheid & Walster, 1978, pp. 3–4).

So attraction may refer to reactions as diverse as a father's love for his child, a son's love for his mother, the passion between two lovers, the intimacy of a long-married couple, the nostalgic feeling for a childhood friend, the liking for a present companion, or the thought that Candidate X would make a fine president. Attraction refers to all these states and many more. Do they have enough in common to march together under the same banner?

The answer is a qualified yes. There are any number of ways that the above examples differ from one another, and later in the chapter we will explore the relationship between liking and loving as two important affective responses. However, we should also remember that because all forms of interpersonal attraction are presumably based on an affective response, they are not completely different. In fact, several studies have found that various measures of interpersonal attraction are correlated. For example, Rubin (1970) discovered that, for a sample of dating couples, measures of liking and love were moderately related. Segal (1979) found generally high correlations among measures of liking, respect, and friendship choice for both basketball teams and groups of police officers. Such results certainly make sense, given that all attraction measures have in common a generalized affective response. Nevertheless, they are also different in important ways.

You should keep this in mind because most of the research discussed in this chapter deals with only one kind of attraction: liking, and usually liking for a stranger. Obviously, it is important to know what produces liking for strangers, and it seems likely that this form of

Although the exact feelings may differ, families and co-workers both show attraction.

attraction forms a basis for other, deeper forms; but still we must be wary of using this one measure to stand for all others.

Most researchers tend to conceptualize attraction as a kind of immediate, affective response, partially because most research has dealt with relatively superficial interpersonal relationships. However, in recent years there has been considerable interest in how relationships form, persist, and break up, and consequently, there has been more interest in what we might call deeper forms of attraction. It is not yet clear how one ought to conceptualize the relationship between liking and deeper forms of attraction, and in a later section of the chapter we discuss this issue in some detail. In Chapter 13 we discuss the nature of relationships, and there too we will have more to say about how attraction changes in the course of one person's relationship with another.

THEORIES OF ATTRACTION

For thousands of years, thinkers have speculated about the mysteries of liking and loving. Why do you like some people more than others? Why don't certain people like the same people you do? Why doesn't everyone like you? There are an enormous number of things that affect liking. Do they have anything in common? In other words, do we have a general theory that suggests why these variables affect attraction? Two major kinds of theories have been used by social psychologists, and both of these will be familiar to you from previous chapters. One is Heider's balance theory, and the other is reward theory, a version of reinforcement or, more generally, hedonistic theory.

Balance Theory Balance theory generally predicts that balanced situations should be better liked than those that are not balanced. As we discussed in Chapter 3, balance theory works with a triad of people and objects, each of which has a sentiment or unit relationship with each of the others. You should show a general preference for balanced situations, in which you and another person agree about something and like one another, or in which you and another disagree and dislike one another.

More generally, the theory clearly predicts that you will like a person if you discover that you have a similar relationship to some third object or person. So you should be inclined to like people who like or dislike the same sports teams, political candidates, and common acquaintances as you. This may also occur if you have a common bond (unit relationship) to some third object. For example, you are likely to take an instant liking to a fellow Texan or Hoosier that you meet in Hong Kong, because you both share a unit relationship to a particular state. Of course, if you were to meet a fellow Buckeye in Cleveland, this common bond would not be salient or differentiating and so would provide little basis for attraction. Conversely, if you were to discover that you disagree with another person over some political issue or if you meet a person from a rival school at your school, the only way for you to maintain balance would be to feel some, perhaps mild, dislike for the other.

Balance theory is very simple and that is part of its appeal. Despite this, the theory is powerful in accounting for some aspects of interpersonal attraction. According to this theory, we should like those who are similar to us or with whom we share some common bond.

Reward Theories   Several psychologists have emphasized that we like others who reward us and dislike those who punish us or provide us with significant costs (Berscheid & Walster, 1978; Byrne, 1971; Homans, 1961; Lott & Lott, 1974; Thibaut & Kelley, 1959). This makes some intuitive sense. Don't you tend to like people who are nice (rewarding) to you and dislike those who are nasty or mean? Would you not prefer to spend your time with someone who could amuse you, make you popular, satisfy your needs?

The theoretical argument is that rewards arouse positive affect or feelings and that punishments arouse negative feelings. Thus, your liking or disliking for another represents positive or negative feelings aroused by rewards and punishments. However, we should be careful not to assume that everyone finds the same things rewarding or punishing. Further, people's reactions to a given reward may be affected by their moods or immediate needs. For example, I find your compliment about my lecture more rewarding on days when everything has gone wrong than on one of those rare days

when everything has gone smoothly. Also, people's reactions to a given reward will be affected by what they are used to. A rich man is probably less likely to feel happy about a $100 gift than you or I would. Similarly, a successful and popular woman will likely find a compliment less rewarding than a person with a history less rich in approval. Thus, reward theory does not assume that all things are equally rewarding to all people under all circumstances.

VARIABLES THAT AFFECT ATTRACTION

SIMILARITY

People have long noted that those who are of like disposition seek one another's company: "Birds of a feather flock together." Of course, there may be many reasons why fellow flockers seem to be similar. One possibility (discussed in Chapter 11) is that group members impose uniformity on one another through conformity pressures. But in this chapter we are interested in another obvious possibility: that people like and associate with one another because they are similar. But why should similarity lead to attraction?

Why Are Similarity and Attraction Related?   Balance theory has one ready explanation. The theory clearly predicts that you will like another if you both like the same object or both dislike it (producing a balanced triad); conversely you should dislike one another if you disagree (again producing a balanced situation).

Alternatively, we could emphasize the rewards that similar others provide. For example, two people with similar attitudes generally have smoother, less effortful interactions, particularly when the attitudes are central to the interaction (Davis, 1981). When I talk to my psychology colleagues, I may prefer those who share my attitudes toward psychology so as to

Similarity of interests facilitates liking because it makes interactions smoother and more rewarding.

avoid stressful arguments, but I hardly even consider whether we have similar religious attitudes or different feelings about the value of space exploration.

Similarity may also produce more cognitive kinds of rewards. As Festinger's social comparison theory suggests (see Chapter 5), similar others tend to reduce uncertainty and to confirm that what one is and believes are good, proper, and correct. Because the reduction of uncertainty is satisfying, we should like the agent of the uncertainty reduction (Byrne, Nelson, & Reeves, 1966).

Another possibility is that we like similar others because we assume they also like us; perhaps it is the expected approval that we find rewarding rather than the similarity as such (Aronson & Worchel, 1966). In support of this proposition, there is evidence that people expect similar people will like them more than dissimilar people will (Gonzales et al., 1983; Insko et al., 1973).

But similarity, like hot fudge sundaes, can be too much of a good thing in large doses, so it is not always rewarding. For example, if your friend always believes the same things you do, she might become boring. Also, sometimes dissimilar others are in a position to be more helpful. Imagine a situation where you are totally confused. To the extent a similar person would be likely to be as confused as you are, you might prefer a dissimilar other who has a different perspective (Russ, Gold, & Stone, 1979).

In addition, sometimes similarity is downright threatening. Imagine that Mr. Obnoxious announces that he agrees with you that social psychology is an interesting course. Wouldn't this be somewhat alarming? Other people might assume that if you and Mr. Obnoxious share this one attitude you may be similar in lots of ways. Therefore while you may like a *nice* person who is similar to you, you would be more likely to dislike the similar person who is socially stigmatized or unpleasant (Novak & Lerner, 1968; Taylor & Mettee, 1971). Indeed, people will sometimes actually change their attitudes rather than appear similar to an obnoxious other (Cooper & Jones, 1969). Thus, the costs of being associated with an obnoxious person may outweigh whatever rewards come from knowing that someone agrees with you. This does not invalidate the general rule that similarity is generally rewarding, but by the same token similarity is not *inevitably* rewarding.

Similarity of Attitudes   Donn Byrne stimulated much of the research on the effects of attitude similarity on liking. In his standard paradigm, a subject fills out an attitude questionnaire and later makes judgments about another person. The experimenter provides certain information about the other person (who is, in fact, a hypothetical person), and it turns out that the attitudes of this other person are more or less similar to the subject's. Finally the subject indicates his or her attraction to this hypothetical stranger.

In one early study (Byrne, 1961), subjects especially liked the stranger when the stranger

TABLE 12.1 MEAN ATTRACTION TO STRANGERS WITH VARYING NUMBER AND PROPORTION OF SIMILAR ATTITUDES. *Higher numbers indicate more attraction. Note that liking increases most consistently as the proportion of similar attitudes increases, but there is a much less consistent relationship between liking and number of agreements.*

| Proportion of Similar Attitudes | Number of Similar Attitudes | | | |
	4	8	16	Mean
1.00	11.14	12.79	10.93	11.62
.67	10.79	9.36	9.50	9.88
.50	9.36	9.57	7.93	8.95
.33	8.14	6.64	6.57	7.12
Mean	9.86	9.59	8.73	

SOURCE: After Byrne and Nelson, 1965.

answered 26 attitude items exactly as the subjects had. However, the interpretation is not clear. Did subjects like the other because he agreed so much (26 times) or because he agreed so consistently (100%)? Later research showed that it is not the number but the proportion of agreements that is crucial (Byrne & Nelson, 1965). For example, the subjects liked a person with 4 similar and 2 dissimilar (67% similar) attitudes more than a person with 8 similar and 8 dissimilar (50% similar), even though the latter had more agreements with the subjects (see Table 12.1).

A great many other studies along the same lines provide variations on the theme: when we meet someone for the first time, an important determinant of liking is similarity of attitudes. The effects of attitude similarity on liking is one of social psychology's best-established and most robust generalizations.

Attitude Similarity in the Development of Relationships   Obviously, attitude similarity affects whether you like someone you have just met. Do these effects persist throughout the development of a friendship? If close friends have similar attitudes, did they become friends because they were similar or did they become similar (through mutual social influence) because they were friends?

To answer questions such as these, we need to study friendship formation over time. In one of the classic studies in modern social psychology, Theodore Newcomb (1961) acquired a house at the University of Michigan and recruited students to live there free in return for being subjects in a research project. None of the students knew one another before they set up housekeeping together. Newcomb determined their similarities before they had met and charted the course of developing friendships. Generally, at the beginning of the semester attitude similarity had little or no influence on friendship patterns, but by the end of the semester those who had had similar attitudes before they knew one another were somewhat more likely to be friends than those who were less similar. However, the predictive power of attitude similarity was not strong. Other studies find that attitude similarity does not predict friendships at all (Levinger, 1972).

Similarity of attitudes is probably not so important for friendship formation as it is for liking at first blush for several reasons. First, similarity may lose some of its rewarding power with longer acquaintanceship because it becomes boring. When you have just met someone, you may want to know whether she is the kind of person you want to get to know better, and for that judgment similarity may well be a good cue. However, you are probably more concerned with how interesting a friend is, and hearing her spout the same attitudes you have may not be so rewarding.

Second, although similarity of attitudes may play some role in friendship formation, it may be swamped by other variables as the friendship develops. Although laboratory experiments show that similarity *can* produce liking, in everyday social interactions it does not always, nor is it the only important variable in why we like someone. Several studies confirm that similarities in attitudes are less important for people who know one another well than is similarity along other dimensions. For example, in a study of almost 2,000 adolescent friendship pairs, Kandel (1978) found low, but statistically significant, similarities in attitudes but much greater similarity for such variables as grade in school, ethnicity, religion, and use of drugs.

Personality Similarity It is easy to make an intuitive case that people with similar personalities—that is, with similar motives, values, needs, and behavioral preferences—ought to become fast friends. Joe, who is rather shy and retiring, probably likes Salli, who is also shy, more than he likes Marti, who prefers large, loud parties. On the other hand, you could make an equally appealing case on intuitive grounds that people with somewhat opposite but complementary needs and behaviors would be close friends. It somehow seems unlikely that an aggressive, domineering man would prefer an equally aggressive woman rather than a submissive woman he could more easily dominate.

Winch et al. (1954) suggested that, in marital choices, complementary needs (such as dominance and submissiveness) might be more important than similarity. However, research does not support this conjecture; happily married couples tend to be similar rather than opposite on a great number of personality dimensions (Buss, 1984; Cattell & Nesselroade, 1967; Katz, Glucksberg, & Krauss, 1960); this is even true for traits such as femininity (Antill, 1983) and dominance (Buss, 1984; Meyer & Pepper, 1977) that ought, on theoretical grounds, to show complementarity. Buss (1984) has shown that such similarity extends even to behaviors. For example, husbands and wives tend to respond similarly to an item such as "I refused to accept the compromise." In summary, personality similarity plays a greater role than complementary needs in the formation of relationships and in one's satisfaction with those relationships.

Ability Similarity It seems reasonable that people with similar abilities would like one another. People with similar intellectual and athletic abilities are often able to provide stimulation and competition to each other. By contrast, when you interact with someone who is superior to you in some ability, you may feel inferior, which is hardly rewarding; when you interact with someone who is not as able as you are at something, you may feel some strain in trying to appear modest without being condescending. Thus, in many cases people with similar abilities can provide more rewards at less cost to one another. In addition, balance theory also predicts that similarity in abilities, like similarity in attitudes, should promote liking. Empirical data from marital choices and friendships reflect similarities in both intelligence and educational level (Buss, 1984; Kandel, 1978).

PROPINQUITY AND FAMILIARITY

Propinquity One of the oldest hypotheses cited in the attraction literature is that people tend to prefer others who are physically close. This is called the *propinquity hypothesis.* It has long been known that marriages are more likely among people who live close rather than far apart (Bossard, 1932). Attraction is also greater among co-workers who work physically close rather than far apart (Kipnis, 1975).

In the MIT housing study discussed in Chapter 11, Festinger, Schachter, and Back (1950) studied the relationship of liking and proximity. Subjects were asked to list the other couples they saw socially. For any given resident, the empirical probability of receiving a choice from one apartment away (next door) was .41; from two apartments away, .23; from three away, .16; and from four away, .10. Sheer physical distance was not the only important variable, however; what Festinger and his colleagues called *functional distance* also played a role. Functional distance might be defined in terms of the likelihood of meeting someone else. For example, those who lived at the bottom of stairways tended to have more friends on the upper floors than did those not living near stairs, presumably because those on the upper floors often passed the apartments of those at the foot of the stairs. Where the apartments were arranged in courtyards, people whose apartments faced into the inner courtyard were more popular than those whose apartments did not, because as they went about their day's business they were more likely to pass other apartments. The wise architect takes such effects into account. If you want to build group loyalties and friendly feelings among people, buildings have to be designed so people will come into contact frequently.

You may be able to think of several reasons why we are more inclined to like those who are close. For one thing, it requires less energy to interact with those who are close than with those who are far away, so those who are close offer more rewards at lower cost.

A second possibility is based on the trivial fact that you are more likely to encounter people who are close rather than far away. If you generally like those you meet, you will tend to have more friends who live and work close by because you encounter many more nearby than faraway people. Propinquity may not, by itself, cause greater liking, but it facilitates finding rewards that do lead to liking. Once you meet someone, you may then be able to structure the conversation to discover mutual interests and other sources of rewards (Insko & Wilson, 1977).

However, if the close-encounters hypothesis is correct, proximity can facilitate *disliking* as well as liking. A nice person is a joy as a roommate but an obnoxious other is far worse as a roommate than as someone you see once in a while. Close neighbors have the capacity to spoil one's environment by providing a good many costs in the form of noise, disagreeable habits, and the like. Ebbesen,

Kjos, and Konečni (1976) confirm that people living in a condominium complex had a greater probability not only of liking but of disliking close rather than far neighbors, and it is surely no accident that crimes of violence are also particularly likely to take place among family and neighbors (see Chapter 15).

A third reason that closeness leads to liking is more cognitive. According to balance theory, we should prefer situations in which unit relationships (such as proximity) and affective relationships (liking) are consistent. Therefore, the mere knowledge that you live close to someone, belong to the same organization, or work in the same place should engender liking. When two people belong to the same organization, they have a similar unit relationship to it, and this similarity will lead to balance if the two people like one another. This, of course, explains why people on vacations far from home honk at drivers from their home state.

Experimental research has documented that merely informing a subject that he or she has been paired with someone else increases the subject's liking for that other person even if there has been no direct contact between the two (Arkin & Burger, 1980; Darley & Berscheid, 1967). Furthermore, people placed into arbitrary groupings show considerable bias toward liking in-group as opposed to out-group others (Brewer, 1979; Wilder, 1981). Thus, it seems that we have a basic positive reaction to those who are close to us or with whom we share group membership.

Familiarity and Exposure   It is possible that propinquity effects are due to decreased effort of interaction, to facilitating rewarding interactions, and to cognitive balance, but there is yet a fourth and more general explanation. Those people who live or work close to us are people we generally see often; they are familiar. A certain amount of folk wisdom suggests that we like things that are familiar (and dislike things that are unfamiliar, strange, or different). Is this true?

Zajonc (1968) has stimulated a large amount of research that shows that mere exposure to stimuli enhances liking for those stimuli. Zajonc felt that it was important to use stimuli that the subjects had never seen before, so he could manipulate precisely their familiarity. He selected realistic but fake Chinese characters and nonsense words on the reasonable assumption that subjects had not been exposed to them. He then varied the number of times these stimuli were presented to the subjects. When subjects were asked to rate the positivity of these characters, the more familiar (more frequen•ly exposed) stimuli were better liked.

Mere exposure effects have also been demonstrated for people as stimuli. Saegert, Swap, and Zajonc (1973) shuttled subjects in and out of experimental rooms in such a way that they saw one another a differential number of times, although they were not allowed to talk to one another or interact in any way. (In everyday life, we may like people we see often because we have pleasant interactions with them. So it was important in the experiment that the familiarity effect be assessed independently of actual interaction.) As shown in Figure 12.1, subjects reported liking those they had seen more often. The experimenters also manipulated how pleasant the experiment was, and the familiarity effect was found in both pleasant and unpleasant situations.

The hypothesis that familiarity promotes liking is an old one in psychology (Grush, 1979; Harrison, 1977). Most explanations of the hypothesis assume that recognition of the stimulus increases with number of exposures and that the increased recognizability mediates liking. However, Moreland and Zajonc (1977) and Wilson (1979) have shown that repeated exposure increases liking even when the subject does not recognize the "familiar" stimuli more than the less familiar stimuli.

Recently, Zajonc (1980) has argued that affective reactions to stimuli are somewhat independent of our cognitive reactions. You need not do much thinking about something to like or dislike it. Zajonc argues that the familiarity–liking relationship is a basic, irreducible fact of human experience. This hypothesis does not, of course, account for *why* we like something; liking is simply a primitive (albeit important) reaction that does not necessarily depend on intermediate cognitive processes.

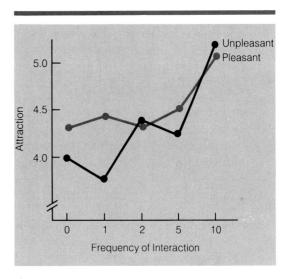

FIGURE 12.1   Attraction to Strangers as a Function of Frequency and Pleasantness or Unpleasantness of Encounters. Note that whether the context was pleasant or unpleasant, the person was liked more the more frequently she was encountered.

PERSONAL CHARACTERISTICS

Perhaps the most obvious set of factors that affects whether or not you will like another person is his or her personal characteristics. Most of us feel that we like another person not so much because he is similar or close, but because he seems to be kind, helpful, or generous. We like people who have a sense of humor, who are tactful, and who are able to provide us with a certain amount of amusement and entertainment. In this section, we review some research on personality traits that affect liking and offer an analysis of physical attractiveness as a variable in attraction.

Personality   Most of us feel that we like others who have pleasant personalities, and there is support for this notion. For example, Lott, Lott, Reed, and Crow (1970) found that, among college students, friends were more likely to be described as energetic, happy, truthful, or intelligent, and less likely to be described as insincere, self-centered, or complaining. Lowenthal, Thurnher, and Chiriboga (1975) asked people of various ages to describe what they looked for in friends. Similarity of interests and values was rated as most important, but interpersonal variables such as being supportive and understanding were also central. Marriage partners report that consideration, being a good companion, honesty, being affectionate and kind, and so on, are highly desirable in a mate (Buss & Barnes, 1986). In Chapter 9, we examined the development of social competence and noted that popular, socially competent children were generally friendlier, more cooperative and helpful, and less aggressive than their less competent peers. We cannot be sure that these traits actually caused liking, but certainly they are reasonable candidates simply because they are the sorts of traits likely to produce rewards for other people.

Physical Attractiveness   Important as personality may be, relatively superficial qualities such as beauty may also be important causes of attraction. The very fact that most of us try to look as attractive as possible suggests that we are at least willing to consider the possibility that being attractive may lead others to like us. Political organizers are jubilant when they have an attractive candidate to work with, and they are doubly happy if he or she has an attractive spouse and (one's cup runneth over) beautiful children. For centuries people who are into the game of finding a spouse have discovered that physical beauty, while only skin deep, was deep enough to land a mate. Whatever your own feelings about its

importance, beauty does affect liking. The first major demonstration of this came from Walster et al. (1966), who set up a dance during "Welcome Week" for freshmen at the University of Minnesota. The students were told that a computer would match them on the basis of personality similarity. Actually, men were assigned to women at random. At the intermission, the subjects were asked to evaluate their partner on a questionnaire. A follow-up study was conducted several months later to see whether there had been any additional dating. Partners rated their date for attractiveness, and four experimenters also rated the attractiveness of each subject.

The best predictor of how much the males liked their date or whether they asked the women out again was the attractiveness of the women. About 10% of the least-attractive women were asked for a second date, whereas about one-third of the most-attractive women were asked out again. The more attractive males were liked best by their dates and were seen as more desirable future dates.

This kind of effect has been replicated often for dating situations (Green, Buchanan, & Heuer, 1984; Shanteau & Nagy, 1979. Physical attractiveness also affects ratings of liking for strangers in a nondating context (Byrne, London, & Reeves, 1968), although subjects seem to take physical beauty into account more when judging how much they would like to date someone than when judging whether they simply like them or whether they think they would be a good marriage partner (Strobe et al., 1971).

We have stressed that we like people who are rewarding or who at least have the potential to provide rewards at reasonable cost. Why is physical beauty rewarding? One possibility is that the sheer joy of being able to contemplate a beautiful person, like looking at a beautiful painting, is a kind of esthetic reward. But a more likely possibility is that we feel we will reap social rewards by being seen with a comely person of the opposite sex. Beauty, like status, a sports car, athletic prowess, and fame, has real worth on the social commodity market. To be seen with a rich or famous person suggests that you yourself must be an outstanding person to be associated with such luster. Because attractiveness, like money, is scarce, it enhances status. The fact that this status can rub off on companions makes it a social reward.

There is direct evidence that people are evaluated more positively if they are seen with an attractive member of the opposite sex and that they feel they will be more positively evaluated in the presence of beauty (Kernis & Wheeler, 1981; Sigall & Landy, 1973). Further, conventional wisdom suggests that attractive people who are apparently in demand as status enhancement companions can be choosy about whom to date and marry. Accordingly, both men (Huston, 1973) and women (Shanteau & Nagy, 1979) are less sure that attractive than unattractive people will go out with them. Finally, high scorers on the self-monitoring scale (see Chapter 8), who tend to worry about the impression they make, are more concerned with the physical beauty of dates than are low self-monitors (Snyder, Berscheid, & Glick, 1985).

Another reason we like attractive people is that we see them as having desirable personality traits. Perhaps a woman is more willing to go out with a handsome man, not so much because he is a hunk, but because she suspects he will be considerate, self-confident, and charming. There is abundant evidence that pretty people are *perceived* to have better traits, especially in the areas of social vitality (they are seen as more outgoing) and traditional gender stereotypes (Bassili, 1981; Gillen, 1981). Furthermore, attractive people are assumed to be more similar to self in attitudes than are unattractive people (Marks & Miller, 1982), and unattractive people are seen as more likely to display mild forms of social deviance, such as homosexuality or radicalism (Unger, Hilderbrand, & Madar, 1982).

One temptation (at least for those of us who are not among the beautiful people) is to assume that, surely, these personality perceptions are in error. However, several studies have found that attractive people actually do have more desirable social traits such as self-confidence and outgoingness (Abbott & Sebastian, 1981; Huston, 1973). In one study, attractive people were even rated as more likeable than unattractive people in a phone conversation by people who could not see them (Goldman & Lewis, 1977). Furthermore, Reis et al. (1982) have shown that attractive males have more social encounters and better social interactions than less-attractive males. Results for females are more complex, but attractive females generally also have better social interactions than less-attractive females.

Assume for the moment that attractive and unattractive people do have different personalities and that these differences may favor the attractive people. How could this happen? Undoubtedly, the process begins early in life. Even when very young, beautiful babies are responded to more positively than less-attractive babies (Stephan & Langlois, 1984). By age 5, attractive and unattractive children have already begun to differ in their social behaviors (Langlois & Down, 1979). So it may well be that pretty babies get more reinforcement for behaving socially; furthermore, the extra attention they may get from adults would likely give them the self-confidence to meet successfully the social demands of early childhood.

Of course, personality differences may continue to be supported by interactions with others throughout life. For example, even as teenagers and adults, attractive people may elicit warmer responses from others, thus creating warmer behavior on their part. Snyder, Tanke, and Berscheid (1977) have shown one way this might work. A male and a female subject who were not allowed to meet were placed in separate rooms and told to carry on a conversation over a phone hookup.

Although the female subject did not know this, her male partner was given a picture, supposedly of her. Actually, these pictures were bogus; half the male subjects got "partner" pictures that were quite attractive and half got unattractive pictures. The conversations were taped and later rated. The men who thought they were talking with attractive women behaved more warmly than those who thought they were talking with the unattractive ones. Interestingly enough, in response to this treatment the "pretty" women became warmer in their own behavior than did the "ugly" women (you might look again at Figure 3.3). Thus, attractive people may elicit greater warmth, which in turn makes them more socially adept, which encourages further social responses from others, and on the cycle goes.

APPROVAL FROM OTHERS

The variables we have already considered—similarity, propinquity, and personal characteristics—might be thought of as facilitating rewards from others, although there are probably other reasons why each causes liking. Similarity, closeness, and beauty are not necessarily rewarding in themselves, but they do facilitate access to rewards. Sometimes, of course, people give us direct rewards in the form of promotions, pay raises, advice, or aid on a difficult task. The most important direct reward others provide is their approval.

Reactions to Approval   We like those who approve of or like us. You probably spend most of your time with others who seem to like and respect you, and you may even find yourself avoiding those who cannot see your better qualities. There is ample experimental evidence that being liked causes liking in return (Berscheid & Walster, 1978; Shrauger, 1975). Furthermore, in actual groups there is reciprocity of liking wherein people like those who like them (Kenny & Nasby, 1980; Wright, Ingraham, & Blackmer, 1984).

There are several possible reasons for this reciprocity effect. One is that we tend to see someone who likes us as being agreeable and as thereby having other positive characteristics. You probably like others who always seem to have smiles on their faces and good words for everyone, even if those behaviors are not directed to you personally (Folkes & Sears, 1977). Of course, there are limits to this kind of thing. You probably would not like someone who liked everything, because he would seem insincere or undiscerning. But still, most of us probably prefer the upbeat person to the chronic cynic or critical person.

Like many other reward variables we have considered, approval from others is usually but not always rewarding. A positive evaluation from another can embarrass you, make you feel that the evaluator is insincere, or force you to change your behavior in ways you may not desire. It is, for example, highly unlikely that a teenager who has just stumbled through his annual piano recital likes his great aunt for her smothering, indiscriminant, and effusive public praise afterwards. Because the rewarding value of positive evaluations is so obvious, most research in this area has been directed to demonstrating conditions that change the reward value of approval.

When Is Approval Not Rewarding? According to Heider's balance theory, you should reject approval if you have a low self-

Elaine Hatfield (Walster)   Ellen Berscheid

concept. The reasoning is that we tend to dislike those who disagree with us; if I feel I am poor at something and you say I am good, we disagree and I should, therefore, tend to dislike you and reject your approval. The classic study in support of this prediction was done by Deutsch and Solomon (1959), who organized subjects into teams and had each subject either succeed or fail on a task. Each subject then received a note from a teammate saying that the other either did or did not want the subject as a teammate. The subjects then indicated how much they liked the evaluator. When the subject had succeeded (and thus had a positive self-evaluation), she liked the positive evaluator more than the negative evaluator—a result predicted by both balance and reward theories. When the subject had a negative self-evaluation, she liked the negative evaluator more—a result that supports balance theory (see Table 12.2).

However, most research in this area has found that people with low self-concepts like rather than dislike the positive evaluator (Jones, 1973), so a low self-concept does not always or even usually make approval unrewarding by itself. Nevertheless, there may be conditions under which low-self-concept people would feel that acceptance of approval would produce negative consequences, and under these circumstances we might expect to find that people with low self-concepts reject the approval, as did Deutsch and Solomon's subjects. One such reason is the risk of subsequent disclosure (Jones & Pines, 1968). If you feel that you are not very good at math, you might be more willing to accept someone telling you that you are a math whiz over summer vacation than the night before the calculus final. In the latter case it is dangerous to accept the compliment because events may soon disclose that you are in fact poor at math, contrary to the compliment. There may also be personal costs in accepting a high evaluation from others. If you are sure you are bad at something, a compliment may seem insincere

TABLE 12.2 LIKING FOR AN EVALUATOR AS A FUNCTION OF PAST SUCCESS OR FAILURE AND POSITIVE OR NEGATIVE EVALUATION. *Low numbers indicate more liking. Note that the subjects liked the evaluator more when her evaluations were consistent with previous success or failure.*

	Negative Evaluation	Positive Evaluation
Success	4.7	2.0
Failure	2.8	3.2

SOURCE: After Deutsch and Solomon, 1959.

and do you little good. If, on the other hand, you are less certain that you are bad at something, you may be more willing to grasp at the straws of praise from others. Research does show that people with low but uncertain self-concepts like approval more than those who are more certain they are poor at something (Dutton, 1972; Jones & Schneider, 1968).

How discerning the approval is may also affect how we respond to it (Mettee & Aronson, 1974). Those who approve everything are doomed to having their compliments viewed as meaningless. On the other hand, approval from those who are generally critical may have considerable effect. Students seem justifiably prouder of good grades from professors who have high standards for work and accomplishment than they are of good grades from professors who are more relaxed.

Consider an attributional perspective on how you think about evaluations (see Chapter 4). Your concern as a perceiver is whether an evaluation of you is caused by the entity—you, in which case you can feel rewarded for your qualities—or is caused by the qualities of the evaluator, which means the evaluation says little about you. One of the factors that leads to entity attributions is high distinctiveness—evaluations that vary across entities. Thus, the discerning evaluator, who can distinguish between people, must be responding to the qualities of those people.

SUMMARY

Of all areas in social psychology, there is perhaps least mystery about interpersonal attraction. That is not to say that the area does not bear continuing scrutiny but only that balance theory and reward models can explain most of what we know about the whys and wherefores of liking others. Balance theory points out that when two people agree in their attitudes, abilities, or almost any other characteristic, their liking one another produces a balanced triad. Similarly, when people have the same unit relationship to something (come from the same state, go to the same school, sit close together), balance requires that they like one another. Reward theories suggest that we like people who provide maximum rewards at minimum costs. Similarity is generally rewarding, and propinquity also lowers the costs of interacting with people. Likewise, people with pleasant personalities or with dispositions to be helpful and nice are liked because they are rewarding. Physically attractive people also tend to produce social rewards in the form of increased status. Finally, we tend to like people who like and praise us. However, there are limitations on the extent to which factors such as similarity and praise are rewarding, and when they are not rewarding they do not produce attraction.

INGRATIATION

THE INGRATIATION MODEL

We have been discussing why one person is attracted to another. Although there may have been a surprise or two, you have probably been impressed with how commonsensical all this has seemed. Most of you have a pretty good idea about why you like someone, and you may have a good sense of how to make the other person like you. For thousands of years, philosophers and amateur psychologists have been giving advice on how to become the sort of person others will like and respect. For

TABLE 12.3   SIX WAYS TO MAKE PEOPLE LIKE YOU.

1. Become genuinely interested in other people.
2. Smile.
3. Remember that a person's name is to him or her the sweetest and most important sound in any language.
4. Be a good listener. Encourage others to talk about themselves.
5. Talk in terms of the other person's interest.
6. Make the other person feel important—and do it sincerely.

SOURCE: From Carnegie, 1936.

example, in Plato's *Republic*, several of the more cynical members of the group give quite good advice on how to maintain appearances of justice. The biographer of the ancients, Plutarch, and the Renaissance social philosopher Machiavelli each outlined strategies for controlling public images. In the twentieth century, such books as Dale Carnegie's *How to Win Friends and Influence People* have provided advice on how to do just that. The fact that Carnegie could reduce his advice to six simple rules (see Table 12.3) should not in any way detract from the fact that his advice is reasonably serviceable.

Surprisingly, social psychologists have only recently taken an interest in the whole question of how we try to make others like us, in what is called *ingratiation*. Edward E. Jones (1964) stimulated much of the research on this topic. According to Jones, ingratiation is "a class of strategic behavior illicitly designed to influence particular other persons concerning the attractiveness of one's personal qualities" (Jones, 1964, p. 11). This definition points to two important characteristics of ingratiation. First, ingratiation is designed to win the approval of other people, to make others think that the ingratiator is an attractive or worthwhile person. Second, the ingratiation behaviors are illicit in the sense that the actor tries to project a set of feelings, attitudes, or behaviors that are not representative of his or her true state.

There are any number of useful ingratiation strategies. The most direct and obvious one is positive self-presentation. By presenting oneself as a paragon of virtue—as being a particularly worthy person—one presumably increases the chances of receiving approval (to the degree that people are obligated to take self-presentations at face values). A second ingratiation strategy is conformity. People like to have others agree with them; people like similar others. A third tactic is other-enhancement. To tell another person that he or she is wonderful is, all things being equal, likely to make that other like you. Finally, there is a range of tactics associated with helping another person—cooperating, doing favors, and the like—behaving in an essentially prosocial manner.

INGRATIATION STRATEGIES

Self-presentation Earlier, we considered evidence that people with socially desirable characteristics such as physical attractiveness, status, wealth, the right friends, and desirable personality traits are liked by others. Thus, if you wish to make others like you, you might try to convince others that you have desirable characteristics.

The attempt to control the information that others have about you is called *self-presentation*. Obviously, by selectively emphasizing positive characteristics and by de-emphasizing negative ones, you may be able to convey to another person that you are an outstanding sort. There are several ways one might control information about oneself (Schneider, 1981). First, you might display some of your possessions. Showing that you have a large car or Gucci loafers suggests that you have more money than the average person and may also be taken as evidence that you have a clear sense of current fashion. Second, you may make some behavioral display that can be taken as evidence of underlying dispositions. You might, for example, demonstrate how clever you are or try to show that you are

friendly and kind. Third, there are various stylistic, mostly nonverbal, strategies for creating a good impression. For example, people who are trying to make others like them tend to talk less but smile, nod, and gaze more (Godfrey, Jones, & Lord, 1986). Fourth, and most commonly, the ingratiator may simply assert that he has certain characteristics.

How might you present yourself if you wanted someone to like you? Given that we like those with positive traits, it might seem the best strategy would be to claim these positive features for oneself. In fact, many studies show that when people want approval they do say positive things about themselves (Gergen, 1965; Jones, Gergen, & Davis, 1962; Schneider, 1969).

However, keep in mind that the target of the self-presentation may be perfectly aware that the ingratiator has a strong motive to be approved, and this may create problems. The ingratiator may, for example, be perceived as lying. A second problem is that tooting your own horn may make others feel less desirable by comparison. Even if the positive presentation is essentially correct, the target will not wish to be reminded of her own limitations by comparison with someone who has greater ability and accomplishment. The ingratiator would defeat his purpose of getting approval

Sometimes we encourage others to judge us for what we own rather than for what we are.

from the target if she feels belittled by the positive presentation. In fact, people who try to promote their own accomplishments may make others dislike them *and* fail to accomplish their goal of making others think they are competent (Godfrey et al., 1986). Third, there are normative rules of presentation. One is that the presentation should be honest. Research confirms that people are better liked when their presentations match their true competencies than when they do not (Schlenker & Leary, 1982). There are also politeness norms that constrain presentations to be neither too modest nor too immodest (Goffman, 1955, 1959).

One way to avoid most of these difficulties is to use a modest (but not too modest) self-description, but this carries the inherent risk that the ingratiation attempt will be unsuccessful. I can hardly convince you that I am smart by claiming to have average intelligence. One possible solution is to mix modest and more positive presentations. If the ingratiator is obviously bad at something, he might as well confess it publicly; at least others will realize that he is not always a braggart. People who acknowledge their disabilities are often better liked than those who do not (Hastorf, Wildfogel, & Cassman, 1979). On the other hand, positive presentations may be more useful in areas where the audience has little opportunity to verify the truth of the presentation (Baumeister & Jones, 1978).

Sometimes even obvious accomplishments might be downplayed. After a great game, sports stars are virtually obligated to say something like "Well, I had a pretty good game, but everything just went right today and I had lots of help from my teammates." Such presentations will not dishonor the obvious great performance but will show that our hero knows social codes about modesty. Done properly, such presentational performances can be downright charming.

On the other hand, sometimes the person cannot afford the luxury of such modesty. A business executive may feel that she must in-spire confidence in her abilities by drawing attention to her recent accomplishments, but she may try to demonstrate her humanness by being more modest about her golf game or tennis skills. In one experiment, subjects who had high status did mix their self-presentations in just this way. They were quite positive about matters central to their status but more modest for less central matters (Jones, Gergen, & Jones, 1963).

The ingratiator must also be concerned about what the audience values. My colleagues might not be impressed with my efforts to eradicate crabgrass, but my neighbors might be more taken with that than with a recent scientific publication. Research confirms that such audience values are taken into account by ingratiators. For example, Zanna and Pack (1975) and Baeyer, Sherk, and Zanna (1981) have shown that women present themselves differently depending on whether a male target values traditional feminine virtues or has a more modern conception of women. Clearly, the ingratiator has to consider a range of tactical problems (see Schlenker, 1980, and Schneider, 1981, for further discussion). But the strategic problem is constant: how to present oneself positively without seeming to brag or without threatening the targets of the ingratiation attempt.

Conformity   Conforming to the opinions of another or doing what she asks is a useful ingratiation strategy for two basic reasons. Most obviously, the actor's expressions of opinions similar to those of the target promotes perceptions of similarity, and, as we have seen, similarity leads to attraction. Second, conforming to the demands of another is often taken as a sign that she is worthy of respect; hence, conformity can be thought of as a form of approval of the target, a confirmation of the worth of the target, which is a factor that also produces attraction.

However, as with self-presentation, there are tactical problems with conformity. Again, the most obvious is that opinion conformity may not be accepted as sincere, that the ingratiator will be found out as an ingratiator. As Jones and Wortman (1973) pointed out, there are several ways of making the attitude expression seem real. One is to conform at times when the need for approval is not obvious, so that the ulterior motive will not be salient. Another is to anticipate what the target is likely to say. Suppose that you have a passion for a certain politician. If I wait for you to announce that you like him, there is every risk that I will be perceived as performing slavishly. However, if I state "my" opinion that the politician is a jewel before you have stated yours, I can at least avoid the appearance of conformity. A third technique is to conform on issues crucial to the ingratiation attempt but to display independence on others. Experiments have shown that people mix conformity and nonconformity in an effort to provide maximum credibility for the conformity (Jones et al., 1963).

Other Enhancement   When you tell another person that you think that she is wonderful, you are practicing ***other enhancement***. Other enhancement is such a familiar and obvious tactic that it is particularly difficult to pull it off successfully. When the ingratiator's motives are obvious, his avowed approval of the other is less credible than when it is not so obvious (Dickoff, 1961; Lowe & Goldstein, 1970).

The problem from the ingratiator's point of view is how he can convey a compliment and have it be believed. One useful strategy is to arrange to have the compliment conveyed by a third party who presumably has no reason to win the favor of the target (Jones & Wortman, 1973). Another strategy is to be an attribution theorist; one can arrange to vary both consistency and distinctiveness information (see Chapter 4) by varying compliments and criticism. For example, the ingratiator might maintain a posture of being very critical about most things and then slip in a compliment to the target. Because the actor has estalished himself

"Bob and Gwen, I mean this terribly seriously. Seriously, we had a wonderful time. I mean that. Seriously."

Drawing by Wm. Hamilton © 1975 by the New Yorker Magazine, Inc.

as a critical sort, the compliment seems all the more convincing—it obviously does not stem simply from a good-natured disposition on the part of the actor. Or the actor may criticize the target on one or more irrelevant points and then slip in the compliment on the more relevant point. This is a technique used by some writers of letters of recommendation who try to maximize the credibility of their positive recommendations by making sure that some negative information is also mentioned.

As Jones and Wortman (1973) point out, there are more subtle and probably more useful ways to make the other think that you like and respect her. You can ask her for advice or help, thus defining her by implication as a competent person. Nonverbal cues such as smiles and closeness of contact are probably also important ways that the ingratiator can convey that he likes the other. Even such subtle things as the use of first names affects how well an ingratiator is liked (Kleinke, Staneski, & Weaver, 1972), as Dale Carnegie suggested.

Rendering Favors   We tend to like those who help us, especially if it is clear that the person intended to help (Nemeth, 1970a). Of course, the favor must be appropriate to the situation to maintain the credibility of the intention, but, assuming these conditions have been met, the favor-doer will generally be liked.

Research on ingratiation suggests that although the basic rules of attraction may be fairly simple, there are a number of complexities about how we can in fact get people to like us. People respond to approval and rewards, but what is rewarding is determined not only by what people generally value but also by particular, contextual factors. Generally, we all like approval from others, but the approval must also seem sincere, appropriate, and based on distinctiveness information. The psychology of making people like you is simple in principle but often difficult in practice.

SUMMARY

Because we like to be liked, most people try to behave in ways that will make them attractive to others. Sometimes, people deliberately seek to do this; such attempts are termed ingratiation. Generally, ingratiators try to present themselves as positively as possible, but ensuring that the presentation remains credible and nonthreatening requires skill. Because we like others who agree with us, conformity to the opinions of others can be a successful strategy. Finally, we may praise others and directly reward them by doing favors for them.

LOVE

Although we know a vast amount about what leads us to like someone, we know much less about the more intense forms of interpersonal attraction. Until recently, there has been almost no empirical research on the most intense form of attraction: love.

There are many reasons why psychologists have not studied love (Rubin, 1973; Walster & Walster, 1979). For one thing, love seems mysterious and romantic—not the sort of thing that can be or ought to be subjected to scientific scrutiny. Also, in some of its manifestations, love is closely linked to sex, and until recently, sex itself was a forbidden topic. But perhaps the most important reason for not giving love scientific attention is that love is a very complex feeling, surely a more complicated form of attraction than liking.

If I asked you to tell me whether you liked a particular other, you might confess to ambivalent feelings, but you would understand what you were being asked and except in rare cases you would be able to give an answer. But love is different. If you were asked whether you love someone you have been seeing in a romantic context, your answer would probably be much less certain. Even after people have known each other or have been married for years, they may not be able to say whether they are truly in love. Recall the various definitions that people gave for love at the beginning of this chapter—it hardly seems as if these people were talking about the same thing.

Love is also hard to study because it can refer to many different feelings; a person reports that she loves her country, parents, children, dog, and husband. It is quite clear that she will not show affection to her country in the same way she does to her husband or child, yet we speak of love in each case. To some extent, social psychologists have gotten around this problem by concentrating their attention on romantic, heterosexual love. Not only is romantic love interesting in its own right, but it is an important element in the building of relationships; we will have more to say about its role in that context in Chapter

13. For the moment, you should be aware that when we talk about love in this chapter we are talking about romantic love.

From a scientific point of view, there is an additional complication in the study of love. Liking develops fairly quickly and can be easily manipulated in experiments; love usually takes longer to develop and responds to factors that are difficult or unethical to manipulate. Therefore, it is hard to do experiments on love, although we may still do naturalistic studies.

LOVING AND LIKING

Is love related to liking? Earlier we argued that all forms of interpersonal attraction have a general affective feeling in common so that we should expect to find that love and liking are at least somewhat related. Several studies have confirmed moderately high correlations between measures of liking and loving (Dermer & Pyszczynski, 1978; Rubin, 1970), and one study by Sternberg and Grajek (1984) found quite high relationships for parents, siblings, and friends. However, loving and liking are not merely two versions of the same thing. For example, although both men and women report that they like their lovers only slightly more than friends, they report loving their romantic companions a great deal more (Rubin, 1973; Sternberg & Grajek, 1984). This suggests that you have to do more than simply like someone a lot to be in love. One can like someone, indeed like him or her very much, without feeling that extra something called love. Thus, loving and liking are not inevitably closely related, and love is not merely liking gone beserk.

MODELS OF LOVE

We can point to some major components of love as most of us understand it. You might think of these as something added to liking to produce romantic love. There have been three general approaches to the social psychology of love. Some have argued that love is a special kind of interpersonal relationship. A second approach argues for the role of intense feelings and passion. A third approach is more integrative in that it discusses several types of romantic love.

Love as a Special Relationship   When we think of two people as being in love, normally we think of some special glue that holds the relationship together. Generally, love exists between people who have known each other for some time. To be sure, there is also the notion of love at first sight; although the ways of love are often mysterious, love at first sight does not seem to be a common experience. This in turn suggests that feelings of love are built on more than superficial characteristics of the other. You can like another person who loves opera as you do or who helps you with your classwork, but it would be odd to say that you love her because she is so similar or helpful. Love is also a more general reaction than liking. You may like a friend for only one thing (say a similar interest in football), but love seems to transcend boundaries of specific interests. When you love someone, it is generally assumed that you want to do many different things with that person.

Love is also fairly discriminating and exclusive (Davis, 1985). Typically, we feel that love should be extended only to family and a few close friends. Furthermore, love relationships tend to exclude other people. You mark off those relatively few people you love from the much greater number of people you like, and you tend to spend more time alone with those you love.

Love relationships usually involve general feelings of dependency. To some extent we depend on many or most of the people we know well, but typically we depend on friends for different things: Joe makes you happy, Mary helps with your work, and so on. Love,

In any society, love relationships are often given an institutional blessing.

on the other hand, implies a general dependency on the partner for a wide range of material and psychological rewards. As we shall see in Chapter 13, there are also strong norms that such rewards should be noncontingently provided in a love relationship. You should not have to beg for security, affection, or help from a loved one, and you help someone you love not because of a sense of duty or expectations of reciprocation but because you want to help. For example, a man may care for his invalid spouse for years out of love even though she can provide few of the rewards normally associated with marriage. Steck et al. (1982) confirmed that most people think a pattern of high caring and relatively low need for the loved one implies a higher level of love than the reverse pattern of low care and high need, which was seen as more consistent with liking.

Love as a Special Feeling   Another obvious way that loving differs from liking is that love typically implies a more intense emotional arousal (Berscheid, 1983). If liking is a pastel feeling, love can be described in vivid reds, pinks, and purples; love is a passion. For one thing, lovers often report a fascination with their partner in the sense of thinking about the partner often, even obsessively (Davis, 1985). The most obvious source of this passion, at least for romantic love, is sexual arousal. It might even be argued that such love is nothing more than liking and sexual passion blended together through some secret recipe. Of course, we must always keep in mind that this kind of model may be appropriate for romantic love but not for other forms such as parental love for children or the love between two close, but sexually nonintimate, friends. Research has implicated sexual arousal as a factor in love. For example, sexual arousal increases people's reported love but not liking for their partners (Dermer & Pyszczynski, 1978).

Berscheid and Walster (1974) have argued that feelings of love may be a misattribution of sexual arousal. According to Schachter's theory of emotion, experienced emotions (including love) are a joint function of arousal and defining cognitions. As we saw in Chapter 5, it is possible to get people to change the emotions they feel by changing cognitive cues. In the present case, arousal (particularly sexual) may be defined as love in the presence of an attractive, likable other.

Although this misattribution idea is hard to test clearly, several experiments are consistent with it. For example, Dutton and Aron (1974) had male and female experimenters interview male subjects as they crossed a high suspension bridge that swayed enough to create some fear arousal. Compared to control subjects not on the bridge, male subjects showed increased affection to the female but not to the male experimenters when they crossed the bridge. Apparently, part of the fear arousal was misattributed to attraction for the opposite-sex person. White, Fishbein, and Rutstein (1981) manipulated arousal in various ways (such as through exercise or listening to a comedy tape) and found that aroused males rated attractive females more positively on romantic items. On the other hand, as we saw in Chapter 5, misattribution effects are often fragile and hard to produce. Some studies fail to confirm the possibility that irrelevant arousal increases romantic attraction (Kenrick & Cialdini, 1977; Riordon & Tedeschi, 1983). However, the general hypothesis remains an intriguing possible explanation of the extra "oomph" that seems a central part of love.

Varieties of Love   Perhaps one reason it has proved so hard to pin love down is that love is not a single feeling or entity. We have already noted that romantic love is different than love of country or of parents, and maybe romantic love itself has many forms or dimensions. There may simply be various kinds of romantic love. Hendrick and Hendrick (1986) designed a questionnaire to measure several styles of love suggested by Lee (1977) on the basis of a careful reading of philosophers and fiction writers and descriptions provided by subjects. Hendrick and Hendrick discovered that each of these types or styles of love has a basic integrity and that the styles are independent of one another. To avoid the evaluative words we use for love, Lee used Greek and Latin terms: (1) *eros*, or erotic love, refers to love with a strong element of sexual passion and an emphasis on ideals of physical beauty; (2) *ludus* (meaning *play*) is a gamelike love without strong commitment or jealousies; (3) *storge* refers to a quiet companionate or friendship type of love with little emphasis on passion; (4) *pragma*, or pragmatic love, has a strong element of rational choice with an emphasis on what the partner can do for self; (5) *mania*, or symptom-based love, is close to what is often called puppy-love with a strong physical component but little in the way of mature commitment; and (6) *agape* refers to a selfless, altruistic caring. Table 12.4 gives some characteristic items for each style from the Hendricks' scale designed to measure styles of love.

Lee and the Hendricks began with the idea that there is probably no single thing called love but rather a series of types of love, and they have begun to explore the factors that seem related to each type of romantic love. In some sense, the opposite approach would be to begin with the basis of love and try to build up

---

TABLE 12.4 SAMPLE ITEMS FROM THE ATTITUDES TOWARD LOVE AND SEX SCALE ILLUSTRATING DIFFERENT STYLES OF LOVE.

EROS (Erotic Love)
   My lover and I have the right physical "chemistry" between us.
   My lover fits my ideal standards of physical beauty.
LUDUS (Interaction Games)
   I try to keep my lover a little uncertain about my commitment to him/her.
   I enjoy playing the "game of love" with a number of different partners.
STORGE (Friendship)
   The best kind of love grows out of a long friendship.
   Genuine love first requires caring for awhile.
PRAGMA (Pragmatic)
   I try to plan my life carefully before choosing a lover.
   An important factor in choosing a partner is whether or not he/she will be a good parent.
MANIA (Puppy Love)
   Sometimes I get so excited about being in love that I can't sleep.
   When things aren't right with my lover and me, my stomach gets upset.
AGAPE (Altruistic)
   I would rather suffer myself than let my lover suffer.
   When my lover gets angry with me, I still love him/her fully and unconditionally.

BOX 12.1

THE TRIANGULAR THEORY OF LOVE

Sometimes, to match the complexity of human behavior, psychological theories are themselves quite complex. On the other hand, the most powerful kinds of models often are those that have relatively few assumptions and that can be easily grasped and readily applied to many phenomena. Cognitive dissonance theory and balance theory are classic cases of theories that most people can understand quickly but that also have broad ramifications. Sternberg's (1986) triangular theory of love also is simple, although it is yet too early to know whether the model will have the predictive power of more complex theories.

Sternberg suggests that love has three major components: intimacy, passion, and commitment. It is not clear how these three components were selected, but they do make a certain amount of intuitive sense. These three components differ in several ways. For example, Sternberg suggests that passion is not very stable across time while intimacy and commitment are. A person usually has control over the decision to get involved and to commit, but typically feels little control over the passionate side of love. Furthermore, the three components tend to have different courses over time. The intimacy component typically increases during the early stages of the relationship as the partners get to know one another, but during the later stages may actually decrease. The passion component is based on arousal and is likely to develop quickly and then decline more slowly. The commitment component is likely to increase gradually and, at least for successful relationships, will continue to increase, although typically with several peaks and valleys along the way.

The three components can be depicted as sides of a triangle (our pictorial representation differs slightly from Sternberg's but the differences are not crucial here). This geometric representation offers several advantages. First, different kinds of love can be represented visually. If we imagine that each of the components can be either very strong or very weak, we could represent this as triangles of different shapes and sizes (Figure B.12.1 shows examples). Second, given this geometric representation, the total amount of love can be represented by the area of the triangle. If we compare two people who have equal commitment and intimacy with their partners, the one with the larger passion component will produce a triangle with a larger area representing the intuitive notion that this person loves her

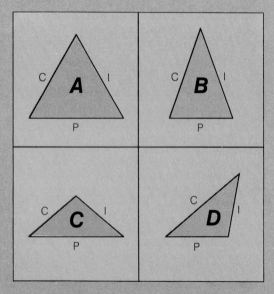

FIGURE B.12.1   Types of Love Varying in Passion, Commitment, and Intimacy.

partner more than her partner loves her. In Figure B.12.1 triangle A is larger and hence shows more love than triangle B because the former has a larger passion component. But, of course, lowering either of the other components also reduces the amount of love.

There are other ways we might compare shapes and sizes of love triangles. For example, in an on-going relationship it might be useful to look at the sizes and shapes of the triangles for the two partners. They might match fairly closely, so that the two show approximately equal amounts of the three components. Alternatively, the triangles might be the same general shape but differ in size because one partner has less intimacy, passion, and commitment than the other, that is, she brings less love to the relationship. Or an even more intriguing possibility is that the two partners have equal amounts of love (the areas of their triangles are equal) but different mixtures of components. John and Stella might love each other equally, but where John's love is strongly passionate for Stella, Stella's total love for John is based more on commitment. Sternberg suggests that satisfaction with the relationship ought to be based on the degree of overlap between the triangles, and data from a study by Sternberg and Barnes (1985) support this idea. Figure B.12.2 shows a reasonably congruent match where the partners have roughly the same amount of love and generally the same balance of components. In the incongruent set, Person A not only loves Person B more than the reverse (A's triangle is larger) but there are substantial mismatches: although they both have strong passion, A's commitment and intimacy are much larger than B's. The incongruence is illustrated by the lack of overlap between the triangles.

Another kind of comparison is between one's ideal love and one's real love. That is, you might desire a relationship with lots of passion but find that your present one is somewhat lacking in that department. Again, we can represent this in terms of different triangles, one for real and one for ideal, and see how well they match. They can differ in total area (one wishes one had more love than one has), in shape (one wants less commitment than one has), or both. Sternberg reports that satisfactory relationships have a greater overlap between the real and ideal triangles than do the less satisfactory ones.

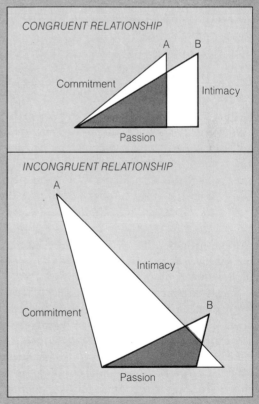

FIGURE B.12.2   Congruent and Incongruent Relationships. Congruent relationships have greater overlap in the triangles representing the two people.

BOX CONTINUED

It is too early to tell how much value the Sternberg model has. But we should make an important point about how theories function in psychology. Some theories are very precise and detailed. From narrow postulates they may generate a multitude of explicit hypotheses that can be tested quite precisely. Such theories are typically found more often in the cognitive than in the social sciences, although certain models of group decision-making and performance as we saw in Chapter 10 often qualify. In Box 4.1 we presented an example of a memory model that has some of these features.

But other sorts of theories have a different contribution to make. The triangular theory of love does not make precise predictions (other than those about overlaps in area), and at present it is not complex in the sense of having many interrelated components. Indeed, it is more a way of representing aspects of love than it is a theory. However, perhaps at this stage of our study of love this is an appropriate kind of theory. And it has one distinct advantage: it orients us to asking all manner of questions. Several spring to mind, and you may be able to invent others: (1) Given a constant amount of love, is there a particular shape that is best in the sense of leading to more satisfying relationships? (Is it better to have more commitment and less passion, for example?) (2) How do the shapes of love triangles change over the course of a relationship? (3) Do homosexual and heterosexual relationships differ in the relative importance of the components? (4) Can we predict the success of a relationship by knowing the shapes of the respective partners' triangles early in the relationship? (5) How might a long-married couple conceptualize the shape of their love 10 or 25 years ago? Do these retrospective accounts predict anything?

One does not need to draw triangles to ask these questions. By the same token, however, once one begins to think of love in this way, these questions seem to spring to mind more readily. So it is important to recognize that even fairly simple and imprecise theories can be important not so much for their abilities to explain but for their abilities to lead to new and interesting research questions. Such theories stimulate inquiry and promote a sense of wonder and excitement.

---

to the various types. In a recent comprehensive theory of love, Robert Sternberg (1986) argues that there are really three dimensions to love. The first is *intimacy*, which is basically a feeling of closeness. In terms of our previous discussion, this would be closest to liking, because we often report feeling close to people we like a great deal, but intimacy also includes feelings of caring, mutual understanding, and support. The second component is *passion*, corresponding to the motivational and arousal components we have been discussing. Finally, Sternberg argues for a *commitment* component. Initially you must make a decision that you are in love and then subsequently work at maintaining that love relationship. Again, this corresponds roughly to the notion of love as a special kind of relationship to which one makes a unique commitment.

Within the Sternberg model, these three components form the vertices of a triangle. One advantage of such a consciously geometric model is that the strength of each of the components can be represented as a length. Two clear implications follow. First, the total area of the triangle represents the total amount of love—obviously, if the length of, say, the passion component increases, so does the area of the triangle. Second, different kinds of love can be represented by triangles of different shapes. For example, if the passion component is strong (as in erotic love), the triangle will be thin and tall. The Sternberg model is still quite new and preliminary but shows some promise as an attempt to integrate what we know about love. Box 12.1 further discusses some implications of the triangular model of love.

SUMMARY

Love and liking are related in that both represent affective reactions to other people. On the other hand, it is clear that love is not merely liking run amok; it is a distinct set of feelings. One possibility is that we use love to refer to the feelings we have in special kinds of relationships. Love involves longer relationships, is based on less-superficial characteristics, and is more exclusive than liking. On the other hand, love may also refer to a special feeling. The most obvious possibility is sexual passion. Finally, there are several kinds of romantic love. Sternberg's theory suggests that love can vary along the three dimensions of intimacy, passion, and commitment.

CHAPTER SUMMARY

- Interpersonal attraction consists of the attitudes we have toward others, and usually the affective aspect is emphasized. Typical forms of attraction include liking, loving, and respecting.

- Balance theory explains attraction in terms of balance tendencies. When two people agree or have the same unit relationship to an object, event, or person, the triad will be balanced if the people like each other.

- Reward theory simply suggests that we like people to the extent they provide psychological or material rewards at relatively low cost.

- Both balance theory and reward theory predict that we should like those who are similar to us in attitudes, personality, and abilities. That proposition has been mostly confirmed, but reward theory suggests that there are circumstances in which similarity might not be rewarding. One is when the similar other is obnoxious.

- We generally like those who are physically close and whom we see frequently. One reason is that familiarity leads to positive affect. Another is that people we encounter frequently give us many opportunities to discover mutually rewarding behaviors. It also follows that people we see often may be intensely disliked if the contact leads to costly encounters.

- We like those who have pleasant personalities and who perform helpful, cooperative behaviors.

- Physically attractive people are also liked more than their unattractive counterparts. One reason is that, because it is scarce, beauty confers status on those who possess it or who are associated with it. Another possibility is that handsome and beautiful people have greater social skills; it is possible that attractive people are encouraged to develop and maintain social skills.

- One of the premier rewards others provide is their approval. We typically like people who like us, unless their approval is tainted or is perceived as insincere.

- Because we want to be liked, we behave in ways likely to gain social approval. Sometimes people explicitly take advantage of others and try to solicit approval through ingratiation. There are several forms of ingratiation: self-presentation, conformity, flattery, and rendering favors. All of these strategies are based on factors that affect liking. The ingratiator has a precarious stance as he tries to win the approval of others without seeming to do so.

- Love is related to liking but is not merely an intense form of liking. One model of love suggests that *love* is a term we use for referring to attraction in certain types of relationships. Typically, love involves long-term relationships with intense and general feelings as well as dependency. Also, love may be a special kind of feeling based on sexual passion.

- Recently it has been suggested that there are several forms of love, and Sternberg has suggested that love relationships vary in dimensions on intimacy, passion, and commitment.

C H A P T E R

13

RELATIONSHIPS

He was a symbol of his age and one of the world's great thinkers. John Stuart Mill was born in 1806 in England. He could read Greek at age 3; based on this and other accomplishments, his IQ has been estimated as close to 200. Mill was raised to be the perfectly rational man, and he became admired for his intellect, logical abilities, rationality, and quiet kindness. He lacked only emotion among admirable human qualities.

In 1826, Mill met the great and only love of his life. Harriet Taylor was attractive, impetuous, emotional, and decisive—in short, all the things John Stuart Mill was not. She was also married. Her husband, John Taylor, was a kind, good-natured, and prosperous businessman, but by the time she met Mill she had decided that marriage was a prison. She particularly objected to her husband's fairly insistent sexual demands. She, like many women of her time, had been totally ignorant of sex before she married, and argued quite openly that it was immoral for women to have to enter into marriage without knowing anything about its sexual aspect.

Harriet and John Stuart soon became warm friends and before long she was spending more time with Mill than with her husband and family. She and Mill even attended social events together, thereby shocking Victorian society. Mr. Taylor, for his part, was hurt but was ultimately understanding enough to buy his wife a separate house where she and Mill could be alone together. Finally, after John Taylor died in 1849, Harriet and John Stuart married and lived together for seven more years before she died.

Theirs has been described as the perfect marriage. As far as anyone could judge, they respected and loved one another without reservation. They never exchanged unkind words, at least in public, and probably not in private.

Francine Hughes goes to trial.

From 1840 on, Harriet was a silent collaborator on Mill's great books on psychology, logic, and political and moral theory. His logical mind combined with her enormous energy, critical abilities, and great feeling for essential moral issues proved to be an intellectual combination for all time. Among his (their) most famous books was one arguing for the equality of men and women, a radical idea indeed for the time. Their marriage was ideal except in one respect. As far as one can judge, the marriage was never consummated sexually. Her extreme distaste for sex combined perfectly with his own excessive (even by Victorian standards) sexual inhibition. It turns out that this was not so uncommon as one might expect. John Ruskin, Thomas Carlyle (probably), and George Bernard Shaw, among famous men of the nineteenth century, probably never had sexual relations with their wives. Happy marriage without sex? Apparently so.

Let us now turn to a more modern example, also not typical but hardly singular. Francine Hughes married her husband, Mickey, in 1963 when she was 16 and he 18. They were reasonably happy in the first few months of their marriage. He was, however, insanely jealous, and shortly after their marriage began hitting her for wearing what he considered to be suggestive clothes.

Mickey often spent his income on other women and drinking. When he drank, he often beat Francine. Gradually her life became a living hell as she had to watch her every word and deed lest she make Mickey angry enough to hit her. Sometimes she called the police but they were usually not helpful, and when they put him in jail he would just return home angrier than ever.

When Francine began taking courses at a local business college, Mickey often taunted her about her attempts to raise her station in life. On March 9, 1977, when Francine came home from her classes and made dinner, Mickey became angry and threw all the food on the floor and made her clean it up. He also complained about her school activities and finally forced her to burn her school notes and papers. He also forced her to have sex with him. In some respects this was an evening like many others, but something gave way in Francine that night. She gathered up her children and left for good. Just before leaving, however, she poured gasoline around the bed in which Mickey was sleeping and set it on fire. He died. She was subsequently tried for murder and acquitted on the grounds of temporary insanity. Francine's life was the subject of a television movie, "The Burning Bed," based on the book of the same title (McNulty, 1980).

It is, of course, interesting and important to know why Mickey beat Francine and to debate the appropriateness of her acquittal. But for our present purposes, the more immediate question is why she stayed in a relationship with a man she hated for 14 years, a miserable relationship about as different from that of the Mills' as one can imagine.

INTRODUCTION

Marriage is, of course, one important kind of social relationship, but we have many other sorts of relationships as well, ranging from superficial and fleeting to deep and lasting. Most relationships involve more than just being with or thinking about another person; we have special feelings about relationships. We care about other people, and we also value the sense of a bond with them. Much of our social behavior exists in the context of various relationships with others. In fact, when we think about social interactions we are apt to think in terms of friendships, marriage, work partners, and the like.

Most important relationships are based on interpersonal attraction, and we will focus on those that do involve liking and loving—friendships and romance. However, relationships vary in many ways, of course. Some are permanent, such as those between parents and their children, although the quality of that relationship typically changes over the years. Others are less permanent, such as the one you have with one of your professors. Some relationships are superficial, others are deep. Some are based solely on rewards and costs whereas others are based more on love and mutuality. Relationships can be informal or formal and legally sanctioned. Some are primarily emotional while others are revolve purely around a particular task. Status is important for some but irrelevant for others. Most of your relationships are probably positive, but surely some have a strong negative flavor. So when we speak about relationships we encompass a wide scope with considerable variety.

THE BASES OF RELATIONSHIPS

Before we can consider differences among relationships and developmental changes, we need to consider some general features of all relationships. We need a psychological foundation on which to build our analysis. There are four such essential building blocks. The first of these is *interpersonal attraction,* which we considered in the last chapter. Normally, close and superficial relationships are distinguished, in part, by the type and intensity of the feelings of the people involved. Second, relationships involve *exchanges* of rewards and costs. The patterning of such exchanges helps to structure relationships. Third, there are sets of important *norms,* such as about equity and reciprocity, that help to structure relationships and that regulate reward–cost exchanges. Fourth, people in relationships generally reveal information about themselves in part through their behavior and in part through explicit verbal statements, what we call *self-disclosure.* We will now consider each of these last three factors in some detail.

EXCHANGE THEORY

Probably the dominant theoretical tradition in the study of relationships has been exchange theory. As you will recall from Chapter 1, exchange theories assume that people are motivated to gain a favorable reward–cost ratio—to turn a profit—from any social exchange. Furthermore, the value of any relationship, how much one likes it, is based largely or entirely on the profits one gains from it.

Taken at face value, this theory makes people out to be selfish, egocentric beasts, and there are such people—Mickey Hughes from the opening example is one. However, the theory also allows for the rewards given to others to be experienced as rewards for self, so that altruism and fellow-feeling are active parts of the theory.

The Nature of Rewards   Exchange theories allow for a full range of material and psychological rewards and costs. So when we say that people in a relationship desire to make a profit, we do not mean that they are merely exchanging money or gifts, although certainly this is common enough. Foa and Foa (1974) have grouped interpersonal rewards and costs into six major categories: (1) material goods, (2) money, (3) services, (4) status, (5) information, and (6) love. Generally, each of these is important in at least some relationships and is more important for some relationships than for others. For example, I am hardly concerned about exchanging love and affection with the person who delivers my morning paper, but I willingly exchange money for his service. But with my wife, love and status may be more important than money as media of exchange. The relative importance of these classes of outcomes also differs from person to person. Because I value his intellectual stimulation, I may continue a relationship with a friend who is always borrowing things he never returns, but another person might well find the costs of the constant borrower more important than I do or value the stimulation less.

Within the exchange perspective, rewards and costs are often more than what they appear on the surface. When I agree to loan you $1,000, I have not only granted you a certain sum of money, which is one kind of reward, but I have also provided you a more symbolic reward by declaring that I value you and trust you enough to loan you the money. Similarly, a party invitation is important not only for the fun it promises, but for the additional reward of being approved. Our social relations are concerned with symbolic exchange, that is, with providing support and indicating worthiness and trust (Haas & Deseran, 1981); often such rewards are implied by other actions rather than being directly granted.

You might want to think about the rewards Mickey and Francine found in their relationship. For Mickey the relationship was highly profitable. He had his meals prepared, his clothes taken care of, easy sexual opportunities, and minimum obligations to his family. It is much more difficult to understand how Francine managed to stay in the relationship. The costs of degradation and pain were very real, but she also obtained some rewards of a sort. There were some good times between them, and she was very scared of being on her own, so having Mickey there was a kind of security. She was also afraid of him, so that the pain was better than the fear of what he might do if she kicked him out. Staying with Mickey was easier than facing the world alone.

We will have much more to say about rewards and costs throughout this chapter. For the moment it is sufficient to keep in mind that relationships vary in the complexity of exchange and in the reward–cost value of behaviors. In general, superficial contacts involve fairly explicit and simple exchanges of rewards—often money for services or smiles for small favors. However, for more important relationships, exchanges will likely be more complex and involve a greater number of the six classes of rewards mentioned earlier.

Interdependency and Control   Two people are in a relationship when their choices of behavior affect one another. My decision as to whether to schedule an exam October 15 will not affect you because we have no relationship; however, my students will be affected. For that matter, what you decide to do October 15 has no effect on me, but a decision by one of my students to vacation in Aspen that day may affect my behavior. Relationships involve interdependent exchanges.

As a single example, consider two roommates, John and Bill, and some of the activities each might prefer. Suppose that on a particular evening John has to decide between going to a movie and studying and that Bill has the same choice. Each, of course, will consider his own rewards and costs in doing one activity as opposed to the other. The question of a relationship arises when Bill and John can affect one another's outcomes as well as their own by their choices.

For the moment, consider matters just from John's perspective. He has his own preferences, say, to go to the movie. That is independent of whatever Bill does. John expects more favorable outcomes, greater pleasure, from going to the movie than from studying.

However, Bill's behavior may also affect the outcomes John expects. John might have a preference for what Bill does. For example, John may want to go to the movies with Bill just to have some companionship; or John may prefer to be alone—to have Bill do the opposite of what he does. Now here is the important point. Because John cares what Bill does, John is dependent on Bill for some of his own rewards and costs. The other side to John's dependency on Bill is Bill's power over John. Bill has the power to make John relatively happy or unhappy by doing what John wants or not.

Up to this point we have been considering matters only from John's point of view. However, Bill will have his own preferences, and we could analyze these in exactly the same way. And to the extent that Bill cares what John does, Bill will be dependent on John. When each person is mutually dependent on the other, we have interdependencies and can say that John and Bill have a relationship.

Mickey and Francine illustrate much the same point. Obviously, Mickey had enormous control over Francine. She preferred him to be nice rather than to beat her, and so she worked very hard to make sure that she did not displease him. Most of us feel that those were not her only two options—to please Mickey or to be beaten—but for her the other options were less clear. In the formal language of Thibaut and Kelley (see Chapter 10), being married to Mickey was below her comparison level (roughly, the level that determines satisfaction) but above the comparison level of her alternatives (the rewards offered by the next-best alternative). She tried to kick him out; that was costly because he would beat her further. Clearly she was also dependent on him in other ways—for a certain sense of self-esteem and love, for example. One problem was that their relationship was extremely one-sided. Mickey had more freedom in the relationship than Francine (or had more power over her than she over him) because he did not allow her behavior to limit his options. If she refused to cook, he ate elsewhere; no sex, well, he had his girlfriends. So whether Francine was a good cook, a nice companion, or sexually satisfying did not make very much difference to Mickey. Because whatever she did made little difference to his outcomes, he was not dependent on her. Therefore Francine lacked much of the power that most people in a relationship have.

Transformations   In their most recent work on relationships, Kelley and Thibaut (1978) have added another feature to the analysis. In most relationships, we care not only about our own outcomes but also about those of the other person. John will not only want what is most pleasing to himself but will also care about what is pleasing to Bill. From the Thibaut and Kelley perspective, however, this must be expressed as a reward or cost to John. So we can say that John's own personal outcomes are transformed by taking into account Bill's outcomes. The simplest kind of transformation would be one in which John's knowledge that Bill wanted to study would make Bill's studying more directly rewarding to John—more rewarding to John because John wants Bill to be happy.

Another common kind of transformation occurs when one party to the relationship becomes upset by the power the other has over her. If your friend tries to manipulate your behavior by promising you a good time if you go to the movies with him and a miserable night if you study while he goes alone to the movies, you might so resent this control that you transform your outcomes to be more positive (say by feeling proud of your moral strength) when you do not give in to his controlling behavior. Such transformations generally create real problems for a relationship because the more Joe tries to control Sonya the more she tries to exert countercontrol by doing the opposite of what he wants.

The important point for our present purposes is that these **transformations,** the ways that each person has of taking account of the desires of others, are important in resolving conflict in relationships. Because most of us want at least some different things than our partners, relationships have inherent potential for conflict. Recall that transformations allow one person to take account of the desires and needs of the other. The kinds of transformations used will affect the potential for conflict in a relationship. Over the course of a relationship, the two people are apt to recognize certain stabilities and continuities in the transformations the other person uses. So the familiar arguments of "You never care what I want," "You're always trying to take advantage of me," or "You don't listen to me" are all really arguments about what kinds of transformations the other person uses. If your friend feels that for a particular kind of issue you rarely, if ever, take her desires into account, she is saying that when the preferences conflict, you fail to transform your outcomes to take account of hers.

From the exchange perspective, the development of relationships is characterized by mutual dependencies and interdependence. If you do only what you want to do without caring about what your partner does, it would hardly seem that you have a real relationship. On the other hand, if you do have a relationship, meaning that your outcomes are affected by your partner's behavior, the partner will have some control over your life. He can make it clear that he will reward you if you do one thing rather than another, and he can also make it clear that your best outcomes depend, in part, on his behavior.

THE NORMATIVE FOUNDATIONS OF EXCHANGE

Exchange theories assume that people are basically hedonistic. We value rewards, dislike costs, and govern our behavior accordingly. Concerns with profits structure our relationships. Yet there is surely more to the story. Exchange theories recognize that there are also important norms that help to regulate interpersonal exchange. Suppose you are responsible for running a small office. You have about 10 workers under you and it is time to hand out annual bonuses. Your boss has told you that you can distribute $10,000 among your 10 employees. How do you do this? You might use several possible rules.

Probably the most obvious possibility is that you hand out bonuses in accordance with how well each of your workers has performed. Surely Jane, who is willing to work overtime, always gets to work on time, is efficient, and has made several useful suggestions, deserves a bonus of $2,000, while John, who is surly, frequently late, and lazy, deserves no bonus at all. Jane has invested more in her job than John and therefore deserves a bigger outcome. If you think along these lines, you are responding to a norm of *equity.*

On the other hand, you may reason that because the bonus has been granted because of the effort of the entire group, you should give everyone the same bonus of $1,000. Such a distribution pattern reflects an *equality* norm.

Or, perhaps you are aware that although Jane is a hard worker and John is not, John has been having a number of family problems. Among other things, one of his children is having a series of operations. Would it not make sense to give John a big bonus to help him through these difficult times? Are we not supposed to help those in need? If you were to give John a big bonus because of his need we would say that you had responded to a norm of *altruism.*

Yet another norm is *reciprocity.* Suppose that although Jim is only an average worker, he did you a big favor by covering up one of your infrequent errors so that your boss did not find out. You are pretty sure that Jim didn't help you for any ulterior motive, but you feel you should show your appreciation now by giving him a big bonus. After all, aren't we supposed to reciprocate favors?

Finally, you may feel bound by previous promises. When Sally came to work for you, you had trouble hiring her because of the low starting salary. But you promised her that you would make it up to her whenever you could. The time has now come. Independent of how good a worker Sally is, don't you feel that you should live up to your promise? Aren't you supposed to keep promises, to conform to a norm of *honesty?*

As you can see, not only does each of these rules make a certain amount of sense in the context (some perhaps more than others) but each may conflict with another from time to time. Sally may not deserve a bonus on merit, but she does according to an honesty norm. You can't reward Jane's hard work if you are going to reward people equally.

The examples we have used are based on economic relationships because everyone understands dollars and cents. However, both exchange models and the norms of exchange apply broadly to all sorts of relationships. Consider a family. Equity norms are quite common in this set of relationships. For example, the person who cooks a meal usually has more to say about what will actually be cooked; his or her greater work input provides the right to choose the outcomes. Equality norms are also quite common. Children are supposed to be treated alike, and most families apportion food approximately equally even though the parents have contributed far more to the costs of buying and preparing it. Children benefit from the norm of altruism: parents help children with all sorts of things with no expectation of direct or immediate help in return. Family members also urge one another to share and trade (reciprocity) and, of course, one is supposed to be honest within a family situation. The norms of equity, equality, altruism, reciprocity, and honesty are thus general norms that apply to a broad range of superficial and deep relationships.

The Functions of Exchange Norms   As long ago as 1651, the social theorist Thomas Hobbes recognized that naked hedonism provides a poor basis for a stable society. If each of us sought only his or her own rewards without concern for others, we would maintain few, if any, relationships with others. So long as you reward me and I reward you, we can be friends. But suppose that we lived in a place with no laws and that each of us has been brought up to think only of our own needs. I admire your new hut and, being conscious of getting rewards at minimum cost, I ask you to turn it over to me. Perhaps I even offer you a bunch of bananas as a payment. You naturally refuse because it took you far more time and effort to build the hut than it would to gather your own bananas. However, I know how to solve this problem—I will simply kill you and take the hut for myself. There is no law to punish me and I am blessed with a perfect selfishness that admits of no guilt for such actions. Indeed, under these conditions I do get maximum rewards (your hut) for minimum efforts (the effort involved in killing you).

Hobbes had something like this in mind when he noted that in such a "state of nature" without laws and norms, people would be in a constant "war of all against all." Today I kill you to get your hut, and tomorrow I will have to defend my life against another person who also wants the hut. Hobbes questioned how we could create a stable society given our basic hedonism. His answer was both simple and profound. I may value your hut, but I value my own life and security against attack even more. So from a purely selfish perspective I will give up my freedom to kill you to get your hut (and this loss of freedom is certainly a cost) in return for the even greater reward of security. In society, people collectively have a vested interest in obeying certain rules of decency and cooperation so that they generally get more rewards than costs. Therefore, because the resultant security makes their own outcomes better over the long run, people will be socialized to harness their own selfishness and to worry some about the common good. Freud would make a similar point nearly 300 years later.

Hobbes' point is well taken. If most people follow these norms of fair play, each of us will be more secure and will achieve profits within this normative framework. Thus, we have basic norms that regulate to some extent what kinds of rewards we should get and how we are supposed to operate in an exchange relationship. They provide the necessary security and predictability of human behavior that allow us to get on with out business without the costs of certain sorts of worry. As such, they function very much like the legal framework of modern business, where certain laws provide for the execution of contracts so that business people have the security of knowing what they can expect from a business deal.

Equity and Equality   The importance of both equality and equity norms is readily apparent. Feelings that everyone should be treated alike and that those who work harder should get more rewards appear fairly early in the lives of children and are strongly held standards for most adults in our society. However, the two norms can sometimes come into conflict. For example, parents may have to decide whether to give equal allowances to their 7- and 10-year-old daughters. If they opt for equality, the older child will complain that she had greater need for money and has more responsibilities within the home; if they opt for equity and give the older child a bigger allowance, the younger child may feel offended that she is not being given equal treatment. And when I hold office hours, should I give everyone equal time or should I devote more time to students who have earned my time by being serious students?

Equity Theory   Equity theory is based on the intuitively appealing proposition that those people who contribute more to a relationship or group should be rewarded more than those who contribute less (Adams, 1965; Walster, Walster, & Berscheid, 1978). There has been some disagreement about how equity should be defined (Alessio, 1980; Farkas & Anderson, 1979; Harris, 1980; Harris, Messick, & Sentis, 1981), but for our purposes equity is an equality of ratios of outcomes to inputs (see Figure 13.1). Thus, the theory suggests that everyone in a group should have the same ratio of rewards (such as pay or approval) to costs or investments (such as time spent). If one person is paid $50 for 10 hours of hard work, then her friend who works 20 hours should get $100.

Research confirms that there are strong tendencies to reward people in an equitable way (more rewards for more work). However, some people in some situations prefer the equality norm. For example, many workers prefer to be rewarded on the basis of equality because equal division of pay is perfectly straightforward and unambiguous (Leventhal, 1976). Rewards based on equity, on the other hand, require that someone determine who has worked hardest or most effectively, thus bringing in a subjective judgment that can be based on personal bias. The boss who rewards Henry more than Jane because Henry works harder also leaves herself open to the charge that Henry has to work harder because he is inefficient or that she must be playing favorites to pretend that Henry really has worked harder.

In general, equality norms tend to favor harmonious group feelings, whereas equity norms promote competition. Therefore it makes sense that equality norms are especially salient when the allocator will have future interactions with the recipient (Greenberg, 1979; Shapiro, 1975). Also, women are often more likely to prefer equal rather than equitable allocations, probably reflecting the fact that women have traditionally been taught to value cooperation

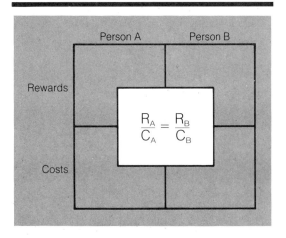

FIGURE 13.1   Factors Involved in Equitable Relationships. Note that equity is defined as an equality of ratios. Thus, if A's outcomes (on the left) increase, B can either increase own outcomes (numerator on right) or decrease inputs (denominator on right) to make B's ratio equal to A's.

and men competition. However, if the situation encourages a competitive, equity orientation, women also prefer equity (Brehm, 1985). It is also important to remember that preferences for equity and equality norms are heavily culturally determined. For example, Leung and Bond (1984) have shown that in Chinese culture, which favors collective values, equality norms are highly favored.

Another major proposition of equity theory is that people in an inequitable relationship should feel some distress. Obviously, almost any psychological theory would predict that a person who is undercompensated for his efforts would feel angry, but equity theory also proposes that those who are overbenefited should feel distress, commonly in the form of guilt. There is supporting evidence. For example, Pritchard, Dunnette, and Jorgenson (1972) had men work on a clerical task for several days. They had been promised a certain wage for their work, but after working for a while some were told they would be paid more, others less, than promised. The equitably paid workers reported they were more satisfied

When people such as these farmers feel they have not been treated justly, they may engage in public protest.

with the work than either the over- or underpaid people.

A third proposition of the theory is that people who are in an inequitable relationship will try to restore equity. This can be done by changing either investments (costs) or outcomes (rewards), and these changes can take place either objectively or psychologically. For example, suppose you worked 30 hours on a paper and got a grade of B+ but your friend worked only 20 hours and got an A−. You might feel angry and cheated because your ratio of rewards (grade) to investments (work) is less than your friend's; according to the theory you would try to restore equity. But how could you change outcomes or investments? One obvious possibility would be to complain to the professor, hoping she will increase your outcomes by raising your grade. Another possibility would be to demean your friend's grade by teasing him; thus you try psychologically to reduce his A to your B or below. Or you might, were you really unkind, try to interfere with his work on the next paper so he gets a lower grade than you do, thus restoring

equity over a longer time period. You might decide to work less hard on your next paper—"If I'm going to get a B anyway, there's no point in working so hard"—thus reducing your investment of work. Or you could find additional rewards. You might reason that, although you got only a B on the paper, you learned a great deal, whereas your friend learned nothing even though he got an A. You could lower your perceived costs by deciding that your friend really hated the 20 hours he spent doing the paper whereas you actually liked the 30 hours you spent. In other words, your investment or costs weren't as great as your friend's, everything considered. In any case, through either objective or subjective means, you might adjust the outcomes and investments of your own ratio or your friend's so that the ratios are more equivalent.

Equity theory is relatively easy to understand, obviously true in many situations, and simple to apply. Therefore it has been used widely to explain people's feelings of satisfaction and how they behave to achieve greater satisfaction (see Walster et al., 1978, for a comprehensive review). We will have occasion to use the theory later in this chapter to explain certain aspects of close relationships. First let us consider another theory of how we perceive fairness of outcomes.

Altruism   Altruism is generally thought of as helpful behavior with no expectation of direct reciprocity. We are taught to help others, especially those in need and those who are dependent on us. This is essential (at least for the kind of society most of us value) because otherwise, relatively powerless people, such as children, older people, and work subordinates would inevitably have greater costs than rewards.

But from society's point of view norms of altruism perform another important function. Acts of altruism are generalized across people, as are expectations of reciprocity. If I help a stranded motorist, I certainly expect him to be thankful, but I hardly have performed the act to get the thanks or because I expect him to loan me his chainsaw if I need it. Instead, norms of altruism tend to ensure that if I am helpful today someone will help me when I am in need. When A helps B and B helps C there will come a point at which C (or D or E) will help A, so that everyone helps and gets helped and no one gets cheated in the game of life over the long run. I do not expect any particular person to help me when I am in need, but the altruism norm means that there will be plenty of people who have been helped in the past who will be willing to engage in costly helping behavior.

Aid freely given without explicit expectation of reciprocity is important in the development of relationships because altruism is a visible symbol of one's unselfish concern for others. Who would not prefer to interact with someone who is consistently helpful than with someone who makes clear that his help is contingent on your paying up and fast? Furthermore, the implication that someone thinks so highly of you that she is willing to incur some immediate costs creates a special kind of reward, the feeling of being a valuable person.

Reciprocity   The reciprocity norm suggests that we pay back in kind those who reward or punish us (Gouldner, 1960). Reciprocity tends to guarantee that we discharge our social debts. If I loan my friend my car, he will recognize that he owes me something and that if I always give and never receive I will, in time, have no reason to continue such an unprofitable relationship. Therefore it will be in his best interest to find a way to pay me back as soon as possible so he can borrow again in the future. I, in turn, have obligations to allow him to do so. It may be considered saintly not to allow others to return favors, but it is bad social form. If I cook dinner for you when you are sick, but then refuse to accept the plant you give me to show your appreciation, I may have made a point about my altruistic nature, but I will have lost a friendship. Although there are many circumstances

when we do not feel obligated to pay someone back for a favor, we generally feel more comfortable when we have a chance to reciprocate.

Norms of reciprocity apply over longer times for closer, more stable relationships and over shorter times for more superficial relationships. If a casual acquaintance does me a favor, I will try to find a fairly immediate way to reciprocate; certainly I will be very effusive in my thanks, this being a reward of sorts in payment for the favor. On the other hand, it would seem odd if I were equally effusive with my wife when she does me a small favor, and certainly I would not be so concerned to find an immediate opportunity to reciprocate. The basis of a long-term relationship ensures that one does not have to keep score; reciprocity will take place over the long run, or so we assume (Clark 1981, 1984; Clark & Mills, 1979).

Honesty   Norms of honesty are important because they provide the basic trust so necessary for security. If you did not trust a person who was buying your car, you would probably demand payment before you turned over the title and keys. If your friend promises to help you with an assignment but fails to show up, the next time she asks you for help you may be more concerned about what's in it for you. Because so many of our exchanges of pay and approval for a job well done, money for goods, and help given for help received are not simultaneous and immediate, we have to be able to trust people to fulfill their parts of legal, financial, and social bargains later. If you do not trust someone, you will find it hard to have any sort of a long-term, meaningful relationship with her just because you will always worry about being cheated. Without honesty and trust we are never sure that reciprocity, altruism, equity, and equality norms will be translated into behavior.

Just World   Norms of honesty, reciprocity, and altruism are important determinants of our sense of fair play in everyday social relations. The norms of equity and equality, dealing even more specifically with questions of what constitutes justice, have been major issues in social, legal, and political philosophy for centuries; the earliest great work of social philosophy, Plato's *Republic,* is, among other things, a treatise on justice. Our feelings of justice and fairness are often affected by whether people in ordinary social relationships as well as in the larger society seem to follow the norms that govern exchange.

Lerner, Miller, and Holmes (1976) have suggested that our everyday conceptions of justice have their roots in the notion of deservingness. In general, one "deserves an outcome if he has met the appropriate 'preconditions' for obtaining it" (Lerner et al., 1976, p. 134). Lerner and his colleagues have suggested that the child learns that he cannot always have what he wants and that he may gain more in the long run by postponing immediate gratification and investing his time and energy in activities that have long-term payoffs. Naturally, the child feels that such investments should have appropriate payoffs, that through his investments he deserves certain rewards or punishments in the future. However, before he can make this sort of investment, he must assume that the social and physical worlds are orderly and predictable. Just as a person would hardly be willing to put his or her hard-earned money into a bank if it paid unpredictable interest or was likely to fail, so the child learns that social stability is necessary before he can benefit from delaying immediate gratification. Thus, the child gradually develops a commitment to a general norm of justice, that everyone should get what he or she deserves.

So long as the child (or an adult) observes that all is right with the world and that everyone does, indeed, get his just deserts, his sense of security is preserved. Quite obviously, however, we all encounter instances of blatant injustice everyday: the man who is paid more than he earns, the hard-working person whose medical bills and family circumstances keep her from getting ahead, the murderer who gets a light sentence, the president who is pardoned

for violating his public trust, and so on. How do we react to injustice?

Most of us feel indignant. The security of a just world is threatened. Our reactions are not limited to indignation, however. Often we try to take action to restore justice. We give time and money to the needy, we write our legislators urging them to rectify unjust conditions, we seek better social and economic conditions. On the other hand, most of us soon come to realize that there is little we can do individually to change most unjust conditions.

How might we react under those circumstances? Lerner suggests that our desires to maintain the belief in a just world are so strong that often we will use psychological means to convince ourselves that the unjust world is just. For example, I read about a mother of five children whose husband deserted her and whose illness keeps her from working and leaves her with huge medical bills she cannot pay. Because I cannot (or am unwilling to) help the unfortunate woman I have read about, I can make the world seem just by assuming that she deserves the outcomes she gets: "If she had taken care of herself she would not now be ill—probably she drinks or is on drugs anyway. She shouldn't have had so many children if she could not take care of them."

Thus, the central notion of the ***just-world theory*** is that, if people cannot take action to restore justice, they will tend to assume that the person deserves his fate. There are several experimental demonstrations of this tendency. In many of these studies, subjects see a victim presumably being harmed and are asked to evaluate the victim. Generally, they derogate the victim as if to say he deserved what he got (Lerner, 1980). However, there are situations in which this derogation does not occur. For example, when subjects expect to share the fate of the victim, the derogation is lessened considerably (Lerner & Matthews, 1967; Sorrentino & Boutilier, 1974).

It may seem that discussions of justice and norms of exchange are far removed from our major concern about the development of relationships. In the chapters that follow, we will make frequent reference to these norms as we attempt to explain altruism, cooperation, competition, and aggression. However, the norms also have a fairly explicit effect on our feelings about relationships. In the first place, we evaluate our relationships, in part, on how well they satisfy these norms. Most of us would feel unhappy having a friend or a spouse who was incapable of altruism or who put us in an inequitable position. Divorce courts are filled with people wanting to break off relationships that seem unfair or unjust.

More to the point, however, these norms of exchange are especially important as relationships develop because they tend to transform tit-for-tat exchanges into less immediate ones. No marriage or deep friendship could long survive in a happy state if exchanges and decisions had to be constantly negotiated or instantly reciprocated. The existence of exchange norms allows for the kind of trust and expanded time perspective that allows us to provide rewards for those we like and love without having to worry about immediate returns. As relationships become closer, one can worry less about immediate rewards and costs and realize that, over the long course of events, things will probably even out. Thus, a commitment to a relationship is both based on the operation of these norms and helps to strengthen them.

SELF-DISCLOSURE

It has been commonly assumed that **self-disclosure**—the personal information a person chooses to share with others—plays an important role in the development of relationships (Altman & Taylor, 1973; Levinger & Snoek, 1972). Quite obviously, after you meet someone, the development of a deeper relationship is likely to be based on gaining additional information about the other person. Most relationships could hardly sustain themselves on the basis of the kind of superficial chatter common in most first encounters. In addition, self-disclosure is based on trust and may even engender trust and attraction to the other, thus playing a crucial role in how a relationship develops.

Definition   There are many aspects to self-disclosure (Chelune, 1979). Altman and Haythorne (1965) made a useful distinction between the breadth and depth of self-disclosure. *Breadth* refers to the sheer amount of self-relevant information shared with another person, whereas *depth* refers to the intimacy of the revelations. There are those who freely describe their attitudes, values, and past behaviors on a wide variety of topics. However, for a man to tell you which professional football teams are his favorites, to describe which sport he likes best, to say which novels he has recently read, and to talk about his education and hobbies may reveal a lot of self-relevant information but only at a rather superficial level. One must, then, distinguish the amount of information from the intimacy value of the information disclosed.

This distinction between breadth and depth may make logical sense, but is it important in everyday situations? Do you think that a person who talks a lot about superficial aspects of

Conversations are primary vehicles for self-disclosure.

himself is as revealing as someone who talks profoundly about only one or two central features of her personality? In one study, subjects listened to tape-recorded interviews and rated the interviewees on their self-disclosure. These ratings were found to be predicted by the intimacy (or centrality) of the information, by the number of self-references per unit time (a measure of amount of disclosure), as well as by whether the interviewee displayed affective congruence between what he said and how he said it. Thus, it appears that both breadth and depth of information affect perceived self-disclosure (Chelune, Skeffington, & Williams, 1981).

Factors Affecting Disclosure   Self-disclosure can be a dangerous business. If I convey information to you about my innermost motives, attitudes, and concerns, I may give you the power to control my behavior. If you know that I desperately want your approval, you can then manipulate my behavior shamelessly by dangling your approval before me like a carrot on a stick. Also, many intimate disclosures involve negative or socially undesirable information that may lead others to reject you. The fact that you were arrested for shoplifting when you were 16 may not say much about the current, inner you, but it might well lead people to prefer not to associate with you.

Thus, it seems clear on theoretical grounds that self-disclosure of intimate information can be dangerous because of the control it gives others and that disclosure of negative information is also risky because it may lead to rejection. Given these dangers, what factors might affect the decision as to whether to reveal information about oneself?

One factor might be the personality of the discloser. Some people seem generally more revealing than others, although there are few consistent personality correlates of self-disclosure (Archer, 1979). One of the most important individual differences variables that predicts disclosure is gender; women generally disclose more than men unless the situation strongly encourages men to disclose (Shaffer & Ogden, 1986).

Perhaps the most important determinant of revealingness is the nature of the target. Most of us would find it easier to talk about an intimate problem with a close friend than with a mere acquaintance. Accordingly, self-disclosure is usually higher to friends and family than to mere acquaintances (Jourard & Lasakow, 1958) and to liked rather than disliked others (Worthy, Gary, & Kahn, 1969). Because disclosure has power and dependency overtones, it is likely that low-power people will both disclose more and seek more disclosures from high-power people than the reverse (Earle, Giuliano, & Archer, 1983). The general rule of thumb is that intimate disclosures will be reserved for those who we can trust and who are unwilling or unable to use the information against us.

The nature and amount of self-disclosure will change as relationships change. When you meet someone it is helpful to disclose enough to provide the basis for conversation, but too much disclosure is likely to be threatening at such an early stage. As the relationship develops, however, more disclosure seems natural. Consequently, in casual encounters people who disclose moderate and appropriate amounts are liked more than those who disclose too much or too little (Kleinke, 1979).

Reciprocity   One of the most reliable findings from social psychology research is that people who are not closely related tend to reciprocate disclosures. If one person becomes more intimate, the other generally does also (Derlega, Harris, & Chaikin, 1973; Schneider, & Eustis, 1972; Wright & Ingraham, 1986). One possible reason is that the initial disclosure sets a tone of trust; if I trust you then you can trust me. It is also possible that disclosures act as a kind of reward, and the norm of reciprocity suggests that one reward (disclosure) should be reciprocated with another. Or perhaps the initial discloser provides a kind of social reality that defines the situation as one in which disclosure is appropriate.

How might reciprocity influence the development of the relationship? Keep in mind that a disclosure conveys not only information about the discloser but also about her trust in and feelings for the target as well as the status of the relationship itself. So intimate disclosures may provide an important symbol that all is well with the relationship. Also, we should not forget that most relationships are fueled in part by both people finding out new things about one another (see Figure 13.2).

Reciprocity is surely more important in the earlier than in the later stages of a relationship (Altman, 1973). Research also confirms that reciprocity of disclosures is more likely for strangers than for friends (Derlega, Wilson, & Chaikin, 1976), although friends *perceive* that they reciprocate more disclosures (Miller & Kenny, 1986). Comparative strangers will respond to the reciprocity norm, social reality factors, and feelings of trust engendered by the first person to disclose. But as the relationship develops, the people will move beyond the need to constantly reaffirm their trust through immediate exchanges of disclosures. This does not mean that a long-married couple ceases to exchange personal feelings but only that such exchanges will take place over a longer period of time and without explicit scorekeeping. So disclosure of information continues to play a role in long-standing relationships, indeed may be a major ingredient that helps to define them, but the meaning of such disclosures changes for such relationships and immediate exchanges are not necessary or even desirable.

SUMMARY

Among social psychologists, the most popular way to conceptualize relationships is as a

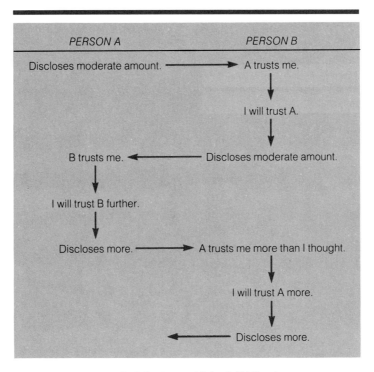

FIGURE 13.2   How Self-disclosure Might Build Trust.

set of mutual dependencies of each partner on the other for pleasant outcomes. People have distinct preferences for what they want to do, but they also realize that their partners' behavior can affect their outcomes. All this is not inevitably selfish because most partners in a relationship transform their own outcomes to take account of those of their partner. However, exchange of rewards and costs is regulated to some extent in relationships, as it is in society, by various norms: equity, equality, altruism, reciprocity, honesty, and justice.

Self-disclosures also play an important role in many relationships. Self-disclosure refers both to the amount of information and the intimacy of information given to another person. Generally, we disclose more to people who are nonthreatening, and we tend to disclose more to people who disclose to us. Disclosure is important in the building of close relationships because of the information each person has about the other and also because of the trust implied by disclosure, which in turn engenders further trust.

THE DEVELOPMENT OF
CLOSE RELATIONSHIPS

At the beginning of this chapter we discussed the fact that we have various kinds of relationships with other people. Student–professor, doctor–patient, parent–child, lovers, and friends are relationships that differ in many ways. However, most social psychologists have been especially concerned with how relationships develop from relatively superficial ones to close ones. One reason for this particular interest is that most people place a great deal of emphasis on their close relationships; we are happy to have many acquaintances, but we particularly value our close friends and relatives.

Most of us consider our close relationships rather special and comforting. However, it is also important to remember that there are large individual differences in the needs people feel for close relationships. Some people are unhappy unless surrounded by many people and they are relatively indifferent to how superficial these relationships are, while others are concerned primarily with relatively fewer close relationships and still others are relatively happy with no friendships at all.

Quite obviously, superficial and intimate relationships differ in many ways. There have been several attempts to characterize these differences (Huston & Burgess, 1979; Levinger & Snoek, 1972; Walster, Walster, & Berscheid, 1978). Table 13.1 presents the list of Huston and Burgess. For our purposes, we can concentrate on fewer, broader distinctions.

FACTORS PROMOTING INTIMACY

As a relationship moves from relatively impersonal or superficial to relatively personal or close, several features of the relationship also change. Mutuality, knowledge and trust, personal norms, and self-investment are important features that distinguish personal from impersonal relationships.

Mutuality   The two participants in a personal relationship are likely to want to have mutually satisfactory outcomes and to account of each other's feelings and desires. Each person is concerned about what the other thinks of the relationship and of him or her. I can perfectly well buy a new drill bit from a hardware dealer without worrying whether the hardware dealer thinks I am stupid or smart, rich, happy, depressed, or what have you. However, when I consider a friend, I do care what he thinks of me. Furthermore, I also assume that he cares what I think of him.

Earlier in this chapter we discussed the concept of mutual dependence, or interdependence. Each person in a relationship is able to affect the other's rewards and is able to induce the other to adjust his or her behavior so that better outcomes are achieved. In that discussion we also noted that the person's outcomes are usually transformed as he or she takes account of the preferences of the other. This willingness to take account of the outcomes of the other is a major characteristic of close relationships. When a casual acquaintance asks me to go with her to a movie I really do not want to see, I am likely to consider only my own preferences and decline the invitation. However, when my wife makes the same request, I am more likely to go with her. I do so, in part, because I care about her pleasures. Being in a close relationship implies a certain subordination of one's own to the other's preferences.

Knowledge and Trust A second feature of personal relationships is that the two people are more knowledgeable about each other. For example, think of a close, personal friend; undoubtedly you have shared experiences with that person, perhaps over a long period of time. Having seen your friend in many situations, you naturally feel that you know a lot about him or her. In addition, there is more self-disclosure in close relationships; as we have noted earlier, self-disclosure tends to engender feelings of mutual trust by the participants. This in turn encourages further disclosures. Mutual secrets and trust are important in structuring relationships and setting them

---

TABLE 13.1 CHANGES CHARACTERIZING THE MOVEMENT FROM SUPERFICIAL TO CLOSE RELATIONSHIPS.

1. The participants interact more often, for longer periods of time, and in a widening array of settings.

2. The participants attempt to restore proximity when separated and feel comforted when proximity is regained.

3. The participants "open up" to each other in the sense that they disclose secrets and share physical intimacies.

4. The participants become less inhibited, more willing to share positive and negative feelings and to praise and criticize each other.

5. The participants develop their own communication system and become ever more efficient in using it.

6. The participants increase their ability to map and anticipate each other's views of social reality.

7. The participants begin to synchronize their goals and behavior and begin to develop stable interaction patterns.

8. The participants increase their investment in the relationship, thus enhancing its importance in their life space.

9. The participants begin increasingly to feel that their separate interests are inextricably tied to the well-being of their relationship.

10. The participants increase their liking, trust, and love for each other.

11. The participants see the relationship as irreplaceable or at least as unique.

12. The participants more and more relate to others as a couple rather than as individuals.

SOURCE: Adapted from Huston and Burgess, 1979, p. 8.

apart from the rest of society (Simmel, 1950).

Of course, much more is involved in trust than knowledge and disclosure. Rempel, Holmes, and Zanna (1985) argue that predictability, dependability, and faith that the partner will be caring and kind are important components of trust. They gave couples several questionnaires including measures of faith (such as "I can rely on my partner to react in a positive way when I expose my weaknesses to him/her"), dependability ("I can rely on my partner to keep the promises he/she makes to me"), and predictability ("My partner behaves in a very consistent manner"). Subjects also filled out a scale measuring love for their partner. The research of Rempel et al. showed that trust, especially the faith component, is correlated with love in couples.

Personal Norms As we noted in Chapter 10, all groups have norms. A feature of personal relationships is that they involve more norms than impersonal dyads do, many of them specific to the relationship. There are a large number of general norms that govern our everyday impersonal interactions with other people. For example, unless provoked, one should always refrain from staring or making a face at another person. These general norms also apply to more intimate and personal relationships, although often the partners will feel freedom to deviate from norms of politeness with close friends.

There are also unique norms that govern close relationships. Families, for example, establish norms about who will do household chores and under what circumstances, what is an appropriate time to eat, what should happen to family members who do not arrive for meals on time, how late one is allowed to sleep on Saturday morning, how often various family members will have access to the family car and TV, and whether or not the family's dog is allowed in the living room. Although all families probably have norms about the allocation of household chores, these norms differ from one family to another. In one family, father may wash the dinner dishes and mother prepare the dinner; in another family, the children may wash the dishes and father may prepare the dinner; and in another family, perhaps mom does both tasks.

Self-investment Finally, and perhaps this sums up all that has gone before, what distinguishes personal from impersonal relationships is that one cares more about the former than about the latter. This goes beyond saying that people are more attracted to personal friends or lovers than to impersonal acquaintances. In personal relationships, one has invested a certain aspect of oneself because of the greater intimacy and trust involved. Because the other person in the relationship knows what you are like, a rejection from that person is a very deep blow to pride and self-esteem. In addition, we usually have strong commitments to the idea of close relationships in and of themselves. Even friends who have grown apart or a long-married couple who have little love left in their relationship will work at maintaining the relationship. Our marriages, love affairs, and close friendships are supported by societal pressures and hold fond memories even after they are over.

FRIENDSHIP

Thus far we have considered the differences between superficial and close relationships. The question still remains of how two people move from one to the other. Most of the research work on this topic concerns the development of romantic relationships, but it should not be forgotten that friendships also have a developmental history.

Bases of Friendship Obviously, we are likely to form friendships among people we like. However, more must be involved than that. I can think of many people I find charming and likable but who are no more than superficial friends, if that. So how do we move from the stage of liking people to forming friendships with them? Certainly, a great deal of what makes for friendship must be accidental. For example, you happen to stumble onto a mutually satisfying topic with Joe at a party or you have an especially pleasant time with someone you have just met. Friendships may also develop as mutual friends or particular social contexts throw you together with the same person on many occasions. But a great many people maintain their primary friendships with people from their work environment, church, or social clubs (Huston & Levinger, 1978). Such social contexts provide situations for the relaxed exploration of mutual interests without the necessity of making a strong commitment to a relationship. You can get to know someone through work pretty well before you have to decide whether to invite her over for dinner, an invitation that is likely to be reciprocated and that may involve too much interdependence too fast.

The basis for friendships varies considerably from social class to social class, from age to age, and from sex to sex. The number of friendships increases dramatically from childhood into early adulthood and then declines during the adult years. The basis of friendships also changes throughout the life cycle.

Friendships throughout the Life Cycle
Given the tremendous cognitive, emotional, and behavioral changes during childhood, it is not surprising that the meaning of friendship also changes during this period. As we saw in Chapter 9, the preadolescent years are generally characterized by a growth out of a purely egocentric perspective to one that includes the capacity to understand mutuality; friendships show a corresponding pattern. Selman (1980) notes that during early childhood, children are friends with anyone they can play with. Subsequently, children learn to take the role of the other and come to understand that friendship involves mutual give and take,

cooperation and reciprocity, even as they continue to value friends for their ability to satisfy their own needs. With the approach of adolescence, friends are valued more for their more personal characteristics, such as loyalty, having a sense of humor, and the like. Friendships begin to take on an exclusive and intimate quality; this is the stage of chums (Berndt, 1982; La Gaipa, 1981).

Despite the growing importance of friendships before 12 or so, most children continue to value their family relationships more than friendships. During adolescence, the greater freedom from family on the one hand and the more exclusive and intimate nature of friendships on the other hand shift the adolescent's relationships toward peers. Self-disclosure is now aimed primarily toward friends rather than toward parents, as many parents discover to their dismay.

During the adult years, until old age at least, the number of friends remains fairly constant (Reisman, 1981). However, the amount of time spent with friends generally declines throughout the adult years (Dickens & Perlman, 1981). This partly reflects reduction in the need for friends as support for identity and for help; for the young adult, a romantic

partner often begins to fill these needs, and the demands of careers and children further restrict the amount of time available for friendship. For the married couple, friendships typically are based on relationships formed at work or in community organizations; somewhat surprisingly, neighbors are not usually considered to be close friends. Also, the exclusivity and primariness of the marriage bond typically restrict most friendships to other couples with similar socioeconomic status, children the same age, and the like (Reisman, 1981).

There are important differences between men and women in how they view friendships (Reisman, 1981). Men tend to pick friends with whom they have common interests and with whom they can share mutually enjoyable activities. Women tend to think of friends as confidants, someone with whom they can talk over problems and obtain support. This may represent a general preference on the part of women, but there may also be situational reasons. When women are not employed outside the home and have primary responsibility for child and home care, they may be both more restricted in their opportunities for friendship and also have a need to find someone who shares their concerns, a function that work partners fill for their working husbands.

ROMANTIC RELATIONSHIPS

Among our most important relationships are those that involve romantic love. In our culture, romantic relationships are typically between two members of the opposite sex, and such heterosexual relationships have been the most intensively studied, although there is no reason to believe that homosexual relationships are radically different in their processes and dynamics (Brehm, 1985). To some extent, romantic relationships are further extensions of friendships. Just as love is built on liking, so romantic involvements may be built on friendships. However, as we saw in the last chapter, love is not merely intensified liking; similarly, most marriages are something more than intense friendships.

Until recently, there have been few studies of how romantic relationships develop. Ideally, one would want to obtain data on a couple from the time of their first meeting to the point at which they make a permanent commitment to one another and ultimately (perhaps) break up. This is an extremely difficult research strategy to effect, not only because of the problems in carrying out such research over a long period of time but also because the vast majority of people that one picks for initial study will ultimately be of no interest because their relationship does not progress beyond their first meeting. For this reason, much of what we know about the development of romantic relationships comes from retrospective reports. However, one longitudinal study of relationships is described in Box 13.1.

There may be several stages in the life cycle of a romantic relationship; for the purposes of discussion we will use the stages proposed by Levinger (1983). First there is the stage of *acquaintanceship* in which the couple first becomes aware of one another as distinct people. This is the stage of impression formation (Chapter 4) and of deciding that the other person is likable or not (Chapter 12). The second stage may be called *courtship*. At this stage, which may be quite lengthy, the couple begins to explore mutual activities and identifies outcomes that can be achieved easily within this particular relationship. In the *continuation* stage, the partners make a commitment to one another and to the relationship. This involves a more or less explicit decision to be more than just close friends. In many cases, this explicit decision results in marriage, but, of course, many relationships last for long periods of time without this legal ratification. Fourth, many, probably most, relationships enter a stage of deterioration, perhaps resulting in *dissolution* of the relationship.

Courtship　　Courtships vary not only in their duration but also in their intensity. Some couples achieve psychological (and perhaps sexual) intimacy within a few days or weeks. Others have more prolonged courtships before one or both people are willing to make a final commitment to themselves as a couple. As you might imagine, the more accelerated courtships have fewer conflicts, and progress toward commitment is generally not only quick but untroubled by reversals. Longer courtships, on the other hand, tend to have some conflicts that are serious enough that one or both partners reduce involvement and commit-

George Levinger

ment to the relationship, at least temporarily (Huston et al., 1981).

Studies by Huston et al. (1981) and Braiker and Kelley (1979) agree that there are certain predictable changes that take place during the courtship. Love and affectionate feelings generally increase during the courtship as it moves from superficial to deeper involvement. One interesting finding reported consistently in studies of romantic relationships is that men tend to fall in love more quickly than women (Rubin et al., 1981). Perhaps men are the more romantic of the sexes. However, there is also a more cynical or at least prosaic possibility. Marriage traditionally represents a larger investment for women than men (women have had to move with their husbands and the wife's social success was dependent on his status) and women might therefore be more cautious about falling in love.

A second dimension of change is behaviors to maintain the relationship. These include self-disclosures, confessing vulnerabilities, offering help and support, reciprocation, and accommodation. Again, as one might expect, these behaviors increase as the relationship gets deeper, but there are some interesting sex differences reported by Huston et al. (1981). Men who fall in love more readily also are more likely to engage in maintenance behaviors early in the relationship. However, once the couple is married, the woman provides more of the maintenance behaviors, even though her love does not proportionately

BOX 13.1

LONGITUDINAL APPROACHES TO THE STUDY OF RELATIONSHIPS

Perhaps the most characteristic feature of relationships is that they develop and change—they are intrinsically dynamic rather than static. Unfortunately, growth, development, and change are hard to capture within a scientific net of experimental techniques.

There are several strategies for studying how relationships change. One would be to take a series of cross-sectional snapshots at various intervals along the way. This is commonly used in the study of childhood development when we study the behavior of 3-year-olds, 5-year-olds, and so on and assume that in 2 years the present 3-year-olds will resemble the present 5-year-olds. A major problem in using this strategy is that relationships do not grow in the same way children do. Children tend to get more proficient as they get older and do not regress to earlier behavior, but relationships do not necessarily grow in any particular direction. A relationship can become more passionate, cool off, and then heat up again. Because relationship development is less obviously progressive and organized into clear stages, it would be hard to know a priori when and where to take the various snapshots.

It would therefore be preferable to study how individual relationships change over time. The *longitudinal study* is a device for examining the changes in a sample of people over a particular time period. This sounds easy enough, but there are major practical difficulties. First, one must select the initial sample and measurement devices quite carefully. It would be a major disaster, for example, to discover in the seventh year of a 10-year study that one has forgot-

ten to ask a particular question in the second year. Second, longitudinal research is usually quite expensive in both money and time. There must be a continuing involvement of the same team of investigators, often over a period of several years. Furthermore, collecting data on hundreds of subjects at regular intervals typically requires many assistants, perhaps payments to the subjects, and major computing resources. Third, there are major problems of subject loss. People move and fail to leave addresses, become bored with their participation, get irritated with the study, refuse to cooperate, or die. This means that the initial sample must be large enough to allow for such shrinkage. In addition, there are real concerns about the effects of such shrinkage on the representativeness of the sample: people who leave or refuse to cooperate may be quite different from those who remain in the sample.

These problems account for why longitudinal research is not more popular. However, there is general agreement that this is the research strategy of choice for studying developmental issues. Ted Huston and his colleagues have begun one of the more important longitudinal studies of marriages. The PAIR project (Process of Adaptation in Intimate Relationships) involved 168 couples who were married in 1981. These couples lived in four rural counties in Pennsylvania. They were interviewed within 3 months of their marriages and then again after 1 year and after 2 years (present plans call for additional follow-ups). Husbands and wives were interviewed separately and responded to various questions about their attitudes, values, and expectations.

The Huston team also wanted information about the typical behavior patterns of the couples; unfortunately, such data are easier to think about than to collect. One traditional way of finding out what people typically do is to ask them. There are many problems with this approach, however. First, people genuinely may not remember how they have behaved in the past, and such estimates require calculations that most of us do not usually make. For example, it is hard to estimate how much household cleaning I do because the task is not well defined and tends not to be done all at one time. Furthermore, husbands and wives might have quite different perspectives—she thinks he doesn't do enough around the house while he thinks he does his share.

Another strategy for collecting such data is to have trained observers observe the couple systematically. Not only is this an expensive way to collect data, but there is no guarantee that the observers would catch the subjects in various meaningful activities. The couple might not clean house during the observation period, for example. In addition, having an observer present is highly intrusive, a condition that may stimulate atypical behavior.

Subjects might be asked to keep diaries about their daily activities, but it is hard for most people to find the time to perform this task in a careful way. Furthermore, it is not always possible for the research team to ask questions about diary entries, so opportunities are lost to get data that shed light on the meaning of the activities.

Because these traditional methods have major limitations, Huston and his colleagues devised yet another strategy (Huston, Robins, Atkinson, & McHale, 1987). Each couple was contacted by telephone nine times during a 2- to 3-week period and the husband and wife were asked separately (and privately) to describe activities that had taken place during the immediately preceding 24 hours. Such a procedure allows subjects to report events while they are still fresh in the memory, and because there were multiple reports of events, the researchers could aggregate the events. For example, over the 2- to 3-week period, the researchers could determine who tended to perform which type of activity and whether the activities were performed exclusively by one person (she always cleans), by either (they take turns doing dishes), or jointly (they go to the grocery store together). Subjects were asked questions about four areas: household tasks, leisure activities, positive interaction events (for example, hugging one another or making the partner laugh), and negative interaction events (for example, criticizing the other or turning down a sexual advance).

This work has provided a rich source of data on the development of the early years of marriage; there have been some expected and some surprising results. We can merely summarize some of the results here. First, as has often been reported, marital satisfaction declines during the initial year of marriage (Huston, McHale, & Crouter, 1985). There are no changes in the total number of joint activities, but a greater proportion are instrumental as opposed to leisure. The couples also report a drop in the amount of time conversing with one another. The number of activities performed to bring the partner pleasure declines by about 40%, although the number of negative activities does not increase—so the marriages become more affectively neutral over time.

Some of the couples had their first child during the first year of marriage. As one might expect, the birth of the baby increases

BOX CONTINUED

instrumental activities (especially for mothers) and decreases leisure activities. As opposed to nonparents, parents tend to focus their companionship around instrumental activities as opposed to leisure ones. Parents reported decreased satisfaction with marriage; however, because the PAIR research team had a comparative sample of childless couples, they were able to show that couples with children had no greater decline than those without children, an important point (McHale & Huston, 1985).

Finally, the PAIR research team examined sex roles in marriage. As one might expect, the women perform most (about two-thirds) of the traditional feminine tasks such as cooking and cleaning house, whereas the men are more apt to perform masculine tasks such as household repairs and car work. Interestingly, attitudes toward women and women's roles did not strongly predict how tasks were divided within the home. The greatest predictor of the division of labor within the home was the extent to which the husband worked more outside the home than did the wife. That is, when the husband worked outside far more than the wife, she performed more of the traditional feminine tasks within the home. This could reflect traditional values, or it could reflect the obvious fact that women who work less outside the home have more time for activities inside the home. The husband's perceived skill at feminine activities predicted his involvement in them, and those husbands who perceived themselves as good at traditional male activities tended

to be less involved in traditional feminine ones. Women tended to work more on traditional male tasks when they felt they were good at them and their husbands were more feminine in orientation.

The tendency for females to be more involved with feminine tasks increases fairly strongly for new mothers (McHale & Huston, 1984). In one sense, then, the birth of the child makes the family more traditional in terms of gender divisions, but this occurs almost entirely because of a dramatic increase in the number of household tasks that mothers end up performing. A mother's involvement with her child is lessened when she works outside the home but, interestingly enough, is not predicted by various measures of sex-role attitudes and values. A father's involvement, on the other hand, is predicted by his perceived competence as a child-care agent and by his desire to be involved with child care.

Many of these results are not at all surprising and have been found by others. Other results are unexpected. In either case, one advantage of such a large-scale longitudinal study is the ability to study relationships among a wide range of variables and to track how they change over time. In future years this study will give us further insights into the causes and consequences of divorce, into changes in family life when wives enter the work force after several years at home, and into how the development of children affects marital relationships, among other interesting and important questions.

---

increase. In related findings, Adams and Shea (1981) have shown that self-disclosure and love are related for both men and women, but that for men, self-disclosure tends to precede

love, whereas women tend to disclose more only after they have fallen in love.

Contrary to romantic ideals, conflict characterizes most deep relationships. Conflict tends

Ted Huston

to increase markedly during the early stages of a relationship, presumably as the partners work out their reciprocation and accommodation patterns, but tends to level out as the couple reaches the point of deeper commitment. Ambivalence is also quite common in the early stages of a relationship but decreases during the later stages. Thus, as a relationship matures, it is characterized by increasing love and maintenance behaviors, by a leveling-off of conflict, and by decreasing ambivalence.

When couples are asked about their actual mutual activities, changes are also found. Generally, mutual instrumental activities (the kind of practical and grubby activities of everyday life such as shopping) and mutual affectional activities both increase with a deepening relationship. Mutual leisure activities also show a marked increase, and there is also a decrease in activities shared with other people (Milardo, Johnson, & Huston, 1983). Thus, a relationship deepens as the partners develop a more exclusive relationship with each other. As romantic relationships develop, a special "we" feeling grows that is absent in most friendships. This feeling of being a part of a special relationship may be fostered by the surrounding social context and social norms. Lovers are treated by others as having special rights and privileges with regard to one another, and romantic unions often are encouraged by families and friends.

Because the romantic relationship is fairly explicit and consciously chosen, the level of involvement in it is likely to have special significance. This suggests that the degree of involvement or commitment ought to predict the course of the relationship. It is now well documented that couples who are more deeply involved with the relationship are more likely to persist in that relationship over time (Berg & McQuinn, 1986; Hill, Rubin, & Peplau, 1976).

Continuation   While people can and have lived together for long periods without being married, most of the research in this area has been conducted on married couples. Substantial changes take place in all marriages over the years: some marriages deepen and grow more secure, others quickly deteriorate, and still others show a gradual loss of vitality. Thus, despite our romantic ideals, there is a great deal of diversity in how marriages change. Married couples find that career pressures, changing interests, and an inevitable lowering of sexual involvement force constant adjustments. Perhaps the most profound change that occurs in most marriages is the arrival of children. Not only does the first child radically change the ways parents spend their time, but typically it leaves less time and energy for wife–husband interactions. It also tends to alter the distribution of household tasks to more traditional gender-linked roles, which is especially distressing to women who

The arrival of the first child often changes the relationships within the marriage.

do not have traditional values (Belsky, Lang, & Huston, 1986). There has been some controversy about whether the birth of children affects marital satisfaction. Some studies have suggested that satisfaction with the marriage declines with the birth of children and increases again when children leave home, but other studies do not find this (Levinger, 1983).

The meaning of a marriage may change in subtle, or sometimes dramatic, ways over a period of time, and we must always keep in mind that there is no perfect form of marriage. Some marriages evolve into a companionate form in which intimacy and commitment are more important than passion; the marriage of Mill and Taylor described at the beginning of the chapter is a classic example of such a marriage. In some marriages, some partner dominates in the sense that his (and it is usually the husband) career dominates not only work but social activities. Other marriages involve a certain amount of parallel activity. She has her career and he has his; or he takes care of making money and she takes care of the house and children.

Many studies have found that marriage partners report declines in satisfaction with the relationship over time, but other studies have

not (Levinger, 1983). In some marriages, arguments over finances, the children, dual careers, the importance of sex, and lack of communication take their toll, and even though the marriage may remain intact, it seems to hang on more out of habit and convenience than considered preference. Other couples seem to be able to find new interdependencies and their marriages seem to grow stronger.

Dissolution   However, romantic relationships, like friendships, frequently end. Obviously, this is fairly common during courtship because most of us have several romantic relationships before getting married or making a more or less permanent commitment to a single partner. About 40% of all current marriages will end in divorce. Ultimately, of course, all romantic relationships end with the death of one partner.

FACTORS PROMOTING SUCCESSFUL ROMANTIC RELATIONSHIPS

There are at least five factors that affect how successful a romantic relationship is: interdependency, exchange factors, equity, self-disclosure and communication, and external factors. We have discussed many of these factors earlier in the chapter in an effort to understand the bases of relationships, and now by way of partial summary we will review their role in making relationships happy and secure.

Interdependency   Increasing closeness in relationships presupposes interdependency. In other words, what one person does will inevitably affect the other. If this interdependency fails to develop (if, for example, the partners decide on independent careers in different cities and have different preferences for spending their leisure time), we can predict that the marriage will have trouble surviving. Not only does behavior coordination become difficult, but the partners may have neither the time nor the inclination to commit as many resources to the relationship and to the other as to self. Furthermore, even in initially successful marriages, a cumulative drifting apart and finding separate activities, as well as children leaving the immediate family environment, take away some of the reasons for interdependency and leave fewer reasons for maintaining the marriage bond.

Exchange Factors   All relationships involve exchanges of material and psychological rewards. Both satisfaction with and commitment to relationships are affected by levels of rewards received from the other (Rusbult, 1983) and affect how interpersonal problems are handled (Rusbult, Zembrodt, & Gunn, 1982). In general, as rewards and, consequently, satisfaction increase, people adopt more constructive methods of dealing with conflict.

Several people have commented on the changing nature of exchange as relationships develop. Hatfield, Utne, and Traupmann (1979) argue that as relationships deepen they have a longer time perspective, which creates changes in the exchanges. For one thing, the value of certain rewards and costs is typically increased in romantic relationships. To some extent the approval of a spouse may be taken for granted, but the simple phrase "I like you a lot" may be more potent coming from a spouse than a friend, and "I wish I had never met you" is surely more devastating when spoken by a lover. Also, more intimate couples are more likely to exchange a variety of rewards (and costs) and to substitute them for one another. When I am invited to a friend's house for dinner, I am more or less obligated to reciprocate in kind, reasonably soon. However, when my wife does me a favor, I do not need to reciprocate immediately or exactly. In fact, Levinger (1979) has argued that concern with the precise details of exchange is usually a danger signal in existing relationships. When a relationship begins to go sour, either or both partners may become obsessed with the level of rewards given and received as well as with equity and equality.

The level of rewards in a relationship may be compared with the best alternative, such as living with another or alone after separation. The person who has an outcome level barely above the next-best alternative (the CL_{alt}) is less dependent on the relationship and may be tempted to explore new alternatives. Thus, the person who is more dependent (that is, whose outcomes are well above the CL_{alt}) may have reason to be jealous (G. L. White, 1980). In addition, people make other kinds of comparisons. For example, discrepancies between how one thinks the partner feels about self and how the ideal partner would feel are strongly predictive of how much one loves the partner (Sternberg & Barnes, 1985). I am not likely to continue to love my spouse if I think she feels much more negatively toward me than the woman of my dreams would.

Equity   Hatfield and her colleagues (1979) have also provided a useful analysis of intimate relationships from the standpoint of equity theory. They note that both partners have investments of time and energy in the relationship, but one person may receive more rewards relative to investments than the other. As equity theory predicts, the partners will feel happier if the relationship is equitable than if it is inequitable (Schafer & Keith, 1980). Presumably people will either leave inequitable relationships or try to restore equity. It seems likely that the person who has the relatively smaller reward-to-investment ratio would at least think about divorce, but this may not always be feasible because of religious values or because the person is extremely dependent on the relationship for a sense of identity or financial security. For example, the traditional wife who feels that her husband does not appreciate her efforts to keep the home fires burning may feel unconfident about beginning a new relationship or establishing her own career. In that case, she might try to restore equity by magnifying the rewards she gets from her husband or by reducing her investments by withdrawing her love or by offering less support for her husband.

"I didn't say I wasn't happily married. I simply said it's been quite some time since my happiness knew no bounds."

Drawing by Geo. Price © 1984 by The New Yorker Magazine, Inc.

Self-disclosure and Communication   Self-disclosure is an important part of romantic relationships. One is supposed to tell one's lover things that one would tell no one else. In addition, merely living with someone gives the other access to special information that no one else has. Hendrick (1981) found that self-disclosure is related to marital happiness but also that levels of self-disclosure tend to decline over years of marriage. This might indicate that long-married couples have less to disclose to one another (the really secret stuff having already come out earlier), that levels of trust are sufficiently high that buttressing from mutual disclosures is no longer necessary, or that people have less involvement with their marriages over time.

There has been a long history of studying marital success as a function of communication, especially concerning areas of conflict. In troubled relationships, a lack of communication may only be a reflection of other difficulties, but one might also argue that lack of communication would also produce or exacerbate other problems. It is important to repeat a point made earlier. Romantic relationships typically involve conflict and tensions. However, the way conflict is handled can be extremely important. There will be times when each partner is insensitive or selfish, but one major problem is that the "bad" behavior of one person is often interpreted dispositionally by the partner; that is, it is attributed to the inherent character or disposition of the "bad" partner (Newman, 1981; Orvis, Kelley, & Butler, 1976). "You hurt my feelings" is one kind of statement, but "You hurt my feelings because you are and always have been an insensitive slob" is a statement of a different order. The latter is likely to be more damaging to the target and to the relationship.

Another problem in communication is that many couples enter conflicts with mutual recriminations (sometimes called cross-complaining) so that when one states a complaint, the other responds with another complaint, often unrelated and of long-standing duration. Couples who function better are more likely to listen to one another's gripes without bringing up their own (Gottman, 1979). Another dysfunctional pattern of responding to complaints is avoidance; one partner may ignore the other or leave the room. Such avoidance not only leaves the conflict unresolved but is perceived as insensitive and uncaring, thus heightening conflicts and disagreements about partners' perceptions of one another (Knudson, Sommers, & Golding, 1980). Patterns of destructive responses to destructive responses are good predictors of relationship distress (Rusbult, Johnson, & Morrow, 1986). In general, better-adjusted couples are more accurate and effective in their communications (Noller, 1980), including having fewer discrepancies among nonverbal cues and between nonverbal and verbal messages (Noller, 1982).

External Factors   To some extent, all romantic relationships encapsulate themselves; to use Levinger's (1979) phrase, they build barriers around themselves. However, external factors frequently intrude. For example, money (or the lack of enough of it) is a frequent source of conflict in most marriages. Also, commitment to romantic relationships is lowered as available alternatives become more attractive, so external friendships (sexual or not) may contribute to a lowered involvement in the romantic relationship.

It is also important to remember that marriages (and to some extent all romantic relationships) are social institutions and therefore exist within a rich normative and social context. There was a day when divorce was considered scandalous, and fear of social disapproval kept many marriages intact. Friends and relatives also bring pressures to bear on a marriage. If letters to advice columnists such as Ann Landers are to be trusted, lack of support for a marriage from friends and in-laws is a significant problem for many. Just the knowledge that friends and relatives think you have made a poor choice is likely to focus some attention on available alternatives.

People who are deeply committed to one another and to their relationship can, of course, withstand such external pressures, but most marriages have less-than-ideal levels of commitment. Furthermore, many people in our society marry at a relatively early age when external pressures of school, money problems, beginning careers, and the like are strong and the wisdom to deal with the problems not fully developed. It is no accident that early marriages are likelier to end in divorce.

We have been emphasizing the reasons for the breakups of romantic relationships, but the more remarkable fact is that so many survive. The interdependencies of close relationships are numerous and complex, and many of us find it difficult to learn to live with another person who brings his or her own repertoire of needs, demands, preferences, and irritating habits to the relationship. Unfortunately, love does not cure all. The fact that most of us will ultimately find a person with whom we share our lives for a lengthy period speaks volumes about our abilities to coordinate our behaviors and desires with those of others.

SUMMARY

Close relationships are important to most people. In general, as relationships become closer and more intimate they increase in mutuality, show greater knowledge and trust, are structured by more personal norms, and involve more self-investment. Romantic relationships have been intensively studied by psychologists. Broadly, such relationships proceed from acquaintanceship through courtship and into a continuation and maintenance stage. Most romantic relationships also eventually deteriorate or even terminate. The factors that make for a successful romantic relationship include substantial interdependency of outcomes, a relative lack of concern for exact and timely exchange of outcomes, feelings of equity, substantial self-disclosure and healthy communication, and external supports.

CHAPTER SUMMARY

- Relationships are built on a foundation of interpersonal attraction but also involve interdependencies among the participants created by exchange of rewards and costs.

- Exchange of rewards can involve material goods and money, but in most relationships services, status, information, and love are more important rewards.

- When one person cares what the other does, he or she becomes dependent on the other. In a relationship, each partner depends on the other for rewards, and this gives each power over the other. In most relationships, each partner also takes account of preferences of the other and finds it rewarding to please the other. Other transformations of the reward structure are also possible, as when one person tries to punish the other and finds such punishment pleasant.

- Most relationships respond to several norms that govern the exchange of rewards and costs. Reciprocity requires one to return rewards and costs in kind; altruism leads one to reward the other with no expectation of return; equity means that rewards should be given only to those who have earned them; equality suggests that rewards be distributed equally; and honesty requires one to live up to one's bargains regarding such exchanges. In addition, people like to feel that the world is a just one and they will sometimes feel that people have deserved their bad fates.

- Self-disclosure refers to information about ourselves that we share with others. Disclosures vary in amount and in intimacy value. Because disclosures can be embarrassing and even dangerous, we usually disclose only to certain people, typically those who can be trusted. Self-disclosure is also reciprocated and is probably an important builder of trust in the formation of relationships.

- Close relationships differ from superficial ones in many ways. Close relationships typically have more interdependencies or mutual exchanges, are based on greater knowledge and trust, have a more elaborate set of personal norms, and have a greater degree of self-investment.

- The nature of friendships changes over the life span. Small children think friends are people who are fun to play with, but gradually children pick friends on the basis of intimacy factors. For adults, especially those who are married, friends become less important.

- Romantic relationships go through a series of stages. First, the people must become acquainted; then there is a buildup to a commitment, followed by a continuation phase and, for some, dissolution.

- The buildup or courtship phase may be quite gradual and is typically marked by conflict and reversals. During this phase, the couple becomes romantically involved, performs more behaviors together, and develops a special "we" feeling.

- The continuation phase (typically marked by marriage) can take a number of courses. Many marriages become less satisfying over time, and some end in divorce or separation. On the other hand, others seem to deepen over time.

- Various factors have been linked to the failure of relationships. Secure relationships involve greater interdependencies, a wider range of reward exchanges, and little need to "keep score" on rewards. Secure relationships are also likely to be perceived as equitable and often involve greater self-disclosure and communication patterns, which help resolve conflict. Finally, marriages may fail because of external factors such as money or in-law problems.

CHAPTER

14

ALTRUISM, COOPERATION, AND COMPETITION

The Ik (pronounced *Eek*) are a tribe of a few thousand people who live in mountainous terrain near the point at which Uganda, Kenya, and Sudan meet. Several decades ago they were forcibly removed from their traditional hunting grounds and they had to adapt to an entirely different way of life. In the middle 1960s, their fragile adaptation was further threatened by drought and famine. The description of the Ik provided by anthropologist Colin Turnbull (1972) makes them prime candidates for the most unpleasant people on the earth. Their close competitors, the Yanomamo, will be described in Chapter 15.

When Turnbull lived with the Ik, they were starving, and this explains some of their seemingly inhuman cultural adaptations. Turnbull observed people taking partially eaten food out of the mouths of dying relatives. Water would be stolen from old people too feeble to defend themselves. People gathered food alone so they would not have to share.

Perhaps the most shocking aspect of the Ik behavior was the almost total lack of family feeling. Relations between husbands and wives were almost nonexistent; there seems to have been little cooperation in the gathering or preparation of food. Men tended to hunt for food and might be gone for several days. However, it would be extremely unlikely that a man would bring food home for his hungry family; more than likely he would have eaten anything he caught before returning home. Wives gathered whatever food could be found closer to home. Sex was seen as mildly pleasant (about the level of defecation, according to one informant), but marriage did not seem to prohibit adultery.

Well, surely the children were a unifying family force? Not so. Children were nursed until about 3 years of age and then were kicked out of the family hut. They slept outside and were responsible for getting their own food. Even sick children did not seem to tug at

Leningrad in 1942.

their parents' hearts. One dying girl begged her parents to take care of her but was barricaded into a hut and allowed to starve to death. In another case a father stole the food intended for his dying son. The children did manage a revenge of sorts. Before going to bed at night, the Ik had to empty their sleeping mats of roaches, lice, and other bugs. The parents naturally shook their mats outside their huts, but the children took great delight in shaking theirs at the doors so the bugs went inside the huts.

The Ik have embraced a culture that is probably highly adaptive in their harsh circumstances. Their selfishness approximates that envisioned by Thomas Hobbes (1651), who saw in primitive society a "war of all against all." In a Hobbesian world, those who are weak and dying must make way for those more likely to survive. Yet, although the Ik culture may be adaptive, it is still shocking to read about a people without religion, laws, norms, values, or the fellow feeling that ordinarily promotes altruism and cooperation. The Ik are not people one would choose to have for neighbors.

The Ik lived under extremely harsh conditions, but other people have lived under even worse conditions without resorting to Hobbesian selfishness. Consider as one example the behavior of the citizens of Leningrad during the early days of World War II. Leningrad was once the most cultured and sophisticated city in the Soviet Union, with a population of about 2,500,000 people. German forces attacked Leningrad in June of 1941 and, though they could not defeat the protecting armies, they managed to blockade the city. During the famous siege of Leningrad, which lasted over 2 years, some 1,500,000 Russian citizens and troops died. In 900 days, more people died in this one city than America has lost in *all* its wars.

The harshest period was the first winter, when little food or fuel could be imported into the city and few people moved out. Food was rationed. During the worst period of the siege, people were allowed only 150 calories of bread (about one slice) a day. The bread itself was made of sawdust in addition to flour. People made jellies from leather items; library paste was another delicacy. In addition, there was almost no fuel to heat this far northern city. During Janaury, the water pipes froze throughout the city. People went for months without baths and normal sanitation was impossible. People died by the thousands every day, and bodies lay in the streets throughout the winter because no one had the energy to dig graves. The physical conditions were horrible and the psychological toll was even greater.

How did the citizens of Leningrad react? In all kinds of ways, actually. Many stole food and fuel; some killed to stay alive. There was even cannibalism; on the black market one could buy meat patties, officially horse meat but more than likely human. Ration cards were stolen, and this doomed the victim to certain death because they could not be replaced until the end of every month.

But in this case there is also another side to the response to extreme adversity. Throughout the long siege, people did cooperate, they did share, they did sacrifice their lives so that oth-

ers could live. The spirit of Leningrad did not die. In the darkest days of the siege, in early 1942, the Hermitage, a famous museum, held a celebration in honor of its 500th anniversary; one of the scholars died just as he finished his address. Poets continued to meet and write poetry. Composers composed, and concerts were held. The library stayed open, and the University of Leningrad continued to hold classes and grant degrees. People who had lost half their body weight, who were too weak to perform even normal everyday tasks, who suffered extreme anxiety about their own fate and that of their country, preserved as much civilization as was humanly possible.

As one reads descriptions of Leningrad during this period one can find plenty of evidence of selfish and competitive behavior, but one can also read of countless acts of cooperation and selfless altruism: children who took their daily slice of bread home for their parents or sick brothers and sisters to eat; mothers who helped not only their own children but those of their friends; people who shared their meager rations with strangers. Indeed, Leningrad has come to stand for the ability of people to withstand the harshest external circumstances and to emerge with their humanity intact.

INTRODUCTION

The point of these examples is to remind us that people can be both cruel and selfish as well as kind and selfless. Freud and Hobbes would have loved knowing about the Ik, but most social scientists feel that the people of Leningrad offer at least as instructive an example of human behavior. In this and the next chapter, we will consider a wide range of social behavior, some of which is close to that of the Ik and some of which is closer to that of the people of Leningrad.

Social behavior is often divided into two large categories: prosocial and antisocial. **Prosocial behavior** is that which is rewarding or helpful to others. In contrast, **antisocial be-havior** harms others or produces negative consequences for others. In this chapter, we consider **altruism** and **cooperation** as two forms of prosocial behavior and **competition** (which is in some ways inseparable from cooperation) as a form of antisocial behavior. In Chapter 15 we will focus on aggression as another major category of antisocial behavior.

ALTRUISM AND HELPING

TWO PERSPECTIVES

Helping others is a common social behavior: a stranger asks you for the time and you tell it to him; you help your friend paint her house; I try to help my daughter with her geometry homework. Sometimes we even expend great effort in helping others: you might spend part of your vacation helping a friend work on his car or you might stop at the scene of an accident and render assistance. Some forms of helping are dramatic while others are almost too trivial to mention. Why do people help others? Two large categories of reasons have been offered. We might help others because we want to gain rewards from helping (we have egoistic reasons for helping) or we might help others because we want to relieve their distress (we are genuine altruists).

The Egoistic Perspective   Those who feel that helping behavior is motivated entirely by self-rewards can look to a rich philosophical tradition in support of their view. Statements of a basic selfish hedonism have been common

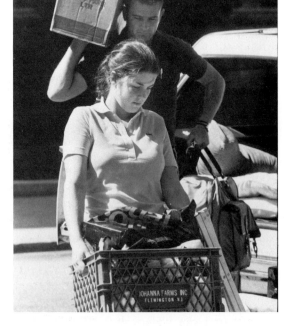

Helping takes many forms.

throughout the ages and reached a height during the Renaissance. With the breakdown of the power of the Church and the rise of nationalism and capitalism, educated people in Europe rediscovered individuality, power, ambition, and even greed in the intellectual as well as the practical ways (Robinson, 1981). By 1500 or so, a number of philosophical justifications for this new individuality had emerged, the most important of which were Machiavelli's *The Prince* and Hobbes' *Leviathan*, which we discussed in Chapter 13.

The new image of humankind was individualistic, hedonistic, and egoistic. We want our rewards, we want them now, and we care precious little about the fate of those around us. To be sure, people have the capacity to help others, but prosocial behavior results from the realization that helping and cooperating with others is an effective means of keeping ahead in the search for power, glory, and pleasure.

The perspective introduced by Hobbes has set the tone for British and American social and political philosophy, which makes it very easy for people of our age and culture to assume that egoism and hedonism are fundamental to human nature and that prosocial behaviors are not innate but learned, and painfully at that. Even Darwin's theory of evolution, which has dominated modern discussions of human nature, is based ultimately on this Hobbesian position; Darwin got his notion of the advantages of competition and survival of the fittest from the great British economist Thomas Malthus, who in turn had been influenced by Hobbes. Thus, our scientific as well as our philosophical heritages conspire to make us feel that prosocial tendencies are learned and grafted onto the more basic, selfish aspects of human nature.

Why do I help my children? Perhaps so they will love and honor me as well as take care of me in my old age. Why do I help students? Perhaps so I can wallow in their praise and high teaching evaluations, which may also get me a pay raise. Why do I help a stranded

Niccolò Machiavelli.

motorist? Again, perhaps his thanks serves as a reward, and I have also learned to experience some inner satisfaction (a reward) from helping others. So, what appears to be genuine altruism is really selfish hedonism in disguise, motivated by desires for praise or other rewards. In the present century, both behaviorist and Freudian perspectives have treated prosocial behavior in exactly this way.

Among psychologists, those who advocate this egoistic position can also point to a large body of research that shows that helping behavior, like most other forms of behavior, is increased by rewards (Staub, 1978). If one is convinced that all helping behavior is motivated by the lust for reward, it is easy to find any number of possible rewards lying about in odd corners of the mind that might motivate helping: you can gain money, fame, or approval, or create obligations that may be called due at a later time.

Genuine Altruism   Those who feel that helping can be a genuinely altruistic act motivated by a desire to help the other rather than the self also have their philosophical backers. The ancient Stoics who preached the essential brotherhood of people, many of the Christian thinkers during the Middle Ages, and more modern philosophers such as Rousseau and Marx have argued passionately that people are naturally social, that unless society and greed corrupt our best impulses we have a natural tendency to help and cooperate.

A boost of sorts for the naturalness of altruism has recently come from certain data and speculations of sociobiologists (see Chapter 1). You will recall that one problem for classic evolutionary theory is why any animal would help its fellow animals, given that helping generally exposes the helper to greater risk. One would assume that if there were such a thing as helping genes, they would tend to die out, because helpers are likely to have a higher rate of death than nonhelpers. Sociobiologists have tried to resolve the dilemma by pointing to genetic selection taking place at the group level rather than selection among individuals. Granted that an altruistic animal (and his altruistic genes) is more likely to die early, his altruism is also likely to help his close kin (who share genes within him, including altruistic genes) survive and reproduce. So altruistic genes would live on after self-sacrifice through closely related kin, especially if the helper's behavior directly helps the kin survive (see Ridley & Dawkins, 1981, for a detailed discussion).

But what of the argument that the desire to help others is really thinly disguised rewarding of self? When I help you, I get thanks and feel morally righteous; when I see your pain, I feel pain of my own, and by relieving your pain, I also unburden myself. In that regard, it is important to make a fundamental distinction between the *consequences* of behavior and the *reasons* for having performed that behavior. Let us look in on a scene played out in many

Lennie Skutnik jumped into the freezing Potomac River to rescue victims of an airplane crash. It is highly unlikely that he did this to win the acclaim that he later received.

American homes. Mom and Dad have just been awakened by Baby, who is showing signs of illness. Dad gets up and spends the remainder of the night comforting Baby. In doing so, he makes his child more comfortable than she otherwise would be and allows his wife to get her much-needed rest. Of course, it is true that all sorts of potential rewards perfume the night air (Mom will thank him next morning, Baby will get well quicker, and Dad wears a crown of pleasurable martyrdom to work the next morning). Dad may even be happy to accept these rewards in lieu of sleep. This does not, however, mean that he went through his comforting routine in order to get such outcomes. In fact, the only thoughts that motivated his behavior might have been his concern for his child and his wife. The rewards for behavior are not always the causes of that behavior.

It would be naive to argue that every act, even most acts, of helping is motivated primarily by the desire to help others, but it seems plausible that at least some are. And we must also remember that the two positions we have discussed are not mutually exclusive. Perhaps no acts are performed without *some* consciousness of self-rewards and self-costs, and few acts are perfectly selfish and totally unconcerned with others.

EMPATHY

Most psychologists who accept the notion that there can be genuine altruism place considerable emphasis on empathy. **Empathy** occurs when you put yourself in another's place and experience vicariously some of what he or she is feeling. Hoffman (1981) has argued that empathy not only mediates altruism but that the capacity to empathize with others may well be the product of evolutionary forces. He notes that empathy seems to be a nearly universal capacity (although a few individuals in every culture may lack it) and that empathy appears very early in the life of a child.

Arousal of Empathy   Imagine the feelings you would have at watching a friend being tortured; at a less dramatic level, few people feel indifferent to the cries of a young baby. In a classic study by Berger (1962), subjects watched a confederate supposedly receiving shocks; and their own emotional arousal increased when they saw obvious evidence of pain. Subjects' emotional arousal also increases when they watch vivid scenes such as a movie of a puberty rite involving circumcision of a young man (Lazarus et al., 1962). There is now considerable evidence that seeing others experiencing pain or distress does create arousal in the observer (Piliavin, Dovidio, Gaertner, & Clark, 1981).

Empathy and Helping   Normally we feel distress when we observe the distress of others. However, it does not follow that this empathetic response necessarily encourages helping. For example, I might observe the victim of a horrible accident screaming and writhing in fear and pain, feel extreme distress myself, and yet flee the scene to avoid further emotional

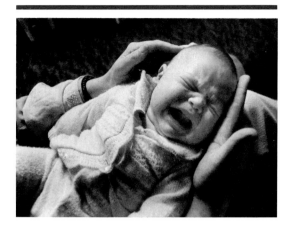

Few people fail to have some empathy with the distress of a crying baby.

strain. Therefore, it is important to show that empathetic arousal can lead to helping *and* under what conditions.

Probably the clearest test to date of the proposition that empathetic arousal can motivate helping was performed by Coke, Batson, and McDavis (1978). Subjects who were given false feedback that they were physiologically aroused at hearing about the plight of someone not only reported more empathetic emotion but were also more likely to help than those who did not have such raised arousal. Coke and his colleagues also reasoned that because empathy results in emotional arousal, standard misattribution techniques (see Chapter 5) should lower empathy and, subsequently, helping to the extent that empathy is necessary for helping. Subjects were encouraged either to observe or to empathize with a person appealing for help. Subjects who had not been encouraged to empathize should help relatively little, because empathy is presumed to be an important cause of helping. In addition, some of the subjects had been given a pill (a placebo), which they had been told would create effects that mimic the arousal symptoms of empathy. Presumably, subjects would feel less empathic emotion whenever their arousal can be misattributed to the pill, and they should therefore have less emotion to motivate their helping. The results shown in Table 14.1 support this reasoning; helping was strongest when the subjects had been encouraged to empathize and the empathy had not been attributed to the pill. These results suggest that empathy is a form of arousal, that it generally motivates behavior, and that if it is explained away it no longer performs this motivational function.

Empathy can motivate helping, but why? One possibility is that when you experience empathic distress, it makes you care enough about the other person to want to reduce her distress. However, the hedonistic, egoistic, reward–cost position quite properly points out that if you are also experiencing distress, perhaps you help not to reduce the other's distress but to reduce your own (Piliavin, Rodin, & Piliavin, 1969). The fact that empathic arousal motivates helping does not necessarily mean that the helping is genuine altruism.

How might we distinguish between these possibilities? If your concern for the other is your major motivation for helping, the only realistic way you can reduce the distress of the other is to help her. However, if your primary concern is to reduce your own distress, you could do that either by helping or by fleeing the scene: out of sight, out of mind; what you don't see won't distress you. In an experiment by Batson et al. (1981), subjects watched a

woman apparently receive painful shocks. Batson and his colleagues reasoned that when empathy with a victim was high, those who were responding to their *own* distress would try to relieve it in the easiest way possible. They would leave the situation if they could, but help if they were not free to leave. If, on the other hand, subjects were primarily motivated by altruistic concerns (that is, by the distress of the victim), they should help even when they could leave. In the experiment, some subjects were told they could leave the experiment, but others were not given this opportunity. The measure of altruism was whether the subjects would agree to take some of the painful shocks to spare the poor victim. The data support the altruistic position: those subjects who reported high empathy for the victim were more likely to agree to take the shocks for her regardless of whether they could escape or not. Their own possible distress did not seem to motivate their behavior as much as the distress of the other did.

The work by Batson and his colleagues strongly suggests that empathy affects helping because of altruistic concerns with the plight of the other. Descriptions of people during the Leningrad siege often revealed helping in response to the evident distress of others even in cases where no help was expected. However, not everyone is so altruistic, and none of us is always a saint. There are clear individual differences in whether people are responsive to altruistic or egoistic forms of empathy (Batson et al., 1983) and more generally in the capacity of empathy to motivate altruistic behavior (Archer et al., 1981).

Moods   Imagine that you have just had one of those miserable days we all experience from time to time: you had a flat tire in the morning and then got a poor grade on an exam and discovered that you will have to do the extra assignment reserved for those who do poorly on exams. Now you see a classmate who seems to be crying. Ordinarily you would

TABLE 14.1   HELP VOLUNTEERED AS A FUNCTION OF EMPATHY AND MISATTRIBUTION. *Note that subjects helped most when they had been encouraged to empathize with the person in distress and that empathy arousal had not been attributed to some other factor.*

	No Misattribution	Misattribution
Empathy	2.60	0.68
Observe	1.27	0.68

SOURCE: Based on Coke, Batson, and McDavis, 1978.

ask if she was having a problem and try to comfort her or do something to help. But today, wouldn't you be tempted to pretend you hadn't seen her? Do you have any pity to spare after expending a fair amount on yourself? On the other hand, it might be argued that you would be especially likely to stop and help because your own problems have made it easier for you to empathize with the problems of others. So do you stop and help or not? The actual research evidence has been remarkably inconsistent, with some studies finding that negative experiences or bad moods enhance helping (Cialdini, Darby, & Vincent, 1973) while others find that they diminish helping (Barden, Garber, Duncan, & Masters, 1981).

Before we discuss some of the ways negative moods affect helping, consider the case of a good mood: imagine that you have been having a good day. Somehow it seems intuitively likely that you would be more willing to help someone after you had received an unexpected good grade or that you would compliment someone after someone had complimented you. Several studies suggest that when people have recently been successful (and thus are presumably in a good mood) they are more likely to be helpful (Isen, 1970). Minor positive experiences, such as finding a dime in a phone booth or receiving an unexpected gift of cookies while studying, lead to increased helping (Isen & Levin, 1972). Even the weather plays a role; most of us feel better when the weather is nice than when it is foul, and Cunningham (1979) found that people are more likely to leave large tips for waitresses and waiters during sunny weather.

The effects of moods on helping have been explained in two basic ways. One possibility is that both good and bad moods affect the rewards and costs of helping; another is that moods affect one's focus of attention and cognitive reactions to events.

Consider first the reward–cost argument. Certainly, when one has had a bad experience or is thinking harsh thoughts about the world,

one way to restore a good mood would be to gain approval from others, and one way to gain approval would be to help another. There are several lines of evidence that support this point of view. One comes from studies that show that people are helpful after failure *unless* they have received other rewards in the interim (Cialdini, Darby, & Vincent, 1973; Kenrick, Baumann, & Cialdini, 1979). Because the other rewards have presumably already restored the person's mood, the motivation to be helpful is reduced. Furthermore, when people are led to believe that their moods cannot change, bad moods do not lead to increased helping, presumably because the helping would be ineffective in raising the mood (Manucia, Baumann, & Cialdini, 1984).

So, being in a bad mood motivates people to help others, thereby getting approval or other rewards and restoring some semblance of a good mood. What incentive then would a person who was already in a good mood have to be helpful? Staub (1978) has suggested that we like to maintain a certain mood balance, so that having more of some commodity (in this case, good feelings) might encourage the person to share the wealth. A good mood might lead to increased hleping because the person feels he should share his good fortunes with others and he can do so at relatively little cost.

Such reward–cost theories can account for the possibilities that both good and bad moods seem to increase helping. However, in recent years more attention has been directed to cognitive mechanisms underlying the effects of moods on helping. Clark and Isen (1982) have argued that good moods generally make the positive features of situations more salient than the negative. For example, people who are in a good mood rate their possessions more favorably (Isen, Shalker, Clark, & Karp, 1978), are more rewarding to self and others (Rosenhan, Underwood, & Moore, 1974), and remember more positive than negative events (see Chapter 3). More to the point, they also have more positive initial reactions to helping situations (Clark & Waddell, 1983).

Another possibility is that moods affect focus of attention, which may then mediate helping behavior. Rosenhan, Salovey, and Hargis (1981) created good moods by asking subjects to think about a nice vacation. One group was asked to think about the vacation as if they themselves were to take it, while the other group was asked to imagine that a friend was to take the vacation. These manipulations created equally good moods, but the self-oriented group was more helpful than the other-oriented group (indeed, this latter group was less helpful than a control group who did not imagine a vacation). Perhaps those who focus on the good experiences of others feel relatively disadvantaged by comparison. At any rate, this study makes clear that good moods may affect helping differently, depending on the focus of attention.

In the case of positive moods, focus on the self seems to increase helping, but intuitively the effects might be different for bad moods. If one focuses on one's own problems, all one's pity and sympathy may be used up on oneself. Focus on self may thus lead to diminished helping (Aderman & Berkowitz, 1983; Gibbons & Wicklund, 1982). On the other hand, having a bad experience may make the problems of others more salient and increase helping because of empathy. Thompson, Cowan, and Rosenhan (1980) found that thinking about negative experiences from the standpoint of self decreased helping, whereas thinking about similar experiences from the standpoint of others increased helping.

Thus, moods would seem to have their effects not only by directing attention to self or others but by their ability to create an empathic mind-set. Merely focusing on another does not create altruism: we might attend to others but view them from our own perspective and feel critical or jealous (Hoover, Wood, & Knowles, 1983; Wegner & Giuliano, 1982). In addition to focusing on others, seeing the situation from their perspective seems to be necessary for helping. Conversely, focusing on self does not necessarily inhibit helping. If such focus increases concentration on one's own normative standards, helping might be increased. However, self-focus can also inhibit helping if the bad mood focuses attention on one's own problems.

THE NORMATIVE FRAMEWORK

People sometimes make great sacrifices for others even though no rational calculation would yield a profitable reward–cost ratio for the behavior. One reason this might occur is genuine altruism: the helper becomes so concerned with the plight of the other that rational calculation ceases. Another reason is that there are powerful norms that suggest we should help others under certain circumstances. In Chapter 13 we argued that exchange norms ameliorate the worst excesses of selfish profit-seeking, and one of the norms we discussed was altruism.

Once norms are in place, they constitute a source of rewards and punishments. We help others in need, we are fair, we obey laws—in part because we expect rewards for obeying the norms and punishment or disapproval for not obeying them. However, most of us have internalized certain norms to such a degree that we obey not so much because we seek approval but because we feel we *ought* to obey. As we saw in Chapter 9, one of the important products of socialization is exactly this internalized feeling of obligation to do what we should do. The starving people of Leningrad helped those in worse shape than themselves simply because they felt that such action was proper and right. Of course, as the example of the Ik people reminds us, not every person or every culture will have internalized norms of helping others.

Reciprocity   Two of the most powerful norms that influence helping in everyday life are reciprocity and social responsibility (Berkowitz, 1972). We have already seen the reciprocity norm in a different context (Chapter 13); in the present context it simply suggests that we should help those who have helped us. Examples from everyday life abound. If your roommate loaned you his car last weekend, you probably feel more obligated to help him out in some way this weekend. If a friend helped you with a tough calculus assignment last week, could you possibly refuse to help her with her chemistry this week? These reciprocity norms are so strong that sometimes we prefer to avoid being helped when we need it just so we won't feel obligated to help someone in return at some inconvenient time in the future. Both our everyday experiences and experimental research suggest reciprocity is a powerful norm, so strong, in fact, that people will even reciprocate help they did not want

and do not appreciate (DePaulo, Brittingham, & Kaiser, 1983).

Social Responsibility   The social responsibility norm simply suggests that we are obligated to help those in need. A well-established norm in most religions, moral philosophies, and the Boy Scout oath, among other possible examples, is that one should help those who cannot help themselves. Experiments confirm that helping is increased when the person in need is dependent on the potential helper (Berkowitz & Daniels, 1964).

Norm Activation   Although such norms are powerful, common experience suggests that they are not sufficient by themselves to engender helping. We have certainly all had the experience of knowing we should help someone but failing to do so. Haven't you sometimes avoided someone you knew was going to ask a favor you did not want to give? Are you sure that you would stop at the scene of an automobile accident?

In Chapter 8 we considered the question of when attitudes lead to behaviors, and here we have a similar problem. When do norms lead to helping? According to Schwartz (1977), when people help they go through an implicit or explicit decision process, and there are four stages in this process: (1) the perception of need and responsibility, where the potential helper must recognize that someone needs help, perceive that he or she is capable of providing the help, and feel some responsibility for helping; (2) there must be activation of norms and feelings of moral obligation; (3) the potential helper has to assess the relevant rewards and costs of the helping behaviors; and (4) the action itself must be performed.

The first stage merely specifies that the situation be perceived as one in which help is necessary or possible. One seemingly trite but important reason for a lack of helping is that the person in need fails to make his problems salient to others. We are often reluctant to ask for help because we fear our request will be seen as a sign of weakness or would otherwise diminish our standing in the eyes of others (Fisher, Nadler, & Whitcher-Alagna, 1982). Furthermore, being helped creates obligations to reciprocate, and such obligations are often unpleasant. At any rate, if the person does not make his needs and desires for help apparent, others may not perceive that their help is needed or may feel that it is not wanted. Even if the potential helper notices that the other needs help, the helper must assess her own abilities to help. For example, if you flunked chemistry last semester, you probably would not volunteer to help the woman down the hall with her assignment, even though you perceive that she is in dire straits.

Our feelings of responsibility may also be affected by our perceptions of the legitimacy of needs. Most of us feel that we are not responsible for helping those who don't try to help themselves. One reason welfare policies have been relatively unpopular in this country is the perception that most poor people are lazy and therefore undeserving. I suspect I would be more likely to help a student who missed an exam if he missed it because his father was ill than if he had been skiing with his family at Aspen. We are most likely to help others when their plight is seen as due to uncontrollable factors rather than to controllable ones such as a lack of effort (Reisenzein, 1986; Weiner, 1980).

The second stage leading from norms to helping behavior involves activation of feelings of moral obligation. Schwartz feels that we can best predict helping behavior by examining individualized norms to help in a particular situation, an argument similar to that of Azjen and Fishbein (1980) that specific attitudes best predict specific behaviors. These personal norms are animated by feelings of internalized obligation and are based on self-expectations. Thus, the person is concerned not so much with what others will think of her as with what she thinks of herself. Such personal norms usually facilitate helping (Schwartz & Fleishman,

1982) although some people may also have personal norms that inhibit helping; for example, if you felt you should not help people who are lazy, we might expect that you would not help the guy down the hall when he asks for help after partying all night.

Several variables are likely to affect the activation of feelings of moral obligation. For example, people are more likely to help when they have observed examples of helping (Rushton, 1979), including examples on television (Berkowitz, 1985). One commonplace example is a mass of cars trying to go through a single exit of a parking lot. I find that if someone kindly lets me cut in, I am much more likely to be a courteous driver for the next several minutes.

It is also likely that how we think of ourselves affects how we activate norms about helping. People who think of themselves as helpful are generally more helpful, provided this self-image is salient at the time of helping. Kraut (1973) exposed subjects to various appeals from charitable organizations. In the first phase of the experiment for those subjects who gave to the charity, the canvasser either labeled them aloud as charitable or said nothing; similarly, for those who did not give, half were labeled as uncharitable and half were not. The dependent measure was response to an appeal by another charity at a later time. In the second solicitation, previous nondonors gave less than the previous donors, suggesting that there are, indeed, some people who are dispositionally more helpful than others. However, the labels also had an impact. For the past donors, those who had been labeled as charitable gave more than those who had not been labeled; for previous nondonors, those who were labeled as noncharitable gave slightly less than those without the label (see Table 14.2).

Other studies have found similar results; people labeled as helpful are more likely to help than those not so labeled (Batson et al., 1979; Strenta & DeJong, 1981). When people have attributed certain characteristics to themselves, in this case charitableness, they will, in the future, act in accord with that attribution. In Chapter 11 a similar explanation was given for compliance; subjects who complied with a small request were more likely to comply with a later large request—they had come to see themselves as likely to comply with requests. Similarly, people who come to see themselves as charitable will probably act on that belief.

In a third stage, people calculate the potential costs of the helping activity. This involves assessing the consequences of the help for the other as well as the costs to the helper. You may want to give a $100 gift to help victims of poverty but you realize also that $100 of help is trivial given the magnitude of the problem. You will also have to calculate costs to yourself. You may have considerable conflict

TABLE 14.2 MEAN MULTIPLE SCLEROSIS CONTRIBUTIONS FOR THE SECOND SOLICITATION. *Note that those who helped previously donated more the second time, especially when they had been labeled as charitable.*

	Labeled	Nonlabeled
Donor	$ .70	$ .41
Nondonor	$ .23	$ .33

SOURCE: After Kraut, 1973.

between your feelings of obligation and the potential costs of the aid. Potential helpers do take into account both costs to themselves and the value of their help to others in deciding whether to help (Dovidio, 1984; Weyant, 1978).

Imagine the following common problem. An aged and senile relative clearly cannot care for herself and could live with you. You feel that you should help her, especially because the alternative will be a nursing home. Yet, you also realize that she will require constant physical care, perhaps for many years, and that her presence will mean great inconvenience for the rest of your family. How might you resolve this conflict between what you know you should do and the costs of that behavior? According to Schwartz, you may well go through a defensive process in which you reassess your costs and obligations. You may, for example, decide that the aged woman would get much better care in the nursing home or that she is so senile that she will not be aware of any special help you give her. You might also invoke other values. For example, you might decide that your family also has important rights and that you have a primary obligation to them.

This is not to suggest that we always or even frequently resolve such conflicts in favor of our own outcomes. There would never be any helping if this were the case. But people often choose not to help because helping is too costly; Schwartz has simply emphasized that such decisions are likely to be accompanied by a certain amount of cognitive activity that reduces perceived obligations to help.

Finally, in the fourth stage, all this cognitive activity must be translated into action. Ordinarily, if the person has decided that she can help, that she has an obligation to do so, and that the rewards of helping are greater than the costs, helping will occur. However, once the helping sequence is initiated, the situation may change or new facts may come to light that change one or more of the above factors. For example, the person in need may become hostile, and the helper may discover that helping is more costly than he or she first thought. In that case, new assessments of the factors might lead to a decision to cease or decrease the helping activity.

EMERGENCY HELPING

For the most part, we have been considering what might be called routine helping behaviors, the kinds where both need and the type of appropriate helping behavior are both fairly obvious. However, there is another type of helping that, although not so common, is important—helping others in an emergency. Research on emergency helping was stimulated by a dramatic incident in New York City. In the spring of 1964, Kitty Genovese was repeatedly stabbed, to death, outside her apartment complex at about 3 A.M. This kind of murder is not itself so unusual, unfortunately, but what made Kitty Genovese's case so riveting was that at least 38 people heard her repeated cries for help, and one man saw her being stabbed, yet no one called the police or tried to save her until it was far too late (Seedman & Hellman, 1974). To many people, this incident provided a vivid example of dehumanization of big-city life, and indeed there is good evidence that people in larger communities are less helpful, especially in this kind of emergency situation (Amato, 1983; Korte, 1981). However, failures to help in emergencies are not limited to citizens of large cities.

Why did the Kitty Genovese bystanders make no effort to help? One approach is to see whether the unwillingness to help in an emergency could be duplicated in controlled laboratory settings. No one would be surprised if it could not since there are many differences between a city street and a social psychology laboratory. Nonetheless, two social psychologists thought the attempt worth making. John Darley and Bibb Latané were able not only to demonstrate the phenomenon in both laboratory and field settings but also to gain some insights into why it occurred.

In a study that closely replicated the Kitty Genovese phenomenon, Darley and Latané's (1968) subjects were placed in a room alone but were connected via an intercom with presumed subjects in other, similar rooms. At some point in a group discussion held over the intercom, one person clearly became very ill; apparently he was having an epileptic seizure. The dependent measure was if people left their rooms to summon help and, if they did, how long it took. There had been a large number of observers in the Kitty Genovese murder, and the researchers wondered whether the size of the group would have an effect on helping. The size variable did have an effect. As Table 14.3 shows, subjects who thought they were alone with the ill confederate responded more often than did subjects who thought they were

TABLE 14.3 HELPING AS A FUNCTION OF GROUP SIZE. *Note that both the percentage of subjects who help and the speed of helping decrease as the group gets larger.*

Group Size	% Subjects Helping	Time to Seek Help (seconds)
2 (subject, victim)	85	52
3 (subject, other, victim)	62	93
6 (subject, four others, victim)	31	166

SOURCE: Darley and Latané, 1968.

Bibb Latané

part of a larger group. Subsequent research has generally confirmed that intervention in emergencies is inhibited by having others present (Latané & Nida, 1981).

There seem to be three general classes of variables that affect helping in emergencies. First, because emergencies are so unexpected and typically develop quickly, there may be considerable ambiguity about what is happening, whether help is needed, and what type of help will be appropriate. Second, in situations where there are many bystanders to an emergency (as with the Kitty Genovese murder), each individual may assume that others will help, so that there is diffusion of responsibility. Third, emergencies, like other situations involving help, involve a range of costs and rewards. A potential helper may be inhibited by perceived costs.

Ambiguity   Emergencies are, obviously, unexpected and unusual. Most people do not have a well-learned set of responses to an emergency. The bystander is likely to be confused about what has happened, whether to help, and what he or she can do (Latané & Darley, 1970). People react to ambiguity in different ways, but most people choose to do nothing if they are unable to determine an appropriate response. There is also additional ambiguity about the rewards and particularly about the costs involved. These ambiguities will be reduced through whatever information is available, particularly the behavior of others. A person who is confused looks to others

to see how they define the situation and how they behave. There is a tragic irony here. Suppose I am confused about what to do. Naturally I look to the behavior of others. But because they are not helping, I conclude either that the situation is not dangerous or that it is too dangerous for me to get involved. In either case, the nonhelping bystanders reduce the ambiguity but also reduce the chances that others will help.

If emergency helping is inhibited because bystanders are not sure whether the situation is actually an emergency, it follows that when the victim clearly defines the situation as one requiring help, bystanders should be more likely to intervene. This has been shown in many studies (Bickman, 1972; Clark & Word, 1972; DeJong, Marber, & Shaver, 1980; Shotland & Heinold, 1985). Darley, Teger, and Lewis (1973) further showed that nonverbal cues from bystanders—such as startle responses, which suggest that the situation is an emergency—tended to reduce inhibitions and increase helping.

Bystanders may be quite clear that a victim needs help, but still be confused about the consequences of helping or about who is best qualified to help. For example, if I am among the first at the scene of an automobile accident, I may not wish to help an obviously seriously hurt passenger because I am not sure what to do, given my lack of first-aid training. I may look around hoping there is another bystander who is better qualified than I to administer first aid. Following this reasoning, Schwartz and Clausen (1970) found that the presence of a supposedly medically trained person inhibited helping by bystanders more than did the presence of a nonmedical person; presumably people reason that the medically trained person is better qualified to help. It is also possible that people who are qualified to help feel less ambiguity about their role and hence are inhibited less. Huston, Ruggiero, Conner, and Geis (1981) interviewed people (almost all males) who had intervened in actual criminal episodes. These interveners were

Sometimes we help in accident situations.

more likely than noninterveners to have had life-saving, first-aid, or medical training; they also saw themselves as physically stronger than controls and as bigger than the criminal offenders they faced. Thus, the men who intervened may well have seen themselves as particularly competent to intervene in emergencies.

In general, then, these studies point to the role of ambiguity in inhibiting bystander intervention. If people are confused about what is happening or what they should do, they will likely do nothing. The presence of other bystanders may inhibit helping because their lack of helping ironically helps define the situation as one not requiring helping behavior. Conversely, factors that either make the situation more clearly an emergency or help define the consequences of acting positively tend to increase the rate of helping.

Diffusion of Responsibility   Diffusion of responsibility can refer to at least two different processes. First, it may mean that as the number of bystanders increases, it becomes increasingly unclear which one of them should be the first to help. When you are alone with a

person who needs help, either you help or the person doesn't get aid. When there are 15 other people, you may be more willing to wait for someone else to make the first move. Bickman (1971, 1972) has shown that when the individual subject knows that other bystanders cannot help, that person is more likely to help than when he or she knows that other bystanders can also help. Ross and Braband (1973) paired subjects with either a blind or a sighted but passive confederate. When the sign of an emergency next door was visual (smoke), subjects with the blind confederate were much more likely to try to aid those next door than were subjects paired with the sighted confederate. When the sign of the emergency was auditory (a scream), however, subjects were equally inhibited from helping by the blind and the sighted confederate. In other words, when it is clear that others cannot help, the individual is more likely to take action. Second, diffusion of responsibility may also refer to a less salutary motivation. Because the presence of lots of other people means that no one person is required to help, the single person in a mass of others may reason that he can't be held accountable for the problem. "No one can blame me, because there were so many others" reflects a more egoistic kind of diffusion of responsibility.

Rewards and Costs   Once the situation is defined as an emergency, there are other inhibitions against helping. The most obvious is that helping may be costly to the bystander. A bystander who tries to break up a fight, for example, runs the risk of being hurt. Furthermore, people may simply be unwilling to risk a public definition of incompetence, lack of "coolness," or inability to behave correctly in the presence of others. To try to help a seriously ill person or a victim of an accident can be time consuming, risky to the health of the victim, and often emotionally trying. Piliavin and Piliavin (1972) have shown that the sight of blood on a victim reduced helping, and Piliavin, Rodin, and Piliavin (1969) found that

We do not always help people, in part because they seem undeserving or because the helping would expose us to significant costs.

people were less likely to help a drunk than a nondrunk. Bloody and drunk victims raise the costs of helping considerably.

This would suggest that when bystanders can see one another and pick up expressions of disapproval, helping should be especially inhibited. Generally, this appears to be the case (Latané & Nida, 1981). However, when bystanders can see one another, this should also help a potential helper learn that others will approve his intervention, if the bystanders do indeed approve (Schwartz & Gottlieb, 1980). In that regard, Rutkowski, Gruder, & Romer (1983) have pointed out that most research on emergency helping has used bystanders who were previously unacquainted with one another (with good reason, because that is probably typical of many, perhaps most, emergency situations). However, with a group of cohesive bystanders, social responsibility norms might be highly salient and cancel out diffusion effects. These authors found that cohesive groups did help more quickly than noncohesive groups.

This was once illustrated to me vividly when, as a classroom demonstration, I set up an emergency helping situation in the laboratory behind the lecture hall. As the taped screams began playing, the entire class, led by the star lineman on the football team, flattened me on the way to the supposed emergency. The class was small and cohesive, and this all took place in a small college where most people know one another. Helping norms were apparently more salient than keeping one's cool image. This was also the first and last time I ran an emergency helping experiment; I was bruised for weeks, but my students, outraged at having been tricked, explained that I deserved it. (See Box 14.1 for further discussion of emergency helping research outside the laboratory.)

When Do People Help?   Given the original impetus of this research in the Kitty Genovese case, it is not surprising that much of the research has sought to identify factors that *inhibit* helping. However, this may obscure the important fact that in many emergencies people do help, and rather quickly. Piliavin, Dovidio, Gaertner, and Clark (1981) have presented a model of emergency helping that is oriented more toward why people help than why they do not. There are some subtle but important differences between this model and what we have already discussed.

Jane Piliavin

BOX 14.1

FIELD RESEARCH ON HELPING

Research on emergency helping has been a blend of observational studies, laboratory experiments, and field research. Latané and Darley wanted to explain why people did not help Kitty Genovese, and although much of their research was performed in a laboratory setting, they tried to investigate the importance of the conditions that existed that evening. However, one can never be quite sure that laboratory conditions faithfully duplicate the everyday world. To reduce this element of doubt, social psychologists sometimes do experiments outside the laboratory—that is, in the field—these are accordingly called field experiments.

A series of famous field experiments on emergency helping was performed by Jane and Irving Piliavin. In the first (Piliavin, Rodin, & Piliavin, 1969), four-person teams worked the New York subways. One of the team members played the role of a victim, one was a helping model, and the remaining two team members recorded data. Sessions were run during the middle part of the day when the subway car was not overly crowded. Also, because people getting on and off the car at stops might make interpretation of results difficult, the experiments were run while the subway would make no stops for 7.5 minutes.

The research team entered the car; the observers sat down but the victim and model remained standing. As the train passed the first station (70 seconds into the ride), the victim staggered forward and collapsed to the floor of the car. The victim was either a black or a white male, and he either walked with a cane or was carrying a

bottle in a bag and smelled of alcohol. In addition, the team member who was the helping model helped either quickly (70 seconds) or much later (150 seconds). So, from the standpoint of a rider of the subway—an unwitting subject in this research—he or she sees either a black or a white man, who appears to be drunk or who is using a cane, fall down. If no one helps within a minute or so, another male (the model) tries to help.

Several dependent measures can be collected in this type of situation. The most obvious is whether the victim is helped at all; one can also record how quickly he is helped. The cane victim was helped in 95% of the cases before the model intervened at 70 seconds. The drunk victim was helped only 50% of the time within 70 seconds. In 60% of the helping episodes, more than one person tried to help. Males were more likely to help than females. Black and white victims were equally likely to get help. There was, however, a slight tendency for victims to be helped more by members of their own race, especially when the victim was drunk. The authors speculate that when the victim uses a cane, helping is mediated entirely by sympathy, which is relatively color blind. However, for the drunk victim, sympathy is combined with feelings of disgust and fear, factors that inhibit helping and that may be higher for white subjects when the victim is black. In Chapter 16 we will further discuss these and other race effects.

Piliavin and Piliavin (1972) ran a second study, this time using the Philadelphia subways. In this case the victim also collapsed, and the major independent variable was

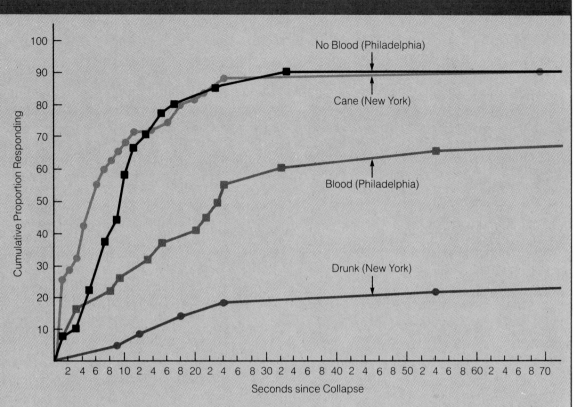

FIGURE B.14.1   Percentage of People Who Help White Male Victims as a Function of Time. Note that there is less helping and slower helping when the victim is bloody or drunk.

Piliavin and Piliavin, 1972.

whether "blood" (actually a red dye) trickled out of his mouth after he fell. In addition, one of the team members was dressed like a medical intern, a priest, or in regular street clothes so that the effects of a competent bystander could be studied.

The data are basically consistent with the New York study. In this case, there was direct help on 80% of the trials; 95% of the bloodless victims were helped but only 65% of the bloody victims got help. The bloodless victims were also helped more quickly. Figure B.14.1 shows the cumulative proportion of help over time for the two studies.

When the victim carried a cane or showed no blood, the proportion of times he was helped rises quickly with time; for example, about 50% of such victims were helped within the first 10 seconds. On the other hand, the victims who might have been more costly to help (those who appeared drunk or bloody) are not only helped less often (their curves are lower) but the help takes longer to arrive (the curves are less steep in the first 20 seconds or so). Finally, the research team was interested in whether the presence of a competent bystander (the intern) would aid diffusion of responsibility

BOX CONTINUED

and thus lower bystander helping, and it did in fact take longer for bystanders to help the bloody victim when the "intern" was present.

This kind of research is fraught with practical complications. In the first study, there were some problems when the teams did not perform as trained, and before the study could be completed a student strike at Columbia University channeled the teams' energies elsewhere. In the Philadelphia study, problems included "harassment" by transit authorities, subway riders who pulled the emergency cord to stop the train, and "impending panic" during some trials. In addition, some trials had to be dropped because a nurse was on board the train and helped quickly. Of course, one does not

have most of these problems in a laboratory situation. Over and above the intrusion of uncontrolled variables into the research, the researchers were limited in their dependent measures. They could not, for example, ask the riders what they thought or why they helped. Still the research produced surprisingly rich data. There are costs and benefits of doing this research, as there are in laboratory experiments. Field experiments are generally more time consuming and frustrating to run and there are always problems with lack of control and with inability to get some measures one would like. However, the benefits of realism and of increased confidence that the results apply to everyday life more than compensate for the limitations of field research.

Piliavin and her colleagues argue that, when people witness an emergency, they will be aroused, and this arousal influences the degree and kind of helping. If the arousal is attributed to the emergency itself, it may actually facilitate helping. Support for this idea comes from a study by Sterling and Gaertner (1984) in which extraneous, exercise-induced arousal facilitated helping when the emergency was clear. Conversely, as we have already seen earlier in the chapter, misattribution of empathic arousal reduces helping and the extra arousal may be so aversive that the person finds it easier and less costly to flee the scene rather than to help.

Piliavin and her colleagues point out that, in many situations, most people help quite rapidly. This impulsive helping generally occurs without giving full consideration to the possible rewards and costs. Impulsive helping is particularly likely when the emergency is clear

and vivid; it is also enhanced when the bystanders have some prior relationship with the victim or are likely to feel positive toward him or her.

The emphasis on impulsive helping is important. Although we may not be surprised that people do not always help in an emergency, we should hardly regard that as the normal state of affairs. Victims of automobile accidents do receive help and often quite quickly, and we have all witnessed many incidents of almost instantaneous helping of the old or the ill or of those who stumble and fall. People do not always take the time to calculate their costs (or rewards) for helping. Even if they do calculate their costs, they may still decide to help, but as our previous discussion indicates, the likelihood is reduced. So it is important to remember Kitty Genovese, but it is equally important to keep in mind that not everyone is likely to have such an unfortunate fate.

SUMMARY

One perspective on helping has been that people help because they feel they will gain rewards by doing so. Alternatively, another perspective is that people help from a genuine concern for others. Those who take the latter position often point to empathy as a mediating link. Empathy has been shown to lead to helping. When people empathize with another, they will help that person even if an easier way of reducing their own empathic distress is available. Those who feel that helping is motivated primarily by a concern for rewards point out that, although there are powerful norms for us to help others, we will not automatically help—norms alone do not lead to helping behavior. In general, helping norms must be activated *and* people must feel that helping will be beneficial for helping to take place. Like other forms of helping, helping in emergencies is affected by perceived rewards and especially by perceived costs of helping. In addition, people in emergencies are often uncertain about what they should do and this reduces helping unless the presence of others helps define the situation as one in which helping is appropriate.

COOPERATION AND COMPETITION

Another important form of prosocial behavior is cooperation. In some respects, this is a weak form of prosocial behavior because there is usually an explicit element of self-gain involved as well. Often this is expressed in explicit bargains—"you scratch my back and I'll scratch yours."

Cooperative behavior is quite common and forms the basis of many, if not all, relationships. A marriage is, among other things, an agreement to work together toward certain goals that both partners can accomplish more efficiently than either can separately. Purely commercial relationships between buyer and seller can be thought of as cooperative, in the sense that each person helps the other so that his own rewards may be maximized.

There is little mystery about why cooperation occurs, although the mechanics of getting an agreement that is mutually beneficial to everyone are often fascinating. Accordingly, most social scientists have been more concerned with why cooperation does *not* occur, with why people compete. That is, if cooperation is such a good deal for everyone concerned, why isn't it more common? Why do we have wars, divorces, arguments, and conflicts in general? Part of the answer is that in a great many situations there is no overlap of interests. If I must get $70,000 for my house and you are willing to pay only $50,000, we are not likely to strike a bargain. Also, scarce resources mean that hard choices may have to be made, and not everyone will

Cooperation makes many jobs easier.

be happy. There may be, for example, no way for a young married couple to pay for both his new stereo and her new car—at least one of them will have to do without.

So, when we have scarce resources and when different people (or groups) want different things, conflict is natural. Still, there are many other situations in which it seems people ought to be able to cooperate but they don't. For example, everyone recognizes that there is something vaguely irrational about spending unimaginably vast sums on yet more military equipment that is necessary only because other countries do the same. If only all the countries would agree to be less belligerent, we could all quit the arms race.

SOCIAL DILEMMAS

Social psychologists have been particularly interested in situations where two or more people have a long-term interest in cooperation but a short-term interest in noncooperation. Such situations are common and important. Let us imagine two countries that are making decisions about how much money to spend on airplanes, boats, bombs, guns, men, and other implements of war. Both countries feel that they should cooperate and spend more of their money on domestic programs and less on military equipment. It is in the long-term interests of each to reduce military expenditures. However, each also recognizes that it is in its short-term interest to try to gain military superiority, to be the first country on the block to have a new (and expensive) weapons system. Unfortunately, each also recognizes what the other recognizes: that from the perspective of Country A the best of all possible worlds would be for Country B to reduce expenditures while A builds the new weapons. Although their long-term interests are served by cooperation, their short-term interests favor competition. And so we have arms races.

Consider a second example, usually called the tragedy of the commons or the **commons dilemma** (Hardin, 1968). In an earlier period of American and English history, residents of small towns grazed their cows and sheep together in a public pasture (the commons). Suppose we have a town of 25 families and a commons that will ideally support exactly 25 cows. On the available land, each cow will produce an average of 500 gallons of milk a year. However, if 30 cows are put in the same area, each gets somewhat less than the optimal amount of grass and produces only 400 gallons per year. With 50 cows the production is only 100 gallons per year, per cow. Each family has equal access to the land, and the total milk output is 12,500 gallons per year for 25 cows. With 30 cows the total output is 12,000 gallons and with 50 cows only 5,000 gallons. The obvious best collective strategy is for each family to graze a single cow on the commons.

This all makes sense from a collective standpoint. But how does it look from the standpoint of a single villager? Suppose Caleb has had a good year making candles and decides he wants 6 cows instead of 1. He adds 5 new cows, which makes for 30 now on the commons. Caleb's 6 cows will produce a total of 2,400 gallons of milk, which provides his family with cream for their coffee, butter with every meal, and a bit left over for a good eggnog at Christmas. Of course, milk production for the village will be down (from 12,500 to 12,000 gallons), but from Caleb's standpoint, his decision to add 5 cows gains him an extra 1,900 gallons of milk. Unfortunately, there are many Calebs in this village, and for each the immediate gain of adding a cow or two is greater than his share of the collective loss. As you might expect, in most villages the commons land was overgrazed and milk production fell.

Finally, there is the problem of public goods. Every year the local public broadcasting station and noncommercial classical music stations appeal for my dollars so they can stay on the air. The problem is that I can afford to give only about $25 to each and obviously that will make no difference to the quality of the stations. On the other hand, if everyone reasons as I do, then none of us will have "Masterpiece Theatre," Mozart, or Mahler. Similarly, although I have voted in elections for over 25 years, I have never voted in one where my single vote came anywhere close to making a difference. Yet, if everyone were to refuse to vote on the grounds that no single vote makes a difference, we would have no electoral process.

Though it may not be immediately apparent, these examples—the arms race, the commons dilemma, the public goods dilemma —have certain basic similarities (Cross & Guyer, 1980; Linder, 1982; Platt, 1973). In each case, the individual always gains his best, immediate outcomes by behaving in a way that produces collective costs. In the arms race, each country gets better outcomes by continuing to arm, and the world suffers; with the commons, each person gains more from grazing an extra cow even though the commons as a whole suffers as a result; for public (broadcasting) goods, I come out ahead if I don't contribute at all but then watch and listen to the stations for free. Other examples are not hard to find. My gas-guzzling car is comfortable and depletes the nation's oil reserves by a trivial amount, but if everyone drives such cars there is risk that the reserves are depleted to the point where no one drives cars. Or, a company pollutes the atmosphere but is unwilling to incur the costs of being the only company to install pollution control devices, and so on and so on.

Social psychologists have devoted special research attention to the commons dilemma, where a common resource available to all may be depleted if individuals do not cooperate in their use of the resource. Typically, groups begin with a resource pool from which each member can withdraw or "harvest" a certain amount on each of several trials. After each group member has made his harvest for each trial, the experimenter adds a certain amount to the pool before the next trial to simulate the regeneration of the resources over time; for example, new grass grows on the commons as the old is consumed, and reservoirs refill with water even as we continue to drink and bathe. The replenishment amount is usually a small percentage of the total pool—if individual members are too greedy the total pool will soon be depleted. For example, suppose you are one of five subjects in an experiment with an initial pool of $220. Each of you makes an individual decision about how much money to take out. When you have each made your decision, the total amount is subtracted from the common pool, and the experimenter puts back 10% of the remaining pool. Obviously, your group of five people can each continue to take $4 (for a total of $20) on each trial for an indefinite number of trials—that is, without depleting the common pool. The group takes $20 and the experimenter puts back 10% of the remaining $200 (or $20), restoring the pool to its original size. However, if the group takes out $40 each time, the pool lasts for only 8 trials; the pool lasts for 12 trials if the group harvests $30 on each trial and 32 trials if the group harvests $21, which is only $1 more than the harvest that can be maintained indefinitely (See Figure 14.1).

Is the collective deficit that generally results from such situations due more to the inherent selfishness of people or to other causes? Individuals usually do better at managing their resources than groups do (Messick & McClelland, 1983), but why? One reason is surely greed; there are some people who exploit group situations. In the resource-pool example above, one individual might reason that if he takes $24 each time while the other four people take their $4 (for a total of $40 on each trial) he will come out way ahead. To be sure, the common resource will be depleted after 6 turns, but our greedy person reasons that he will have made $144 in that time and it would

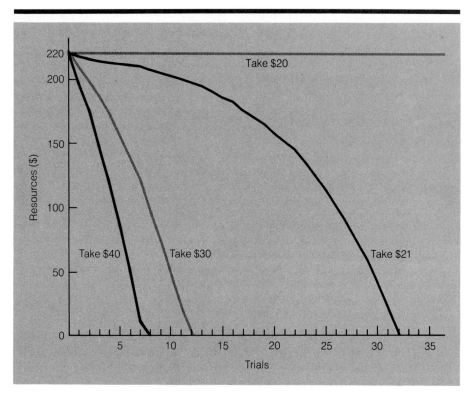

FIGURE 14.1   Depletion of Resources in a Commons Dilemma. The depletions shown here are a function of how much the group members harvest with 10% replenishment after each harvest.

take him 36 trials to amass that amount if he were to take only his "fair" $4 per trial. But, of course, he is not likely to be the only person in the group who can figure that out, and sooner or later the entire group will take large harvests and deplete the resource even faster.

There is clear evidence that some people do have personalities that incline them toward such selfish or at least collectively irresponsible behavior (Liebrand & van Run, 1985). You know the type—the guy who waters his lawn during a time of voluntary water conservation. On the other hand, the research evidence suggests that other factors are also important. One is whether the people think of themselves as part of a group. It is a common stereotype that people in small towns and communities

cooperate and help one another because they think of themselves as part of the common group whereas people in big cities are cold and cruel to one another because they have no sense of groupness with others. Kramer and Brewer (1984) have shown that when group identity is made salient, there is less individual exploitation of the common resource. Communication is also important; the resource pool tends to be depleted less when the subjects can communicate with one another (Brechner, 1977). Such communication may make subjects more aware of the needs of each other and thus reduce purely selfish motives, and it is also likely that the ability to talk to one another helps establish a common, nonexploitive strategy.

On the other hand, Schroeder et al. (1983) have shown that when group members can observe the behavior of others, the pool is depleted more rapidly. There could be two reasons for this. First, a given subject may wish to take only her fair share and not deplete the general pool, but she may find that others are not so cooperative. Thus she might become more selfish herself so as to get her share and not appear to be a sucker. Alternatively, each person may be somewhat confused about the best strategy and use the behavior of others as a guide. When subjects were given explicit instructions on the optimal strategy, their harvests were not affected by the harvests of the others. If subjects had been merely being selfish, then they should not have let the instructions deter them from following the greedy lead of their fellow subjects.

It is worth noting that even when individual subjects withdraw resources from their own private pools, they often deplete the pool (Messick & McClelland, 1983). This suggests that mere selfishness is not the only culprit and that people have some trouble understanding the necessity of conserving resource pools. Experiences and training that help people understand the importance of conserving resources produce better management of the common pool (Allison & Messick, 1985). In actual social situations, it is hard to get people to understand that their own behavior may detract from the common good because typically it does so only in minimal (but collectively crucial) ways. Furthermore, even if people recognize this fact, they might well reason that their own sacrifices in the absence of similar sacrifices by others will help the problem only a trivial amount and may lead to their being exploited.

In many instances, the government or some other external agency has to step in to provide the direction that is hard to achieve in large communities with the lack of communication. The government may also enforce cooperation when trust is lacking. For example, no individual car manufacturer would want to charge customers an extra (say) $500 for pollution devices because customers would simply switch to less-expensive cars by competitors. Therefore, it is necessary to have a federal law that mandates such devices for *all* manufacturers if any one of them is to add the devices.

Under some circumstances, people may willingly give up their freedoms to exploit (and be exploited) for the common good. Messick et al. (1983) showed that when the group overused the common resource, they were more willing to elect a leader to guide their choices than when they did not overuse the resource. Thus, as the effects of lack of cooperation become apparent, subjects are more willing to submit to control for the common good—a common good that benefits each person, albeit less directly than an individualistic, exploitive strategy by each subject.

Thus, for the worst effects of social dilemmas to be diminished, several features must be present. People must be able to communicate both to facilitate understanding and to formulate effective strategies. People must trust one another not to exploit the common good for their own selfish interests. In some cases an effort has to be made to ensure that cooperation is publicly recognized and rewarded. Finally, it is sometimes helpful to assign overall management of common resources to an impartial agency or leader to reduce exploitation and to ensure effective trust.

PRISONER'S DILEMMA

Much of the research on cooperation has been conducted with the use of various games. This may seem curious at first, because we normally think of games as competitive. Indeed, many of the most popular games we play are what game theorists call *zero-sum games:* the sum of winnings and losses must equal zero. For example, after an evening's play of poker, the losses of the losers equal the winnings of the winners. Many other games, such as chess, checkers, and bridge, are also effectively zero-sum, because winners win by the same amount the losers lose. We might call such zero-sum games examples of pure competition, because each player can achieve his or her best outcomes only by beating the other player or players.

Although games of pure competition are popular and well known, it is also possible to create games in which wins and losses do not have to balance out. One of the most popular games of this type is the *Prisoner's Dilemma,* named from the following story. Two men have been arrested for a crime and locked in separate cells where they cannot communicate with each other. The district attorney points out that each can either confess or not confess. If neither confesses, both will be given moderate sentences (say, 1 year); if one confesses and the other does not, the one who confesses will go free while his comrade gets a stiff sentence (7 years). Finally, if both confess, their sentences will be moderately heavy (5 years). Thus, collectively, the two are better off not confessing, but it is tempting to confess and get off with a really light sentence while leaving the poor comrade to suffer.

If we think of each prisoner's choice as analogous to a play in a game, we can reduce the situation to a matrix of rewards and costs dependent on the choices or plays that are made. Table 14.4 gives an example for the situation we have just described. In the actual situation confronting the two prisoners in the last paragraph, neither can really win anything, but only keep from losing; however, it is quite easy to create matrices where each person can win something, and an example is given in Table 14.5. The essential dilemma in this case is that Alice and Carol each have a preferred course of action, but if both choose it, they will both get relatively poor outcomes. In the situation confronting the prisoners, each is individually better off by confessing, but if both do this, then both end up with less-than-optimal outcomes. In the example given in Table 14.5, each player is better off playing B, but if they both do so they get less reward than if both play A. Obviously, it is to each player's advantage to have the other make a cooperative response (A) while she makes a noncooperative one (B). If each player acts only in her own self-interest by playing B, both players achieve less-than-ideal outcomes. On the other hand, quite favorable outcomes can be achieved if both make a cooperative response, which unfortunately leaves each open to exploitation from the other. Thus, each player must ask herself whether she can afford to trust the other to cooperate when the temptations for noncooperation are so great.

The essential dilemma of the game is also important in everyday life. In a great many situations, the collective good is gained only if

---

TABLE 14.4 PRISONER'S DILEMMA. *In this version of the game, neither participant can really win anything (compare Table 14.5).*

| | | Prisoner B | |
		Not Confess (Cooperation)	Confess (Competition)
Prisoner A	Not Confess (Cooperation)	Prisoner A gets 1 year Prisoner B gets 1 year	Prisoner A gets 7 years Prisoner B goes free
	Confess (Competition)	Prisoner A goes free Prisoner B gets 7 years	Prisoner A gets 5 years Prisoner B gets 5 years

TABLE 14.5 PRISONER'S DILEMMA. *In this version of the game, favorable outcomes can be achieved if both participants make a cooperative effort (compare Table 14.4).*

		Carol		
		A (Cooperation)		B (Competition)
A (Cooperation)		Alice 5		Alice − 5
Alice		Carol 5		Carol 10
B (Competition)		Alice 10		Alice − 2
		Carol − 5		Carol − 2

everyone is willing to trust one another not to exploit their prosocial orientations. As the example of the Ik indicates, once this trust disappears there is a perverse sort of rationality in looking out for one's own interests. It is often hard to get people to give up their short-term gains for the collective good, and when people play the Prisoner's Dilemma game, the rate of cooperation is generally quite low. Usually, fewer than 50% of the total choices are cooperative. Social psychologists have expended a fair amount of time to uncover the conditions that might increase this rate of cooperation.

Other-concern Increasing the concern that people have with one another tends to increase cooperation in the Prisoner's Dilemma. For example, students coming from a small college are more cooperative than those from a large university, presumably because those in the small college are more likely to know and be concerned about one another (Oskamp & Perlman, 1965). Cooperation is also more likely with people subjects know (McClintock & McNeil, 1967) or like (Swingle & Gillis, 1968) or with whom they have had favorable experiences (Harrison & McClintock, 1965). Perhaps such positive involvement produces greater empathy or perhaps prosocial norms such as honesty and altruism are more salient when we interact with those about whom we care.

Public Image Most of us do not like to be identified as exploitive and selfish. Thus, cooperation increases when people make choices in public rather than in private (Oskamp & Perlman, 1965). This tendency to pay attention to one's public image should be especially high among high self-monitors (see Chapter 8), those people who are generally concerned with social rewards and who are willing to change their social behavior according to situational demands to get such rewards. Danheiser and Graziano (1982) confirmed that high self-monitors (those concerned with their social standing) were more cooperative when they expected future interaction with their partner than when they did not; this was not the case for the low self-monitors.

Communication Communication often improves cooperation. It helps establish bonds between people and it helps ensure that everyone understands the consequences of various behaviors. Ability to communicate also affects rate of cooperation in the Prisoner's Dilemma. Imagine that you are playing the game without being able to communicate with your partner. Your immediate concern would be what your partner intends to do. If you are inclined to be competitive yourself, you will probably assume that the other is also going to be competitive (Kelley & Stahelski, 1970a) and hence play the competitive choice to protect yourself. But even if you are inclined to trust your partner and assume she is going to cooperate, it is likely that one or the other of you will soon stray and play the competitive choice. When one or both players have given evidence that they will compete rather than cooperate, it is very hard to generate the trust necessary to make the cooperative choice. Remember that if you do cooperate, you are open to exploitation from a competitive partner.

Several studies have found that the rate of cooperation is higher when the people can communicate their intentions directly (Brechner, 1977; Caldwell, 1976; Dawes, McTavish

& Shaklee, 1977; Jorgenson & Papciak, 1981). Note that communication does not *guarantee* cooperation, but it should facilitate it. If two people can talk to one another, they might agree to play the cooperative choice. However, such agreement does not guarantee cooperation—one of the players could lie and make a competitive choice.

The Behavior of the Other   One of the more obvious things to vary in a Prisoner's Dilemma situation is whether the other person is cooperative or competitive. This can be accomplished either by having one of the players be a confederate of the experimenter or by having the experimenter control what each subject thinks the other has played. Interestingly enough, pure cooperation on the part of a confederate does not necessarily result in cooperation on the part of the other player (Bixenstine & Wilson, 1963; McClintock et al., 1963). A glance at the Prisoner's Dilemma matrix (Table 14.5) will make it clear why this might happen. Obviously, if another player is going to be cooperative no matter what I do, I can maximize my rewards by performing the competitive response. With an invariably cooperative other, tendencies to reciprocate are cancelled out by the opportunity to exploit. Saints are rarely wealthy.

Deutsch et al. (1967) investigated the effects of several strategies of the other player. One of the most successful strategies is the *reformed sinner* strategy in which the programmed

player plays very competitively during the first phase of the experiment, but then begins to play in a more cooperative manner. This action elicited a large increase in the amount of cooperative play from the other person. Another cooperation-induced strategy was the *deterrent* strategy, in which the confederate responded in a threatening way to any noncooperative act of the subject and also counterattacked when the subject attacked; however, when the subject played cooperatively, the programmed confederate also played cooperatively. The results from these and other experiments suggest that cooperation is best enhanced not by unilateral cooperation, but by responding to cooperation with cooperation and to threat with counterthreat.

Threat   Another variable that might be expected to increase cooperation, at least in the short run, is threat. Obviously, in a Prisoner's Dilemma game, each player can threaten to defect if the other does not cooperate. To study the nature of threat more closely, Deutsch and Krauss (1960) used the Trucking Game, which, although not properly the Prisoner's Dilemma, shares some features with it (Figure 14.2). Rewards were promised to subjects on the basis of how quickly they could get their truck to the destination. But in this situation the shortest route to the destination for both players is across a one-lane road that both players cannot use simultaneously. If both players begin at the same time and head toward the destination, they will meet in the middle and a deadlock will ensue. There are two possible solutions. One is for Acme to wait before getting to the one-lane road for Bolt to get through, which then frees the road for Acme to use. This will, of course, result in Bolt's getting to his destination more quickly. Over a series of trials, the people might agree to cooperate, such that on the first trial one player would wait, on the second trail the other player would wait, and so on. The other possibilities are for either player to take the

Morton Deutsch

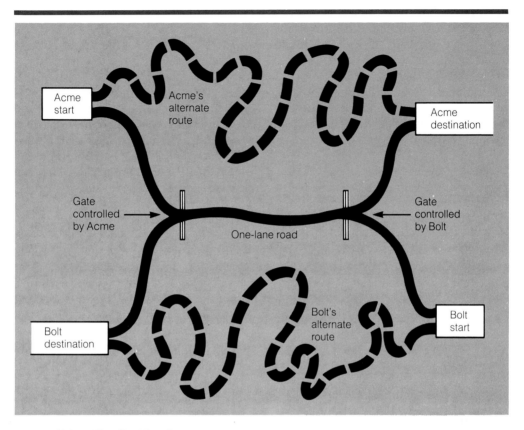

FIGURE 14.2   The Trucking Game. The shortest route for both players (and the only route that makes money) is through a one-lane road that either player can block with gates.

Deutsch and Krauss, 1960.

longer route or for both players to take the longer route; the latter course would result in a loss for both players.

However, suppose both players meet in the middle of the road and sit there. As time passes and each player begins to lose money, the situation becomes frustrating. If Acme decides to back off, she allows Bolt to reach his destination before Acme; although both may lose money because they sat in the middle of the road glaring at each other for some time, Bolt would lose less money than the cooperative Acme would. To back off at this stage of the game, then, means losing not only money relative to the other person, but also face.

In what Deutsch and Krauss described as a no-threat condition, which is essentially the one just described, the players tended to make money in the course of playing several games. This must have resulted from their having taken turns at going over the road, because any players who used the alternate route would lose at least 10¢ per trial. Threat was introduced into this situation by creating gates that could block the route. In the unilateral-threat condition, only Acme controlled a gate; in the bilateral-threat condition, both subjects controlled gates. The players lost money under the threat conditions, and they lost somewhat more money when the threat was bilateral—

that is, when both players controlled gates—than when only one subject could control the gate.

The psychology of threat is complex (see Tedeschi, 1970), but such variables as how the threat is perceived (Mogy & Pruitt, 1974) and how the target responds to threat (Tedeschi, Bonoma, & Lindskold, 1970) are important in determining how threats affect cooperation.

Criticisms   Some social psychologists have argued that the Prisoner's Dilemma paradigm is too simple to be of any significant value. The fact that so little cooperation is exhibited in Prisoner's Dilemma studies, perhaps less than in the real world, has led some social psychologists to conclude that the Prisoner's Dilemma is not an adequate representation of the real world. Nemeth (1970b, 1972) and Abric (1982), among others, have been particularly critical of the Prisoner's Dilemma research. Nemeth feels that the Prisoner's Dilemma situation is ambiguous for the subjects involved. They are not quite sure what is expected of them, and they are cut off from most of the ways that they generally use to find out, such as talking to the other, asking other people who have been in similar situations, and the like. When the subjects cannot talk to one another, they have little way of making their intentions and the meaning of their behavior clear. For example, when the other has made a competitive response in the last trial, is the subject to interpret this as boredom, as a punishment for the subject's past competitiveness, as a threat, or as an attempt at exploitation? Obviously, the subject's behavior might be different, depending on how he or she interprets the other's behavior.

Although it is true that the Prisoner's Dilemma and other games are quite artificial, it is also true that they simulate many features of real-life conflict situations. The most unfortunate aspect of this research is that researchers have sometimes lost sight of the real-life issues that stimulated the research in the first place.

SUMMARY

Cooperation is another form of prosocial behavior but one in which the person and at least one other person both realize some immediate benefits from their action. Although it would seem natural for cooperation to occur, it is often not easy for people to agree how to cooperate. Social psychologists have been especially interested in situations in which the individual's short-term interests hurt the larger community interests. In such situations, it is often hard to get people to not exploit the common good. However, communication and group identity are two factors that improve cooperation in this situation. A closely related situation is the Prisoner's Dilemma, in which if each person takes advantage of the other, both suffer. In actual games, the rate of competition is quite high, and again explicit communication, clarity of options, and fellow feeling often improve cooperation. Threats and the ability to punish are sometimes also valuable options.

CHAPTER SUMMARY

- Prosocial behavior is behavior that is helpful or rewarding to others, whereas antisocial behavior is behavior that produces harmful consequences to others.

- Some theorists emphasize that even behavior that helps others is performed only to achieve rewards for the self, rewards that can include pride and feelings of satisfaction as well as social approval. Other theorists have argued that people have a genuine regard for one another and that we help others because we are genuinely concerned about them.

- For those who subscribe to the genuine altruism position, the role of empathy is important. Empathy is experiencing an emotion when observing another display it, and experiments show that most people feel empathic distress at watching another in distress. Empathy increases helping; when empathy arousal is misattributed, helping declines. It has been argued that people help in order to reduce their own empathic distress, but evidence suggests that even when the potential helper's distress can be reduced by withdrawal, helping still occurs.

■ People in good moods help more than those in neutral moods, because helping helps to preserve their good mood, because good moods increase the positive features of situations, or because a good mood alters the focus of attention. Bad moods may increase or decrease helping, depending on whether the helping can restore a good mood and focus of attention.

■ There are several norms that we should help others. In general, these norms must be activated before they lead to helping behavior. The person must see the norms as relevant to the situation and must assess the potential costs and rewards of helping and not helping.

■ People do not always help in emergencies, and this seems to be true more in larger groups. One explanation is that it is costly to help others in an emergency. Another is that bystanders often are unsure about the appropriate action to perform. A third is that when there are many people present there is diffusion of responsibility such that each person feels less responsibility for helping.

■ Cooperation is another form of prosocial behavior. It is similar to altruism in that rewards are provided for others, but usually in cooperation there is greater focus on mutual rewards for all people.

■ The short-term interests of individuals often conflict with the long-term interests of the group. Specifically, if most people behave only in their own self-interest, the group suffers. Individual greed, the lack of collective feeling, and the inability to communicate—all promote individual over group interests. Sometimes people will accept leadership or legislation to make them behave in the collective interest.

■ The Prisoner's Dilemma is a class of games in which two people compete in such a way that if each tries to exploit the other, they both lose. In such situations, it is hard to achieve stable cooperation, because both players are tempted to exploit the other for self-gain. Again, collective spirit and communication are important means to achieving greater cooperation. Threat can also sometimes be effective in getting cooperation.

CHAPTER

15

AGGRESSION

The Yanomamo live in lowland jungles in Southern Venezuela and Northern Brazil. Descriptions provided by the first anthropologist to study them in detail, Napolean Chagnon (1968, 1974), make clear that they are a fierce and violent people, mean-spirited and selfish. The Yanomamo engage in almost constant warfare with other villages, and fights and arguments within villages are also common. Fierceness is therefore the quality most valued in males.

The most common way the Yanomamo resolve conflicts is the chest-pounding duel. One man plants his feet and the other pounds him in the chest as hard as he can with his fist until the first says he has had enough. Then the first is allowed to retaliate on the second. Participants cough up blood for days afterward. If the chest-pounding duel does not produce a solution to the problem, the disputants might take turns hitting one another over the head with 10-foot poles. These hits invariably open major wounds on the head and sometimes result in death. Yanomamo men proudly display their scarred heads, some keeping them shaved just so others can see how fierce they are. Finally, there are occasions for spear duels, where men throw spears at one another.

There are also wars and raids between villages. Chagnon (1974) estimates that something like one-third of all males in this culture die violently. Raids usually occur for the purpose of stealing women, although killing enemies is considered good sport too. There is a scarcity of girls and marriageable women because girls are often killed at birth and because some men have multiple wives. Males and females do marry within villages, but when a young man wishes to marry a woman he will usually be required to do bride-service, which involves working his in-law's gardens for a period of several years. When all is said and done, young males are often better off stealing

Yanomamo: the fierce people.

their wives rather than winning them in the ordinary courting ways. The women themselves do not relish being taken away from their villages as the booty of war, and they play an active role in encouraging their men to be tough and belligerent. In addition, women are beaten regularly by their husbands, and a woman measures the extent of her husband's love (or possessiveness) by the harshness of the beatings she receives.

The political life of the Yanomamo is built around alliances devoted to protecting villages from raids. A village smaller than, say, 75 or so has a hard time fielding raiding parties while still leaving men at home to protect the females from raids. But when the villages get to be over 100 people or so, internal bickering tends to become excessive and eventually there is a split into two new and mutually hostile villages. The intervillage alliances that the Yanomamo form for mutual protection are very fragile. It is not unknown for one village to invite a nominal ally to a feast and then attack their guests during the festivities.

The Yanomamo are unpleasant and violent in small and large ways. Why? One possibility is genetic. If (and this is a very big if) there is a genetic basis for aggression, then the Yanomamo culture would surely select for it, given that marriage and begetting children are reserved for the most violent males. But a more likely explanation is ecological. In a society in which aggression permeates every action, no person can afford to be pacific. Any male who is nonaggressive moves directly to the bottom of the status hierarchy, with no compensating rewards. There is no incentive to inhibit aggression and there are a great many rewards to increase it. This is one of the fundamental facts about aggression. Once the level of mutual aggression in any group reaches a certain point, it begins to feed upon itself; no one can afford to back down.

Early in the morning of February 16, 1970, Green Beret captain (and physician) Jeffrey MacDonald called for an ambulance to be sent to his home on base at Ft. Bragg, North Carolina. When the ambulance and military police arrived, they found that MacDonald's wife, Colette, and two daughters had been brutally murdered; each had been stabbed several times. MacDonald had passed out next to his wife with relatively superficial stab wounds. When MacDonald had recovered sufficiently to talk, he told a terrifying story of having been awakened from sleep on the living room couch by screams from one of his daughters and then seeing several hippies standing over him shouting "Kill the pigs" and "Acid is groovy." He fought them off but was stabbed in the chest and lost consciousness. Subsequently, investigators discovered the word *PIG* written in blood on the headboard in the master bedroom.

MacDonald was a man easy to feel sorry for under the circumstances. He was a gifted athlete, a good student at Princeton, a competent physician, and was handsome and articulate to boot. He and Colette had what seemed to be an ideal marriage. However, it subsequently became clear that the pity was misplaced. Investigations failed to turn up independent evidence of the hippie band, and it was suspicious

that MacDonald had received only superficial wounds (which could have been self-inflicted) in a situation where three other people had been brutally stabbed multiple times. Moreover, certain details of his story did not check out. MacDonald was tried for the crimes in August of 1975. He was found guilty of the three murders and after exhausting various appeals is now in prison for the crimes.

We may never know what happened that night because MacDonald has refused to admit that he was the murderer. But it seems clear (see McGinniss, 1983, for a full account) that beneath the all-American exterior, MacDonald was a troubled man. He was not mentally ill by any reasonable definition, but on that night hidden frustrations and tensions erupted. One of the children was killed first, probably while he was in a rage because she had wet the bed. Next, Colette was killed try-

Jeffrey MacDonald.

ing to defend her daughter, and finally he killed the younger daughter to make the killings seem like the work of outsiders.

MacDonald is not a typical killer, but his case illustrates one fascinating type of murder. He was not the sort of person anyone would have identified as a potential killer. He kept a rein on his anger; he did not beat his wife, get in fights, or argue with his neighbors. He was a seemingly normal man whose defenses broke down just this once.

INTRODUCTION

The vast majority of people will never murder anyone. Yet we are all aggressive from time to time—aggressive behavior is universal. We may deplore it, applaud its socialized forms, and design social systems that mitigate it, but we cannot ignore it. Aggression is common, manifestly social, and as fundamental to social relations as is love or sex.

What is aggression? *Aggression* is commonly defined as behavior intended to harm another person (Baron, 1977; Zillmann, 1979), and this harm can be either physical or psychological. Thus, aggression is not limited to physical actions such as hitting, stabbing, pushing, or shooting but would also include such things as starting vicious rumors or even failing to correct them, if these actions were intended to hurt someone. Sometimes a distinction is made between two types of aggressive behavior. *Emotion-based aggression* refers to the familiar case where an angry or hostile person hits or shouts at another. *Instrumental* (or **incentive-based**) *aggression* refers to instances where one person intends to harm another to get some rewards. As best we can determine, Jeffrey MacDonald killed his first child and wife when he lost control of his temper—emotion-based aggression—but the killing of the second child seems to have been a more instrumental attempt to make the first two killings look like the work of outsiders.

THEORIES OF AGGRESSION

HUMAN NATURE AND BIOLOGY

For centuries, aggression has been seen as both basic and natural. Many theorists have used biological arguments to claim that aggression is as much a part of our biological heritage as sex or hunger.

The Darwinian Heritage   Darwin's theory of evolution provided a firm rationale for biological models of aggression. Darwin saw intraspecies fighting as a major mechanism in evolution. Males may fight for breeding privileges with females and many animals fight for favored food or nesting territories. In such fighting, the strongest or craftiest animals are likely to survive and any genetic bases for these superior tendencies will be passed along to offspring. From an evolutionary perspective, it is clear that aggression is functional both for individual and for group survival.

So there are strong theoretical reasons for believing that aggressive behavior might have an innate component. But how do we conceive this biological aspect? One popular answer has been that aggression is an instinct with its own sources of energy and directive powers. Just as we are born with the desire to seek food when we are hungry or to seek sexual release when we are sexually aroused, so we are born with the urge to be aggressive periodically.

Freud   One of the most popular instinct theories of aggression was developed in a somewhat unsystematic way by Sigmund Freud. Early in his career, Freud suggested that aggression was an innate response to frustration, but after 1920 he ranked aggression equally with sex as an instinct that motivated all human behavior. The child is born, says Freud, with a powerful aggressive drive that is initially directed inward and must be channeled outward toward other people if the infant is to survive. And the aggressive instinct is just like sexual urges that build up over time and increasingly demand release. We need periodic aggressive outbursts against others to keep from destroying ourselves.

However, no society can tolerate unrestrained aggression any more than it can tolerate unbridled lust. So overt physical aggression is inhibited, and most aggression observed in well-socialized adults is subtle and at least thinly disguised: jokes, friendly kidding, and competition are everyday examples. One of the reasons cultures encourage sexual and other positive emotional ties among individuals is that such ties tend to inhibit overt fighting. The depressing aspect of all this is that, as societies become larger and more impersonal, much of our emotional energy that would ideally be invested in highly charged relationships with a few other people is now spread so thinly that modern people have lost the capacity to love and experience real pleasure.

Modern Instinct Theories   Several more recent theorists have preserved the flavor of Freud's theories while trying to find support for aggressive instincts in observations of animal behavior. Konrad Lorenz (1967) has ar-

Konrad Lorenz receives the Nobel Prize.

gued that intraspecies fighting has important survival functions for the species. For example, it spreads animals out over a larger food range, which helps conserve food and ensure that the strongest males will sire offspring. Therefore, members of many animal species are born with a natural inclination to fight. Lorenz agrees with Freud that this instinctual energy builds up over time and requires periodic release.

Lorenz also argued that many animal species had built-in restraints against indiscriminate killing. For example, dogs who are getting the worst of a fight will often adopt a submissive stance that inhibits the other's attacks. For certain other species, such restraints are unnecessary because there is no easy way for one individual to kill another and fleeing is sufficient to stop the fight. For example, it is hard to imagine a fight to the death between two robins. If one bird aggressively pecked another, a weak victim disinclined to peck back could simply fly away. In that sense humans are like robins. Lacking impressive claws and teeth, people never had to develop innate inhibitions against aggression; running would do. Unfortunately, modern technology has upset the biological applecart. We have aggressive instincts and no effective inhibitions against killing and maiming, but running is no longer effective when someone has a gun or bomb.

Lorenz is a Nobel laureate in biology, and his theory rests on his acute observations of animal behavior. Robert Ardrey, a playwright, has less immediate claim on our attention, although his several books on aggression have commanded a wide audience. His first book, *African Genesis*, argues that because fossil records of early human predecessors suggest death by weapons, there must be a basic (in the sense of evolutionarily early) aggressive instinct in humans. In another book, *The Territorial Imperative*, Ardrey marshals evidence on the tendencies of animals to defend home territories. Because such tendencies are quite common in the animal kingdom and because parallels can be found in human behavior, Ardrey suggests that wars and other territorially based fights have a strong instinctual basis.

Biological Evidence   Can these arguments be correct? Is there something like an aggressive instinct? Almost all modern biologists and psychologists would claim that Freud, Lorenz, and Ardrey have simply misread and overgeneralized their data. For example, even though some animal species are quite aggressive, others are not. Among the closest relatives of humans, chimpanzees are relatively aggressive and actually commit murder, whereas gorillas are quite nonaggressive, despite appearances. Some animal species defend their territories to the death whereas others seem as content to settle one place as another. It is hard to find the universal aggressive tendencies among animals that must therefore implicate the human animal as innately aggressive. What about the argument that animals seem to need to release their pent-up aggressions periodically? There is little or no evidence for such tendencies at the level of neural and physiological data, and the evidence we have for such tendencies comes almost entirely from fanciful interpretations of animal behavior.

This is not, however, to suggest that aggression has no biological basis. In fact, research data strongly suggest otherwise (Brain, 1984; Moyer, 1976). For example, within many species animals can be bred for fighting ability and ferociousness. Aggression can also be affected through various biological interventions. For thousands of years, farmers have known that gelding a stallion, neutering a tomcat, or making a bull a steer reduces physical aggression, and injection of male sex hormones can increase aggression, although the effects of hormones depend heavily on situational, developmental, and other biological factors. Finally, stimulation of certain areas of the brain tends to increase fighting and general irritability among animals (Moyer, 1976).

There is certainly a biology of aggression, but it is far too complex to be reduced to simple instincts. Almost no biologist or psychologist would accept the idea that humans are subject to a blind, powerful, mechanical, unremitting aggressive instinct. We are no more puppets on the end of an aggression string than we are robots controlled by sexual urges. Certainly no one would doubt that sexual urges have strong foundations in biology, but the vast majority of people learn to control such urges, and for most people, sexual behavior has a clear sense of time and place. The effects biology has on aggression are typically not direct or controlling but are mediated by the culture and the situation.

FRUSTRATION–AGGRESSION

Whatever the role biology plays in human aggression, psychological factors are especially critical in determining when and to whom we are aggressive. Each of us has at some time or another taken out our frustrations on someone else by yelling or even hitting. The hypothesis that frustration can cause aggression is ancient, but within modern psychology it was developed formally by a group of Yale University psychologists (Dollard et al., 1939). Their hypothesis was quite straightforward: frustration was caused by having a goal blocked, frustration always leads to aggression, and all aggression results from frustration. The authors were clear that the degree of frustration increases as the blocked goal becomes more important and as the blockage becomes more extensive; frustrations also build up over time, creating the potential for an explosive aggressive display, as with Captain MacDonald.

Although at first glance this theory seems to reveal much truth, some reflection will quickly suggest limitations. For one thing, not all aggression results from frustration, at least not when we define frustration as goal blockage. I have been known to be quite aggressive when I stub my toe in the middle of the night, but it seems theoretically perverse to define the sudden pain of a stubbed toe as frustrating my achievement of some goal. Indeed, much aggression results from pain, threat, or disputes over property, and these may be defined as frustrations only if we make frustration such a broad term as to be useless.

Moreover, much aggression is instrumental in the sense of being used to seek money, status, and approval in the complete absence of any frustration. The woman who spreads a vicious rumor about her work colleague in an effort to secure an important promotion for herself is not motivated by frustration but by cold-blooded calculation of reward. Laboratory research confirms that aggression can be motivated by purely instrumental concerns and that this form of aggression may be even more common than aggression based on frustration (Buss, 1966).

Frustration–aggression theory was an important milestone in the history of social psychology, although we now recognize that the strong statement of a basic, inevitable link between frustration and aggression is incorrect. We need a broader framework.

REVISED FRUSTRATION–AGGRESSION: BERKOWITZ

Anger   Such a broader framework was provided by Berkowitz's (1962, 1969) attempt to rescue frustration–aggression theory. Berkowitz noted that, because there is no one-to-

In some situations, and for some people, aggression is valued.

one correspondence between frustration and aggression, there must be a mediating link, something else besides frustration that causes aggression. He proposed anger as this important mediator. Only when frustration leads to anger will it also lead to aggression; thus frustration causes aggression but only indirectly and not always. More recently, Berkowitz (1983) has contended that aggression is stimulated by anger-producing aversive events, such as pain and threat, in addition to frustration.

Cues   Berkowitz takes the general position that anger or anger-induced arousal primes the person for aggressive behavior. The occurrence and form of aggressive behavior are then determined by cue properties of the situation. In particular, *aggressive cues*— stimuli in the environment that have been associated with aggression in the past—prompt the aggressive behavior from the person who has been primed by anger. Thus, anger creates the need or precondition to be aggressive, while the aggressive cues are necessary to elicit the particular aggressive behavior. For exam-

Leonard Berkowitz

ple, you might become angry at a friend but not burst out at her until she says something that sets you off. On the other hand, some people, such as the Yanomamo, live in a social environment that is filled with aggression cues.

SOCIAL LEARNING: BANDURA

Bandura (1973) has provided a comprehensive analysis of aggression in terms of social learning theory. Recall that, for social learning theorists, the person tries to maximize his or her outcomes and so scrutinizes the environment for information about whether particular behaviors will yield approval or other rewards. Aggression is not different from other behavior in this regard.

Bandura agrees with Berkowitz that situational cues are important, but he does not feel that anger (or any other emotion) is *necessary* for aggression to occur, although it may play a role. For example, anger as a form of arousal might facilitate dominant aggressive responses. However, Bandura's theory emphasizes that we hurt other people, just as we help them or get out of their way, because we feel it is in our self-interest to do so.

We learn aggression in two senses. First, we must learn how to perform aggressive behaviors; we are not born knowing how to shoot a gun or stab someone. Second, we must also learn what consequences are likely to follow from performing aggressive behaviors. Social learning theorists make clear that much of

Albert Bandura

Berkowitz suggests that anger is an important cause of aggression.

our knowledge about such matters comes from observation of others. I do not have to insult a policeman to learn what happens to people who do so. And although I have never been in a knife fight, I have seen enough TV versions to know that sometimes people get hurt.

The values we learn through socialization will affect the consequences we expect from behavior. For example, like the Yanomamo, you may have learned to value toughness and aggression, and you may have learned that aggression pays off when you bully others into doing what you want them to. On the other hand, most of us also learn inhibitions and restraints. If you are angry at your psychology professor, you might well find some rewards in hitting him—you might feel better and prove to yourself and your friends that you are a tough person who cannot be pushed around. But presumably, there are costs as well: perhaps you will feel guilty or think poorly of yourself for having lost your cool; perhaps you will be arrested for assault; perhaps the professor will hit you back; or perhaps your friends will ostracize you. We generally do not hit others because the various costs generally far outweigh the rewards. However, not everyone shares our values. We can imagine someone who is so large that no one hits him back and whose friends praise rather than criticize his violent exploits. Presumably, he gets into a good many more barroom fights than you or I do.

Keep in mind that for modern social learning theorists, external rewards and punishments are often less important than internal feelings generated by guilt, shame, and pride. For example, men who have been imprisoned for violent behavior typically place a great deal of emphasis on their toughness, and this becomes an important aspect of their self-esteem and their public image. Many of us prefer to build our self-images around more pacific pursuits and are actually proud of ourselves when we inhibit aggression. Obviously, internally based rewards and punishments differ markedly from person to person. In any case, Bandura and other social learning theorists argue that aggressive behavior, like other kinds of behavior, is controlled largely by expectations of internal and external rewards and punishments.

SUMMARY

Aggression is a complex form of behavior; therefore it is not surprising that several theories point to different causes of aggression. Biological models suggest that there are natural, biologically mandated reasons for aggression. It is surely true that humans are born with the capacity to be aggressive, but beyond that it is hard to know how to conceptualize the biological component of aggression. Frustration–aggression theory, on the other hand, sees the causes of aggression as almost entirely situational, although the theory does suggest that people are born with a "natural" tendency to respond to environmentally induced frustrations with aggression. Although frustration sometimes causes aggressive behavior, it is not the only or even most important cause. Other theories, such as that of

Berkowitz, have argued that anger is the immediate cause of aggression and that frustration as well as other conditions such as pain may create the anger that leads to aggression. Berkowitz also argues that although anger primes the person to be aggressive, situational aggressive cues are necessary to elicit the aggressive behavior. Bandura argues that emotion is not necessary for aggression, although it may facilitate it; all aggression is instrumental in the sense that the aggressor thinks that the behavior will yield favorable consequences.

EMPIRICAL ISSUES

MOTIVATION

Theories of aggression are divided as to what they see as the main instigators or causes of aggression: instinct theories propose a biological source of energy waiting to be released by environmental events; frustration–aggression theory proposes frustration as a cause; Berkowitz's model argues for the centrality of anger and cues; while social learning theories see expected rewards and costs as crucial to aggressive behavior.

It might be helpful to think about some occasions when you have been hostile or aggressive. Why did you behave this way? Perhaps such things as frustrations, threats, insults, or even attacks from others led you to be aggressive. Research has confirmed that each of these can produce aggression (Baron, 1977).

But clearly you are not always aggressive, even when someone irritates you. If your friend insults you in a kidding way, you might not be especially happy, but you are unlikely to hit him. You may be frustrated when your mother's sudden illness keeps you from going to the movies with friends, but you are unlikely to yell at poor Mom as a result. On the other hand, if you believe that your friend's jab was intended to hurt you, you will want to retaliate, and you might be very angry with your mother if you discover she faked her illness to keep you home. Deliberate, arbitrary, or inconsiderate harm generally produces more aggression than harm perceived as accidental or unintended (Baron, 1977). For example, Kulik and Brown (1979) had subjects call people to solicit for a charity. Frustration occurred when the people who were called (actually confederates of the experimenters) refused to contribute. In a condition of legitimate frustration, the people refused to give because they claimed they were unemployed or had given to another charity. With illegitimate frustration, the people refused because they claimed they thought charities were a waste of time. There were several measures of aggression, including what the subject–caller said and how hard he or she banged the receiver down at the end of the conversation. As expected, the greatest amount of aggression was found when the frustration was illegitimate.

Unfortunately, behaviors of others are often, indeed usually, ambiguous. We might expect to find individual differences in how aversive behavior from others is interpreted. Someone who generally interprets the behavior of others negatively should be especially aggressive. Kenneth Dodge (1980) has shown that aggressive boys are especially prone to see ambiguous behavior as aggressive and hostile. By the same token, others perceive the behavior of aggressive boys as particularly hostile, and such boys are, in fact, picked on and teased a great deal by their peers (Dodge & Frame, 1982). Thus, aggressive boys are caught in a vicious circle. They perceive the behavior of others as aggressive, which causes them to retaliate, which in turn leads others to see them as aggressive and to behave aggressively toward them, which in turn leads the boys to be sensitive to aggressive overtures.

SITUATIONAL CUES

Even those who believe that anger is a central cause of aggression recognize that we are not always aggressive when we are angry. Berkowitz's argument is that anger primes ag-

gression but that cues direct the behavior; thus, without appropriate directive cues, aggression is not likely. These cues are stimuli that have become associated with aggressive behavior. Surely for most of us the sight of blood, a machine gun, or a man holding a knife in a menacing way are such cues.

As a demonstration of situational cues that provoke aggression, consider the classic Bob and Kirk study (Berkowitz & Geen, 1966). In this experiment, subjects participated with a partner (actually a confederate) who, during a preliminary phase, either did or did not anger the subjects. Following the anger manipulation, subjects were exposed to aggressive or nonaggressive cues. Some subjects watched a (nonaggressive) film about track runners while others watched a boxing film in which a familiar actor, Kirk Douglas, was beaten to a pulp. Then subjects got a chance to shock the confederate, and this was taken as a measure of aggression. The prediction from the Berkowitz model would be that the maximum aggression should occur when the subjects were angry and when they had also been exposed to the aggressive movie (a situational cue). To make sure the subjects associated the film with their current situation some confederates were named Kirk (like Kirk Douglas). As a control, other confederates were named Bob. This leads to the further refined prediction that aggression will be highest when the subject is angry, has watched the aggressive film, and associates the film with the person he is about to shock (that is, when the confederate is named Kirk). As Table 15.1 (p. 440) shows, the data strongly confirm the prediction.

AROUSAL

There is another possibility for why cues associated with aggression and anger interact to produce high levels of aggression. Earlier (in Chapters 1 and 11) we noted that general arousal facilitates dominant behaviors. Anger, like any emotion, is a form of arousal and may facilitate aggressive behavior that has been

TABLE 15.1   MEAN NUMBER OF SHOCKS GIVEN TO ACCOMPLICE.   *Note that angry subjects give more shocks than nonangry subjects, but that the combination of anger, exposure to an aggressive film, and the aggressive cue, Kirk, produces the most aggression.*

Accomplice's Name	Aggressive Film		Track Film (control)	
	Angered	Nonangered	Angered	Nonangered
Kirk	6.09	1.73	4.18	1.54
Bob	4.55	1.45	4.00	1.64

SOURCE: Berkowitz and Geen, 1966.

made dominant by situational cues for aggression. This would suggest that the crucial thing about being angry is not the specific feelings of anger but the general fact of arousal.

There are several demonstrations that general arousal can facilitate aggressive behavior when aggressive cues are strong. Perhaps the clearest is also one of the earliest. Geen and O'Neal (1969) used white noise (similar to static on your radio between stations), which at an appropriate level of loudness is arousing but not irritating. Aroused subjects who saw an aggressive film were more aggressive than those who were not aroused (see Table 15.2). Thus, the combination of arousal and aggressive movie cues seems to raise the general level of aggression, which is exactly what one might expect.

The Three-factor Theory   Although the Geen–O'Neal experiment did not manipulate anger, most subsequent investigators have manipulated arousal for subjects who are already angered. In these studies, it seems as if arousal adds something to the arousal already existing from the anger. The details of how this might occur have been spelled out by Zillmann (1979).

Zillman's three-factor theory, which is an elaboration of Schachter's theory of emotion, proposes three components of an emotion: dispositional, excitatory, and experiential. First, whatever stimulus makes you angry is also likely to produce some behavioral tendency or *disposition*. For example, you may have learned that when someone insults you, you should respond with a counterinsult or something more physical, such as hitting. This learned disposition guides the behavior. Second, the stimulus (say an insult) will also produce some arousal or *excitation* that serves to energize the behavior. If you are not strongly aroused, your disposition will likely result in moderate behavior, but with increasing levels of arousal your behavior will become more vigorous. Third, you will use information about the level of your arousal as well as about your behavioral tendencies to label or *experience* some emotion. So, the insult will provide a feeling in the pit of your stomach (the arousal) as well as dispose you to hit (the disposition to be aggressive), both of which will lead you to experience anger (see Figure 15.1).

According to this theory, the aggressive responses to annoyances will depend both on

TABLE 15.2   TOTAL SHOCKS GIVEN BY A SUBJECT. *Note that the aggressive film increased violence only for those subjects aroused by the white noise.*

Arousal Treatment	Film Condition	
	Aggressive	Control
Arousal	22.25	10.33
No arousal	12.75	14.75

SOURCE: Geen and O'Neal, 1969.

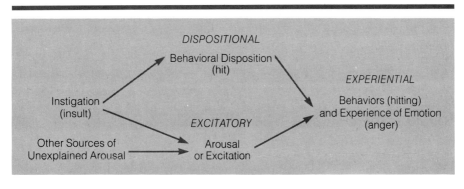

FIGURE 15.1   Zillmann's Three-factor Theory.

the behaviors typical of a given individual in such a situation and on the magnitude of the arousal. There are several important implications of this model. The degree of arousal is important in determining how much aggression will be displayed, and this arousal can be affected in many ways. In the first place, anger-based arousal may dissipate fairly rapidly, although there are surely individual differences in the extent to which this occurs: some people seem to stay angry (aroused) for a long time while others seem to get over insults, threats, and frustrations easily. Various external and internal stimuli may also affect how fast the arousal dissipates. Exposure to continued annoyance, thinking about or brooding over the threat, and exposure to aggressive models may keep the arousal from dissipating; conversely, distraction, counting to 10, and other such devices may facilitate reduction of arousal.

There is another important implication of this three-factor theory. You will recall that arousal is theoretically an undifferentiated state. Zillmann argues that people attribute arousal to its actual source when that source is clear. However, unexplained or ambiguously caused arousal will tend to be attributed to the most salient source. So, for example, if a person has unambiguously been insulted by a person standing before her, the resultant arousal will clearly be attributed to the obnoxious

other and the arousal will be experienced as anger. However, there may be other sources of arousal that are less clear. The caffeine in coffee and certain cola drinks, marijuana, exercise, sexual excitement, and hunger are some obvious examples. The arousal from these sources will add to the arousal from the insult, but since the source of these other forms of arousal may be less clear than that from the insult, all the arousal will be misattributed to the clearest source, the insult.

Suppose you have had three strong cups of coffee and are feeling highly aroused and jumpy. Now suppose someone insults you and your natural disposition is to make a nasty remark. The arousal from the insult by itself might instigate only a mild retaliatory insult. However, because you are also aroused from the coffee, your remark may be even quicker and more vicious than it otherwise would be. But keep in mind that the caffeine-induced arousal will facilitate your aggression only if you have no ready explanation for the arousal, and often when we drink coffee we do not especially reflect on how it has aroused us. On the other hand, if you had just been engaged in a conversation about how coffee makes you nervous, so that the cause of this extraneous arousal is salient to you, you would not attribute your arousal to anger and your caffeine-induced arousal would therefore not facilitate aggression.

In an experiment by Zillmann, Johnson, and Day (1974), subjects were angered by a confederate and then engaged in exercise. Subsequently, subjects were given a chance to aggress against the confederate. Should the exercise increase aggression? It depends. If the subject is aware that part of his or her general arousal is due to the exercise, then the extra (in addition to the anger) arousal should not facilitate the aggressive behavior; when the aggressive opportunity comes immediately after the exercise, the subject ought to know exactly why his or her heart is racing, and such easily explained arousal should not lead to aggression. But suppose he or she waited several minutes (six in this study). Most of us would still have some residual arousal from the exercise, but it would be diffuse and not easily attributed to the prior exercise. Because this extra (in addition to the anger) arousal is now unexplained, it may be misattributed to anger and thereby facilitate aggression. The results supported the hypothesis: exercise arousal that could easily be explained had no effects on aggression, but the less easily explained arousal facilitated aggression.

Sexual Arousal   A considerable body of research suggests that sexual arousal can also facilitate aggression. In such research, subjects are angered and then exposed either to sexually arousing or to sexually neutral material. As Figure 15.2 shows, exposure to erotic stimuli can increase subsequent aggression (Donnerstein, 1980; Zillmann, 1971), although there are also reports that exposure to erotic arousal may lower aggression (Baron, 1974c). Part of the problem is that erotic stimuli do many things in addition to arousing people. For example, when one has been made angry, exposure to relatively mild erotic stimuli (say, pictures from *Playboy*) might raise arousal somewhat but also distract the subjects from maintaining anger (Donnerstein, Donnerstein, & Evans, 1975).

Sexual arousal may facilitate aggression under some circumstances, but there is also

another reason to be concerned with the effects of sexual materials on hostile behavior (Malamuth & Donnerstein, 1982). In certain types of pornography men rape women, and often the women are depicted as enjoying their brutalization. In such cases, we might expect that exposure to aggressive pornography facilitates aggression against females but not necessarily against males. And indeed, exactly this sort of effect has been found (Donnerstein & Berkowitz, 1981). In general, there are major individual differences among males as to whether they find sexual aggression stimulating (Malamuth, Check, & Briere, 1986). Most males find depictions of rape unarousing or only mildly so, but those who are aroused are also likely to report that they employ force in their sexual relations (Malamuth, 1986).

The effects of sexual arousal on aggressive behavior are obviously complex, but the im-

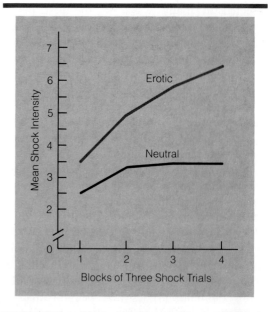

FIGURE 15.2   Mean Intensity of Shocks Given to Confederates. The shocks were measured over blocks of trials by subjects exposed to sexually arousing or sexually neutral materials. Those subjects exposed to the sexually arousing materials were more aggressive than those exposed to the neutral materials.

portant point is that sexual arousal can facilitate aggression under certain circumstances. Part of this facilitation comes from the addition of sexual arousal to whatever annoyance-based arousal is already present, and part from certain erotic materials that provide models of sexual aggression against women.

Other Forms of Arousal   Other forms of arousal also contribute to aggression. For example, crowding can lead to negative feelings and aggression (Sundstrom, 1978). Crowding is not inevitably aversive, nor does it always lead to hostile reactions, but the arousal produced by the close presence of others, combined with frustrations and inconveniences of being close to others, may lead to hostilities.

In addition, such factors as air pollution (Rotton & Frey, 1985) and heat (Anderson & Anderson, 1984) have been implicated in the commission of violent crimes. Both heat and pollutants can produce arousal directly but may also act by increasing anger or frustration, which are also forms of arousal. When you are hot and uncomfortable, you do not usually initiate aggression against the nearest person, but the arousal may make you more easily provoked into aggression if that person somehow makes you angry.

TELEVISION and AGGRESSION

Bandura and other social learning theorists have emphasized that we learn both how to perform aggressive acts and what the consequences of those acts will be from watching others. Clearly, television provides highly salient models for many people, especially children, and we know that American television contains a high amount of aggression. In 1979, 80% of all TV programs contained some violence, and there was an average of over 5 violent acts per program (Signorielli, Gross, & Morgan, 1982). Thus, the conditions are favorable for stimulation of aggression by television, though we would want to demonstrate carefully a connection between modeling

of behavior and prevalence of media violence in a real-life context before we made any grand claims for a causal connection between the two.

It should be pointed out that, although the vast amount of research in this area has concerned the role of television, there is probably nothing privileged about the television medium in facilitating violence. Movies, books, or newspapers may work just as well. Indeed, research has shown that violent events can affect subsequent hostility and physical aggression for those who observe them. For example, people are more hostile after watching violent sporting events such as football and hockey (Arms, Russell, & Sandilands, 1979; Goldstein & Arms, 1971) and the homicide rate in the country as a whole increases after well-publicized prize fights (Phillips, 1983). At any rate, television is not the only culprit, if a culprit is to be found, but most research has concentrated on television because it is such a salient feature of modern life.

Correlational Results   Several studies have examined the relationship between the amount of violent television watched and the amount of aggressive behavior displayed, particularly among children. Although such studies provide mixed results, generally they have found modest but statistically significant correlations (Comstock et al., 1978; Huesmann, 1982).

However, as we saw in Chapter 2, the existence of an empirical correlational relationship between two variables does not indicate which of the possible connections are causal ones. Television violence may cause aggressive behavior, but the causal direction might also be reversed—children who are aggressive prefer to watch violent TV. There are supporting data for the latter possibility. For example, Diener and DeFour (1978) found that people who have aggressive dispositions prefer violent TV programs, and Fenigstein (1979) has shown that male subjects who had recently been induced to fantasize about aggression or to behave aggressively had increased preferences for viewing aggressive movies.

So it is possible that the observed relationship between violent TV watching and actual aggressive behavior occurs because aggression creates a desire to watch violence rather than the reverse. It is also possible that some third variable (or variables) causes both TV preferences and aggressiveness. For example, aggressive boys who watch lots of action programs may have parents who encourage their sons both to be aggressive and to watch violent fare on TV.

Several approaches have been used to try to get at the question of causality. One approach is to look carefully at the relationships between variables over time. If TV preferences at one time predict aggressiveness at a later time, but aggressiveness does not predict later TV preferences, one would feel more confident that the casual direction goes from violent TV to aggressive behavior, given that causes must precede effects. One such study was done by Eron and his colleagues. In the first study reported by Eron (1963), programs typically watched by third-grade children were classified by adult raters as either violent or nonviolent. Parents were asked which programs their children watched, and each child was given a

score for how many violent programs he or she watched. Aggression scores were determined for each child by classmates' ratings. The results showed quite clearly that the aggressiveness ratings for boys—but not for girls—increased with the number of violent programs watched. Perhaps the girls did not identify with the aggressive male models—there were few female models for aggression on TV at that time—or perhaps the girls were not as often placed in situations where they could make use of the behavior they had seen on TV.

A follow-up study ten years later on these same children helps support the proposition that TV watching causes aggression (Eron, Lefkowitz, Huesmann, & Walder, 1972). For boys, there was a significant relationship between aggression at ages 9 and 19. Moreover, there was a relationship between the number of violent programs watched at age 9 and aggression at age 19. However, there was no relationship between aggression at age 9 and TV watching at age 19. Thus, early TV watching predicted later aggression more strongly than early aggression predicted later TV watching, which suggests that the causal direction is more likely to go from TV to behavior than the reverse.

Laboratory Research   Because ambiguities are bound to remain in correlational studies, there has been a fair amount of experimental research devoted to this topic. The easiest way to do this research is in a well-controlled laboratory situation. In one study that can serve as an example of the many that have been done, Liebert and Baron (1972) used children who were 5–8 years of age. When the children arrived for the experiment, they were asked to wait in a room where a TV set was showing actual TV programs that were either violent or nonviolent. The children had no reason to believe that this was part of the experiment. Then they were taken to another room where they were allowed to press either a hurt button, which they thought would administer pain to another child in the next room, or a help button. The children who watched the violent TV programs pressed the hurt button more than did the children who watched the nonviolent programs. Although one might wish for a measure of aggression that had more real-life validity, it is worth noting that the children were not precisely imitating the TV models, none of whom had done anything remotely like pressing a hurt button. Thus, it would seem that the effects of TV violence may not be limited to pure imitation. Several other laboratory studies provide similar results. Nonetheless, it might be (and has been) argued that well-controlled laboratory studies inevitably lack some generalizability to the real world.

Field Studies   A number of investigators have tried to extend such experimental research to the field. Ideally, one would like two large and comparable samples of people, some of whom are told to watch violent TV programs while others are told to watch nonviolent programs. However, most American families would resent having their TV watching dictated to them, even for a short time, and there would be inevitable problems in making sure no one cheated.

Fortunately for researchers, there are groups of people for whom some control over the television diet can be exercised. Several studies with captive populations have been done, and although the results are inconsistent (Freedman, 1984), the studies generally support the hypothesis of a causal relationship between violent TV and agressive behavior. Consider an example by Parke et al. (1977). American boys in minimum security detention centers were shown movies in the evening. Some of the boys saw violent movies and some saw neutral ones. Outside observers then rated the boys' behavior over a period of several weeks. Generally, aggression increased during the week the movies were shown (and in subse-

quent weeks) for those boys who saw violent movies, and there was no corresponding increase for nonviolent movie conditions (see Figure 15.3). These results were also replicated with a Belgian sample. Although this research is not perfect, it strongly suggests that watching TV violence increases aggression.

However, we must take into account many other variables before we can come to definitive conclusions. For example, the viewing context is probably quite important. If a boy watches TV with his parents, their comments on the fare may have an effect on his subsequent behavior. There is more imitation of TV models when children watch with adults who approve rather than disapprove of the model's behavior (Hicks, 1968). Also, when children are given explicit instructions about the unreality of television and the dangers of imitation, such imitation is lessened (Huesmann, et al., 1983).

Social Policy   The evidence is fairly strong that watching violent TV can lead to aggression. This does not mean that the effects of violent television are strong; in fact, some (such as Freedman, 1984) would argue that they are weak indeed. Box 15.1 discusses Freedman's criticisms in some detail. For most children and adults, there may well be more important causes of aggression, including frustration and anger, general cultural values, and the rewards they've experienced for aggressive behavior.

However, television and the mass media in general may have other, more important, indirect effects. We live in a culture that tends to glorify violence and aggressive solutions to social problems. Dirty Harry, the tough cop; Rambo, the macho hero; J. R. Ewing, the aggressive businessman—these are standard folk heros in our society. In one sense, violent television merely reflects existing cultural values. But reflection is also tacit approval. We provide many models of violent solutions to problems, but we are not nearly so clever at

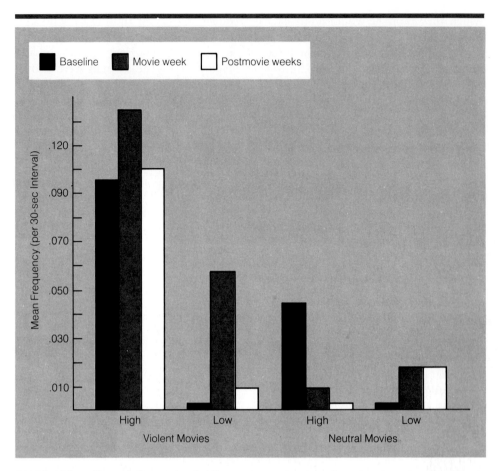

FIGURE 15.3 General Aggression for Boys. Aggression here is a function of type of movie watched, whether the boys were initially high or low in tendency to be aggressive, and whether aggression was measured before the movies were shown (baseline), during the movie week, or in the weeks after the movies were shown. Note that the boys high in initial aggressiveness are more aggressive than the boys who were low in initial aggressiveness, but, more important, aggression increased for the boys who had watched the aggressive movie (but not for those who watched the neutral movie) during the week the movies were shown.

providing salient nonviolent models. The danger of violent television may be not so much the existence of models for aggression as the lack of alternative, pacific models.

Television is a part of a larger cultural context, and it is difficult to change long-cherished cultural values. At the same time, one makes changes where one can. Although the effect of television *may* be slight, it is one potential cause of aggression we can do something about.

If we can assume for the moment that television does cause aggressive behavior, we still have to assess this fact against our values. Do we think such aggression is bad? Even if we assume that such aggression is bad, do we then

BOX 15.1

DOES TELEVISED VIOLENCE AFFECT AGGRESSION?

Most experts believe that media portrayals of aggression contribute directly and indirectly to aggressive behavior. However, there remains some dissent. Recently, social psychologist Jonathan Freedman (1984, 1986) has argued that the support for the causal link between televised violence and aggression is actually meager, and we must therefore regard the hypothesized relationship as unsupported. Is this issue simply a matter of opinion?

Let us examine Freedman's criticisms in some detail. First, he accepts the now well-documented conclusion that televised violence can affect aggression in laboratory situations. However, he quite reasonably argues that generalization from the laboratory to the real world is never fully guaranteed. In particular he sees three major reasons to doubt the external validity (see Chapter 17) of such studies: (1) the measures of aggression are sometimes quite artificial and do not represent the kinds of aggression of interest in the outside world, such as hitting, yelling, and stabbing; (2) because the television programs have been chosen by the experimenter, subjects who view the violent films may feel that the experimenter approves violence, a condition that may not obtain outside; and (3) the films used in laboratory studies and the viewing conditions are not representative of those found in real life.

Friedrich-Cofer and Huston (1986) have argued that Freedman is, at best, only partially correct in these criticisms. In the first place, although hitting a doll or pressing a hurt button is clearly not the same as hitting or yelling at a person, it is not clear that these laboratory measures are fundamentally different from real-life ways of being hostile. There is also no evidence that aggression in the laboratory is a response to assumed experimental approval, and it would be hard to account for some results of laboratory studies with this argument. Finally, several studies have used representative movies, so it is hard to argue that the effects are limited to made-for-experiment movies.

Although Freedman's specific criticisms of laboratory studies are not compelling, his larger point, that we need to be sure that laboratory findings do generalize, is. In other words, we may have no special reason to believe that laboratory findings lack external validity, but we would still feel most comfortable knowing that the results could be generalized.

Freedman's criticisms of correlational studies are fairly standard. Despite the fact that behavioral aggression and amount of violent television watched are positively correlated, it is hard to pin down causal direction with these data. However, Eron et al. (1972) showed that TV watching in the third grade predicted aggression ten years later but that aggression in the third grade did not predict later TV watching. Freedman acknowledges that finding, but notes that it only occurred for boys, is found only for some measures, and has not always been found in subsequent studies. However, data from other studies generally support the idea that TV watching causes aggression (Huesmann, Lagerspetz, & Eron, 1984; Milavsky, Stipp, Kessler, & Rubens, 1982), although it is also possible that the reverse

BOX CONTINUED

also occurs. Freedman is correct that the effects are not powerful.

To some extent there will always be doubts about laboratory experiments and correlational studies. That is why it is important to perform well-controlled field studies. Such research is hard to do well. The major problem is that the scientist does not have the control in the field that he or she enjoys in the laboratory. For example, Feshbach and Singer (1971) made boys in residential schools watch either violent or nonviolent television programs for six weeks. They found no evidence that those who watched the violent programs were more aggressive. However, the boys liked the aggressive programs more, and the boys who watched the nonaggressive programs may well have been more frustrated. Therefore Feshbach and Singer may have been comparing a group of happy boys who watched violent TV with a group of frustrated boys who watched nonviolent TV. The two groups could have been equally aggressive but for different reasons. There were other ways in which the two groups of boys were noncomparable, which makes interpretation of the results problematic.

The research by Parke and his colleagues (1977) discussed in the text is a cleaner effort. In their samples (two American and one Belgian), boys watched a movie every night for a week; some movies were violent and some were not. Then the boys' behaviors were assessed by trained observers. The most important measures of aggression used were verbal aggression, physical aggression, and a general index of aggression. The results generally show that those boys who watched the aggressive TV were more aggressive. If this result were to be trusted, we would then have our required demonstration.

But Freedman has his doubts. In the first place, he notes that in all three studies, the boys exposed to the violent movies lived in cottages of boys who were more aggressive to begin with than those exposed to the neutral films. Boys who are more aggressive to begin with may also be more affected by violent movies. Thus, when the findings show that these boys are more aggressive, one cannot be sure how much is due to the movies and how much is due to the boys' dispositions.

A more serious problem is that all the boys who lived in a single cottage were in the same experimental condition; that is, all 30 boys in Cottage A saw the same violent or same neutral movies. Yet, the aggression measures were taken for individual boys. But consider that aggression is an interper-

want to censor the airwaves to eliminate television programs that may stimulate aggression? I happen to dislike censorship even more than I dislike the aggressive effects of television, so I am wary of attempts to regulate television programming for the public good. On the other hand, you may order your values differently, and you might also point out that television is already heavily censored and a bit more won't make much difference. The point is this, however: facts do not dictate social policy—values do. Even if we were to agree that violent TV causes aggression, we would still have to decide how to deal with those facts in the arena of social policy, an arena in which values share center stage with facts.

sonal event: if you have 30 aggressive boys in one cottage and the movie stimulates one of the boys to become more aggressive, his aggression will affect the other 29 boys when they fight back. Although the violent movie affected only 1 boy directly, the statistical results of the experiment will show that the violent TV program affects all 30 boys. There is a big difference between having a violent movie affect 1 person and having it affect 30 people. There is no evidence this actually happened, but it would have been sounder statistically to have used cottages rather than boys as the unit of analysis; unfortunately, there were not enough cottages to have done this.

Freedman also notes that the results were somewhat inconsistent from measure to measure and study to study. That is a correct but somewhat unfair criticism. Generally, across the three studies the results are that the violent movies affect aggression, although this shows up in slightly different ways. It would, of course, be nice if the results had been perfectly consistent across studies, but they were not and rarely are in psychological research. Also, the strongest results were for the general measure of aggression, the measure that included most of the others.

Is all this simply a matter of opinion then? To some extent, it is. Freedman's criticisms are legitimate but overly stringent. Each of the many studies has a major flaw or two, and these flaws should not be ignored. On the other hand, the impressive thing is that a number of studies, each with somewhat different flaws, all point in the same direction. We know that people who watch a great deal of violent TV are more aggressive, we know from laboratory research that TV watching could cause the aggression, and we have at least some data from field experiments that suggest that TV watching does cause aggression. The convergence of several studies on the same general conclusion gives more confidence than could any single study, however well-designed and -executed that study might be.

Freedman's criticisms are useful, even if only to remind us that the case on the effects of television is still open to some extent. In areas where it is difficult to do the kind of well-controlled research we would like to see, we must work with the consensus of experts. At present that consensus favors the proposition that watching violent television causes violence. Later research may change that concensus, and that is why we need the additional research.

SUMMARY

Several empirical issues have dominated research on aggression. One traditional question concerns the prime instigators of hostile behavior. Frustration, threats, pain—indeed, almost any aversive experience—can lead to aggressive behavior to the extent that it creates anger or arousal. Situational cues that have been associated with aggression or that suggest approval of aggressive behavior also encourage aggression. When cues make aggressive behavior dominant in a given situation, arousal from any source will make that aggressive behavior more likely. Finally, there has been extensive analysis of the role played by the mass media, especially television, in causing aggression. Most studies support the hypothesis that television violence is a cause of aggressive behavior.

CONTROL OF AGGRESSION AND VIOLENCE

We have been dealing primarily with factors that *facilitate* aggressive behavior, but this is only half the story. We also need to consider factors that actively *inhibit* such behavior. These are theoretically and practically important. If you agree that aggressive behavior, especially in its more extreme forms, is generally undesirable, you will probably be concerned with how it can be eliminated or at least controlled.

One obvious strategy for such control would be to eliminate the factors that facilitate aggression. Yet, if you reflect on the matter, you will soon realize that as a general strategy it is both impractical and undesirable to eliminate such factors. For example, frustration is unpleasant, but it is inevitable for anyone who is trying to extend herself, trying to accomplish more. To eliminate frustration is to eliminate ambition and striving. Anger leads to mischief, but it also has useful functions. Would you want to live in a society in which people did not feel angry at injustice or the misdeeds of others? If we were to eliminate the factors that cause aggression, we would probably cut the very soul from our culture in doing so. At the least, it would be a less interesting place to live.

The same is true for aggressive stimuli and models. We must remember that aggressive models are often only exaggerated versions of other desirable values. We value competition, making money, maintaining individuality, and being able to look out for our own interests. It should come as no surprise that professional football players become highly aggressive,

given the stakes involved, or that people in highly competitive professions discover the value of occasionally stabbing their colleagues in the back. Obviously, this is not necessarily to defend such practices, but we should also not ignore the fact that while we decry certain forms of aggression, these are often not so far removed from other models of aggression that are culturally accepted and even normative.

Presumably, we could reduce facilitating factors through education, better child-rearing practices, reductions of media aggressive models, and new laws, but we are not likely ever to eliminate them entirely. Thus, theorists have paid careful attention to inhibitions and other means of reducing aggression.

INHIBITIONS

Self-controls   Self-controls in the form of guilt, shame, and self-punishment are important for most of us, and may be aided by the motivation to match our standards induced by self-observation (Scheier, Fenigstein, & Buss, 1974). Although there may be some argument about whether such internalized inhibitions would long persist in the absence of external disapproval and fears of punishment, everyday observation suggests that people often are not aggressive even when they would suffer no external sanctions for being aggressive. Most of us do have considerable internal controls; we would feel guilty if we hurt someone else, intentionally or unintentionally, and we do not go about killing irritating neighborhood dogs even when we could do so undetected. Thus, socialization directed toward increased internal inhibitions is important (see Chapter 9).

Threats and Punishments   Although Western culture places a great deal of emphasis on internal controls over aggression, there are also many external costs imposed by society for aggression. Common sense and all theories of aggression point to punishment and threat of punishment as major inhibitors. Several experiments confirm that when people are punished for behaving aggressively they tend to be less aggressive in the future, at least around the punishing agent (Zillmann, 1979). Furthermore, threat of punishment, whether physical punishment or the disapproval of others, reduces the probability of aggression. One especially important form of punishment is retaliation or the threat thereof. Generally, people are less likely to aggress or express hostility against high-status or high-power others (Worchel, 1957) or against someone who has the ability and intention to retaliate (Baron, 1973; Wilson & Rogers, 1975). However, fear-based inhibitions may become less effective as anger increases (Baron, 1973, 1974b). When someone has insulted you and really made you angry, you may be more concerned with saving face or dispensing primitive justice than with fear for your own physical safety. Thus, threats and punishments are likely to inhibit aggression unless there are rewards associated with the hostile behavior that outweigh the threats.

It is also important to realize that the threat of punishment will not always be effective. As many parents have learned to their dismay, they can threaten all they wish, but to stop undesirable behavior they first have to catch the culprit in the act and then administer the punishment. Conditions that favor not being caught, such as anonymity or deindividuation, tend to render threats of punishment ineffective (Donnerstein, Donnerstein, Simon, & Ditrichs, 1972; Mann, Newton, & Innes, 1982; Rogers & Prentice-Dunn, 1981). In addition, punishment can backfire when the punishment itself sets an example of dealing with frustrating circumstances through aggression.

Pain Cues   In Chapter 14 we emphasized the role of empathy in facilitating prosocial behavior, and it seems likely that empathy might also inhibit antisocial behavior. Suppose, for example, that a parent is spanking a child for some horrible misdeed. The child makes it obvious that he is being hurt. Would not most people feel some empathy with the child and stop the spanking? Some research does indeed show that expression of pain by the target of aggression tends to lower aggression (Baron, 1971).

However, there are also theoretical reasons to expect that pain cues should sometimes facilitate rather than inhibit aggression. The parent who spanks her child (to teach him a lesson) will be satisfied only if she does inflict some harm; otherwise the spanking is futile. Thus, the feedback may act as a kind of reinforcement for the behavior, or, more generally, it provides information that goals are being met. If a person is really angry, a state that presumably leads him or her to want to inflict harm on others, we should expect pain cues to facilitate aggression. On the other hand, if the aggressor is only mildly angry, the desire to hurt the other may be quite small and consequently the pain cues should inhibit aggression. Several experiments show that pain cues raise aggression for angry subjects but lower it for those who are not angry (Baron, 1974a, 1977; Swart & Berkowitz, 1976).

CATHARSIS

Perhaps the most popular suggestion for control of aggression is the notion that one should not bottle up frustrations and anger but rather "let it all out." The technical term for this is *catharsis* (from a Greek word meaning to cleanse or clean). That symbolic aggression—for example, through sports, exercise, or watching violence at the theater or on TV—is an effective way to drain aggressive energy is an ancient notion, dating at least to Aristotle. In our century, Freud, Lorenz, Ardrey, and others have argued that aggressive energy builds up and must be drained periodically. Even the frustration–aggression theorists feel that frustrations accumulate over time and that the frustration-based instigations to be aggressive need release. On the other hand, theorists such as Bandura and Berkowitz do not postulate any aggressive energy, so there is nothing to drain away. Because there is nothing to "let out," symbolic or substitute aggression should have no effects on subsequent aggression—there should be no catharsis effect. Thus, research on catharsis has served as a testing ground for various aggression theories.

Important, real-life implications for control of aggression rest on the debate over catharsis. If, in fact, aggressive energy can be drained away through any form of aggression, it follows that major forms of violence can be controlled by allowing people a series of milder substitute activities. Thus, if we encouraged people to punch a punching bag, jog, and yell, we might be able to cut down the rate of murder and assault.

There are actually several parts to the catharsis hypothesis; let us consider the evidence for each part systematically. First, Freud and others argued that aggressive energy builds up by itself so that periodic aggression is necessary for all of us. But there is no clear empiri-

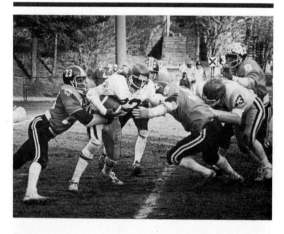

Some have argued that contact sports provide a good catharsis for aggressive energy, but available data do not support this idea.

cal support for the idea of aggressive energy that builds up by itself (Zillmann, 1979).

However, this does not rule out the kind of process suggested by frustration–aggression theory, namely, that frustrations from the environment can accumulate over time. We have all experienced times when nothing seems to go right, and we become more and more tense, frustrated, angry with each new blow to pride, self-esteem, and feelings of control. Thus, a modern version of this theory might predict that (1) aversive events lead to increases in anger or general arousal (a form of energy), (2) a catharsis experience such as hitting a punching bag should lower this arousal, and (3) once this arousal is lowered the motivation for aggression should be lowered and the person should be less aggressive. Let us examine each of these predictions.

Arousal Factors   The first hypothesis, that aversive events should increase arousal, is well supported by the research literature. Hokanson and his colleagues have used systolic blood pressure as a measure of arousal, and they consistently find that frustration leads to a rise in blood pressure (Hokanson & Burgess, 1962).

What about the second hypothesis, that subsequent aggression should lead to lowered arousal? When a person is frustrated and angry and blood pressure goes up markedly, aggression can lead to a rapid reduction in blood pressure (Hokanson & Burgess, 1962). However, this is not inevitable. Many people feel guilty about being aggressive, even in mild, supposedly cathartic ways, and such guilt raises rather than lowers arousal. For example, females (at least those of several years ago) do not show the drop in blood pressure after catharsis that males show, possibly because they feel more guilty about being aggressive or have been socialized to fear reactions of others when they are aggressive (Eagly & Steffen, 1986; Hokanson & Edelman, 1966). Aggressing against a high-status person also fails to produce a drop in blood pressure, presumably because most of us fear (a form of arousal) being hostile to those who have higher status. So aggression can lower arousal but only when it is not accompanied by guilt or fear that will increase arousal (Geen & Quanty, 1977).

Behavioral Effects   So aversive events increase arousal, and subsequent aggression lowers arousal, at least under circumstances when the aggression does not produce guilt or fear. What about the third hypothesis, that lowered arousal should lower aggressive behavior? We would hardly be interested in catharsis as a way of reducing aggression if it had no behavioral effects.

It would be nice and simple if aggression directed toward inanimate objects such as punching bags provided a catharsis and reduced subsequent aggression toward people. Unfortunately, the data provide almost no support for the hypothesis that this form of catharsis—aggression directed toward substitute, inanimate objects—effectively reduces interpersonal aggression (Geen & Quanty, 1977; Zillmann, 1979).

What happens when the catharsis is directed toward an actual person? Here the hypothesis receives some support. Doob and Wood (1972) had a confederate annoy subjects, and then in a cathartic phase the subjects either were or were not allowed to shock the confederate. To get measures of actual aggression, all subjects were allowed to shock the confederate in a third and final phase. Table 15.3 shows the actual number of shocks given in the last phase. The subjects who were angered (annoyed) and had no catharsis (that is, who did not shock the confederate in the second, cathartic phase of the study) were clearly more aggressive in the final phase than those who had previously shocked the confederate in the catharsis stage. Konečni and Doob (1972) showed that when the catharsis consisted of shocking an irrelevant bystander, shocks to the original annoyer were also reduced.

TABLE 15.3 MEAN NUMBER OF SHOCKS DELIVERED. *Subjects gave shocks after they had been annoyed or not annoyed and after catharsis or no catharsis. Note that, as expected with no catharsis, the annoyed subjects were more aggressive than the nonannoyed subjects, but that the catharsis reduced the aggression of the annoyed group considerably.*

Condition	Catharsis (previous shock)	No Catharsis
Annoy	6.80	10.67
No annoy	8.07	6.60

SOURCE: After Doob and Wood, 1972.

Although other explanations of these results are also possible (Geen & Quanty, 1977), these experiments stand as the best examples of catharsis effects in experimental research. Note, however, that although the results have some theoretical value, the nature of the particular effects precludes any practical significance. The appeal of the catharsis hypothesis is that we hope to reduce harm to people by having the angry person channel aggressive energy into some less-harmful substitute activity. Yet, in the Doob experiments, the results show that cathartic aggression against a person reduces later aggression against a person. In other words, someone must be hurt to keep someone from being hurt; this hardly constitutes a major breakthrough in our ability to control aggression.

SUMMARY

Although social scientists have a clear understanding of the major factors that cause aggressive behavior, it is immoral and impractical or impossible to remove most of them as a way to control aggression. One cannot eliminate frustrations, threats, or anger and would not want to if one could. Aggression can be inhibited by threats and strong internal controls such as guilt. It has also been suggested that aggression can be controlled by giving people opportunities to drain away aggressive impulses, but this catharsis model has limited support in the available research. It is also based on a false premise, namely, that aggression results from accumulation of some particular energy that can be drained away.

VIOLENT CRIME

During the 1960s and 1970s, the American public became obsessed with violence. The political assassinations, riots, and acts of civil disobedience of the 1960s seemed to many to open a new chapter in American history. Furthermore the mass media focused our attention on seemingly irrational and often bizarre murders: the Boston Strangler, Charles Manson and his "family," the Son of Sam, the Hillside Strangler of Los Angeles, and the murders of several black youngsters in Atlanta are cases in point. We have even "discovered" new crimes of violence—such as spouse and child abuse—that we preferred to ignore before, and we have come to see spousal rape and incest as having aggressive motivation.

In this chapter, we have had a great deal to say about various causes of aggression. For obvious ethical reasons, research psychologists must use in their experiments aggression measures that are pale reflections of real-life violence, and the question naturally arises as to whether we have anything to say about the causes of these more important forms of aggression. Let us see.

VIOLENCE IN CONTEXT

Public opinion polls consistently show that Americans rate crime as one of the most important issues facing American society, and these fears are partially justified. There has been a substantial rise in crime, especially violent crime, from the early 1960s to the early 1980s, with a leveling off of sorts in recent years. However, we might put this into a

Americans are concerned about the increase in violent crime.

broader context. Although our current rate of violence is high, especially by standards of other industrialized societies, it is probably not so high compared to other periods of American history. As many have pointed out, Americans have a violent history (Brown, 1969; Silberman, 1978). The Wild West really was wild; millions were killed in our brutal policies against Native Americans and black slaves; and most American cities of the nineteenth century far outdid their modern equivalents in violent crime. During the first 30 years of this century, murder rates increased dramatically—we are just now exceeding the murder rates of the 1930s. In some sense, the question ought to be why the 1940s and 1950s were so nonviolent, not why we are so violent today.

CRIME STATISTICS

Most of what we know about crime rates comes from the Uniform Crime Statistics collected and published every year by the Federal Bureau of Investigation (FBI). The FBI records information for eight major or index crimes: larceny, car theft, burglary, arson, murder, as-

TABLE 15.4   CRIMES FOR 1985 FROM UNIFORM CRIME STATISTICS.

	No. Offenses	Rate/100,000	% Change 1984–1985	Clearance Rate*
VIOLENT CRIMES				
Murder	18,976	7.9	0.0	72%
Assault	723,246	302.9	4.4	62%
Rape	87,340	36.6	2.5	54%
Robbery	497,874	208.5	1.5	25%
NONVIOLENT CRIMES				
Burglary	3,073,348	1287.3	1.9	14%
Larceny	6,926,380	2901.2	3.9	20%
Motor Vehicle Theft	1,102,862	462.0	5.7	15%

*Roughly, a measure of the percentage of crimes that are solved.
SOURCE: Uniform Crime Reports 1985.

sault, robbery, and rape. The last four of these are classified as *violent crimes*. The data are reported in terms of total crimes and number of crimes committed per 100,000 people; the latter is a measure of *crime rate*. There are classic problems with these data. Not all crimes are reported to the police, and police departments exercise some discretion in how they classify and report crimes. To get a better idea of true crime rates, the Census Bureau began in the 1960s to sponsor victimization surveys, in which people are asked whether they have been the victim of certain crimes in the past year (Hindelang, Gottfredson, & Garafalo, 1978). Such surveys (which are themselves subject to many forms of bias) suggest that the true crime rate is substantially higher than the FBI statistics suggest.

It is also important to recognize that the vast majority (nearly 90%) of major crimes are property crimes that do not involve violence. Table 15.4 gives the 1985 FBI statistics for major crimes.

VIOLENT PEOPLE

Every significant demographic group of people in America commits violent crimes. Yet the arrest statistics show that some groups commit more than their share of violence. In particular, violent crimes are more likely to be com-

mitted by those who are below the age of 25 than by those who are older, by males rather than females, by the poor rather than the rich, and by blacks more than whites (even when income differences are adjusted). Although these data are based mostly on arrest statistics, which may be biased (Tittle, Villemez, & Smith, 1978), it appears likely that there are real social class, gender, and race differences in crime rates (Hindelang, Hirschi, & Weis, 1979). However, remember that white, middle-class women also abuse children and murder their husbands and that the majority of young, poor, black males are not violent criminals.

Individual Difference Explanations Most of us get no further than privately relishing the thought of harm coming to our enemies. What, therefore, can we make of those who carry such thoughts into action? Some people seem to feel that there is a special psychology of the criminal, especially of the violent offender, and two common misconceptions are that violent offenders are mentally deranged and that they carry out their acts in a cold-blooded, calculated, unfeeling fashion. Such mentally ill and cold-blooded killers do exist, but they are far from representative of murderers (who can, for the moment, stand for violent offenders generally). In reality, most murders take place after arguments, typically among people already acquainted or related; the victim often plays a major role in his fate by provoking an argument or being the first to use a weapon; the murderer is usually drunk or has been drinking; and the murderer is usually sorry for what he has done after the fact.

Case studies of murderers usually find family backgrounds with a history of economic strain, family hostility, and inadequate parenting (Lester & Lester, 1975; Lunde, 1976). There are at least two general ways such backgrounds might affect violence proneness. First, children from pathological home backgrounds may experience massive numbers of aversive events that lead to aggression. In one interesting study, Palmer (1960) compared the histories of murderers with their brothers who were not murderers. The murderers had more frustrations in their early childhoods. For example, they were more likely to have had serious childhood illnesses, operations, and accidents and were more apt to have visible deformities. The mothers were more punitive and rigid with the murderers than with their brothers. So the murderers seem to have had harsher childhoods, although, of course, not every frustrated child becomes a murderer.

Another possibility is that the early home environment may discourage the development of inhibitions against violence. One study of violence-prone adolescents found that their parents actually encouraged them to be aggressive (Bandura & Walters, 1959). However, not all murderers have insufficient inhibitions. For example, Jeffrey MacDonald, the Green Beret captain, could hardly be described as lacking such inhibitions. Megargee (1966) has suggested that while some murderers have too few inhibitions, others have learned inhibitions so well that they tend to stifle legitimate expressions of anger. Such a person often appears to be a proverbial nice boy, but at some point the rigid controls are overwhelmed by suppressed anger, and the person may erupt in

a massive rage and kill loved ones. So, although most killers probably find it hard to control their violence, there are others who control it all too well until they can control it no longer.

Biological Explanations   Biology and heredity have long been popular explanations for criminality. The early criminologist, Cesare Lombroso, argued that criminals had the facial and bodily characteristics of lower primates and that they thus were a throwback to an earlier evolutionary stage. Surely Lombroso was incorrect in his assumptions about evolution, but there are clear data that criminals tend as a group to have a particular body-type, one high in muscularity and low in thinness (Wilson & Herrnstein, 1985).

More recently Jacobs, Brunton, and Melville (1965) reported that male prison inmates were strikingly more likely than noncriminals to have an extra Y chromosome. Because the Y chromosome is the determinant of being a male (normal males have an X and a Y; females have two Xs), it might be argued that XYY men have an extra dose of masculinity and are thereby more likely to be aggressive, keeping in mind that physical aggression is more typically a male activity than a female activity. However, the XYY men in prisons were not by and large incarcerated for violent crimes but, for example, for crimes against property (Price & Whatmore, 1967; Witkin et al., 1976). It is true that XYY men have more problems with the law than XY men do, but not because they are more aggressive.

Another proposal is that criminals have underreactive arousal systems that make learning of guilt and inhibitions difficult, a condition that seems to have an hereditary component (Mednick, 1977). Other data suggest that there may be a genetic component to criminal behavior (Wilson & Herrnstein, 1985), but as with all such data it is hard to pin down exactly which inherited constitutional factors are associated with criminality.

Psychosocial Explanations   Personality and biology aside, what insights can we gain into the psychology of the criminal from the material presented earlier in this chapter? One popular sociological theory of criminality is social strain theory (Cloward & Ohlin, 1960; Merton, 1938). According to this model, exposure to cultural ideals teaches us all that such things as a big car, a nice house, and a secure job are highly desirable. But some people, especially those who are poor and those from various minority groups, are discriminated against or do not develop the resources necessary to achieve these goals. Thus, they feel a strain between what they want and what they can obtain through legitimate means. Consequently, they choose what most of us consider to be illegitimate means to these goals, a response that is reinforced by a cultural milieu in which a certain amount of illegal hustling is encouraged. Whether or not this particular model is correct, it seems obvious that many of those who grow up poor will be subject to material frustration and will experience anger at people who have more than they do or at a system that perpetuates what they consider injustice. It is also likely that the greater problems experienced by poorer families, such as economic hardship, unstable family relations, and relatively poor psychological adjustment, handicap them in the task of raising children to uphold values the children may not see as immediately beneficial.

Social learning theory stresses that many people find that violence pays, if not in material then in psychological ways (Bandura, 1973, 1979). In particular, violence-prone people often have a vested interest in appearing to be tough, and this self-presentational strategy naturally leads to fighting. But why then do some people value toughness while others value a more pacific demeanor? One possible answer comes from subculture of violence theories (Cohen, 1955; Miller, 1958; Wolfgang & Ferracuti, 1967). According to such theories, violent offenders live in areas (often,

Youth gangs often provide a subculture that glorifies and encourages violence.

but not inevitably, poor) where youth subcultures value toughness, physical responses to verbal insults, and the like. Thus, young men (and, to an extent, young women) are socialized to feel that violence is not only a permissible but a valued solution to certain interpersonal problems.

Hans Toch (1969) developed a typology of violent offenders based on what psychological rewards come from aggressive behavior. His subject population was violent prison inmates and recent parolees: he found he could classify them into one of ten categories. The most common category was self-image compensating (41%). These men get into fights to punish those who have either insulted them or cast aspersions on their worth as persons. The second largest category (14%) is reputation defending. Men in this category are those whose public role is one of aggressiveness; gang leaders and people whom others look up to as "enforcers" would fall into this group. Twelve percent of the men fell into the category of pressure removing, men who tend to explode with violence when they encounter situations with which they cannot deal effectively. There are also a variety of categories encompassing men whose violence is an effective means to achieve their own selfish ends. Such men (who make up about one-quarter of the total) may be bullies who derive pleasure from hurting others, those who feel that others exist only to satisfy their own needs, those who tend to resort to violence when others frustrate them, and those who manipulate others to do their bidding through violence and threats of violence.

According to Toch, violent men have learned that violence pays as a solution to interpersonal problems. When a young man learns that beating up others makes him feel powerful and worthwhile or gives him considerable status and respect in his peer group, he will be inclined to use this solution often. "Violence is habit-forming" precisely because it yields rewards (Toch, 1969, p. 186). Not only do people learn from their own experiences about the rewards of extremely aggressive behavior, but cultural heroes and the mass media provide many examples of payoffs for aggressive behavior. Naturally, most children learn in time that getting ahead, being popular, and the like require some control over aggressive tendencies, but some children learn that the rewards they gain through aggression are more important than those gained through more socially desirable means.

CONTROL OF VIOLENT CRIME

We know very little about how to control violent crime (or any other kind for that matter). Most of the popular "get tough" solutions are either silly, seriously misleading, or counterproductive. Control involves several steps. To change a violent offender, we must identify, arrest, convict, and rehabilitate him or her. Each of these stages presents problems, and therefore fewer than 10% of all crimes result in conviction, with perhaps fewer than 3% resulting in prison terms (Silberman,

1978). This is shocking, but there is no simple way to raise the rate. Consider some of the variables that affect the process.

Arrest and Conviction   One of the major problems in crime control is arresting the guilty. Most crimes do not lead to arrest, although the rate of arrest is higher for most violent crimes (especially murder) than for nonviolent crimes. The reasons for relatively low arrest rates are fairly obvious. Before the police can arrest a perpetrator, citizens must report crimes quickly, and many citizens are reluctant to do so for a variety of reasons, including fear of the police, fear of the criminal, simple indifference, or the desire to seek private solutions (Greenberg & Ruback, 1982). Moreover, contrary to the image projected on countless television programs, the police are not very good at solving crimes in which immediate evidence is lacking. The main reason most murderers are caught is because they are either present at the murder scene, weapon in hand, or because the murder was witnessed by others.

Even if the criminal is arrested, he or she faces a long road through the criminal justice system. An increasingly popular image is that many criminals manage to go free or get light sentences because they have a good lawyer, because the courts are hampered by restrictive rulings and legal technicalities, or because prosecutors and judges are soft on crime. These may be problems, but they are not the major ones. Two other problems are actually more important.

The first problem is that the criminal justice system is simply overwhelmed. In some courts there may be as much as a year or two between arrest and final judgment. In this context, it is natural that most convictions result from plea bargaining, in which the defendant is given a reduced sentence but does not clog up the system with a jury trial. There is some debate about whether plea bargaining is necessary or desirable, but it is likely to remain the major way criminals are sentenced in the foreseeable future unless the public is willing to subsidize massive expansion of the criminal justice system.

A second, even more major, problem is what we ought to do with people who have been convicted of crimes. The standard solution is, of course, that people who commit major crimes should go to jail. There are many purposes that might be served by jail sentences, but the two most commonly given are deterrence and rehabilitation. We put people in prison either to show them and others that crime does not pay or to help them learn to mend their ways through counseling and job training.

Deterrence and Rehabilitation   However, the goals of deterrence and rehabilitation are somewhat contradictory. Long prison sentences might serve the deterrence function reasonably well, but they are inconsistent with rehabilitation. Prisons are unsafe, provide little privacy, offer little or no effective counseling, social skills, or job training, and they keep the criminal in the company of criminals. In such an environment, a long prison term may increase bitterness, lead to adjustments that are not effective in the outside world, and expose the prisoner to more effective models of criminal activity. So, given the realities of what prisons can do, when a judge hands down a light sentence, especially to a first offender, this may be less an expression of a do-gooder philosophy than of a 'hard-headed realization that prison does more harm than good.

We raise these issues about problems in sentencing because they have major implications for the control of crime. Precise data are hard to come by, but a large number of crimes (certainly 50%, perhaps as many as 80%) are committed by repeat offenders, so that the issue of rehabilitation is a central one. Unfortunately, most observers of the system have become quite pessimistic about the possibilities of rehabilitation, at least given present funding levels for prisons and rehabilitation programs. There is very little evidence that prison (or any

other less harsh option) significantly inhibits convicted criminals from relapsing into crime. About half of the people convicted of crimes will commit future crimes regardless of whether they are imprisoned, set free, or given some form of psychological treatment (Silberman, 1978; J. Q. Wilson, 1975). We not only do not know how to change criminals into law-abiding citizens; we cannot predict which criminals will commit further crimes and which will not.

However, in addition to rehabilitation, there are other cogent reasons for prison sentences. It seems reasonable that stiff sentences deter other people from crime. After all, isn't one of the reasons you do not rob banks your fear of being sent to prison? Earlier in this section we saw that fear of punishment is one of the major inhibiting factors for aggression in general. So although prison may have bad effects on the people in them and hamper their rehabilitation, this very fact may deter other people from committing crime.

Sanctions for criminal activity do play a role in keeping crime rates down. Most of us are deterred by fear of going to jail. But what about the average criminal? There is reason to

believe that for some people such fears are not especially relevant. For one thing, the deterrence function of punishment depends heavily on the potential offender's belief that he will be caught, convicted, and punished. Yet, as we have seen, the probabilities are that for any particular crime this will not happen.

Furthermore, we must not fall into the trap of assuming that everyone weighs the costs of prison sentences the same way. I fear prison because I would resent the restrictions on my freedom and I would be incredibly ashamed before my friends and family. But suppose someone finds prison not much worse than his present living conditions. Or maybe he doesn't have a family to worry about or doesn't worry about the one he has. And, of course, it is quite possible that many offenders consider prison sentences a badge of honor rather than shame, at least within the circles in which they travel. This is not to suggest that all criminals have no fear of prison or are not ashamed of their status, but only that the costs involved may not be the same for them as for those of us who do not break major laws.

Toch (1969) has argued that most violent men are so obsessed with their own low self-esteem that they are not deterred by prison sentences.

> But are Violent Men not deterred by prison? Nothing in our picture suggests that they would be. To the contrary, in fact: Violence feeds on low self-esteem and self-doubt, and prison un-mans and dehumanizes; violence rests on exploitation and exploitiveness and prison is a power-centered jungle. . . . The rewards and punishments are measured in increments and decrements to the ego, rather than in terms of future well-being. The perspective of violence is short-term and impulsive, rather than calculated and future-oriented. The Violent Man measures his worth by the distorted criterion of his physical impact, rather than by his ability to pursue a life plan. He has no career to be threatened, no stake to be impaired by prospective imprisonment. . . . It is curiously true that deterrence is potentially most effective with those who least require its impact—with rational, career-oriented,

future-invested individuals of the kinds who populate the ranks of the non-violent, law-abiding middle-class. (Toch, 1969, pp. 220–21)

Crimes of violence are frequently impulsive and motivated by anger. In such circumstances of high arousal, the aggressor may not consider the full range of costs connected with his action. It is highly unlikely that the man who attacks his wife in the midst of a drunken family argument is thinking much about prison. Further, we have suggested earlier that in arguments people may be temporarily obsessed with the costs associated with loss of honor or pride, and the costs of prison may be outweighed by the costs of not assaulting the other. More to the point, however, there is practically nothing that we can do to keep arguments from happening, and this is the most frequent source of murder and assault. Although some people are deterred by the possibility of strong punishment, it is obvious that others are not. And those who are not are the very people we most want to deter.

SUMMARY

There are several explanations for why people commit violent crimes. Violent offenders may have underactive autonomic nervous systems, and they often come from groups that favor violent solutions to problems. Social learning approaches emphasize that most people are violent because they have learned that violence pays. There is no easy way to lower violent crime. Violent criminals must be caught, must be convicted, and must be punished and rehabilitated, yet there are major problems at each of these stages.

CHAPTER SUMMARY

■ Because Darwin emphasized the importance of competition and violence as mechanisms in evolution, it has been easy to assume that human nature contains an aggressive imperative. Several theorists, including Freud, have argued that there is an instinct for aggression. However, there is no evidence for such an instinct. Biology plays a role in aggression, but its effect is tempered, constrained, or overshadowed by cultural and environmental factors.

■ Frustration–aggression theory argues that frustrations cause aggression. However, frustration does not always cause aggression and is probably not even the most important cause of aggressive behavior.

■ Berkowitz argues that anger is the operative cause of aggression: anger primes the person to be aggressive, and situational cues associated with aggression draw out the behavior.

■ Bandura argues that emotional factors such as anger are not essential causes of aggression, although they may facilitate hostile behaviors. Social learning theory suggests that aggressive behavior is performed because the person thinks it will be in his or her best interests to be aggressive.

■ Almost all events that are aversive (such as threat, frustration, or pain) can lead to aggression. However, even when these events lead to anger, aggression may not occur. Bandura argues that anger may accompany aggression but not cause it. There is, however, general agreement that anger facilitates aggression, especially when there are situational cues that encourage aggressive behavior.

■ Social facilitation theory argues that general arousal facilitates behavior that is dominant in a particular situation. It follows that when a person is inclined to be aggressive, extraneous arousal from sex or exercise, for example, may cause the person to be even more aggressive, and research generally supports that idea.

■ Laboratory research strongly suggests that media presentations of violence could cause people to become more aggressive, but this has been hard to document clearly in the everyday world. However, most experts feel that televised violence does cause aggression.

■ Although the causes of aggressive behavior are reasonably well understood, one cannot control aggression simply by eliminating such things as frustration, anger, threats, and aggressive cues. A more practical solution would be to encourage development of self-controls such as guilt for aggressive behavior, but it may be difficult to instil such controls in an adult who lacks them. Alternatively, punishment and other external controls can inhibit aggression, but cannot eliminate it.

■ Many people feel that aggression could be eliminated by allowing the person to drain away aggressive energy through catharsis. However, there is no evidence for any sort of specifically aggressive energy, and research generally suggests that catharsis is ineffective in controlling aggression.

■ Violent crime is increasing in our society. Several theories have attempted to explain why people kill and hurt others. Violent offenders usually come from family backgrounds with little emphasis on building internalized controls and with considerable family pathology and frustration.

■ Most biological theories of violence have been found wanting, although there is some evidence that criminals have trouble learning self-controls over behavior.

■ Other theories emphasize the fact that violent criminals usually come from backgrounds in which violence is encouraged. Furthermore, violent criminals often value toughness and find that violence pays.

■ Control of violent crime is difficult. The perpetrator must be apprehended, convicted, and either rehabilitated or punished sufficiently to deter future crime. There are problems at each of these stages. Prisons do not rehabilitate most criminals and also do not serve as effective deterrents.

CHAPTER
16
PREJUDICE AND DISCRIMINATION

attended a small school in a rural area outside Indianapolis. There were about 50 in my graduating high school class, and probably well over half of that group had attended class together in the same building for all 12 years of their schooling. So a new student was therefore an event of major proportions.

Especially a black student. One year, a black girl, whom I will call Joanna, entered my fifth-grade class. As far as I can remember, Joanna was the only black student in all 12 grades among 500 white students.

I would like to report that after an initial period of suspicion, Joanna became fully accepted by our little band, that she changed forever our attitudes about blacks, that she became a great scientist. But it didn't work out that way. My most vivid recollections of Joanna are that she cried all the time and that she was our favorite target of gossip and mean comments. Joanna was slow in the classroom and that didn't help her standing much. The teacher once talked to us about Joanna on one of the many days she was absent. Her condescending message was something like the following: We shouldn't be so mean to those who were less fortunate than ourselves, Joanna couldn't help it that she was slow, and it wasn't her fault that her parents had moved her away from her own kind and into an area where she really couldn't compete. But, of course, we continued to giggle at her mistakes, to make fun of her behind her back, and to tease one another that anyone who sat near her would get cooties and unspeakable diseases.

Joanna left after that one year, and I have often wondered what happened to her. She was not totally the victim of childish (but horribly cruel) racism. In a fairly tightknit group, any stranger is subjected to close scrutiny, and it is likely that even had Joanna been white she would have been rejected as stupid, ugly, or whatever—she was not the only of our classmates who "had cooties." But there is also no denying the fact that race was crucial. Although Indianapolis had a sizeable black population, blacks were rigidly segregated into their own part of town, and many of the white people living in the rural areas outside the city had moved there to escape the spread of blacks into white areas of the city. Most of us 10-year-olds had never talked to a black person other than maids (even middle-class people could afford maids in those days, especially when the maids were underpaid black women). There was no sense that blacks had anything other than a highly inferior culture (although it was readily granted that they made good basketball players, a nontrivial attribute in Indiana). It was taken for granted that the Joannas of the world did not have the same mental equipment as we white youngsters had.

INTRODUCTION

The study of prejudice and discrimination has an old and honorable history within the field of social psychology. Indeed, much of the early empirical work by social psychologists during the 1920s and 1930s dealt explicitly with prejudice and attitudes toward ethnic groups. One reason we will consider the topic is that people from various racial, ethnic, and gender groups interact with one another in terms of group identities, and intergroup behavior is manifestly social. So even if we did not care about the moral and practical implications of racism and sexism for our society, the topic would still be a legitimate part of social psychology. But we do care. Some people suffer a great deal from the prejudices of others, and such prejudices cost our society morally in terms of our sense of justice and pragmatically in terms of our failures to realize the talents of millions of people. Prejudice and discrimination are politically, economically, and morally important topics.

We have already made passing reference in almost every chapter to prejudice and discrimination. You will be reminded of Chapter 3 ("Social Cognition") when we consider stereotyping. You may wish to reread the opening example of a conversation with a student about Mexican-Americans and how he perceived them to be lazy. The implications of person perception (Chapter 4) for discussions of prejudice, especially stereotyping, are obvious; both attribution and impression formation ideas will appear in this chapter again. The self (Chapter 5) is relevant because of the ways that race, religion, and gender (among other categories) affect how we think about ourselves. You will recall that we explicitly discussed gender schemata, and many of the same points presumably apply to race, religion, and occupational categories. In Chapter 6, we discussed language, communication, and categorization. Again, one example was that of a teacher who could not understand that

Negro and *black* had different meanings for black students. But more generally, the ways in which people talk to one another and communicate are both influenced by racial and gender groupings and contribute to the maintenance of those groupings. Chapter 7 dealt with attitudes, and because prejudice is, among other things, an attitude, much of what we learned about the development and change of attitudes has ready applications. In Chapter 8, we discussed how attitudes are translated into behaviors. In that chapter, many of our examples concerned race explicitly, but in the present chapter we will further consider when prejudiced attitudes become actualized as overt discrimination. In the socialization chapter (9), we explicitly discussed the nature of sex differences and how they are maintained in part by cultural values and overt discrimination. We could just as easily have used race or religion to make the same point. Socialization also explains how people grow up prejudiced in this and other societies.

Because racial, gender, economic, religious, and other categories often constitute groups, we will draw on the material of Chapter 10 to discuss how groups interact. In Chapter 11, we discussed social influence. Much discrimination is based on conformity to group norms, as was evident especially in our consideration of the mass psychology of race riots and lynchings. Chapters 12 and 13 dealt with attraction and relationships. Again, given the fact that prejudice is based in part on attraction responses, these chapters are generally relevant. Finally, when we considered cooperation, altruism, and aggression in Chapters 14 and 15, we noted that race is often relevant to these categories of behaviors.

DEFINITIONS

In this chapter, we consider a family of related terms: *prejudice, ethnocentrism, stereotypes, discrimination, racism,* and *sexism.* These terms have been used in a variety of ways by both scientists and lay people, and, not surprisingly, it is now difficult to keep straight all the meanings. Definitions are, of course, conventions and are therefore neither true nor false but only more or less useful. Therefore, for the purposes of this chapter, let us propose some definitions that will aid our further discussion.

Prejudice   *Prejudice* is in some ways the easiest of the terms to define, if only because its root meaning is so clear. It comes from the Latin *praejudicium,* literally meaning "before judgment." In English the term means the same: a prior judgment, that is, a judgment prior to direct experience or knowledge of facts. Gordon Allport (1954) defined **prejudice** as "a feeling, favorable or unfavorable, toward a person or thing, prior to, or not based on, actual experience" (Allport, 1954, p. 7). There are some remaining unclarities with that definition, but it will suit us for the moment. A related term is **ethnocentrism,** which is a general feeling of superiority of one's own group over others. Commonly, *ethnocentrism* applies to a prejudice or discrimination toward other ethnic or national groups.

Stereotypes   Prejudice is usually based on a **stereotype,** "a set of beliefs about the personal attributes of a group of people" (Ashmore & Del Boca, 1981, p. 16). So stereotypes represent generalizations about people based on their social, racial, or ethnic categories. Stereotypes, like prejudices, can be either positive or negative. A belief that students are smart and hard working is as much a stereotype as a belief that students are lazy and ill mannered.

Discrimination   *Discrimination* refers to overt behaviors. Again, the Latin root, *discriminare,* which means to make a distinction, suggests the modern meaning. There are notions of discrimination that refer only to cognitive variables, such as when we say a certain woman is a discriminating art collector, mean-

ing that she has learned to make distinctions between good and bad art, but generally discrimination has behavioral overtones. *Discrimination* may be defined as behavior that denies "to individuals or groups of people equality of treatment which they may wish" (Allport, 1954, p. 50).

Racism   *Racism* and *sexism* refer to broader constellations of attitudes, feelings, and behaviors. **Racism** "results from the transformation of race prejudice and/or ethnocentrism through the exercise of power against a racial group defined as inferior, by individuals and institutions with the intentional or unintentional support of the entire culture" (Jones, 1972, p. 117). According to this definition, racism requires both prejudice and discrimination but further requires the support of the entire culture. By extension, **sexism** is the use of power against one gender group with the support of the culture. Some have argued that racism and sexism include the added belief that the presumed inferiority is genetic, or biologically determined. It is true that those who have been the most overt racists and sexists have often believed that other racial groups, women, and minority groups were biologically inferior, but this hardly seems central to the definition and may even be overly restrictive. For example, we might want to examine similar uses of power against religious groups, and few would claim that people are Methodists by biological command.

Gordon Allport

Jones (1972) argues that there are really three kinds of racism. The first, **individual racism,** is close to what we have been calling prejudice. It is conscious or unconscious discrimination because of prejudiced attitudes. The second, **institutional racism,** is more complex. Institutional racism (or sexism or other discrimination) occurs when the economic, educational, political, and social institutions of a society favor one group over another. There are thousands of ready examples. Until recently, many states effectively kept blacks from voting by imposing a poll tax that most blacks could not easily afford. Many business firms expect their employees to move frequently or to travel, which effectively makes it difficult for single mothers to work for these companies. Other examples are more subtle. For example, a company might use aptitude tests for hiring, and members of minority groups might do less well on these tests than middle-class whites. If these tests predict job performance, a case can be made for using them. But often the tests do such a poor job of predicting job performance that their use constitutes clear, if indirect, discrimination. On the other hand, even if the tests do a good job of predicting job performance, we still have to ask why members of one group do better than members of another. Could it be that poorer schools or past discrimination play a role? In other words, if members of one group are ill prepared to do a particular job, the whole institutional structure of the society may be at fault for their poor preparation. It is surely not the immediate fault of an employer that minority-group applicants are ill prepared to do the job he offers, but by the same token he and his company participate in and benefit from a larger society that tolerates discrimination and produces such problems.

Cultural racism is based on two factors. The first is the recognition that different ethnic and racial groups have somewhat different cultures; the second is the implicit or explicit feeling that one's own culture is better than other

The American Nazi Party illustrates one extreme form of cultural racism.

cultures. Again, examples abound. When you next go to an art museum, look at the amount of space devoted to European art and that devoted to African art. And why is it that many of us, and especially the better educated, generally think that "classical music" is somehow on a higher plane than black-influenced jazz or rock music? Why do we favor Standard American English over its black counterparts? And to use a cultural sexism example, why is raising children, a traditional feminine enterprise, less valued than making money?

The point is not that all achievements of all cultures are somehow equal or that there are no standards of achievement. Nor is the argument that one should have no culturally based preferences. We are allowed to like what we like so long as we keep an open mind toward the achievements of others with different experiences and cultural backgrounds. I will continue to prefer Mozart to Scott Joplin (although I like both), but if I make fun of the achievements of blacks (or Jews or Japanese), then I am flirting with racism, and if I use my position of authority to ensure that products of other cultures are devalued, simply because they come from another culture, then I am surely being a cultural racist.

RELATIONSHIPS AMONG COMPONENTS

Stereotypes are cognitive; they are a set of beliefs. When affect is added to these beliefs, we have prejudice. When this prejudice is activated into behaviors, we may speak of discrimination. However, these do not follow one another inevitably. One can have a stereotype without a prejudice; I believe that men are, on the average, physically stronger than women, but I am not aware that I have any negative feelings toward either group because of that generalization or stereotype. Conversely, prejudices occur without stereotypes. My dog has a quite negative prejudice toward people who come to our door, but there is no evidence that he has any accompanying beliefs. Similarly, discrimination may occur without prejudice and prejudice may exist without discrimination. For example, if I were to decide that every fifth name in my grade book for a course gets an A regardless of performance, that would be discrimination, even though I have no conscious bias for or against such people. On the other side, a person may be quite prejudiced but, because of social or legal pressures, fail to act on the basis of his prejudice. Still, normally we would expect there to be some correspondence between beliefs, affect, and behaviors.

We also need not assume that the three factors always build on one another in a temporal way. People may begin with stereotypes and add affect and then behavioral discrimination, but it is quite possible for people to grow up disliking another group and then form stereotypes to justify the negative affect. Or perhaps a person who discriminates may come to dislike those she has offended.

Stereotypes are inevitable products of our cognitive activities and everyone has some stereotypes (see Chapters 3 and 4). However, affect, discrimination, and racism or sexism usually involve a larger degree of cultural and social influence. As we move from beliefs to racism we will also subtly shift the focus from the individual to the culture. Another way to put this is that, as we move from stereotypes to racism, we continue to hold the individual at the center of our picture but we gradually use a wider-angle lens to take in more of the cultural landscape.

STEREOTYPES

In Chapter 4, we discussed person perception and impression formation. Stereotypes are one kind of impression we have about others. My fifth grade cohorts and I had a negative stereotype about blacks before and certainly after our experience with Joanna. However, stereotypes are not restricted to ethnic groups, nor are they always negative. Furthermore, recent approaches to the topic have suggested that stereotypes are often products of common person-perception activities.

Most of the stereotype research done before 1975 or so concentrated on the content of stereotypes toward ethnic groups and the relationships of such stereotypes to prejudice (Brigham, 1971). Social psychologists now tend to approach stereotypes as generalizations with the same cognitive underpinnings as other generalizations and to stress the links to implicit personality theories and general schema-based processing of information. The focus has shifted from the *content of stereotypes* to the *processes of stereotyping*.

STEREOTYPES AND CATEGORIES

Categorization   Before you can rely on your stereotype of professors, you must first see a person in her role as a professor rather than as a woman, mother, or Democrat. Such categorization is, of course, a fundamental aspect of processing information of any sort and may (but need not) lead to stereotyping (Taylor, 1981). Categorization often makes salient both the similarities of objects within a

We sometimes put people into categories based on their appearance.

category and the differences between those objects and objects from other categories (Tajfel, 1970). To label a person as a basketball player may emphasize the ways he is like other players and unlike other students. This raises the possibility that we may see *too much* similarity among members of groups (and too much difference between members of different groups). This is especially likely to be a problem when the group in question is one to which we do not belong.

In-groups versus Out-groups   All of us belong to certain groups, and these are *in-groups;* groups to which we do not belong are *out-groups.* There is abundant evidence that we tend to see members of other groups as different from us and members of our in-group (Wilder, 1986). In everyday life this may, of course, be a realistic perception. Methodists may, in fact, have a great deal in common with each other and differ from Catholics in fundamental ways. Given different cultural experiences, blacks share some characteristics not generally shared with whites. However, it is clear that mere categorization—apart from actual experience—creates similar effects; even

in arbitrarily formed groups, people tend to assume that the members of their own group are similar to themselves and that the members of out-groups are different from them (Allen & Wilder, 1979).

Another fundamental consequence of such categorization is that we tend to assume that members of out-groups are similar to one another and that they are homogeneous in attitudes, values, and behaviors (Linville, Salovey, & Fischer, 1986). The age-old "they all look alike" phenomenon has been shown experimentally: people are better at recognizing faces for their own racial groups (Brigham & Malpass, 1985). Sometimes this simply reflects differential experience and knowledge. Most of us spend more time with people in our ethnic, cultural, political, and special-interest groups than with "outsiders." Thus, it should be no surprise that we know more about our own groups than other groups and that we seem to have more complex beliefs about in-groups than out-groups (Linville, 1982).

In particular, we may be more aware of differences among individuals in our own than in other groups (Quattrone & Jones, 1980). To a student at the University of Texas, the student body at Austin may seem almost infinitely diverse while Texas A&M students all seem to be unsophisticated farmers or engineers. Of course, the A&M Aggie will find it easier to see diversity among his comrades and might view all UT students as party people and tea-sippers. But, again, more seems to be involved than experience—categorization alone seems to lead to perceptions of similarity among group members. For example, Park and Rothbart (1982) examined perceptions of the opposite sex by both males and females, and it is hard to argue that most of us lack experiences with members of the opposite sex. In this study, people saw members of their own gender as having fewer stereotypical traits than members of the other gender. We tend to magnify differences between our own and other groups and to see members of other groups as less differentiated or more stereo-typed than members of our own groups.

Memory   Categorization can also affect how we organize information about people and their behaviors in our memories. It seems perfectly natural to remember behaviors in terms of who performed them (Joe poured the wine, Mary told the silly joke, Hazel made the rude remark). However, there is nothing inevitable about this. Ostrom, Pryor, and Simpson (1981) have argued that behavioral information will be organized by person at some times and by other themes, such as event or category of person, at other times. That is, you might remember that wine was poured at the cocktail party and that the silly joke was told by a woman rather than remember specifically who did what. Generally, organization by person is strongest when the people are familiar, and other ways of organizing are favored when you are remembering unfamiliar people (Pryor et al., 1982) or the people are similar to one another (McCann, Ostrom, Tyner, & Mitchell, 1985).

So we might have some concern that once a relatively unfamiliar person (say, a member of an out-group) is categorized into some group, the individuality of his or her behavior will be lost because behaviors may be organized by group rather than person. Such an effect was shown in research by Taylor, Fiske, Etcoff, and Ruderman (1978). Subjects saw a discussion involving both blacks and whites, and because race is a salient social category, it is not surprising that the subjects remembered fairly well whether a black or a white had made a particular comment. However, subjects also frequently made errors in ascribing the comments within the groups, not being able to remember which white or which black had made the remark. Thus, behaviors were apparently better remembered by ethnic group than by individual. People are also prone to make within-gender memory errors, and this tendency is strongest when strongly sex-typed

Marilynn Brewer

perceivers view members of the opposite sex. Thus, a person who sees himself as a super-macho male may have trouble remembering which of several women performed a particular behavior (Frable & Bem, 1985).

Subcategories   The categorization approach reminds us that there are many ways a person could be categorized. We could see a particular woman as a woman, a black woman, a black housewife, a black middle-class housewife, and so on. Social psychologists have mostly been concerned with high-order social categories such as race or gender in their studies of stereotyping, yet evidence suggests that stereotyping may actually be somewhat richer for subcategories (Ashmore, 1981). For example, Brewer, Dull, and Lui (1981) found that more stereotyping occurs for narrower categories such as "senior citizen" or "grandmother type" than for the broader category of "older person." Similarly, Eagly and Steffen (1984) found that subjects held certain stereotypes for women who do not have jobs outside the home (namely, that such women were more social and less forceful than men) but that these stereotypes did not apply to women in general. So when we talk about stereotypes, we must try to be clear about the generality and limitations of the stereotypes, to make sure that stereotypes about blacks are not really stereotypes about, for example, lower-class blacks, or that stereotypes about women are not, for example, stereotypes about homemakers.

Problems   The real problem with categorization is not that it occurs; we can hardly avoid putting people into cognitive pigeonholes of one sort or another and then generalizing about the categories. The real problem occurs when we allow the mere act of categorization to lead us to a relative inability or unwillingness to think about individuals. One of the major dangers of generalizing about categories of people is that we let such generalizations do our thinking for us. This is certainly not inevitable, but categorization needs careful and continual scrutiny lest our generalizations lead us into discrimination and prejudice.

STEREOTYPES AS IMPLICIT PERSONALITY THEORIES

One of the first major studies that emphasized the processing approach to stereotyping was explicitly tied to research on implicit personality theories. Recall that implicit personality theories are those we all have about

which characteristics go together. Hamilton and Gifford (1976) assumed that, just as you might feel that warm people were happy, you might also feel that professors are lazy or students at your university are hard working. In other words, race, gender, group membership, and so on could be thought of as major traits related to other traits in an implicit personality theory. Then why is it so common for negative traits to be attached to minority groups? Hamilton and Gifford picked up on Chapman and Chapman's (1967) idea of illusory correlation. As you may recall from Chapter 3, the Chapmans discovered that traits that were uncommon or distinctive tend to be seen as cooccurring or going together more than experience would support. So Hamilton and Gifford argued that, for the average white person, members of minority groups and negative behaviors are both fairly uncommon and hence are likely to be seen as cooccurring. The experiments were able to show that subjects were biased toward remembering uncommon negative behaviors as going with people from a less-common group; this led to a more negative evaluation of the "minority" group. In general, then, on the assumption that people from our own group are more familiar and common, we may have cognitive tendencies to see uncommon out-group members as having more uncommon behaviors, behaviors that are often negative (Hamilton, Dugan, & Trolier, 1985; Hamilton & Trolier, 1986).

STEREOTYPES AS HYPOTHESES

Rigidity   Although some people probably have stereotypes that allow no exceptions, most people readily admit exceptions to their stereotypes (McCauley, Stitt, & Segal, 1980). So I may state my generalization (stereotype, if you prefer) that women make better grades in Introductory Psychology (they do in my classes—I checked) without meaning to suggest that it is unusual for a male to do well. Nor are stereotypes necessarily used in the face of competing evidence. Some studies have shown that

"You six-year-olds are all alike."

Drawing by Joe Mirachi © 1984 by the New Yorker Magazine, Inc.

people use stereotypes to judge others primarily when they do not have other information about their behaviors, roles, or traits (Deaux & Lewis, 1984; Locksley, Borgida, Brekke, & Hepburn, 1980; Locksley, Hepburn, & Ortiz, 1982). Such individuating information is used when it is available. These studies suggest, then, that for many of us stereotypes are not rigid and unyielding but fairly flexible schemata for thinking about others.

Maybe it is best to think of stereotypes as provisional hypotheses about what people are like. If you have never met someone before, you might imagine what she would be like from noting her appearance, gender, age, and the like. But unless your stereotype is rigid, you would probably not defend your inferences in the face of compelling contrary evidence. In your experience, most middle-aged women are warm and friendly, but this particular middle-aged woman is not. That does not destroy the validity of the generalization or create cognitive chaos; you simply recognize that your hypothesis was wrong for this particular woman.

On the other hand, having hypotheses about people because of their race, gender, or occupation is not without its dangers. As we saw in Chapter 3, a great deal of our processing of information consists of using schemata (and stereotypes are one kind of schema) to organize incoming information. This leads to efficient but sometimes biased processing. Therefore, when you begin your interaction with a stranger with certain hypotheses, you may come away with biased conclusions.

Labeling   One possibility is that you will label ambiguous behaviors in terms of your stereotypes. We saw one example with the Duncan (1976) study of how white subjects labeled the same shoving behavior of blacks and whites differently (see Chapter 3). Probably a person who believes women are poor drivers would be inclined to see an attempt to change lanes during rush hour as evidence of bad driving by a woman driver but as aggressive, skillful driving by a man. In an experiment by Darley and Gross (1983), subjects were told that a child came from either a lower- or a middle-class background. Subjects who predicted intellectual ability knowing only the social class of the child did not infer that the poor child was less gifted than the middle-class child (which is what you might expect if they had stereotypes that lower-class children were less smart). Other subjects saw a videotape of the child performing in an academic situation, and those who thought the child was lower class rated her as having lower ability than did those who thought she was middle class. Both groups of subjects had seen exactly the same tape; apparently their differing information about social class led to hypotheses about performance that then led the subjects to see and interpret behavioral information selectively.

Behavioral Effects   Your stereotypes may also affect how you behave to the other person, which in turn might affect her behavior. In Chapter 3, we discussed various ways that people bias their information search. One way is through self-fulfilling prophecies. For example, if you think someone dislikes you, you may behave in a hostile manner that then leads her to behave in an unfriendly manner, in turn leading you to conclude that your hypothesis is confirmed: she doesn't like you. In an experiment by Word, Zanna, and Cooper (1974), white college student subjects interviewed black and white job candidates, who were actually confederates programmed to behave in a consistent manner. The nonverbal behavior of the interviewers was rated and in general was less positive to black than to white interviewees. For example, the interviewers sat farther away from the black than from the white interviewees.

It is possible that interviewees who were naive might pick up these subtle cues and mirror the behavior of the interviewer. This was tested in a second study in which trained interviewers duplicated the nonverbal styles of behavior displayed by the interviewers of the first study. Subjects interviewed by the relatively more positive interviewer were judged (by independent judges) to have performed better in the interview than those interviewed by the negative interviewer. Thus, white interviewers might interview black candidates in a way that encourages them to do worse. Then, of course, the interviewer can claim confirming evidence for his stereotype that black candidates seem to show less ability. What he fails to realize is that his own behavior may virtually have forced such a confirmation.

Memory   Memory biases may also support stereotypes. In Chapter 3, we reviewed evidence that people are likely to remember schema-consistent information. Because stereotypes are one kind of schema, the same should be and is true for stereotypes (Hamilton & Rose, 1980; Lui & Brewer, 1983). But you will also recall that we have especially good memories for schema- (or stereotype-) inconsistent information. This presents a theoretical problem: if we tend to remember the inconsistent material, how do stereotypes persist? If you think men are insensitive slobs, you should particularly remember instances of sensitivity by men, evidence that should undercut your stereotype. Yet this doesn't seem to happen. One reason may be that we create separate categories for exceptions (Weber & Crocker, 1983). So if you have a stereotype that men are insensitive slobs, you may develop a category of neat, sensitive men into which you place all the exceptions you encounter. Thus, you can still say that most men are slobs, but there are exceptions.

Our memories for stereotype material may be biased in more subtle ways. Rothbart et al. (1978) have argued that people's impressions of groups may be heavily affected by extreme examples of behavior, because such extreme examples are highly available in memory. For example, suppose you try to compare the laziness of professors and bankers. Assume for the sake of argument that 30% of both groups are lazy, but that the lazy professors seem to be

more extreme in their laziness. When you try to recall examples of lazy behavior, you may find it easier to recall examples of lazy professor behavior (because they are readily available in memory) and hence feel that a higher percentage of professors are lazy.

Many people seem to feel that stereotypes are inevitably simpleminded, wrong, prejudicial, and negative. Although there are some people who rigidly hold stereotypes that are manifestly wrong and that clearly reveal more about the subject than the object of the beliefs, most people use their stereotypes in reasonable ways. The problem is that most of us let our stereotypes think for us on occasion. The point is not to defend the existence of stereotypes, especially those that are negative, but merely to point out how hopeless it is to eliminate them entirely. Our best strategy is to try to respond to people as much as we can in terms of their individual qualities and to be always vigilant so that our stereotypes will not lead to erroneous and costly judgments.

SUMMARY

Stereotypes are generalizations about groups of people. In recent years, social psychologists have emphasized the cognitive underpinnings of the process of stereotyping others. Because they are generalizations, stereotypes naturally arise when we place people into categories. We are especially likely to see members of groups to which we do not belong (out-groups) in terms of generalized characteristics. Our memories of social events tend to be organized around group memberships, so that we recall that a member of a group did something but we don't recall which member. Such categorization effects need not lead to negative stereotypes, but work by Hamilton suggests that we tend to remember infrequent negative traits as correlated with infrequent minority groups. It is also important to remember that stereotypes are not always rigid; nor do most people think that all members of groups have the same characteristics. Therefore, it is useful to think about stereotypes as provisional hypotheses that may or may not be confirmed by individual contact. However, a stereotype-based hypothesis about what a person is like may bias cognitive processing enough that the stereotype is confirmed, despite contrary evidence.

PREJUDICE

PREJUDICE IS AN ATTITUDE

Prejudice is both an attitude and a form of interpersonal attraction, a special kind of liking or disliking. Recall that attitudes have cognitive (belief), affective (feeling), and behavioral components and that interpersonal attraction (liking or disliking) can be thought of as an attitude toward a person in which the affective dimension is given special emphasis. Prejudice then is a special kind of attraction in which a person is liked or disliked on the basis of his or her gender, occupation, race, ethnic group, sexual preferences, religion, region of the country, or other basis of categorization.

Our definition of prejudice also incorporates the notion that this must be a prejudgment, a judgment before the fact or without referring to basic factual information. That is, if you were to dislike dogs because they frequently have fleas, your reaction at least has the virtue of being based on some factual information, though there may be an occasional flealess dog who might resent being rejected. This exhibits the root problem with prejudice. When is there ever a basis of rejecting a person or thing on the basis of incomplete evidence? I religiously avoid movies starring Sylvester Stallone because I saw *Rocky* and I didn't like it. Does this mean I would also hate his Rambo series of movies? In my own mind I am justified in prejudging whether I would like a movie I have never seen on the basis of what I know about it. Still, there is the possibility that my judgment has been in error and that I would truly enjoy *Rambo XXIII* or whatever. If you like Rambo movies, you will probably see me

as prejudiced, but if you agree with me, you probably feel I have enough evidence for my evaluation.

Prejudice, then, is a matter of degree and exists to some extent in the eye of the beholder. At one extreme are those who reject everyone in a designated group on the basis of no real evidence but only because of a vague emotional unease; we all agree they are prejudiced. At the other extreme are those who reject individuals on the basis of lots of experience. Consider the man who has worked all his life with Hispanics and who feels that they are lazy. I may argue that he fails to allow for individual differences and that he takes his stereotypes as fact rather than as provisional hypotheses, but he does have *some* basis, even if biased, for his opinion.

Keep in mind that *prejudice* can technically refer to positive as well as negative prejudgments. It is as much a prejudgment for me to say I like all redheads as it is for me to say I hate all Bulgarians. However, most people think of prejudice as a negative evaluation, even when it is supported by factual evidence (Rodin & Harari, 1986).

THEORIES OF PREJUDICE

Scapegoating One of the oldest theories of prejudice rests on the notion that people need a scapegoat to explain their own failures. According to the frustration–aggression hypothesis discussed in Chapter 15, aggression results from frustration, but because aggression often cannot be expressed directly toward the cause of the frustration, it may be displaced toward a substitute target. In American society until recently, racial minorities were an ideal displacement target because they were relatively powerless to get back at those who attacked. Thus, prejudice against blacks (and other minorities) was a convenient way to vent frustration.

There are abundant circumstantial data to support this point of view. For example, Hovland and Sears (1940) showed that there was

One of the early effects of state-sanctioned anti-Semitism in Nazi Germany was the destruction of Jewish-owned businesses.

once a high negative correlation between the price of cotton and lynchings in the South. As the price of cotton went down, frustration presumably increased and aggression (indexed as the number of lynchings) went up. In another study (Campbell, 1947), a negative correlation was found between satisfaction with one's economic status and prejudice against Jews. Historically, prejudice against minorities tends to be higher among working-class and poor people (who are presumably economically frustrated), which might again be taken as evidence of displacement or scapegoating (Allport, 1954).

There is some truth to the scapegoating hypothesis. Often we try to explain our failures by blaming someone else. However, most social scientists now feel that the scapegoating theory is incomplete and misleading. For one thing, most of the evidence that supports this point of view is correlational and could be explained in other ways. For example, working-class and poor people are also typically less educated, and education generally decreases prejudice (Schuman, Steeh, & Bobo, 1985). Also, the scapegoating model does not accurately and precisely predict which groups will

be selected as objects of prejudice. Finally, the theory fails to take account of cultural supports for prejudice. There are many minority groups in every society, and not just frustration but cultural values must play a major role in determining which of these groups are selected as targets.

Authoritarian Personality   Perhaps the single most important theory of prejudice was developed in the late 1940s by a group of social scientists who set out to study anti-Semitism and ended up with a theory of authoritarianism (Adorno et al., 1950). Their theory shares some features in common with the scapegoating model (because of a similar ancestry in Freudian theory) in that both propose that prejudice is anger directed outward toward other groups. However, whereas the scapegoating model emphasizes the selection of specific groups as targets, the concept of the authoritarian personality is built on the idea that prejudice is a general personality characteristic. The researchers discovered that anti-Semitic attitudes were often associated with negative attitudes toward other groups (ethnocentrism) and with political conservatism. For example, prejudice against Jews and Negroes correlated highly. More recently, Weigel and Howes (1985) showed that racial prejudice was correlated with prejudice against homosexuals and the elderly. Earlier research by Hartley (1946) showed that people prejudiced against conventional minority groups also rejected nonexistent groups. So prejudice cannot be based entirely on direct experience; it seems to be a more generalized attitude toward all out-groups. Prejudice is but one—important —part of the more general syndrome the researchers called authoritarianism. Table 16.1 shows some examples of the Ethnocentrism Scale and the F-Scale used by Adorno et al. to measure authoritarianism.

The authoritarian personality (best exemplified by the television character Archie Bunker) is characterized by prejudiced atti-

TABLE 16.1 ITEMS FROM THE ETHNOCENTRISM SCALE AND F-SCALE.

Items from the Ethnocentrism Scale

One trouble with Jewish businessmen is that they stick together and prevent other people from having a fair chance in competition.

Manual labor and unskilled jobs seem to fit the Negro mentality and ability better than more skilled or responsible work.

The worst danger to real Americanism during the last 50 years has come from foreign ideas and agitators.

The people who raise all the talk about putting Negroes on the same level as whites are mostly radical agitators trying to stir up conflicts.

Certain religious sects who refuse to salute the flag should be forced to conform to such a patriotic action, or else be abolished.

America may not be perfect, but the American way has brought us about as close as human beings can get to a perfect society.

Items from the F-Scale

Obedience and respect for authority are the most important virtues children should learn.

What this country needs most, more than laws and political programs, is a few courageous, tireless, devoted leaders in whom the people can put their faith.

Most of our social problems would be solved if we could somehow get rid of the immoral, crooked, and feebleminded people.

The wild sex life of the old Greeks and Romans was tame compared to some of the goings-on in this country, even in places where people might least expect it.

Every person should have complete faith in some supernatural power whose decisions he obeys without question.

SOURCE: Adorno et al., 1950.

tudes, a rigid perspective on ethics and traditional values, the feeling that authorities know best, and a negative reaction to sex and sexual pleasure. Authoritarians are rigid and intolerant of people who do not think or act as they do.

The study of prejudice was long dominated by work on the authoritarian personality. It is an attractive theory. For one thing, everyone knows one or two Archie Bunker types who really do seem to hate everyone. For another, it seems to explain how people could succumb to such silly beliefs: prejudiced people have warped personalities. And there is a good deal of support for the model. People who score high in authoritarianism *are* more prejudiced (Allport, 1954).

However, social scientists came to realize that personality is not sufficient to account for racism and prejudice. Although individual au-

thoritarianism scores do predict prejudice, generally those parts of the country that are most prejudiced are not most authoritarian (Pettigrew, 1958). Moreover, it is obvious that even people who do not have warped personalities can be prejudiced and can discriminate. It is hard to imagine that *all* the citizens of Little Rock or Montgomery who so strongly resisted integrated schools were authoritarian. Some had racist views, but these racial beliefs were not necessarily a part of their integral personality pattern. Many spoke in prejudiced ways and actively discriminated for the same reasons that they wore the latest fashions and watched the TV programs everyone watched—they were simply conforming uncritically to what others expected. So the concept of the authoritarian personality can no longer be accepted as a complete explanation for prejudice.

Thomas Pettigrew

Belief Similarity   One feature common to the scapegoating and authoritarian personality theories is an emphasis on individual differences. Basically, both models argue that certain people (these who are frustrated or those with particular flaws in their personalities) are prone to being prejudiced while the rest are not. A more recent emphasis, however, suggests that certain social and cognitive circumstances create the conditions for all of us to be prejudiced, at least sometimes.

One thing that seems to encourage prejudice is the feeling that people from other groups have bad values and unacceptable attitudes. Rokeach, Smith, and Evans (1960) have suggested that a person may dislike people from another ethnic group because those people are perceived as holding different values and attitudes. Thus, prejudice becomes a manifestation of the similarity-leads-to-attraction rule. Many whites argue that they are not prejudiced against blacks because of skin color as such, but reject black people because they don't have "our" values and behavior patterns. Research confirms the proposition that we *assume* members of our own ethnic and racial groups are more similar to us than are members of other groups (Hendrick, Bixenstein, & Hawkins, 1971; Stein, Hardyck, & Smith, 1965), although the actual similarities between groups may be much closer than most people think.

Is assumed dissimilarity of beliefs sufficient to account for prejudice? Most studies find that perceived belief similarity is more important than race similarity for friendship judgments, but that for a closer relationship such as marriage, race is more important than belief similarity. For example, Moe, Nacoste, and Insko (1981) gave black and white teenagers in a Southern town questionnaires supposedly filled out by other whites and blacks showing attitudes similar or dissimilar to the subjects'. For most measures of attraction (such as willingness to work with the person or being partners in an athletic contest), belief similarity was more important than race similarity; however, both black and white teenagers showed that race was more important than attitudes when asked whether they would be willing to have the person as a close kin by marriage. For marriage there are powerful social norms that regulate social distance and support prejudice.

Prejudice, particularly in its most institutional-racist forms, cannot be reduced to perceived belief dissimilarity. However, some prejudice, particularly those forms that control everyday contact, reflects the correct or incorrect perception that people of different racial groups have different beliefs. Thus, reduction of prejudice may involve correcting erroneous beliefs about the extent of between-group differences in attitudes and values as well as weakening the similarity–attraction relationship within groups.

Out-group Rejection   Some have argued that people have a basic, almost primitive tendency to favor members of their own groups over those of other groups, even to the point of actively discriminating in favor of the ingroup. Perhaps the classic demonstration of this was by Sherif and Sherif (1953). In working with boys at a summer camp, they arbitrarily divided the boys into two groups that later had a competition. During the competition two striking things occurred. First, the boys strengthened an already existing feeling of we-ness; the competition seemed to engender considerable in-group feeling and loyalty. Second, this in-group loyalty was accompanied by a dramatic increase in hostility toward the out-group. This was expressed not only in terms of a competitive spirit but in name-calling and subsequently actual fights between the two groups. Most people who have worked with younger people (and not just boys) have noted the extraordinary tendency of youngsters to form cliques and groups that sometimes seem to exist for the sole purpose of discrimination, of keeping others out.

Henri Tajfel (1970) stimulated a great deal of the subsequent research in this area by showing that the effects occur even for arbitrary groups. In the Tajfel paradigm, unacquainted subjects are arbitrarily placed into two groups on the basis of artistic preferences or simply are placed into groups with different labels having no intrinsic meaning (such as greens versus blues). Subsequently, the subjects work on tasks unrelated to the basis of the grouping (if there ever was a basis) and in due course they are given opportunities to divide rewards or are asked about preferences among all the people. Such studies usually show in-group favoritism; when rewards are allocated, subjects tend to assign proportionally more to members of their own group.

Note two features of this research paradigm. The first is that subjects show preference for their own group even when the basis of that group has no essential meaning. If we get such effects with arbitrary groups, imagine what we might get with existing groups who have had opportunities to interact over many years and develop stereotypes about one another. Second, note that the effects occur even though the groups are not essentially competing with one another. Competition is not a prerequisite for this effect.

Attributions   In almost every society the major targets of prejudice are those with low status and economic position. In a technological society such as ours, members of targeted groups such as blacks, Hispanics, and women are more often out of work, are paid lower salaries, have lower-status jobs, and are less educated than are white, Anglo males. Although to some extent prejudice and discrimination create these conditions, for the moment we want to emphasize that the conditions can also feed prejudice.

When we considered attribution, we discussed the fundamental attribution error (Chapter 4), the tendency to see the causes of others' behavior as dispositional. This is especially evident in the explanations people give for the lowered status of members of minority groups. Why are blacks more likely to be unemployed? Because of something about them—they are lazy. Why do we not find women in more executive positions in business? Because they are not tough or smart enough. Or so the arguments go.

Obviously, some blacks are lazy and some women cannot run the executive suite, though we have to be sure to compare those cases with lazy or inept white males. There are, however, several problems with this sort of attribution. First, such attributions are often too simplistic and overgeneralized. Some unemployed blacks (and whites) are lazy, but some are not. Some women are incapable of running major companies, but some have not been given the training and opportunities to try. It is sometimes accurate, but often dangerous, to infer only dispositional reasons for behaviors.

Second, such attributions often function as convenient excuses that have the effect of focusing attention away from other causes. If women are not present in high numbers in executive positions, it is convenient for those already there to assume that it is the fault of women rather than of their own prejudices or company policies. And even if there are at present no qualified women to elevate, some consideration should probably be given to why and how this can be remedied quickly.

Attributing problems to the dispositions of the afflicted is a way to blame the victim

(Ryan, 1971). Such cognitive strategies make those in the majority feel good, but they almost always ignore the subtle interplay of factors that affect our behavior, are frequently overgeneralized and simply inaccurate, and do nothing to solve the problem.

Culture   Heretofore we have been considering a variety of individual emotional and cognitive processes that might give rise to prejudice. Yet it is unlikely that these would create the kinds of problems prejudice encourages without also receiving considerable support from the larger culture. Certainly, for all its preaching about equality, American society has had, at best, ambivalent attitudes toward its various minorities. Until comparatively recently, it was simply an article of social reality that blacks, Hispanics, women, and so on were inferior to white males. Incidentally, America was far from alone in such beliefs; almost every society has one or more minority groups generally considered to be deficient by the dominant majority.

It is, of course, no secret how such prejudice is learned. In many families prejudice is taught explicitly and in others certain experiences will lead to prejudice. The child who encounters only black maids and Joannas is not likely to have the basis for positive attitudes toward blacks or to understand that he is seeing an unrepresentative sample. Moreover, the mass media may exert a major role in supporting if not actually creating prejudice. For example, until the consciousness of American whites was raised dramatically during the 1960s, media portrayal of blacks was largely negative. Blacks were portrayed primarily as criminals or servants (Liebert, Sprafkin, & Davidson, 1982). Only recently have blacks occupied roles in television dramas where their race was largely irrelevant, "The Cosby Show" being a prime example.

Cultures also play a powerful if indirect role in encouraging prejudice by making some activities and achievements more valued than

Such radio and television programs as "Amos 'n' Andy" played heavily on stereotypes of minority groups.

others. Western society in general places far more emphasis on those things men have traditionally done well than those things at which women have excelled. Would you rather spend the day with the president of a major company or with the winner of a Homemaker of the Year contest? Well, the former is likely to be more interesting, you say. But only, you should realize, in terms of the values of this culture. Why does a newspaper feature a day in the life of a wealthy socialite but not a day in the life of a black welfare mother struggling to raise a family under much less attractive circumstances? If you think about why the life of the former seems more interesting to most people, it may help you understand some of the implicit values our culture has about what is valuable and important.

Earlier we cautioned against the too-easy assumption that prejudice is a matter of flawed personalities or cognitive processes gone astray. We need to consider also the cultural factors that create and maintain prejudice. However, by the same token, we must beware of trying to reduce all prejudice to cultural racism. The notion that prejudice is a cultural problem is attractive both intellectually and morally, but again, taken by itself the model is too simplistic. There is no doubt that American culture has encouraged overt prejudice and discrimination against a wide range of people. On the other hand, it is also obvious that within a given culture there are wide individual differences in degrees of prejudice. Some people manage to transcend, at least to a degree, their cultural backgrounds. Our histories and cultures strongly influence us but they do not control us.

SUMMARY

Prejudice is an attitude with belief (stereotype), affective, and behavioral (discrimination) components. Several major theories of prejudice each emphasize different aspects of this complex state. For example, the scapegoating model suggests that people who are frustrated will blame a convenient minority group for their problems. The theory of authoritarian personality also sees prejudice as an individual problem; in this case, certain people are thought to have warped personalities that lead them to blame others for their own shortcomings. The major problem with both of these models is that they ignore the cultural and societal causes of prejudice and they assume that prejudice is a special feeling possessed only by some people. However, several features of life common to us all also promote prejudice. For example, we tend to favor members of our own group over those of other groups, even when the "groups" are entirely artificial. We tend to assume that people from other groups have values different from our own. Because members of targeted groups often are economically and educationally disadvantaged, we tend to attribute the causes of their disadvantage to something about themselves as persons, a manifestation of the fundamental attribution error. Cultural theories suggest that our general culture prepares us to dislike and distrust other groups of people. In some cases, this comes through direct socialization that some people are inferior; in other cases it happens because the culture emphasizes the achievements of some people more than others.

DISCRIMINATION

Stereotypes are the belief component and prejudices are the affective component of racism; discrimination is the behavioral aspect of racism. In some respects, discrimination is the most important of the three components. We may feel that stereotypes are somehow wrong and we may deplore prejudice, but until these are activated into concrete behavioral discrimination they are private and do not directly damage other people. You may hate college professors as much as you wish, but until you either state your prejudices or discriminate against professors, your stereotypes and prejudices create no problems for that group.

WHEN DO PEOPLE DISCRIMINATE?

Throughout this text we have made the point that our social behavior is a joint product of our values and motives on the one hand and our perceptions of situational forces on the other. We have, for example, suggested that people often try to maximize their rewards but that situations often determine what will be rewarding and costly. In Chapter 8 on internal and external controls over behavior, we explicitly noted that attitudes and values often have less control over behavior than do situational forces (as mediated by our thoughts).

Thus, it should come as no surprise to you to learn that our feelings and thoughts about other people do not inevitably lead to corresponding behaviors. Just as LaPierre's prejudiced hotel managers (Chapter 8) did not usually reject a Chinese couple, so in everyday life many people with firm prejudices do not overtly discriminate. At the same time, some people who do not have deep-seated prejudices may nevertheless actively discriminate if such behavior seems appropriate to them. For example, a person who has no prejudice against women may still refuse to hire a woman for a construction job because of perceptions that other workers might care. Or a person who has no fundamental bias against blacks might still prefer that blacks not join her club because it might drive away members she likes. We do not hold such people up as paragons of virtue or moral courage, but for what follows it is crucial to remember that prejudice does not inevitably lead to discrimination, nor does discrimination inevitably result from prejudice.

It is useful to examine this question in terms of the reasoned theory of action developed by Fishbein and Ajzen discussed in Chapter 8. You will recall that the major determinant of behavior (in this case, discrimination) is intention (to discriminate). Intentions in turn are caused by two major classes of variables: attitudes toward the act and subjective norms. Specifically, the intention to discriminate is caused by prejudice (attitude) and norms about discriminating. The subjective-norm component has two subparts. The first is the normative beliefs themselves and the second is the motivation to comply with these beliefs. The normative beliefs correspond to all the pressures brought to bear on a person by family, friends, culture, and society (and internalized values) to discriminate or not, and the motivational component refers to how strongly the person wants to conform to these demands. Although this component may also include internalized norms, it generally corresponds to external pressures.

Thus, discrimination is produced by intentions, which are in turn produced by a combination of prejudice and societal pressures. These latter two components are additively related, so either can produce the relevant intention if strong enough. This is why the intensely racist Ku Klux Klan member will still march in the streets to voice his prejudices despite strong legal and community pressures not to. Conversely, the nonprejudiced person (for whom the attitude component is low) will nevertheless discriminate if societal pressures are strong enough. For example, one of the tragedies of a totally racist society (such as the present one in South Africa) is that it becomes almost impossible to have friendships across racial lines just because the legal and peer pressures are too strong. It may seem to outsiders that an individual white should be willing to overcome such pressures for friendship and compassion. But to do so puts one in a position of possibly having to go to jail and losing all one's friends; the force of the unprejudiced attitudes must be very strong to overcome the immense norm component.

The model that we developed extensively in Chapter 8 does not explain all discrimination. It does, however, provide an important orientation. It suggests that prejudice alone will not lead to discrimination if there are strong external pressures in the form of informal norms and laws that counteract the prejudice. It also suggests that reducing prejudice is not likely to eliminate discrimination if there are strong built-in cultural and institutional pressures that support the prejudice. Prejudice is an important cause of discrimination, but it is not the only, and frequently not even the most important, cause.

KINDS OF DISCRIMINATION

One thing that makes it so difficult to deal with discrimination is that discrimination is not always blatantly obvious nor intended. We would all agree that the person who refuses to give a female student an A because females are stupid (yes, I once had a colleague who made exactly that argument) is engaging in blatant sexism and discrimination. Or the person who refuses to hire blacks because he claims they smell funny has certainly translated his racist views into overt discrimination. But what about the person who merely administers a policy that is indirectly discriminating; for example, what about the admissions director who uses admissions criteria (such as SAT tests) that favor whites over blacks (for whatever reasons)? In such cases (and they are numerous), there has been no conscious attempt to discriminate and in some sense the causes reside not in the immediate administrator of the policy but in larger historical and institutional forces. Naturally, the admissions director resents being accused of discrimination, but just as naturally those who are victimized by the admissions criteria are frustrated and look to blame the most visible cog in a very large wheel. A full discussion of discrimination thus involves more than psychology, because institutional and cultural factors must also be considered.

Subtle Forms   Discrimination is not always overt: there are subtle ways it can be displayed. Let us cite some examples, some of which have been discussed earlier in this and other chapters. One indirect form of discrimination is to refuse to do something for one group that one might do for another. For example, I was once accused (unjustly I thought) of being biased against Hispanics because I did not give a Hispanic student a chance to redo a miserable term paper. In fact, I give no one second chances on term papers (as one student said, "He's equally mean to everyone"), but the charge did make me think about whether I inadvertently gave more help to Anglo students. Did I have a nonconscious feeling that Hispanic students couldn't write well to begin with and hence couldn't do well on papers despite any help I might give? If I harbored

such a feeling (and I don't think I did), I might be more inclined to help Anglo students than Hispanic students.

One experimental demonstration of subtle discrimination has been called the "wrong number technique." Gaertner and Bickman (1971) had confederates with obviously black or white speech patterns call black and white subjects. The caller said he was trying to get a garage to repair his stalled car, and he had obviously dialed the wrong number. Because he had just used his last coin to make the call, he asked the subject to call the garage for him. While two-thirds of the subjects were willing to call for the white, more blacks (60%) than whites (53%) were willing to make the call for the black stranded motorist. Put another way, whites were more willing to help a white, whereas blacks did not discriminate as much. Members of minority groups often find themselves subjected to these annoying and sometimes important forms of bias.

It is common for people to be more formal and less friendly with people they do not like, and members of minority groups may find themselves the victims of this kind of coolness. Earlier in the chapter we discussed work by Word, Zanna, and Cooper that suggested that white interviewers often adopt a more negative nonverbal demeanor with black interviewees. At other times, whites may try to act more friendly toward blacks in an effort to hide or compensate for prejudices, which only leads them to feel uncomfortable in the situation (Ickes, 1984) and probably provides leakage cues (Chapter 5) for real feelings and contributes to perceptions by the blacks of hypocrisy by the whites.

Other studies suggest that discrimination may be withheld under some circumstances but prevail under others. Gaertner and Dovidio (1986) have argued that most people genuinely hold egalitarian values but also have negative racial attitudes. Such people will be motivated to behave in an unbiased way to fulfill their values and will do so when there is strong support for nondiscrimination. However, when the normative structure is less clear or pressing, such people will be less concerned about presenting a public image of fairness, and the underlying negative racial attitudes may lead to discrimination. This model suggests that people will behave positively toward blacks and members of other minority groups when they think this is what will be approved, but they will behave more negatively when such normative standards are weak.

For example, Frey and Gaertner (1986) have shown that whites help blacks as much as they help whites when norms support helping, but whites help blacks less in the absence of such norms. Norms are usually less active as controls over behavior when the behavior is more private. Donnerstein and Donnerstein (1973) showed that aggression directed toward blacks by whites in an experimental setting was less when a record of the subjects' responses was to be kept than when a record was not to be kept. In fact, subjects were less aggressive to blacks than to whites in the record condition but more aggressive in the nonrecord condition (see Figure 16.1). Presumably, subjects worried more about what others would think when their behavior was to be recorded and open to scrutiny. Also, discrimination may be more powerful when the object of the behavior has no chance to retaliate. Donnerstein, Donnerstein, Simon, and Ditrichs (1972) found that whites were less aggressive to blacks than to whites when the target could retaliate, but that the opposite was true when no retaliation was possible.

The Gaertner and Dovidio approach emphasizes conflict between culturally provided values of egalitarianism and a more diffuse negative affect toward blacks. Katz (1981) has argued that many white people have a largely unconscious ambivalence between positive and negative feelings toward blacks. When the white person who has such a conflict of feelings performs a negative behavior toward a black person (such as refusing to hire him), this conflict will demand resolution. One reso-

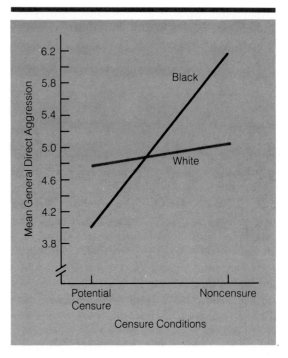

FIGURE 16.1   Mean Aggression toward Black and White Targets by White Subjects as a Function of Whether the Aggressive Responses Were Recorded or Not. Note that the white subjects were less aggressive to the black target than to the white target when their responses could be recorded and they were presumably subject to public censure for their behavior. However, when the responses were not recorded, and subjects could not be held responsible for their behavior, subjects were more aggressive toward the black target.

lution is to devalue the black person ("He wasn't qualified for the job"). Another resolution is to help the person by way of compensation, say, by sending the applicant to another employer with a job opening. Situational norms and availability of responses will determine which course is chosen, but the prediction that those white people with ambivalent attitudes toward blacks will behave more extremely to blacks than to whites has been confirmed (Katz, Wackenhut, & Hass, 1986).

Members of minority groups may also not get the benefit of the doubt often. For example, in one classic study, Pheterson, Kiesler, and Goldberg (1971) found that prize-winning paintings were rated equally high when ascribed to male and female painters, but that nonprize paintings were rated more favorably when ascribed to males. Those who excel may not suffer as much from discrimination as those who are merely competent. In that regard, people may attribute the causes of male and female success differently. Males are seen as succeeding because of high ability whereas females are seen as succeeding because of hard work (Taynor & Deaux, 1973). This may not seem to be particularly damaging to women until you realize that hard work is considered a more variable quality than ability. The woman who achieves success with hard work may be working hard today, but we cannot be sure about tomorrow. In contrast, the man with high ability will continue to have ability.

Futhermore, members of minority groups may be concerned that their stereotypic behaviors may trigger inferences of additional stereotypic traits. Research by Schneider and Blankmeyer (1986) suggests that people will infer stereotypic behaviors and traits only (1) when stereotypes are salient (which loads an inference gun) and (2) when the target person exhibits some stereotypic behaviors (which pulls the inference trigger). For example, a former mental patient will be given the benefit of the doubt by most people, but when he begins to exhibit some symptoms of mental illness, people tend to infer that he will perform many others. This would suggest that members of stigmatized groups might carefully watch their behavior lest they give others ammunition for assuming they are just like the typical whatever.

Interpersonal Mischief   When discrimination is subtle, there will be inevitable conflicts between overt and subtle messages. The victims of prejudice may have learned from long and bitter experience that others are insincere in their protestations of being unprejudiced. The prejudiced person may not—

probably does not—realize that he is in fact giving off abundant cues that reveal what he is trying so hard to hide. Of course, the problems are not all one-sided. The black, Hispanic, former mental patient, woman, or whoever may adopt the kind of defensive stance that leads her to see prejudice where none was intended or conveyed (insofar as this can be judged). The fact that this is understandable does not make matters easier for those who have to interact with defensive targets. All of this creates a large amount of interpersonal mischief and makes one wonder how it is that victims of prejudice and their former tormenters can ever make peace. We now turn, then, to the issue of reducing prejudice.

SUMMARY

Discrimination refers to behavior usually based on prejudice. Fishbein and Ajzen's theory of reasoned action suggests that an intention to discriminate is based both on prejudice (an attitude) and on norms that favor or inhibit discrimination. Thus, prejudiced people do not always discriminate if norms favor fairness, but the relatively nonprejudiced person may discriminate if norms favor such behavior. One problem with discrimination is that many of its forms may be quite subtle, such as not being as helpful to targets of prejudice, helping or hurting them only under certain circumstances, and communicating negative affect in subtle, nonverbal ways. Unfortunately, such people often feel they are unprejudiced but their behavior appears hypocritical to the targets of their discrimination.

REDUCING PREJUDICE

HAVE WE MADE PROGRESS?

We have explored many of the causes of prejudice and discrimination. But what can we do to eliminate these negative aspects of our social life? In Chapter 15, we saw that there are a variety of practical, political, and moral reasons for why aggression cannot be stopped simply by removing the factors that facilitate it. The same is true for prejudice. We cannot easily change the fact that some people are economically insecure and blame convenient victims, nor can we change prejudiced personalities and families who preach racial and ethnic-group hatred, short of massive psychotherapy. Racism is a part of the life of our culture as it has been of nearly every culture, and cultures do not change overnight.

Changes in Prejudice   Nonetheless, progress is possible. Many (including the present author) would argue that we have made substantial progress within the past 50 years, especially within the past 25 or so. The *Brown* decision by the Supreme Court in 1954 was followed by other Court decisions that made overt discrimination more difficult, and the Civil Rights Act of 1964 abolished most of the remaining legal bases for discrimination. With fits and starts, the courts and legislative bodies, in combination with active pressure by various groups, have moved American society toward equality of opportunity, if not yet equality of achievement. There are those who

We have made progress in abolishing at least blatant forms of discrimination.

would argue that we have moved too fast, that discrimination against minority groups has been replaced by discrimination against majorities, that various solutions to institutional racism are neither fair nor useful in the long run. But whatever your feelings about the solutions, no one can deny that we have seen a lot of change in the past few decades.

Consider: in the 1940s many major universities had few Jewish or black students (and no women). In the South there were *no* black students at most universities, including state universities that were paid for in part by black taxpayers. Jackie Robinson, the first black major-league baseball player, joined the Brooklyn Dodgers in the late 1940s. Most college athletic teams were completely white until well into the 1950s, and most Southern universities had no black athletes until the 1960s. Until the middle 1960s, blacks sat in the backs of buses in the South and had their own drinking fountains and restrooms. In the North as well as in the South, almost all black children attended all-black or nearly all-black schools. The only blacks one saw in law firms and major corporations were the janitors.

Let us beware of painting too rosy a picture—we have a long way to go before we have racial equality in economic, political, and educational achievement, and even further to go before race becomes as irrelevant as height or hair color (which is to say that it is noticed but not made much of). Indeed, recent analyses of census data on health, education, and income suggest that gaps between white and black Americans are still wide and in some areas may be growing (Dovidio & Gaertner, 1986; Jones, 1986). Still, there have been advances. Few if any societies in history have reduced so much overt discrimination in such a short period. But we have only done the easy work. It will be harder to root out the more subtle and institutionalized forms of racism.

Have these changes been accompanied by corresponding reductions in stereotypes and attitudes? On the surface, yes. For stereotypes, we have data from Princeton students in the

TABLE 16.2   PERCENTAGE OF PRINCETON UNIVERSITY STUDENTS WHO CHECKED THAT VARIOUS TRAITS WERE CHARACTERISTIC OF JEWS AND NEGROES, AT THREE DIFFERENT TIMES.

	Jews				*Negroes*		
	1933	*1952*	*1969*		*1933*	*1951*	*1969*
Shrewd	79	47	30	Superstitious	84	41	13
Mercenary	49	28	15	Lazy	75	31	26
Sly	20	14	07	Ignorant	38	24	11
Intelligent	29	37	37	Musical	26	33	47
Ambitious	21	28	48				

SOURCE: Karlins, Coffman, & Walters, 1969.

early 1930s, the 1950s, and the late 1960s (Gilbert, 1951; Karlins, Coffman, & Walters, 1969; Katz & Braly, 1933). As Table 16.2 shows, there have been fairly sharp declines in the attribution of negative traits to Jews and Negroes; those traits for which there are still substantial stereotypes are generally positive.

For attitudes, we also have a series of public opinion polls for nearly the past 50 years (Schuman, Steeh, & Bobo, 1985). On most such measures there have been real and substantial reductions. For example, in 1942 only 36% of national respondents said that having a black move into the same block would make no difference to them, compared to 85% in 1972. From 1942 to 1982, the percentage of people who endorsed a statement that blacks and whites should go to the same rather than racially separate schools increased from 32% to 90%. From 1958 to 1983, the percentage of people who claimed they would vote for a well-qualified black for president increased from 37% to 81%. Agreement with a statement that blacks and whites were equally intelligent increased from 47% to 77% from 1942 to 1968. The same studies, however, also show limited and basically nonincreasing support for particular social and legal policies, such as bussing and government intervention in employment. For example, fewer than 40% of Americans support the idea that the federal government should help ensure equal job treatment for blacks.

What was caused this change? No one knows for sure. One possibility is that educational levels have improved, and we know that people with more education tend to be less prejudiced. Another possibility is that white Americans have become more aware of the pervasive discrimination in the society and have been forced to reexamine their own attitudes in terms of their proclaimed values. Perhaps blacks and other minorities have been granted more favorable treatment in the mass media, especially television. Still another possibility is that reductions in prejudice do not represent individual change but the replacement of older prejudiced people by younger unprejudiced ones in survey samples. It is also possible that the changes result from more and better contacts between members of racial groups. Given increasing school desegregation and more blacks working beside whites, there certainly have been opportunities for such contact. We will consider that possibility in more detail shortly. Finally, perhaps changes in laws have helped to change prejudice through self-perception and social influence processes. We should note that these explanations are not mutually exclusive.

Superficial Change and Symbolic Racism
Yet another possible explanation for the apparent reductions in stereotypes and prejudices is that all these changes are only superficial and not real. It is clear that, at least among

reasonably well-educated people, it is no longer admirable to be prejudiced, and people who participate in public opinion polls may be reluctant to give their real attitudes. Although we can always be thankful for whatever improvements we find (including even superficial politeness and a decline in public use of racial and ethnic-group jokes and epithets), we ought not to identify superficial change with the fundamental change we want. Subtle measures of prejudice and discrimination reveal real evidence of continuing discrimination (Crosby, Bromley, & Saxe, 1980). Some have argued that these cosmetic changes have even been negative in the long run because they drive prejudice underground where it festers, out of contact with others who might change it.

David Sears, John McConahay, and their colleagues (Kinder & Sears, 1981, McConahay, 1982, 1986; Sears, Hensler, & Speer, 1979) have argued that overt prejudice and racism have become transformed into **symbolic racism** (McConahay now prefers the term *modern racism*). According to this model, many white people grow up with prejudiced attitudes that are learned early in life without much direct experience with black people. Such diffuse, underground attitudes are hard to change and may be hard to express openly because of social pressures. These prejudices can, however, be indirectly expressed by opposing social policies such as bussing or by opposing black political candidates. Such prejudice may be fueled by fears of aggression or fears of losing one's economic position, as well as by adherence to traditional American values of hard work, obedience, and discipline, so that the opposition to certain policies is symbolic of both prejudice and deeper concerns. Table 16.3 gives some items from McConahay's old-fashioned and modern racism scales.

The strongest argument for this position comes from data showing that opposition to social policies designed to benefit minorities has little relationship to self-interest. So opposition to bussing and minority job quotas is often as strong among people who are retired or have no children as among people who will be directly affected by these policies. In a study of voting in the 1969 and 1973 Los Angeles mayoral elections, which pitted a black candidate against a white candidate, indices of symbolic racism (essentially, opposition to social policies perceived to favor blacks) predicted voter preferences quite well. In addition, symbolic racism predicted voting far better than did personal vulnerabilities to the policies (Kinder & Sears, 1981), although others have argued that opposition to racially relevant policies is affected more by the whites' fear that

---

TABLE 16.3   ITEMS FROM MODERN AND OLD-FASHIONED RACISM SCALES.

Old-fashioned Racism

Generally speaking, I favor full racial integration. (disagree)
I am opposed to open or fair housing laws. (agree)
It is a bad idea for blacks and whites to marry one another. (agree)
Black people are generally not as smart as whites. (agree)

Modern Racism

Over the past few years, the government and news media have shown
  more respect to blacks than they deserve. (agree)
It is easy to understand the anger of black people in America. (disagree)
Blacks are getting too demanding in their push for equal rights. (agree)
Discrimination against blacks is no longer a problem in the United States. (agree)

SOURCE: From McConahay, 1986.

their higher status and greater access to resources are being threatened than by racist attitudes as such (Bobo, 1983).

On the other hand, symbolic racism does not predict even a majority of the variance in voting preferences. Weigel and Howes (1985) have further argued that symbolic racism and overt prejudice are not so discrepant as the Sears analysis suggests. They found that symbolic racism and direct measures of prejudice correlated quite highly with each other, and both measures were associated with adherence to traditional views of marriage and to religiosity, which suggests that prejudice against minority groups may be fueled by perceptions that they violate traditional values. (Other interpretations are also possible—for example, both prejudice and religious values may stem from more basic personality processes.)

Although many among us might find it acceptable and convenient to express our prejudices indirectly as opposition to certain social policies, we must be cautious in labeling opposition to such policies as symbolic racism. For one thing, there is reason to doubt that such opposition is a *disguised* version of racism—it may be perfectly overt racism. Second, there may be perfectly valid, nonracist reasons for opposing certain policies. One does not have to be racist to resent having one's children bussed several miles when one picked a particular neighborhood to live in because it was close to a good school. Opposition to bussing and other pro-equality policies may be based on many factors, although racism in either its overt or its disguised form is likely to be one of the important ones.

FACTORS IN CHANGE

The Contact Hypothesis   Perhaps the most frequently cited strategy for diminishing prejudice and discrimination is to establish better and more frequent contact between groups. Many of the hypotheses we considered for the causes of prejudice (such as stereotyping, misperceptions of dissimilarity, and cultural socialization) rest directly or indirectly on the notion that people from different groups do not have sufficient contact with one another to prevent misperceptions from occurring. It might be argued that if we could just engender more contact between groups we would dispel stereotypes and misperceptions. More formally, the *contact hypothesis* rests on three general assumptions: "(a) initial perceptions are unrealistic and potentially disconfirmable, (b) contact provides the evidence necessary to disconfirm these unrealistic beliefs, and (c) the disconfirming attributes of members generalize to the group as a whole" (Rothbart & John, 1985, p. 82). This hypothesis sounds reasonable, and so contact ought to work. But be careful. You can surely think of examples where contact increases rather than decreases hostilities. Returning to the example of Joanna at the beginning of the chapter, I doubt that my prejudices or those of anyone else were reduced by our year with her. Actually, we have known for many decades that mere contact between groups does not necessarily reduce prejudice (Allport, 1954).

Factors That Enhance the Power of Contact There has been general consensus that several conditions facilitate the ability of contact to reduce prejudice (Allport, 1954; Amir, 1969; Stephan, 1985). One is that members of the groups must have equal status at least within and perhaps outside the intergroup situation. As we have seen (Chapter 10), unequal power can distort relationships and lead to a variety of misperceptions, especially of the lower-status person by the higher. As one example, people who order others around are not ideally situated to conclude that the others have high competence.

Second, the members of the groups should be able to interact with one another in a nonstereotypic context; they should have opportunities to discover that they share many of the same problems and a common humanity that transcends their group membership. Miller,

Brewer, and Edwards (1985) have argued that if members of mutually hostile groups react to one another as interchangeable members of the group, stereotypes will likely be strengthened rather than diminished. Individualized interaction is important.

Third, there should be support by authority figures for the interaction and for reduction of prejudice. If members of both groups are mocked by others they respect for their changing attitudes, we could expect that the new, less prejudiced attitudes would never have the opportunity to jell.

Fourth, the basis of the interaction must be cooperative rather than competitive. Competition engenders hostility and hostility can lead to selective labeling, interpretations, and memory of behaviors, leading to support rather than disconfirmation of stereotypes.

Factors That Reduce the Power of Contact
In Chapter 3, we reviewed theories and data that suggest that schemata (of which stereotypes are one variety) are often extremely hard to change (see also Rothbart & John, 1985). For one thing, some traits and psychological characteristics are more closely tied to behavioral data than others (Rothbart & Park, 1986). One could easily determine whether a person is "brave" or "intelligent" by observing a sample of behavior; however, "lazy" (which is generally attributed to all minority groups by all majorities) is hard to document. Recall the conversation with my student (Chapter 3) in which he claimed that Mexican-Americans were lazy because they worked hard only when they were told to. One suspects that almost any behavior can be interpreted as evidence of laziness for this particular, prejudiced person.

Second, we often find ourselves in circumstances where behavioral disconfirmation of stereotypes is difficult. If you work only with blacks who have menial jobs, you are unlikely to discover that some blacks are smart, if only because the job does not readily encourage smart behaviors.

Third, you may recall the fundamental attribution error (Chapter 4), in which we tend to assume that the behavior of others reflects their dispositions. Put another way, we are insufficiently attentive to situational causes of behavior for other people. This may also make stereotype disconfirmation difficult (Pettigrew, 1979). I have always thought of myself as hard-working, but I used to have jobs during summers that were so grubby and boring that I found myself looking for excuses to slack off. There are some jobs that no one much enjoys, and that should be taken into account before we make attributions of laziness to people who hold these jobs. Similarly, members of minority groups may frequently find themselves in situations in which anger is appropriate and hostility hard to inhibit. For example, in some cities, police officers stop more black motorists than white motorists for seemingly random reasons. The police officer who stops more blacks than whites will discover that he gets more grief from blacks purely because he stops more of them. If he does not take account of the base-rates, he will attribute too much of the reaction to the person and race.

Fourth, recall that sometimes we set the stage for confirmation of our stereotypes through self-fulfilling prophecies. The university system in which I work tends to treat faculty as though they were lazy and unwilling to work hard without the stimulus of various bureaucratic prods. As a result, many professors perform their jobs strictly as defined and do little more. The police officer who is scared of a black man because he assumes he will be hostile may behave gruffly and engender that very hostility.

Fifth, even if one discovers that a particular member of another group does not fit the stereotype, one still has to generalize to the broader category, and this is often problematic. The person who sees a smart, hard-working Hispanic doctor may come to think of him as a doctor rather than as a Mexican-American or Cuban-American. This will allow her to confirm her stereotype that doctors are smart and hard-working while leaving the stereotype of Hispanics unmolested. Or she may create a subcategory of exceptions: "Well, he is one of the 'good ones.' I never said that *all* Hispanics were lazy." It is important to recall that we think of people in terms of prototypes. For many whites, the prototypical black is the fat welfare mother with six children or the drug dealer who is too lazy to look for honest work. Such people do exist, but they are not representative of the larger class of blacks. A prejudiced person finds it easy to dismiss the "good" examples as exceptions; they are exceptions to his or her prototype but not to the real category.

This is far from a complete list of ways that one can go wrong cognitively in trying to disconfirm stereotypes, but it should be sufficient to indicate that mere contact between groups is not sufficient to reduce stereotypes or prejudice. As Rothbart and John (1985) indicate, mere behavioral contact is likely to be ineffective unless active steps are taken to change the ways people process information about others.

Desegregation   It has been one of the unfortunate lessons of the massive school desegregation in our society during the past 20 years that desegregation does not necessarily lead to integration. In the original *Brown* decision, the Supreme Court relied to some extent on the testimony of psychologists and other social scientists that segregation fostered prejudice between blacks and whites, caused low self-esteem among blacks, and led to poor academic performance on the part of blacks. Presumably, desegregation could be expected to reverse these problems.

It has not quite worked out that way (Gerard, 1983). Several major studies have examined the consequences of desegregation, and the results have been disappointing. There is some evidence that black self-esteem rises in a desegregated environment, and mixed evidence that academic performance by blacks rises in desegregated schools (Stephan, 1978). But our

Schools are now mostly desegregated, but increased contact between black and white children does not necessarily reduce prejudice.

concern here is with reducing prejudice in the sense of fostering more positive attitudes toward members of other groups or increasing friendships across racial boundaries. There is real doubt that this has worked; indeed, some studies find substantial increases in prejudice when schools are integrated racially (Gerard & Miller, 1975; Stephan, 1978). Does that mean that desegregation has not worked? Possibly. Does that mean that it cannot work? Not necessarily.

Before we can conclude that desegregated schools cannot work, we need to be sure that the best possible strategies for getting it to work have been used. Several large-scale programs have shown that desegregation in conjunction with planning can reduce prejudice (Slavin, 1985). One of the most famous is the so-called jig-saw classroom (Aronson et al., 1978). Students are divided into teams to study a particular project. Each member of the team is assigned the role of being the expert on some facet of the project and brings his or her expertise back to the team. This technique seems to promote enjoyment of school, effective cooperation among team members, and liking for other members of the team, even

BOX 16.1

WHEN A BLACK FAMILY MOVES INTO THE NEIGHBORHOOD

It is no secret that many white people do not want to have black families and members of other minority groups live in their neighborhoods. Part of this reaction is probably based on racism, whether of the old-fashioned or the symbolic variety. In addition, many white people fear that when a neighborhood is desegregated, property prices may fall and their investments in their houses will be undercut. On the other hand, when neighborhoods are desegregated slowly enough to avoid panic selling of homes by whites, desegregation may have a positive effect on prejudice.

David Hamilton and his student George Bishop (Hamilton & Bishop, 1976) were interested in exactly what happens when a black family moves into a previously all-white neighborhood. They located eight all-white neighborhoods in towns around New Haven into which a black family was about to move. They then attempted to interview someone in every house in what they termed the microneighborhood of the target house. This consisted of the two houses on either side of the target house, the five closest houses across the street, and the three closest houses behind the target house. They were able to interview about

David Hamilton

half of such houses. They also interviewed families in 10 other neighborhoods in which a similar house was being sold but to a white family. These two types of neighborhoods were comparable on most measures taken before the new families moved in. Some families were interviewed before the new families moved in, whereas others were interviewed 1 month, 3 months, or 1 year later. It is important to examine such time effects because prejudice and racism may take time to develop and dissipate.

In an interview study, one of the toughest problems is deciding what to ask and how to ask it. Ideally, Hamilton and Bishop would have asked the white respondents how prejudiced they were and how much they resented having a black family move in. However, most of the respondents would probably have been unwilling to admit prejudice directly. So the researchers used a scale of symbolic racism that is less subject to desires to "look good" (McConahay, 1986). The researchers also did not want to alert the families to the purposes of the study, because the respondents might display more liberal attitudes than they felt. So the researchers did not ask directly about the new families. Instead they asked more indirect questions, such as, "Have there been any changes in the nature of the neighborhood in the last year or so?" and recorded whether the new family and its race were mentioned. Then, if the new family was mentioned, the interviewer could go on to ask questions about the new neighbor and the neighborhood in a natural way.

Several results were of major interest. First, even before the new family had moved in, the new black family was often mentioned in response to questions about changes in the neighborhood. Before the family moved in, 52% mentioned the new black family, and 1 month later 80% mentioned them; even 3 months later 76% of the interviewees mentioned the new family. By contrast, only 18% mentioned the new white family before the move, 71% a month after, and 37% 3 months later. In other words, the salience of the black families stayed high longer than did the salience of the white families. The fact of mention alone does not necessarily represent prejudice; having a black family move into a white area *is* a highly salient event. However, most of the neighborhood discussion about the new family had been quite negative. In general, there were no race differences in how much neighbors knew about the new family, although fewer people reported interactions with the new black family than with the new white family after a year (31% versus 50%). This suggests that there was more discussion about the black neighbor but more direct interaction with the white. There were no major differences on ratings of the nature of the neighborhood for those with the new black and new white neighbors. So the general results suggest that the neighborhoods were not much affected by whether the new family was black or white. What about prejudice? Symbolic racism scores were affected by the race of the family. Although respondents were equivalent before the new move-in, a year later the desegregated neighborhoods showed less prejudice.

In a follow-up study, Hamilton, Carpenter, and Bishop (1984) examined the economic and sociological consequences of the desegregation. Did property values decline in the integrated neighborhoods? Did the introduction of one black family lead to an exodus of white families? These authors examined available data a decade after the original study: there was no evidence that the desegregation had any economic or social effects at all. The integrated neighborhoods did not have a greater rate of turnover in the decade following, and all the neighborhoods had remained predominantly white. Some 2.9% of the homes in the originally desegregated neighborhoods were owned by blacks; the comparable figure for the segregated (10 years before) neighborhoods was 2.0%. There were no differences in property values in the two neighborhoods: resale values of houses sold in the 10-year period were not affected by segregation or integration.

Thus, we can summarize the results of this set of analyses quite simply. Having a black family move into a formerly all-white neighborhood is a highly salient event. The residents are fairly negative about this event, and they are cautious about meeting the new black neighbor; so the response could be characterized as cool but not hostile. Prejudice scores actually decline when a black family moves in. There are no discernible effects on property values or the nature of the neighborhood. We cannot claim that neighborhood desegregation never has bad effects and always reduces prejudice, but in this case the effects were generally minor and mostly positive.

The Hamilton–Bishop research illustrates another methodological point: interview data can be used to test basic hypotheses. It also illustrates some problems in doing interview studies. Only about half the families could be interviewed, and, of those, the researchers could not always ask the most direct forms of the questions they wanted to ask. Nonetheless, the data speak to important questions about the effects of desegregation.

when they are from different social, racial, or ethnic groups. Other similar programs that make use of cooperative learning have shown increases, sometimes dramatic, in such friendships, in achieving real integration (Slavin, 1985).

Another place where contact may have important effects is in integrating neighborhoods. What happens when a black family moves into a previously all-white neighborhood? According to data collected by Hamilton and Bishop (1976), such contact can reduce prejudice. Box 16.1 discusses their research in some detail.

Other Factors   We have paid special attention to contact between groups (mostly races) as one way in which prejudice can be reduced. Yet it seems clear that, however valuable contact may be, it does not fully account for the reductions in prejudice that seem to have occurred in the past 20–40 years. To conclude, we mention an additional factor worthy of discussion if only because there is a certain amount of commonsense misunderstanding about it. It used to be said in the early days of the civil rights movement that passing laws was ineffective because one can-

not change the hearts (and prejudices) of people by passing laws.

This is a mistaken attitude on at least two counts. In the first place, to some extent it misses the main moral argument. When people are overtly discriminated against in hiring and education, not to mention in politics, the most relevant concern is not with attitudinal prejudice but with putting a stop to the behavioral discrimination.

But what about the seeming commonsense notion that laws will not change the ways people think? We have, of course, no direct evidence one way or another as to whether the wave of civil rights legislation and court rulings that began in the mid-1950s actually played a role in changing attitudes and prejudice. It is true that white attitudes toward specific programs aimed at achieving equality have not improved much in the past 10 or 20 years, but at the same time other indices of prejudice have declined during that same period. So at a minimum it would seem that laws do not interfere with reducing prejudice and may actually enhance such reductions.

How could that happen? We do not know for certain, but there are several hypotheses

In recent years, the Equal Rights Amendment and other attempts to change the legal status and rights of women have generated enormous controversy.

that social psychologists might advance to explain such putative effects. First, from a self-perception point of view, attitudes are often based on behaviors. Whites who find themselves sitting on the bus beside blacks may eventually change their attitudes to match their behaviors.

Second, the actual legal changes may have been buttressed by support from political, religious, and economic leaders. It may or may not be an accident that civil rights legislation occurred at about the same time that the South (at which most such laws were directed) was trying to achieve economic parity with the rest of the country. Under such circumstances, state and community leaders may have found it advisable to submerge their own racist feelings in favor of a good public image. There were strong economic and political (not to mention moral) reasons for community leaders to make the best of the situation. Laws that have at least the tacit support of leaders may be effective in changing attitudes.

Prejudice and discrimination are hard to change because they exist at so many levels. People hold stereotypes that give rise to prejudices; these beliefs and feelings both stem from experiences within a given culture and are continually supported by that culture in small and sometimes large ways, both covertly and overtly. Yet, at some level, it is hard to know how we might change the values and norms of an entire culture, given that beliefs and values are, after all, products of individual thought processes. So we cannot change the individual without changing the society and the society cannot be changed without dealing with the individual. Perhaps all we can hope for is to make changes at one level (say the legal), wait for changes at another (say in terms of people's behaviors), which in turn may help to change attitudes and contribute to a climate conducive to additional cultural and societal change. This is not to say that we are doing or have done all that we can, but merely to recognize that change of the magnitude we are discussing will take time no matter how hard we push.

SUMMARY

Available data suggest that considerable progress has been made in the past 25 years or so in reducing both prejudice and discrimination. This may have resulted from greater education, more interracial contact, better media presentation of members of minority groups, and laws designed to reduce discrimination. Another possibility is that the changes are superficial; some data suggest that certain forms of discrimination have become more subtle rather than less frequent. The most commonly mentioned strategy for changing prejudice and discrimination is to provide more and better contact among members of minority groups. However, mere contact is not sufficient. For increased contact to have a chance to reduce prejudice, the contact must involve people with approximately equal status in a nonstereotypic context, must be supported by authority figures, and must be cooperative. Even under such favorable circumstances, however, a variety of social and cognitive factors work against real changes.

CHAPTER SUMMARY

■ Several terms refer to intergroup relations. *Prejudice* refers to a feeling toward a person or thing prior to or not based on actual experience. A *stereotype* is a set of beliefs about the personal attributes of a group of people. *Discrimination* is behavior that denies to individuals or groups of people equality of treatment that they may wish. Finally, *racism* is the use of power against a racial group defined as inferior: *individual racism* is close to prejudice; *institutional racism* occurs when the institutions of an entire society foster differences among groups; and *cultural racism* is the tendency to use the cultural values of people in the majority to devalue the accomplishments of those in minority groups.

- Stereotypes lead to prejudice, which in turn leads to discrimination and racism. However, these factors are loosely related and each can occur without the support of the others. Sometimes racism and discrimination lead to prejudice and stereotypes.

- Recently, social psychologists have focused on the cognitive underpinnings of stereotyping rather than on the content of stereotypes as such. The tendency has been to see stereotyping as an inevitable aspect of cognitive processing. When we place people into categories, we often see people within the category as having more similarities to each other than they do and we often play up the ways they differ from people in other groups. This is especially likely when the category is a group to which we do not belong.

- Illusory correlations occur when we see minority groups associated more with negative behaviors than we should. We may make this association because both negative behaviors and people from minority groups are distinctive stimuli.

- Most people do not think that their stereotypes apply to all people. Therefore, it might be preferable to construe stereotypes as hypotheses people have about members of groups. Although such hypotheses may be disconfirmed, a variety of cognitive and social factors conspire to confirm them.

- There are several theories of prejudice. Some, such as scapegoating and the theory of the authoritarian personality, suggest that prejudice is largely found among people who are frustrated or who have flawed personalities. Other theories emphasize common cognitive and social processes. For example, we all have a tendency to reject people in groups not our own, and we

also reject people whom we see as having different values and attitudes. In addition, we often attribute the negative behaviors of others to their own character. These factors need not lead to prejudice, but they often do, particularly when there is cultural support for negative images of certain groups in society.

- Discrimination is often based on negative attitudes (prejudice), but a full understanding of discrimination also requires understanding cultural, social, and situational norms.

- Overt discrimination may be inhibited for many reasons, but people may discriminate in more subtle ways, such as by helping people from certain groups less, being more negative toward them when equality norms are weak or nonsalient, or not giving them the benefit of the doubt. This leads to misunderstandings when a prejudiced person claims his or her behavior is nondiscriminating but others responding to the subtle cues see a larger amount of discrimination.

- Several studies show lessening prejudice and discrimination in the past 25 years. However, whites have not fully accepted policies designed to reduce inequalities that still persist in health, education, and economic areas. One suggestion has been that people remain prejudiced but cannot express these attitudes overtly, so they do so in symbolic ways by opposing school bussing, hiring policies and quotas, and minority politicians.

- The most popular suggestion for reducing prejudice has been to increase contact between groups. However, this does not always work and may even increase prejudice unless several conditions are met: people from the two groups should have equal power, the context of interaction should not be stereotypical, people should respond to one another in individualized ways, and there must be support from authority figures. Even with favorable contact, several cognitive and social factors may undercut changes in prejudice.

■ Desegregation as a tool to lower racial tensions has not been a resounding success. This results at least in part from less-than-optimal implementations, though several programs within schools have been shown to make desegregation more effective.

■ It is probable, though far from definitively proven, that changes in laws lessen both prejudice and overt discrimination.

PART FOUR

AFTERWORD

CHAPTER
17

SOCIAL PSYCHOLOGY AND LIFE

ike many social psychologists, I am sometimes contacted by reporters or asked to appear on talk shows and the like. Sometimes this works out well, but sometimes it does not. Here is a recent episode. The precipitating incident was the discovery by San Antonio police of a teenage hideout where devil worship allegedly took place, complete with animal sacrifices. I was called by a reporter for one of the local newspapers to answer questions about whether satanic music had caused this episode and more generally about the effects of listening to satanic music. Now, I have survived raising two teenagers without ever having been exposed to such music, and I told the reporter this. She then read me some lyrics and asked whether I approved of this sort of thing. What follows is a reconstructed conversation (I took some notes as I do in these situations).

DJS: My approval hardly matters, but I don't care for the lyrics and probably wouldn't care for the music that goes with it. I would be happier if such music did not exist, but that doesn't make it bad.

R: Could these lyrics influence children?

DJS: They could, but I doubt if they influence most kids.

R: Well, why not? How can you say that?

DJS: Several things would have to happen before the lyrics could have such an impact. First, kids would have to hear and pay attention to the lyrics. In my limited experience, rock lyrics are often hard to hear and kids don't seem to pay that much attention to their specifics.

R: But the lyrics could seep into their consciousness.

DJS: That's possible, but normally influence doesn't work quite that way.

R: But it's a proven fact, isn't it, that hidden messages played on tapes have a "subliminal" impact?

DJS: Such influence is far from a proven fact; I doubt that there is anything special about subliminal influence. Either you hear the message or you don't. If you don't then it has no effect, but if you do, then it might just have some influence—like any message you hear.

R: Well, what about those records where they put secret messages on backwards so they can work on your unconscious? It's a fact, isn't it, that these kind of hidden messages can make people do things?

DJS: That's pretty clearly nonsense. In the first place, I would have to have someone prove to me that record manufacturers went to the trouble to put lyrics on the records backward. It seems like a lot of work. Second, I would have to have someone prove to me that people can *hear* the backward words over all the music on the record itself. Third, I would want to be assured that people could *understand* backward speech; in my experience it's hard, even impossible, to know what is being said. Then we would still have to show that possibly nonexistent lyrics that no one can hear or understand can still influence behavior. I think the possibilities are quite remote.

R: (in an exasperated tone of voice) So what you are saying is that this kind of influence doesn't occur.

DJS: Exactly. That's just what I am saying.

R: I just wish you experts would get your acts together. I read in a magazine that some psychologist had shown that these backwards lyrics definitely influenced people. I have to give him some credibility because he was quoted in a national magazine.

DJS: Lots of fools are quoted by reporters. If the man said what you claim he said, he is probably a quack. I'd love to see the evidence for these assertions.

R: You just can't get a straight answer from psychologists—they want to make everything so complicated. And they never agree.

DJS: You can believe whomever you want, but I think you owe it to your readers to get the best information before them. I'll be happy to lay out my arguments in more detail if you wish. It's really quite logical and straightforward. Then you can present both points of view.

R: Well, I have a deadline, and I'm not sure I can get the article that I read. Suppose we talk about something else. You said that it's possible some kids would be influenced by rock lyrics. What kind of kids would be?

DJS: I really don't know, and I don't think anyone else does either.

R: Well, I just talked to Dr. P. [a local psychiatrist], and he had said that he had two or three troubled adolescent patients recently who had shown clear bad effects of listening to rock music all day.

DJS: But that isn't compelling evidence.

R: Why not?

DJS: Well, first, I would want to know what effects the psychiatrist was talking about—had these youngsters maimed old ladies or mutilated dogs, or just done more of what they had been doing? It's also possible that these effects might be in the eye of the beholder. Furthermore, we have to be careful about what's causing what. When kids sit around all day

doing the same thing—whether listening to satanic rock or Beethoven—they might be negatively affected. Furthermore, before drawing any conclusions, I would want to know something about what the more typical experiences are for his patients: do his patients who listen to a certain kind of rock music get into more trouble than his patients who do not? And a sample of troubled adolescents who were seeking psychiatric care is not an appropriate sample for drawing conclusions about adolescents at large. I'm not saying that he is wrong—some people are probably affected by the music—but I am saying that you can't conclude much from a few unrepresentative cases.

R: You sure are argumentative. Why do you have to make everything so complex? It's common sense that this kind of music would harm kids, and I don't know why you resist such an obvious conclusion.

DJS: I don't think I'm resisting anything. I've already said that such music could influence kids, but that the effects are likely to be subtle, confined to only a few, and hardly the mechanical, robotlike influence you are suggesting.

R: Then you're saying that you can't make a definitive statement.

DJS: Correct.

R: Then you're saying that it's really a matter of opinion.

DJS: Incorrect.

R: But every time I bring up someone else's opinion you tell me they are wrong. Now who am I supposed to believe?

DJS: I appreciate that this is frustrating, but that's why we have scientific journals, so that people can lay out the evidence for their conclusions and let other people criticize.

R: And meanwhile these kids are mutilating dogs in their satanic rituals, and they could start on people next.

DJS: I hardly think we face a crisis situation here.

R: Probably not, but it's still frustrating. You're lucky to be in a business where you have the luxury of looking at things from all sides. I have to keep things simple for my readers.

This is a good place to stop. The conversation went on for some time and actually became quite friendly. We chatted some about whether we should ban satanic records or put warnings on the labels, and I explained that certain theories (such as Brehm's reactance theory) would predict that this would only make people want to buy the forbidden records. She wondered about a national law to censor lyrics, and we discussed the possibility that censorship here, as in most places, would not solve the problem it tries to eradicate and would create many others. We also discussed whether these adolescents had the right to participate in a satanic cult in view of our freedom of religion in this country. We finally ended the conversation after an hour or so. As far as I know the article never appeared.

We have surveyed the terrain of social psychology and have even stopped to look at some of the scenery. Now is a good time to ask whether this has all been worthwhile. Is it all a matter of opinion? Does all this scientific endeavor lead to any sort of worthwhile conclusions about human behavior? There are at least three important questions we might ask ourselves. First, have we learned anything at all? Is social psychology a cumulative science, one that within its short lifetime can show obvious signs of progress in what we know and how we know it? Second, is what we know worth knowing? Is it relevant, applicable, useful in any meaningful sense? And third, have our theoretical and methodological approaches limited us in important ways?

HAVE WE LEARNED ANYTHING?

Have we moved beyond that degree of knowledge common to all people that we might identify with common sense? Have you specifically learned some things about social behavior in this course that you did not know before or could not have learned from studying great novels or social philosophy? Naturally I cannot answer that question for you, but I would certainly hope that the answer is yes.

COMMON SENSE

The claim is often made that so much of what we have learned in social psychology is about what any intelligent grandmother would know: "It's all common sense" or "Everybody knows that." I would not want to take anything away from common sense; socially adept people know many things about how to get along in the social world that we have yet to capture in our laboratories. But I also think social psychologists have some wisdom that is not commonsensical.

Validation   Common sense sometimes is self-contradictory: "absence makes the heart grow fonder" but "out of sight, out of mind." Not only do our distillations of common sense come into conflict, but sometimes they are downright wrong. I think I need not remind you of all the silly things people have believed throughout the ages: the world is flat, witches cast spells, black people are hardly more intelligent than apes, women cannot benefit from education, children are incapable of learning unless they are beaten for their mistakes, the sun revolves around the earth—the list goes on. Such beliefs were part of common sense and were held by the brightest and best-educated people of the times.

There was a period, perhaps not fully over, when social psychologists seemed particularly enamored of explanations that were counterintuitive, that explicitly violated everyday understandings (Ring, 1967). The idea seems to be that science must undermine common sense to buttress its own position. But social psychology need not take as its mission the overthrow of common sense; sometimes grandmothers are right. Nor is there any reason to devalue the generalizations of social psychology because they are what nearly everyone seems to know; sometimes grandmothers are wrong. We therefore need ways of discovering which brands and whose brands of common sense are correct. Although empirical research is not an infallible guide to truth, it is surely better than taking a public opinion poll. Common sense has been wrong often enough that we need the added confidence provided by research. We should monitor common sense for the same reasons that the public health departments check the water supply—to make sure it is safe for consumption. Opinions, no matter how expert they may be, are no substitute for hard evidence.

The Value of Theory   Another major advantage of striving for scientific wisdom is that science helps us integrate knowledge and place it within a larger, more understandable context. For example, everyone knows at some level that similarity leads to attraction, but most people do not know why. But when one examines this "rule" in the context of a theory that similarity is rewarding, one can immediately begin to think of circumstances when similarity is *not* rewarding. Similarly, a good theory about the effects of mass media (including satanic music) on behavior would help us understand who is influenced by what under which circumstances. The social psychologist's theory helps us to understand more deeply and fully, to see exceptions, to be more precise, to know what further questions to ask.

Salience   Because of theories and research, a good many "rules" of behavior have been discovered in social psychological laboratories, and social psychology research has opened new areas of inquiry. It is, for example, unlikely that the role of televised violence on aggression would have been given the attention it has been given if we merely depended on common sense. Nor is it likely that we would have investigated the biases produced by our cognitive schemata without benefit of our research and theories, because common sense suggests that our sensory organs provide us with reliable information about the world. The idea that there are advantages to having psychological characteristics of both genders is not a new idea and is perfectly obvious once you hear it, but clearly the attention that has been given to that idea

has been stimulated by an outpouring of empirical research. I can't speak for your grandmother, but mine would not have known that sometimes people change their attitudes to match their behaviors; she would have taken the commonsensical position that attitudes cause behavior and not the reverse. Of course, the cognitive dissonance and self-perception theory predictions *seem* perfectly sensible when they are explained, but these ideas have not been a part of the common wisdom.

I may seem to have belabored an obvious point, but I suspect it is not obvious to everyone. Students are typically impressed with the number of commonsense truths they find in social psychology texts, and they often reject those generalizations that do not fit their preconceived beliefs. It does not diminish the social psychology enterprise to either confirm or disconfirm common sense. It diminishes common sense to refuse to consider the best scientific consensus about social behavior.

COMPLEXITY

What can we do about the reporter's frustration (and perhaps yours as well) that by abandoning common sense we enter a realm where all generalizations have an iffy quality, where nothing is straightforward, where every conclusion is qualified, where, in short, explanations seem too complex? This is, I think, a serious problem, and one that greatly undercuts public confidence in social psychology.

There are really two quite separate issues involved here. The first is why our explanations seem so complex. The other is what effects our complex explanations have on our abilities to apply what we have learned to the problems we face in real life.

Why Explanations Are Complex   There are two major reasons why social psychology produces seemingly complex and indefinite explanations for events. The first is that human behavior *is* complex. We sometimes have the

Steven J. Sherman　　　Harry Reis　　　　Thomas Ostrom　　　David Messick

Scientific research is published in journals after evaluation by other scientists and editors who decide if the research makes a significant contribution to our knowledge. Steven "Jim" Sherman and Harry Reis are editors of the *Journal of Personality and Social Psychology,* and Thomas Ostrom is the immediate past editor and David Messick the present editor of the *Journal of Experimental Social Psychology.*

expectation that things we experience immediately ought to be easy to understand, but generally this is not true. Explanations in the physical and biological sciences are also quite complex, but most people do not dwell on the complexity of those explanations, because they spend little of their free time thinking about molecules or DNA. It is probably no easier to explain simply which teenagers will be affected by rock music than to explain why some people get cancer and others do not. So our explanations are complex because that's the way the world is.

Second, as a new science, psychology, and especially social psychology, does not have the highly developed theories necessary to integrate a wide range of phenomena under a few basic laws. So at times when we psychologists say that we don't know, we should be taken at our word. Case in point. We know almost nothing about how listening to rock music affects people's thoughts and behaviors because, to the best of my knowledge, there has been little research on the topic. With the reporter, I struggled to apply what we *do* know about social influence and the effects of television on behavior to a perhaps far-different domain. If our theories had been

more highly developed or more extensively integrated, I could have made this translation with more confidence. Let me be clear: I am not suggesting that we close up shop and declare an intellectual bankruptcy sale. We can and should work with the theories we have, but sometimes we will falter. And so we hedge, and appropriately so. Nevertheless, as the history of other sciences has shown, we can find the results of science highly useful long before we know all the answers to important questions.

Applications This raises the whole question of how we can apply the theories and generalizations we have. We consider this in more detail in the next section, but for now let us focus briefly on how complexity affects application. Given that there are many psychological principles that can apply to a given bit of behavior, how do we decide which to apply? As one example, consider the popular (in some circles) proposal that some rock albums should be censored, accompanied by warning labels concerning the lyrics, or that the sale of such albums be restricted to those 18 years and older. What would social psychologists predict about the effectiveness of such policies?

Reactance theory predicts that the denial of freedom to buy the albums of one's choice would make them even more appealing, thus defeating the very purpose of the law. On the other hand, cognitive dissonance theory predicts that if the penalties were barely strong enough to keep people from buying the albums, favorability toward the albums would decrease as people reduced their dissonance between liking the albums and not buying them. The theory of reasoned action (Chapter 8) points out that if external, normative pressures are strong enough, behavior may not match attitudes—in other words, even favorable attitudes toward the albums could be overcome by strong legal pressure. On the other hand, the censorship might make attitudes toward the albums positive enough to overcome these legal forces by making the albums seem even more interesting. Because attitudes are often changed more when people comprehend the message (Chapter 7), censorship could also indirectly make attitudes toward the music more favorable by encouraging people to listen more carefully to the lyrics; if that happened, and to the extent that attitudes affect behavior, the censorship might thereby actually produce behavior more in line with the lyrics. So which principles win?

There is no easy answer, but I have two observations. The first is that successful applications require a certain amount of experience. One does not master social psychology or physics by taking a single course. We take for granted the fact that experts in the physical and biological sciences must have a high degree of training before they are qualified to make pronouncements about what will or will not fly or explode. We do not turn over the launching of spaceships or the invention of new computer chips to garage hobbyists, otherwise savvy grandmothers, or students with an introductory physics course fresh under their belts. Yet, in the behavioral sciences the silliest people, the equivalent of garage hobbyists, often get cited for their expert opinions. Anyone can write a book and even get it pub-

Signs such as these may or may not be effective advertising techniques; theories about such effects would help guide research to find out.

lished by some press, and it is not all that hard to get your name cited in a mass-circulation magazine, but this does not guarantee wisdom. Personally, I am very suspicious of anyone who believes that the answers to almost any problem of consequence are simple. Any solution that is only "ten easy steps" is likely to be a very trivial solution to a very trivial problem. Real experts, the kinds we can trust, recognize that knowledge and its application are not easy.

Second, in many cases we need more direct research on the issues we want to solve. Because so many theories can be brought to bear on whether kids are affected by satanic music, we need direct, focused research to investigate the issue. As we saw when we considered the issue of whether television affected violence, we did the research to find out; several theories and their supporting data suggested that watching TV violence *could* affect behavior, but we needed research "in the field"—in real-life settings—to be confident that everything would fall into place. Applied research is hard to do, and it may be frustrating to wait around for its completion. But this is the only way to get the answers we want.

SUMMARY

Some have argued that social psychology has shown little to us not already available as common sense. But common sense is not always correct, and much of the wisdom of the field is not consistent with common sense. Moreover, even if the generalizations of social psychology research turn out to be no more than versions of common sense, it is still important to have validated those beliefs scientifically. In addition, theory and research provide a broader context for understanding and make certain issues salient for further inquiry and research.

Another criticism has been that social psychological theories are far too complex. This results in part from the complexity of human behavior but also from the relatively underdeveloped theories in use. It also requires a fair amount of experience to be able to apply the results of psychological research to human behavior appropriately.

IS WHAT WE HAVE LEARNED RELEVANT?

Let's assume for the moment that we agree that social psychologists have enriched our understanding of human behavior. We have *not* said that they have uncovered eternal truths or even that they are moving in that direction rapidly, but only that social psychology has taught us some things we would not have otherwise learned.

Next question: is what we have learned useful in any sense? Science may or may not be a more valid road to supreme knowledge than philosophy, but clearly one of the reasons science is better supported by the public is that there is payoff in the form of applications. There is, in fact, very little doubt that the rapid rise in our level of comfort, freedom from disease, and the like is due to the remarkable advances in science over the past two centuries or so. Science may or may not arrive at

ultimate truths, but it arrives at ones that work. Airplanes fly, medicines heal, space vehicles get to the moon, bridges support enormous loads, and cars, telephones, TVs, and microwaves make our lives easier (as well as more complex) because scientists managed to rope in a bit of reality. I would not want to claim that we have a well-developed technology of social psychology, but we do have our successes in application. For example, in the last chapter we discussed the jig-saw classroom, a technique making use of social psychological ideas on cooperation and interpersonal attraction to help make racial integration a success. Janis' work on groupthink stands as another example of an analysis based on sound social psychological principles that has led to greater understanding of group decisions. Research on juries and jury selection also has ready applicability.

This is not to suggest that the ultimate justification of science or anything else is that it works in some crude and vulgar sense. If science helps us understand the universe we live in, then it is valuable, whatever else it may or may not do. However, if science can prove immediately useful, that is icing on the cake. Can psychology, especially social psychology, help alleviate social problems, show us the way to the good life, make our everyday social worlds more tractable and enjoyable?

PROBLEMS WITH APPLICATIONS

A Young Science   I think that social psychology has major contributions to make toward these goals, but it would be silly to claim that we are always in a position to make the kinds of direct contributions made by, say, biology. There are several reasons for this. One is that psychology, and especially social psychology, is a young science. Whereas physicists have regularly been subjecting their ideas to empirical tests for over 200 years, social psychology has been an empirical science for only 50, perhaps 75, years.

Behavior Is Complex   A second reason is that human behavior is inherently more complex than the behavior of physical objects. Nearly everyone would agree that it is more difficult to predict the behavior of a person than of a ball dropped from a tower.

Conditions of Application   Third, physical and biological scientists typically have much greater control over the conditions of application than do social scientists. It is a mighty feat to be able to make a spaceship hit the moon, but this is accomplished only after the vehicle itself is built to rigid specifications, the launch conditions are ideal, and potential unpredictable events are minimized as much as possible. It is also a mighty feat to be able to predict several months in advance, on the basis of demographic data, who will win a presidential election, and usually social scientists maintain a larger margin of error in such a task than do rocket scientists in theirs. But in part this is because there is no control over the test conditions. Whereas the physical scientist can design his or her ideal spaceship, I cannot design my ideal voter; the physical scientist can safely avoid all sorts of extraneous variables, such as weather conditions, by launching only on days with favorable weather, but elections will be held on certain days no matter what the psychological weather. If we have a rule that says that, under ideal circumstances, with no other conditions operating, black union members are almost certain to vote for the Democratic candidate, then, for purposes of predicting voting behavior, we have to hope that such extraneous, "unideal" factors as economic hard times, scandals, and wars, which surely influence voting behavior, do not occur. Yet, of course we have no such control. I do not deny that natural scientists have an exactitude of knowledge that makes their predictions almost inherently more accurate than ours. What I would claim, however, is that our failures to make inevitably accurate predictions about human behavior do not damn our scientific quest; such failures often

reveal how much less control we have than other scientists over extraneous variables *in application,* in contrast to our understanding in principle.

Generality of Theory   There is little doubt also that there is a gap between our theories and everyday situations that does not exist in the natural sciences. The natural sciences typically bridge this gap with precise (typically mathematical) rules of turning abstract theories into concrete applications. As one critic has put it: "the [social psychology] theorist furnishes the practitioner with a set of abstractions for which there are ambiguous particulars" (Gergen, 1982, p. 77). In the social sciences, there are so many theories with imprecise reference that it is often hard even to know which one should be applied. Our theories are too abstract and insufficiently tied to events in the everyday world. It remains to be seen whether this results from the immaturity of social psychology or is intrinsic to the study of human behavior.

APPLIED RESEARCH

Applied Experiments   But there may be other important reasons for our mixed record. Several social psychologists would argue that one reason we do not better predict concrete human behavior in complex social situations is that our whole research effort is misguided. There are many versions of this argument, but one of the best reasoned might go something like the following: "real scientists" not only develop theories and test them in well-controlled laboratory situations, but they also have a long history of testing them in the field. Only in this situation can the generalizations be tested as variables interact with one another in complex ways. Just as we need an applied physics, we also need an applied social psychology.

Usually this contention is coupled with a more or less strong attack on social psychology laboratory experiments as hopelessly artificial. We will consider the arguments for and against the artificiality of laboratory experiments in social psychology shortly. But for now let us confess that there is some justice to these charges. At a minimum, it is necessary to test our generalizations in the crucible of the real world. No engineer would design a space vehicle and try to launch it solely on the basis of theory and without various tests along the way. Similarly, it is not possible to know what will and will not work in the social world without concrete empirical tests. For example, I happen to think that the research on small-group decision-making is important and informative, but I would not apply it to jury behavior before testing it either with real juries or with simulated ones that had as much correspondence to real juries as possible (see Hastie, Penrod, and Pennington, 1983).

This position does not, however, further commit us to the notion that useful psychological principles can come *only* from experiments done with real people in real contexts. All we have said is that we would want *verification* of these rules there before trying to sell them to the public.

Applications as a Focus   It has also been argued that social psychologists have not been fully responsive to social and major everyday issues because they have not taken these concerns as their primary focus. The argument is that psychologists test theories that may or may not map onto important everyday concerns—they do not use everyday relevance as their criterion for study. For example, suppose you set about studying interpersonal attraction. For years this area was dominated by research on whether similarity (especially of attitudes) leads to attraction. Now this is an issue of some theoretical interest, but perhaps one of less-than-striking practical importance. If you ask people on the street why they like others, similarity is not likely to be high on the list. So if we had begun with the question of what is important in everyday life, we might have spent far more time on questions such as what makes people seem interesting and charming, questions to which we have almost no answers. By the same token, people interested in interpersonal conflict would not have spent so much time using Prisoner's Dilemma–type games had they been required to use the corporate boardroom or a troubled marriage as their point of departure.

Such criticisms are just, up to a point. It is a simple fact that most psychological reactions and behaviors of interest to us are caused by many factors, far too many to study within a single research program. And so scientists must make some choices. If critics argue that the typical social psychologist looks to theory and past research rather than to the real world for guidance, they are probably empirically correct; if critics argue that the issues we studied would be different if psychologists placed more emphasis on the real world, they are also correct in the trivial sense that whatever we concentrate on determines what we study. But when they further argue that we *ought* to spend more time thinking about social issues and the concerns of the everyday person, we are in for a substantial debate. Social issues are important, but so are theories. And, in reality, the temperaments of most scientists, physicists as well as psychologists, lie more toward the testing of theories than the solving of social issues. Only rarely do scientific communities allow their attention to the everyday world to dictate their research programs. Social psychologists are no different from other scientists in their desire to test theories rather than alter the mundane, everyday world. In fact, I rather suspect that the average social psychologist is much *more* concerned with mapping her research results onto existing issues than the average biologist is in applying his research to the cure of disease.

One of the many reasons for the success of American science has been the willingness of the American public and its institutions to support scientists in pure research. People are at their most creative and insightful when they are working on problems in their own ways that interest them. This is enormously inefficient if you feel the goal of science is to produce immediately applicable knowledge. The vast amount of science turns out to be peripheral, wrong, forgotten. Clearly, if most of us knew how to produce the research that would be important, classic, and remembered, we would do so. Until we know how to do this, perhaps the best recipe is to allow scientists to do what they want in methodically sound ways.

There is another side to this as well. Often, applied research is terribly short-sighted and parochial. If I am asked to do research on whether teenagers are affected by satanic music (and assuming there is some socially relevant and compelling reason to do the research), I might be able to answer that question at some cost in terms of my time and taxpayers' money. However, it is unlikely, or at least not immediately obvious, that what I have learned will readily apply to the effects of other kinds of music or media. The research will have turned out to be quite expensive in the sense that it has little applicability to similar issues.

Moreover, even to tackle such a seemingly simple problem (although such problems rarely are as simple as they first seem), I must rely to some extent on psychological theories that have been supported and defined through basic, nonapplied research. Sometimes basic research produces unexpected dividends. One of the best examples in social psychology has been the research on forced compliance. You may recall from Chapter 5 that Festinger and Carlsmith (1959) wanted to see whether people's liking for a task could be affected by their having said it was interesting. The original motives for this research were many, but one of the most important was to test a major prediction from cognitive dissonance theory that was nonobvious and therefore inconsistent with common sense and other psychological theories. It was a clever experiment, justifiably one of the most famous in all of social psychology. Yet, although this experiment

was devoid of mundane realism and immediate applicability to the real world, it has led to a huge body of research on how our behavior affects our attitudes, self-perception of emotion, intrinsic motivation, and so on. And it arguably has been the most important insight of modern social psychology; it has transformed our ideas about the relationships of internal and external controls over behavior. More to the point for present purposes, it has led to insights about all manner of issues in education, psychotherapy, prejudice, advertising and consumer behavior, and even international relations and negotiations. The research did not begin with any sort of practical focus, but it has changed the ways we think about the social world. So sometimes there is nothing so practical as a good theory (to paraphrase Kurt Lewin) and sometimes good "pure" research turns out to be far more important and practical than research more narrowly oriented toward immediate applications.

None of the above is meant to suggest that there is anything wrong with or second rate about applied research. My own preference would be to have a greater emphasis on applied issues in research and more time, money, and energy devoted to training future social psychologists to do applied research well. The need is great. On the other hand, in its short history, social psychology has contributed more than enough applications to social issues to justify its existence according to a criterion of relevance to the real world.

SUMMARY

There are several reasons why sometimes it has proved hard to apply the results of social psychological research to everyday issues. The science is young and behavior is complex, but the most important reason is that we often do not have control over vital extraneous factors during application. Also, the specific nature of many social psychological theories makes application difficult. Before we can be confident of our applications, we need to do applied research, and social psychologists need to focus more on applications of their research to the everyday world.

CRITICISMS OF TRADITIONAL EXPERIMENTAL APPROACHES

Recently, the whole social psychological enterprise as represented in this text has come under attack for a variety of reasons. Basically, it is argued that the theories we use and the research methods we employ are based on false premises and are unethical. The criticisms range all the way from concrete issues having to do with how subjects approach social psychology experiments to abstract issues of human nature.

ETHICAL ISSUES

Of all the issues involved in experimentation, perhaps none is so vexing as that of ethics. Do we have the right to do what we do to people in experiments? There have been three major concerns. The first is threat and the use of manipulations or situations that expose subjects to physical or psychological harm. The second concerns giving subjects possibly harmful self-insights. The third is the use of deception in the research itself.

Before we discuss some ethical issues, you should understand that psychologists themselves have been deeply concerned about ethics. In the early 1970s, the American Psychological Association published a set of guidelines for conducting research that has been periodically revised, and various agencies of the federal government that provide money for psychological research also require federally funded research to be approved by an institutional review board within each institution. The net result of these changes has been that ethically intolerable or dubious research is now much less common. Neither the APA nor the federal guidelines *forbid* potentially harmful research or that which employs deception, but the benefits of such research now have to be assessed against the potential gains in knowledge. As a beginning, let us consider some concrete cases.

Harm to Subjects   Some of the classic experiments in social psychology have involved potential harm to the subjects. Let us consider two as paradigm cases. The famous Schachter and Singer studies on emotional definition involved giving subjects injections of epinephrine, or adrenaline. This is not normally a harmful substance in the doses administered, and it was administered in these studies by a physician. Nonetheless, the potential did exist for side effects and adverse reactions. Other types of experiments that might involve physical harm include those in which shocks are administered as a way of creating anxiety or fear. Some would argue that experimenters do not have the right to hurt other people and, in addition, there is the admittedly remote possibility that the shock itself or the fear of getting shocked might lead to such side effects as a heart attack.

Another case is the classic Milgram experiments on obedience. Here the potential harm was psychological rather than physical. As you will recall, subjects in that study were required to give strong, possibly lethal, doses of shock to a person they thought was actually being hurt by their actions. Of course, the subjects had the right to refuse to participate or go along, but most of them continued to give the shocks. The behavior of subjects indicated that they were extremely troubled and anxious, as most of us would be if we thought we were severely harming another person. Other studies employ success and failure manipulations as a way of creating moods or changes in self-concepts. Most of us receive our share of both successes and failures in a given day, and presumably most of us have learned to live with such ups and downs. Still, for a subject to be told that he or she is terrible at social sensitivity (to use an example from my own research of several years ago) may be a strong blow to pride. And, given what we know about people's relative unwillingness to change back to their previous beliefs even when they have been told that the feedback in the experiment was bogus, one could easily argue that these changes are significant. Another type of potential harm occurs when people are exposed to something that violates their values. For example, some people may refuse to watch violence on principle, and others might feel that exposure to pornography goes against their deep-seated values.

Many (including this author) would argue that there is no way to reduce completely the ethical problems with such research. However, experimenters routinely take two steps to mitigate the problems. The first is to debrief subjects at the end of the experiment, to inform them of the nature of the manipulations. Of course, this does not make the pain of having been shocked go away, but it can help to reduce psychological effects. Sensitive experimenters also talk to subjects and explore the subjects' feelings about their experience in the experiment. Second, it is standard practice (and required by most universities) that subjects sign an informed consent form before they take part in experiments. Before signing, subjects should be told of possible harm they might experience ("Some subjects in this experiment may be asked to look at X-rated or pornographic movies"; "In this study you will be taking several tests which may be scored; you will be given feedback on your performance and the possibility exists, of course, that you may perform well below average or well above average"). Subjects are then asked whether they understand what might happen to them, and their signature indicates that they have agreed to subject themselves to the designated risk. It is also standard practice to tell subjects that they may leave the experiment at any time they wish. Although informed consent is an important protection for subjects, it does not completely exonerate researchers. For example, it is quite probable that some subjects would agree to let experimenters cut off their index fingers in the name of science. Although one's sympathy may be muted for people who behave so stupidly, morality does not reside in opinion. If it is wrong to hurt someone, then it is wrong whatever that person may feel.

Self-knowledge   Another kind of harm subjects can experience is gaining knowledge about their own proclivities. For example, it is possible that some subjects in the Milgram situation discovered that they enjoyed shocking others; after all, daily life provides few opportunities for such revelations. As another example, consider the following study by Malamuth, Heim, and Feshbach (1980). Subjects were exposed to various kinds of violent pornography and their sexual arousal was monitored. In one condition, the woman victim was portrayed as experiencing pain but enjoying the rape experience, and for male viewers this led to the highest level of arousal. There are two problems here that create ethical concern. The first is that this particular condition is rare; most women do not enjoy being raped. The second is that subjects may have discovered that they were aroused by this particular form of violence and consequently might want to perform this activity. Although the experimenters informed subjects after the fact that women do not enjoy rape, questions remain about the effectiveness of this debriefing and its consequences (Sherif, 1980).

Are psychologists ever justified in harming others? The argument in favor of practices that do lead to harm is almost entirely pragmatic, namely, that benefits in the form of knowledge are more important than the relatively minor costs of individual harm. And experimenters usually take considerable pains to reduce the potential harm and ameliorate the effects through debriefings. Those who take a pragmatic stance argue that harm is inevitable in human relations (we harm others when we give them low grades, take a job away from them, and so on) and that in most circumstances we are willing psychologically and ethically to tolerate small amounts of potential harm for the greater good of truth and knowledge. It might also be argued that subjects in many of these experiments might learn valuable lessons. For example, the Milgram subject who learns that he is willing to give strong shock to another, even though this violates his deepest values, may well learn to be more vigilant and less obedient in the future. In addition, subjects' own reports often indicate that they feel they have benefited from the study. Milgram (1964) reports that 84% of the subjects in an obedience study said they were glad they had been in the experiment.

However, one needs to be neither cynical nor a psychoanalytic theorist to doubt the complete validity of such reports, given what we know about the effects of external variables on our feelings and attitudes. Moreover, such reports do not speak to one additional issue. If we take the subject reports at face value, they indicate that subjects do not experience as much harm as we might imagine. But this is not total justification to those who argue that the ethical quality of acts resides at least to some extent in the motives and intentions of the actor. The drug dealer makes the lives of his customers happier at some level, and most users would report that they are happy to do business with him; still, most of us would condemn the pusher as immoral. Similarly, it can be argued that experimenters do not have the right to routinely harm people, even if the people claim to like it. The important question is whether you feel that the ethical dilemma revolves around absolute moral issues or is reducible to a cost–benefit analysis.

Deception   The other major ethical concern in social psychology research is the use of deception. In many of the studies discussed in this book, subjects were deceived about vari-

ous aspects of the research situation. They may have been told that the study concerned getting acquainted and meeting another person when in reality it dealt with reactions to physical beauty. In the Milgram obedience studies, subjects thought the study involved the effectiveness of shock on learning. Or subjects may have been misinformed about one or more of the manipulations. For example, in the Schachter studies, some subjects were given false information about the effects of the drugs on their physiological responses. In other studies, one or more supposed other subjects may actually be programmed confederates of the experimenter. Recent surveys suggest that somewhere in the vicinity of 60% of published papers in major social psychology journals use deception in some way (Adair, Dushenko, & Lindsay, 1985; Gross & Fleming, 1982).

There are many strong arguments against the use of such practices (see Baumrind, 1964, 1985; Kelman, 1967). One is that lying to another person is always wrong, no matter what the justification, because it abuses the trust we try to encourage between individuals. A more pragmatic argument is that professors and their assistants ought to be dedicated to truth, and lying to subjects in experiments is inconsistent with the notion of being truthful in the classroom. Furthermore, deception research may be bad public relations. People may leave social psychology experiments thinking that social psychologists enjoy manipulating their feelings (Kelman, 1967, 1968). Such an image is inconsistent with our high purposes, is generally false, and is certainly not the image we would choose others to have of us.

These arguments against deception are strong ones, but, depending on one's moral stance, they may not be decisive. If one is willing to weigh various benefits of science against the costs to the subjects and the profession, the benefits may win. There is research evidence that subjects are not as bothered by being deceived as some have feared (Schwartz & Gottlieb, 1981; Smith & Richardson,

1983). And the fact is that it is almost impossible to do some research without employing at least mild deceptions. For example, if subjects in the Milgram study had been fully informed that the study concerned obedience, they probably would have been much less obedient and their responses would have been far less valid. Knowledge of the hypotheses of studies can affect how subjects respond (Kruglanski, 1975). There have been some suggestions that some research projects could be conducted with role-playing (Kelman, 1968), but most social psychologists feel that subjects are thus inclined to say what they think they would do rather than what they actually would (Freedman, 1969; Miller, 1972; but see also Yardley, 1982). Some deception will continue to be used in social psychology research because it is necessary to the research enterprise as we currently construe it.

EXTERNAL VALIDITY

Perhaps the strongest criticism of many experiments is that they lack external validity. **External validity** deals with the question of whether the results of an experiment can be generalized to conditions and circumstances outside the experimental situation (Campbell & Stanley, 1963). Although this is usually raised as an issue with regard to laboratory research, where we all agree that conditions are different than in most other situations, in reality it refers to all situations in which data are collected. That is, if we do a helping experiment in a shopping mall, we can still raise questions about whether results from shopping mall behavior generalize to behavior in other situations. Indeed, there is evidence that much research conducted in "real-world" settings has no more external validity than that conducted in the formal laboratory (Dipboye & Flanagan, 1979).

Criticisms of the external validity of experiments come in various forms. One is that the subjects are an unrepresentative sample of real-life people. Another is that the experimental situation produces behavior unrepresentative of the real world: the stimuli of the experiment may be artificial and contrived, or subjects, knowing they are in an experiment, may make responses that are not good analogs of behaviors in everyday life.

Consider as an example my own PhD research project (Schneider, 1969). I use this example not for the sake of vanity but because it is always best to begin criticism at home. Male student subjects signed up (or were called) to participate in an experiment on personality tests, a title that was both slightly intriguing and vague enough to convey no information about what would happen. Each subject was then given a battery of personality tests and was told that the experiment really dealt with validation of social sensitivity tests. He took a quite plausible test of his social sensitivity (which was perfectly bogus). It was scored and the subject was either given no feedback on his performance or was told that he had done well or poorly. Then the subject was told that he would be interviewed by another student who would also be assessing social sensitivity (a plausible story was given for why this was necessary). The interviewer either would or would not give him feedback on his assessment of his sensitivity. The interviewer (a confederate, of course) entered, engaged the subject in conversation, and then asked him to describe himself on a series of self-relevant items. This latter was the real dependent measure in the study and was taken as a measure of self-presentation and desire to impress the interviewer. Although the exact results need not concern us here, subjects generally described themselves more positively after failure than after success, but only when the interviewer would give them feedback on their presentation.

This was quite an elaborate procedure, but all quite necessary. I worked for several weeks to fine-tune the experiment and make all the cover stories believable. With few exceptions, the subjects were convinced that the study was on the level. But we would all agree that there are some highly artificial elements in this situation. First, the typical subject in this study was a middle-class, bright undergraduate male at a prestigious university and was in the experiment either to earn money or to meet a course requirement. Most were fairly blasé, but a few were hostile and some enjoyed being in research. Most showed some signs of apprehension about what would happen to them, and this apprehension was magnified when they discovered that they would be tested for social sensitivity. Quite a number were suspicious that they were about to be deceived, because the lab where this took place was famous on campus for deception research, so a fair amount of my opening explanation was designed to make the cover story convincing.

Subjects were then told what to do; it is highly unlikely that most would otherwise have taken tests or subjected themselves to interviews. The testing procedures themselves probably made them quite uncomfortable and focused more attention on self than is usual. The interview was highly constrained, and the measure of self-presentation may or may not have been representative of the kinds of things the subjects would usually talk about.

Can the subjects' behaviors in this situation tell us anything about everyday life? I think so, but it is clear that such a contention would need to be supported. Those who criticize social psychology research note that college-student subjects are unrepresentative of other people and that when subjects enter experiments their behavior may be quite atypical of their behavior in everyday situations. In this case people entered the experiment with a mixture of hostility, suspicion, and apprehension that may not be readily duplicated elsewhere. We do not know that this made any difference, but it might have. The situation itself was contrived. The success and failure were much more explicit than successes and failures usually are; the subjects confronted a person in an academic environment where such successes and failures may be more important than in other areas of life. The interview was rather sterile, and people usually do not try to impress others by answering such explicit questions. One can easily find analogs of any of the above conditions in the nonlaboratory world, but overall one is struck by the artificial nature of the situation.

Subject Samples   There is little doubt that most of what we know about social psychology is based on the behavior of college students in experimental laboratories (Higbee, Lott, & Graves, 1976; Higbee, Millard, & Folkman, 1982; Sears, 1986). Such subjects

Much of what we know about human behavior comes from experiments using subjects like these college students.

are in many respects ideal. They tend to be cooperative and smart enough to understand some of the complex instructions they are given; moreover they are readily available. However, this ideal is obviously a practical and not a scientific one, because college students may also be unrepresentative of other people.

College students differ from people in the general population in many ways. Students are, on the average, younger, brighter, richer, whiter, freer from major adult responsibilities, and so on. Now it is important to note that these and other factors need not spoil the generalizability of research. It is, in the final analysis, an empirical question as to whether smarter people respond differently to variables in experiments than do those who are less bright. In many cases I suspect they do not, and therefore many of our findings probably do generalize to the larger American population. However, Sears (1986) has pointed out some alarming possibilities. For example, college-age students have less-well-developed attitudes on many issues than those who have lived longer. This may make college students more likely to conform, less likely to exhibit attitude–behavior consistency, and especially prone to infer attitudes from behavior. Obviously, older people also conform and infer attitudes from behavior, but we may have overestimated the power of such effects because we have used populations of subjects who show them so strongly. So subject selection is one of those potential problems that may or may not be serious but that we have chosen to ignore by and large. (This is an observation of fact and not a defense of common subject-selection practices.)

Another potentially serious problem is that subjects are usually volunteers. Even those students who are required to participate in experiments as a part of the Introductory Psychology subject pool usually have some freedom of choice about which experiments they will participate in. Rosenthal and Rosnow (1969) have shown that volunteers tend to differ from

random samples in characteristic ways, being richer, more intelligent, and higher in need for approval, among other things. Furthermore, subjects who volunteer for an experiment with one description differ in their responses from subjects who volunteer for the same experiment but with a different description (Saunders, Fisher, Hewitt, & Clayton, 1985), suggesting that how subjects are recruited may affect their responses. Again, this is a potentially polluting factor in experimental research, but for a given experiment we usually cannot tell how important it is.

Experimenter Bias   Independent of its purported research topic, the social psychology experiment is social in the sense that one or more experimenters interact with one or more subjects (and confederates). These interactions may not be profound. For example, the experimenter may simply explain the use of a computer terminal, ask subjects to watch the screen and type in their answers to questions, and leave the room. At the other extreme, the experimenter may be an active part of the social environment. For example, in the Milgram studies the experimenter actually encouraged the subjects to perform one kind of behavior over another. But in any event, the experiment itself is a social situation.

Why should this be a problem? There are really two separate but interrelated worries. The first is that the experimenter will inadvertently influence the subjects' responses. The second, discussed in the next section, is that subjects enter the experiment with peculiar motivations and cognitions not fully representative of those they normally have.

Robert Rosenthal (1966) has shown that experimenters can and probably do unintentionally bias the results of their experiments, an effect known as *experimenter bias.* For example, in an experiment by Rosenthal and Fode (1963), several students were recruited to be experimenters in a study where subjects were to rate pictures as to whether the person pictured was experiencing success or failure. The

Robert Rosenthal

student–experimenters were encouraged to get "good results" and were given specific hypotheses their subjects should confirm. Specifically, half the experimenters were told that the subjects should rate the persons pictured as successful and the other half that the persons pictured should be rated as failing. The subjects tended to give results in line with the hypotheses held by their experimenters.

These kinds of effects have been replicated often. When experimenters know in advance what it is that they want or expect, the results tend to come out that way. Various possibilities exist for how experimenters affect the behavior of the subjects. For example, the experimenter may frown when subjects give the "wrong" response or may inadvertently use vocal stress to indicate the "right" response (Duncan & Rosenthal, 1968). However, just because such effects can be produced does not mean that they are an inevitable part of research. Fortunately for this particular problem, there exists a range of solutions (Aronson, Brewer, & Carlsmith, 1985). One possibility is to keep the experimenter ignorant of the actual hypothesis of the research. However, this is not practical when the person performing the research invented the hypotheses, and even if naive experimenters are used, they may well discover the true hypothesis or invent one that will bias the results. Usually a better alternative is to keep the experimenter ignorant of the experimental condition (in this case, the experimenter would not know if a given subject was supposed to rate pictures as

successes or as failures). Obviously, if the experimenter does not know a subject's experimental condition, he or she cannot bias the results in the "correct" direction. But this precaution is not always possible (for example, in a study involving gender, the experimenter will usually have some sense of whether the subject is male or female), but in many situations the instructions that provide the manipulation of independent variables can be given in written form or in some other way so the experimenter does not know the experimental condition. Such precautions have become standard practice and ought to be employed as a safeguard whenever possible.

Subject Roles   We have discussed the possibility that experimenters can bias the results of experiments, but subjects also enter experiments with their own concerns. It is reasonable to believe that they develop hypotheses about what is going on, what they are expected to do, and how they should behave; such factors may affect their behavior. In addition, subjects may have particular reasons to behave one way or another.

Four general conceptions of subject motivations have emerged (Weber & Cook, 1972). The *good* subject tries to confirm what she thinks is the experimental hypothesis, probably because she wants to help science. Some subjects may also act out a *negativistic* role, where they try to disconfirm the hypothesis, perhaps because they are angry at having to participate in research or at having been deceived in previous research projects. The *faithful* subject may develop clear ideas about the hypotheses of the study but bend over backwards to avoid acting on them for fear of invalidating the results. Finally, an *apprehensive* subject may be concerned that he is under a psychological microscope and his primary motivation is to avoid looking foolish.

Research confirms that these sources of motivation do exist, at least under some circumstances (Adair & Schachter, 1972; Fillenbaum, 1966; Fillenbaum & Frey, 1970; Sigall,

Aronson, & Van Hoose, 1970), but direct evidence for their importance is limited (Kruglanski, 1975). In one controversial attempt, Carlston and Cohen (1980) found that subjects could be given explicit instructions to play these roles and subject behaviors were then often consistent with their roles. The researchers also found that subjects who were not instructed to play a role gave responses that were less biased than those of the instructed subjects. This suggests that although the roles may have a psychological reality, they may not be important in the average experiment, because the uninstructed subjects showed little bias. On the other hand, others have argued that this research may say more about what subjects can do than about what they do do in the typical experimental situation and that uninstructed subjects can show bias under some circumstances (Carlopio, Adair, Lindsay, & Spinner, 1983; Christensen, 1982).

There are no general solutions for subject-role problems. Subjects have every right to formulate hypotheses and to try to act on them. However, at present there is no strong reason to believe that subject-role motivations constitute such a powerful source of bias that they inevitably corrupt subject responses.

Artificial Stimuli and Responses   Perhaps the most obvious threat to external validity is that in most experiments the actual stimuli and responses are quite far removed from those encountered in everyday life. You can find relevant examples on almost every page of this text or our leading research journals. In my own experiment, described earlier, subjects took a test that may or may not have been meaningful to them, were interviewed by someone who may or may not have seemed like a typical person they might encounter, and had their self-presentations measured by scales that may or may not have been relevant in a format that may have seemed more like an oral examination than a conversation.

Dependent measures are also frequently pale imitations of their real-life counterparts. For

example, since we cannot use real measures of hitting, aggression studies frequently measure shocks given by an angered person to another. It can and has been suggested that pushing a button in a laboratory is a long way from hitting a person in a barroom. Bandura's research that measured children's hitting a toy doll has been extensively criticized on the grounds that hitting a doll is not the same as hitting a person.

In Artificiality a Problem?   The main case against the external validity of laboratory research is that it is hard to know how one would "prove" that results from a given experiment do or do not generalize to the everyday world. However, this limitation is bound to be a matter of degree. For almost every artificial laboratory experiment there is probably a corresponding real-life situation, somewhere, that matches it reasonably closely, at least in surface details. On the other hand, such correspondences are probably rare enough to be of no real importance. More to the point, however, there are *always* going to be differences between any research setting and the domains of application; hence, there will always be arguments about how close the correspondences are. The critic who claims that shock measures are not valid measures of aggression because they do not represent most forms of aggression is then open to the charge that shooting someone in a robbery is equally invalid because it is not at all like other forms of aggression, such as hitting or arguing. There is, in short, no easily definable way to know when a particular setting has or lacks external validity.

If one adopts the notion that people's behaviors are controlled by their reactions to situations, then the crucial variable in any experiment is how the subject sees the situation (Berkowitz & Donnerstein, 1982). If a subject perceives the laboratory situation as threatening, then his behavior there may well generalize to other threatening situations, no matter how dissimilar the kind of threat. If a subject feels that she is hurting someone when she presses a shock button, then her behavior may generalize to outside situations involving aggression, no matter how dissimilar the aggressive behaviors.

Moreover, there is a basic philosophical and philosophy of science issue involved. *One* purpose of basic research—but not the only one—is to find results that generalize immediately to the real world. Basic experimental research also aids the discovery of variables that might make a causal difference (Henshel, 1980), and it helps us test the validity of generalizations (Mook, 1983). So, for example, if a researcher wants to know whether the marital status of a rape victim can make a difference in the evaluation of the crime, it makes perfect sense to vary this status in the description of the crime read by the subject. The researcher does not want to claim that marital status is more important than other variables or that it usually makes a difference, but only that it *can*. Similarly, everyone understands that the Milgram studies involve a highly limited situation—how many times have you been in a situation where an authority figure ordered you to shock someone? But the value of that research was in demonstrating that people *sometimes* comply with extreme requests, not in suggesting that they *always* do under *any and all* circumstances.

In Chapter 2 we indicated that an essential feature of well-designed experimental research is control of extraneous variables. Unfortunately, such control involves controlling the variables in unnatural ways or, often, eliminating them altogether. Consider the situation facing a biologist who wants to discover the causes of a particular form of cancer. In her research, she is likely to employ cell cultures that are not only divorced from a particular organism but that may not appear naturally in the real world. She does this so she can have control over the growth and "behavior" of these cells. Similarly, the social psychologist who studies, say, aggression may well want to manipulate certain variables (such as television

watching) in a sterile context not at all like that of everyday TV watching. We all understand that the average living room after dinner is not the same as the average laboratory in the morning, but the researcher wants to study the effects of TV watching uncontaminated by these other real-life variables.

This is important because, among other reasons, some causes may be camouflaged in the real world (Greenwood, 1982). For example, news and entertainment media may affect propensities to be aggressive, but these inclinations may be swamped by other, more important variables most of the time. It is hard to make general statements about which causes are the most important because different ones are likely to be active in different situations. If we study only those that seem most obviously important, we may fail to appreciate the subtle aspects of social behavior. Under any circumstances, causes (such as media violence) that may be relatively unimportant in some contexts (such as in the average family) might be crucial in others (say, in a troubled family).

Taken to an extreme, the demand for external validity destroys the basis of all generalization. If all our experiments were conducted in exactly the situation of their application we would have two terribly damaging problems. The first would be that we would have almost no control over important variables and hence we probably would not be able to come to any conclusions about what had caused what. Second, we would be able to generalize only to extremely similar situations but not to others—which is not generalization at all. Science seeks to find *general* answers, whatever else it may do.

A NEW PHILOSOPHY OF SCIENCE

Many of the issues about external validity are pragmatic ones and have been widely discussed for years. Recently, however, a number of social psychologists have gone further to argue that experimental research is based on a false premise about how to uncover truth

(Gergen, 1973; Harré, 1979; Harré & Secord, 1972; Kukla, 1982; Sampson, 1977). Not all of these critics would eschew experimental research altogether, but they are all suspicious of the high claims that experimentation is the royal road to truth. They would accept most of the criticisms about the lack of external validity in laboratory research but would go further and deeper in their criticisms.

The Human Machine   The experiment presupposes a model of human nature as well as a philosophy of how to get at truth. Whatever else they do, experiments try to get at causal relations, and the critics have suggested that human behavior does not fit a physical causality model. The first experimental psychologists were mostly physiologists and physicists, and when they began to do psychological research, they naturally took the model of physical science experimentation, which tries to isolate causes. However, such researchers as Hermann von Helmholtz and Wilhelm Wundt clearly believed that experimental approaches in psychology were limited to basic sensory and physiological systems. They not only felt that experimentation on higher mental processes and behavior was practically difficult, they believed that much of human psychology was not amenable to causal analysis. One could not make meaningful *causal* statements about how people behave, and therefore experimental approaches were doomed to failure.

One way of viewing the history of psychology in this century is as a series of pitched battles over the issue of how much human behavior can be brought under experimental scrutiny. Without doubt we have widened the scope immensely, so we now do experiments in areas the early psychologists considered taboo. However, the basic challenge remains. Perhaps all our causal analyses are for naught simply because human thought and behavior are not caused in the ways our research presupposes.

When the physicist shows the workings of a fundamental law such as the law of gravitation, he assumes that under well-controlled conditions (such as in a vacuum) all objects dropped from the same height will reach the ground at the same time. He would be quite perturbed if this happened only on the average and only some of the time. It must happen inevitably because gravitation is the only effective cause of the behavior of the falling objects in a controlled environment. So the psychologist who adopts this same basic model of causality must assume that human behavior also can be exactly predicted if we have perfect control over causes. In the ideal case, all subjects would be alike in all relevant ways and the situation would be so well controlled that all subject responses to a given set of independent variables would be identical. That this does not happen should be a major clue that the behavior of people is not caused in the same ways that the behavior of falling objects is. Trying to impose a causal framework on the behavior of people makes about at much sense as trying to outfit a chimpanzee in a dress. It can be done, but it's pointless and looks silly.

More generally it has been argued that, in everyday life, events must and will be interpreted by the people involved (Georgoudi & Rosnow, 1985; Gergen, 1982; Harré, 1979). That point has been made throughout this text, but the critics go further. Not the events themselves but the events as mediated by our interpretations serve as influences on behavior. Because such interpretations are subject to a host of historical, cultural, and contextual frames, there can never be an objective stimulus that causes behaviors. One can, and sometimes does, constrain interpretations within the laboratory, but only at the risk of cutting the heart from the reality of social behavior.

Isn't all this a semantic quibble? If we can "make" subjects do our bidding in the laboratory, does it matter whether their behavior is caused by manipulated variables or by subject interpretations? If we confine our interest in behavior to the laboratory, it may not make much difference. The problem occurs when we try to generalize to the outside world. If laboratory behavior is caused by manipulated variables, then, if those variables reoccur in the nonlaboratory world, we should expect the same behavior to occur. Psychological causes, like gravitational ones, do not take vacations or choose when to operate. On the other hand, if the behavior results from how the subject sizes up the situation, we would expect similar behavior only in a situation where the subject assesses the situation in the same way. But such similarities may be quite rare, given that the social psychological laboratory is quite different from most other situations. Indeed, because social stimuli and events "mean" only what the context says they should mean, it may be difficult indeed to find similarities between the laboratory and the outside world, given the differences in contexts (Greenwood, 1982).

The Historical Context of Social Behavior
There are additional criticisms. In a famous paper, Ken Gergen (1973) argued forcefully that a general, universal psychology was impossible because our laws of human behavior change over time. Indeed, other people have commented on the extent to which, even within short periods, the "laws" of social psychology seem to have changed. Eagly (1978)

Kenneth Gergen

presents one well-known example in a summary of research on sex differences. Many studies done before 1970 found that women were more conforming and likely to change attitudes than men, but studies done after 1970 find fewer differences. It is, of course, likely that the women's movement has affected women's propensities to conform, although there may be other explanations for this change as well. There are other examples of psychological generalizations that seem to have lost their validity over time (Gergen, 1982).

There may be several reasons for this. The most obvious and noncontroversial is that cultural changes may change relationships among variables. Second, as free and intelligent beings, people react to what psychologists and other thinkers discover. It might, for example, be likely that after the huge publicity accorded the Milgram obedience studies, people are a lot less willing to be obedient, at least in that kind of simplified situation. So the very popularity of psychology may undercut its validity by changing the psychology of the people who are studied. Third, Gergen suggests that what we consider important, what variables we emphasize in our research, and what values we place on our results change from one time to another. It is no accident that the study of sex roles became popular at just the time many women were trying to break free from traditional roles or that conformity was a popular topic during the 1950s, a period of bland uniformity in American life.

More recently, Gergen (1985) has argued that the very organization of human behavior is temporal. Most of us guide our behavior with regard to future goals that are themselves a result of a lengthy cultural history. You are presently reading this textbook, in part, I assume, because you think that this will help you get along with your life. You want a good grade so you can get a good job or get into graduate school. But, of course, those desires to do well result from your socialization into and experiences with a larger culture that did not begin the day you were born. Thus, when social psychologists study your behavior in the laboratory, they are really examining a single time slice that has little meaning outside this larger context. Before we can fully understand your behavior in the present, we must understand how your past affects how you think about your future. This suggests that the models of physical science that demand that behavior be stripped, at least momentarily, of its temporal and situational contexts for study will not work well for the psychological world.

At this point, Gergen's historical analysis joins forces with the beliefs of those who feel that experimentally based knowledge is faulty, limited, or wrong because experimental variables must be interpreted and thus are not objective in the usual sense of that term. The typical experimental study, then, is simply misguided, making no more sense than trying to capture the beauty of a Titian painting by using modern chemical analysis of the paints. One can do the analysis, but it doesn't speak to the questions we ask. Social psychologists then find themselves in the position of the drunk man who lost his keys along a dark street but looked for them under the streetlamp because that is the only place he could see. Our investigations are conditioned by what we have been trained to do and not by any reasoned or reasonable attempts to find truth.

Values and Facts   Most of the recent critics of social psychology have also argued that social psychologists are not as objective as their lusting after scientific status would suggest. In particular, Sampson (1978) has questioned the whole premise of objectivity of scientific psychology. It is silly to attempt to study objective facts because social psychologists deal with a nonfactual domain, one made up of interpretations rather than objective facts. In the world of Everyperson, fact and value, the objective and the subjective, are

hopelessly intertwined and it is folly for the scientist to attempt to separate the one from the other. An objective account of human nature is impossible, and whatever accounts we offer are bound to be heavily biased in certain directions. For example, Sampson (1977) has suggested that much American social psychology is built around the ideal of what he calls *self-contained individualism*. There is an implicit and none-too-subtle value judgment in most social-influence research that conformity is bad and independence good; yet, in many cultures the opposite would be assumed. Does this influence the ways the research program is carried out? Perhaps and perhaps not, but it surely affects the problems that are studied and the conclusions that are drawn.

A Reply   These critics of the social psychology enterprise are not without their own critics. What might be called mainstream, establishment social psychology has not lacked for defenders (such as Schlenker, 1974, 1977). The issues are complex, but we can clarify a few points.

First, the critics have often overstated their case. It is true that people are not robots whose behavior can be predicted by virtue of its being mechanically caused. It is also true that, because of cultural and physiological factors, there is an essential predictability about some, perhaps most, human behavior. For example, I attend all the classes I am supposed to teach with great regularity, and each time I get up to go teach I do so after creating some meaning for the situation. My meaning may be quite different than that of the person in the office next door, who also meets her classes regularly, but the behaviors of both of us are predictable.

I agree with the critics that human behavior is context sensitive. We respond to the situations we are in, and our responses are affected by cultural understandings, knowledge, and the like, which change over time. I personally would be willing to concede that this makes a *complete* science of human behavior impossible, although others would feel that these changes themselves can be incorporated within a scientific framework (Schlenker, 1974). Although my weaker claim would mean that human behavior will never have the essential predictability and controllability of physical objects, it does not mean that behavior has no predictability. The question is not about models of causality but about whether our laboratory research enhances our abilities to predict behavior outside as well as inside the laboratory. I think it does. I have no special proof for this statement, but as I look at what we have learned and what we do, I am simply more optimistic than the critics. They have the right to point to our failures, which are substantial and obvious, but I feel they have also slighted our successes.

The issue of facts and values, objectivity and subjectivity, is a vexing one. In everyday life, most of us subscribe to a naive realism that suggests that what we see and believe is dictated by the status of the things around us. And physical science built a very large church of sorts on those grounds by claiming to get at deeper and deeper realities of things and events. However, such claims have long been philosophically suspect, and many modern philosophers of science would reject them out of hand (Manicas & Secord, 1983). The essential reality of things must be forever hidden from view; hence, according to this line of argument, science represents only one, albeit a pragmatically useful, approach to constructing knowledge. Although such claims are subject to much debate, the lesson for our purposes is that claims for facts, reality, and objectivity cannot be supported by appeal to a particular method.

Science is not perfectly objective, and values surely do intrude into the scientific enterprise at various points. Values affect what issues we think are important to study, what things we take as so indubitably true as to be unworthy of study, whether someone is willing to fund the research, what significance scientific colleagues assign to the research, and how the research can be applied to the world at large. Few people have denied that science is so affected. Still, we must recognize that different kinds of statements about the world embody different mixtures of objectivity, subjectivity, and value.

There are some kinds of statements that, all reasonable people agree, have some nonfactual (for want of a better term) basis. Smart people do not debate the *empirical basis* of God's existence. That does not mean facts are irrelevant, but only that the issues will not be decided on the basis of who has the most facts at his or her disposal. Even if we agree that a theological account of predestination is psychologically satisfying (and this would not get universal agreement), we still would recognize that there is no empirical evidence supporting such an account.

Then there are those "facts" for which empirical proof is largely irrelevant because they are matters of obvious cultural agreement. "Ronald Reagan was president of the United States on September 15, 1986" is one example, and "the book is blue" is another. Such statements depend on cultural understandings and the use of words for their validity. On the assumption that we can agree on the referents for *Ronald Reagan* (presumably there are other men with that name around and about) and *president* and that we agree how to assign dates, the first statement is about as true as anything can be. It is so obvious a fact that normally we would not know what empirical data would be useful for convincing someone who did not accept the validity of the statement. Likewise, the validity of the color of the book depends in large part on what we mean by terms such as *book* and *blue* and ultimately on a cultural consensus about how to label aspects of experience. The book does, of course, reflect light of a particular wavelength, but when I call a book blue I do not refer to a physicist's reality but to the fact that most people in my culture would also call the book blue.

Thus, we have statements that are incapable of proof in the ordinary sense and those that are true by definition or by consensual agreement as to the meaning of words. While "the book is blue" and "God exists" are statements that differ in a good many ways, in both cases empirical support is difficult and beside the point. People do not believe in God or in the blueness of books because of experimental data. However, there is a broad range of statements that most people accept as susceptible to empirical justification. "Ronald Reagan's economic policies have been a disaster" may lie toward "God exists" in being mostly a matter of faith and value, but at least one could imagine some economic indices that would support or contradict the proposition. Similarly, "men are taller than women on the average" is close to "the book is blue" in that it seems almost a part of the definition of men that they are on average taller than women, but again empirical observation can help solve the issue if one chooses to make it an issue. Statements such as "watching violent TV causes aggression" seem even more a matter of empirical justification. These kinds of statements are not totally objective, are not totally free of values, but they are the sorts of statements for which empirical data count.

Obviously, there are many issues for which empirical support is useful. Most of us readily recognize that propositions supported by experimental data are bound to be more convincing than those without such support (see Gergen, 1982, for more extensive argument along these lines). That is, of course, a cultural matter; one could easily imagine a culture—indeed several now exist—for which such empirical support would not be telling. But, in this culture, systematically collected data are important, and they are important in part because they help us predict human behavior. A statement that students who have trouble reading and writing also have trouble graduating from college may seem to some to be ideologi-

cal in the sense that it embodies a number of assumptions about status, education, wisdom, and the like. And I would be willing to agree that the statement is not value neutral. On the other hand, if I find the statement pertinent at some level to predicting the success of students, I see no reason to apologize for accepting it because it is based on systematic data. Some of the critics of social science, social psychology in this case, have been prone to assume that because few statements are totally objective, empirical data are fairly worthless. My reply would be simply that a lot depends on the kind of statement and how it will be used. I see no reason to throw out the baby of scientific method because the bathwater of objective reality is sometimes clouded by values and subjectivity.

Finally, I would assert the right to feel that science gives us the feeling of understanding phenomena. I am perfectly willing to grant the critics their notion that such feelings are not privileged, and I will readily grant the notion that understanding may be enhanced by fiction, philosophy, and history as well as by empirical research. I personally do not claim a sacred spot for science and experimentally based knowledge. But scientific understanding is important to the ways I and others think about the world, and I do not feel I live in a fool's paradise when I feel enriched by reading about a successful research program.

Social psychology has been the target of criticism since its inception. First it was attacked by the rest of psychology for lacking scientific status and for its inability to do experimental research. Then, as it became a part of the science establishment, it was attacked for being irrelevant and an ivory tower. The most recent waves of criticism have attacked it for both sets of reasons, and the arguments are philosophically sophisticated and worthy of attention. There has not been space here to outline fully and more convincingly the critical arguments or possible responses.

The critics have raised interesting issues and they are correct in many of their criticisms.

But I feel they have gone too far and have not paid sufficient attention to what has been valuable about the field. In this book, I have tried to present the best case I can for the value of social psychology as it is currently practiced. Ultimately, I must rest my own case on the last several hundred pages. If they have convinced you that the enterprise, flawed as it may be, is worthwhile, then I can only suggest that you read the critics for another point of view. If you have not been convinced, then I'm afraid I can do no more. I happen to feel both happy and privileged to be an experimental social psychologist, and naturally I would be delighted to have others see as much value in the enterprise as I do.

I could defend the field in many ways, but finally I would argue that in a world where some seek to manipulate and control others, a knowledge of social psychology is essential for freedom. And at a period when many of us are perhaps inclined to take a bit too much credit for our accomplishments, it is important to appreciate the *social* context of what we do. Our friends make us happy and make us sad; it's enriching to understand both. It remains endlessly fascinating to me that we are both nurtured and constrained by our social contexts, and it is my conviction that the material summarized in this book can help each of us better understand that context and learn to chart our ways through the very rocky waters that are modern civilization. I can only hope you agree.

SUMMARY

Traditional laboratory research in social psychology has been heavily criticized. Ethical issues are often involved, because subjects are sometimes subjected to harmful manipulations or are deceived about the experiment and their role in it. The fundamental argument in favor of such procedures is that well-controlled research would be impossible otherwise, and that the benefits of increased knowledge outweigh possible harms to subjects. The counter-argument is that deception and harm-

ing another person are always or nearly always wrong and that such wrongs are not mitigated by other benefits.

Another source of concern has been external validity, which refers to the ease of generalizing results to situations outside the research context. There is no doubt that many experiments employ artificial stimuli and place subjects in unusual situations that seem to be quite different from those in the external world. In addition, dependent measures sometimes do not seem representative of their parallels in the outside world. However, it is important to remember that these issues cannot be settled by argument. It is always an empirical issue whether behavior in any situation—whether in the laboratory or in the real world—generalizes to other situations.

A third kind of criticism has been that subject samples are biased. There is no doubt that the student subjects used in most research are unlike most other people in many ways, but again it is an empirical issue whether these differences are important. Other research on experimenter bias has suggested that experimenters may influence subjects to respond in particular ways, but fortunately there are ways to protect against this. Some critics have maintained that subjects play roles in experiments that may not be like the roles they play in everyday life. However, despite the fact that several such roles have been identified, there are few convincing data that this is a major problem affecting the validity of the research.

In general, it must be remembered that artificiality of stimuli and responses in the laboratory has its advantages and its disadvantages. Experimenters need to exert as much control as possible, and this inevitably leads to a certain amount of artificiality. It is also important to remember that major purposes of research are to uncover important variables and to validate generalizations. For such purposes it is not necessary for the research setting to resemble the outside world.

Recent attacks on the nature of social psychology as a science have revolved around the nature of science as a means to gaining truth. One argument has been that experiments assume that the behavior of people is caused like that of a robot, but this criticism misses the point that research in the laboratory often allows better prediction of outside behavior whether or not behavior is mechanically caused. Others have suggested that the historical context of human behavior is fundamental but ever changing, making prediction impossible. Finally, some critics claim that values and facts cannot be separated in everyday life and hence the attempts to separate them in the laboratory are doomed to failure. One response to such criticisms is that they are overgeneralized and do not apply to many research efforts.

CHAPTER SUMMARY

- It sometimes seems that social psychology is nothing more than common sense. However, many of the generalizations from social psychological research are not consistent with common sense. Furthermore, common sense is often wrong, so it is important to validate it through research efforts. Social psychological theories also place our understandings in a broader framework and lead to work on important problems that are not always salient in everyday life.

- Social psychological theories are sometimes complex because human behavior is complex and because our theories do not have as much unifying force as theories in the more-developed sciences.

- Many people feel that the real test of a science is whether the results of research can be applied to problems in everyday life. The results of social psychological research do not always easily apply, and sometimes it is difficult to know which theories can be used to explain a concrete event. Perhaps the most important reason application is so imprecise is that social psychologists

typically do not have the same amount of control over the conditions of prediction and application as do their counterparts in the physical sciences.

- Some feel that social psychology needs more applied research. Such research is essential if we are to feel confident in applying the results of basic research.

- One of the major criticisms of social psychology research has been that subjects are treated unethically. One concern is that subjects are subjected to physically and psychologically harmful manipulations. Another is that subjects are sometimes provided with insights about their own proclivities to commit antisocial behavior. A third is that the deceptions employed in a research project break an implicit bond of trust and that lying to subjects is inconsistent with the commitment of scientists to truth. The major defense of such practices is that subjects are not harmed as much as is feared and that the potential gains in understanding outweigh the possible harm to individuals. Others argue in return that such practices are bad in and of themselves and that morality is not a matter of balancing costs and benefits.

- External validity refers to whether the results of research in one setting can be generalized to another setting. Because the stimuli, responses, and setting of so much laboratory research are artificial, the external validity of much laboratory research seems quite low. However, this is really an empirical matter and is not to be decided through debate.

- Subject samples are usually heavily drawn from college student populations and are therefore unrepresentative of the larger population of people. However, it is again an empirical issue as to how much difference this makes.

- Research on experimenter bias suggests that experimenters can bias the responses of subjects. This can be a serious problem, but fortunately there are several ways to alleviate such bias.

- Subjects in experiments may play roles that would make their behavior unrepresentative of their behavior in other situations. However, although many such roles have been identified, the data do not suggest that this is a major problem in most research.

- Laboratory experiments involve artificiality, but this is sometimes necessary for good control. Artificiality is a problem to the extent that the research is to be generalized to the external world, but much research is conducted to discover important variables that affect behavior and to validate possible theoretical relationships. For such purposes, artificiality is less of a problem.

- One recent criticism has been that experiments assume cause–effect relationships, yet human behavior is not caused in the same way that a model of mechanical causality would imply. One response to this criticism has been that behavior in the laboratory has led to better predictions of human behavior outside, so that in a pragmatic sense the issue is moot.

- Gergen has claimed that human behavior has an essential temporal context that is violated in the typical experiment. He claims that research can help us understand human behavior, but that the changing nature of laws of human behavior over time forbid a complete science of human behavior.

- An additional criticism has been that, because values and facts cannot be rigorously separated in the outside world, the attempts of scientists to separate them in the laboratory are doomed to failure. This criticism has some validity but rests on a failure to distinguish the different ways that facts and values interact.

GLOSSARY

A

Abnormal conditions test The tendency to assign causal responsibility to the condition that seems most abnormal in a given situation.

Action identification theory Vallacher and Wegner's theory that the level at which we label behavior and the type of label we choose affect our behavior.

Actor attribution Attribution that assigns the causes of behavior to internal characteristics of the person. *See also* **Dispositional forces; Internal force.**

Affiliation Being in the company of or with other people.

Agenda setting A theory that the mass media play a major role in public perceptions of the importance of political issues.

Aggression Behavior that is intended to hurt another person. *See also* **Emotion-based aggression; Instrumental (incentive-based) aggression.**

Aggressive cues According to Berkowitz's theory, people who are angry will be more aggressive when they are around cues or stimuli they have learned to associate with aggression.

Altruism Behavior that is motivated primarily by the desire to help another person without regard for one's own outcomes.

Altruism norm The belief that we should help those in need even without expectation of reward in return.

Androgynous Having both masculine and feminine interests and values.

Anticipatory belief change The tendency of people to change toward a communication before they have heard it as a way of convincing themselves that they are not changed by the communication.

Antisocial behavior Behavior that harms or produces negative consequences for others. Common forms of antisocial behavior are aggression and competition. *See also* **Aggression; Competition.**

Arousal A hypothetical construct representing generalized activation of the nervous system. Arousal is the sum of all drives and stimulation; it energizes but does not direct behavior. *See also* **Generalized drive.**

Assimilation effect Displacement of judgments about some stimulus toward (assimilated to) some previous judgment. *See also* **Contrast effect.**

Attachment A relatively enduring emotional tie to a specific other person. With children, a distinction is sometimes made between *secure attachment*, where the child is not fearful at mother's leaving and is glad when she returns, and *insecure* or *anxious attachment*, where the child seems unsure about its ties to mother.

Attitude   An evaluative reaction to persons, objects, or events.

Attraction   The tendency or predisposition to evaluate another person or symbol of the person in a positive or negative way.

Attribution   An inference about the cause of behavior, typically expressed in terms of motives, values, attitudes, abilities, personality characteristics, situational pressures, norms, laws, and circumstances. *See also* **Actor attribution; Circumstance attribution; Entity attribution.**

Authoritarian personality   A syndrome of attitudes that includes prejudice against minorities, hostility toward out-groups, political conservatism, moral rigidity, and emphasis on authority.

Automatic cognitive processing   Well-practiced cognitive processes, such as adding simple numbers, that take place largely outside awareness. *See also* **Controlled cognitive processing.**

Availability heuristic   The tendency to judge frequency or probability of occurrence on the basis of how easy it is to remember relevant instances.

B

Basic categories   A level of categorization that allows informative differentiation among instances without producing irrelevant distinctions.

Body language   Stylistic features of bodily behavior, such as gestures, facial expressions, and eye contact.

Bogus pipeline   A technique for encouraging subjects to be honest about their attitudes by convincing them that the experimenter has a machine that can detect true attitudes.

Brainwashing   Informally, radical and extreme changes of attitudes and values after intense pressure.

C

Catharsis   The releasing or purging of aggressive energy; if people release aggressive energy through substitute aggressive behaviors, perhaps they will be less aggressive toward others.

Choice shift   The tendency for group decisions and behavior to be more extreme than the average of the members within the group. *See also* **Group polarization; Risky shift.**

Circumstance attribution   Attribution that suggests that a person's behavior is due primarily to peculiar, situationally and personally nonstable causes such as fatigue, luck, or mood.

Coalition formation   Two or more people uniting to exercise power in a group.

Coercive power   The ability to affect people because of threats and punishments.

Cohesiveness   Generally, how well people in a group get along; used in a slightly different sense by Festinger and his colleagues to refer to pressures, such as liking for the group and its activities, that keep people in a group.

Commons dilemma   A social dilemma in which individuals are motivated to exploit a common resource because it is in their selfish interest to do so, but the resource is soon depleted if everyone exploits it.

Comparison level   A standard that determines whether we like or dislike a particular group or relationship. Typically, this is an average of outcomes gained from other group memberships. *See also* **Comparison level of alternatives.**

Comparison level of alternatives   The standard, based on the outcomes of the next-best alternative, that determines whether group membership will be maintained. *See also* **Comparison level.**

Competition   Hurting or working against other people primarily for self-gain.

Compliance   Behavioral change in response to social pressure without accompanying private change or convictions. *See also* **Conformity; Internalization.**

Concrete case bias   Preference to use concrete cases rather than abstract category probabilities to make decisions because the former seem representative. *See also* **Representativeness heuristic.**

Confederate A person who is trained to play a particular part in an experiment, typically that of another subject.

Conformity Changes in behavior that result from the explicit or implicit demands of others. *See also* **Compliance; Internalization.**

Conjunction error The tendency to see the conjunction of two events as more probable than either taken separately because the conjunction of the two events is more representative of some stereotype. *See also* **Representativeness heuristic.**

Connotative meaning Implicit and largely emotional and affective meanings of terms.

Consensus information Information about whether other people behave the same as a given person toward a particular entity.

Consistency information Information that tells the perceiver whether a given person behaves toward an entity the same way (consistently) over situations and circumstances.

Contact hypothesis The idea that more frequent and better contact between members of racial groups would reduce prejudice.

Content-free schemata Schemata and theories about logical and causal relationships among events and things. *See also* **Schema.**

Content-specific schemata Schemata or theories about specific classes of people, events, and things. *See also* **Schema.**

Contingency model of leadership Fiedler's model that leadership effectiveness is contingent on a match between leader characteristics and task demands.

Contrast effect Displacement of judgments about some stimulus away from (contrasted with) previous judgments. *See also* **Assimilation effect.**

Controlled cognitive processing Cognitive processes that are largely conscious and require planning and control. *See also* **Automatic cognitive processing.**

Convention A rule about what a particular society, culture, or group considers good and proper. Conventions are based on behavioral regularities. *See also* **Moral rule; Pragmatic rule.**

Conversion Changes in private attitudes and values that accompany public compliance to social pressures. *See also* **Compliance; Conformity.**

Cooperation Helping or working with other people primarily for self-gain.

Correlational research Research in which two or more variables are correlated with or related to one another. In such research, the independent variables are not manipulated and there is limited control over extraneous variables; this makes difficult any interpretation in terms of cause–effect. *See also* **Experimental research; Quasi-experimental design.**

Cultural racism Discrimination based on a recognition that different groups have different cultures and the feeling that the culture of one's own group is superior to that of others. *See also* **Racism.**

D

Deindividuation The state or feeling that arises when one cannot be identified as an individual. Deindividuation allows a person to behave in a less normative and more impulsive way because normative restraints on behavior are relaxed.

Dependent variable A variable that is predicted by one or more independent variables. In an experiment, the dependent variable is considered the effect, or the caused variable. *See also* **Independent variable.**

Dilution effect The tendency of nondiagnostic information to lower the prediction of information based on diagnostic information.

Direct speech act An utterance whose form and meaning are directly related, such as when a question is asked in question form. *See also* **Indirect speech act.**

Discount The tendency to dismiss or to be unconfident about any information that a potential (internal or external) cause of behavior was the *actual* cause when in fact many such potential causes are present.

Discrimination Behavior that denies to individuals or groups equality of treatment that they may wish.

Dispositional forces Personality traits, abilities, motives, values, attitudes—factors internal to the person—that dispose the person to behave in particular ways. *See also* **Actor attribution; Internal force.**

Distinctiveness information Information about whether a person's behavior toward an entity is the same toward similar entities at different times and in different circumstances.

Door-in-the-face technique A compliance strategy that relies on the fact that people who have refused to do a large favor are more likely to perform a small one.

Dramaturgical perspective An approach that emphasizes the similarities between actors who enact roles by following scripts and people in everyday life who also have roles and a sense of how to play them properly.

Drive A biologically based motive assumed by Hull and his students to have a strong basis in survival needs. *See also* **Generalized drive.**

Dyad A group of two people.

E

Egocentric Perceptions and evaluations that are overly influenced by the standpoint of self.

Emblem A nonverbal behavior that has a clear and stable meaning within a given culture.

Emergent norm theory Norms about what is proper and permissible that arise from crowd behavior.

Emotion-based aggression Aggression that is accompanied or caused by strong emotion, typically anger.

Empathy Experiencing an emotion because of watching another person experience it.

Entity attribution Attribution that assigns the causes of behavior to the power of a particular external person, thing, or event. *See also* **External force.**

Equality norm The belief that the outcomes, especially rewards, obtained from some activity should be distributed equally among group members. *See also* **Equity norm.**

Equity norm The belief that the ratio of outcomes to inputs for some activity should be approximately equal for the different people in a group or relationship. *See also* **Equality norm.**

Ethnocentrism A general feeling of superiority of one's own group over others.

Exchange theory A class of theories that suggest that social interactions are structured by and evaluated in terms of the rewards and costs experienced by participants. *See also* **Hedonism, psychological.**

Experimental research Research in which the experimenter manipulates one or more independent variables, observes the effects on one or more dependent variables, and controls extraneous variables, typically through randomization procedures. *See also* **Correlational research.**

Experimenter bias When experimenters interact with subjects in experiments, they may bias the subjects' responses toward their hypothesis.

Expert power The ability to influence others because of superior wisdom or knowledge.

External force A cause of behavior, such as a social pressure, law, norm, or role, that is imposed on people. *See also* **Induced force.**

External validity Whether the results of an experiment in one setting generalize to (that is, are valid in) other settings (those external to the experimental one).

Extraneous variable A variable that is irrelevant to the cause–effect relationship being explored. An important property of experimental research is the attempt to control or neutralize the effects of extraneous variables.

F

F-scale Stands for potential fascist, a scale designed to measure authoritarianism. *See also* **Authoritarian personality.**

False consensus effect   Overestimating the number of people who agree with one's own position.

Field experiment   An experiment conducted outside the laboratory, in everyday, nonartificial settings. *See also* **Experimental research.**

Foot-in-the-door technique   A compliance strategy that relies on the fact that people who have complied with a small request may be more inclined to comply with a later, larger request.

Fundamental attribution error   The tendency to overattribute causality for the behavior of others to internal, dispositional factors.

G

Generalized drive   According to Hull, all biological drives add together to produce a general drive (D) that energizes but does not direct behavior. *See also* **Arousal; Drive.**

Group   A collection of people whose behavior is interdependent and who recognize a degree of mutual relationship.

Group dynamics   An approach to social influence, pioneered by Lewin, that emphasizes conformity pressures in existing groups.

Group polarization   The tendency for group decisions and behavior to be more extreme or polarized than the average of the members within the group. *See also* **Choice shift; Risky shift.**

Groupthink   The tendency for decision-making groups to reach less-than-optimal decisions because of in-group pressures.

H

Halo effect   The tendency to see characteristics as going together on the basis of evaluative similarity: positive characteristics imply other positive characteristics and negative characteristics imply other negative characteristics. *See also* **Implicit personality theory.**

Hedonism, psychological   A theory that human behavior is motivated solely by seeking pleasure and avoiding pain. *See also* **Exchange theory.**

Heuristic processing   Relatively automatic, nonthoughtful processing of message and communicator information (typically based on obvious cues) in attitude change. Sometimes called *peripheral processing. See also* **Systematic processing.**

Heuristics   Cognitive shortcut rules for making decisions. *See also* **Availability heuristic; Representativeness heuristic.**

Hindsight bias   The tendency to assume that events that actually occur should have seemed likely beforehand.

Honesty norm   The belief that we should keep promises made to others.

I

Idiosyncrasy credit   The freedom that high-status people have to deviate from the group on certain issues.

Illusory correlation   The tendency to perceive things that should go together as going together to a larger extent than is justified by empirical evidence.

Implicit personality theory   Implicit ideas perceivers have about which traits and other characteristics tend to go together.

Impression formation   The process of organizing information about another person into a coherent image.

Independent variable   A variable that predicts other (dependent) variables. In an experimental situation, the independent variable is the cause. *See also* **Dependent variable.**

Indirect speech act   An utterance whose form and meaning do not correspond directly, such as the use of a question ("Would you pass the salt?") to express a command. *See also* **Direct speech act.**

Individual racism   Conscious or unconscious discrimination based on prejudiced attitudes. *See also* **Prejudice; Racism.**

Induced force   A conformity pressure from

others that is not congruent with one's own desires. *See also* **External force.**

Induction strategy   An attempt to control the behavior of children through reasoning and explanation. *See also* **Power-assertion strategy.**

Informational social influence   Conformity resulting from information provided by others that is accepted as valid. *See also* **Normative social influence.**

Ingratiation   Strategic behavior illicitly designed to influence the judgment of particular other persons concerning the attractiveness of one's personal qualities.

In-group   A group to which one belongs.

Innuendo effect   People associated with negative events are evaluated negatively—even when their relationship with the event is denied—because people remember the content of the allegation longer than they remember the disclaimer.

Inoculation effect   People can resist persuasive communication to a greater extent when they have had to resist previous, weaker communications.

Instinct   An innate survival need that early psychologists assumed was the driving force behind certain behavioral tendencies.

Institutional racism   Racial discrimination that is supported and fostered by the economic, political, and social institutions of a society. *See also* **Racism.**

Instrumental (incentive-based) aggression   Aggressive behavior that is motivated by the desire to get some reward.

Internal force   A cause of behavior, such as an attitude, value, ability, motive, or personality characteristic, that seems to be part of the psychological makeup of a person. *See also* **Dispositional forces; Own force.**

Internalization   The process of acquiring internal controls over behavior.

Interrole conflict   *See* **Role conflict.**

Intrarole conflict   *See* **Role conflict.**

J

Just-world theory   Lerner's theory that when our notions of a just world are violated, we often try to restore feelings of justice by assuming that people deserve their unjust fate.

L

Leadership   The power of a person to influence others in a group.

Leakage hypothesis   The presumption that information about lies leaks out in bodily behavior when people try to control vocal and facial cues for deceit.

Learned helplessness   The tendency to cease trying after failure even when subsequent effort might lead to success.

Legitimate power   The ability to influence others because they accept the higher-status person's right to exert power.

Life space   Refers, in Lewin's theory, to people's psychological environments, which consist of their perceptions of the physical world around them as well as of social and cultural demands.

Longitudinal study   The study of a group of people over a period of time in order to assess developmental changes.

M

Mindlessness   The tendency to perform well-scripted and practiced behavior without thinking about it in a reasoned way.

Misattribution   The strategy of attempting to change emotions or beliefs by directing attention to alternative possible causal factors.

Moral rule   A rule of behavior that is obligatory, general, important, not changed by whether particular people agree with it, not changed for convenience, and not tied to a particular historical and cultural content.

N

Norm   An informal rule that governs group-related activity.

Normative social influence   Conformity resulting from concerns with the rewards and punishments (often approval and disapproval) that others control. *See also* **Informational social influence.**

O

Objective self-awareness   The state of consciousness when attention is focused on the self as an object. In the state of objective self-awareness, people try to meet standards of social acceptability. *See also* **Subjective self-awareness.**

Other enhancement   Complimenting and approving other people in an effort to win their approval—a form of ingratiation. *See also* **ingratiation.**

Out-group   A group to which one does not belong; often, but not always, a group in competition with one's own group or in-group.

Overjustification   Task performance that is overrewarded, leading to a decrease in task enjoyment.

Own force   A motive to behave in certain ways that stems from one's own needs and values. *See also* **Internal force.**

P

Paralanguage   Nonsemantic aspects of speech, such as rate of speaking, pitch, and hesitations; vocal behavior without the words.

Person perception   The study of how we infer the causes of behavior and form integrated impressions of self and others.

Personal space   An envelope of space around a person that when intruded upon leads to discomfort.

Perspective-taking   The ability to see a given situation from the standpoint of another person.

Phenomenological approach   A theoretical framework that suggests that people's perceptions and interpretations of their environments are the primary causes of their behavior.

Power-assertion strategy   An attempt to control the behavior of children through the use of threat, force, and superior power. *See also* **Induction strategy.**

Pragmatic rule   A rule that children learn during socialization, specifying how one should behave to be successful and to avoid physical harm and social disapproval. *See also* **Convention; Moral rule.**

Prejudice   A favorable or unfavorable feeling about a person, group, or thing that is not based on actual experience.

Primacy effect   To give more weight to information that comes first than to information that comes later in forming impressions of others. *See also* **Recency effect.**

Prisoner's Dilemma   A class of games in which both players have moderate winnings if they cooperate but both lose a large amount if each tries to exploit the other by being competitive.

Propinquity hypothesis   We are attracted to those who are physically close.

Prosocial behavior   Behavior that produces rewarding consequences for others. Common forms of prosocial behavior are cooperation and altruism. *See also* **Altruism; Cooperation.**

Prototype   An instance of a category that is "average" in the sense of being the most representative of the other category members.

Proxemics   The study of messages conveyed by the use of space and touch.

Q

Quasi-experimental design   A research design in which, although the independent variables are not manipulated by the researcher and extraneous variables are not controlled through randomization, causal direction and control of extraneous variables are assessed statistically. *See also* **Correlational research.**

R

Racism   The exercise of power against a racial group defined as inferior by individuals and institutions with the intentional or unintentional support of the entire culture.

Randomization A strategy for controlling extraneous variables by assigning subjects to experimental conditions randomly. If done successfully, this strategy ensures that the experimental conditions do not differ except in ways controlled by the experimenter.

Reactance, psychological When people feel their freedom to behave or think as they wish is threatened, they react by trying to restore that freedom psychologically.

Reasoned action theory Fishbein and Ajzen's theory that people consider the implications of their behavior before they act; in particular, behavior results from a combination of attitudes toward an act and from normative pressures.

Recency effect To give more weight to information that comes last than to information that comes first in forming impressions of others. *See also* **Primacy effect.**

Reciprocity norm The belief that we should return rewards and costs to others in degree if not in kind.

Referent power The ability to influence others based on superior prestige or status.

Relative deprivation The feeling of being deprived that depends less on objective circumstances than on whether one is deprived relative to salient others. *See also* **Social comparison theory.**

Representativeness heuristic The judging of events on the basis of whether they are representative of familiar categories of events.

Reward power The ability to affect people because of the promise of rewards.

Risky shift The tendency for group decisions to be riskier than the average decision of the members within the group. *See also* **Choice shift; Group polarization.**

Role In a group, a specific position that carries expectations of certain behaviors.

Role conflict The psychological state that arises when roles prescribe conflicting behaviors. *Intrarole conflict* occurs when the same role prescribes conflicting behaviors; *interrole conflict* occurs when two or more roles the person occupies demand conflicting behaviors.

S

Schema (plural schemata) Implicit theories or models about people and things that direct attention, aid recognition and labeling, lead to inferences about missing information, and affect memory about stimuli.

Script Schemalike theories about the temporal organization of common behavioral sequences. *See also* **Schema.**

Selective exposure Preferences for seeing or hearing information consistent with one's prior beliefs or theories.

Selective social interaction The tendency to interact with others who will confirm our attitudes and values and especially our self-conceptions.

Self-disclosure The personal information a person chooses to share with another. *See also* **Self-presentation.**

Self-efficacy The belief that one is able to perform some behavior or accomplish some goal.

Self-fulfilling prophecy An hypothesis of ours about people or events that leads us to behave in ways that make the hypothesis come true.

Self-handicapping The creation of attributional ambiguity for potential failure by providing an alternative attribution for the failure, such as illness, drug use, or personality.

Self-monitoring The tendency to monitor the environment for evidence of the success of one's own behavior. People who are high in this tendency change behavior to suit situational demands, whereas those who are low in self-monitoring tend to be more consistent from situation to situation.

Self-presentation Attempts to control the information that others have of oneself. *See also* **Self-disclosure.**

Semantic differential A technique used to measure the connotative meanings of terms by rating them on several scales. *See also* **Connotative meaning.**

Semantics The study of the meaning of words.

Sexism The exercise of power against a gender group defined as inferior, with the support of the culture. *See also* **Racism.**

Sleeper effect Refers to situations in which attitude change toward a noncredible communicator becomes greater over time because information about credibility of the communicator is forgotten more quickly than information about the communication.

Snap judgment Nonreflective, often nonconscious, judgment about others based on easily perceived physical appearance and behavioral cues.

Social comparison theory Festinger's theory that, in the absence of a physical reality, we compare with others to evaluate our opinions and abilities.

Social competence The ability, often indexed by popularity or status, to adapt to the social world.

Social facilitation The tendency for the mere presence of other people to enhance performance on certain types of tasks, especially those that have been well learned and practiced.

Social impact theory Latané's theory that the amount of social influence is a function of the strength, immediacy, and number of sources exerting influence.

Social influence Generally, the effects that people have over the thoughts and behaviors of others. *See also* **Compliance; Conformity; Internalization.**

Social learning theory Theories that stress the social context of learning, especially through observation of others.

Social loafing The tendency for people in groups to work less hard than they would as individuals.

Social psychology The study of how people think about, evaluate, and respond to their social experiences.

Social reality Those beliefs we take for granted that are acquired from the larger culture and from other people.

Socialization The process of learning how to behave effectively in groups and to adjust to particular cultures.

Sociobiology A modern version of evolutionary theory that emphasizes social mechanisms for survival of genetic potential, especially for behaviors such as altruism that are difficult to explain within classic Darwinian theory.

Socioemotional specialist A type of group leader who is oriented toward morale, making sure that people feel happy within the group.

Socratic effect Changes in attitudes that result from changing logically associated beliefs.

Stereotype A set of beliefs about the personal attributes of a group of people.

Subjective self-awareness The state of consciousness when the self is a subject and attention is focused on other objects. *See also* **Objective self-awareness.**

Symbolic racism (also called **modern racism**) Racist behavior that manifests itself as opposition to policies favoring racial minorities because direct discrimination and prejudice are not permitted.

Systematic processing Detailed and conscious processing of message and communicator information in attitude change. Sometimes called *central processing. See also* **Heuristic processing.**

T

Task specialist A type of group leader who is oriented to making sure that the group accomplishes its goals efficiently.

Template A pattern of personality characteristics that represents ways people achieve success in particular situations.

Transformation In the exchange theory of Thibaut and Kelley, the immediate rewards and costs one experiences in a relationship may be transformed by taking account of the other's outcomes, as when one person finds an activity more pleasant simply because the other wants to do it.

W

Weighted averaging model *Averaging* models suggest that we average information in making judgments about others; *weighted* averaging models suggest that some information is weighted more than other information in making those judgments.

Werther effect The tendency for well-publicized suicides to increase suicide rates.

Z

Zero-sum game A game in which the total winnings by all players must equal the total losses. Poker is one example.

REFERENCES

A

Abbott, A.R., & Sebastian, R.J. (1981). Physical attractiveness and expectations of success. *Personality and Social Psychology Bulletin, 7,* 481–486.

Abelson, R.P. (1976). Script processing in attitude formation and decision making. In J.S. Carroll & J.W. Payne (Eds.), *Cognition and social behavior.* Hillsdale, NJ: Erlbaum.

Abelson, R.P., Kinder, D.R., Peters, M.D., & Fiske, S.T. (1982). Affective and semantic components in political person perception. *Journal of Personality and Social Psychology, 42,* 619–630.

Abramovitch, R., & Grusec, J.E. (1978). Peer imitation in a natural setting. *Child Development, 49,* 60–65.

Abramson, L.Y., Garber, J., & Seligman, M.E.P. (1980). Learned helplessness in humans: An attributional analysis. In J. Garber & M.E.P. Seligman (Eds.), *Human helplessness: Theory and application.* New York: Academic Press.

Abric, J.C. (1982). Cognitive processes underlying cooperation: The theory of social representations. In V.J. Derlega & J. Grzelak (Eds.), *Cooperation and helping behavior.* New York: Academic Press.

Adair, J.G., Dushenko, T.W., & Lindsay, R.C.L. (1985). Ethical regulations and their impact on research practice. *American Psychologist, 40,* 59–72.

Adair, J.G., & Schachter, B.S. (1972). To cooperate or look good? The subject's and experimenter's perceptions of each others' intentions. *Journal of Experimental Social Psychology, 8,* 74–85.

Adair, J.G., & Spinner, B. (1981). Subjects' access to cognitive processes: Demand characteristics and verbal reports. *Journal for the Theory of Social Behavior, 11,* 31–52.

Adams, G.R., & Shea, J.A. (1981). Talking and loving: A cross-lagged panel investigation. *Basic and Applied Social Psychology, 2,* 81–88.

Adams, J.S. (1965). Inequity in social exchange. In L. Berkowitz (Ed.), *Advances in experimental social psychology* (Vol. 2). New York: Academic Press.

Aderman, D., & Berkowitz, L. (1983). Self-concern and the unwillingness to be helpful. *Social Psychology Quarterly, 46,* 293–301.

Adorno, T.W., Frenkle-Brunswick, E., Levinson, D., & Sanford, N. (1950). *The authoritarian personality.* New York: Harper.

Ainsworth, M.D.S. (1967). *Infancy in Uganda: Infant care and the growth of attachment.* Baltimore, MD: The Johns Hopkins Press.

Ainsworth, M.D.S. (1985). Patterns of infant–mother attachments: Antecedents and effects on development. *Bulletin of the New York Academy of Medicine, 61,* 772–790.

Ainsworth, M.D.S., Blehar, M.C., Waters, E., & Wall, S. (1978). *Patterns of attachment: A psychological study of the strange situation.* Hillsdale, NJ: Lawrence Erlbaum.

Ajzen, I., & Fishbein, M. (1970). The prediction of behavior from attitudinal and normative variables. *Journal of Experimental Social Psychology, 6,* 466–487.

Ajzen, I., & Fishbein, M. (1973). Attitudinal and normative variables as predictors of specific behaviors. *Journal of Personality and Social Psychology, 27,* 41–57.

Ajzen, I., & Fishbein, M. (1977). Attitude–behavior relations: A theoretical analysis and review of empirical research. *Psychological Bulletin, 84,* 888–918.

Ajzen, I., & Fishbein, M. (1980). *Understanding attitudes and predicting social behavior.* Englewood Cliffs, NJ: Prentice-Hall.

Alessio, J.C. (1980). Another folly for equity theory. *Social Psychology Quarterly, 43,* 336–340.

Alexander, C.N., Zuker, L.G., & Brody, C.L. (1970). Experimental expectations and autokinetic experiences: Consistency theories and judgmental convergence. *Sociometry, 33,* 108–122.

Alker, H. (1977). Beyond ANOVA psychology in the study of person–situation interactions. In D. Magnusson & N.S. Endler (Eds.), *Personality at the crossroads: Current issues in interactional psychology.* Hillsdale, NJ: Lawrence Erlbaum.

Allen, V.L., & Levine, J.M. (1969). Consensus and conformity. *Journal of Experimental Social Psychology, 5,* 389–399.

Allen, V.L., & Wilder, D.A. (1979). Group categorization and attribution of belief similarity. *Small Group Behavior, 10,* 73–80.

Allison, G.T. (1971). *Essence of decision: Explaining the Cuban missile crisis.* Boston: Little Brown.

Allison, S.T., & Messick, D.M. (1985). Effects of experience on performance in a replenishable resource trap. *Journal of Personality and Social Psychology, 49,* 943–948.

Allport, F.H. (1924). *Social psychology.* Cambridge: Houghton Mifflin.

Allport, G.W. (1954). *The nature of prejudice.* Garden City, NJ: Doubleday.

Allyn, J., & Festinger, L. (1961). The effectiveness of unanticipated persuasive communication. *Journal of Abnormal and Social Psychology, 62,* 35–41.

Altman, I., (1973). Reciprocity of interpersonal exchange. *Journal for the Theory of Social Behavior, 3,* 249–261.

Altman, I., & Haythorne, W.W. (1965). Interpersonal exchange in isolation. *Sociometry, 28,* 411–426.

Altman, I., & Taylor, D. (1973). *Social penetration: The development of interpersonal relationships.* New York: Holt, Rinehart & Winston.

Amabile, T.M. (1983). *The social psychology of creativity.* New York: Springer-Verlag.

Amabile, T.M., DeJong, W., & Lepper, M.R. (1976). Effects of externally imposed deadlines on subsequent intrinsic motivation. *Journal of Personality and Social Psychology, 34,* 92–98.

Amato, P.R. (1983). Helping behavior in urban and rural environments: Field studies based on a taxonomic organization of helping episodes. *Journal of Personality and Social Psychology, 45,* 571–586.

Amir, Y. (1969). Contact hypothesis in ethnic relations. *Psychological Bulletin, 71,* 319–342.

Andersen, S.M. (1984). Self-knowledge and social inference: II. The diagnosticity of cognitive/affective and behavioral data. *Journal of Personality and Social Psychology, 46,* 294–307.

Andersen, S.M., & Ross, L. (1984). Self-knowledge and social inference: I. The impact of cognitive/affective and behavioral data. *Journal of Personality and Social Psychology, 46,* 280–293.

Anderson, C.A. (1982). Inoculation and counterexplanation: Debiasing techniques in the perseverance of social theories. *Social Cognition, 1,* 126–139.

Anderson, C.A. (1983). The causal structure of situations: The generation of plausible causal attributions as a function of type of event situation. *Journal of Experimental Social Psychology, 19,* 185–203.

Anderson, C.A. (1985). Actor and observer attributions for different types of situations: Causal-structure effects, individual differences, and the dimensionality of causes. *Social Cognition, 3,* 323–340.

Anderson, C.A., & Anderson, D.C. (1984). Ambient temperature and violent crime: Tests of the linear and curvilinear hypotheses. *Journal of Personality and Social Psychology, 46,* 91–97.

Anderson, C.A., & Arnoult, L.H. (1985). Attributional style and everyday problems in living: Depression, loneliness, and shyness. *Social Cognition, 3,* 16–35.

Anderson, C.A., Horowitz, L.M., & French, R.D. (1983). Attributional style of lonely and depressed people. *Journal of Personality and Social Psychology, 45,* 127–136.

Anderson, C.A., Lepper, M.R., & Ross, L. (1980). Perseverance of social theories: The role of explanation in the persistence of discredited information. *Journal of Personality and Social Psychology, 39,* 1037–1049.

Anderson, C.A., New, B.L., & Speer, J.R. (1985). Argument availability as a mediator of social theory perseverance. *Social Cognition, 3,* 235–249.

Anderson, C.W., Nagle, R.J., Roberts, W.A., & Smith, J.W. (1981). Attachment to substitute caretakers as a function of center quality and caretaker involvement. *Child Development, 52,* 53–61.

Anderson, N.H. (1965). Adding versus averaging as a stimulus combination rule in impression formation. *Journal of Experimental Psychology, 70,* 394–400.

Anderson, N.H., & Hubert, S. (1963). Effects of concomitant verbal recall on order effects in personality impression formation. *Journal of Verbal Learning and Verbal Behavior, 2,* 379–391.

Antill, J.K. (1983). Sex role complementarity versus similarity in married couples. *Journal of Personality and Social Psychology, 45,* 145–155.

Apple, W., & Hecht, K. (1982). Speaking emotionally: The relation between verbal and vocal communication of affect. *Journal of Personality and Social Psychology, 42,* 864–875.

Apple, W., Streeter, L.A., & Krauss, R.M. (1979). Effects of pitch and speech rate on personal attributions. *Journal of Personality and Social Psychology, 37,* 715–727.

Archer, R.L. (1979). Role of personality and the social situation. In G.J. Chelune (Ed.), *Self-disclosure.* San Francisco: Jossey-Bass.

Archer, R.L., Diaz-Loving, R., Gollwitzer, P.M., Davis, M.H., & Foushee, H.C. (1981). The role of dispositional empathy and social evaluation in the empathic mediation of helping. *Journal of Personality and Social Psychology, 40,* 786–796.

Ardrey, R. (1961). *African genesis.* New York: Dell.

Ardrey, R. (1966). *The territorial imperative.* New York: Dell.

Aries, P. (1962). *Centuries of childhood.* New York: Vintage.

Arkin, R.M., Appelman, A.J., & Burger, J.M. (1980). Social anxiety, self-presentation, and the self-serving bias in causal attribution. *Journal of Personality and Social Psychology, 38,* 23–35.

Arkin, R.M., & Burger, J.M. (1980). Effects of unit relation tendencies on interpersonal attraction. *Social Psychology Quarterly, 43,* 380–390.

Arms, R.L., Russell, G.W., & Sandilands, M.L. (1979). Effects on the hostility of spectators of viewing aggressive sports. *Social Psychology Quarterly, 42,* 275–279.

Aronson, E. (1961). The effect of effort on the attractiveness of rewarded and unrewarded stimuli. *Journal of Abnormal and Social Psychology, 63,* 375–380.

Aronson, E., Blaney, N., Stephan, C., Sikes, J., & Snapp, M. (1978). *The jigsaw classroom.* Beverly Hills, CA: Sage.

Aronson, E., Brewer, M., & Carlsmith, J.M. (1985). Experimentation in social psychology. In G. Lindzey & E. Aronson (Eds.), *Handbook of social psychology* (3rd edition, Vol. I). New York: Random House.

Aronson, E., & Carlsmith, J.M. (1962). Performance expectancy as a determinant of actual performance. *Journal of Abnormal and Social Psychology, 65,* 178–183.

Aronson, E., & Carlsmith, J.M. (1963). Effect of the severity of threat on the devaluation of forbidden behavior. *Journal of Abnormal and Social Psychology, 66,* 584–588.

Aronson, E., & Mills, J. (1959). The effects of severity of initiation on liking for a group. *Journal of Abnormal and Social Psychology, 59,* 177–182.

Aronson, E., & Worchel, P. (1966). Similarity versus liking as determinants of interpersonal attractiveness. *Psychonomic Science, 5,* 157–158.

Asch, S.E. (1946). Forming impressions of personalities. *Journal of Abnormal and Social Psychology, 41,* 258–290.

Asch, S.E. (1948). The doctrine of suggestion, prestige, and imitation in social psychology. *Psychological Review, 55,* 250–276.

Asch, S.E. (1952). *Social psychology.* Englewood Clifts, NJ: Prentice-Hall.

Asch, S.E., & Zukier, H. (1984). Thinking about persons. *Journal of Personality and Social Psychology, 46,* 1230–1240.

Asher, S.R. (1979). Referential communication. In G.J. Whitehurst & B.J. Zimmerman (Eds.), *The functions of language and cognition.* New York: Academic Press.

Asher, S.R. (1984). Social competence and peer status: Re-

cent advances and future directions. *Child Development, 54,* 1427–1434.

Ashmore, R.D. (1981). Sex stereotypes and implicit personality theory. In D.L. Hamilton (Ed.), *Cognitive processes in stereotyping and intergroup behavior.* Hillsdale, NJ: Lawrence Erlbaum.

Ashmore, R.D., & Del Boca, F.K. (1981). Conceptual approaches to stereotypes and stereotyping. In D. L. Hamilton (Ed.), *Cognitive processes in stereotyping and intergroup behavior.* Hillsdale, NJ: Lawrence Erlbaum.

Atkinson, J., & Huston, T.L. (1984). Sex role orientation and division of labor early in marriage. *Journal of Personality and Social Psychology, 46,* 330–345.

Austin, J.L. (1962). *How to do things with words.* Oxford: Oxford University Press.

Austin, W., McGinn, N.C., & Susmilch, C. (1980). Internal standards revisited: Effects of social comparisons and expectancies on judgment of fairness and satisfaction. *Journal of Experimental Social Psychology, 16,* 426–441.

B

Back, K. (1951). Influence through social communication. *Journal of Abnormal and Social Psychology, 46,* 9–23.

Back, K.W., Bunker, S., & Dunnagan, C.B. (1972). Barriers to communication and measurement of semantic space. *Sociometry, 35,* 347–356.

Backman, C.W. (1983). Toward an interdisciplinary social psychology. In L. Berkowitz (Ed.), *Advances in experimental social psychology* (Vol. 16). New York: Academic Press.

Backman, C.W., & Secord, P.F. (1962). Liking, selective interaction, and misperception in consequent interpersonal relations. *Sociometry, 25,* 321–335.

Baeyer, C.L., Sherk, D.L., & Zanna, M.P. (1981). Impression management in the job interview: When the female applicant meets the male (chauvinist) interviewer. *Personality and Social Psychology Bulletin, 7,* 45–51.

Bagozzi, R.P. (1981). Attitudes, intentions, and behavior: A test of some key hypotheses. *Journal of Personality and Social Psychology, 41,* 607–627.

Bakeman, R., & Brownlee, J.R. (1982). Social rules governing object conflicts in toddlers. In K.H. Rubin & H.S. Ross (Eds.), *Peer relationships and social skills in childhood.* New York: Springer-Verlag.

Bales, R.F. (1958). Task roles and social roles in problem-solving groups. In E.E. Maccoby, T.M. Newcomb, & E.L. Hartley (Eds.), *Readings in social psychology.* New York: Holt, Rinehart & Winston.

Bandura, A. (1969). *Principles of behavior modification.* New York: Holt, Rinehart & Winston.

Bandura, A. (1973). *Aggression: A social learning analysis.* Englewood Cliffs, NJ: Prentice-Hall.

Bandura, A. (1977). Self-efficacy: Toward a unifying theory of behavioral change. *Psychological Review, 84,* 191–215.

Bandura, A. (1979). The social learning perspective: Mechanisms of aggression. In H. Toch (Ed.), *Psychology of crime and criminal justice.* New York: Holt, Rinehart & Winston.

Bandura, A., Adams, N.E., & Beyer, J. (1977). Cognitive processes mediating behavioral change. *Journal of Personality and Social Psychology, 35,* 125–139.

Bandura, A., & Cervone, D. (1983). Self-evaluative and self-efficacy mechanisms governing the motivational effects of goal systems. *Journal of Personality and Social Psychology, 45,* 1017–1028.

Bandura, A., Ross, D., & Ross, S.A. (1963a). Imitation of film-mediated aggressive models. *Journal of Abnormal and Social Psychology, 66,* 3–11.

Bandura, A., Ross, D., & Ross, S.A. (1963b). A comparative test of the status envy, social power, and secondary reinforcement theories of identificatory learning. *Journal of Abnormal and Social Psychology, 41,* 527–534.

Bandura, A., & Schunk, D.H. (1981). Cultivating competence, self-efficacy, and intrinsic interest through proximal self-motivation. *Journal of Personality and Social Psychology, 41,* 586–598.

Bandura, A., & Walters, R.H. (1959). *Adolescent aggression.* New York: Ronald Press.

Barash, D.P. (1977). *Sociobiology and behavior.* New York: Elsevier.

Barclay, J.R., Bransford, J.D., Franks, J.J., McCarrell, N.S., & Nitsch, K. (1974). Comprehension and semantic flexibility. *Journal of Verbal Learning and Verbal Behavior, 13,* 471–481.

Barden, R.C., Garber, J., Duncan, S.W., & Masters, J.C. (1981). Cumulative effects of induced affective states in children: Accentuation, inoculation, and remediation. *Journal of Personality and Social Psychology, 40,* 750–760.

Barenboim, C. (1981). The development of person perception in childhood and adolescence: From behavioral comparisons to psychological constructs to psychological comparisons. *Child Development, 52,* 129–144.

Bargh, J.A. (1982). Attention and automaticity in the processing of self-relevant information. *Journal of Personality and Social Psychology, 43,* 425–436.

Bargh, J.A. (1984). Automatic and conscious processing of social information. In R.S. Wyer & T.K. Srull (Eds.), *Handbook of social cognition* (Vol. 3). Hillsdale, NJ: Lawrence Erlbaum.

Bargh, J.A., & Thein, R.D. (1985). Individual construct accessibility, person memory, and the recall–judgment link: The case of information overload. *Journal of Personality and Social Psychology, 49,* 1129–1146.

Barnard, C.I. (1938). *The functions of the executive.* Cambridge, MA: Harvard University Press.

Baron, R.A. (1971). Magnitude of victim's pain cues and level of prior anger as determinants of adult aggressive behavior. *Journal of Personality and Social Psychology, 17,* 236–243.

Baron, R.A. (1973). Threatened retaliation from the victim as an inhibitor of physical aggression. *Journal of Research in Personality, 7,* 103–115.

Baron, R.A. (1974a). Aggression as a function of victim's pain cues, level of prior anger arousal, and exposure to an aggressive model. *Journal of Personality and Social Psychology, 29,* 117–124.

Baron, R.A. (1974b). Threatened retaliation as an inhibitor of human aggression: Mediating effects of the instrumental value of aggression. *Bulletin of the Psychonomic Society, 3,* 217–219.

Baron, R.A. (1974c). The aggression-inhibiting influence of heightened sexual arousal. *Journal of Personality and Social Psychology, 30,* 318–322.

Baron, R.A. (1977). *Human aggression.* New York: Plenum.

Bartlett, F.C. (1932). *Remembering: A study in experimental and social psychology.* New York: Macmillan.

Bassili, J.N. (1981). The attractiveness stereotype: Goodness or glamour. *Basic and Applied Social Psychology, 2,* 235–252.

Bassili, J.N., & Smith, M.C. (1986). On the spontaneity of trait attribution: Converging evidence for the role of cognitive strategy. *Journal of Personality and Social Psychology, 50,* 239–245.

Bassok, M., & Trope, Y. (1983–1984). People's strategies for testing hypotheses about another's personality: Confirmatory or diagnostic? *Social Cognition, 2,* 199–216.

Batson, C.D., Duncan, B.D., Ackerman, P., Buckley, T., & Birch, K. (1981). Is empathic emotion a source of altruistic motivation? *Journal of Personality and Social Psychology, 40,* 290–302.

Batson, C.D., Harris, A.C., McCaul, K.D., Davis, M., & Schmidt, T. (1979). Compassion or compliance: Alternative dispositional attributions for one's helping behavior. *Social Psychology Quarterly, 42,* 405–409.

Batson, C.D., O'Quin, K., Fultz, J., Vanderplas, M., & Isen, A.M. (1983). Influence of self-reported distress and empathy on egoistic versus altruistic motivation for help. *Journal of Personality and Social Psychology, 45,* 706–718.

Baumeister, R.F. (1982). A self-presentational view of social phenomena. *Psychological Bulletin, 91,* 3–26.

Baumeister, R.F. (1984). Choking under pressure: Self-consciousness and paradoxical effects of incentives on skillful performance. *Journal of Personality and Social Psychology, 46,* 610–620.

Baumeister, R.F. (1986). *Identity: Cultural change and the struggle for self.* New York: Oxford University Press.

Baumeister, R.F., Cooper, J., & Skib, B.A. (1979). Inferior

performance as a selective response to expectancy: Taking a dive to make a point. *Journal of Personality and Social Psychology, 37*, 424–432.

Baumeister, R.F., & Jones, E.E. (1978). When self-presentation is constrained by the target's knowledge: Consistency and compensation. *Journal of Personality and Social Psychology, 36*, 608–618.

Baumeister, R., & Steinhilber, A. (1984). Paradoxical effects of supportive audiences on performance under pressure: The home field disadvantage in sports championships. *Journal of Personality and Social Psychology, 47*, 85–93.

Baumeister, R.F., & Tice, D.M. (1984). Role of self-presentation and choice on cognitive dissonance under forced compliance: Necessary or sufficient cause. *Journal of Personality and Social Psychology, 46*, 5–13.

Baumrind, D. (1964). Some thoughts on ethics of research: After reading Milgram's "Behavioral study of obedience." *American Psychologist, 19*, 421–423.

Baumrind, D. (1967). Child care practices anteceding three patterns of preschool behavior. *Genetic Psychological Monographs, 75*, 43–88.

Baumrind, D. (1971). Current patterns of parental authority. *Developmental Psychology Monographs, 4*, part 2.

Baumrind, D. (1985). Research using intentional deception: Ethical issues revisited. *American Psychologist, 40*, 165–174.

Bavelas, A., Hastorf, A.H., Gross, A.E., & Kite, W.R. (1965). Experiments on the alteration of group structure. *Journal of Experimental Social Psychology, 1*, 55–70.

Beaman, A.L., Cole, C.M., Preston, M., Klentz, B., & Steblay, N.M. (1983). Fifteen years of foot-in-the-door research: A meta- analysis. *Personality and Social Psychology Bulletin, 9*, 181–196.

Becker, F.D. (1973). Study of spatial markers. *Journal of Personality and Social Psychology, 26*, 439–445.

Bell, R.Q. (1968). A reinterpretation of the direction of effects in studies of socialization. *Psychological Review, 75*, 82–95.

Bellezza, F.S. (1984). The self as a mnemonic device: The role of internal cues. *Journal of Personality and Social Psychology, 47*, 506–516.

Belsky, J., Lang, M., & Huston, T.L. (1986). Sex typing and division of labor determinants of marital change across the transition to parenthood. *Journal of Personality and Social Psychology, 50*, 517–522.

Bem, D.J. (1965). An experimental analysis of self-persuasion. *Journal of Experimental Social Psychology, 1*, 199–218.

Bem, D.J. (1967). Self-perception: An alternative interpretation of cognitive dissonance phenomena. *Psychological Review, 74*, 183–200.

Bem, D.J. (1968). The epistemological status of interpersonal simulations: A reply to Jones, Linder, Kiesler,

Zanna, & Brehm. *Journal of Experimental Social Psychology, 4*, 270–274.

Bem, D.J. (1972). Self-perception theory. In L. Berkowitz (Ed.), *Advances in experimental social psychology* (Vol. 6). New York: Academic Press.

Bem, D.J., & Allen, A. (1974). On predicting some of the people some of the time: The search for cross-situational consistencies in behavior. *Psychological Review, 81*, 506–520.

Bem, D.J., & Funder, D.C. (1978). Predicting more of the people more of the time: Assessing the personality of situations. *Psychological Review, 85*, 485–501.

Bem, S.L. (1974). The measurement of psychological androgyny. *Journal of Consulting and Clinical Psychology, 42*, 155–162.

Bem, S.L. (1981). Gender schema theory: A cognitive account of sex-typing. *Psychological Review, 88*, 354–364.

Bem, S.L., & Lenney, E. (1976). Sex typing and the avoidance of cross-sex behavior. *Journal of Personality and Social Psychology, 33*, 48–54.

Bentler, P.M., & Speckart, G. (1979). Models of attitude–behavior relations. *Psychological Review, 86*, 452–464.

Bentler, P.M., & Speckart, G. (1981). Attitudes "cause" behaviors: A structural equation analysis. *Journal of Personality and Social Psychology, 40*, 226–238.

Berg, J.H., & McQuinn, R.D. (1986). Attraction and exchange in continuing and noncontinuing dating relationships. *Journal of Personality and Social Psychology, 50*, 942–952.

Berger, J., Conner, T.L., & Fisek, M.H. (Eds.) (1974). *Expectation states theory: A theoretical research program.* Cambridge, MA: Winthrop Publishers.

Berger, S.M. (1962). Conditioning through vicarious instigation. *Psychological Review, 69*, 450–466.

Berk, R.A. (1974). A gaming approach to crowd behavior. *American Sociological Review, 39*, 355–373.

Berkowitz, L. (1962). *Aggression: A social psychological analysis.* New York: McGraw-Hill.

Berkowitz, L. (1969): The frustration–aggression hypothesis revisited. In L. Berkowitz (Ed.), *Roots of aggression.* New York: Atherton.

Berkowitz, L. (1972). Social norms, feelings, and other factors affecting helping and altruism. In L. Berkowitz (Ed.), *Advances in experimental social psychology* (Vol. 6). New York: Academic Press.

Berkowitz, L. (1983). Aversively stimulated aggression: Some parallels and differences in research with animals and humans. *American Psychologist, 38*, 1135–1144.

Berkowitz, L. (1985). Some effects of thoughts on anti- and prosocial influence of media events: A cognitive-neoassociation analysis. *Psychological Bulletin, 95*, 410–427.

Berkowitz, L., & Daniels, L.R. (1964). Affecting the salience of the social responsibility norm. *Journal of Abnormal and Social Psychology, 68,* 275–281.

Berkowitz, L., & Donnerstein, E. (1982). External validity is more than skin deep: Some answers to criticisms of laboratory experiments. *American Psychologist, 37,* 245–257.

Berkowitz, L., & Geen, R.G. (1966). Film violence and the cue properties of available targets. *Journal of Personality and Social Psychology, 3,* 525–530.

Berkowitz, L., & Macaulay, J. (1971). The contagion of criminal violence. *Sociometry, 34,* 238–260.

Berlin, B., & Kay, P. (1969). *Basic color terms: Their universality and evolution.* Berkeley, CA: University of California Press.

Berman, J.S., & Kenny, D.A. (1976). Correlational bias in observer ratings. *Journal of Personality and Social Psychology, 34,* 263–273.

Berndt, T.J. (1982). The features and effects of friendship in early adolescence. *Child Development, 53,* 1447–1460.

Berndt, T.J., McCartney, K., Caparulo, B.K., & Moore, A.M. (1983–1984). The effects of group discussions on children's moral decisions. *Social Cognition, 2,* 343–359.

Bernstein, B. (1967). Social structure, language, and learning. In J.P. DeCecco (Ed.), *The psychology of language, thought, and instruction.* New York: Holt, Rinehart & Winston.

Bernstein, M., & Crosby, F. (1980). An empirical examination of relative deprivation theory. *Journal of Experimental Social Psychology, 16,* 442–456.

Berscheid, E. (1983). Emotion. In H.H. Kelley et al., *Close relationships.* New York: Freeman.

Berscheid, E., & Walster, E. (1974). A little about love. In T.L. Huston (Ed.), *Foundations of interpersonal attraction.* New York: Academic Press.

Berscheid, E., & Walster, E. (1978). *Interpersonal attraction,* 2nd edition. Reading, MA: Addison-Wesley.

Berscheid, E., Graziano, W., Monson, T., & Dermer, M. (1976). Outcome dependency: Attention, attribution, and attraction. *Journal of Personality and Social Psychology, 34,* 978–989.

Bickman, L. (1971). The effect of another bystander's ability to help on bystander intervention in an emergency. *Journal of Experimental Social Psychology, 7,* 367–379.

Bickman, L. (1972). Social influence and diffusion of responsibility in an emergency. *Journal of Experimental Social Psychology, 8,* 438–445.

Bishop, G.D., & Myers, D.G. (1974). Informational influence in group discussion. *Organizational Behavior and Human Performance, 12,* 92–104.

Bixenstine, V.E., & Wilson, K.V. (1963). Effects of level of cooperative choice by the other players on choices in a prisoner's dilemma game, Part II. *Journal of Abnormal and Social Psychology, 67,* 139–147.

Blasi, A. (1980). Bridging moral cognition and moral action: A critical review of the literature. *Psychological Bulletin, 88,* 1–45.

Blau, P.M. (1964). *Exchange and power in social life.* New York: Wiley.

Block, J.H. (1983). Differential premises arising from differential socialization of the sexes: Some conjectures. *Child Development, 54,* 1335–1354.

Bobo, L. (1983). Whites' opposition to bussing: Symbolic racism or realistic group conflict? *Journal of Personality and Social Psychology, 45,* 1196–1210.

Boggiano, A.K., Harackiewicz, J.M., Bessette, J.M., & Main, D.S. (1985). Increasing children's interest through performance-contingent reward. *Social Cognition, 3,* 400–411.

Boggiano, A.K., Ruble, D.N., & Pittman, T.S. (1982). The mastery hypothesis and the overjustification effect. *Social Cognition, 1,* 38–49.

Bollen, K.A., & Phillips, D.P. (1982). Imitative suicides: A national study of the effects of television news stories. *American Sociological Review, 47,* 802–809.

Bond, C.F., Jr. (1982) Social facilitation: A self-presentational view. *Journal of Personality and Social Psychology, 42,* 1042–1050.

Bond, C.F., Jr., Kahler, K.N., & Paolicelli, L.M. (1985). The miscommunication of deception: An adaptive perspective. *Journal of Experimental Social Psychology, 21,* 331–345.

Bond, C.F., Jr., & Titus, L.J. (1983). Social facilitation: A meta-analysis of 241 studies. *Psychological Bulletin, 94,* 265–292.

Borstelmann, L.J. (1983). Children before psychology: Ideas about children from antiquity to the late 1800s. In P.H. Mussen (Ed.), *Handbook of child psychology* (4th edition, Vol. 1). New York: Wiley.

Bossard, J.H.S. (1932). Residential propinquity as a factor in mate selection. *American Journal of Sociology, 38,* 219–224.

Bourhis, R.Y., & Giles, H. (1977). The language of intergroup distinctiveness. In H. Giles (Ed.), *Language, ethnicity, and intergroup relations.* London: Academic Press.

Bower, G. (1981). Mood and memory. *American Psychologist, 36,* 129–148.

Bower, G.H., & Gilligan, S.G. (1979). Remembering information related to one's self. *Journal of Research in Personality, 13,* 420–432.

Bowers, K.S. (1973). Situationalism in psychology: An analysis and a critique. *Psychological Review, 80,* 307–336.

Bowlby, J. (1969). *Attachment and loss.* New York: Basic Books.

Bowlby, J. (1973). *Separation.* New York: Basic Books.

Brackbill, Y. (1958). Extinction of the smiling response in infants as a function of reinforcement schedule. *Child Development, 29,* 114–124.

Bradley, G.W. (1978). Self-serving biases in the attribution process: A reexamination of the fact or fiction question. *Journal of Personality and Social Psychology, 36,* 56–71.

Braiker, H.B., & Kelley, H.H. (1979). Conflict in the development of close relationships. In R.L. Burgess & T.L. Huston (Eds.), *Social exchange in developing relationships.* New York: Academic Press.

Brain, P.F. (1984). Biological explanations of human aggression and the resulting therapies offered by such approaches: A critical evaluation. In R.J. Blanchard & D.C. Blanchard (Eds.), *Advances in the study of aggression* (Vol. 1). Orlando, FL: Academic Press.

Bramel, D.A. (1962). A dissonance theory approach to defensive projection. *Journal of Abnormal and Social Psychology, 69,* 121–129.

Braver, S.L., Linder, D.E., Corwin, T.T., & Cialdini, R.B. (1977). Some conditions that affect admissions of attitude change. *Journal of Experimental Social Psychology, 13,* 565–576.

Brechner, K.C. (1977). An experimental analysis of social traps. *Journal of Experimental Social Psychology, 13,* 552–564.

Breckler, S.J. (1984). Empirical validation of affect, behavior, and cognition as distinct components of attitude. *Journal of Personality and Social Psychology, 47,* 1191–1206.

Brehm, J.W. (1960). Attitudinal consequences of commitment to unpleasant behavior. *Journal of Abnormal and Social Psychology, 60,* 379–383.

Brehm, J.W. (1966). *A theory of psychological reactance.* New York: Academic Press.

Brehm, S.S. (1985). *Intimate relationships.* New York: Random House.

Brewer, M.B. (1979). In-group bias in the minimal intergroup situation: A cognitive-motivational analysis. *Psychological Bulletin, 86,* 307–324.

Brewer, M.B., Dull, V., & Lui, L. (1981). Perceptions of the elderly: Stereotypes as prototypes. *Journal of Personality and Social Psychology, 41,* 656–670.

Brickman, P., Coates, D., & Janoff-Bulman, R. (1978). Lottery winners and accident victims: Is happiness related? *Journal of Personality and Social Psychology, 36,* 917–927.

Brigham, J.C. (1971). Ethnic stereotypes. *Psychological Bulletin, 76,* 15–38.

Brigham, J.C., & Malpass, R.S. (1985). The role of experience and contact in the recognition of faces of own- and other-race persons. *Journal of Social Issues, 41,* 139–156.

Brodt, S.E., & Zimbardo, P.G. (1981). Modifying shyness-related social behavior through symptom misattribution. *Journal of Personality and Social Psychology, 41,* 437–444.

Brookhart, J., & Hock, E. (1976). The effects of experimental context and experiential background on infants' behavior toward their mothers and a stranger. *Child Development, 47,* 333–340.

Brown, R. (1965). *Social psychology.* New York: Free Press.

Brown, R., & Ford, M. (1961). Address in American English. *Journal of Abnormal and Social Psychology, 62,* 375–385.

Brown, R., & Lenneberg, E.H. (1954). A study in language and cognition. *Journal of Abnormal and Social Psychology, 49,* 254–262.

Brown, R.M. (1969). Historical patterns of violence in America. In H.D. Graham & T.R. Gurr (Eds.), *Violence in America: Historical and comparative perspectives.* New York: Bantam Books.

Brunner, L.J. (1979). Smiles can be back channels. *Journal of Personality and Social Psychology, 37,* 728–734.

Bryan, J.H., & Test, M.A. (1967). Models of helping: Naturalistic studies in aiding behavior. *Journal of Personality and Social Psychology, 6,* 400–407.

Buck, R. (1984). *The communication of emotion.* New York: Guilford.

Burton, R.V. (1963). The generality of honesty reconsidered. *Psychological Review, 70,* 481–499.

Buss, A. (1966). Instrumentality of aggression, feedback, and frustration as determinants of physical aggression. *Journal of Personality and Social Psychology, 3,* 153–162.

Buss, D.M. (1981). Sex differences in the evolution and performance of dominant acts. *Journal of Personality and Social Psychology, 40,* 147–154.

Buss, D.M. (1984). Toward a psychology of person–environment (PE) correlation: The role of spouse selection. *Journal of Personality and Social Psychology, 47,* 361–377.

Buss, D.M., & Barnes, M. (1986). Preferences in human mate selection. *Journal of Personality and Social Psychology, 50,* 559–570.

Buss, D.M., & Craik, K.H. (1983a). Act prediction and the conceptual analysis of personality scales: Indices of act density, bipolarity, and extensity. *Journal of Personality and Social Psychology, 45,* 1081–1095.

Buss, D.M., & Craik, K.H. (1983b). The act frequency approach to personality. *Psychological Review, 90,* 105–126.

Bussey, K., & Bandura, A. (1984). Influence of gender constancy and social power on sex-linked modeling. *Journal of Personality and Social Psychology, 47,* 1292–1302.

Byrne, D. (1961). Interpersonal attraction and attitude similarity. *Journal of Abnormal and Social Psychology, 62,* 713–715.

Byrne, D. (1961). Interpersonal attraction and attitude similarity. *Journal of Abnormal and Social Psychology, 62,* 713–715.

Byrne, D. (1971). *The attraction paradigm*. New York: Academic Press.

Byrne, D., London, O., & Reeves, K. (1968). The effects of physical attractiveness, sex, and attitude similarity on interpersonal attraction. *Journal of Personality, 36,* 259–271.

Byrne, D., & Nelson, D. (1965). Attraction as a linear function of proportion of positive reinforcements. *Journal of Personality and Social Psychology, 1,* 659–663.

Byrne, D., Nelson, D., & Reeves, K. (1966). Effects of consensual validation and invalidation on attraction as a function of verifiability. *Journal of Experimental Social Psychology, 2,* 98–107.

C

Cacioppo, J.T., & Petty, R.E. (1979). Attitudes and cognitive response: An electrophysiological approach. *Journal of Personality and Social Psychology, 37,* 2181–2199.

Cacioppo, J.T., & Petty, R.E. (1981). Effects of extent of thought on the pleasantness ratings of P-O-X triads: Evidence for three judgmental tendencies in evaluating social situations. *Journal of Personality and Social Psychology, 40,* 1000–1009.

Cacioppo, J.T., Petty, R.E., Losch, M.E., & Kim, H.S. (1986). Electromyographic activity over facial muscle regions can differentiate the valence and intensity of affective reactions. *Journal of Personality and Social Psychology, 50,* 260–268.

Cairns, R.B. (1979). *Social development*. San Francisco: W.H. Freeman.

Calder, B.J., Insko, C.A., & Yandell, B. (1974). The relation of cognitive and memorial processes to persuasion in a simulated jury trial. *Journal of Applied Social Psychology, 4,* 62–93.

Caldwell, M.D. (1976). Communication and sex effects in a five-person prisoner's dilemma game. *Journal of Personality and Social Psychology, 33,* 273–280.

Campbell, A.A. (1947). Factors associated with attitudes toward Jews. In T.M. Newcomb & E.L. Hartley (Eds.), *Reading in social psychology*. New York: Holt.

Campbell, D.T. (1975). On the conflicts between biological and social evaluation and between psychology and moral tradition. *American Psychologist, 30,* 1103–1126.

Campbell, D.T., & Stanley, J.C. (1963). *Experimental and quasi-experimental designs for research*. Chicago: Rand-McNally.

Campos, J.J., Barrett, K.C., Lamb, M.E., Goldsmith, H.H., & Stenberg, C. (1983). Socioemotional development. In P.H. Mussen (Ed.), *Handbook of child psychology* (4th edition, Vol. 2). New York: Wiley.

Canon, L. (1964). Self-confidence and selective exposure to information. In L. Festinger (Ed.), *Conflict, decision, and dissonance*. Stanford, CA: Stanford University Press.

Cansler, D.C., & Stiles, W.B. (1981). Relative status and interpersonal presumptuousness. *Journal of Experimental Social Psychology, 17,* 459–471.

Cantor, N., Mackie, D., & Lord, G. (1983–1984). Choosing partners and activities: The social perceiver decides to mix it up. *Social Cognition, 2,* 256–272.

Cantor, N., & Mischel, W. (1977). Traits as prototypes: Effects on recognition memory. *Journal of Personality and Social Psychology, 35,* 38–48.

Carlopio, J., Adair, J.G., Lindsay, R.C.L., & Spinner, B. (1983). Avoiding artifact in the search for bias: The importance of assessing subjects' perceptions of the experiment. *Journal of Personality and Social Psychology, 44,* 693–701.

Carlston, D.E. (1980). The recall and use of traits and events in social inference processes. *Journal of Experimental Social Psychology, 16,* 303–328.

Carlston, D.E., & Cohen, J.L. (1980). A closer examination of subject roles. *Journal of Personality and Social Psychology, 38,* 857–870.

Carter, D.B., & McCloskey, L.A. (1983–1984). Peers and the maintenance of sex-typed behavior: The development of children's conceptions of cross-gender behavior in their peers. *Social Cognition, 2,* 294–314.

Carver, C. (1974). Facilitation of physical aggression through objective self-awareness. *Journal of Experimental Social Psychology, 10,* 365–370.

Carver, C.S. (1979). A cybernetic model of self-attention processes. *Journal of Personality and Social Psychology, 37,* 1251–1281.

Carver, C.S., Blaney, P.H., & Scheier, M.F. (1979a). Reassertion and giving up: The interactive role of self-directed attention and outcome expectancy. *Journal of Personality and Social Psychology, 37,* 1859–1870.

Carver, C.S., Blaney, P.H., & Scheier, M.F. (1979b). Focus of attention, chronic expectancy, and responses to a feared stimulus. *Journal of Personality and Social Psychology, 37,* 1186–1195.

Carver, C.S., Ganellen, R.J., Froming, W.J., & Chambers, W. (1983). Modeling: An analysis in terms of category accessibility. *Journal of Experimental Social Psychology, 19,* 403–421.

Carver, C.S., & Scheier, M.F. (1978). Self-focusing effects of dispositional self-consciousness, mirror presence, and audience presence. *Journal of Personality and Social Psychology, 36,* 324–332.

Cattell, R.B., & Nesselroade, J.R. (1967). Likeness and completeness theories examined by sixteen personality factor measures on stably and unstably married couples. *Journal of Personality and Social Psychology, 7,* 351–361.

Chagnon, N.A. (1968). *Yanomamo: The fierce people*. New York: Holt, Rinehart & Winston.

Chagnon, N.A. (1974). *Studying the Yanomamo*. New York: Holt, Rinehart & Winston.

Chaiken, S. (1979). Communicator physical attractiveness and persuasion. *Journal of Personality and Social Psychology, 37*, 1387–1397.

Chaiken, S. (1980). Heuristic versus systematic information processing and the use of source versus message cues in persuasion. *Journal of Personality and Social Psychology, 39*, 752–766.

Chaiken, S. (1986). Physical appearance and social influence. In C.P. Herman, M.P. Zanna, & E.T. Higgins (Eds.), *Physical appearance, stigma, and social behavior: The Ontario Symposium* (Vol. 3). Hillsdale, NJ: Lawrence Erlbaum.

Chaiken, S. (1987). The heuristic model of persuasion. In M.P. Zanna, J.M. Olson, & C.P. Herman (Eds.), *Social influence: The Ontario Symposium* (Vol. 5). Hillsdale, NJ: Lawrence Erlbaum.

Chaiken, S., & Baldwin, M.W. (1981). Affective-cognitive consistency and the effect of salient behavioral information on the self-perception of attitudes. *Journal of Personality and Social Psychology, 41*, 1–12.

Chaiken, S., & Eagly, A.H. (1976). Communication modality as a determinant of message persuasiveness and message comprehensibility. *Journal of Personality and Social Psychology, 34*, 605–614.

Chaiken, S., & Eagly, A.H. (1983). Communication modality as a determinant of persuasion: The role of communicator salience. *Journal of Personality and Social Psychology, 45*, 241–256.

Chaiken, S., & Stangor, C. (1987). Attitudes and attitude change. In M.R. Rosenzweig & L. Porter (Eds.), *Annual Review of Psychology* (Vol. 38). Palo Alto, CA: Annual Reviews.

Chaiken, S., & Yates, S. (1985). Affective-cognitive consistency and thought-induced attitude polarization. *Journal of Personality and Social Psychology, 49*, 1470–1481.

Chaplin, W.F., & Goldberg, L.R. (1985). A failure to replicate the Bem and Allen study of individual differences in cross-situational consistency. *Journal of Personality and Social Psychology, 47*, 1074–1090.

Chapman, L.J., & Chapman, J.P. (1967). Genesis of popular but erroneous psychodiagnostic observation. *Journal of Abnormal Psychology, 72*, 193–204.

Chapman, L.J., & Chapman, J.P. (1969). Illusory correlation as an obstacle to the use of valid psychodiagnostic signs. *Journal of Abnormal Psychology, 74*, 271–280.

Chelune, G.J. (1979). Measuring openness in interpersonal communication. In G.J. Chelune (Ed.), *Self-disclosure*. San Francisco: Jossey-Bass.

Chelune, G.J., Skiffington, S., & Williams, C. (1981). Multidimensional analysis of observers' perceptions of self-disclosing behavior. *Journal of Personality and Social Psychology, 41*, 599–606.

Chemers, M.M., & Skrzypek, G.J. (1972). Experimental test of the contingency model of leadership effectiveness. *Journal of Personality and Social Psychology, 24*, 172–177.

Chemers, M.M., Hays, R.B., Rhodewalt, F., & Wysocki, J. (1985). A person–environment analysis of job stress: A contingency model explanation. *Journal of Personality and Social Psychology, 49*, 628–635.

Christensen, L. (1982). Examination of subject roles: A critique of Carlston and Cohen. *Personality and Social Psychology Bulletin, 8*, 579–583.

Cialdini, R. (1985). *Influence: Science and practice*. Glenview, IL: Scott, Foresman and Company.

Cialdini, R.B., Borden, R.J., Thorne, A., Walker, M.R., Freeman, S., & Sloan, L.R. (1976). Basking in reflected glory: Three (football) field studies. *Journal of Personality and Social Psychology, 34*, 366–375.

Cialdini, R.B., Braver, S.L., & Lewis, S.K. (1974). Attributional bias and the easily persuaded other. *Journal of Personality and Social Psychology, 30*, 631–637.

Cialdini, R.B., Darby, B.L., & Vincent, J.E. (1973). Transgression and altruism: A case for hedonism. *Journal of Experimental Social Psychology, 9*, 502–516.

Cialdini, R.B., Petty, R.E., & Cacioppo, J.T. (1981). Attitude and attitude change. In M.R. Rosenzweig & L.W. Porter (Eds.), *Annual review of psychology* (Vol. 32). Palo Alto, CA: Annual Reviews.

Cialdini, R.B., & Richardson, K.D. (1980). Two indirect tactics of image management: Basking and blasting. *Journal of Personality and Social Psychology, 39*, 406–415.

Cialdini, R.B., Vincent, J.E., Lewis, S.K., Catalan, J., Wheeler, D., & Darby, B.L. (1975). Reciprocal concessions procedure for inducing compliance: The door-in-the-face technique. *Journal of Personality and Social Psychology, 31*, 206–215.

Clark, H.H. (1985). Language use and language users. In G. Lindzey & E. Aronson (Eds.), *The handbook of social psychology* (3rd ed.). New York: Random House.

Clark, H.H., & Clark, E.V. (1977). *Psychology and language: An introduction to psycholinguistics*. New York: Harcourt Brace Jovanovich.

Clark, H.H., & Haviland, S.E. (1974). Psychological processes as linguistic explanation. In D. Cohen (Ed.), *Explaining linquistic phenomena*. Washington, DC: Hemisphere Publishing.

Clark, M.S. (1981). Noncomparability of benefits given and received: A cue for the existence of friendship. *Social Psychology Quarterly, 44*, 375–381.

Clark, M.S. (1984). Record keeping in two types of relationship. *Journal of Personality and Social Psychology, 47*, 549–557.

Clark, M.S., & Isen, A.M. (1982). Toward understanding the relationship between feeling states and social behavior. In A.H. Hastorf & A.M. Isen (Eds.), *Cognitive social psychology*. New York: Elsevier.

Clark, M.S., & Mills, J. (1979). Interpersonal attraction in exchange and communal relationships. *Journal of Personality and Social Psychology, 37,* 12–24.

Clark, M.S., & Waddell, B.A. (1983). Effects of moods on thoughts about helping, attraction, and information seeking. *Social Psychology Quarterly, 46,* 31–35.

Clark, R.D., III, & Word, L.E. (1972). Why don't bystanders help? Because of ambiguity? *Journal of Personality and Social Psychology, 24,* 392–400.

Clarke-Stewart, K.A. (1978). And daddy makes three: The father's impact on mother and young child. *Child Development, 49,* 466–478.

Cloward, R., & Ohlin, L.E. (1960). *Delinquency and opportunity: A theory of delinquent gangs.* Glencoe, IL: Free Press.

Coch, L. & French, J.R.P. (1948). Overcoming resistance to change. *Human Relations, 1,* 512–532.

Cohen, A. (1955). *Delinquent boys.* Glencoe, IL: Free Press.

Cohen, L.J. (1982). Are people programmed to commit fallacies? Further thoughts about the interpretation of experimental data on probability judgment. *Journal for the Theory of Social Behavior, 12,* 251–274.

Coke, J.S., Batson, C.D., & McDavis, K. (1978). Empathic mediation of helping: A two-stage model. *Journal of Personality and Social Psychology, 36,* 752–766.

Collins, W.A. (1983). Social antecedents, cognitive processing, and comprehension of social portrayals on television. In E.T. Higgins, D.N. Ruble, & W.W. Hartup (Eds.), *Social cognition and social development: A sociocultural perspective.* Cambridge: University of Cambridge Press.

Comer, R.J., & Piliavin, J.A. (1972). The effects of physical deviance upon face-to-face interaction. The other side. *Journal of Personality and Social Psychology, 23,* 33–39.

Comstock, G., Chaffee, S., Katzman, N., McCombs, M., & Roberts, D. (1978). *Television and human behavior.* New York: Columbia University Press.

Conley, J.J. (1984). Relation of temporal stability and cross-situational consistency in personality: Comment on the Mischel–Epstein debate. *Psychological Review, 91,* 491–496.

Conquest, R. (1968). *The great terror: Stalin's purge of the Thirties.* New York: Macmillan.

Constantinople, A. (1973). Masculinity–femininity: An exception to a famous dictum? *Psychological Bulletin, 80,* 389–407.

Conway, M., & Ross, M. (1984). Getting what you want by revising what you had. *Journal of Personality and Social Psychology, 47,* 738–748.

Cook, M. (1969). Anxiety, speech disturbances and speech rate. *British Journal of Social and Clinical Psychology, 8,* 13–21.

Cook, T.D. (1969). Competence, counterarguing, and attitude change. *Journal of Personality, 37,* 342–358.

Cooper, H.M. (1979). Statistically combining independent studies: A meta-analysis of sex differences in conformity research. *Journal of Personality and Social Psychology, 37,* 131–146.

Cooper, J., & Jones, E.E. (1969). Opinion divergence as a strategy to avoid being miscast. *Journal of Personality and Social Psychology, 13,* 23–30.

Cooper, J., Zanna, M.P., & Goethals, G.R. (1974). Mistreatment of an esteemed other as a consequence affecting dissonance reduction. *Journal of Experimental Social Psychology, 10,* 224–233.

Cooper, W.H. (1981). Ubiquitous halo. *Psychological Bulletin, 90,* 218–244.

Cottrell, N.B. (1968). Performance in the presence of other human beings: Mere presence, audience and affiliation effects. In E.C. Simmel, R.A. Hoppe, & G.A. Milton (Eds.), *Social facilitation and imitative behavior.* Boston: Allyn & Bacon.

Cottrell, N.B., Wack, D.L., Sekerak, G.O., & Rittle, R.H. (1968). Social facilitation of dominant responses by the presence of an audience and the mere presence of others. *Journal of Personality and Social Psychology, 9,* 245–250.

Crano, W.D., & Sivacek, J. (1982). Social reinforcement, self-attribution, and the foot-in-the-door phenomenon. *Social Cognition, 1,* 110–125.

Crocker, J., Hannah, D.B., & Weber, R. (1983). Person memory and causal attributions. *Journal of Personality and Social Psychology, 44,* 55–66.

Crockett, W.H. (1982). Balance, agreement, and positivity in the cognition of small social structures. In L. Berkowitz (Ed.), *Advances in experimental social psychology* (Vol. 15). New York: Academic Press.

Crook, J.H. (1981). The evolutionary ethology of social processes in man. In H. Kellerman (Ed.), *Group cohesion.* New York: Grune & Stratton.

Crosby, F., Bromley, S., & Saxe, L. (1980). Recent unobtrusive studies of black and white discrimination and prejudice: A literature review. *Psychological Bulletin, 87,* 546–563.

Cross, J.G., & Guyer, M.J. (1980). *Social traps.* Ann Arbor, MI: University of Michigan Press.

Crowne, D., & Marlowe, D. (1964). *The approval motive: Studies in evaluative dependence.* New York: Wiley.

Croyle, R.T., & Cooper, J. (1983). Dissonance arousal: Physiological evidence. *Journal of Personality and Social Psychology, 45,* 782–791.

Crutchfield, R.S. (1955). Conformity and character. *American Psychologist, 10,* 191–198.

Cunningham, J.D., Starr, P.A., & Kanouse, D.E. (1979). Self as actor, active observer, and passive observer: Implications for causal attributions. *Journal of Personality and Social Psychology, 37,* 1146–1152.

Cunningham, M.R. (1979). Weather, mood, and helping behavior: Quasi-experiments with the sunshine Samaritan. *Journal of Personality and Social Psychology, 37,* 1947–1956.

D

D'Andrade, R.G. (1974). Memory and the assessment of behavior. In T. Blalock (Ed.), *Measurement in the social sciences.* Chicago: Aldine-Atherton.

Damon, W. (1975). Early conceptions of positive justice as related to the development of logical operations. *Child Development, 46,* 301–312.

Damon, W. (1977). *The social world of the child.* San Francisco: Jossey-Bass.

Damon, W., & Hart, D. (1982). The development of self-understanding from infancy through adolescence. *Child Development, 53,* 841–864.

Danheiser, P.R., & Graziano, W.G. (1982). Self-monitoring and cooperation as a self-presentation strategy. *Journal of Personality and Social Psychology, 42,* 497–505.

Darley, J.M., & Berscheid, E. (1967). Increased liking as a result of the anticipation of personal contact. *Human Relations, 20,* 29–40.

Darley, J.M., & Fazio, R.H. (1980). Expectancy confirmation processes arising in the social interaction sequence. *American Psychologist, 35,* 867–881.

Darley, J.M., & Gross, P.H. (1983). A hypothesis-confirming bias in labeling effects. *Journal of Personality and Social Psychology, 44,* 20–33.

Darley, J.M., & Latané, B. (1968). Bystander intervention in emergencies: Diffusion of responsibility. *Journal of Personality and Social Psychology, 8,* 377–383.

Darley, J.M., Teger, A.I., & Lewis, L.D. (1973). Do groups always inhibit individuals' responses to potential emergencies? *Journal of Personality and Social Psychology, 26,* 395–399.

Darwin, C. (1859). *The origin of species by means of natural selection, or the preservation of favored races in the struggle for life.* New York: Modern Library.

Darwin, C. (1872). *The expression of emotions in man and animals.* London: John Murray.

Darwin, C. (1877). A biological sketch of an infant. *Mind, 11,* 286–294.

Davies, J.C. (1962). Toward a theory of revolution. *American Sociological Review, 27,* 5–19.

Davies, N. (1981). *Human sacrifice: In history and today.* New York: Morrow.

Davis, D. (1981). Implications for interaction versus effectance as mediators of the similarity–attraction relationship. *Journal of Experimental Social Psychology, 17,* 96–116.

Davis, D., & Holtgraves, T. (1984). Perceptions of unresponsive others: Attributions, attraction, understandability, and memory of their utterances. *Journal of Experimental Social Psychology, 20,* 383–408.

Davis, J.H., Kerr, N.L., Atkin, R.S., Holt, R., & Meek, D. (1975). The decision processes of 6- and 12-person mock juries assigned unanimous and two-thirds majority rules. *Journal of Personality and Social Psychology, 32,* 1–14.

Davis, K.E. (1985). Near and dear: Friendship and love compared. *Psychology Today, 19,* 22–30.

Dawes, R.M., McTavish, J., & Shaklee, H. (1977). Behavior, communication, and assumptions about other people's behavior in a commons dilemma situation. *Journal of Personality and Social Psychology, 35,* 1–11.

Deaux, K., & Lewis, L.L. (1984). Structure of gender stereotypes: Interrelationships among components and gender label. *Journal of Personality and Social Psychology, 46,* 991–1004.

Deci, E. (1971). Effects of externally mediated rewards on intrinsic motivation. *Journal of Personality and Social Psychology, 18,* 105–115.

Deci, E. (1975). *Intrinsic motivation.* New York: Plenum.

Deci, E.L., & Ryan, R.M. (1980). The empirical exploration of intrinsic motivation processes. In L. Berkowitz (Ed.), *Advances in experimental social psychology* (Vol. 13). New York: Academic Press.

Deci, E.L., & Ryan, R.M. (1985). *Motivation and self-determination in human behavior.* New York: Plenum.

Deffenbacher, K.A. (1980). Eyewitness accuracy and confidence: Can we infer anything about their relationship? *Law and Human Behavior, 4,* 243–260.

DeFleur, M.L., & Westie, F.A. (1958). Verbal attitudes and overt acts: An experiment in the salience of attitudes. *American Sociological Review, 23,* 667–673.

DeJong, W. (1979). An examination of self-perception mediation of the foot-in-the-door effect. *Journal of Personality and Social Psychology, 37,* 2221–2239.

DeJong, W., Marber, S., & Shaver, R. (1980). Crime intervention: The role of a victim's behavior in reducing situational ambiguity. *Personality and Social Psychology Bulletin, 6,* 113–118.

DePaulo, B.M., Brittingham, G.L., & Kaiser, M.K. (1983). Receiving competence-relevant help: Effects on reciprocity, affect, and sensitivity to the helper's nonverbally expressed needs. *Journal of Personality and Social Psychology, 45,* 1045–1060.

DePaulo, B.M., Rosenthal, R., Green, C.R., & Rosenkrantz, J. (1982). Diagnosing deceptive and mixed messages from verbal and nonverbal cues. *Journal of Experimental Social Psychology, 18,* 433–446.

Derlega, V.J., Harris, M.S., & Chaikin, A.L. (1973). Self-disclosure reciprocity, liking, and the deviant. *Journal of Experimental Social Psychology, 9,* 277–284.

Derlega, V.J., Wilson, M., & Chaikin, A.L. (1976). Friendship and disclosure reciprocity. *Journal of Personality and Social Psychology, 37,* 578–582.

Dermer, M., Cohen, S.J., Jacobsen, E., & Anderson, E.A. (1979). Evaluative judgments of aspects of life as a function of vicarious exposure to hedonic extremes. *Journal of Personality and Social Psychology, 37,* 247–260.

Dermer, M., & Pyszczynski, T.A. (1978). Effects of erotica upon men's loving and liking responses for women they love. *Journal of Personality and Social Psychology, 36,* 1302–1309.

DeSoto, C.B., Hamilton, M.M., & Taylor, R.B. (1985). Words, people, and implicit personality theory. *Social Cognition, 3,* 369–382.

Deutsch, M., & Gerard, H.B. (1955). A study of normative and informational social influences upon individual judgement. *Journal of Abnormal and Social Psychology, 51,* 629–636.

Deutsch, M., Epstein, Y., Canavan, P., & Gumpert, P. (1967). Strategies of inducing cooperation. *Journal of Conflict Resolution, 11,* 345–360.

Deutsch, M., & Krauss, R.M. (1960). The effect of threat upon interpersonal bargaining. *Journal of Abnormal and Social Psychology, 61,* 181–189.

Deutsch, M., & Solomon, L. (1959). Reactions to evaluations by others as influenced by self-evaluations. *Sociometry, 22,* 93–112.

Deutschmann, P.J. (1962). Viewing, conversation, and voting intentions. In S. Kraus (Ed.), *The great debates.* Bloomington: Indiana University Press.

Dickens, W.J., & Perlman, D. (1981). Friendship over the life-cycle. In S. Duck & R. Gilmour (Eds.), *Personal relationships. 2: Developing personal relationships.* New York: Academic Press.

Dickoff, H. (1961). Reactions to evaluations by others as a function of self-evaluation and the interaction context. Unpublished Ph.D. thesis, Duke Univeristy.

Diener, E. (1979). Deindividuation, self-awareness, and disinhibition. *Journal of Personality and Social Psychology, 37,* 1160–1171.

Diener, E. (1980). Deindividuation: The absence of self-awareness and self-regulation in group members. In P. Paulus (Ed.), *The psychology of group influence,* Hillsdale, NJ: Lawrence Erlbaum.

Diener, E., & DeFour, D. (1978). Does television violence enhance program popularity? *Journal of Personality and Social Psychology, 36,* 333–341.

Diener, E., Larsen, R.J., & Emmons, R.A. (1984). Person × situation interactions: Choice of situations and congruence response models. *Journal of Personality and Social Psychology, 47,* 580–592.

Diener, E., Lusk, R., DeFour, D., & Flax, R. (1980). Deindividuation: Effects of group size, density, number of observers, and group member similarity on self-conscious and disinhibited behavior. *Journal of Personality and Social Psychology, 39,* 449–459.

Dienstbier, R.A., & Munter, P.O. (1971). Cheating as a function of the labeling of natural arousal. *Journal of Personality and Social Psychology, 17,* 208–213.

Dipboye, R.L., & Flanagan, M.F. (1979). Research set-

tings in industrial and organizational psychology: Are findings in the field more generalizable than in the laboratory? *America Psychologist, 34,* 141–150.

DiVitto, B., & McArthur, L.Z. (1978). Developmental differences in the use of distinctiveness, consensus, and consistency information for making causal attributions. *Developmental Psychology, 14,* 474–482.

Dix, T., & Grusec, J.E. (1983). Parental influence techniques: An attributional analysis. *Child Development, 54,* 645–652.

Dodge, K.A. (1980). Social cognition and children's aggressive behavior. *Child Development, 51,* 162–170.

Dodge, K.A. (1983). Behavioral antecedents of peer social status. *Child Development, 54,* 1386–1399.

Dodge, K.A., & Frame, C.L. (1982). Social cognitive biases and deficits in aggressive boys. *Child Development, 53,* 620–635.

Dollard, J., Doob, L.W., Miller, N., Mowrer, O.H., & Sears, R.R. (1939). *Frustration and aggression.* New Haven, CT: Yale University Press.

Donnerstein, E. (1980). Aggressive erotica and violence against women. *Journal of Personality and Social Psychology, 39,* 269–277.

Donnerstein, E., & Berkowitz, L. (1981). Victim reactions in aggressive erotic films as a factor in violence against women. *Journal of Personality and Social Psychology, 41,* 710–724.

Donnerstein, E., & Donnerstein, M. (1973). Variables in interracial aggression: Potential in-group censure. *Journal of Personality and Social Psychology, 27,* 143–150.

Donnerstein, E., Donnerstein, M., & Evans, R. (1975). Erotic stimuli and aggression: Facilitation or inhibition. *Journal of Personality and Social Psychology, 32,* 237–244.

Donnerstein, E., Donnerstein, M., Simon, S., & Ditrichs, R. (1972). Variables in interracial aggression: Anonymity, expected retaliation and a riot. *Journal of Personality and Social Psychology, 22,* 236–245.

Doob, A.N., & Macdonald, G.E. (1979). Television viewing and fear of victimization: Is the relationship causal? *Journal of Personality and Social Psychology, 37,* 170–179.

Doob, A.N., & Wood, L.E. (1972). Catharsis and aggression: Effects of annoyance and retaliation on aggressive behavior. *Journal of Personality and Social Psychology, 22,* 156–162.

Dovidio, J.F. (1984). Helping behavior and altruism: An empirical and conceptual overview. In L. Berkowitz (Ed.), *Advances in experimental social psychology* (Vol. 17). Orlando, FL: Academic Press.

Dovidio, J.F., & Ellyson, S. L. (1982). Decoding visual dominance: Attributions of power based on relative percentages of looking while speaking and looking while listening. *Social Psychology Quarterly, 45,* 106–113.

Dovidio, J.F., & Gaertner, S.L. (1986). Prejudice, discrimination, and racism: Historical trends and contemporary approaches. In J.F. Dovidio & S.L. Gaertner (Eds.), *Prejudice, discrimination, and racism.* Orlando, FL: Academic Press.

Dreben, E.K., Fiske, S.T., & Hastie, R. (1979). The independence of evaluative and item information: Impression and recall order effects in behavior-based impression formation. *Journal of Personality and Social Psychology, 37,* 1758–1768.

Dreitzel, H.P. (1970). *Recent sociology. 2: Patterns of communicative behavior.* New York: Macmillan.

Duncan, B.L. (1976). Differential social perception and attribution of intergroup violence: Testing the lower limits of stereotyping of blacks. *Journal of Personality and Social Psychology, 34,* 590–598.

Duncan, S. (1972). Some signals and rules for taking speaking turns in conversations. *Journal of Personality and Social Psychology, 23,* 283–292.

Duncan, S., Brunner, L.J., & Fiske, D.W. (1979). Strategy signals in face-to-face interaction. *Journal of Personality and Social Psychology, 37,* 301–313.

Duncan, S., & Fiske, D. (1977). *Face-to-face interaction.* Hillsdale, NJ: Lawrence Erlbaum.

Duncan, S., & Rosenthal, R. (1968). Vocal emphasis in experimenters' instruction reading as unintended determinant of subjects' responses. *Language and Speech, 11,* 20–26.

Dutton, D.G. (1972). Effect of feedback parameters on congruency versus positivity effects in reactions to personal evaluations. *Journal of Personality and Social Psychology, 24,* 366–371.

Dutton, D.G., & Aron, A.P. (1974). Some evidence for heightened sexual attraction under conditions of high anxiety. *Journal of Personality and Social Psychology, 30,* 510–517.

Duval, S., & Wicklund, R.A. (1972). *A theory of objective self-awareness.* New York: Academic Press.

E

Eagly, A.H. (1974). Comprehensibility of persuasive arguments as a determinant of opinion change. *Journal of Personality and Social Psychology, 29,* 758–773.

Eagly, A.H. (1978). Sex differences in influenceability. *Psychological Bulletin, 85,* 86–116.

Eagly, A.H. (1981). Recipient characteristics as determinants of responses to persuasion. In R. E. Petty, T. M. Ostrom, & T. C. Brock (Eds.), *Cognitive responses in persuasion.* Hillsdale, NJ: Lawrence Erlbaum.

Eagly, A.H. (1983). Gender and social influence: A social psychological analysis. *American Psychologist, 38,* 971–981.

Eagly, A.H., & Carli, L.L. (1981). Sex of researchers and sex-typed communications as determinants of sex differences in influenceability: A meta-analysis of social influence studies. *Psychological Bulletin, 90,* 1–20.

Eagly, A.H. & Chaiken, S. (1984). Cognitive theories of persuasion. In L. Berkowitz (Ed.), *Advances in experimental social psychology* (Vol. 17). New York: Academic Press.

Eagly, A.H., & Crowley, M. (1986). Gender and helping behavior: A meta-analytic review of the social psychological literature. *Psychological Bulletin, 100,* 283–308.

Eagly, A.H., & Steffen, V.J. (1984). Gender stereotypes stem from the distribution of women and men into social roles. *Journal of Personality and Social Psychology, 46,* 735–754.

Eagly, A.H., & Steffen, V.J. (1986). Gender and aggressive behavior: A meta-analytic review of the social psychological literature. *Psychological Bulletin, 100,* 309–330.

Eagly, A.H., Wood, W., & Chaiken, S. (1978). Causal inferences about communicators and their effect on opinion change. *Journal of Personality and Social Psychology, 36,* 424–435.

Earle, W.B., Giuliano, T., & Archer, R.L. (1983). Lonely at the top: The effect of power on information flow in the dyad. *Personality and Social Psychology Bulletin, 9,* 629–637.

Easterbrooks, M.A., & Goldberg, W.A. (1984). Toddler development in the family: Impact of father involvement and parenting characteristics. *Child Development, 55,* 740–752.

Ebbesen, E.B., & Bowers, R.J. (1974). Proportion of risky to conservative arguments in a group decision and choice shift. *Journal of Personality and Social Psychology, 29,* 316–327.

Ebbesen, E.B., Kjos, G.L., & Konečni, V.J. (1976). Spatial ecology: Its effects on the choice of friends and enemies. *Journal of Experimental Social Psychology, 12,* 505–518.

Eckerman, C.O., & Stein, M.R. (1982). The toddler's emerging interactive skills. In K. H. Rubin & H. S. Ross (Eds.), *Peer relationships and social skills in childhood.* New York: Springer-Verlag.

Edinger, J.A., & Patterson, M.L. (1983). Nonverbal involvement and social control. *Psychological Bulletin, 93,* 30–56.

Edwards, J.R. (1979). Judgments and confidence reactions to disadvantaged speech. In H. Giles & R. N. St. Clair (Eds.), *Language and social psychology.* Oxford: Basil Blackwell.

Efran, M.G., & Cheyne, J.A. (1974). Affective concomitants of the invasion of shared space: Behavioral, physiological, and verbal indicators. *Journal of Personality and Social Psychology, 29,* 219–228.

Egeland, B., & Farber, E.A. (1984). Infant–mother attachment: Factors related to its development and changes over time. *Child Development, 55,* 753–771.

Einhorn, H.J., & Hogarth, R.M. (1986). Judging probable cause. *Psychological Bulletin, 99*, 3–19.

Eisenberg, N., & Lennon, R. (1983). Sex differences in empathy and related capacities. *Psychological Bulletin, 94*, 100–131.

Eisenberg, N., Pasternack, J.F., Cameron, E., & Tryon, K. (1984). The relation of quantity and mode of prosocial behavior to moral cognitions and social style. *Child Development, 55*, 1479–1485.

Eisenberg-Berg, N., & Hand, M. (1979). The relationship of preschoolers' reasoning about prosocial moral conflicts to prosocial behavior. *Child Development, 50*, 356–363.

Eiser, J.R. (1980). *Cognitive social psychology*. London: McGraw-Hill.

Ekman, P., & Friesen, W.V. (1969). Nonverbal leakage and cues to deception. *Psychiatry, 32*, 88–108.

Ekman, P., & Friesen, W.V. (1971). Constants across cultures in the face and emotion. *Journal of Personality and Social Psychology, 17*, 124–129.

Ekman, P., & Friesen, W.V. (1974). Detecting deception from the body or face. *Journal of Personality and Social Psychology, 29*, 288–298.

Ekman, P., Friesen, W., & Ellsworth, P. (1972). *Emotion in the human face*. New York: Pergamon Press.

Ekman, P., Friesen, W.V., & Scherer, K.R. (1976). Body movement and voice pitch in deceptive interaction. *Semiotica, 16*, 23–27.

Elkin, R.A., & Leippe, M.R. (1986). Physiological arousal, dissonance, and attitude change: Evidence for a dissonance–arousal link and a "don't remind me" effect. *Journal of Personality and Social Psychology, 51*, 55–65.

Elliott, G.C. (1979). Some effects of deception and level of self-monitoring on planning and reacting to a self-presentation. *Journal of Personality and Social Psychology, 37*, 1282–1292.

Ellsworth, P.C., Carlsmith, J.M., & Henson, A. (1972). The stare as a stimulus to flight in human subjects: A series of field experiments. *Journal of Personality and Social Psychology, 21*, 302–311.

Ellyson, S.L., Dovidio, J.F., & Fehr, B.J. (1981). Visual behavior and dominance in women and men. In C. Mayo & N.M. Henley (Eds.), *Gender and nonverbal behavior*. New York: Springer-Verlag.

Ember, C.R. (1981). A cross-cultural perspective on sex differences. In R.H. Munroe, R.L. Munroe, & B.B. Whiting (Eds.), *Handbook of cross cultural psychology*. New York: STPM Press.

Endler, N.S., Hunt, J.M., & Rosenstein, A.J. (1962). An S–R inventory of anxiousness. *Psychological Monograph, 76*, #17 (Whole #536).

Epley, S.W. (1974). Reduction of the behavioral effects of aversive stimulation by the presence of companions. *Psychological Bulletin, 81*, 271–283.

Epstein, S. (1979). Explorations in personality today and tomorrow: A tribute to Henry A. Murray. *American Psychologist 34*, 649–653.

Epstein, S. (1980). The stability of behavior: II. Implications for psychological research. *American Psychologist, 35*, 790–806.

Epstein, S. (1983). The stability of confusion: A reply to Mischel and Peake. *Psychological Review, 90*, 179–184.

Epstein, S., & O'Brien, E.J. (1985). The person–situation debate in historic and current perspective. *Psychological Bulletin, 98*, 513–537.

Ericsson, K.A., & Simon, H.A. (1980). Verbal reports as data. *Psychological Review, 87*, 215–251.

Eron, L.D. (1963). Relationship of TV viewing habits and aggressive behavior in children. *Journal of Abnormal and Social Psychology, 67*, 193–196.

Eron, L.D., Lefkowitz, M.M., Huesmann, L.R., & Walder, L.Q. (1972). Does television violence cause aggression? *American Psychologist, 27*, 253–263.

Evans, G.W. (1978). Human spatial behavior: The arousal model. In A. Baum & Y.M. Epstein (Eds.), *Human response to crowding*. Hillsdale, NJ: Lawrence Erlbaum.

Exline, R. (1963). Explorations in the process of person perception: Visual interaction in relation to competition, sex, and nAff. *Journal of Personality, 31*, 1–20.

Exline, R., & Winters, L. (1965). Affective relations and mutual glances in dyads. In S. Tomkins & C. Izard (Eds.), *Affect, cognition, and personality*. New York: Springer.

F

Farkas, A.J., & Anderson, N.H. (1979). Multidimensional input in equity theory. *Journal of Personality and Social Psychology, 37*, 879–896.

Faunce, W.A. (1984). School achievement, social status, and self-esteem. *Social Psychology Quarterly, 47*, 3–14.

Fazio, R.H., Chen, J-M., McDonel, E.C., & Sherman, S.J. (1982). Attitude accessibility, attitude–behavior consistency, and the strength of the object–evaluation association. *Journal of Experiemental Social Psychology, 18*, 339–357.

Fazio, R.H., Herr, P.M., & Olney, T.J. (1984). Attitude accessibility following a self-perception process. *Journal of Personality and Social Psychology, 47*, 277–286.

Fazio, R.H., & Zanna, M.P. (1981). Direct experience and attitude–behavior consistency. In L. Berkowitz (Ed.), *Advances in experimental social psychology* (Vol. 14). New York: Academic Press.

Fazio, R.H., Zanna, M.P., & Cooper, J. (1977). Dissonance and self-perception: An integrative view of each theory's proper domain of application. *Journal of Experimental Social Psychology, 13*, 464–479.

Feinberg, J. (1965). Action and responsibility. In M. Black (Ed.), *Philosophy in America*. London: Allen & Unwin.

Feldman, N.S., Higgins, E.T., Karlovac, M., & Ruble, D.N. (1976). Use of consensus information in causal attributions as a function of temporal presentation and availability of direct information. *Journal of Personality and Social Psychology, 34*, 694–698.

Feldman, N.S., Klosson, E.C., Parsons, J.E., Rholes, W.S., & Ruble, D.N. (1976). Order of information presentation and children's moral judgments. *Child Development, 47*, 556–559.

Felson, R.B. (1981). Self and reflected appraisal among football players: A test of the Meadian hypothesis. *Social Psychology Quarterly, 44*, 116–126.

Fenigstein, A. (1979). Does aggression cause a preference for viewing media violence? *Journal of Personality and Social Psychology, 37*, 2307–2317.

Fenigstein, A. (1984). Self-consciousness and the overperception of self as a target. *Journal of Personality and Social Psychology, 47*, 860–870.

Fenigstein, A., Scheier, M.F., & Buss, A.H. (1975). Public and private self-consciousness: Assessment and theory. *Journal of Consulting and Clinical Psychology, 4*, 522–527.

Feshbach, S., & Singer, R.D. (1971). *Television and aggression: An experimental field study*. San Francisco: Jossey-Bass.

Festinger, L. (1950). Informal social communication. *Psychological Review, 57*, 271–282.

Festinger, L. (1954). A theory of social comparison process. *Human Relations, 7*, 117–140.

Festinger, L. (1957). *A theory of cognitive dissonance*. New York: Row, Peterson.

Festinger, L., & Carlsmith, J.M. (1959). Cognitive consequences of forced compliance. *Journal of Abnormal and Social Psychology, 58*, 203–210.

Festinger, L., Gerard, H.B., Hymovitch, B., Kelley, H.H., & Raven, B. (1952). The influence process in the presence of extreme deviates. *Human Relations, 5*, 327–346.

Festinger, L., & Maccoby, N. (1964). On resistance to persuasive communications. *Journal of Abnormal and Social Psychology, 68*, 359–366.

Festinger, L., Pepitone, A., & Newcomb, T.M. (1952). Some consequences of de-individuation in a group. *Journal of Abnormal and Social Psychology, 47*, 382–389.

Festinger, L., Riecken, H., & Schachter, S. (1956). *When prophecy fails*. Minneapolis: University of Minnesota Press.

Festinger, L., Schachter, S., & Back, K. (1950). *Social pressures in informal groups*. New York: Harper.

Festinger, L., & Thibaut, J. (1951). Interpersonal communication in small groups. *Journal of Abnormal and Social Psychology, 46*, 92–100.

Fiedler, F.E. (1978). The contingency model and the dynamics of the leadership process. In L. Berkowitz (Ed.), *Advances in experimental social psychology* (Vol. 11). New York: Academic Press.

Fillenbaum, S. (1966). Prior deception and subsequent experimental performance: The "faithful" subject. *Journal of Personality and Social Psychology, 4*, 532–553.

Fillenbaum, S., & Frey, R. (1970). More on the "faithful" behavior of suspicious subjects. *Journal of Personality, 38*, 43–51.

Fincham, F.D., & Jaspers, J.M. (1980). Attribution of responsibility: From man the scientist to man as lawyer. In L. Berkowitz (Ed.), *Advances in experimental social psychology* (Vol. 13). New York: Academic Press.

Fischhoff, B., & Beyth-Marom, R. (1983). Hypothesis evaluation from a Bayesian perspective. *Psychological Review, 90*, 239–260.

Fishbein, M. (1967a). A behavioral theory approach to the relations between beliefs about an object and the attitude toward the object. In M. Fishbein (Ed.), *Attitude theory and measurement*. New York: Wiley.

Fishbein, M. (1967b). Attitude and the prediction of behavior. In M. Fishbein (Ed.), *Attitude theory and measurement*. New York: Wiley.

Fishbein, M., & Ajzen, I. (1974). Attitudes towards objects as predictors of single and multiple behavioral criteria. *Psychological Review, 81*, 59–74.

Fishbein, M., & Ajzen, I. (1975). *Belief, attitude, intention, and behavior: An introduction to theory and research*. Reading, MA: Addison-Wesley.

Fisher, J.D., Nadler, A., & Whitcher-Alagna, S. (1982). Recipient reactions to aid. *Psychological Bulletin, 91*, 27–54.

Fishkin, J., Keniston, K., & MacKinnon, C. (1973). Moral reasoning and political ideology. *Journal of Personality and Social Psychology, 27*, 109–119.

Fishman, J.A. (1977). Language and ethnicity. In H. Giles (Ed.), *Language, ethnicity, and intergroup relations*. London: Academic Press.

Fiske, S.T. (1980). Attention and weight in person perception: The impact of negative and extreme behavior. *Journal of Personality and Social Psychology, 38*, 889–901.

Fiske, S.T., & Taylor, S.E. (1984). *Social cognition*. Reading, MA: Addison-Wesley.

Flaherty, J.F., & Dusek, J. (1980). An investigation of the relationship between psychological androgyny and components of self-concept. *Journal of Personality and Social Psychology, 38*, 984–992.

Flavell, J.H. (1978). The development of knowledge about visual perception. In C.B. Keasey (Ed.), *Nebraska Symposium on Motivation 1977*. Lincoln: University of Nebraska Press.

Flavell, J.H., Botkin, P.T., Fry, C.L., Jr., Wright, J.W., & Jarvis, P.E. (1968). *The development of role-taking and communication skills in children*. New York: Wiley.

Fleischer, R.A., & Chertkoff, J.M. (1986). Effects of dominance and sex on leader selection in dyadic work groups. *Journal of Personality and Social Psychology, 50,* 94–99.

Flowers, M.L. (1977). A laboratory test of some implications of Janis' groupthink hypothesis. *Journal of Personality and Social Psychology, 35,* 888–896.

Foa, U.G., & Foa, E.B. (1974). *Societal structures of the mind.* Springfield, IL: Charles C. Thomas.

Fodor, E.M., & Smith, T. (1982). The power motive as an influence on group decision making. *Journal of Personality and Social Psychology, 42,* 178–185.

Folkes, V.S., & Sears, D.O. (1977). Does everybody like a liker? *Journal of Experimental Social Psychology, 13,* 505–519.

Fong, G.T., & Markus, H. (1982). Self-schemas and judgments about others. *Social Cognition, 1,* 191–204.

Ford, M.E. (1979). The construct validity of egocentrism. *Psychological Bulletin, 86,* 1169–1188.

Forgas, J.P., Bower, G.H., & Krantz, S.E. (1984). The influence of mood on perceptions of social interaction. *Journal of Experimental Social Psychology, 20,* 497–513.

Foss, R.D. (1981). Structural effects in simulated jury decision making. *Journal of Personality and Social Psychology, 40,* 1055–1062.

Frable, D.E.S., & Bem, S.L. (1985). If you are gender schematic, all members of the opposite sex look alike. *Journal of Personality and Social Psychology, 49,* 459–468.

Fredricks, A.J., & Dossett, D.L. (1983). Attitude–behavior relations: A comparison of the Fishbein–Azjen and the Bentler–Speckart models. *Journal of Personality and Social Psychology, 45,* 501–512.

Freedman, J.L. (1969). Role playing: Psychology by consensus. *Journal of Personality and Social Psychology, 13,* 107–114.

Freedman, J.L. (1984). Effect of television violence on aggression. *Psychological Bulletin, 96,* 227–246.

Freedman, J.L. (1986). Television violence and aggression: A rejoinder. *Psychological Bulletin, 100,* 372–378.

Freedman, J.L., Birsky, J., & Cavoukian, A. (1980). Environmental determinants of behavioral contagion: Density and number. *Basic and Applied Social Psychology, 1,* 155–161.

Freedman, J.L., & Fraser, S. (1966). Compliance without pressure: The foot-in-the-door technique. *Journal of Personality and Social Psychology, 4,* 195–202.

Freedman, J.L., & Perlick, P. (1979). Crowding, contagion, and laughter. *Journal of Experimental Social Psychology, 15,* 295–303.

French, J.R.P., & Raven, B. (1959). The bases of social power. In D. Cartwright (Ed.), *Studies in social power.* Ann Arbor: University of Michigan Press.

Freud, S. (1922, original 1921). *Group psychology and the analysis of the ego.* London: Hogarth.

Freund, T., Kruglanski, A.W., & Shpitzajzen, A. (1985). The freezing and unfreezing of impressional primacy: Effects of the need for structure and the fear of invalidity. *Personality and Social Psychology Bulletin, 11,* 479–488.

Frey, D. (1981). Postdecisional preference for decision-relevant information as a function of the competence of its source and the degree of familiarity with its information. *Journal of Experimental Social Psychology, 17,* 51–67.

Frey, D. (1986). Recent research on selective exposure to information. In L. Berkowitz (Ed.), *Advances in experimental social psychology* (Vol. 19). New York: Academic Press.

Frey, D.L., & Gaertner, S.L. (1986). Helping and the avoidance of inappropriate interracial behavior: A strategy that perpetrates a nonprejudiced self-image. *Journal of Personality and Social Psychology, 50,* 1083–1090.

Friedman, L. (1981). How affiliation affects stress in fear and anxiety situations. *Journal of Personality and Social Psychology, 40,* 1102–1117.

Friedrich-Cofer, L., & Huston, A.C. (1986). Television violence and aggression: The debate continues. *Psychological Bulletin, 100,* 364–371.

Fromm, E. (1941). *Escape from freedom.* New York: Rinehart and Company.

Funder, D.C. (1982). On the accuracy of dispositional versus situational attributions. *Social Cognition, 1,* 205–222.

Furman, W., & Bierman, K.L. (1983). Developmental changes in young children's conceptions of friendship. *Child Development, 54,* 549–556.

G

Gabrielcik, A., & Fazio, R.H. (1984). Priming and frequency estimation: A strict test of the availability heuristic. *Personality and Social Psychology Bulletin, 10,* 85–89.

Gaertner, S.L., & Bickman, L. (1971). Effects of race on the elicitation of helping behavior: The wrong number technique, *Journal of Personality and Social Psychology 20,* 218–222.

Gaertner, S.L., & Dovidio, J.F. (1986). The aversive form of racism. In J.F. Dovidio & S.L. Gaertner (Eds.), *Prejudice, discrimination, and racism.* Orlando, FL: Academic Press.

Gaes, G.G., Kalle, R.J., & Tedeschi, J.T. (1978). Impression management in the forced compliance situation. *Journal of Experimental Social Psychology, 14,* 493–510.

Gara, M.A., & Rosenberg, S. (1981). Linguistic factors in implicit personality theory. *Journal of Personality and Social Psychology, 41,* 450–457.

Garfinkel, H. (1967). *Studies in ethnomethodology*. Englewood Cliffs, NJ: Prentice-Hall.

Garvey, C. (1974). Some properties of social play. *Merrill-Palmer Quarterly, 20*, 163–180.

Geen, R.G. (1981). Evaluation apprehension and social facilitation: A reply to Sanders. *Journal of Experimental Social Psychology, 17*, 252–256.

Geen, R.G., & O'Neal, E.C. (1969). Activation of cue-elicited aggression by general arousal. *Journal of Personality and Social Psychology, 11*, 289–292.

Geen, R.G., & Quanty, M.B. (1977). The catharsis of aggression: An evaluation of a hypothesis. In L. Berkowitz (Ed.), *Advances in experimental social psychology* (Vol. 10). New York: Academic Press.

Geertz, C. (1973). *The interpretation of cultures*. New York: Basic Books.

Georgoudi, M., & Rosnow, R.L. (1985). Notes toward a contextualist understanding of social psychology. *Personality and Social Psychology Bulletin, 11*, 5–22.

Gerard, H.B. (1963). Emotional uncertainty and social comparison. *Journal of Abnormal and Social Psychology, 66*, 568–573.

Gerard, H.B. (1983). School desegregation: The social science role. *American Psychologist, 38*, 869–877.

Gerard, H.B., & Fleischer, L. (1967). Recall and pleasantness of balanced and unbalanced cognitive structures. *Journal of Personality and Social Psychology, 7*, 332–337.

Gerard, H.B., & Miller, N. (1975). *School desegregation: A long-term study*. New York: Plenum Press.

Gerard, H.B., & Rabbie, J.M. (1961). Fear and social comparison. *Journal of Abnormal and Social Psychology, 62*, 568–592.

Gergen, K.J. (1965). The effects of interaction goals and personalistic feedback on presentation of self. *Journal of Personality and Social Psychology, 1*, 413–425.

Gergen, K.J. (1973). Social psychology as history. *Journal of Personality and Social Psychology, 26*, 309–320.

Gergen, K.J. (1982). *Toward transformation in social knowledge*. New York: Springer-Verlag.

Gergen, K.J. (1985). The social constructionist movement in modern psychology. *American Psychologist, 40*, 266–275.

Gibb, C.A. (1969). Leadership. In G. Lindzey & E. Aronson (Eds.), *The handbook of social psychology* (2nd edition, Vol. IV), Reading, MA: Addison-Wesley.

Gibbons, F.X., & Wicklund, R.A. (1982). Self-focused attention and helping behavior. *Journal of Personality and Social Psychology, 43*, 462–474.

Gilbert, D.T., & Jones, E.E. (1986). Perceiver-induced constraint: Interpretations of self-generated reality. *Journal of Personality and Social Psychology 50*, 269–280.

Gilbert, G.M. (1951). Stereotype persistence and change among college students. *Journal of Abnormal and Social Psychology, 46*, 245–254.

Gilbert, S.J. (1981). Another look at the Milgram obedience studies: The role of the graduated series of shocks. *Personality and Social Psychology Bulletin, 7*, 690–695.

Giles, H., & Powesland, P.F. (1975). *Speech style and social evaluation*. London: Academic Press.

Gillen, B. (1981). Physical attractiveness: A determinant of two types of goodness. *Personality and Social Psychology Bulletin, 7*, 277–281.

Gillig, P.M., & Greenwald, A.G. (1974). Is it time to lay the sleeper effect to rest? *Journal of Personality and Social Psychology, 29*, 132–139.

Gilovich, T. (1981). Seeing the past in the present: The effect of associations to familiar events on judgments and events. *Journal of Personality and Social Psychology, 40*, 797–808.

Gilovich, T. (1983). Biased evaluation and persistence in gambling. *Journal of Personality and Social Psychology, 44*, 1110–1126.

Ginsburg, H.J., & Miller, S.M. (1982). Sex differences in children's risk-taking behavior. *Child Development, 53*, 426–428.

Glucksberg, S., Krauss, R.M., & Weisberg, R. (1966). Referential communication in nursery school children: Method and some preliminary findings. *Journal of Experimental Child Psychology, 3*, 333–342.

Godfrey, D.K., Jones, E.E., & Lord, C.G. (1986). Self-promotion is not ingratiating. *Journal of Personality and Social Psychology, 50*, 106–115.

Goethals, G.R., Cooper, J., & Naficy, A. (1979). Role of foreseen, foreseeable, and unforeseen behavioral consequences in the arousal of cognitive dissonance. *Journal of Personality and Social Psychology, 37*, 1179–1185.

Goffman, E. (1955). On face-work: An analysis of ritual elements in social interaction. *Psychiatry, 18*, 213–231.

Goffman, E. (1959). *The presentation of self in everyday life*. New York: Doubleday/Anchor.

Goffman, E. (1963a). *Stigma: Notes on the management of spoiled identity*. Englewood Cliffs, NJ: Prentice-Hall.

Goffman, E. (1963b). *Behavior in public places*. New York: Free Press.

Goffman, E. (1974). *Frame analysis*. New York: Harper & Row.

Goldman, W., & Lewis, P. (1977). Beautiful is good: Evidence that the physically attractive are more socially skilled. *Journal of Experimental Social Psychology, 13*, 125–130.

Goldstein, J.H., & Arms, R.L. (1971). Effects of observing athletic contests on hostility. *Sociometry, 34*, 83–90.

Gonzales, M.H., Davis, J.M., Loney, G.L., Lukens, C.K., & Junghans, C.M. (1983). Interactional approach to interpersonal attraction. *Journal of Personality and Social Psychology, 44*, 1192–1197.

Gormly, J. (1983). Predicting behavior from personality test scores. *Personality and Social Psychology Bulletin, 9*, 267–270.

Gottman, J.M. (1979). *Martial interaction*. New York: Academic Press.

Gouldner, A. (1960). The norm of reciprocity: A preliminary statement. *American Sociological Review, 25,* 161–178.

Graesser, A.C., Woll, S.B., Kowalski, D.J., & Smith, D.A. (1980). Memory for typical and atypical actions in scripted activities. *Journal of Experimental Psychology: Human Learning and Memory, 6,* 503–515.

Gray-Little, B., & Appelbaum, M.I. (1979). Instrumentality effects in the assessment of racial differences in self-esteem. *Journal of Personality and Social Psychology, 37,* 1221–1229.

Green, K.D., Forehand, R., Beck, S.J., & Vosk, B. (1980). An assessment of the relationship among measures of children's social competence and children's academic achievement. *Child Development 51,* 1149–1156.

Green, S.K., Buchanan, D.R., & Heuer, S.K. (1984). Winners, losers, and choosers: A field investigation of dating initiation. *Personality and Social Psychology Bulletin, 10,* 502–511.

Greenberg, J. (1979). Group vs. individual equity judgments: Is there a polarization effect? *Journal of Experimental Psychology, 18,* 504–512.

Greenberg, M.S., & Ruback, R.B. (1982). *Social psychology of the criminal justice system.* Monterey, CA: Brooks/Cole Publishing Company.

Greenwald, A.G. (1980). The totalitarian ego: Fabrication and revision of personal history. *American Psychologist, 35,* 603–618.

Greenwald, A.G., & Pratkanis, A.R. (1984). The self. In R.S. Wyer, Jr., & T.K. Srull (Eds.), *Handbook of social cognition* (Vol. 3). Hillsdale, NJ: Lawrence Erlbaum.

Greenwood, J.D. (1982). On the relation between laboratory experiments and social behavior: Causal explanation and generalization. *Journal for the Theory of Social Behavior, 12,* 225–250.

Gregory, W.L., Cialdini, R.B., & Carpenter, K.M. (1982). Self-reliant scenarios as mediators of likelihood estimates and compliance: Does imagining make it so? *Journal of Personality and Social Psychology, 43,* 89–99.

Grice, H.P. (1975). Logic and conversation. In P. Cole & J. L. Morgan (Eds.), *Syntax and semantics. 3: Speech acts.* New York: Academic Press.

Grice, H.P. (1978). Some further notes on logic and conversation. In P. Cole (Ed.), *Syntax and semantics. 9: Pragmatics.* New York: Academic Press.

Gross, A.E., & Fleming, I. (1982). Twenty years of deception in social psychology. *Personality and Social Psychology Bulletin, 8,* 402–408.

Gruder, C.L. (1977). Choice of comparison persons in evaluating oneself. In J.M. Suls & R.L. Miller (Eds.), *Social comparison processes: Theoretical and empirical perspectives.* Washington, DC: Hemisphere.

Gruder, C.L., Cook, T.D., Hennigan, K.M., Fry, B.R., Alessis, C., & Halamaj, J. (1978). Empirical tests of the absolute sleeper effect predicted from the discounting cue hypothesis. *Journal of Personality and Social Psychology, 36,* 1061–1074.

Grueneich, R. (1982). The development of children's integration rules for making moral judgments. *Child Development, 53,* 887–894.

Grumperz, J.J., & Wilson, R. (1971). Convergence and creolization: A case from the Indian–Aryan/Dravidian border in India. In D.H. Hymes (Ed.), *Pidginization and creolization of language.* Cambridge: Cambridge University Press.

Grush, J.E. (1979). A summary review of mediating explanations of exposure phenomena. *Personality and Social Psychology Bulletin, 5,* 154–159.

Gunderson, E.K.E. (1965). Body size, self-evaluation, and military effectiveness. *Journal of Personality and Social Psychology, 2,* 902–906.

H

Haan, N., Smith, M.B., & Block, J. (1968). Moral reasoning of young adults: Political–social behavior, family background, and personality correlates. *Journal of Personality and Social Psychology, 10,* 183–201.

Haas, D.F., & Deseran, F.A. (1981). Trust and symbolic exchange. *Social Psychology Quarterly, 44,* 3–13.

Hackman, J.R., & Morris, C.G. (1975). Group tasks, group interaction process, and group performance effectiveness: A review and proposed integration. In L. Berkowitz (Ed.), *Advances in experimental social psychology* (Vol. 8). New York: Academic Press.

Halberstam, D. (1972). *The best and the brightest.* New York: Random House.

Hall, E.T. (1959). *The silent language.* New York: Doubleday.

Hall, E.T. (1966). *The hidden dimension.* New York: Doubleday.

Hall, J.A. (1978). Gender effects in decoding nonverbal cues. *Psychological Bulletin, 85,* 845–857.

Hall, J.A. (1979). Gender, gender roles, and nonverbal communication skills. In R. Rosenthal (Ed.), *Skill in nonverbal communication.* Cambridge, MA: Oelgeschlager, Gunn, & Hain.

Hamilton, D.L., & Bishop, G.D. (1976). Attitudinal and behavioral effects of initial integration of white suburban neighborhoods. *Journal of Social Issues, 32,* 47–67.

Hamilton, D.L., Carpenter, S., & Bishop, G.D. (1984). Desegregation of a suburban neighborhood. In N. Miller & M.B. Brewer (Eds.), *Groups in contact: The psychology of desegregation.* New York: Academic Press.

Hamilton, D.L., Dugan, P.M., & Trolier, T.K. (1985). The formation of stereotypic beliefs: Further evidence for the distinctiveness-based illusory correlations. *Journal of Personality and Social Psychology, 48,* 5–17.

Hamilton, D.L., & Gifford, R.K. (1976). Illusory correlation in interpersonal perception: A cognitive basis of stereotype judgments. *Journal of Experimental Social Psychology, 12,* 392–407.

Hamilton, D.L., Katz, L.B., & Leirer, V.O. (1980). Cognitive representation of personality impressions: Organizational processes in first impression formation. *Journal of Personality and Social Psychology, 39,* 1050–1063.

Hamilton, D.L., & Rose, T.L. (1980). Illusory correlation and the maintenance of stereotypic beliefs. *Journal of Personality and Social Psychology, 39,* 832–845.

Hamilton, D.L., & Trolier, T.K. (1986). Stereotypes and stereotyping: An overview of the cognitive approach. In J. Dovidio & S.L. Gaertner (Eds.), *Prejudice, discrimination, and racism.* Orlando, FL: Academic Press.

Hamilton, D.L., & Zanna, M.P. (1974). Context effects in impression formation: Changes in connotative meaning. *Journal of Personality and Social Psychology, 29,* 649–654.

Hamilton, V.L. (1980). Intuitive psychologist or intuitive lawyer? Alternative model of the attribution process. *Journal of Personality and Social Psychology, 39,* 767–772.

Hammen, C., Marks, T., deMayo, R., & Mayol, A. (1985). Self-schemas and risk for depression: A prospective study. *Journal of Personality and Social Psychology, 49,* 1147–1159.

Harackiewicz, J.M., Manderlink, G., & Sansone, C. (1984). Rewarding pinball wizardry: Effects of evaluation and cue value on intrinsic interest. *Journal of Personality and Social Psychology, 47,* 287–300.

Harari, H., Mohr, D., & Hosey, K. (1980). Faculty helpfulness to students: A comparison of compliance techniques. *Personality and Social Psychology Bulletin, 6,* 373–377.

Hardin, G. (1968). The tragedy of the commons. *Science, 162,* 1243–1248.

Harkins, S.G., & Jackson, J.M. (1985). The role of evaluation in eliminating social loafing. *Personality and Social Psychology Bulletin, 11,* 457–466.

Harkins, S.G., & Petty, R.E. (1982). Effects of task difficulty and task uniqueness on social loafing. *Journal of Personality and Social Psychology, 43,* 1214–1229.

Harlow, H.F. (1958). The nature of love. *American Psychologist, 13,* 673–685.

Harlow, H.F. (1962). The heterosexual affectional system in monkeys. *American Psychologist, 17,* 1–9.

Harré, R. (1979). *Social being.* Oxford: Blackwell.

Harré, R., & Secord, P.F. (1972). *The explanation of social behavior.* Oxford: Blackwell.

Harrington, D.M., & Andersen, S.M. (1981). Creativity,

masculinity, femininity, and three models of psychological androgyny. *Journal of Personality and Social Psychology, 41,* 744–751.

Harris, R.J. (1980). Equity judgments in hypothetical four-person partnerships. *Journal of Experimental Social Psychology, 16,* 96–115.

Harris, R.J., Messick, D.M., & Sentis, K.P. (1981). Proportionality, linearity, and parameter constancy: Messick and Sentis reconsidered. *Journal of Experimental Social Psychology, 17,* 210–225.

Harrison, A.A. (1977). Mere exposure. In L. Berkowitz (Ed.), *Advances in experimental social psychology* (Vol. 10). New York: Academic Press.

Harrison, A.A., & McClintock, C.G. (1965). Previous experience within the dyad and cooperative game behavior. *Journal of Personality and Social Psychology, 1,* 671–675.

Hart, D., & Damon, W. (1986). Developmental trends in self-understanding. *Social Cognition, 4,* 388–407.

Hart, H.L.A., & Honoré, A.M. (1959). *Causation in the law.* London: Oxford University Press.

Hart, L.M., & Goldin-Meadow, S. (1984). The child as nonegocentric art critic. *Child Development, 55,* 2122–2129.

Harter, S. (1983). Developmental perspectives on the self-system. In P.H. Mussen (Ed.), *Handbook of child psychology* (4th edition, Vol. 4). New York: Wiley.

Hartley, E.L. (1946). *Problems in prejudice.* New York: King's Crown Press.

Hartshorne, H., & May, M. (1928–1930). *Studies in the nature of character.* New York: Macmillan.

Hartup, W.W. (1970). Peer interaction and social organization. In P. Mussen (Ed.), *Carmichael's manual of child psychology* (3rd edition). New York: Wiley.

Hartup, W.W. (1983). Peer relations. In P. H. Mussen (Ed.), *Handbook of child psychology* (4th edition, Vol. 4). New York: Wiley.

Hass, R.G. (1981). Effects of source characteristics on the cognitive processing of persuasive messages and attitude change. In R. Petty, T. Ostrom, & T. Brock (Eds.), *Cognitive responses in persuasion.* Hillsdale, NJ: Lawrence Erlbaum.

Hass, R.G., & Grady, K. (1975). Temporal delay, type of forewarning, and resistance to influence. *Journal of Experimental Social Psychology, 11,* 459–469.

Hastie, R. (1980). Memory for behavioral information that confirms or contradicts a personality impression. In R. Hastie, T.M. Ostrom, E.B. Ebbesen, R.S. Wyer, Jr., D. L. Hamiliton, & D. E. Carlston (Eds.), *Person memory: The cognitive basis of social perception.* Hillsdale, NJ: Lawrence Erlbaum.

Hastie, R. (1983). Social inference. In M.R. Rosenzweig & L.W. Porter (Eds.), *Annual review of psychology* (Vol. 34). Palo Alto, CA: Annual Reviews, Inc.

Hastie, R. (1984). Causes and effects of causal attributions. *Journal of Personality and Social Psychology, 46,* 44–56.

Hastie, R., & Kumar, P.A. (1979). Person memory: Personality traits as organizing principles in memory for behaviors. *Journal of Personality and Social Psychology, 37,* 25–38.

Hastie, R., Park, B., & Weber, R. (1984). Social memory. In R.S. Wyer & T.K. Srull (Eds.), *Handbook of social cognition* (Vol. 3). Hillsdale, NJ: Lawrence Erlbaum.

Hastie, R., Penrod, S.D., & Pennington, N. (1983). *Inside the jury.* Cambridge, MA: Harvard University Press.

Hastorf, A.H., Wildfogel, J., & Cassman, T. (1979). Acknowledgment of handicap as a tactic in social interaction. *Journal of Personality and Social Psychology, 37,* 1790–1797.

Hatfield, E., Utne, M.K., & Traupmann, J. (1979). Equity theory and intimate relationships. In R.L. Burgess & T.L. Huston (Eds.), *Social exchange in developing relationships.* New York: Academic Press.

Hay, D.F., Pedersen, J., & Nash, A. (1982). Dyadic interaction in the first year of life. In K. H. Rubin & H. S. Ross (Eds.), *Peer relationships and social skills in childhood.* New York: Springer-Verlag.

Hayduk, L.A. (1983). Personal space: Where we now stand. *Psychological Bulletin, 94,* 293–335.

Heider, E.R. (1972). Universals in color naming and memory. *Journal of Experimental Psychology, 93,* 10–20.

Heider, F. (1958). *The psychology of interpersonal relations.* New York: Wiley.

Heilbrun, A.B., Jr. (1981). Gender differences in the functional linkage between androgyny, social cognition, and competence. *Journal of Personality and Social Psychology, 41,* 1106–1118.

Hendrick, C., Bixenstine, V.E., & Hawkins, G. (1971). Race versus belief similarity as determinants of attraction: A search for a fair test. *Journal of Personality and Social Psychology, 17,* 250–258.

Hendrick, C., & Hendrick, S. (1986). A theory and method of love. *Journal of Personality and Social Psychology, 50,* 392–402.

Hendrick, S.S. (1981). Self-disclosure and marital satisfaction. *Journal of Personality and Social Psychology, 40,* 1150–1159.

Henley, N.M. (1977). *Body politics: Power, sex, and nonverbal communication.* Englewood Cliffs, NJ: Prentice-Hall.

Henshel, R.L. (1980). The purposes of laboratory experimentation and the virtues of deliberate artificiality. *Journal of Experimental Social Psychology, 16,* 466–478.

Heshka, J., & Nelson, Y. (1972). Interpersonal speaking distance as a function of age, sex, and relationship. *Sociometry, 35,* 491–498.

Heslin, R., & Boss, D. (1980). Nonverbal intimacy in airport arrival and departure. *Personality and Social Psychology Bulletin, 6,* 248–252.

Hicks, D.J. (1968). Effects of co-observers' sanctions and adult presence on imitative aggression. *Child Development, 39,* 303–309.

Higbee, K.L. (1969). Fifteen years of fear arousal: Research on threat appeals 1953–1968. *Psychological Bulletin, 72,* 426–444.

Higbee, K.L., Lott, W.J., & Graves, J.P. (1976). Experimentation and college students in social-personality research. *Personality and Social Psychology Bulletin, 2,* 239–241.

Higbee, K.L., Millard, R.J., & Folkman, J.R. (1982). Social psychology research during the 1970s: Predominance of experimentation and college students. *Personality and Social Psychology Bulletin, 8,* 180–183.

Higgins, E.T. (1976). Social class differences in verbal communicative accuracy: A question of "which question?" *Psychological Bulletin, 83,* 695–714.

Higgins, E.T. (1981a). The "communication game": Implications for social cognition and persuasion. In E.T. Higgins, C.P. Herman, & M.P. Zanna (Eds.), *Social cognition: The Ontario Symposium* (Vol. 1). Hillsdale, NJ: Lawrence Erlbaum.

Higgins, E.T. (1981b). Role taking and social judgment: Alternative developmental perspectives and processes. In J. H. Flavell & L. Ross (Eds.), *Social cognitive development: Frontiers and possible futures.* Cambridge: Cambridge University Press.

Higgins, E.T., & Bargh, J.A. (1987). Social cognition and social perception. In M.R. Rosenzweig & L.W. Porter (Eds.), *Annual review of psychology* (Vol. 38). Palo Alto, CA: Annual Reviews, Inc.

Higgins, E.T., & Bryant, S.L. (1982). Consensus information and the fundamental attribution error: The role of development and in-group versus out-group knowledge. *Journal of Personality and Social Psychology, 43,* 889–900.

Higgins, E.T., & King, G.A. (1981). Accessibility of social constructs: Information-processing consequences of individual and contextual variability. In N. Cantor & J.F. Kihlstrom (Eds.), *Personality, cognition, and social interaction.* Hillsdale, NJ: Lawrence Erlbaum.

Higgins, E.T., King, G.A., & Mavin, G.H. (1982). Individual construct accessibility and subjective impressions and recall. *Journal of Personality and Social Psychology, 43,* 35–47.

Higgins, E.T., & Parsons, J.E. (1983). Social cognition and the social life of the child: Stages as subculture. In E.T. Higgins, D.N. Ruble, & W.W. Hartup (Eds.), *Developmental social cognition: A sociocultural perspective.* New York: Cambridge University Press.

Higgins, E.T., Rholes, W.S., & Jones, C.R. (1977). Category accessibility and impression formation. *Journal of Experimental Social Psychology, 13*, 141–154.

Higgins, E.T., & Wells, R.S. (1986). Social construct availability and accessibility as a function of social life phase: Emphasizing the "how" versus the "can" of social cognition. *Social Cognition, 4*, 201–226.

Hill, C.T., Rubin, Z., & Peplau, L.A. (1976). Breakups before marriage: The end of 103 affairs. *Journal of Social Issues, 32*, 147–168.

Hilton, D.J., & Slugoski, B.R. (1986). Knowledge-based causal attribution: The abnormal conditions focus model. *Psychological Review, 93*, 75–88.

Hilton, J.L., & Darley, J.M. (1985). Construing other persons: A limit on the effect. *Journal of Experimental Social Psychology, 21*, 1–18.

Hindelang, M.J., Gottfredson, M.R., & Garafalo, J. (1978). *Victims of personal crime: An empirical foundation for a theory of personal victimization.* Cambridge: MA: Ballinger Publishing.

Hindelang, M.J., Hirschi, T., & Weis, J.G. (1979). Correlates of delinquency: The illusion of discrepancy between self-report and official measures. *American Sociological Review, 44*, 995–1014.

Hinsz, V.B., & Davis, J.H. (1984). Persuasive arguments theory, group polarization, and choice shifts. *Personality and Social Psychology Bulletin, 10*, 260–268.

Hirschberg, N., & Jennings, S.J. (1980). Beliefs, personality, and person perception: A theory of individual differences. *Journal of Research in Personality, 14*, 235–249.

Hoffman, C., Mischel, W., & Mazze, K. (1981). The role of purpose in the organization of information about behavior: Trait-based versus goal-based categories in person cognition. *Journal of Personality and Social Psychology, 40*, 211–225.

Hoffman, M.L. (1970). Moral development. In P. Mussen (Ed.), *Carmichael's manual of child psychology* (3rd edition). New York: Wiley.

Hoffman, M.L. (1977). Moral internalization: Current theory and research. In L. Berkowitz (Ed.), *Advances in experimental social psychology* (Vol. 10). New York: Academic Press.

Hoffman, M.L. (1981). Is altruism part of human nature? *Journal of Personality and Social Psychology, 40*, 121–137.

Hoffman, M.L. (1983). Affective and cognitive processes in moral internalization. In E.T. Higgins, D.N. Ruble, & W.W. Hartup (Eds.), *Social cognition and social development: A sociocultural perspective.* Cambridge: University of Cambridge Press.

Hogan, R. (1973). Moral conduct and moral character: A psychological perspective. *Psychological Bulletin, 79*, 217–233.

Hokanson, J., & Burgess, M. (1962). The effects of status, type of frustration, and aggression on vascular processes. *Journal of Abnormal and Social Psychology, 65*, 232–237.

Hokanson, J., & Edelman, R. (1966). Effects of three social responses on vascular processes. *Journal of Personality and Social Psychology, 3*, 442–447.

Hollander, E.P. (1958). Conformity, status, and idiosyncracy credit. *Psychological Review, 65*, 117–127.

Hollander, E.P. (1978). *Leadership dynamics: A practical guide to effective relationships.* New York: The Free Press.

Hollander, E.P., & Julian, J.W. (1970). Studies in leader legitimacy, influence, and innovation. In L. Berkowitz (Ed.), *Advances in experimental social psychology* (Vol. 5). New York: Academic Press.

Holmes, D.S. (1970). Differential change in affective intensity and the forgetting of unpleasant personal experience. *Journal of Personality and Social Psychology, 15*, 234–239.

Holtzworth-Munroe, A., & Jacobson, N.S. (1985). Causal attributions of married couples: When do they search for causes? What do they conclude when they do? *Journal of Personality and Social Psychology, 48*, 1398–1412.

Holyoak, K.S., & Gordon, P.C. (1983). Social reference points. *Journal of Personality and Social Psychology, 44*, 881–887.

Homans, G.C. (1961). *Social behavior: Its elementary forms.* New York: Harcourt, Brace & World.

Hoover, C.W., Wood, E.E., & Knowles, E.S. (1983). Forms of social awareness and helping. *Journal of Experimental Social Psychology, 19*, 577–590.

Hornstein, G.A. (1985). Intimacy in conversational style as a function of the degree of closeness between members of a dyad. *Journal of Personality and Social Psychology, 49*, 671–681.

House, J.S. (1977). The three faces of social psychology. *Sociometry, 40*, 161–177.

Hovland, C.I. (1959). Reconciling conflicting results derived from experiments and survey studies of attitude change. *American Psychologist, 14*, 8–17.

Hovland, C.I., Harvey, O.J., & Sherif, M. (1957). Assimilation and contrast effects in reactions to communication and attitude change. *Journal of Abnormal and Social Psychology, 55*, 244–252.

Hovland, C.I., Janis, I.L., & Kelly, H.H. (1953). *Communication and persuasion. New Haven: Yale University Press.

Hovland, C.I., & Pritzker, H.A. (1957). Extent of opinion change as a function of amount of change advocated. *Journal of Abnormal and Social Psychology, 54*, 257–261.

Hovland, C.I., & Sears, R.R. (1940). Minor studies in aggression. VI: Correlation of lynchings with economic indices. *Journal of Psychology, 9,* 301–310.

Hovland, C., & Weiss, R. (1951). The influence of source credibility on communication effectiveness. *Public Opinion Quarterly, 15,* 635–650.

Hudson, R.A. (1980). *Sociolinguistics.* Cambridge: Cambridge University Press.

Huesmann, L.R. (1982). Television violence and aggressive behavior. In D. Pearl, L. Bouthilet, & J. Lazar (Eds.), *Television and behavior: Ten years of scientific progress and implications for the eighties.* Washington, DC: Government Printing Office.

Huesmann, L.R., Eron, L.D., Klein, R., Brice, P., & Fisher, P. (1983). Mitigating the imitation of aggressive behaviors by changing children's attitudes about media violence. *Journal of Personality and Social Psychology, 44,* 899–910.

Huesmann, L.R., Lagerspetz, K., & Eron, L.D. (1984). Intervening variables in the TV violence–aggression relationship. *Developmental Psychology, 20,* 746–775.

Huston, A.C. (1983). Sex-typing. In P.H. Mussen (Ed.)., *Handbook of child psychology* (4th edition, Vol. 4). New York: Wiley.

Huston, T.L. (1973). Ambiguity of acceptance, social desirability, and dating choice. *Journal of Experimental Social Psychology, 9,* 32–42.

Huston, T.L., & Burgess, R.L. (1979). Social exchange in developing relationships: An overview. In R.L. Burgess & T.L. Huston (Eds.), *Social exchange in developing relationships.* New York: Academic Press.

Huston, T.L., & Levinger, G. (1978). Interpersonal attraction and relationships. In M.R. Rosenzweig & L.W. Porter (Eds.), *Annual review of psychology* (Vol. 29). Palo Alto, CA: Annual Reviews, Inc.

Huston, T.L., McHale, S.M., & Crouter, A.C. (1985). When the honeymoon's over: Changes in the marriage relationship over the first year. In R. Gilmour & S. Duck (Eds.), *The emerging science of personal relationships.* Hillsdale, NJ: Lawrence Erlbaum.

Huston, T.L., Robins, E., Atkinson, J., & McHale, S.M. (1987). Surveying the landscape of marital behavior: A behavioral self-report approach to studying marriage. In S. Oskamp (Ed.), *Family processes and problems: Social psychological aspects.* Beverly Hills, CA: Sage.

Huston, T.L., Ruggiero, M., Conner, R., & Geis, G. (1981). Bystander intervention into crime: A study based on naturally occurring episodes. *Social Psychology Quarterly, 44,* 14–23.

Huston, T.L., Surra, C.A., Fitzgerald, N.M., & Cate, R.M. (1981). From courtship to marriage: Mate selection as an interpersonal process. In S. Duck & R. Gilmour (Eds.), *Personal relationships 2: Developing personal relationships.* London: Academic Press.

Ickes, W. (1984). Compositions in black and white: Determinants of interaction in interracial dyads. *Journal of Personality and Social Psychology, 47,* 330–341.

Ingham, A.G., Levinger, G., Graves, J., & Peckham, V. (1974). The Ringelmann effect: Studies of group size and group performance. *Journal of Experimental Social Psychology, 10,* 371–384.

Insko, C.A., Drenan, S., Solomon, M.R., Smith, R., & Wade, T.J. (1983). Conformity as a function of the consistency of positive self-evaluation with being liked and being right. *Journal of Experimental Social Psychology, 19,* 341–358.

Insko, C.A., Thibaut, J.W., Moehle, D., Wilson, M., Diamond, W.D., Gilmore, R., Solomon, M.R., & Lipsitz, A. (1980). Social evaluation and the emergence of leadership. *Journal of Personality and Social Psychology, 39,* 431–448.

Insko, C.A., Thompson, V.D., Stroebe, W., Shaud, K.F., Pinner, B.E., & Layton, B.D. (1973). Implied evaluation and the similarity–attraction effect. *Journal of Personality and Social Psychology, 25,* 297–308.

Insko, C.A., & Wilson, M. (1977). Interpersonal attraction as a function of social interaction. *Journal of Personality and Social Psychology, 35,* 903–911.

Isen, A.M. (1970). Success, failure, attention, and reaction to others: The warm glow of success. *Journal of Personality and Social Psychology, 15,* 294–301.

Isen, A.M. (1984). Toward understanding the role of affect in cognition. In R.S. Wyer & T.K. Srull (Eds.), *Handbook of social cognition* (Vol. 3), Hillsdale, NJ: Lawrence Erlbaum.

Isen, A.M., Johnson, M.M.S., Mertz, E., & Robinson, G.F. (1985). The influence of positive affect on the unusualness of word associations. *Journal of Personality and Social Psychology, 48,* 1413–1426.

Isen, A.M., & Levin, P.F. (1972). Effect of feeling good on helping: Cookies and kindness. *Journal of Personality and Social Psychology, 21,* 384–388.

Isen, A.M., & Means, B. (1983). The influence of positive affect on decision-making strategy. *Social Cognition, 2,* 18–31.

Isen, A.M., & Shalker, T.E. (1982). The effect of feeling state on evaluation of positive, neutral, and negative stimuli: When you "accentuate the positive" do you "eliminate the negative"? *Social Psychology Quarterly, 45,* 58–63.

Isen, A.M., Shalker, T.E., Clark, M., & Karp, L. (1978). Affect, accessibility of material in memory and behavior: A cognitive loop? *Journal of Personality and Social Psychology, 36,* 1–12.

Iyengar, S., Kinder, D.R., Peters, M.D., & Krosnick, J.A. (1984). The evening news and presidential evaluations. *Journal of Personality and Social Psychology, 46,* 778–787.

J

Jablin, F.M. (1979). Superior–subordinate communication: The state of the art. *Psychological Bulletin, 86,* 1201–1222.

Jackson, D.N., & Paunonen, S.V. (1985). Construct validity and the predictability of behavior. *Journal of Personality and Social Psychology, 49,* 554–570.

Jackson, J.M., & Harkins, S.G. (1985). Equity in effort: An explanation of the social loafing effect. *Journal of Personality and Social Psychology, 49,* 1199–1206.

Jackson, J.M., & Latané, B. (1981). All alone in front of all those people: Stage fright as a function of number and type of co-performers and audience. *Journal of Personality and Social Psychology, 40,* 73–85.

Jacobs, P.A., Brunton, M., & Melville, M.M. (1965). Aggressive behavior, mental subnormality, and the XYY male. *Nature, 208,* 1351–1352.

Jacobs, R.C., & Campbell, D.T. (1961). The perpetuation of an arbitrary tradition through several generations of laboratory microculture. *Journal of Abnormal and Social Psychology, 62,* 649–658.

James, W. (1884). What is emotion? *Mind, 4,* 188–204.

James, W. (1950, original, 1890). *The principles of psychology.* New York: Dover.

Janis, I.L. (1967). Effects of fear arousal on attitude change: Recent developments in theory and experimental research. In L. Berkowitz (Ed.), *Advances in experimental social psychology* (Vol. 3). New York: Academic Press.

Janis, I.L. (1982). *Groupthink.* Boston: Houghton Mifflin.

Janis, I.L., & Feshbach, S. (1953). Effects of fear-arousing communications. *Journal of Abnormal and Social Psychology, 48,* 78–92.

Janis, I.L., Kaye, D., & Kirschner, P. (1965). Facilitating effects of "eating-while-reading" on responsiveness to persuasive communications. *Journal of Personality and Social Psychology, 1,* 181–186.

Janis, I.L., & King, B.T. (1954). The influence of role-playing on opinion change. *Journal of Abnormal and Social Psychology, 49,* 211–218.

Janoff-Bulman, R. (1979). Characterological versus behavioral self-blame: Inquiries into depression and rape. *Journal of Personality and Social Psychology, 37,* 1798–1809.

Janoff-Bulman, R., Timko, C., & Carli, L.L. (1985). Cognitive biases in blaming the victim. *Journal of Experimental Social Psychology, 21,* 161–177.

Janowitz, M. (1969). Patterns of collective racial violence. In H.D. Graham & T.R. Gurr (Eds.), *The history of violence in America.* New York: Bantam Books.

Jellison, J.M. (1981). Reconsidering the attitude concept: A behavioristic self-presentation formulation. In J.T. Tedeschi (Ed.), *Impression management theory and social psychological research.* New York: Academic Press.

Jellison, J.M., & Arkin, R.M. (1977). Social comparison of abilities: A self-presentational approach to decision making in groups. In J.M. Suls & R.L. Miller (Eds.), *Social comparison processes.* New York: Halsted Press.

Jellison, J.M., & Riskind, J. (1970). A social comparison of abilities interpretation of risk-taking behavior. *Journal of Personality and Social Psychology, 15,* 375–390.

Jennings, J., Geis, F.L., & Brown, V. (1980). Influence of television commercials on women's self-confidence. *Journal of Personality and Social Psychology, 38,* 203–210.

Jennings, M.K., & Niemi, R.G. (1981). *Generations and politics: A panel study of young adults and their parents.* Princeton, NJ: Princeton University Press.

Jervis, R. (1976). *Perception and misperception in international relations.* Princeton, NJ: Princeton University Press.

Johnson, H.G., Ekman, P., & Friesen, W.V. (1975). Communicative body movements: American emblems. *Semiotica, 15,* 335–353.

Johnson, J.T., Jemmott, J.B., & Pettigrew, T.R. (1984). Causal attribution and dispositional inference: Evidence of inconsistent judgments. *Journal of Experimental Social Psychology, 20,* 567–585.

Jones, E.E. (1964). *Ingratiation.* New York: Appleton-Century-Crofts.

Jones, E.E., & Berglas, S. (1978). Control of attributions about the self through self-handicapping strategies: The appeal of alcohol and the role of underachievement. *Personality and Social Psychology Bulletin, 4,* 200–206.

Jones, E.E., & Davis, K.E. (1965). From acts to dispositions: The attribution process in person perception. In L. Berkowitz (Ed.), *Advances in experimental social psychology* (Vol. 2). New York: Academic Press.

Jones, E.E., Davis, K.E., & Gergen, K.J. (1961). Role playing variations and their informational value for person perception. *Journal of Abnormal and Social Psychology, 63,* 302–310.

Jones, E.E., Gergen, K.J., & Davis, K.E. (1962). Some determinants of reactions to being approved or disapproved as a person. *Psychological Monographs, 76,* Whole #521.

Jones, E.E., Gergen, K.J., & Jones, R.G. (1963). Tactics of ingratiation among leaders and subordinates in a status hierarchy. *Psychological Monographs, 77,* Whole #566.

Jones, E.E., & Goethals, G.R. (1972). Order effects in impression formation: Attribution context and the nature of the entity. In E.E. Jones et al. (Eds.), *Attribution: Perceiving the causes of behavior*. Morristown, NJ: General Learning Press.

Jones, E.E., & Harris, V.E. (1967). The attribution of attitudes. *Journal of Experimental Social Psychology, 3,* 1–24.

Jones, E.E., & Nisbett, R. (1972). The actor and observer: Divergent perceptions of the causes of behavior. In E. E. Jones et al. (Eds.), *Attribution: Perceiving the causes of behavior*. Morristown, NJ: General Learning Press.

Jones, E.E., Rhodewalt, F., Berglas, S., & Skelton, J.A. (1981). Effects of strategic self-presentation on subsequent self-esteem. *Journal of Personality and Social Psychology, 41,* 407–421.

Jones, E.E., Riggs, J.M., & Quattrone, G. (1979). Observer bias in the attitude attribution paradigm: Effect of time and information order. *Journal of Personality and Social Psychology, 37,* 1230–1238.

Jones, E.E., Rock, L., Shaver, K.G., Goethals, G.R., & Ward, L.M. (1968). Pattern of performance and ability attribution: An unexpected primacy effect. *Journal of Experimental Social Psychology, 10,* 317–341.

Jones, E.E., & Sigall, H. (1971). The bogus pipeline: A new paradigm for measuring affect and attitude. *Psychological Bulletin, 76,* 349–364.

Jones, E.E., Wells, H.H., & Torrey, R. (1958). Some effects of feedback from the experimenter on conforming behavior. *Journal of Abnormal and Social Psychology, 57,* 207–213.

Jones, E.E., Worchel, S., Goethals, G.R., & Grumet, J.F. (1971). Prior expectancy and behavioral extremity as determinants of attitude attribution. *Journal of Experimental Social Psychology, 7,* 59–80.

Jones, E.E., & Wortman, C. (1973). *Ingratiation: An attributional approach*. Morristown, NJ: General Learning Press.

Jones, J.M. (1972). *Prejudice and racism*. Reading, MA: Addison-Wesley.

Jones, J.M. (1986). Racism: A cultural analysis of the problem. In J.F. Dovidio & S.L. Gaertner (Eds.), *Prejudice, discrimination, and racism*. Orlando, FL: Academic Press.

Jones, S.C. (1973). Self and interpersonal evaluations: Esteem theories versus consistency theories. *Psychology Bulletin, 79,* 185–199.

Jones, S.C. & Pines, H.A. (1968). Self-revealing events and interpersonal evaluations. *Journal of Personality and Social Psychology, 8,* 277–281.

Jones, S.C., & Schneider, D.J. (1968). Certainty of self-appraisal and reactions to evaluations from others. *Sociometry, 31,* 395–403.

Jorgenson, D.O., & Papciak, A.S. (1981). The effects of communication, resource feedback, and identifiability on behavior in simulated commons. *Journal of Experimental Social Psychology, 17,* 373–385.

Jourard, S.M. (1968). *Disclosing man to himself*. Princeton, NJ: Van Nostrand.

Jourard, S.M., & Lasakow, P. (1958). Some factors in self-disclosure. *Journal of Abnormal and Social Psychology, 57,* 91–98.

Judd, C.M., & Harackiewicz, J.M. (1980). Contrast effects in attitude judgment: An examination of the accentuation hypothesis. *Journal of Personality and Social Psychology, 38,* 390–398.

Judd, C.M., & Milburn, M.A. (1980). The structure of attitude systems in the general public: Comparisons of a structural equation model. *American Sociological Review, 45,* 627–643.

K

Kagen, J. (1982). *Psychological research on the human infant: An evaluation summary*. New York: W.T. Grant Foundation.

Kahneman, D., & Tversky, A. (1972). Subjective probability: A judgment of representativeness. *Cognitive Psychology, 3,* 430–454.

Kalven, H., & Zeisel, H. (1966). *The American jury*. Boston: Little, Brown.

Kandel, D. (1978). Similarity in real-life adolescent friendship pairs. *Journal of Personality and Social Psychology, 36,* 306–312.

Kanter, R.M. (1972). *Commitment and community: Communes and utopias in sociological perspective*. Cambridge, MA: Harvard University Press.

Karabenick, S.A. (1983). Sex-relevance of content and influenceability. *Personality and Social Psychology Bulletin, 9,* 243–252.

Karlins, M., Coffman, T.L., & Walters, G. (1969). On the fading of social stereotypes: Studies in three generations of college students. *Journal of Personality and Social Psychology, 13,* 1–16.

Karniol, R. (1978). Children's use of intention cues in evaluating behavior. *Psychological Bulletin, 85,* 76–85.

Karniol, R., & Ross, M. (1976). The development of causal attributions in social perception. *Journal of Personality and Social Psychology, 34,* 455–464.

Kassin, S.M. (1979). Consensus information, prediction, and causal attribution: A review of the literature and issues. *Journal of Personality and Social Psychology, 37,* 1966–1981.

Katz, D., & Braly, K.W. (1933). Racial stereotypes of one hundred college students. *Journal of Abnormal and Social Psychology, 28,* 280–290.

Katz, D., & Stotland, E. (1959). A preliminary statement

to a theory of attitude structure and change. In S. Koch (Ed.), *Psychology: A study of a science* (Vol. 3). New York: McGraw-Hill.

Katz, I. (1981). *Stigma: A social psychological analysis.* Hillsdale, NJ: Lawrence Erlbaum.

Katz, I., Glucksberg, S., & Krauss, R. (1960). Need satisfaction and Edwards PPS scores in married couples. *Journal of Consulting Psychology, 24,* 205–208.

Katz, I., Wackenut, J., & Hass, R.G. (1986). Racial ambivalence, value duality, and behavior. In J.F. Dovidio & S.L. Gaertner (Eds.), *Prejudice, discrimination, and racism.* Orlando, FL: Academic Press.

Keenan, J.M., & Baillet, S.D. (1980). Memory for personality and socially significant events. In R.S. Nickerson (Ed.), *Attention and performance VIII.* Hillsdale, NJ: Lawrence Erlbaum.

Kelley, H.H. (1967). Attribution theory in social psychology. In D. Levine (Ed.), *Nebraska symposium on motivation 1967.* Lincoln: University of Nebraska Press.

Kelley, H.H. (1972). Attribution in social interaction. In E.E. Jones et al. (Eds.), *Attribution: Perceiving the causes of behavior.* Morristown, NJ: General Learning Press.

Kelley, H.H., & Stahelski, A.J. (1970). Errors in perception of intentions in a mixed-motive game. *Journal of Experimental Social Psychology, 6,* 379–400.

Kelley, H.H., & Thibaut, J.W. (1978). *Interpersonal relations: A theory of interdependence.* New York: Wiley.

Kelley, H.H., & Woodruff, C. (1956). Members' reactions to apparent group approval of counternorm communication. *Journal of Abnormal and Social Psychology, 52,* 67–74.

Kelman, H.C. (1967). Human use of human subjects: The problem of deception in social psychological experiments. *Psychological Bulletin, 67,* 1–11.

Kelman, H.C. (1968). *A time to speak.* San Francisco: Jossey-Bass.

Kenny, D.A. (1979). *Correlation and causality.* New York: Wiley.

Kenny, D.A., & Nasby, W. (1980). Splitting the reciprocity correlation. *Journal of Personality and Social Psychology, 38,* 249–256.

Kenrick, D.T., Baumann, D.J., & Cialdini, R.B. (1979). A step in the socialization of altruism as hedonism: Effects of negative mood on children's generosity under public and private conditions. *Journal of Personality and Social Psychology, 37,* 747–755.

Kenrick, D.T., & Cialdini, R.B. (1977). Romantic attraction: Misattribution versus reinforcement explanations. *Journal of Personality and Social Psychology, 35,* 381–391.

Kenrick, D.T., & Gutierres, S.E. (1980). Contrast effects and judgments of physical attractiveness: When beauty

becomes a social problem. *Journal of Personality and Social Psychology, 38,* 131–140.

Kernis, M.H., & Wheeler, L. (1981). Beautiful friends and ugly strangers: Radiation and contrast effects in perceptions of same-sex pairs. *Personality and Social Psychology Bulletin, 7,* 617–620.

Kerr, N.L. (1983). Motivation losses in small groups: A social dilemma analysis. *Journal of Personality and Social Psychology, 45,* 819–828.

Kerr, N.L., Atkin, R.S., Strasser, G., Meek, D., Holt, R.W., & Davis, J.H. (1976). Guilt beyond a reasonable doubt: Effects of concept definition and assigned decision rule on the judgments of mock jurors. *Journal of Personality and Social Psychology, 34,* 282–294.

Kerr, N.L., & MacCoun, R.J. (1985). The effects of jury size and polling method on the process and product of jury deliberation. *Journal of Personality and Social Psychology, 48,* 349–363.

Kiesler, C.A. (1971). *The psychology of commitment.* New York: Academic Press.

Kihlstrom, J.F., & Cantor, N. (1984). Mental representations of the self. In L. Berkowitz (Ed.), *Advances in experimental social psychology* (Vol. 17). New York: Academic Press.

Kilham, W., & Mann, L. (1974). Level of destructive obedience as a function of transmitter and executant roles in the Milgram obedience paradigm. *Journal of Personality and Social Psychology, 29,* 696–702.

Kinder, D.R., & Sears, D.O. (1981). Prejudice and politics: Symbolic racism versus racial threats to the good life. *Journal of Personality and Social Psychology, 40,* 414–431.

Kinder, D.R., & Sears, D.O. (1985). Public opinion and political action. In G. Lindzey & E. Aronson (Eds.), *Handbook of social psychology* (3rd edition, Vol. 2). New York: Random House.

Kipnis, D. (1957). Interaction between members of bomber crews as a determinant of sociometric choice. *Human Relations, 10,* 263–270.

Kleck, R., Buck, P.L., Goller, W.L., London, R.W., Pfeiffer, J.R., & Vukcevic, D.P. (1968). Effect of stigmatizing conditions on the use of personal space. *Psychological Reports, 23,* 111–118.

Klein, S.B., & Kihlstrom, J.F. (1986). Elaboration, organization, and the self-reference effect in memory. *Journal of Experimental Psychology: General, 115,* 26–38.

Kleinke, C.L. (1979). Effects of personal evaluations. In G.J. Chelune (Ed.), *Self-disclosure.* San Francisco: Jossey-Bass.

Kleinke, C.L., Staneski, R.A., & Weaver, P. (1972). Evaluation of a person who uses another's name in ingratiating and noningratiating situations. *Journal of Experimental Social Psychology, 8,* 457–466.

Knight, J.A., & Vallacher, R.R. (1981). Interpersonal engagement in social perception: The consequences of getting into the action. *Journal of Personality and Social Psychology, 40,* 990–999.

Knudson, R.M., Sommers, A.A., & Golding, S.L. (1980). Interpersonal perception and mode of resolution in marital conflict. *Journal of Personality and Social Psychology, 38,* 751–763.

Kohlberg, L. (1966). A cognitive-developmental analysis of children's sex role concepts and attitudes. In E. Maccoby (Ed.), *The development of sex differences.* Stanford, CA: Stanford University Press.

Kohlberg, L. (1969). Stage and sequence: The cognitive-developmental approach to socialization. In D. Goslin (Ed.), *Handbook of socialization theory and research.* Chicago: Rand-McNally.

Kolditz, T.A., & Arkin, R.M. (1982). An impression management interpretation of the self-handicapping strategy. *Journal of Personality and Social Psychology, 43,* 492–502.

Komorita, S.S., & Chertkoff, J.M. (1973). A bargaining theory of coalition formation. *Psychological Review, 80,* 149–162.

Konečni, V.J., & Doob, A.N. (1972). Catharsis through displacement of aggression. *Journal of Personality and Social Psychology, 23,* 379–387.

Korte, C. (1981). Constraints on helping behavior in an urban environment. In J.P. Rushton & R.M. Sorrentino (Eds.), *Altruism and helping behavior.* Hillsdale, NJ: Lawrence Erlbaum.

Kramer, R.M., & Brewer, M.B. (1984). Effects of group identity on resource use in a simulated commons dilemma. *Journal of Personality and Social Psychology, 46,* 1044–1057.

Krauss, R., Geller, V., & Olson, C. (1976). Modalities and cues in the detection of deception. Paper presented at the American Psychological Association Convention.

Krauss, R.M., Vivekananthan, P.J., & Weinheimer, S. (1968). "Inner speech" and "external speech": Characteristics and communication effectiveness of socially and non-socially encoded messages. *Journal of Personality and Social Psychology, 9,* 295–300.

Kraut, R.E. (1973). Effects of social labeling on giving to charity. *Journal of Experimental Social Psychology, 9,* 551–562.

Kraut, R.E. (1978). Verbal and nonverbal cues in the perception of lying. *Journal of Personality and Social Psychology, 36,* 380–391.

Kraut, R.E., & Johnston, R.E. (1979). Social and emotional messages of smiling: An ethological approach. *Journal of Personality and Social Psychology, 37,* 1539–1553.

Kraut, R.E., & Lewis, S.H. (1982). Person perception and self-awareness: Knowledge of influences on one's own judgment. *Journal of Personality and Social Psychology, 42,* 448–460.

Kraut, R.E., Lewis, S.H., & Swezey, L.W. (1982). Listener responsiveness and the coordination of conversation. *Journal of Personality and Social Psychology, 43,* 718–731.

Krebs, D., & Gillmore, J. (1982). The relationship among the first stages of cognitive development, role-taking abilities, and moral development. *Child Development, 53,* 877–886.

Krisher, H.P., Darley, S.A., & Darley, J.M. (1973). Fear-provoking recommendations, intentions to take preventive actions, and actual preventive action. *Journal of Personality and Social Psychology, 26,* 301–308.

Kroger, R.O. (1982). Explorations in ethogeny: With special reference to the rules of address. *American Psychologist, 37,* 810–820.

Kruglanski, A.W. (1975). The human subject in the psychology experiment: Fact and artifact. In L. Berkowitz (Ed.), *Advances in experimental social psychology* (Vol. 8). New York: Academic Press.

Kruglanski, A.W., Friedland, N., & Farkash, E. (1984). Lay persons' sensitivity to statistical information: The case of high perceived applicability. *Journal of Personality and Social Psychology, 46,* 503–518.

Kuiper, N.A., & Derry, P.A. (1981). The self as a cognitive prototype: An application to person perception and depression. In N. Cantor & J.F. Kihlstrom (Eds.), *Personality, cognition, and social interaction.* Hillsdale, NJ: Lawrence Erlbaum.

Kuiper, N.A., & Macdonald, M.R. (1982). Self and other perception in mild depressives. *Social Cognition, 1,* 223–239.

Kuiper, N.A. Olinger, L.J., Macdonald, M.R., & Shaw, B.F. (1985). Self-schema processing of depressed and nondepressed content: The effects of vulnerability to depression. *Social Cognition, 3,* 77–93.

Kuiper, N.A., & Rogers, T.B. (1979). Encoding of personal information: Self–other differences. *Journal of Personality and Social Psychology, 37,* 499–514.

Kukla, A. (1982). Logical incoherence of value-free science. *Journal of Personality and Social Psychology, 43,* 1014–1017.

Kulik, J.A. (1983). Confirmatory attribution and the perpetuation of social beliefs. *Journal of Personality and Social Psychology, 44,* 1171–1181.

Kulik, J.A., & Brown, R. (1979). Frustration, attribution of blame, and aggression. *Journal of Experimental Social Psychology, 15,* 183–194.

Kunda, Z., & Schwartz, S.H. (1983). Undermining intrinsic moral motivation: External reward and self-presentation. *Journal of Personality and Social Psychology, 45,* 763–771.

Kurtines, W., & Greif, E.B. (1974). The development of moral thought: Review and evaluation of Kohlberg's approach. *Psychological Bulletin, 81*, 453–470.

L

LaGaipa, J.J. (1981). Children's friendships. In S. Duck & R. Gilmour (Eds.), *Personal relationships. 2: Developing personal relationships*. London: Academic Press.

Lalljee, M., & Abelson, R.P. (1983). The organization of explanations. In M. Hewstone (Ed.), *Attribution theory: Social and functional extensions*. Oxford: Basil Blackwell.

Lamb, M.E., & Roopnarine, J.L. (1979). Peer influences on sex-role development in preschoolers. *Child Development, 50*, 1219–1222.

Lambert, W.E. (1967). The social psychology of bilingualism. *Journal of Social Issues, 23*, 91–109.

Lamke, L.K. (1982). The impact of sex-role orientation on self-esteem in early adolescence. *Child Development, 53*, 1530–1535.

Lamm, H., & Myers, D.G. (1978). Group induced polarization of attitudes and behavior. In L. Berkowitz (Ed.), *Advances in experimental social psychology* (Vol. 11). New York: Academic Press.

Landy, D., & Aronson, E. (1969). The influence of the character of the criminal and his victim on the decisions of simulated jurors. *Journal of Experimental Social Psychology, 5*, 141–152.

Lane, H. (1979). *The wild boy of Aveyron*. Cambridge, MA: Harvard University Press.

Langer, E.J. (1975). The illusion of control. *Journal of Personality and Social Psychology, 32*, 311–328.

Langer, E., Blank, A., & Chanowitz, B. (1978). The mindlessness of ostensibly thoughtful action: The role of "placibic" information in interpersonal interaction. *Journal of Personality and Social Psychology, 36*, 635–642.

Langlois, J.H., & Downs, A.C. (1979). Peer relations as a function of physical attractiveness: They eye of the beholder or behavioral reality. *Child Development, 50*, 409–418.

Langlois, J.H., & Downs, A.C. (1980). Mothers, fathers, and peers as socialization agents of sex-typed play behaviors in young children. *Child Development, 51*, 1237–1247.

Langlois, J.H., & Stephan, C.W. (1981). Beauty and the beast: The role of physical attractiveness in the development of peer relations and social behavior. In S.S. Brehm, S.M. Kassin, & F.X. Gibbons (Eds.), *Developmental social psychology*. New York: Oxford University Press.

LaPiere, R.T. (1934). Attitude vs. actions. *Social Forces, 13*, 230–237.

LaRue, A., & Olejnik, A.B. (1980). Cognitive "priming" of principled moral thought. *Personality and Social Psychology Bulletin, 6*, 413–416.

Latané, B. (1981). Psychology of social impact. *American Psychologist, 36*, 343–356.

Latané, B., & Darley, J.M. (1970). *The unresponsive bystander: Why doesn't he help?* New York: Appleton-Century- Crofts.

Latané, B., & Nida, S. (1981). Ten years of research on group size and helping. *Psychological Bulletin, 89*, 308–324.

Latané, B., Williams, K., & Harkins, S. (1979). Many hands make light the work: The causes and consequences of social loafing. *Journal of Personality and Social Psychology, 37*, 822–832.

Latané, B., & Wolf, S. (1981). The social impact of majorities and minorities. *Psychological Review, 88*, 438–453.

Laughlin, P.R., & Adamopoulos, J. (1980). Social combination processes and individual learning for six-person cooperative groups on an intellectual task. *Journal of Personality and Social Psychology, 38*, 941–947.

Laughlin, P.R., Kerr, N.L., Davis, J.H., Halff, H.M., & Marciniak, K.A. (1975). Group size, member ability, and social decision schemes on an intellectual task. *Journal of Personality and Social Psychology, 31*, 522–535.

Lay, C.H., & Jackson, D.N. (1969). Analysis of the generality of trait-inferential relationships. *Journal of Personality and Social Psychology, 12*, 12–21.

Lazarus, R.S., Spersman, J.C., Mordkoff, A.M., & Davison, L. (1962). A laboratory study of psychological distress produced by a motion picture film. *Psychological Monographs, 76*, Whole #553.

LeBon, G. (1968, original 1895). *The crowd*. New York: Ballantine.

Lee, J.A. (1977). A typology of styles of loving. *Personality and Social Psychology Bulletin, 3*, 173–182.

Lee, M.T., & Ofshe, R. (1981). The impact of behavioral style and status characteristics on social influence: A test of two competing theories. *Social Psychology Quarterly, 44*, 73–82.

Leffler, A., Gillespie, D.L., & Conaty, J.C. (1982). The effects of status differentiation on nonverbal behavior. *Social Psychology Quarterly, 45*, 153–161.

Lefkowitz, M., Blake, R.R., & Mouton, J. (1955). Status factors in pedestrian violations of traffic signals. *Journal of Abnormal and Social Psychology, 51*, 704–705.

Leippe, M.R. (1980). Effects of integrative memorial and cognitive processes on the correspondence of eyewitness accuracy and confidence. *Law and Human Behavior, 4*, 261–274.

Lepper, M. (1973). Dissonance, self-perception, and

honesty in children. *Journal of Personality and Social Psychology, 25,* 65–74.

Lepper, M.R., & Greene, D. (1975). Turning play into work: Effects of adult surveillance and extrinsic rewards on children's intrinsic motivation. *Journal of Personality and Social Psychology, 31,* 479–486.

Lepper, M.R., Greene, D., & Nisbett, R.E. (1973). Undermining children's intrinsic interest with extrinsic reward: A test of the "overjustification" hypothesis. *Journal of Personality and Social Psychology, 28,* 129–137.

Lerner, M.J. (1980). *The belief in a just world: A fundamental delusion.* New York: Plenum.

Lerner, M.J., & Matthews, G. (1967). Reactions to suffering of others under conditions of indirect responsibility. *Journal of Personality and Social Psychology, 5,* 319–325.

Lerner, M.J., Miller, D.T., & Holmes, J.G. (1976). Deserving and the emergence of forms of justice. In L. Berkowitz & E. Walster (Eds.), *Equity theory: Toward a general theory of social interaction. Advances in experimental social psychology* (Vol. 9). New York: Academic Press.

Lester, D., & Lester, G. (1975). *Crimes of passion: Murder and the murderer.* Chicago: Nelson-Hall.

Leung, K., & Bond, M.H. (1984). The impact of cultural collectivism on reward allocation. *Journal of Personality and Social Psychology, 47,* 793–804.

Leventhal, G.S. (1976). The distribution of rewards and resources in groups and organizations. In L. Berkowitz & E. Walster (Eds.), *Equity theory: Toward a general theory of social interaction. Advances in experimental social psychology* (Vol. 9). New York: Academic Press.

Leventhal, H. (1970). Findings and theory in the study of fear communications. In L. Berkowitz (Ed.), *Advances in experimental social psychology* (Vol. 5). New York: Academic Press.

Levine, J.M. (1980). Reaction to opinion deviance in small groups. In P.B. Paulus (Ed.), *Psychology of group influence.* Hillsdale, NJ: Lawrence Erlbaum.

Levine, J.M., Saxe, L., & Harris, H.J. (1976). Reaction to attitudinal deviance: Impact of a deviate's direction and distance of movement. *Sociometry, 39,* 97–107.

Levinger, G. (1972). Little sandbox and big quarry: Comment on Byrne's paradigmatic spade for research in interpersonal attraction. *Representative Research in Social Psychology, 3,* 3–19.

Levinger, G. (1979). A social exchange view on the dissolution of pair relationships. In R.L. Burgess & T.L. Huston (Eds.), *Social exchange in developing relationships.* New York: Academic Press.

Levinger, G. (1983). Development and change. In H.H. Kelley et al. (Eds.), *Close relationships.* New York: Freeman.

Levinger, G., & Schneider, D.J. (1969). Test of the "risk is a value" hypothesis. *Journal of Personality and Social Psychology, 11,* 165–169.

Levinger, G., & Snoek, D. (1972). *Attraction in relationship: A new look at interpersonal attraction.* Morristown, NJ: General Learning Press.

Lewicki, P. (1983). Self-image bias in person perception. *Journal of Personality and Social Psychology, 45,* 384–393.

Lewicki, P. (1984). Self-schemata and social information processing. *Journal of Personality and Social Psychology, 47,* 1177–1190.

Lewicki, P. (1985). Nonconscious biasing effects of single instances on subsequent judgments. *Journal of Personality and Social Psychology, 48,* 563–574.

Lewin, K., (1935). *A dynamic theory of personality.* New York: McGraw-Hill.

Lewin, K., (1947). Frontiers in group dynamics. *Human Relations, 1,* 143–153.

Lewin, K., (1951). *Field theory in social science.* New York: Harper.

Lewis, M., & Brooks-Gunn, I. (1979). *Social cognition and the acquisition of self.* New York: Plenum.

Liebert, R.M., & Baron, R.A. (1972). Short-term effects of televised aggression on children's aggressive behavior. In G.A. Comstock, E.A. Rubinstein, & J.P. Murray (Eds.), *Television and social behavior* (Vol. 2): *Television and social learning.* Washington, DC: Government Printing Office.

Liebert, R.M., Sprafkin, J.N., & Davidson, E.S. (1982). *The early window: The effects of television on children and youth* (2nd edition). Elmsford, NY: Pergamon.

Liebrand, W.B.G., & van Run, G.J. (1985). The effects of social motives on behavior in social dilemmas in two cultures. *Journal of Experimental Social Psychology, 21,* 86–102.

Linder, D.E. (1982). Social trap analysis: The tragedy of the commons in the laboratory. In V.J. Derlega & J. Grzelak (Eds.), *Cooperation and helping behavior.* New York: Academic Press.

Linder, D.E., Cooper, J., & Jones, E.E. (1967). Decision freedom as a determinant of the role of incentive magnitude in attitude change. *Journal of Personality and Social Psychology, 6,* 245–254.

Lingle, J.H., Geva, N., Ostrom, T.M., Leippe, M.R., & Baumgardner, M.H. (1979). Thematic effects of person judgments on impression organization. *Journal of Personality and Social Psychology, 37,* 674–687.

Lingle, J.H., & Ostrom, T.M. (1981). Principles of memory and cognition in attitude formation. In R.E. Petty, T.M. Ostrom, & T.C. Brock (Eds.), *Cognitive responses in persuasion.* Hillsdale, NJ: Lawrence Erlbaum.

Linville, P.W. (1982). The complexity–extremity effect and age-based stereotyping. *Journal of Personality and Social Psychology, 42,* 193–211.

Linville, P.W., Salovey, P., & Fischer, G.W. (1986). Stereotyping and perceived distributions of social characteristics: An application to ingroup–outgroup perception. In J. Dovidio & S.L. Gaertner (Eds.), *Prejudice, discrimination, and racism*. Orlando, FL: Academic Press.

Lippa, R. (1976). Expressive control and the leakage of dispositional introversion–extroversion during role-playing teaching. *Journal of Personality, 44*, 541–559.

Liska, A.E. (1974). Emergent issues in the attitude–behavior consistency controversy. *American Sociological Review, 39*, 261–272.

Livesley, W.J., & Bromley, D.B. (1973). *Person perception in childhood and adolescence*. New York: Wiley.

Lloyd-Bostock, S. (1983). Attributions of cause and responsibility as social phenomena. In J. Jaspers, F.D. Fincham, & M. Hewstone (Eds.), *Attribution theory and research: Conceptual, developmental, and social dimensions*. London: Academic Press.

Locke, J. (1693). *Some thoughts concerning education*. London: A. & J. Churchill.

Locksley, A., Borgida, E., Brekke, N., & Hepburn, C. (1980). Sex stereotypes and social judgment. *Journal of Personality and Social Psychology, 39*, 821–831.

Locksley, A., Hepburn, C., & Ortiz, V. (1982). Social stereotypes and judgments of individuals: An instance of the base rate fallacy. *Journal of Experimental Social Psychology, 18*, 23–42.

Loftus, E.F., Miller, D.G., & Burns, H.J. (1978). Semantic integration of verbal information into a visual memory. *Journal of Experimental Psychology: Human Learning and Memory, 4*, 19–31.

Loftus, E.F., & Palmer, J. (1974). Reconstruction of automobile destruction. *Journal of Verbal Learning and Verbal Behavior, 13*, 585–589.

Lord, C.G. (1980). Schemas and images as memory aids: Two modes of processing social information. *Journal of Personality and Social Psychology, 38*, 257–269.

Lord, C.G. (1982). Predicting behavioral consistency from an individual's perception of situational similarities. *Journal of Personality and Social Psychology, 42*, 1076–1088.

Lord, C.G., Lepper, M.R., & Mackie, D. (1984). Attitude prototypes as determinants of attitude–behavior consistency. *Journal of Personality and Social Psychology, 46*, 1254–1266.

Lord, C.G., Lepper, M.R., & Preston, E. (1984). Considering the opposite: A corrective strategy for social judgment. *Journal of Personality and Social Psychology, 47*, 1231–1243.

Lord, C.G., Ross, L., & Lepper, M.R. (1979). Biased assimilation and attitude polarization: The effects of prior theories on subsequently considered evidence. *Journal of Personality and Social Psychology, 37*, 2098–2109.

Lorenz, K. (1967). *On aggression*. New York: Bantam.

Lott, A.J., & Lott, B.E. (1974). The role of reward in the formation of positive interpersonal attitudes. In T.L. Huston (Ed.), *Foundations of interpersonal attraction*. New York: Academic Press.

Lott, A.J., Lott, B.R., Reed, T., & Crow, T. (1970). Personality trait descriptions of differentially liked persons. *Journal of Personality and Social Psychology, 16*, 284–290.

Lowe, C.A., & Goldstein, J.W. (1970). Reciprocal liking and attribution of ability: Mediating effects of perceived intent and personal involvement. *Journal of Personality and Social Psychology, 16*, 291–297.

Lowenthal, M.F., Thurnher, M., & Chiriboga, D. (1975). *Four stages of life: A comparative study of women and men facing transitions*. San Francisco: Jossey-Bass.

Lubinski, D., Tellegen, A., & Butcher, J.N. (1981). The relationship between androgyny and subjective indicators of emotional well-being. *Journal of Personality and Social Psychology, 40*, 722–730.

Lubinski, D., Tellegen, A., & Butcher, J.N. (1983). Masculinity, femininity, and androgyny viewed and assessed as distinct concepts. *Journal of Personality and Social Psychology, 44*, 428–439.

Lui, L., & Brewer, M.B. (1983). Recognition accuracy as evidence of category-consistency effects in person memory. *Social Cognition, 2*, 89–107.

Lunde, D.T. (1976). *Murder and madness*. New York: W.W. Norton.

M

Maass, A., & Clark, R.D. (1984). Hidden impact of minorities: Fifteen years of minority influence research. *Psychologic Bulletin, 95*, 428–450.

McArthur, L.Z. (1972). The how and what of why: Some determinants and consequences of causal attribution. *Journal of Personality and Social Psychology, 22*, 171–193.

McArthur, L.Z. (1981). What grabs you? The role of attention in impression formation and causal attribution. In E.T. Higgins, C.P. Herman, & M.P. Zanna (Eds.), *Social cognition: The Ontario Symposium* (Vol. 1). Hillsdale, NJ: Lawrence Erlbaum.

McArthur, L.Z., & Apatow, K. (1983–1984). Impressions of baby-faced adults. *Social Cognition, 2*, 315–342.

McArthur, L.Z., & Baron, R.M. (1983). Toward an ecological theory of social perception. *Psychological Review, 90*, 215–238.

McArthur, L.Z., & Burstein, B. (1975). Field dependent eating and perception as a function of weight and sex. *Journal of Personality, 43*, 402–419.

McCann, C.D., Ostrom, T.M., Tyner, L.K., & Mitchell,

M.L. (1985). Person perception in heterogeneous groups. *Journal of Personality and Social Psychology, 49,* 1449–1459.

McCauley, C., Stitt, C.L., & Segal, M. (1980). Stereotyping: From prejudice to prediction. *Psychological Bulletin, 87,* 195–208.

McClintock, C.G., Harrison, A.A., Strand, S., & Gallo, P. (1963). Internationalism–isolationism, strategy of the other player, and two-person game behavior. *Journal of Abnormal and Social Psychology, 67,* 631–636.

McClintock, C.G., & McNeil, S.P. (1967). Prior dyadic experience and monetary reward as determinants of cooperative and competitive game behavior. *Journal of Personality and Social Psychology, 5,* 282–294.

Maccoby, E. (1980). *Social development: Psychological growth and the parent–child relationship.* New York: Harcourt Brace Jovanovich.

Maccoby, E., & Jacklin, C.N. (1974). *The psychology of sex differences.* Stanford, CA: Stanford University Press.

Maccoby, E.E., & Martin, J.A. (1983). Socialization in the context of the family: Parent–child interaction. In P. Mussen (Ed.), *Handbook of child psychology* (4th edition, Vol. 4). New York: Wiley.

McConahay, J.B. (1982). Self-interest versus racial attitudes as correlates of anti-bussing attitudes in Louisville: Is it the buses or the blacks? *Journal of Politics, 44,* 692–720.

McConahay, J.B. (1986). Modern racism, ambivalence, and the modern racism scale. In J.F. Dovidio & S.L. Gaertner (Eds.), *Prejudice, discrimination, and racism.* Orlando, FL: Academic Press.

McDougall, W. (1960, original 1908). *Introduction to social psychology.* New York: University Paperbacks.

McFarland, C., & Ross, M. (1982). Impact of causal attributions on affective reactions to success and failure. *Journal of Personality and Social Psychology, 43,* 937–946.

McGinnies, E., & Ward, C.D. (1980). Better liked than right: Trustworthiness and expertise as factors in credibility. *Personality and Social Psychology Bulletin, 6,* 467–472.

McGinniss, J. (1983). *Fatal vision.* New York: G.P. Putnam's Sons.

McGraw, K.O. (1978). The detrimental effects of reward on performance: A literature review and a prediction model. In M.R. Lepper & D. Greene (Eds.), *The hidden costs of reward: New perspectives on the psychology of human motivation.* Hillsdale, NJ: Lawrence Erlbaum.

McGuire, W.J. (1960). A syllogistic analysis of cognitive relationships. In M. Rosenberg et al. (Eds.), *Attitude organization and change.* New Haven: Yale University Press.

McGuire, W.J. (1983). A contextualist theory of knowledge: Its implications for innovation and reform in psychological research. In L. Berkowitz (Ed.), *Advances in experimental social psychology* (Vol. 16). New York: Academic Press.

McGuire, W.J. (1985). Attitudes and attitude change. In G. Lindzey & E. Aronson (Eds.), *Handbook of social psychology* (3rd edition, Vol. 2). New York: Random House.

McGuire, W.J., McGuire, C.V., Child, P., & Fujioka, T. (1978). Salience of ethnicity in the spontaneous self-concept as a function of one's ethnic distinctiveness in the social environment. *Journal of Personality and Social Psychology, 36,* 511–520.

McGuire, W.J., & Millman, S. (1965). Anticipating belief-lowering following forewarning of a persuasive attack. *Journal of Personality and Social Psychology, 2,* 471–480.

McGuire, W.J., & Padawer-Singer, A. (1976). Trait salience in the spontaneous self-concept. *Journal of Personality and Social Psychology, 33,* 743–754.

McGuire, W.J., & Papageorgis, D. (1961). The relative efficacy of various types of prior belief-defense in producing immunity against persuasion. *Journal of Abnormal and Social Psychology, 62,* 327–337.

McGuire, W.J., & Papageorgis, D. (1962). Effectiveness of forewarning in developing resistance to persuasion. *Public Opinion Quarterly, 26,* 24–34.

McHale, S.M., & Huston, T.L. (1984). Men and women as parents: Sex role orientations, employment, and parental roles with infants. *Child Development, 55,* 1349–1361.

McHale, S.M., & Huston, T.L. (1985). The effect of the transition to parenthood on the marriage relationship: A longitudinal study. *Journal of Family Issues, 6,* 409–433.

McHugh, P. (1968). *Defining the situation.* Indianapolis, IN: Bobbs-Merrill.

McHugo, G.J., Lanzetta, J.T., Sullivan, D.G., Masters, R.D., & Englis, B.G. (1985). Emotional reactions to a political leader's expressive displays. *Journal of Personality and Social Psychology, 49,* 1513–1529.

Mackie, J.L. (1974). *The cement of the universe.* London: Oxford University Press.

McKirnan, D.J., Smith, C.E., & Hamayan, E.V. (1983). A sociolinguistic approach to the belief-similarity model of racial attitudes. *Journal of Experimental Social Psychology, 19,* 434–447.

McNeill, D. (1966). Speaking of space. *Science, 152,* 875–880.

McNeill, D. (1985). So you think gestures are nonverbal? *Psychological Review, 92,* 350–371.

McNulty, F. (1980). *The burning bed.* San Francisco: Harcourt Brace Jovanovich.

McPherson, K. (1983). Opinion-related information seeking: Personal and situational variables. *Personality and Social Psychology Bulletin, 9,* 116–124.

Maddux, J.E., & Rogers, R.W. (1980). Effects of source expertness, physical attractiveness, and arguments on persuasion: A case of brains over beauty. *Journal of Personality and Social Psychology, 39,* 235–244.

Maddux, J.E., & Rogers, R.W. (1983). Protection motivation and self-efficacy: A revised theory of fear appeals and attitude change. *Journal of Personality and Social Psychology, 19,* 469–479.

Mahl, G.F., & Schulze, G. (1964). Psychological research in the extralinguistic area. In T.A. Sebeok, A.S. Hayes, & M.C. Bateson (Eds.), *Approach to semiotics.* The Hague: Mouton.

Major, B., Carnevale, P.J.D., & Deaux, K. (1981). A different perspective on androgyny: Evaluations of masculine and feminine personality characteristics. *Journal of Personality and Social Psychology, 41,* 988–1001.

Malamuth, N.M. (1986). Predictors of naturalistic sexual aggression. *Journal of Personality and Social Psychology, 50,* 953–962.

Malamuth, N.M., Check, J.V.P, & Briere, J. (1986). Sexual arousal in response to aggression: Ideological, aggressive, and sexual correlates. *Journal of Personality and Social Psychology, 20,* 330–340.

Malamuth, N.M., & Donnerstein, E. (1982). The effects of aggressive-pornographic mass media stimuli. In L. Berkowitz (Ed.), *Advances in experimental social psychology* (Vol. 13). New York: Academic Press.

Malamuth, N.M., Heim, M., & Feshbach, S. (1980). Sexual responsiveness of college students to rape depictions: Inhibitory and disinhibitory effects. *Journal of Personality and Social Psychology, 38,* 399–408.

Mandler, G. (1962). Emotion. In R. Brown, E. Galanter, E. Hess, & G. Mandler (Eds.), *New directions in psychology.* New York: Holt, Rinehart & Winston.

Mandler, G. (1984). *Mind and body: Psychology of emotion and stress.* New York: Norton.

Manicas, P.T., & Secord, P.F. (1983). Implications for psychology of the new philosophy of science. *American Psychologist, 38,* 399–413.

Manis, M., Cornell, S.O., & Moore, J.C. (1974). Transmission of attitude-relevant information through a communication chain. *Journal of Personality and Social Psychology, 30,* 81–94.

Manis, M., & Paskewitz, J.R. (1984). Judging psychopathology: Expectation and contrast. *Journal of Experimental Psychology, 20,* 363–381.

Mann, L., Newton, J.W., & Innes, J.M. (1982). A test between deindividuation and emergent norm theories of crowd aggression. *Journal of Personality and Social Psychology, 42,* 260–272.

Manucia, G.K., Baumann, D.J., & Cialdini, R.B. (1984). Mood influences on helping: Direct effects or side effects. *Journal of Personality and Social Psychology, 46,* 357–364.

Marks, G., & Miller, N. (1982). Target attractiveness as a mediator of assumed attitude similarity. *Personality and Social Psychology Bulletin, 8,* 728–735.

Markus, H. (1977). Self-schemata and processing information about the self. *Journal of Personality and Social Psychology, 35,* 63–78.

Markus, H. (1981). The drive for integration: Some comments. *Journal of Experimental Social Psychology, 17,* 257–261.

Markus, H., Crane, M., Bernstein, S., & Siladi, M. (1982). Self-schemata and gender. *Journal of Personality and Social Psychology, 42,* 38–50.

Markus, H., & Smith, J. (1981). The influence of self-schema on the perception of others. In N. Cantor & J.F. Kihlstrom (Eds.), *Personality, cognition, and social interaction.* Hillsdale, NJ: Lawrence Erlbaum.

Markus, H., Smith, J., & Moreland, R.L. (1985). Role of self-concept in the perception of others. *Journal of Personality and Social Psychology, 49,* 1494–1512.

Markus, H., & Zajonc, R.B. (1985). The cognitive perspective in social psychology. In G. Lindzey & E. Aronson (Eds.), *Handbook of social psychology* (3rd edition, Vol. 1). New York: Random House.

Marshall, G.Q., & Zimbardo, P.G. (1979). Affective consequences of inadequately explained physiological arousal. *Journal of Personality and Social Psychology, 37,* 970–988.

Maslach, C. (1979). Negative emotional biasing of unexplained arousal. *Journal of Personality and Social Psychology, 37,* 953–969.

Mathes, E.W., & Kahn, A. (1975). Diffusion of responsibility and extreme behavior. *Journal of Personality and Social Psychology, 31,* 881–886.

Mead, G.H. (1934). *Mind, self and society.* Chicago: University of Chicago Press.

Mednick, S.A. (1977). A biosocial theory of the learning of law-abiding behavior. In S.A. Mednick & K.O. Christiansen (Eds.), *Biosocial bases of criminal behavior.* New York: Gardner Press.

Megargee, E.I. (1966). Undercontrolled and overcontrolled personality types in extreme antisocial aggression. *Psychological Monographs, 80,* Whole #611.

Mehlman, R.C., & Snyder, C.R. (1985). Excuse theory: A test of the self-protective role of attributions. *Journal of Personality and Social Psychology, 49,* 994–1001.

Meltzer, L., Morris, W., & Hayes, D.P. (1971). Interruption outcomes and vocal amplitude: Exploration in social psychophysics. *Journal of Personality and Social Psychology, 18,* 392–402.

Merton, R. (1938). Social structure and anomie. *American Sociological Review, 3,* 672–682.

Messick, D.M., & McClelland, C.L. (1983). Social traps and temporal traps. *Personality and Social Psychology Bulletin, 9,* 105–110.

Messick, D.M., Wilke, H., Brewer, M.B., Kramer, R.M., Zemke, P.E., & Lui, L. (1983). Individual adaptations and structural change to social dilemmas. *Journal of Personality and Social Psychology, 44,* 294–309.

Mettee, D.R., & Aronson, E. (1974). Affective reactions to appraisal from others. In T.L. Huston (Ed.), *Foundations of interpersonal attraction.* New York: Academic Press.

Meyer, J.P., & Pepper, S. (1977). Need compatibility and marital adjustment in young married couples. *Journal of Personality and Social Psychology, 35,* 331–342.

Michener, H.A., & Lawler, E.J. (1975). Endorsement of formal leaders: An integrative model. *Journal of Personality and Social Psychology, 31,* 216–223.

Milardo, R.M., Johnson, M.P., & Huston, T.L. (1983). Developing close relationships: Changing patterns of interactions between pair members and social networks. *Journal of Personality and Social Psychology, 44,* 964–976.

Milavsky, J.R., Stipp, H.H., Kessler, R.C., & Rubens, W.S. (1982). *Television and aggression: A panel study.* New York: Academic Press.

Milgram, S. (1963). Behavioral study of obedience. *Journal of Abnormal and Social Psychology, 67,* 371–378.

Milgram, S. (1964). Issues in the study of obedience: A reply to Baumrind. *American Psychologist, 19,* 848–852.

Milgram, S. (1975). *Obedience to authority.* New York: Harper Colophon.

Miller, A.G. (1972). Role playing: An alternative to deception? A review of the evidence. *American Psychologist, 27,* 623–636.

Miller, A.G., Jones, E.E., & Hinkle, S. (1981). A robust attribution error in the personality domain. *Journal of Experimental Social Psychology, 17,* 587–600.

Miller, C.T. (1982). The role of performance-related similarity in social comparison of abilities: A test of the related attributes hypothesis. *Journal of Experimental Social Psychology, 18,* 513–523.

Miller, L.C., & Kenny, D.A. (986). Reciprocity of self-disclosure at the individual and dyadic levels: A social relations analysis. *Journal of Personality and Social Psychology, 50,* 713–719.

Miller, N., Brewer, M.B., & Edwards, K. (1985). Cooperative interaction in desegregated settings: A laboratory analogue. *Journal of Social Issues, 41,* 63–80.

Miller, W. (1958). Lower class culture as a generating milieu of gang delinquency. *Journal of Social Issues, 14,* 5–19.

Mills, C.J. (1983). Sex-typing and self-schemata effects on memory and response latency. *Journal of Personality and Social Psychology, 45,* 163–172.

Mills, J., & Jellison, J.M. (1967). Effect on opinion change of how desirable the communication is to the audience the communicator addressed. *Journal of Personality and Social Psychology, 6,* 98–101.

Mineka, S., & Suomi, S.J. (1978). Social separation in monkeys. *Psychological Bulletin, 85,* 1376–1400.

Mischel, W. (1968). *Personality and assessment.* New York: Wiley.

Mischel, W. (1973). Toward a cognitive social learning reconceptualization of personality. *Psychological Review, 80,* 252–283.

Mischel, W. (1977). The interaction of person and situation. In D. Magnusson & N.S. Endler (Eds.), *Personality at the crossroads: Current issues in interactional psychology.* Hillsdale, NJ: Lawrence Erlbaum.

Mischel, W. (1981a). Personality and cognition: Something borrowed, something new. In N. Cantor & J.F. Kihlstrom (Eds.), *Personality, cognition, and social interaction.* Hillsdale, NJ: Lawrence Erlbaum.

Mischel, W. (1981b). Metacognition and the rules of delay. In J.H. Flavell & L. Ross (Eds.), *Social cognition development.* Cambridge: Cambridge University Press.

Mischel, W., & Baker, N. (1975). Cognitive appraisals and transformation in delay behavior. *Journal of Personality and Social Psychology, 31,* 254–261.

Mischel, W., Ebbesen, E.B., & Zeiss, A.R. (1972). Cognitive and attentional mechanisms in delay of gratification. *Journal of Personality and Social Psychology, 21,* 204–218.

Mischel, W., & Peake, P.K. (1982). Beyond deja vu in the search for cross-situational consistency. *Psychological Review, 89,* 730–755.

Mischel, W., & Peake, P.K. (1983). Some facts of consistency: Replies to Epstein, Funder, and Bem. *Psychological Review, 90,* 394–402.

Moe, V.L., Nacoste, R.W., & Insko, C.A. (1981). Belief versus race as a determinant of discrimination: A study of southern adolescents in 1966 and 1979. *Journal of Personality and Social Psychology, 41,* 1031–1050.

Mogy, R.B., & Pruitt, D.G. (1974). Effects of a threatener's enforcement costs of threat credibility and compliance. *Journal of Personality and Social Psychology, 29,* 173–180.

Monson, T.C., & Hesley, J.W. (1982). Causal attributions for behaviors consistent or inconsistent with an actor's personality traits: Differences between those offered by actors and observers. *Journal of Experimental Social Psychology, 18,* 416–432.

Monson, T.C., Hesley, J.W., & Chernick, L. (1982). Specifying when personality traits can and cannot predict behavior: An alternative to abandoning the attempt to predict single-act criteria. *Journal of Personality and Social Psychology, 43,* 385–399.

Monson, T.C., Keel, R., Stephens, D., & Genung, V. (1982). Trait attributions: Relative validity, covariation with behavior, and prospect of future interaction. *Journal of Personality and Social Psychology, 42,* 1014–1024.

Monson, T.C., & Snyder, M. (1977). Actors, observers,

and the attribution process: Toward a reconceptualization. *Journal of Experimental Social Psychology, 13,* 89–111.

Mook, D.G. (1983). In defense of external invalidity. *American Psychologist, 38,* 379–387.

Moos, R. (1976). *The human context: Environmental determinants of behavior.* New York: Wiley.

Moreland, R.L., & Zajonc, R.B. (1977). Is stimulus recognition a necessary condition for the occurrence of exposure effects? *Journal of Personality and Social Psychology, 35,* 191–199.

Morgan, M. (1982). Television and adolescent's sex role stereotypes: A longitudinal study. *Journal of Personality and Social Psychology, 43,* 947–955.

Moscovici, S. (1976). *Social influence and social change.* New York: Academic Press.

Moscovici, S. (1980). Toward a theory of conversion behavior. In L. Berkowitz (Ed.), *Advances in experimental social psychology* (Vol. 13). New York: Academic Press.

Moskowitz, D.S. (1982). Coherence and cross-situational generality in personality: A new analysis of old problems. *Journal of Personality and Social Psychology, 43,* 754–768.

Moyer, K.E. (1976). *The psychobiology of aggression.* New York: Harper & Row.

Mullen, B., Atkins, J.L., Champion, D.S., Edwards, C., Hardy, D., Story, J.E., & Vanderklok, M. (1985). The false consensus effect: A meta-analysis of 115 hypothesis tests. *Journal of Experimental Social Psychology, 21,* 262–283.

Murnighan, J.K. (1978). Models of coalition behavior: Game theoretic, social psychological, and political perspectives. *Psychological Bulletin, 85,* 1130–1153.

Myers, D.G., & Bishop, G.D. (1970). Discussion effects on racial attitudes. *Science, 169,* 778–789.

Myers, D.G., & Bishop, G.D. (1971). Enhancement of dominant attitudes in group discussion. *Journal of Personality and Social Psychology, 20,* 386–391.

Myers, D.G., & Lamm, H. (1976). The group polarization phenomenon. *Psychological Bulletin, 83,* 602–627.

Myers, M.A. (1980). Social contexts and attributions of criminal responsibility. *Social Psychology Quarterly, 43,* 405–419.

N

Nail, P.R. (1986). Toward an integration of some models and theories of social response. *Psychological Bulletin, 100,* 190–206.

Napolitan, D.A., & Goethals, G.R. (1979). The attribution of friendliness. *Journal of Experimental Social Psychology, 15,* 105–113.

Nassi, A.J., Abramowitz, S.I., & Youmans, J.E. (1983). Moral development and politics a decade later: A replication and extension. *Journal of Personality and Social Psychology, 45,* 1127–1135.

Natale, M., & Hantas, M. (1982). Effect of temporary mood states on selective memory about the self. *Journal of Personality and Social Psychology, 42,* 927–934.

Neisser, U. (1976). *Cognition and reality.* San Francisco: Freeman.

Neisser, U. (1981). John Dean's memory: A case study. *Cognition, 9,* 1–22.

Nelson, S.A. (1980). Factors influencing young children's use of motives and outcomes as moral criteria. *Child Development, 51,* 823–829.

Nemeth, C.J. (1970a). Effects of free versus constrained behavior on attraction between people. *Journal of Personality and Social Psychology, 15,* 302–311.

Nemeth, C.J. (1970b). Bargaining and reciprocity. *Psychological Bulletin, 74,* 297–308.

Nemeth, C.J. (1972). A critical analysis of research utilizing the prisoner's dilemma paradigm for the study of bargaining. In L. Berkowitz (Ed.), *Advances in experimental social psychology* (Vol. 6). New York: Academic Press.

Nemeth, C.J. (1981). Jury trials: psychology and law. In L. Berkowitz (Ed.), *Advances in experimental social psychology* (Vol. 14). New York: Academic Press.

Nemeth, C.J. (1986). Differential contributions of majority and minority influence. *Psychological Review, 93,* 23–32.

Nemeth, C.J., & Wachtler, J. (1973). Consistency and modification of judgment. *Journal of Experimental Social Psychology, 9,* 65–79.

Nemeth, C.J., Wachtler, J., & Endicott, J. (1977). Increasing the size of the minority: Some gains and some losses. *European Journal of Social Psychology, 7,* 15–27.

Newcomb, T.M. (1943). *Personality and social change.* New York: Dryden.

Newcomb, T.M. (1961). *The acquaintance process.* New York: Holt, Rinehart & Winston.

Newman, H. (1981). Communication within ongoing intimate relationships: An attributional perspective. *Personality and Social Psychology Bulletin, 7,* 59–70.

Newton, J.W., & Mann, L. (1980). Crowd size as a factor in the persuasion process: A study of the religious crusade meetings. *Journal of Personality and Social Psychology, 39,* 874–883.

Newtson, D., & Rindner, R.J. (1979). Variation in behavior perception and ability attribution. *Journal of Personality and Social Psychology, 37,* 1847–1858.

Niedenthal, P.M., Cantor, N., & Kihlstrom, J.F. (1985). Prototype matching: A strategy for social decision making. *Journal of Personality and Social Psychology, 48,* 575–584.

Nielsen, S.L., & Sarason, I.G. (1981). Emotion, personality, and selective attention. *Journal of Personality and Social Psychology, 41,* 945–960.

Nisbett, R.E. (1968). Determinants of food intake in obesity. *Science, 159,* 1254–1255.

Nisbett, R.E., & Bellows, N. (1977). Verbal reports about causal influence on social judgments: Private access versus public theories. *Journal of Personality and Social Psychology, 35,* 613–624.

Nisbett, R.E., Krantz, D.H., Jepson, C., & Kunda, Z. (1983). The use of statistical heuristics in everyday inductive reasoning. *Psychological Review, 90,* 339–363.

Nisbett, R.E., & Ross, L. (1980). *Human inference: Strategies and shortcomings of social judgment.* Englewood Cliffs, NJ: Prentice-Hall.

Nisbett, R.E., & Schachter, S. (1966). Cognitive manipulation of pain. *Journal of Experimental Psychology, 2,* 227–236.

Nisbett, R.E., & Wilson, T.D. (1977a). Telling more than we can know: Verbal reports on mental processes. *Psychological Review, 84,* 231–259.

Nisbett, R.E., & Wilson, T.D. (1977b). The halo effect: Evidence for unconscious alteration of judgments. *Journal of Personality and Social Psychology, 35,* 250–256.

Nisbett, R.E., Zukier, H., & Lemley, R.E. (1981). The dilution effect: Nondiagnostic information weakens the implications of diagnostic information. *Cognitive Psychology, 13,* 248–277.

Noller, P. (1980). Misunderstandings in marital communication: A study of couples' nonverbal communication. *Journal of Personality and Social Psychology, 39,* 1135–1148.

Noller, P. (1982). Channel consistency and inconsistency in the communication of married couples. *Journal of Personality and Social Psychology, 43,* 732–741.

Novak, D.W., & Lerner, M.J. (1968). Rejection as a consequence of perceived similarity. *Journal of Personality and Social Psychology, 9,* 147–152.

Nucci, L.P., & Nucci, M.S. (1982a). Children's social interactions in the context of moral and conventional transgressions. *Child Development, 53,* 403–412.

Nucci, L.P., & Nucci, M.S. (1982b). Children's responses to moral and conventional transgressions in free-play settings. *Child Development, 53,* 1337–1342.

Nyquist, L.V., & Spence, J.T. (1986). Effects of dispositional dominance and sex role expectations on leadership behaviors. *Journal of Personality and Social Psychology, 50,* 87–93.

O

Olson, J.M., & Zanna, M.P. (1979). A new look at selective exposure. *Journal of Experimental Social Psychology, 15,* 1–15.

Olweus, D. (1977). A critical analysis of the "modern" interactionist position. In D. Magnusson & N.S. Endler (Eds.), *Personality at the crossroads: Current issues in interactional psychology.* Hillsdale, NJ: Lawrence Erlbaum.

O'Malley, P.M., & Bachman, J.G. (1979). Self-esteem and education: Sex and cohort comparisons among high school seniors. *Journal of Personality and Social Psychology, 37,* 1153–1159.

O'Neill, P., & Levings, D.E. (1979). Inducing biased scanning in a group setting to change attitudes toward bilingualism and capital punishment. *Journal of Personality and Social Psychology, 37,* 1432–1438.

Orvis, B.R., Kelley, H.H., & Butler, D.D. (1976) Attributional conflict in young couples. In J.H. Harvey, W.J. Ickes, & R.F. Kidd (Eds.), *New directions in attribution research* (Vol. 1). Hillsdale, NJ: Lawrence Erlbaum.

Osgood, C.E., Suci, G.J., & Tannenbaum, P.H. (1957). *The measurement of meaning.* Urbana: University of Illinois Press.

Oskamp, S., & Perlman, D. (1965). Factors affecting cooperation in prisoner's dilemma games. *Journal of Conflict Resolution, 9,* 358–374.

Osterhouse, R.A., & Brock, T.C. (1970). Distraction increases yielding to propaganda by inhibiting counterarguing. *Journal of Personality and Social Psychology, 15,* 344–358.

Ostrom, T.M., & Davis, D. (1979). Idiosyncratic weighting of trait information in impression formation. *Journal of Personality and Social Psychology, 37,* 2025–2043.

Ostrom, T.M., Pryor, J.B., & Simpson, D.D. (1981). The organization of social information. In E.T. Higgins, C.P. Herman, & M.P. Zanna (Eds.), *Social cognition: The Ontario Symposium* (Vol. 1). Hillsdale, NJ: Lawrence Erlbaum.

Owen, M.T., Easterbrooks, M.A., Chase-Lansdale, L., & Goldberg, W.A. (1984). The relationship between maternal employment status and the stability of attachments to mother and to father. *Child Development, 55,* 1894–1901.

Owens, J., Bower, G.H., & Black, J.B. (1979). The "soap opera" effect in story recall. *Memory and Cognition, 7,* 185–191.

P

Pallak, S.R. (1983–1984). Salience of a communicator's physical attractiveness and persuasion: A heuristic versus systematic processing interpretation. *Social Cognition, 2,* 158–170.

Pallak, S.R., & Davies, J.M. (1982). Finding fault versus attributing responsibility: Using facts differently. *Personality and Social Psychology Bulletin, 8,* 454–459.

Pallak, S.R., Murroni, E., & Koch, J. (1983–1984). Communicator attractiveness and expertise, emotional versus rational appeals, and persuasion: A heuristic versus systematic processing interpretation. *Social Cognition, 2,* 122–141.

Palmer, S. (1960). *A study of murder.* New York: Crowell.

Park, B., & Rothbart, M. (1982). Perception of out-group homogeneity and levels of social categorization: Memory for the subordinate attributes of in-group and out-group members. *Journal of Personality and Social Psychology, 42,* 1051–1068.

Parke, R.D. (1969). Effectiveness of punishment as an interaction of intensity, timing, agent nurturance, and cognitive structuring. *Child Development, 40,* 213–235.

Parke, R.D. (1979). Perspectives on father–infant interactions. In J.D. Osofsky (Ed.), *Handbook of infant development.* New York: Wiley.

Parke, R.D., Berkowitz, L., Leyens, J.P., West, S.G., & Sebastian, R.J. (1977). Some effects of violent and nonviolent movies on the behavior of juvenile delinquents. In L. Berkowitz (Ed.), *Advances in experimental social psychology* (Vol. 10). New York: Academic Press.

Parke, R.D., & Slaby, R.G. (1983). The development of aggression. In P.H. Mussen (Ed.), *Handbook of child psychology* (4th edition, Vol. 4). New York: Wiley.

Paulhus, D. (1982). Individual differences, self-presentation, and cognitive dissonance: Their concurrent operation in forced compliance. *Journal of Personality and Social Psychology, 43,* 838–852.

Paulus, P.B., & Murdock, P. (1971). Anticipated evaluation and audience presence in the enhancement of dominant responses. *Journal of Experimental Social Psychology, 7,* 280–291.

Paunonen, S.V., & Jackson, D.N. (1985). Idiographic measurement strategies for personality and prediction: Some unredeemed promissory notes. *Psychological Review, 92,* 486–511.

Pearl, D., Bouthilet, L., & Lazar, J. (Eds.) (1982). *Television and behavior: Ten years of scientific progress and implications for the eighties* (Vols. 1 & 2). Washington, DC: Government Printing Office.

Peevers, B.H., & Secord, P.F. (1973). Developmental changes in attribution of descriptive concepts to persons. *Journal of Personality and Social Psychology, 27,* 120–128.

Pendleton, M.G., & Batson, C.D. (1979). Self-presentation and the door-in-the-face technique for inducing compliance. *Personality and Social Psychology Bulletin, 5,* 77–81.

Pennebaker, J.W. (1980). Perceptual and environmental determinants of coughing. *Basic and Applied Social Psychology, 1,* 83–92.

Penrod, S., & Hastie, R. (1979). Models of jury decision making: A critical review. *Psychological Bulletin, 86,* 462–492.

Pepitone, A., & DiNubile, M. (1976). Contrast effects in judgments of crime severity and the punishment of crime violators. *Journal of Personality and Social Psychology, 33,* 448–459.

Perry, D.G., & Bussey, K. (1979). The social learning theory of sex differences: Imitation is alive and well. *Journal of Personality and Social Psychology, 37,* 1699–1712.

Perry, D.G., White, A.J., & Perry, L.C. (1984). Does early sex typing result from children's attempts to match their behavior to sex role stereotypes? *Child Development, 55,* 2114–2121.

Peters, L.H., Hartke, D.D., & Pohlmann, J.T. (1985). Fiedler's contingency theory of leadership: An application of the meta-analysis procedures of Schmidt and Hunter. *Psychological Bulletin, 97,* 274–285.

Peterson, C. (1980). Recognition of noncontingency. *Journal of Personality and Social Psychology, 38,* 727–734.

Peterson, C., & Seligman, M.E.P. (1984). Causal explanation as a risk factor for depression: Theory and evidence. *Psychological Review, 91,* 347–374.

Peterson, L., & Gelfand, D.M. (1984). Causal attributions of helping as a function of age and incentive. *Child Development, 55,* 504–511.

Pettigrew, T.F. (1958). Personality and sociocultural factors in intergroup attitudes: A cross-national comparison. *Journal of Conflict Resolution, 2,* 29–42.

Pettigrew, T.F. (1979). The ultimate attribution error: Extending Allport's cognitive analysis of prejudice. *Personality and Social Psychology Bulletin, 5,* 461–476.

Petty, R.E., & Cacioppo, J.T. (1977). Forewarning, cognitive responding, and resistance to persuasion. *Journal of Personality and Social Psychology, 35,* 645–655.

Petty, R.E., & Cacioppo, J.T. (1979). Issue involvement can increase or decrease persuasion by enhancing message-relevant cognitive responses. *Journal of Personality and Social Psychology, 37,* 1915–1926.

Petty, R.E., & Cacioppo, J.T. (1981). *Attitudes and persuasion: Classic and contemporary approaches.* Dubuque, IA: William C. Brown.

Petty, R.E., & Cacioppo, J.T. (1984). The effects of involvement on responses to argument quality and quantity: Central and peripheral routes to persuasion. *Journal of Personality and Social Psychology, 46,* 69–81.

Petty, R.E., & Cacioppo, J.T. (1986). The elaboration likelihood model of persuasion. In L. Berkowitz (Ed.), *Advances in experimental social psychology* (Vol. 19). New York: Academic Press.

Petty, R.E., Cacioppo, J.T., & Goldman, R. (1981). Personal involvement as a determinant of argument-based persuasion. *Journal of Personality and Social Psychology, 41,* 847–855.

Petty, R.E., Harkins, S.G., Williams, K.D., & Latané, B. (1977). The effects of group size on cognitive effort and evaluation. *Personality and Social Psychology Bulletin,* *3,* 579–582.

Petty, R.E., Ostrom, T.M., & Brock, T.C. (Eds.) (1981). *Cognitive responses in persuasion.* Hillsdale, NJ: Lawrence Erlbaum.

Pheterson, G.I., Kiesler, S.B., & Goldberg, P.A. (1971). Evaluation of the performance of women as a function of their sex, achievement, and personal history. *Journal of Personality and Social Psychology, 19,* 114–118.

Phillips, D.P. (1974). The influence of suggestion on suicide: Substantive and theoretical implications of the Werther effect. *American Sociological Review, 39,* 340–354.

Phillips, D.P. (1977). Motor vehicle fatalities increase just after publicized suicide stories. *Science, 196,* 1464–1465.

Phillips, D.P. (1979). Suicide, motor vehicle fatalities, and the mass media: Evidence towards a theory of suggestion. *American Journal of Sociology, 84,* 1150–1174.

Phillips, D.P. (1983). The impact of mass media violence on U.S. homicides. *American Sociological Review, 48,* 560–568.

Phillips, D.P. (1986). Natural experiments on the effects of mass media violence on fatal aggression: Strengths and weaknesses of a new approach. In L. Berkowitz (Ed.), *Advances in Experimental Social Psychology* (Vol. 19). Orlando, FL: Academic Press.

Phillips, D.P., & Hensley, J. (1984). When violence is rewarded or punished: The impact of mass media stories on homicide. *Journal of Communication, 34,* 101–116.

Piaget, J. (1932). *The moral judgment of the child.* New York: Harcourt, Brace.

Piaget, J. (1958). *The language and thought of the child.* New York: World (Meridian).

Piaget, J., & Inhelder, B. (1956). *The child's conception of space.* London: Routledge and Kegan Paul.

Pietromonaco, P.R. (1985). The influence of affect on self-perception in depression. *Social Cognition, 3,* 121–134.

Piliavin, I.M., Rodin, J., & Piliavin, J.A. (1969). Good samaritanism: An underground phenomenon. *Journal of Personality and Social Psychology, 13,* 289–299.

Piliavin, J.A., Dovidio, J.F., Gaertner, S.L., & Clark, R.D., III (1981). *Emergency intervention.* New York: Academic Press.

Piliavin, J.A., & Piliavin, I.M. (1972). Effect of blood on reactions to a victim. *Journal of Personality and Social Psychology, 23,* 353–361.

Pittman, N.L., & Pittman, T.S. (1979). Effects of amount of helplessness training and internal–external locus of control on mood and performance. *Journal of Personality and Social Psychology, 37,* 39–47.

Platt, J. (1973). Social traps. *American Psychologist, 28,* 641–651.

Pool, D.L., Shweder, R.A., & Much, N.C. (1983). Culture as a cognitive system: Differentiating rule understandings in children and other savages. In E.T. Higgins, D.N. Ruble, & W.W. Hartup (Eds.), *Social cognition and social development: A sociocultural perspective.* Cambridge: Cambridge University Press.

Porter, L.W., & Roberts, K.H. (1976). Communication in organizations. In M.D. Dunnette (Ed.), *Handbook of industrial and organizational psychology.* Chicago: Rand McNally.

Powell, M.C., & Fazio, R.H. (1984). Attitude accessibility as a function of repeated attitudinal expression. *Personality and Social Psychology Bulletin, 10,* 139–148.

Powers, P.C., & Geen, R.G. (1972). Effects of the behavior and the perceived arousal of a model on instrumental aggression. *Journal of Personality and Social Psychology, 23,* 175–183.

Price, R.H., & Bouffard, D.L. (1974). Behavioral appropriateness and situational constraint as dimensions of social behavior. *Journal of Personality and Social Psychology, 30,* 579–586.

Price, W.H., & Whatmore, P.B. (1967). Behavior disorders and patterns of crime among XYY males identified at a maximum security hospital. *British Medical Journal, 1,* 533–536.

Pritchard, R.D., Dunnette, M.D., & Jorgenson, D.O. (1972). Effects of perceptions of equity and inequity on worker performance and satisfaction. *Journal of Applied Psychology Monographs, 56,* 75–94.

Pruitt, D.G. (1971). Choice shifts in group discussion: An introductory review. *Journal of Personality and Social Psychology, 20,* 339–360.

Pryor, J.B., & Kriss, M. (1977). The cognitive dynamics of salience in the attribution process. *Journal of Personality and Social Psychology, 35,* 49–55.

Pryor, J.B., Simpson, D.D., Mitchell, M., Ostrom, T.M., & Lydon, J. (1982). Structural selectivity in the retrieval of social information. *Social Cognition, 2,* 336–357.

Purvis, J.A., Dabbs, J.M., & Hopper, C.H. (1984). The "opener": Skilled user of facial expression and speech pattern. *Personality and Social Psychology Bulletin, 10,* 61–66.

Pyszczynski, T.A., & Greenberg, J. (1981). Role of disconfirmed expectancies in the instigation of attributional processing. *Journal of Personality and Social Psychology, 40,* 31–38.

Pyszczynski, T., Greenberg, J., & LaPrelle, J. (1985). Social comparison after success and failure: Biased search for information consistent with a self-serving conclusion. *Journal of Experimental Social Psychology, 21,* 195–211.

Q

Quattrone, G.A., & Jones, E.E. (1980). The perception of variability within in-groups and out-groups: Implications for the law of small numbers. *Journal of Personality and Social Psychology, 38,* 141–152.

R

Radke-Yarrow, M., Zahn-Waxler, C., & Chapman, M. (1983). Children's prosocial dispositions and behavior. In P.H. Mussen (Ed.), *Handbook of child psychology* (4th edition, Vol. 4). New York: Wiley.

Rakover, S.S. (1983). Hypothesizing from introspections: A model for the role of mental entities in psychological explanation. *Journal for the Theory of Social Behavior, 13,* 211–230.

Raper, A.F. (1933). *The tragedy of lynching.* Durham: University of North Carolina Press.

Rausch, H.L. (1977). Paradox levels, and junctures in person–situation systems. In D. Magnusson & N.S. Endler (Eds.), *Personality at the crossroads: Current issues in interactional psychology.* Hillsdale, NJ: Lawrence Erlbaum.

Read, S.J., & Rosson, M.B. (1982). Rewriting history: The biasing effects of attitudes on memory. *Social Cognition, 1,* 240–255.

Reed, S.K. (1972). Pattern recognition and categorization. *Cognitive Psychology, 3,* 382–407.

Reeder, G.D., & Brewer, M.B. (1979). A schematic model of dispositional attribution in interpersonal perception. *Psychological Review, 86,* 61–79.

Reeder, G.D., & Coovert, M.D. (1986). Revising an impression of mortality. *Social Cognition, 4,* 1–17.

Reeder, G.D., Messick, D.M., & Van Avermaet, E. (1977). Dimensional asymmetry in attributional inference. *Journal of Experimental Social Psychology, 13,* 46–57.

Regan, D.T. (1971). Effects of favor and liking on compliance. *Journal of Experimental Social Psychology, 7,* 627–639.

Regan, D.T., & Cheng, J.B. (1973). Distraction and attitude change. *Journal of Experimental Social Psychology, 9,* 138–147.

Reis, H.T., Wheeler, L., Spiegel, N., Kernis, M.H., Nezlek, J., & Perri, M. (1982). Physical attractiveness in social interaction. II: Why does appearance affect social experience? *Journal of Personality and Social Psychology, 43,* 979–986.

Reisenzein, R. (1983). The Schachter theory of emotion: Two decades later. *Psychological Bulletin, 94,* 239–264.

Reisenzein, R. (1986). A structural equation analysis of Weiner's attribution–affect model of helping behavior. *Journal of Personality and Social Psychology, 50,* 1123–1133.

Reisman, J.M. (1981). Adult friendships. In S. Duck & R. Gilmour (Eds.), *Personal relationships. 2: Developing personal relationships.* London: Academic Press.

Rempel, J.K., Holmes, J.G., & Zanna, M.P. (1985). Trust in close relationships. *Journal of Personality and Social Psychology, 49,* 95–112.

Renshaw, P.D., & Asher, S.R. (1982). Social competence and peer status: The distinction between goals and strategies. In K.H. Rubin & H.S. Ross (Eds.), *Peer relationships and social skills in childhood.* New York: Springer-Verlag.

Report of the Presidential Commission on the Space Shuttle Challenger Accident. (1976). Washington, DC: Government Printing Office.

Rest, J.R. (1983). Morality. In P.H. Mussen (Ed.), *Handbook of child psychology* (4th edition, Vol. 3). New York: Wiley.

Rholes, W.S., & Pryor, J.B. (1982). Cognitive accessibility and causal attribution. *Personality and Social Psychology Bulletin, 8,* 719–727.

Rholes, W.S., & Ruble, D.N. (1984). Children's understanding of dispositional characteristics of others. *Child Development, 55,* 550–560.

Rice, R.W. (1978). Construct validity of the least preferred co-worker score. *Psychological Bulletin, 85,* 1199–1237.

Rice, R.W., Marwick, N.J., Chemers, M.M., & Bentley, J.C. (1982). Task performance and satisfaction: Least preferred coworker (LPC) as a moderator. *Personality and Social Psychology Bulletin, 8,* 534–541.

Richardson, D.C., Bernstein, S., & Taylor, S.P. (1979). The effect of situational contingencies on female retaliative behavior. *Journal of Personality and Social Psychology, 37,* 2044–2048.

Ridley, M., & Dawkins, R. (1981). The natural selection of altruism. In J.P. Rushton & R.M. Sorrentino (Eds.), *Altruism and helping behavior.* Hillsdale, NJ: Lawrence Erlbaum.

Riggio, R.E., & Friedman, H.S. (1983). Individual differences and cues to deception. *Journal of Personality and Social Psychology, 45,* 899–915.

Ring, K. (1967). Experimental social psychology: Some sober questions about some frivolous values. *Journal of Experimental Social Psychology, 3,* 113–123.

Riordan, C.A., & Tedeschi, J.T. (1983). Attraction in aversive environments: Some evidence for classical conditioning and negative reinforcement: *Journal of Personality and Social Psychology, 44,* 683–692.

Roberts, D.F., & Maccoby, N. (1985). Effects of mass communication. In G. Lindzey & E. Aronson (Eds.), *Handbook of social psychology* (3rd edition, Vol. 2). New York: Random House.

Robinson, D.N. (1981). *An intellectual history of psychology* (revised edition). New York: Macmillan.

Rodin, J. (1981). Current status of the internal–external hypothesis for obesity: What went wrong? *American Psychologist, 36,* 361–372.

Rodin, J., & Slochower, J. (1974). Fat chance for a favor:

Obese–normal differences in compliance and incidental learning. *Journal of Personality and Social Psychology, 29,* 557–565.

Rodin, M., & Harari, H. (1986). Fact, belief, and the attribution of prejudice. *Social Cognition, 4,* 437–445.

Rodrigues, A. (1967). Effects of balance, positivety, and agreement in triadic social relations. *Journal of Personality and Social Psychology, 5,* 472–476.

Rofé, Y. (1984). Stress and affiliation: A utility theory. *Psychological Review, 91,* 235–250.

Rogers, T.B. (1981). A model of the self as an aspect of the human information processing system. In N. Cantor & J. Kihlstrom (Eds.), *Personality, cognition, and social interaction.* Hillsdale, NJ: Lawrence Erlbaum.

Rogers, T.B., Kuiper, N.A., & Kirker, W.S. (1977). Self-reference and the encoding of personal information. *Journal of Personality and Social Psychology, 35,* 677–688.

Rogers, R.W. (1983). Cognitive and physiological processes in fear appeals and attitude change: A revised theory of protection motivation. In J. Cacioppo & R. Petty (Eds.), *Social psychophysiology.* New York: Guilford.

Rogers, R.W., & Prentice-Dunn, S. (1981). Deindividuation and anger-mediated interracial aggression: Unmasking regressive racism. *Journal of Personality and Social Psychology, 41,* 63–73.

Rokeach, M., Smith, P.W., & Evans, R.I. (1960). Two kinds of prejudice or one? In M. Rokeach, *The open and closed mind.* New York: Basic Books.

Romer, D., & Revelle, W. (1984). Personality traits: Fact or fiction? A critique of the Shweder and D'Andrade systematic distortion hypothesis. *Journal of Personality and Social Psychology, 47,* 1028–1042.

Ronis, D.L., & Lipinski, E.R. (1985). Value and uncertainty as weighting factors in impression formation. *Journal of Experimental Social Psychology, 21,* 47–60.

Rosch, E. (1973). Natural categories. *Cognitive Psychology, 4,* 328–350.

Rosch, E. (1978). Principles of categorization. In E. Rosch & B.B. Lloyd (Eds.), *Cognition and categorization.* Hillsdale, NJ: Lawrence Erlbaum.

Rosch, E., Simpson, C., & Miller, R.S. (1976). Structural bases of typicality effects. *Journal of Experimental Psychology: Human Perception and Performance, 2,* 491–502.

Rosenberg, M. (1979). *Conceiving the self.* New York: Basic Books.

Rosenhan, D.L., Salovey, P., & Hargis, K. (1981). The joys of helping: Focus of attention mediates the impact of positive affect on altruism. *Journal of Personality and Social Psychology, 40,* 899–905.

Rosenhan, D.L., Underwood, B., & Moore, B. (1974). Affect mediates self-gratification and altruism. *Journal of Personality and Social Psychology, 30,* 546–552.

Rosenhan, D.L., & White, G.M. (1967). Observation and rehearsal as determinants of prosocial behavior. *Journal of Personality and Social Psychology, 5,* 424–431.

Rosenthal, R. (1966). *Experimenter effects in behavioral research.* New York: Appleton-Century-Crofts.

Rosenthal, R., & DePaulo, B.M. (1979). Sex differences in eavesdropping on nonverbal cues. *Journal of Personality and Social Psychology, 37,* 273–285.

Rosenthal, R., & Fode, K. (1963). Three experiments in experimenter bias. *Psychological Reports, 12,* 183–189.

Rosenthal, R., & Rosnow, R.L. (1969). The volunteer subject. In R. Rosenthal & R.L. Rosnow (Eds.), *Artifact in behavioral research.* New York: Academic Press.

Ross, A., & Braband, J. (1973). Effect of increased responsibility on bystander intervention. II: The cue value of a blind person. *Journal of Personality and Social Psychology, 25,* 254–258.

Ross, H.S., Lollis, S.P., & Elliott, C. (1982). Toddler–peer communication. In K.H. Rubin & H.S. Ross (Eds.), *Peer relationships and social skills in childhood.* New York: Springer-Verlag.

Ross, L. (1977). The intuitive psychologist and his shortcomings: Distortions in the attribution process. In L. Berkowitz (Ed.), *Advances in experimental social psychology* (Vol. 10). New York: Academic Press.

Ross, L., Amabile, T.M., & Steinmetz, J.L. (1977). Social roles, social control, and biases in social-perception processes. *Journal of Personality and Social Psychology, 35,* 485–494.

Ross, L., & Anderson, C.A. (1982). Shortcomings in the attribution process: On the origins and maintenance of erroneous social assessments. In D. Kahneman, P. Slovic, & A. Tversky (Eds.), *Judgment under uncertainty: Heuristics and biases.* Cambridge: Cambridge University Press.

Ross, L., Greene, D., & House, A. (1977). The "false consensus effect": An egocentric bias in social perception and attribution processes. *Journal of Experimental Social Psychology, 13,* 279–301.

Ross, L., Lepper, M.R., & Hubbard, M. (1975). Perseverance in self-perception and social perception: Biased attributional processes in the debriefing paradigm. *Journal of Personality and Social Psychology, 32,* 880–892.

Ross, L., Rodin, J., & Zimbardo, P. (1969). Toward an attribution therapy: The reduction of fear through induced cognitive-emotiqnal misattribution. *Journal of Personality and Social Psychology, 12,* 279–288.

Ross, M., McFarland, C., Conway, M., & Zanna, M.P. (1983). Reciprocal relation between attitudes and behavior recall: Committing people to newly formed attitudes. *Journal of Personality and Social Psychology, 45,* 257–267.

Ross, M., McFarland, C., & Fletcher, G.F.D. (1981). The effect of attitude on the recall of personal histories. *Journal of Personality and Social Psychology, 40,* 627–634.

Ross, M., & Sicoly, F. (1979). Egocentric biases in availability and attribution. *Journal of Personality and Social Psychology, 37,* 322–336.

Rotenberg, K.J. (1980). Children's use of intentionality in judgments of character and disposition. *Child Development, 51,* 282–284.

Rotenberg, K.J. (1982). Development of character constancy of self and other. *Child Development, 53,* 505–511.

Rothbart, M. (1981). Memory processes and social beliefs. In D.L. Hamilton (Ed.), *Cognitive processes in stereotyping and intergroup behavior.* Hillsdale, NJ: Lawrence Erlbaum.

Rothbart, M., Evans, M., & Fulero, S. (1979). Recall for confirming events: Memory processes and the maintenance of social stereotypes. *Journal of Experimental Social Psychology, 15,* 343–355.

Rothbart, M., Fulero, S., Jensen, C., Howard, J., & Birrell, P. (1978). From individual to group impressions: Availability heuristics in stereotype formation. *Journal of Experimental Social Psychology, 14,* 237–255.

Rothbart, M., & John, O.P. (1985). Social categorization and behavioral episodes: A cognitive analysis of the effects of intergroup contact. *Journal of Social Issues, 41,* 81–104.

Rothbart, M., & Park, B. (1986). On the confirmability and disconfirmability of trait concepts. *Journal of Personality and Social Psychology, 50,* 131–142.

Rotton, J., & Frey, J. (1985). Air pollution, weather, and violent crimes: Concomitant time-series analysis of archival data. *Journal of Personality and Social Psychology, 49,* 1207–1220.

Rousseau, J.J. (1964, original 1763). *Emile.* Woodbury, NY: Barron's Educational Series.

Rubin, J.Z., Provenzano, F.J., & Luria, Z. (1974). The eye of the beholder: Parents' views on sex of newborns. *American Journal of Orthopsychiatry, 44,* 512–519.

Rubin, K.H., Fein, G.G., & Vandenberg, B. (1983). Play. In P.H. Mussen (Ed.), *Handbook of child psychology* (4th edition, Vol. 4). New York: Wiley.

Rubin, Z. (1970). Measurement of romantic love. *Journal of Personality and Social Psychology, 16,* 265–273.

Rubin, Z. (1973). *Loving and liking.* New York: Holt, Rinehart & Winston.

Rubin, Z., Peplau, L.A., & Hill, C.T. (1981). Loving and leaving: Sex differences in romantic attachments. *Sex Roles, 7,* 821–835.

Rubinstein, E.A. (1983). Television and behavior: Research conclusions of the 1982 NIMH Report and their policy implications. *American Psychologist, 38,* 820–825.

Rubinstein, J. (1973). *City police.* New York: Ballantine Books.

Ruble, D.N., & Rholes, W.S. (1982). The development of children's perceptions and attributions about their social

world. In J.H. Harvey, W. Ickes, & R.F. Kidd (Eds.), *New directions in attribution research* (Vol. 3). Hillsdale, NJ: Lawrence Erlbaum.

Rusbult, C.E. (1983). A longitudinal test of the investment model: The development (and deterioration) of satisfaction and commitment in heterosexual involvements. *Journal of Personality and Social Psychology, 45,* 101–117.

Rusbult, C.E., Johnson, D.J., & Morrow, G.D. (1986). Impact of couple patterns of problem solving on distress and nondistress in dating relationships. *Journal of Personality and Social Psychology, 50,* 744–753.

Rusbult, C.E., Zembrodt, I.M., & Gunn, L.K. (1982). Exit, voice, loyalty, and neglect: Responses to dissatisfaction in romantic involvements. *Journal of Personality and Social Psychology, 43,* 1230–1242.

Rushton, J.P. (1979). Effects of prosocial television and film material on the behavior of viewers. In L. Berkowitz (Ed.), *Advances in experimental social psychology* (Vol. 12). New York: Academic Press.

Russ, R.C., Gold, J.A., & Stone, W.F. (1979). Attraction to a dissimilar stranger as a function of level of effectance arousal. *Journal of Experimental Social Psychology, 15,* 481–491.

Rutkowski, G.K., Gruder, C.L., & Romer, D. (1983). Group cohesiveness, social norms, and bystander intervention. *Journal of Personality and Social Psychology, 44,* 545–552.

Ryan, E.B., & Carranza, M.A. (1975). Evaluative reactions of adolescents toward speakers of Standard English and Mexican-American accented English. *Journal of Personality and Social Psychology, 31,* 855–863.

Ryan, E.B., & Carranza, M.A. (1977). Ingroup and outgroup reactions to Mexican-American language varieties. In H. Giles (Ed.), *Language, ethnicity, and intergroup relations.* London: Academic Press.

Ryan, R.M., Mims, V., & Koestner, R. (1983). Relation of reward contingency and interpersonal context to intrinsic motivation: A review and test using cognitive evaluation theory. *Journal of Personality and Social Psychology, 45,* 736–750.

Ryan, W. (1971). *Blaming the victim.* New York: Pantheon.

Ryckman, R.M., Robbins, M.A., Thornton, B., & Cantrell, P. (1982). Development and validation of a physical self-efficacy scale. *Journal of Personality and Social Psychology, 42,* 891–900.

S

Sabini, J., & Silver, M. (1981). Introspection and causal accounts. *Journal of Personality and Social Psychology, 40,* 171–179.

Sacks, H., Schegloff, E.A., & Jefferson, G. (1974). A simplest systematics for the organization of turn-taking for conversation. *Language, 50,* 596–735.

Saegert, S., Swap, W., & Zajonc, R.B. (1973). Exposure, context, and interpersonal attraction. *Journal of Personality and Social Psychology, 25,* 234–242.

Sagar, H.A., & Schofield, J.W. (1980). Racial and behavioral cues in black and white children's perceptions of ambiguously aggressive acts. *Journal of Personality and Social Psychology, 39,* 590–598.

Saks, M.J. (1977). *Jury verdicts: The role of group size and social decision rule.* Lexington, MA: Lexington Books.

Saks, M.J., & Hastie, R. (1978). *Social psychology in court.* New York: Van Nostrand Reinhold.

Sampson, E.E. (1977). Psychology and the American ideal. *Journal of Personality and Social Psychology, 35,* 767–782.

Sampson, E.E. (1978). Scientific paradigms and social values: Wanted—a scientific revolution. *Journal of Personality and Social Psychology, 36,* 1332–1343.

Sanders, G.S. (1981). Driven by distraction: An integrative review of social facilitation theory and research. *Journal of Experimental Social Psychology, 17,* 227–251.

Sarnoff, I., & Zimbardo, P. (1961). Anxiety, fear, and social affiliation. *Journal of Abnormal and Social Psychology, 62,* 356–363.

Saunders, D.M., Fisher, W.A., Hewitt, E.C., & Clayton, J.P. (1985). A method for empirically assessing volunteer selection effects: Recruitment procedures and responses to erotica. *Journal of Personality and Social Psychology, 49,* 1703–1712.

Schachter, S. (1951). Deviation, rejection, and communication. *Journal of Abnormal and Social Psychology, 46,* 190–208.

Schachter, S. (1959). *The psychology of affiliation.* Stanford, CA: Stanford University Press.

Schachter, S. (1964). The interaction of cognitive and physiological determinants of emotional state. In L. Berkowitz (Ed.), *Advances in experimental social psychology* (Vol. 1). New York: Academic Press.

Schachter, S., & Gross, L. (1968). Manipulated time and eating behavior. *Journal of Personality and Social Psychology, 10,* 98–106.

Schachter, S., & Singer, J. (1962). Cognitive, social, and physiological determinants of emotion. *Psychological Review, 69,* 379–399.

Schachter, S., & Singer, J. (1979). Comments on the Maslach and Marshall–Zimbardo experiments. *Journal of Personality and Social Psychology, 37,* 989–995.

Schafer, R.B., & Keith, P.M. (1980). Equity and depression among married couples. *Social Psychology Quarterly, 43,* 430–435.

Schank, R.C., & Abelson, R.P. (1977). *Scripts, plans, goals, and understanding.* Hillsdale, NJ: Lawrence Erlbaum.

Schegloff, E.A., & Sacks, H. (1973). Opening up closings. *Semiotica, 8,* 289–327.

Scheier, M.F., Fenigstein, A., & Buss, A.H. (1974). Self-awareness and physical aggression. *Journal of experimental social psychology, 10,* 264–273.

Schein, E. (1956). The Chinese indoctrination program for prisoners of war: A study of attempted "brainwashing." *Psychiatry, 19,* 149–172.

Schifter, D.E., & Ajzen, I. (1985). Intention, perceived control, and weight loss: An application of the theory of planned behavior. *Journal of Personality and Social Psychology, 49,* 843–851.

Schlenker, B.R. (1974). Social psychology and science. *Journal of Personality and Social Psychology, 29,* 1–15.

Schlenker, B.R. (1977). On the ethogenic approach: Etiquette and revolution. In L. Berkowitz (Ed.), *Advances in experimental social psychology* (Vol. 10). New York: Academic Press.

Schlenker, B.R. (1980). *Impression management: The self-concept, social identity, and interpersonal relations.* Monterey, CA: Brooks/Cole.

Schlenker, B.R., & Leary, M.R. (1982). Social anxiety and self-presentation: A conceptualization and model. *Psychological Bulletin, 92,* 641–669.

Schneider, D.J. (1969). Tactical self-presentation after success and failure. *Journal of Personality and Social Psychology, 13,* 262–268.

Schneider, D.J. (1973). Implicit personality theory: A review. *Psychological Bulletin, 79,* 294–309.

Schneider, D.J. (1981). Tactical self-presentations: Toward a broader conception. In J.T. Tedeschi (Ed.), *Impression management theory and social psychological research.* New York: Academic Press.

Schneider, D.J., & Blankmeyer, B.L. (1983). Prototype salience and implicit personality theories. *Journal of Personality and Social Psychology, 44,* 712–722.

Schneider, D.J., & Blankmeyer, B. (1986). The triggering hypothesis in stereotypes of the mentally ill. Unpublished paper.

Schneider, D.J., & Eustis, A. (1972). Effects of ingratiation motivation, target positiveness, and revealingness on self-presentation. *Journal of Personality and Social Psychology, 22,* 149–155.

Schneider, D.J., Hastorf, A.H., & Ellsworth, P.C. (1979). *Person perception.* Reading, MA: Addison-Wesley.

Schneider, D.J., & Miller, R. (1975). The effects of enthusiasm and quality of arguments on attitude attribution. *Journal of Personality, 43,* 693–708.

Schroeder, D.A., Jensen, T.D., Reed, A.J., Sullivan, D.K., & Schwab, M. (1983). The actions of others as determinants of behavior in social trap situations. *Journal of Experimental Social Psychology, 19,* 522–539.

Schroeder, H.E. (1973). The risky shift as a general choice shift. *Journal of Personality and Social Psychology, 27,* 297–300.

Schul, Y., & Burnstein, E. (1985). The informational basis of social judgments: Using past impression rather than the trait description in forming a new impression. *Journal of Experimental Social Psychology, 21,* 421–439.

Schultz, D.P. (Ed.) (1964). *Panic behavior.* New York: Random House.

Schuman, H., Steeh, C., & Bobo, L. (1985). *Racial attitudes in America: Trends and interpretations.* Cambridge, MA: Harvard University Press.

Schwartz, B., Tesser, A., & Powell, E. (1982). Dominance cues in nonverbal behavior. *Social Psychology Quarterly, 45,* 114–120.

Schwartz, S.H. (1977). Normative influences on altruism. In L. Berkowitz (Ed.), *Advances in experimental social psychology* (Vol. 10). New York: Academic Press.

Schwartz, S.H., & Clausen, G.T. (1970). Responsibility, norms, and helping in an emergency. *Journal of Personality and Social Psychology, 16,* 299–310.

Schwartz, S.H., & Fleishman, J.A. (1982). Effects of negative personal norms on helping behavior. *Personality and Social Psychology Bulletin, 8,* 81–86.

Schwartz, S.H., & Gottlieb, A. (1980). Bystander anonymity and reactions to emergencies. *Journal of Personality and Social Psychology, 39,* 418–430.

Schwartz, S.H., & Gottlieb, A. (1981). Participants' post-experimental reactions and the ethics of bystander research. *Journal of Experimental Social Psychology, 17,* 396–407.

Searle, J.R. (1969). *Speech acts.* Cambridge: Cambridge University Press.

Sears, D.O. (1983). The person-positivity bias. *Journal of Personality and Social Psychology, 44,* 233–250.

Sears, D.O. (1986). College sophomores in the laboratory: Influences of a narrow data base on social psychology's view of human nature. *Journal of Personality and Social Psychology, 51,* 515–530.

Sears, D.O., Hensler, C.P., & Speer, L.K. (1979). Whites' opposition to "bussing": Self-interest or symbolic politics? *American Political Science Review, 73,* 369–384.

Sears, R.R., Rau, L., & Alpert, R. (1965). *Identification and child rearing.* Stanford, CA: Stanford University Press.

Seedman, A., & Hellman, P. (1974). Why Kitty Genovese haunts New York: The untold story. *New York,* July 29, pp. 7, 32–41.

Segal, M.W. (1979). Varieties of interpersonal attraction and their interrelationships in natural groups. *Social Psychology Quarterly, 42,* 253–261.

Seligman, M.E.P. (1975). *Helplessness: On depression, development, and death.* San Francisco: Freeman.

Selman, R.L. (1980). *The growth of interpersonal understanding: Developmental and clinical analyses.* New York: Academic Press.

Selman, R.L., & Byrne, D.F. (1974). A structural-developmental analysis of levels of role taking in middle childhood. *Child Development, 45,* 803–806.

Shaffer, D.R., & Ogden, J.K. (1986). On sex differences in self-disclosure during the acquisition process: The role of anticipated future interaction. *Journal of Personality and Social Psychology, 51,* 92–101.

Shanteau, J., & Nagy, G.F. (1979). Probability of acceptance in dating choice. *Journal of Personality and Social Psychology, 37,* 522–533.

Shantz, C.U. (1983). Social cognition. In P.H. Mussen (Ed.), *Handbook of child psychology* (4th edition, Vol. 3). New York: Wiley.

Shapiro, E.G. (1975). Effect of expectations of future interaction on reward allocations in dyads: Equity or equality? *Journal of Personality and Social Psychology, 31,* 873–880.

Shaver, K.G. (1985). *The attribution of blame.* New York: Springer-Verlag.

Shaw, M.E. (1932). A comparison of individuals and small groups in the rational solution of complex problems. *American Journal of Psychology, 44,* 491–504.

Sheppard, B.H., & Vidmar, N. (1980). Adversary pretrial procedures and testimonial evidence: Effects of lawyer's role and Machiavellianism. *Journal of Personality and Social Psychology, 39,* 320–332.

Sherif, C.W. (1980). Comment on ethical issues in Malamuth, Heim, and Feshbach's "Sexual responsiveness of college students to rape depictions: Inhibitory and disinhibitory effects." *Journal of Personality and Social Psychology, 38,* 409–412.

Sherif, M. (1936). *The psychology of social norms.* New York: Harper.

Sherif, M., & Hovland, C. (1961). *Social judgment.* New Haven: Yale University Press.

Sherif, M., & Sherif, C.W. (1953). *Groups in harmony and conflict.* New York: Harper & Row.

Sherman, R., & Titus, W. (1982). Covariation information and cognitive processing: Effects of causal implications on memory. *Journal of Personality and Social Psychology, 42,* 989–1000.

Sherman, S.J. (1980). On the self-erasing nature of errors of prediction. *Journal of Personality and Social Psychology, 39,* 211–221.

Sherman, S.J., Presson, C.C., & Chassin, L. (1984). Mechanisms underlying the false consensus effect: The special role of threats to the self. *Personality and Social Psychology Bulletin, 10,* 127–138.

Sherman, S.J., Presson, C.C., Chassin, L., Corty, E., & Olshavsky, R. (1983). The false consensus effect in estimates of smoking prevalence: Underlying mechanisms. *Personality and Social Psychology Bulletin, 9,* 197–207.

Sherman, S.J., Zehner, K.S., Johnson, J., & Hirt, E.R. (1983). Social explanation: The role of timing, set, and recall on subjective likelihood estimates. *Journal of Personality and Social Psychology, 44,* 1127–1143.

Shotland, R.L., & Heinold, W.D. (1985). Bystander response to arterial bleeding: Helping skills, the decision-making process, and differentiating the helping response. *Journal of Personality and Social Psychology, 49,* 347–356.

Shrauger, J.S. (1975). Responses to evaluations as a function of initial self-perceptions. *Psychological Bulletin, 82,* 581–596.

Shrauger, J.S., & Patterson, M.B. (1974). Self-evaluation and the selection of dimensions for evaluating others. *Journal of Personality, 42,* 569–585.

Shrauger, J.S., & Schoeneman, T.J. (1979). Symbolic interactionist view of self-concept: Through the looking glass darkly. *Psychological Bulletin, 86,* 549–573.

Shultz, T.R., & Schleifer, M. (1983). Towards a refinement of attribution concepts. In J. Jaspers, F.D. Fincham, & M. Hewstone (Eds.), *Attribution theory and research: Conceptual, developmental, and social dimensions.* London: Academic Press.

Shweder, R.A., & D'Andrade, R. (1979). Accurate reflection or systematic distortion? A reply to Block, Weiss, and Thorne. *Journal of Personality and Social Psychology, 37,* 1075–1084.

Shweder, R.A., Turiel, E., & Much, N.C. (1981). The moral intuitions of the child. In J.H. Flavell & L. Ross (Eds.), *Social cognitive development.* Cambridge: Cambridge University Press.

Sigall, H., & Landy, D. (1973). Radiating beauty: Effects of having a physically attractive partner on person perception. *Journal of Personality and Social Psychology, 28,* 218–224.

Sigall, H.E., Aronson, E., & Van Hoose, T. (1970). The cooperative subject: Myth or reality? *Journal of Experimental Social Psychology, 6,* 1–10.

Signorielli, N., Gross, L., & Morgan, M. (1982). Violence in television programs: Ten years later. In D. Pearl, L. Bouthilet, & J. Lazar (Eds.), *Television and behavior: Ten years of scientific progress and implications for the eighties.* Washington, DC: Government Printing Office.

Silberman, C.E. (1978). *Criminal violence, criminal justice.* New York: Random House.

Simmel, G. (1950). *The sociology of Georg Simmel.* Glencoe, IL: Free Press.

Singer, J.L., & Singer, D.G. (1981). *Television, imagination, and aggression: A study of preschoolers.* Hillsdale, NJ: Lawrence Erlbaum.

Sistrunk, F., & McDavid, J.W. (1971). Sex variable in conforming behavior. *Journal of Personality and Social Psychology, 17,* 200–207.

Sivacek, J., & Crano, W.D. (1982). Vested interest as a moderator of attitude–behavior consistency. *Journal of Personality and Social Psychology, 43,* 210–221.

Slavin, R.E. (1985). Cooperative learning: Applying contact theory in desegregated schools. *Journal of Social Issues, 41,* 45–62.

Slovic, P., Fischhoff, B., & Lichtenstein, S. (1982). Facts versus fears: Understanding perceived risk. In D. Kahneman, P. Slovic, & Tversky, A. (Eds.), *Judgment under uncertainty: Heuristics and biases.* Cambridge: Cambridge University Press.

Smelser, N.J. (1963). *Theory of collective behavior.* New York: Free Press.

Smith, E.R., & Kluegel, J.R. (1982). Cognitive and social bases of emotional experience: Outcome, attribution, and affect. *Journal of Personality and Social Psychology, 43,* 1129–1141.

Smith, E.R., & Lerner, M. (1986). Development of automatism of social judgments. *Journal of Personality and Social Psychology, 50,* 246–259.

Smith, E.R., & Miller, F.D. (1978). Limits on perception of cognitive processes: A reply to Nisbett and Wilson. *Psychological Review, 85,* 355–361.

Smith, E.R., & Miller, F.D. (1979). Attributional information processing: A response time model of causal subtraction. *Journal of Personality and Social Psychology, 37,* 1723–1731.

Smith, M.B., Bruner, J.S., & White, R.W. (1956). *Opinions and personality.* New York: Wiley.

Smith, S.S., & Richardson, D. (1983). Amelioration of deception and harm in psychological research: The important role of debriefing. *Journal of Personality and Social Psychology, 44,* 1075–1082.

Smith, T.W., Snyder, C.R., & Perkins, S.C. (1983). The self-serving function of hypochondriacal complaints: Physical symptoms as self-handicapping strategies. *Journal of Personality and Social Psychology, 44,* 787–797.

Snarey, J.R. (1985). Cross-cultural universality of social–moral development: A critical review of Kohlbergian research. *Psychological Bulletin, 97,* 202–232.

Snow, M.E., Jacklin, C.N., & Maccoby, E.E. (1983). Sex-of-child differences in father–child interaction at one year of age. *Child Development, 54,* 227–232.

Snyder, C.R. (1985). The excuse: An amazing grace. In B.R. Schlenker (Ed.), *The self and social life.* New York: McGraw-Hill.

Snyder, C.R., Smith, T.W., Augelli, R.W., & Ingram, R.E. (1985). On the self-serving function of social anxiety: Shyness as a self-handicapping strategy. *Journal of Personality and Social Psychology, 48,* 970–980.

Snyder, M. (1974). Self-monitoring of expressive behavior. *Journal of Personality and Social Psychology, 30,* 526–537.

Snyder, M. (1976). Attribution and behavior: Social perception and social causation. In J.H. Harvey, W.J. Ickes,

& R.F. Kidd (Eds.), *New directions in attribution research* (Vol. 1). Hillsdale, NJ: Lawrence Erlbaum.

Snyder, M. (1979). Self-monitoring processes. In L. Berkowitz (Ed.), *Advances in experimental social psychology* (Vol. 12). New York: Academic Press.

Snyder, M. (1981a). Seek, and ye shall find: Testing hypotheses about other people. In E.T. Higgins, C.P. Herman, & M.P. Zanna (Eds.), *Social cognition: The Ontario Symposium* (Vol. 1). Hillsdale, NJ: Lawrence Erlbaum.

Snyder, M. (1981b). On the influence of individuals on situations. In N. Cantor & J.F. Kihlstrom (Eds.), *Personality, cognition, and social interaction*. Hillsdale, NJ: Lawrence Erlbaum.

Snyder, M., Berscheid, E., & Glick, P. (1985). Focusing on the exterior and the interior: Two investigations of the initiation of personal relationships. *Journal of Personality and Social Psychology, 48,* 1427–1439.

Synder, M., & Cantor, N. (1979). Testing hypotheses about other people: The use of historical knowledge. *Journal of Experimental Social Psychology, 15,* 330–342.

Snyder, M., Gangestad, S., & Simpson, J.A. (1983). Choosing friends as activity partners: The role of self-monitoring. *Journal of Personality and Social Psychology, 45,* 1061–1072.

Snyder, M., & Kendzierski, D. (1982). Acting on one's attitudes: Procedures for linking attitude and behavior. *Journal of Experimental Social Psychology, 18,* 165–183.

Snyder, M., & Monson, T.C. (1975). Persons, situations, and the control of social behavior. *Journal of Personality and Social Psychology, 32,* 637–644.

Snyder, M., & Swann, W.B., Jr. (1976). When actions reflect attitudes: The politics of impression management. *Journal of Personality and Social Psychology, 34,* 1034–1042.

Snyder, M., & Swann, W.B., Jr. (1978a). Hypothesis-testing processes in social interaction. *Journal of Personality and Social Psychology, 36,* 1202–1212.

Snyder, M., & Swann, W.B., Jr. (1978b). Behavioral confirmation in social interaction: From social perception to social reality. *Journal of Experimental Social Psychology, 14,* 148–162.

Snyder, M., Tanke, E.D., & Berscheid, E. (1977). Social perception and interpersonal behavior: On the self-fulfilling nature of social stereotypes. *Journal of Personality and Social Psychology, 35,* 656–666.

Sommer, R., & Becker, F.D. (1969). Territorial defense and the good neighbor. *Journal of Personality and Social Psychology, 11,* 85–92.

Sorrentino, R.M., & Boutilier, R.G. (1974). Evaluation of a victim as a function of fate similarity/dissimilarity. *Journal of Experimental Social Psychology, 10,* 84–93.

Sorrentino, R.M., & Boutillier, R.G. (1975). The effect of

quantity and quality of verbal interaction on ratings of leadership ability. *Journal of Experimental Social Psychology, 11,* 403–411.

Spence, J.T., & Helmreich, R.L. (1978). *Masculinity and femininity: Their psychological dimensions, correlates, and antecedents.* Austin: University of Texas Press.

Spiro, R.J. (1980). Accommodative reconstruction in prose recall. *Journal of Verbal Learning and Verbal Behavior, 19,* 84–95.

Srull, T.K. (1981). Person memory: Some tests of associative storage and retrieval models. *Journal of Experimental Psychology: Human Learning and Memory, 7,* 440–463.

Srull, T.K. (1983). Organizational and retrieval processes in person memory: An examination of processing objectives, presentation format, and the possible role of self-generated retrieval cues. *Journal of Personality and Social Psychology, 44,* 1157–1170.

Srull, T.K., & Gaelick, L. (1983). General principles and individual differences in the self as a habitual reference point: An examination of self–other judgments of similarity. *Social Cognition, 2,* 108–121.

Srull, T.K., Lichtenstein, M., & Rothbart, M. (1985). Associative storage and retrieval processes in person memory. *Journal of Experimental Psychology: Learning, Memory, and Cognition, 11,* 316–345.

Staub, E. (1978). *Positive social behavior and morality.* New York: Academic Press.

Steck, L., Levitan, D., McLane, D., & Kelley, H.H. (1982). Care, need, and conceptions of love. *Journal of Personality and Social Psychology, 43,* 481–491.

Stein, D.D., Hardyck, J.A., & Smith, M.B. (1965). Race and belief: An open and shut case. *Journal of Personality and Social Psychology, 1,* 281–289.

Stein, R.T., & Heller, T. (1979). An empirical analysis of the correlation between leadership states and participation rates reported in the literature. *Journal of Personality and Social Psychology, 37,* 1993–2002.

Stein, R.T., Hoffman, L.R., Cooley, S.J., & Pearse, R.W. (1979). Leadership valence: Modeling and measuring the process of emergent leadership. In J.G. Hunt & L.L. Larson (Eds.), *Crosscurrents in leadership.* Carbondale, IL: Southern Illinois University Press.

Steiner, I.D. (1968). Reactions to adverse and favorable evaluations of one's self. *Journal of Personality, 36,* 553–563.

Steiner, I.D. (1972). *Group processes and productivity.* New York: Academic Press.

Steiner, I.D. (1986). Paradigms and groups. In L. Berkowitz (Ed.), *Advances in experimental social psychology* (Vol. 19). Orlando, FL: Academic Press.

Stephan, C.W., & Langlois, J.H. (1984). Baby beautiful: Adult attributions of infant competence as a function of infant attractiveness. *Child Development, 55,* 576–585.

Stephan, W., Berscheid, E., & Walster, E. (1971). Sexual arousal and heterosexual perception. *Journal of Personality and Social Psychology, 20,* 93–101.

Stephan, W.G. (1978). School desegregation: An evaluation of prediction made in *Brown* v. *Board of Education. Psychological Bulletin, 85,* 217–238.

Stephan, W.G. (1985). Intergroup relations. In G. Lindzey & E. Aronson (Eds.), *Handbook of social psychology* (3rd edition, Vol. 2). New York: Random House.

Sterling, B., & Gaertner, S.L. (1984). The attribution of arousal and emergency helping: A bidirectional process. *Journal of Experimental Social Psychology, 20,* 586–596.

Stern, D.N. (1977). *The first relationship.* Cambridge, MA: Harvard University Press.

Stern, L.D., Marrs, S., Millar, M.G., & Cole, E. (1984). Processing time and the recall of inconsistent and consistent behaviors of individuals and groups. *Journal of Personality and Social Psychology, 47,* 253–262.

Sternberg, R.J. (1986). A triangular theory of love. *Psychological Review, 93,* 119–135.

Sternberg, R.J., & Barnes, M.L. (1985). Real and ideal others in romantic relationships: Is four a crowd? *Journal of Personality and Social Psychology, 49,* 1586–1608.

Sternberg, R.J., & Grajek, S. (1984). The nature of love. *Journal of Personality and Social Psychology, 47,* 312–329.

Stier, D.S., & Hall, J.A. (1984). Gender differences in touch: An empirical and theoretical review. *Journal of Personality and Social Psychology, 47,* 440–459.

Stogdill, R.M. (1974). *Handbook of leadership.* New York: Macmillan/Free Press.

Storms, M.D. (1973). Videotape and the attribution process: Reversing actors' and observers' points of view. *Journal of Personality and Social Psychology, 27,* 165–175.

Stouffer, S.A., Lumsdaine, A.A., Lumsdaine, M.H., Williams, R.M., Smith, M.B., Janis, I.L., Star, S.A., & Cothell, L.S. (1949). *The American soldier: Combat and its aftermath* (Vol. II). Princeton: Princeton University Press.

Strasser, G., & Davis, J.H. (1981). Group decision making and social influence: A social interaction sequence model. *Psychological Review, 88,* 523–551.

Streeter, L., Krauss, R., Geller, V., Olson, C., & Apple, W. (1977). Pitch changes during attempted deception. *Journal of Personality and Social Psychology, 35,* 345–350.

Strenta, A., & DeJong, W. (1981). The effect of a prosocial label on helping behavior. *Social Psychology Quarterly, 44,* 142–147.

Strickland, L.H., Lewicki, R.J., & Katz, A.M. (1966). Temporal orientation and perceived control as deter-

minants of risk-taking. *Journal of Experimental Social Psychology, 2,* 143–151.

Stroebe, W., Insko, C.A., Thompson, V.D., & Layton, B.D. (1971). Effects of physical attractiveness, attitude similarity, and sex on various aspects of interpersonal attraction. *Journal of Personality and Social Psychology, 18,* 79–91.

Strube, M.J., & Garcia, J.E. (1981). A meta-analytic investigation of Fielder's contingency model of leadership effectiveness. *Psychological Bulletin, 90,* 307–321.

Struke, M.J., Miles, M.E., & Finch, W.H. (1981). The social facilitation of a single task: Field tests of alternative explanations. *Personality and Social Psychology Bulletin, 7,* 701–707.

Stryker, S. (1983). Social psychology from the standpoint of a structural symbolic interactionism: Toward an interdisciplinary social psychology. In L. Berkowitz (Ed.), *Advances in experimental social psychology* (Vol. 16). New York: Academic Press.

Stults, D.M., Messé, L.A., & Kerr, N.L. (1984). Belief discrepant behavior and the bogus pipeline: Impression management or arousal attribution? *Journal of Experimental Social Psychology, 20,* 47–54.

Sundstrom, E. (1978). Crowding as a sequential process: Review of research on the effects of population density on humans. In A. Baum & Y.M. Epstein (Eds.), *Human response to crowding.* Hillsdale, NJ: Lawrence Erlbaum.

Surgeon General's Scientific Advisory Committee on Television and Social Behavior (1972). *Television and growing up: The impact of televised violence.* Washington, DC: Government Printing Office.

Swann, W.B., Jr., & Hill, C.A. (1982). When our identities are mistaken: Reaffirming self-conceptions through social interaction. *Journal of Personality and Social Psychology, 43,* 59–66.

Swann, W.B., Jr., & Predmore, S.C. (1985). Intimates as agents of social support: Sources of consolation or despair? *Journal of Personality and Social Psychology, 49,* 1609–1617.

Swann, W.B., Jr., & Read, S.J. (1981a). Acquiring self-knowledge: The search for feedback that fits. *Journal of Personality and Social Psychology, 41,* 1119–1128.

Swann, W.B., Jr., & Read, S.J. (1981b). Self-verification processes: How we sustain our self-conceptions. *Journal of Experimental Social Psychology, 17,* 351–372.

Swart, C., & Berkowitz, L. (1976). Effects of a stimulus associated with a victim's pain on later aggression. *Journal of Personality and Social Psychology, 33,* 623–631.

Sweeney, P.D., & Gruber, K.L. (1984). Selective exposure: Voter information preferences and the Watergate affair. *Journal of Personality and Social Psychology, 46,* 1208–1221.

Swingle, P.G., & Gillis, J.S. (1968). Effects of the emotional relationship between protagonists in the prisoner's dilemma. *Journal of Personality and Social Psychology, 8,* 160–165.

T

Tajfel, H. (1970). Experiments in intergroup discrimination. *Scientific American, 223,* 96–102.

Talmon, Y. (1972). *Family and community in the kibbutz.* Cambridge, MA: Harvard University Press.

Tanford, S., & Penrod, S. (1984). Social influence model: A formal integration of research on majority influence processes. *Psychological Bulletin, 95,* 189–225.

Taylor, M.C., & Hall, J.A. (1982). Psychological androgyny: Theories, methods, and conclusions. *Psychological Bulletin, 92,* 347–366.

Taylor, S.E. (1981). A categorization approach to stereotyping. In D.L. Hamilton (Ed.), *Cognitive processes in stereotyping and intergroup behavior.* Hillsdale, NJ: Lawrence Erlbaum.

Taylor, S.E., & Fiske, S.T. (1975). Point of view and perception of causality. *Journal of Personality and Social Psychology, 32,* 439–445.

Taylor, S.E., & Fiske, S.T. (1978). Salience, attention, and attribution: Top of the head phenomena. In L. Berkowitz (Ed.), *Advances in experimental social psychology* (Vol. 11). New York: Academic Press.

Taylor, S.E., Fiske, S.T., Etcoff, N.L., & Ruderman, A.J. (1978). The categorical and contextual bases of person memory and stereotyping. *Journal of Personality and Social Psychology, 36,* 778–793.

Taylor, S.E., & Mettee, D.R. (1971). When similarity breeds contempt. *Journal of Personality and Social Psychology, 20,* 75–81.

Taynor, J., & Deaux, K. (1973). When women are more deserving than men: Equity, attribution, and perceived sex differences. *Journal of Personality and Social Psychology, 28,* 360–367.

Tedeschi, J.T. (1970). Threats and promises. In P. Swingle (Ed.), *The structure of conflict.* New York: Academic Press.

Tedeschi, J.T. (Ed.) (1981). *Impression management theory and social psychological research.* New York: Academic Press.

Tedeschi, J.T., Bonoma, T., & Lindskold, S. (1970). Threatener's reaction to peer announcement of behavioral compliance on defiance. *Behavioral Science, 15,* 171–179.

Tedeschi, J.T., & Rosenfeld, P. (1981). Impression management theory and the forced compliance situation. In J.T. Tedeschi (Ed.), *Impression management theory and social psychology research.* New York: Academic Press.

Tesser, A. (1978). Self-generated attitude change. In L. Berkowitz (Ed.), *Advances in experimental social psychology* (Vol. 11). New York: Academic Press.

Tesser, A., & Campbell, J. (1980). Self-definition: The impact of the relative performance and similarity of others. *Social Psychology Quarterly, 43,* 341–347.

Tesser, A., & Conlee, M.C. (1975). Some effects of time and thought on attitude polarization. *Journal of Personality and Social Psychology, 31,* 262–270.

Tesser, A., & Leone, C. (1977). Cognitive schemas and thought as determinants of attitude change. *Journal of Experimental Social Psychology, 13,* 340–356.

Tesser, A., & Paulhus, D. (1983). The definition of self: Private and public self-evaluation management strategies. *Journal of Personality and Social Psychology, 44,* 672–682.

Tesser, A., & Rosen, S. (1975). The reluctance to transmit bad news. In L. Berkowitz (Ed.), *Advances in experimental social psychology* (Vol. 8). New York: Academic Press.

Tetlock, P.E. (1979). Identifying victims of groupthink from public statements of decision makers. *Journal of Personality and Social Psychology, 37,* 1314–1324.

Tetlock, P.E. (1981). The influence of self-presentation goals on attributional reports. *Social Psychology Quarterly, 44,* 300–311.

Tetlock, P.E. (1983). Accountability and complexity of thought. *Journal of Personality and Social Psychology, 45,* 74–83.

Tetlock, P.E., & Manstead, A.S.R. (1985). Impression management versus intrapsychic explanations in social psychology: A useful dichotomy? *Psychological Review, 92,* 59–77.

Thibaut, J.W., & Kelley, H.H. (1959). *The social psychology of groups.* New York: Wiley.

Thompson, W.C., Cowan, C.L., & Rosenhan, D.L. (1980). Focus of attention mediates the impact of negative affect on altruism. *Journal of Personality and Social Psychology, 38,* 291–300.

Thorndike, E.L. (1920). A constant error in psychological ratings. *Journal of Applied Psychology, 4,* 25–29.

Tilker, H.A. (1970). Socially responsible behavior as a function of observer responsibility and victim feedback. *Journal of Personality and Social Psychology, 14,* 95–100.

Tisak, M.S., & Turiel, E. (1984). Children's conceptions of moral and prudential rules. *Child Development, 55,* 1030–1039.

Tittle, C.R., Villemez, W.J., & Smith, D.A. (1978). The myth of social class and criminality: An empirical assessment of the empirical evidence. *American Sociological Review, 43,* 643–656.

Toch, H. (1969). *Violent men.* Chicago: Aldine.

Trainer, F.E. (1977). A critical analysis of Kohlberg's contribution to the study of moral thought. *Journal for the Theory of Social Behavior, 7,* 41–64.

Tucker, L.A. (1983). Muscular strength and mental health. *Journal of Personality and Social Psychology, 45,* 1355–1360.

Tulving, E., & Thompson, D.M. (1973). Encoding specificity and retrieval processes in episodic memory. *Psychological Review, 80,* 352–373.

Turiel, E. (1978a). Distinct conceptual and developmental domains: Social convention and morality. In C.B. Keasey (Ed.), *Nebraska symposium on motivation 1977.* Lincoln: University of Nebraska Press.

Turiel, E. (1978b). The development of concepts of social structure: Social convention. In J. Glick & K.A. Clarke-Stewart (Eds.), *The development of social understanding.* New York: Gardner Press.

Turiel, E. (1983). *The development of social knowledge: Morality and convention.* Cambridge: Cambridge University Press.

Turnbull, C.M. (1972). *The mountain people.* New York: Simon & Schuster.

Turner, R.H., & Killian, L.M. (1972). *Collective behavior* (2nd edition). Englewood Cliffs, NJ: Prentice-Hall.

Tversky, A., & Gati, I. (1978). Studies in similarity. In E. Rosch & B.B. Lloyd (Eds.), *Cognition and categorization.* Hillsdale, NJ: Lawrence Erlbaum.

Tversky, A., & Kahneman, D. (1971). Belief in the law of small numbers. *Psychological Bulletin, 76,* 105–110.

Tversky, A., & Kahneman, D. (1973). Availability: A heuristic for judging frequency and probability. *Cognitive Psychology, 5,* 207–232.

Tversky, A., & Kahneman, D. (1978). Causal schemata in judgments under uncertainty. In M. Fishbein (Ed.), *Progress in social psychology.* Hillsdale, NJ: Lawrence Erlbaum.

Tversky, A., & Kahneman, D. (1983). Extensional versus intuitive reasoning: The conjunction fallacy in probability judgment. *Psychological Review, 90,* 293–315.

U

Underwood, B., & Moore, B.S. (1981). Sources of behavioral consistency. *Journal of Personality and Social Psychology, 40,* 780–785.

Unger, R.K., Hilderbrand, M., & Madar, T. (1982). Physical attractiveness and assumptions about social deviance: Some sex-by-sex comparisons. *Personality and Social Psychology Bulletin, 8,* 293–301.

V

Vallacher, R.R., & Wegner, D.M. (1985). *A theory of action identification.* Hillsdale, NJ: Lawrence Erlbaum.

Van der Pligt, J. (1984). Attributions, false consensus, and valence: Two field studies. *Journal of Personality and Social Psychology, 46,* 57–68.

Vinokur, A., & Burnstein, E. (1974). Effects of partially shared persuasive arguments on group-induced shifts: A group problem- solving approach. *Journal of Personality and Social Psychology, 29,* 305–315.

Vygotsky, L. (1962). *Thought and language.* Cambridge, MA: M.I.T. Press.

W

Wagner, W. (1984). Recognition of own and others' utterances in a natural conversation. *Personality and Social Psychology Bulletin, 10,* 596–604.

Walker, L.J. (1980). Cognitive and perspective taking prerequisites for moral development. *Child Development, 51,* 131–139.

Walster, E., Aronson, E., Abrahams, D., & Rottman, L. (1966). Importance of physical attractiveness in dating behavior. *Journal of Personality and Social Psychology, 4,* 508–516.

Walster, E., Walster, G.W., & Berscheid, E. (1978). *Equity: Theory and research.* Boston: Allyn and Bacon.

Walster, E.H., & Walster, W. (1979). *A new look at love.* Reading, MA: Addison-Wesley.

Warshaw, P.R., & Davis, F.D. (1985). Disentangling behavioral intention and behavioral expectation. *Journal of Experimental Social Psychology, 21,* 213–228.

Waters, E., Wippman, J., & Sroufe, L.A. (1979). Attachment, positive affect, and competence in the peer group: Two studies in construct validation. *Child Development, 50,* 821–829.

Watkins, M.J., & Peynircioglu, Z.F. (1984). Determining perceived meaning during impression formation: Another look at the meaning change hypothesis. *Journal of Personality and Social Psychology, 46,* 1005–1016.

Watson, D. (1982). The actor and the observer: How are their perceptions of causality divergent? *Psychological Bulletin, 92,* 682–700.

Watts, W.A., & Holt, L.E. (1979). Persistence of opinion change induced under conditions of forewarning and distraction. *Journal of Personality and Social Psychology, 37,* 778–789.

Weary, G., Harvey, J.H., Schwieger, P., Olson, C.T., Perloff, R., & Pritchard, S. (1982). Self-presentation and the moderation of self-serving attributional biases. *Social Cognition, 1,* 140–159.

Weber, R., & Crocker, J. (1983). Cognitive processes in the revision of stereotypic beliefs. *Journal of Personality and Social Psychology, 45,* 961–977.

Weber, S.J., & Cook, T.D. (1972). Subject effects in laboratory research: An examination of subject roles, demand characteristics, and valid inference. *Psychological Bulletin, 77,* 273–295.

Wegner, D.M., Coulton, G.F., & Wenzlaff, R. (1985). The transparency of denial: Briefing in the debriefing paradigm. *Journal of Personality and Social Psychology, 49,* 338–346.

Wegner, D.M., & Giuliano, T. (1980). Arousal-induced attention to self. *Journal of Personality and Social Psychology, 38,* 719–726.

Wegner, D.M., & Giuliano, T. (1982). The forms of social awareness. In W. Ickes & E.S. Knowles (Eds.), *Personality, roles, and social behavior.* New York: Springer-Verlag.

Wegner, D.M., & Giuliano, T. (1983). Social awareness in story comprehension. *Social Cognition, 2,* 1–17.

Wegner, D.M., & Vallacher, R.R. (1986). Action identification. In R.M. Sorrentino & E.T. Higgins (Eds.), *Handbook of cognition and motivation.* New York: Guilford Press.

Wegner, D.M., Vallacher, R.P., Kiersted, G.W., & Dizadji, D. (1986). Action identification in the emergence of social behavior. *Social Cognition, 4,* 18–38.

Wegner, D.M., Vallacher, R.R., Macomber, G., Wood, R., & Arps, K. (1984). The emergence of action. *Journal of Personality and Social Psychology, 46,* 269–279.

Wegner, D.M., Wenzlaff, R., Kerker, R.M., & Beattie, A.E. (1981). Incrimination through innuendo: Can media questions become public answers? *Journal of Personality and Social Psychology, 40,* 822–832.

Weick, K.E., & Gilfillan, D.P. (1971). Fate of arbitrary traditions in laboratory microculture. *Journal of Personality and Social Psychology, 17,* 179–191.

Weigel, R.H., & Howes, P.W. (1985). Conceptions of racial prejudice: Symbolic racism reconsidered. *Journal of Social Issues, 41,* 117–138.

Weinberg, H.I., & Baron, R.S. (1982). The discredible eyewitness. *Personality and Social Psychology Bulletin, 8,* 60–67.

Weiner, B. (1980). A cognitive (attribution)-emotion-action model of motivated behavior: An analysis of judgments of help-giving. *Journal of Personality and Social Psychology, 39,* 186–200.

Weiner, B. (1985). "Spontaneous" causal thinking. *Psychological Bulletin, 97,* 74–84.

Weiner, B., Frieze, I., Kukla, A., Reed. L., Rest, S., & Rosenbaum, R.M. (1972). Perceiving the causes of success and failure. In E.E. Jones et al. (Eds.), *Attribution: Perceiving the causes of behavior.* Morristown, NJ: General Learning Press.

Weinstein, N.D. (1980). Unrealistic optimism about future life events. *Journal of Personality and Social Psychology, 39,* 806–820.

Weintraub, M., Clemens, L.P., Sockloff, A., Ethridge, T., Gracely, E., & Myers, B. (1984). The development of

sex role stereotypes in the third year: Relationships to gender labeling, gender identity, sex-typed toy preference, and family characteristics. *Child Development, 55,* 1493–1503.

Wells, G.L. (1982). Attribution and reconstructive memory. *Journal of Experimental Social Psychology, 18,* 447–463.

Wells, G.L., Lindsay, R.C.L., & Tousignant, J.P. (1980). Effects of expert psychological advice on human performance in judging the validity of eyewitness testimony. *Law and Human Behavior, 4,* 275–286.

Werner, C.M., Brown, B.B., & Damron, G. (1981). Territorial marking in a game arcade. *Journal of Personality and Social Psychology, 41,* 1094–1104.

Wetzel, C.G., Wilson, T.D., & Kort, J. (1981). The halo effect revisited: Forewarned is not forearmed. *Journal of Experimental Social Psychology, 17,* 427–439.

Weyant, J.M. (1978). Effects of mood states, costs, and benefits on helping. *Journal of Personality and Social Psychology, 36,* 1169–1176.

Wheeler, L., & Caggiula, A.R. (1966). The contagion of aggression. *Journal of Experimental Social Psychology, 2,* 1–10.

Wheeler, L., Shaver, K.G., Jones, R.A., Goethals, G.R., Cooper, J., Robinson, J.E., Gruder, C.L., & Butzine, K.W. (1969). Factors determining the choice of a comparison other. *Journal of Experimental Social Psychology, 5,* 219–232.

White, G.L. (1980). Physical attractiveness and courtship progress. *Journal of Personality and Social Psychology, 39,* 660–668.

White, G.L., Fishbein, S., & Rutstein, J. (1981). Passionate love and the misattribution of arousal. *Journal of Personality and Social Psychology, 41,* 56–62.

White, J.D., & Carlston, D.E. (1983). Consequence of schemata for attention, impressions, and recall in complex social interactions. *Journal of Personality and Social Psychology, 45,* 538–549.

White, P. (1980). Limitations on verbal reports of internal events: A refutation of Nisbett and Wilson and of Bem. *Psychological Review, 87,* 105–112.

White, P. (1984). A model of the layperson as pragmatist. *Personality and Social Psychology Bulletin, 10,* 333–348.

Whitely, B.E. (1983). Sex role orientation and self-esteem: A critical meta-analysis. *Journal of Personality and Social Psychology, 44,* 765–778.

Whorf, B. (1956). *Language, thought, and reality* (ed. J.B. Carroll). New York: Wiley and M.I.T.

Wicklund, R.A. (1975). Objective self-awareness. In L. Berkowitz (Ed.), *Advances in experimental social psychology* (Vol. 8). New York: Academic Press.

Wilder, D.A. (1981). Perceiving persons as a group: Categorization and intergroup relations. In D.L. Hamilton (Ed.), *Cognitive processes in stereotyping and inter-group behavior.* Hillsdale, NJ: Lawrence Erlbaum.

Wilder, D.A. (1986). Social categorization: Implications for creation and reduction of intergroup bias. In L. Berkowitz (Ed.), *Advances in experimental social psychology* (Vol. 19). Orlando, FL: Academic Press.

Williams, K., Harkins, S., & Latané, B. (1981). Identifiability as a deterrent to social loafing: Two cheering experiments. *Journal of Personality and Social Psychology, 40,* 303–311.

Wilson, E.O. (1975). *Sociobiology: The new synthesis.* Cambridge: Harvard University Press.

Wilson, J.Q. (1975). *Thinking about crime.* New York: Basic books.

Wilson, J.Q., & Herrnstein, R.J. (1985). *Crime and human nature.* New York: Simon & Schuster.

Wilson, L., & Rogers, R.W. (1975). The fire this time: Effects of race of target, insult, and potential retaliation on black aggression. *Journal of Personality and Social Psychology, 32,* 857–864.

Wilson, T.D., & Capitman, J.A. (1982). Effects of script availability on social behavior. *Personality and Social Psychology Bulletin, 8,* 11–20.

Wilson, T.D., Dunn, D.S., Bybee, J.A., Hyman, D.B., & Rotondo, J.A. (1984). Effects of analyzing reasons on attitude–behavior consistency. *Journal of Personality and Social Psychology, 47,* 5–16.

Wilson, W.R. (1979). Feeling more than we can know: Exposure effects without learning. *Journal of Personality and Social Psychology, 37,* 811–821.

Winch, R.F., Ktsanes, T., & Ktsanes, V. (1954). The theory of complementary needs in mate-selection: An analytic and descriptive study. *American Sociological Review, 19,* 241–249.

Winter, L., & Uleman, J.S. (1984). When are social judgments made? Evidence for the spontaneousness of trait inferences. *Journal of Personality and Social Psychology, 47,* 237–252.

Winter, L., Uleman, J.S., & Cunniff, C. (1985). How automatic are social judgments? *Journal of Personality and Social Psychology, 49,* 904–917.

Wishner, J. (1960). Reanalysis of "impressions of personality." *Psychological Review, 67,* 96–112.

Witkin, H.A., Mednick, S.A., Schulsinger, F., Bakkestrom, E., Christiansen, K.O., Goodenough, D.R., Hirschhorn, K., Lundsteen, C., Oweb, D.R., Philip, J., Rubin, D.B., & Stocking, M. (1976). Criminality in XYY and XXY men. *Science, 196,* 547–555.

Wittgenstein, L. (1958). *Philosophical investigations.* London: Basil Blackwell.

Wolf, S. (1985). Manifest and latent influence of majorities and minorities. *Journal of Personality and Social Psychology, 48,* 899–908.

Wolf, S., & Latané, B. (1983). Majority and minority

influence on restaurant preference. *Journal of Personality and Social Psychology, 45,* 282–291.

Wolfgang, M., & Ferracuti, F. (1967). *The subculture of violence: Toward an integrated theory in criminology.* London: Tavistok.

Woll, S.B., Weeks, D.G., Fraps, C.L., Pendergrass, J., & Vanderplas, M.A. (1980). Role of sentence context in the encoding of trait descriptors. *Journal of Personality and Social Psychology, 39,* 59–68.

Wood, W. (1982). Retrieval of attitude-relevant information from memory: Effects on susceptibility to persuasion and on intrinsic motivation. *Journal of Personality and Social Psychology, 42,* 798–810.

Wood, W., Kallgren, C.A., & Preisler, R.M. (1985). Access to attitude-relevant information in memory as a determinant of persuasion: The role of message attributes. *Journal of Experimental Social Psychology, 21,* 73–85.

Wood, W., & Karten, S.J. (1986). Sex differences in interaction style as a product of perceived sex differences in competence. *Journal of Personality and Social Psychology, 50,* 341–347.

Worchel, P. (1957). Catharsis and the relief of hostility. *Journal of Abnormal and Social Psychology, 55,* 238–243.

Word, C.D., Zanna, M.P., & Cooper, J. (1974). The nonverbal mediation of self-fulfilling prophecies in interracial interaction. *Journal of Experimental Social Psychology, 10,* 109–120.

Worthy, M., Gary, A.L., & Kahn, G. (1969). Self-disclosure as an exchange process. *Journal of Personality and Social Psychology, 10,* 109–120.

Wortman, C.B., Panciera, L., Shusterman, L., & Hibscher, J. (1976). Attribution of causality and reactions to uncontrollable outcomes. *Journal of Experimental Social Psychology, 12,* 301–316.

Wright, J., & Mischel, W. (1982). Influence of affect on cognitive social learning person variables. *Journal of Personality and Social Psychology, 43,* 901–914.

Wright, J.C., & Huston, A.C. (1983). A matter of form: Potentials of television for young viewers. *American Psychologist, 38,* 835–843.

Wright, P., & Rip, P.D. (1981). Retrospective reports on the causes of decisions. *Journal of Personality and Social Psychology, 40,* 601–614.

Wright, T.L., & Ingraham, L.J. (1986). Partners and relationships influence self-perceptions of self-disclosures in naturalistic interactions. *Journal of Personality and Social Psychology, 50,* 631–635.

Wright, T.L., Ingraham, L.J., & Blackmer, D.R. (1984). Simultaneous study of individual differences and relationship effects in attraction. *Journal of Personality and Social Psychology, 47,* 1059–1062.

Wyer, R.S., Jr. (1970). Quantitative prediction of belief

and opinion change: A further test of a subjective probability model. *Journal of Personality and Social Psychology, 16,* 559–570.

Wyer, R.S., Jr., Bodenhausen, G.V., & Gorman, T.F. (1985). Cognitive mediators of reactions to rape. *Journal of Personality and Social Psychology, 48,* 324–338.

Wyer, R.S., Jr., & Carlston, D.E. (1979). *Social cognition, inference, and attribution.* Hillsdale, NJ: Lawrence Erlbaum.

Wyer, R.S., Jr., & Srull, T.K. (1981). Category accessibility: Some theoretical and empirical issues concerning the processing of social stimulus information. In E.T. Higgins, C.P. Herman, & M.P. Zanna (Eds.), *Social cognition: The Ontario Symposium* (Vol. 1). Hillsdale, NJ: Lawrence Erlbaum.

Wyer, R.S., Jr., Srull, T.K., Gordon, S.E., & Hartwick, J. (1982). Effects of processing objectives on the recall of prose material. *Journal of Personality and Social Psychology, 43,* 674–688.

Y

Yardley, K.M. (1982). On distinguishing role plays from conventional methodologies. *Journal for the Theory of Social Behaviour, 12,* 125–139.

Z

Zablocki, B. (1973). *The joyful community.* Baltimore: Pelican.

Zahn-Waxler, C., Iannotti, R., & Chapman, M. (1982). Peers and prosocial development. In K.H. Rubin & H.S. Ross (Eds.), *Peer relationships and social skills in childhood.* New York: Springer-Verlag.

Zahn-Waxler, C., Radke-Yarrow, M., & King, R.A. (1979). Child rearing and children's pro-social initiations toward victims of distress. *Child Development, 50,* 319–330.

Zajonc, R.B. (1965). Social facilitation. *Science, 149,* 269–274.

Zajonc, R.B. (1968). Attitudinal effects of mere exposure. *Journal of Personality and Social Psychology Monographs, 9* (2, part 2), 1–27.

Zajonc, R.B. (1980). Feeling and thinking: Preferences need no inferences. *American Psychologist, 35,* 151–175.

Zajonc, R.B., & Burnstein, E. (1965). The learning of balanced and unbalanced social structures. *Journal of Personality and Social Psychology, 33,* 153–163.

Zajonc, R.B., & Nieuwenhuyse, B. (1964). Relationship between word frequency and recognition: Perceptual

process or response bias. *Journal of Experimental Social Psychology, 67,* 267–285.

Zajonc, R.B., & Sales, S.M. (1966). Social facilitation of dominant and subordinate responses. *Journal of Experimental Social Psychology, 2,* 160–168.

Zander, A.F. (1977). *Groups at work.* San Francisco: Jossey-Bass.

Zanna, M.P., & Cooper, J. (1974). Dissonance and the pill: an attributional approach to studying the arousal properties of dissonance. *Journal of Personality and Social Psychology, 29,* 703–709.

Zanna, M.P., Goethals, G.R., & Hill, J.F. (1975). Evaluating a sex-related ability: Social comparison with similar others and standard setters. *Journal of Experimental Social Psychology, 11,* 86–93.

Zanna, M.P., Higgins, E.T., & Taves, P.A. (1976). Is dissonance phenomenologically aversive? *Journal of Experimental Social Psychology, 12,* 530–538.

Zanna, M.P., Kiesler, C.A., & Pilkonis, P.A. (1970). Positive and negative attitudinal affect established by classical conditioning. *Journal of Personality and Social Psychology, 14,* 321–328.

Zanna, M.P., Olson, J.M., & Fazio, R.H. (1980). Attitude–behavior consistency: An individual difference perspective. *Journal of Personality and Social Psychology, 38,* 432–440.

Zanna, M.P., Olson, J.M., & Fazio, R.H. (1981). Self-perception and attitude–behavior consistency. *Personality and Social Psychology Bulletin, 7,* 252–256.

Zanna, M.P., & Pack, S.J. (1975). On the self-fulfilling nature of apparent sex differences in behavior. *Journal of Experimental Social Psychology, 11,* 583–591.

Zillmann, D. (1971). Excitation transfer in communication mediated aggressive behavior. *Journal of Experimental Social Psychology, 7,* 419–434.

Zillmann, D. (1979). *Hostility and aggression.* Hillsdale, NJ: Lawrence Erlbaum.

Zillmann, D., Johnson, R.C., & Day, K.D. (1974). Attribution of apparent arousal and proficiency of recovery from sympathetic activation affecting excitation transfer to aggressive behavior. *Journal of Experimental Social Psychology, 10,* 503–515.

Zimbardo, P. (1970). The human choice: Individuation, reason, and order versus deindividuation, impulse, and chaos. In W.J. Arnold & D. Levine (Eds.), *Nebraska Symposium on motivation, 1969.* Lincoln: University of Nebraska Press.

Zingg, R.M. (1940). Feral man and extreme cases of isolation. *American Journal of Psychology, 530,* 487–517.

Zuckerman, M., DeFrank, R.S., Hall, J.A., Larrance, D.T., & Rosenthal, R. (1979). Facial and vocal cues of deception and honesty. *Journal of Experimental Social Psychology, 15,* 378–396.

Zuckerman, M., DeFrank, R.S., Spiegel, N.H., & Larrance, D.T. (1982). Masculinity–femininity and encoding of nonverbal uses. *Journal of Personality and Social Psychology, 42*, 548–556.

Zuckerman, M., DePaulo, B.M., & Rosenthal, R. (1981). Verbal and nonverbal communication of deception. In L. Berkowitz (Ed.), *Advances in experimental social psychology* (Vol. 14). New York: Academic Press.

Zuckerman, M., Kernis, M.R., Driver, R., & Koestner, R. (1984). Segmentation of behavior: Effects of actual deception and expected deception. *Journal of Personality and Social Psychology, 46*, 1173–1182.

Zukier, H., & Jennings, D.L. (1983–1984). Nondiagnosticity and typicality effects in prediction. *Social Cognition, 2*, 187–198.

CREDITS

Photo Credits

3: Richard Wood/The Picture Cube; 8 (left): National Library of Medicine; 9: © Sigmund Freud Copyrights, Ltd; 14: © Elizabeth Crews; 17: Michael Pirrocco, 1985; 18: Archives of the History of American Psychology; 21: © Steve Whelan/Zephyr Pictures; 24: Owen Franken/Stock, Boston; 27: © Elizabeth Crews; 32: Carey Wolinsky/Stock, Boston; 37 (left): Mike Boroff/TexaStock; (right): Charles Gatewood/The Image Works; 42: Richard Wood, 1982/The Picture Cube; 49: Howard Dratch/The Image Works; 51 (left): © Elizabeth Crews; (right): Yale University Office of Public Information; 54: Jean-Claude Lejeune/Stock, Boston; 62: Fred Ward/Black Star; 67: Charles Gatewood/Image Works; 73: David S. Strickler/Picture Cube; 76: James B. Adair/Sygma; 84: UPI/Bettmann Newsphotos; 91: Gale Zucker/Stock, Boston; 93: François Sully from Black Star; 95: Lionel J. M. Delevigne/Stock, Boston; 98: Jaye R. Phillips/Picture Cube; 99: UPI/Bettmann Newsphotos; 105 (left): © Susan Holtz; (right): Dan Walsh/Picture Cube; 115: Jim Fox/Anthrophoto; 116: Archives of the History of American Psychology; 118: © Jack Spratt/Image Works; 122: Frances M. Cox/Stock, Boston; 124: © Elizabeth Crews; 125: Pamela R. Schuyler/Stock, Boston; 138: Shirley Zieberg/Taurus Photos; 140: Melanie Carr/Zephyr Pictures; 146: Phyllis Graber Jensen/Stock, Boston; 160: Charles Gatewood/Image Works; 161: Robert Kalman/Image Works; 163: © Eric Roth/Picture Cube; 165: © Paul Ekman; 174: John R. Maher/EKM-Nepenthe; 179: © Ken Karp; 180: UPI/Bettmann Newsphotos; 185: Ellis Herwig/Picture Cube; 189 (top left): David Powers/Stock, Boston; 206: UPI/Bettmann Newsphotos; 211: Owen Franken/Stock, Boston; 219: Laimute Druskis/Stock, Boston; 224: Jerry Berndt/Stock, Boston; 227 (left): Harvey Stein; (right): © Bill Hayward for American Health; 229: Michael Austin/Photo Researchers; 231: Christopher Johnson/Stock, Boston; 238: Peter Vandermark/Stock, Boston; 243: T. C. Fitzgerald/Picture Cube; 246: © Sponholtz. University of Wisconsin Primate Laboratory; 248: J. Berndt/Picture Cube; 251: Bettmann Archive; 254: © Elizabeth Crews; 269: © Elizabeth Crews; 273: Wide World Photos; 275: Frances M. Cox/Stock, Boston; 276: UPI/Bettmann Newsphotos; 282: Armel Brucelle/Sygma; 284: Wide World Photos; 288: © David Welcher/Sygma; 291: Macdonald Photography/Picture Cube; 300: UPI/Bettmann Newsphotos; 305: UPI/Bettmann Newsphotos; 307: Archives of the History of American Psychology; 309: William Vandievert; 311: Eric A. Roth/Picture Cube; 314: © Karen Zebulon; 317: © 1965 by Stanley Milgram. From the film *Obedience*, distributed by New York University Film Library. Estate of Stanley Milgram, Alexandra Milgram, Executrix; 321: Owen Franken/Stock, Boston; 323: Alan Copeland/Black Star; 330: Tim Carlson/Stock, Boston; 339: Wide World Photos; 343 (top): Chester Higgins/Photo Researchers; (bottom): P. Davidson/The Image Works; 345 (left): Alan Carey/The Image Works; (right): Robert V. Eckert/EKM-Nepenthe; 347: Porterfield-Chickering/Photo Researchers; 354 (left): © Bruce Fritz; 357: George Gardner/The Image Works; 362: Lionel Delevigne/Stock, Boston; 370: UPI/Bettmann Newsphotos; 378: Michael Siluk/EKM-Nepenthe; 381: Mark Antman/The Image Works; 384: Paul Conklin; 387: Paul Conklin; 388 (left): Nancy Durrell McKenna/Photo Researchers; 388 (right): © Thomas Hopker/Woodfin Camp & Associates; 393 (right): Mark Antman/The Image Works; 394: Paul Mozell/Stock, Boston; 400: Wide World Photos; 402 (left): Donald C. Dietz/Stock,

Boston; (right): Stock, Boston; **403**: Culver Pictures; **404**: Wide World Photos; **405**: Jerry Howard/Stock, Boston; **407**: Billy E. Barnes/Stock, Boston; **410**: Bernard Pierre Wolff/Photo Researchers; **414**: Miriam Reinhart/Photo Researchers; **415**: Harry Wilkes/Stock, Boston; **419**: Alan Carey/The Image Works; **431**: Napoleon Chagnon/Anthrophoto; **432**: UPI/Bettmann Newsphotos; **434**: Wide World Photos; **436** (right): George Gardner/The Image Works; **437** (right): Robert V. Eckert, Jr./EKM-Nepenthe; **443**: Mark Antman/The Image Works; **452**: Alan Carey/The Image Works; **454**: Jerry Berndt/Stock, Boston; **457**: J. P. Laffont/Sygma; **459**: Paul Conklin; **463**: Elizabeth Crews/Stock, Boston; **465**: Archives of the History of American Psychology; **466**: Paul Sequeira/Photo Researchers; **468**: Hazel Hankin/Stock, Boston; **474**: HBJ collection; **476**: Photo by Don Fukuda/Instructional Services, University of California, Santa Cruz; **478**: Wide World Photos; **484**: Bettmann Archive; **489**: Paul Conklin; **490**: Learning Resources/Photographic Services, University of California, Santa Barbara; **492** (left): Paul Conklin; (right): Wide World Photos; **499**: Paul Natkin/Photo Reserve, Inc.; **503** (far right): Photo by D. Farrell/Learning Resources Photographic Services, University of California, Santa Barbara; **504**: Patricia Hollander Gross/Stock, Boston; **513**: Paul Conklin; **519**: Photo by Bachrach.

Figure Credits

3-3: Bower, G., (1981). Mood and Memory. *American Psychologist* 36: 129–148. Copyright 1981 by the American Psychological Association. Adapted by permission of the publisher and author. **4-1**: Jones, Rock, Shaver, Goethals, and Ward, (1968). Pattern of performance and ability attribution: An unexpected primacy effect. *Journal of Personality and Social Psychology* 10: 317–340. Copyright 1968 by the American Psychological Association. Adapted by permission of the publisher and author. **B4-1**: Winter, L. and Uleman, J. S., (1984). When are social judgements made? Evidence for the spontaneousness of trait inferences. *Journal of Personality and Social Psychology* 47: 237–252. Copyright 1984 by the American Psychological Association. Adapted by permission of the publisher and the author. **5-1**: Markus, H., (1977). Self-schemata and processing information about the self. *Journal of Personality and Social Psychology* 35: 63–78. Copyright 1977 by the American Psychological Association. Adapted by permission of the publisher and author. **6-2**: From Carroll, John B., *Language and Thought*. Copyright 1964, University of Illinois Press, p. 104. **7-1**: Adapted from Petty, R. E. and Cacioppo, J. T.,

(1986). The elaboration likelihood model of persuasion. In Berkowitz, L., (ed.), *Advances in Experimental Psychology*, vol. 19. **7-2**: Adapted by permission Elsevier Science Publishing Co., Inc. from The influence of source credibility on communication effectiveness, by C. I. Hoveland and W. Weiss, *Public Opinion Quarterly*, vol. 15, p. 646. Copyright 1951 by the Trustees of Columbia University. **B7-1**: Pallack, S. R., (1983–84). Salience of a communicator's physical attractiveness and persuasion: A neuristic versus systematic processing interpretation. *Social Cognition* 2: 158–170. **10-1**: From Ingham, A. G., Levinger, G. Graves, J., and Peckham, V., (1974). The Ringelmann Effect: Studies in group size and group performance. *Journal of Experimental Social Psychology* 10: 371–383. **11-1**: Sherif, M., *The Psychology of Social Norms*. New York: Harper and Row, 1986. **11-2**: Latané, B., (1981). The psychology of social impact. *American Psychologist* 36: 343–356. Copyright 1981 by the American Psychological Association. Adapted by permission of the publisher and author. **11-3**: Milgram, S., *Obedience to Authority*. New York: Harper and Row, 1975. **11-4**: Zajonc, R. B. and Sales, S. M., (1964). Social facilitation of dominant and subordinant responses. *Journal of Experimental Social Psychology* 2: 164. **11-5**: Cottrel, N. B., (1968). Performance in the presence of other human beings: Mere presence, audience, and affiliation effects. In Simmel, E. C., Hoppe, R. A., and Milton, G. A., (eds.) *Social Facilitation and Imitative Behavior*. Boston: Allyn and Bacon, 1968, p. 102. **B11-1**: Phillips, David P., The influence of suggestions on suicide: Substantive and theoretical implications of the Werther Effect, *American Sociological Review*, Vol. 39, Figure 1, p. 343. **12-1**: Saegert, S., Swap, W., and Zajonc, R. B., (1973). Exposure, context and interpersonal attraction. *Journal of Personality and Social Psychology* 25: 234–242. Copyright 1973 by the American Psychological Association. Adapted by permission of the publisher and author. **B12-1**: Sternberg, (1986). A triangular theory of love. *Psychological Review* 93: 119–135. Copyright 1986 by the American Psychological Association. Adapted by permission of the publisher and the author. **B14-1**: Piliavin, J. A. and Piliavin, I. M., (1972). Effect of blood on reactions to a victim. *Journal of Personality and Social Psychology* 23: 353–361. Copyright 1972 by the American Psychological Association. Adapted by permission of the publisher and author. **14-2**: Deutsch, M. and Krauss, R., (1960). The effect of threat upon interpersonal bargaining. *Journal of Abnormal and Social Psychology* 61: 55. Copyright 1960 by the American Psychological Association. Adapted by permission of the publisher and author. **15-2**: Zillman, D., (1971). Excitation transfer in communication-mediated aggressive behavior. *Journal of Experimental Social Psychology* 7: 419–434. **15-3**: Parke, R. D., Berkowitz, L., Leyens, J. P., West, S. G., and Sebastian, R. J. Some effects of violent and non-violent movies on the behavior of juvenile delinquents. In Berkowitz, L., (ed.), *Advances in Experimental Social Psychology*, Vol. 10. **16-1**: Donnerstein, E. and Donnerstein, M., (1973). Variables in interracial aggression potential in group censure. *Journal of Personality and Social Psychology* 27: 143–150. Copyright 1973 by the American Psychological Association. Adapted by permission of the publisher and author.

NAME INDEX

SUBJECT INDEX